PHILOSOPHY OF S

Philosophy of Science: A Unified Approach combines a general introduction to philosophy of science with an integrated survey of all its important subfields. As the book's subtitle suggests, this excellent overview is guided methodologically by "a unified approach" to philosophy of science: behind the diversity of scientific fields one can recognize a methodological unity of the sciences. This unity is worked out in this book, revealing all the while important differences between subject areas.
Structurally, this comprehensive book offers a two-part approach, which makes it an excellent introduction for students new to the field and a useful resource for more advanced students. Each chapter is divided into two sections. The first section assumes no foreknowledge of the subject introduced, and the second section builds upon the first by bringing into the conversation more advanced, complementary topics.

Definitions, key propositions, examples, and figures overview all of the core material. At the end of every chapter there are selected readings and exercises (with solutions at the end of the book). The book also includes a comprehensive bibliography and an index.

Gerhard Schurz is Professor of Theoretical Philosophy and Director of the Center for Logic and Philosophy of Science at the University of Duesseldorf.

PHILOSOPHY OF SCIENCE
A Unified Approach

GERHARD SCHURZ

Routledge
Taylor & Francis Group
NEW YORK AND LONDON

First published 2014
by Routledge
711 Third Avenue, New York, NY 10017

and by Routledge
2 Park Square, Milton Park, Abingdon, Oxon OX14 4RN

Routledge is an imprint of the Taylor & Francis Group, an informa business

© 2014 Taylor & Francis

The right of Gerhard Schurz to be identified as author of this work has been asserted by him in accordance with sections 77 and 78 of the Copyright, Designs and Patents Act 1988.

All rights reserved. No part of this book may be reprinted or reproduced or utilised in any form or by any electronic, mechanical, or other means, now known or hereafter invented, including photocopying and recording, or in any information storage or retrieval system, without permission in writing from the publishers.

Trademark notice: Product or corporate names may be trademarks or registered trademarks, and are used only for identification and explanation without intent to infringe.

Library of Congress Cataloging in Publication Data
Schurz, Gerhard.
  [Einführung in die Wissenschaftstheorie. English.]
  Philosophy of science : a unified approach / Gerhard Schurz.
  pages cm
  Includes indexes.
  1. Science—Philosophy. I. Title.
  Q175.S413414 2013
  501—dc23
  2013016467

ISBN: 978-0-415-82934-2 (hbk)
ISBN: 978-0-415-82936-6 (pbk)
ISBN: 978-0-203-36627-1 (ebk)

Typeset in Minion Pro
by Swales & Willis Ltd, Exeter, Devon, UK

Printed and bound in the United States of America by Sheridan Books, Inc. (a Sheridan Group Company).

CONTENTS

List of Figures, Definitions and Key Propositions   x
List of Symbols   xv
Foreword   xvii

1. Introduction: Where Do We Stand?   1
1.1 Tasks and Aims of Philosophy of Science   1
1.2 On the Historical Development of Philosophy of Science   3
1.3 Philosophical Positions in Contemporary Philosophy of Science   5
1.3.1 Logical Empiricism 5; 1.3.2 Critical Rationalism 7; 1.3.3 The Historical Account and Relativism 8; 1.3.4 Metaphysical and Scientific Realism 10; 1.3.5 Snapshots of Further Positions 12
1.4 Introductory Literature and Exercises   15

2. The Question of Unity: In Search of Common Foundations of the Sciences   16
2.1 Normative or Descriptive? The Method of Rational Reconstruction   16
2.2 Common Epistemological Assumptions   22
2.3 Common Methodological Features   25
2.4 Scientific Disciplines and Their Classification   27
2.4.1 The Special Status of Mathematical Sciences 30; 2.4.2 Testing the Common Foundations of Science 31; 2.4.3 Two Further Classifications of Sciences 34
2.5 The Question of Value-Neutrality   37
2.5.1 Max Weber's Value-Freedom Postulate and Its Critics 37; 2.5.2 Value-Neutrality and Means-End Inferences 39; 2.5.3 Explication of the Value-Neutrality Requirement 41

2.6 The Demarcation Problem and the Methodological
Unity of Sciences   44
2.6.1 Demarcation 44; 2.6.2 Methodological Unity Instead of Physical
Reductionism 46
2.7 Scientific Inference and Argumentation   49
2.7.1 Deduction and Induction 49; 2.7.2 Popper and the Significance of
Inductive Inference in the Sciences 52; 2.7.3 Abduction and Inference to the
Best Explanation 55; 2.7.4 Monotonic and Non-Monotonic Inferences 58

Complementary and Advanced Topics
2.8 How Much Metaphysics is Presupposed byScience?   59
2.8.1 Truth, Idealism and Realism 59; 2.8.2 Constructive Realism versus
Radical Constructivism 61
2.9 On the Theory (In)dependence of Observation   63
2.9.1 Theory-Dependency of Observation—Pros and Cons 65;
2.9.2 A Definition of Theory-Neutral Observation Concepts 72
2.10 Value-Neutrality in the Context of Contemporary Debates   75
2.10.1 The Role of Values in Science 75; 2.10.2 Value-Neutrality in the Context
of Meta-Ethics 77; 2.10.3 On the Difference between Sense Experiences and
Value "Experiences" 78
2.11 The Justification of Induction: An Unsolvable Problem?   80
2.12 Introductory Literature and Exercises   85

3 The Conceptual Toolkit: Language, Logic and Probability   **88**
3.1 Kinds and Classification of Concepts   88
3.1.1 The Logical Type of Concepts 88; 3.1.2 Formalization: Syntax and
Semantics, Statements and Models 92; 3.1.3 The Content Type of Concepts 96;
3.1.4 The Gradation (Scale) Type of Concepts 99
3.2 Classification of Sentences According to Their Content Type   105
3.2.1 Descriptive versus Prescriptive Sentences 106; 3.2.2 Observation and
Basic Sentences, Empirical and Theoretical Sentences 107
3.3 Logical Truth and Deductive Logic   110
3.4 Conventions of Meaning and Definitional Truths   113
3.5 Classification of Sentences According to Their Generality   117
3.6 General Sentences, Lawlikeness, Determinism and
Indeterminism   122
3.7 Content of Sentences and Kinds of Content   126
3.8 Verification, Falsification, Confirmation and Disconfirmation   128
3.9 Probability   129
3.9.1 Objective (Statistical) versus Epistemic (Subjective) Probability 129;
3.9.2 Mathematical Laws of Probability 133

Complementary and Advanced Topics
3.10 Disposition Concepts   135
3.11 Challenges to the Logical-Definitional-Synthetic Distinction   140

3.12 Relevance and Irrelevance in Logical Inferences   143
3.13 More on Probability   147
3.13.1 Construction of Probability Models and Sigma-Additivity 147;
3.13.2 Binomial Distribution and Law of Large Numbers 150; 3.13.3 Problems of Objective-Statistical Probability Concepts 152; 3.13.4 Problems of Subjective-Epistemic Probability Concepts 158; 3.13.5 Connections between Objective and Epistemic Probabilities: a Dualist Account 161
3.14 Introductory Literature and Exercises   168

4 A Question of Fit: Law Hypotheses and Their Empirical Testing   172
4.1 The Condition of Relevance   173
4.1.1 Relevance of Strict Laws 173; 4.1.2 Relevance of Statistical Laws 176
4.2 Testing of Strict Law Hypotheses for Truth and Relevance   181
4.2.1 The Method of Agreement and Difference 181; 4.2.2 Methodological Induction: How to Discover Strict Law Hypotheses 185
4.3 Testing Statistical Laws   188
4.3.1 Testing for Likely Truth and Acceptance Intervals 188; 4.3.2 Discovery of Statistical Hypotheses and Confidence Intervals 191; 4.3.3 Testing for Relevance and Significant Differences 193; 4.3.4 Statistical Representativity 196; 4.3.5 Test Statistics and Inference Statistics 198; 4.3.6 Sources of Error in Statistical Methods 200; 4.3.7 Applying Statistical Hypotheses to Individual Cases 203
4.4 Correlation and Causality   204
4.4.1 Hidden Variables 204; 4.4.2 Causal Direction 211

Complementary and Advanced Topics
4.5 Ceteris Paribus and Normic Laws   214
4.5.1 Comparative versus Exclusive CP Laws 214; 4.5.2 Normic Laws and Their Evolution-Theoretic Foundation 219
4.6 Probability Distributions for Continuous Variables   221
4.7 Bayesian Statistics   226
4.7.1 The Likelihood-Intuition: Objections and Replies 226; 4.7.2 The Bayesian Justification of the Likelihood-Intuition 229; 4.7.3 Objective Bayesianism and the Principle of Indifference 232; 4.7.4 Subjective Bayesianism and Convergence of Opinions 235
4.8 Introductory Literature and Exercises   238

5 Going Beyond Experience: Theories and Their Empirical Evaluation   242
5.1 Theoretical Concepts and Multiple Laws of Correspondence   242
5.2 The Example of Newtonian Physics   255
5.3 Theory Statics: The Structure of Scientific Theories   263
5.3.1 Components of Scientific Theories 263; 5.3.2 Theory Nets and Intertheoretical Relations 266

viii • Contents

5.4 Methodological Features of (Good) Scientific Theories 268
5.4.1 System Character: Holism of Meaning, Content, and Theory Testing (Duhem's Thesis) 268; 5.4.2 Empirical Creativity, Global Unification, and Novel Predictions: Answers to Hempel's Dilemma 270
5.5 The Example of Piaget's Theory of Cognitive Development 272
5.6 Theory Dynamics 278
5.6.1 Lakatos' Model of Theory Revision 278; 5.6.2 Theory Evaluation and Theory Progress 281

Complementary and Advanced Topics
5.7 Instrumentalism and Realism: The Ontology of Scientific Theories 291
5.7.1 Versions of Instrumentalism and Realism 291; 5.7.2 No Miracles Argument versus Pessimistic Meta-Induction 294; 5.7.3 Empirical Underdetermination and Use-Novel Evidence 295; 5.7.4 Intertheoretical Correspondence, Structural Realism and the Justification of Abduction 296
5.8 The Ramsey Sentence of a Theory: (Non-) Eliminability of Theoretical Concepts 299
5.8.1 Ramsey Sentence and Carnap Sentence 299; 5.8.2 Instrumentalist Interpretation of the Ramsey Sentence 301; 5.8.3 The Realist Interpretation of the Ramsey Sentence 303; 5.8.4 Lewis Definitions 305
5.9 Criteria for Theoreticity and Empirical Significance 307
5.9.1 Pre-Theoretical and Theoretical Concepts 307; 5.9.2 Empirical Significance 311
5.10 General Accounts of Confirmation 313
5.10.1 Hypothetico-Deductive Confirmation 314; 5.10.2 Bayesian Probabilistic Confirmation 318; 5.10.3 Bayesian Pseudo-Confirmation through Content-Cutting 320; 5.10.4 Latent Variables, Parameter Fitting and Use-Novel Evidence 322; 5.10.5 Curve Fitting 326; 5.10.6 Genuine Probabilistic Confirmation 329; 5.10.7 Goodman's Paradox 331; 5.10.8 Confirmation and Acceptance 333
5.11 Non-Confirmational Accounts of Theory Evaluation 336
5.11.1 Truthlikeness 336; 5.11.2 Unification, Coherence and Simplicity 340; 5.11.3 The Problem of Language Dependence 342
5.12 Introductory Literature and Exercises 345

6 In Search of Causes: Explanation and All That Goes With It 348
6.1 The Deductive-Nomological Model of Explanation 348
6.2 Explanation versus Prediction and Justification 351
6.2.1 Predictions without Explanatory Function 352; 6.2.2 Causality and Lawlikeness 353; 6.2.3 Explanations without Predictive Function 355; 6.2.4 Logical Problems of Irrelevance and Redundancy 356
6.3 Probabilistic Explanation Models 357
6.3.1 Inductive-Statistical Explanation 357; 6.3.2 Maximal Specificity 359; 6.3.3 Probabilistic and Causal Relevance Models 361; 6.3.4 Conflicting Intuitions about the Height of Explanatory Probabilities 362

6.4 Normic Explanations and the Explanation of Human Actions 365
6.5 Expectation, Causation and Unification: Explanation as a
Prototype Concept 367

Complementary and Advanced Topics
6.6 Lawlikeness 370
6.6.1 Laws of Nature versus System Laws 371; 6.6.2 Lawlikeness in the Wide versus Narrow Sense 372; 6.6.3 Lawlikeness i.w.s., Counterfactuals and Inductive Projectibility 373; 6.6.4 Spatiotemporal Universality and Maxwell's Condition 375; 6.6.5 The Best System Account 377; 6.6.6 Physical Necessity and Independent Possibility Knowledge 380

6.7 Causality 382
6.7.1 Singular and General Causality 382; 6.7.2 Regularity Accounts 384; 6.7.3 Counterfactuals and Causal Powers 385; 6.7.4 Causation and the Direction of Time 386; 6.7.5 Causal Processes and Mechanisms 387; 6.7.6 Interventionist Accounts 388; 6.7.7 Causality as a Theoretical Concept 389; 6.7.8 Axioms of Causality: C-connection, Productivity and Faithfulness 395; 6.7.9 Causal Discovery 402; 6.7.10 Empirical Content of GTC 403; 6.7.11 From Variables to Events: Overdetermination and Causal Pre-emption 406

6.8 Introductory Literature and Exercises 407

Bibliography 411

Solutions to Selected Exercises 435

Index of Names 440

Index of Subjects 447

LIST OF FIGURES, DEFINITIONS AND KEY PROPOSITIONS

Figures

2.1–1	The method of rational reconstruction	21
2.3–1	The three levels of the scientific method	28
2.4–1	Scientific disciplines	28
2.4–2	Classification of the factual sciences	35
2.5–1	Schematic representation of the value-neutrality requirement	43
2.7–1	The inductive-deductive scheme	51
2.7–2	Interaction of epistemic induction and abduction	57
2.9–1	Duck-rabbit	66
2.9–2	Mueller-Lyer-illusion	66
2.9–3	Expected learning curves in ostensive learning experiments	75
3.1–1	Division of concepts according to their logical type	89
3.1–2	Classification of concepts according to their content type	97
3.1–3	Classification of concepts according to their gradation type	99
3.1–4	Ordinal scale	101
3.2–1	Classification of sentences according to their content type	105
3.5–1	Classification of sentences according to their generality	118
3.5–2	Statistical generalizations	119
3.8–1	Testability of generalizations	129
3.9–1	Non-monotonicity of conditional probabilities	131

List of Figures, Definitions and Key Propositions • xi

3.13–1	Binomial distributions	152
4.1–1	Irrelevance and joke	177
4.3–1	Acceptance interval	189
4.3–2	Relationship between acceptance and confidence interval	192
4.3–3	Probability distribution of sample differences and significant difference	194
4.4–1	C is a common cause of A and B	205
4.4–2	Common cause vs. intermediate cause	207
4.4–3	Spurious causal independence	210
4.4–4	What is the direction of causality?	212
4.6–1	Normal distribution	222
4.7–1	Shortest 70% interval and two longer 70% intervals	228
4.7–2	A uniform density over μ (frequency) leads to a non-uniform density for λ (wavelength)	233
5.1–1	One theoretical feature causes many empirical dispositions	244
5.1–2	Beam balances and spring scales on Earth and Jupiter	249
5.2–1	Theory lattice in classical mechanics and its manifold applications	259
5.3–1	Subdivision of T according to T's language	265
5.3–2	Subdivision of T according to the logical and the conceptual nature of T's sentences	265
5.3–3	Subdivision of the axioms of T according to their epistemic status	265
5.3–4	Part of the theory net of physical and chemical theories	267
5.6–1	Historical theory sequence	281
5.6–2	T_1 is empirically more successful than T_2	285
5.6–3	Empirically complementary theories	286
5.6–4	Theories of optics	287
5.10–1	Curve fitting and independent evidence	328
6.7–1	Explanation of screening-off by binary causal relations	392
6.7–2	Linking-up	395
6.7–3	Three combinations of screening-off and linking-up	397
6.7–4	Non-faithfulness due to compensation of influences	401
6.7–5	Three strongly statistically indistinguishable graphs	403
6.7–6	Causal graph of variables and related graphs of values	407

Definitions

2.1–1	Method of rational reconstruction	20
2.5–1	General scheme of means-end inferences	39
2.7–1	Monotonicity	58

xii • List of Figures, Definitions and Key Propositions

2.9–1	Theory-neutral observation concepts	74
3.2–1	Descriptive versus prescriptive sentences	106
3.2–2	Observational, empirical, and (T-) theoretical sentences	108
3.3–1	Logical truth	110
3.3–2	Logical validity	112
3.4–1	Definitional truth	113
3.5–1	Essential sentence types	121
3.7–1	Logical and empirical content	126
3.8–1	Verification, falsification, confirmation and disconfirmation	128
3.9–1	Statistical and subjective probability	130
3.9–2	Conditional probability	131
3.9–3	Principle of narrowest reference class	132
3.10–1	Bilateral reduction sentence	137
3.10–2	Nomological definition of dispositions	137
3.12–1	Relevance in logical inferences	144
3.12–2	Relevant elements	146
3.12–3	Relevant content	147
3.12–4	Irreducible representation	147
4.1–1	Relevance for strict law hypotheses	173
4.1–2	Statistical relevance for conjunctive antecedents	180
4.3–1	Acceptance interval	190
4.3–2	Significant difference	194
4.6–1	Mean, variance and standard deviation	223
5.8–1	Ramsey sentence	299
5.8–2	Carnap sentence	300
5.8–3	Ramsey-Lewis sentence	305
5.9–1	Pre-theoreticity and T-theoreticity	307
5.9–2	External theoreticity	308
5.10–1	Classical HD-confirmation	314
5.10–2	Relevant HD-confirmation	317
5.10–3	Bayesian confirmation	318
5.10–4	Genuine confirmation	330
5.10–5	Goodman's grue predicate	331
5.11–1	Popper-truthlikeness	337
5.11–2	Formal Popper-truthlikeness	337
5.11–3	Schurz/Weingartner-truthlikeness	339
6.6–1	Spatiotemporal universality	375
6.7–1	Causal connection axiom	396
6.7–2	Causal Markov condition	398
6.7–3	Faithfulness	400
6.7–4	Productivity axiom	400

6.7–5	Empirical content of GTC	404
6.7–6	Cause-effect relation between values of variables	406

Key Propositions

2.1–1	Supreme epistemic goal of science	19
2.5–1	Value neutrality requirement	42
2.7–1	General pattern of abduction	56
2.7–2	Inference to the best explanation	56
2.7–3	Application rule for monotonic inferences	59
2.7–4	Application rule for non-monotonic inferences	59
3.1–1	Translation between logic and set-theory	95
3.1–2	Linguistic and model-theoretic theory representation	96
3.4–1	Empirical non-creativity	116
3.5–1	Important logical relationships	120
3.9–1	Basic axioms of probability	134
3.9–2	Theorems of unconditional probability	134
3.9–3	Theorems of conditional probability	135
3.12–1	Relevant elements	147
3.13–1	Binomial formula	151
3.13–2	Subjective probabilities as fair betting quotients	159
3.13–3	Single case principal principle	161
3.13–4	Statistical principal principle	162
3.13–5	Exchangeable probability functions	165
3.13–6	Uniform inductive learning	165
3.13–7	Rule of strict conditionalization	167
4.1–1	Statistical relevance for binary properties	178
4.2–1	Method of agreement and difference	185
4.3–1	Testing statistical law hypotheses	195
4.4–1	Reichenbach conditions for screening-off	206
4.5–1	Comparative CP law	214
4.5–2	Exclusive CP assertion	215
4.5–3	CP-laws explicated in terms of variables	216
4.5–4	Normic interpretation of eCP laws	219
4.6–1	Mean value and standard deviation of sample means	224
4.7–1	Principle of Bayes statistics	230
4.7–2	Bayesian justification of the likelihood-intuition	231
4.7–3	Posterior probability	231
4.7–4	Probabilities obtained from indifference	233
4.7–5	Continuous convergence	236
4.7–6	Simple convergence results	237
4.7–7	Biased priors	238

5.1–1	Synthetic nature of laws of correspondence	246
5.1–2, 3	Biased indicators	254/5
5.4–1	Holism of testing	269
5.4–2	Empirical creativity	270
5.6–1	Falsification of theory versions	282
5.6–2, 3	Successes and failures of theory versions	282
5.6–4	Confirmation of theory versions	283
5.6–5	Dynamical truthlikeness	284
5.6–6	Theory comparison and progress	285
5.6–7	Rational acceptability of theory versions	288
5.6–8	Empirical excess content	289
5.6–9	Confirmation of theory cores	290
5.6–10	Preference between theory cores	290
5.6–11	Rational acceptability of theory cores	290
5.7–1	Correspondence theorem	297
5.8–1	Newman's problem	302
5.9–1	Direct laws of correspondence	308
5.9–2	Empirically well-founded theory nets	309
5.10–1	HD- and Bayes-confirmation	319
5.10–2	Bayesian pseudo-confirmation	321
5.10–3	Spread of probability increase	330
6.1–1	DN-explanation of events	348
6.1–2	DN-explanation of laws	351
6.2–1	Lawlikeness and causality in DN-explanations	355
6.2–2	Predictive function	355
6.2–3	Logical relevance of DN-explanations	357
6.3–1	Inductive-statistical explanation	358
6.3–2	Maximal specificity	359
6.4–1	Normic explanation	367
6.5–1	Unification condition	369
6.6–1	Spatiotemporal universality	376
6.6–2	Maxwell's condition	377
6.6–3	Physical necessity	381
6.7–1	Connection between singular and general causality	383
6.7–2	Causal Markov and causal connection condition	398
6.7–3	Productivity and minimality	400
6.7–4	Faithfulness and parameter-stability	401
6.7–5	Causal discovery algorithm	402
6.7–6, 7, 8	Empirical content of general causality theory	404/5/6

LIST OF SYMBOLS

$\neg$	not
$\wedge$	and
$\vee$	or
$\rightarrow$	if-then
$\leftrightarrow$	equivalent (if-and-only-if)
$\leftrightarrow_{def}$	equivalent by definition
$\forall x$	for all x
$\exists x$	there exists an x
$\exists! x$	there exists exactly one x
$=$	identical
$\neq$	not identical
$=_{def}$	identical by definition
$\Box$	necessary
$\in$	is an element of
$\{a_1,\ldots,a_n\}$	set of individuals
$(a_1,\ldots,a_n)$	ordered sequence of individuals
$\{x: Fx\}$	set of individuals which possess property F
$\subseteq$	proper or improper subset
$\subset$	proper subset
$\cap$	intersection
$\cup$	union
$-$	applied to sets: set-theoretical complement
$\times$	Cartesian product between sets
$\cdot$	ordinary product between numbers
$/$	divided by (example: $x \cdot y/z$ = x times y divided by z)
$\emptyset$	empty set

$\Sigma_{i \in I} x_i$ and $\Pi_{i \in I} x_i$	sum and product (respectively) over all x_i with i in I
D	domain
D^n	n-fold Cartesian product of D
I	interpretation function
$\mathcal{L}$	formal language
$M(\mathcal{L})$	set of models for language L
$\leq$	smaller than or equal to
$\geq$	greater than or equal to
$\equiv$	equivalence relation
f:A→B	function from domain A into set of values B
$\models$	verifies (makes true)
$\vdash$	is derivable from
$\Vdash$	follows logically from
$\nVdash$	does not follow logically from
$\dashv\Vdash$	is logically equivalent with
p	statistical probability
P	epistemic probability
C(S) and C_r(S)	logical content and relevant logical content of a sentence set S
E(S) and E_r(S)	empirical content and relevant empirical content of a sentence set S
Ω	possibility space
AL	algebra
$\|A\|$	semantic extension of formula A
df(x)/dx	first derivative of f(x)
$\sqrt{}$	square root
$\int$	integral
$\lim_{n \to \infty}$	limit for n going to infinity
R(T)	Ramsey sentence of theory T
(IN)DEP(X,Y)	variables X and Y are probabilistically (in)dependent

FOREWORD

I have written *Philosophy of Science: A Unified Approach* for beginners as well as for graduate students and experts. This twofold orientation is reflected in the major structure of the chapters, which start with introductory sections for beginners, followed by sections entitled "complementary and advanced topics," in which these topics are explained in a condensed way, including presentations of my own accounts. In this way, the book attempts to offer not only an introduction, but also a detailed overview of the various areas of the Philosophy of Science and their interrelations, which will help the reader familiarize him- or herself with the present state of the art in this field.

The book addresses itself both to philosophers and to scientists of all disciplines. By way of bridging Philosophy of Science with neighboring fields such as statistics, hermeneutics, cognitive science, the debate on science and values, and detailed examples of contemporary theories in sciences and humanities, this book tries to convey a deep understanding of the sciences and their methods. The book is *self-contained* and written without presuppositions about the readers. On rare occasions formulas are used, but I have always explained them in a clear and easy-to-follow language.

Although this book introduces the reader into all major areas of Philosophy of Science, it also has a bias and a general philosophical message. Concerning the bias, the author understands himself as a follower of logically and empirically oriented philosophers of science such as Carnap, Hempel, Reichenbach, and Stegmüller in the German-speaking area. The book's general message is reflected in its subtitle, "A Unified Approach." Behind the diversity of phenomena investigated in disciplines as different as elementary particle physics and social sciences, or chemistry and linguistics, one can recognize a deep common ground which unites all of the sciences. This unity, however, is not so much a unity at the level of objects (as was claimed by the proponents of physical reductionism), but rather a *methodological unity*. Chapter 2 of the book is concentrated on finding the common methodological features of the sciences and their epistemological presuppositions. The remaining chapters will not only work out these common features in detail, but will reveal also some important differences between characteristic groups of disciplines, such as the physical sciences versus special sciences (e.g. biology, psychology or social sciences).

Use in teaching: Restricting the teaching materials to Chapters 1–5, and omitting all sections on advanced topics, will give the basis for a semester-long, two hour per week course. Covering all of the material contained in the book will fill two such courses. The *core materials* of this book are highlighted in the form of *definitions* and *key propositions*.

Conventions for numbering: The numbering of figures follows the following pattern: "Fig. SecNo.-No.," where "SecNo." is the two-digit section-number, and "No." the number of the figure within the section. Example: "Fig. 2.1-2" is the 2nd figure of sec. 2.1. In the same way *definitions* are numbered with "(Def. SecNo.-No.)," *key propositions* with "(Prop. SecNo.-No.)," and *examples* or other *indented* passages with "(SecNo.-No.)." Example: "(Def. 4.2-2)" is the 2nd definition of sec. 4.2; "(3.1-4)" is the 4th example of sec. 3.1.

At the end of every chapter the reader finds hints on selected literature, and exercises. The book concludes with a comprehensive bibliography and several indices.

This textbook is a revised and significantly extended English elaboration of my German Introduction to Philosophy of Science (*Einführung in die Wissenschaftstheorie*). The introduction has been developed from a series of lectures in the Philosophy of Science that I have given at the Universities of Salzburg, Erfurt, Düsseldorf and, less frequently, at other universities, including California at Irvine, Yale, Vienna, Helsinki, Graz, and Fribourg.

Parts of the text of the German edition have been pre-translated into English by Fergal Treanor. For valuable help concerning matters of content I am indebted to Ioannis Votsis, Paul Thorn, Hannes Leitgeb, Wolfgang Spohn, Martin Carrier, Franz Huber, Markus Werning, Oliver Scholz, Andreas Hüttemann, Markus Schrenk, Hans Rott, Wolfgang Balzer, Gernot Kleiter, Theo Kuipers, Ilkka Niiniluoto, Erik Olsson, Stephan Hartmann, Jon Williamson, Igor Douven, Ken Gemes, James Ladyman, John Worrall, Stathis Psillos, James Hawthorne, Alan

Musgrave, Mathias Frisch, Clark Glymour, Kevin Kelly, Horacio Arló-Costa, and Alvin Goldman. What remains on my side is to wish the readers of this book that it shall bring them much fun and intellectual profit.

Gerhard Schurz, Düsseldorf, March 2013

1
INTRODUCTION: WHERE DO WE STAND?

1.1 Tasks and Aims of Philosophy of Science

Science plays a determining role in the life of today's society. In what sense and to what degree can we trust the results of science? There is a scientific discipline, which examines such questions systematically: the *Philosophy of Science*, which in the German language is called "Wissenschaftstheorie" ("Theory of Science"). Following the German usage of the word, I always understand "science" ("Wissenschaft") in its *broad* meaning—including, besides natural sciences, also social sciences, humanities, etc.

The discipline of philosophy (or theory) of science investigates how scientific knowledge works—its goals and its methods, its achievements and its limitations. Like any other scientific discipline, philosophy of science has historically developed out of philosophy. In the present days it is practiced both by philosophers and by scientists of various disciplines.

One distinguishes between the *general* philosophy of science, and philosophies of *particular* sciences. The latter ones are concerned with special kinds of disciplines such as philosophy of physics, biology, psychology, the social sciences or the humanities. The general philosophy of sciences discovers those components of knowledge that are more or less common to all scientific disciplines. Its main questions are:

1   How is a scientific language constructed?
2   What are the rules of correct scientific reasoning, or argument?

2 • Philosophy of Science

3   What are the distinctive features of a scientific observation or "datum"?
4   What is a scientific law, and what does a scientific theory consist of?
5   How are law hypotheses and theories empirically tested? When do they count as confirmed, and when as refuted? What are the criteria for scientific progress?
6   What is achieved by a scientific explanation and what is causality?

This book focuses on these questions of the general philosophy of science, and the following chapters are arranged in corresponding order to the above questions. At the same time, we shall also deal with applications and topics of the philosophies of particular sciences, and examine characteristic *differences* between different branches of science. The most *general* questions of philosophy of science include:

7   Is there an objectively discoverable reality, and an objective truth?
8   What connection exists between science and value judgments?

Question 7 lies on the border between philosophy of science and epistemology (see sec. 2.8), and question 8 on the border with meta-ethics (see sec. 2.5, 2.10).

Beyond its fundamental significance, which consists in providing answers to the above questions, philosophy of science also has a number of significant *applications*, both inside and outside science.

The *internal* applications of philosophy of science consist of the supply of foundational knowledge, which aids the scientist's decisions concerning new or controversial questions. Internal applications also consist of working out *interdisciplinary* common ground and providing *argumentative* competence in critical reflection. Not least, philosophy of science has often paved the way for new scientific disciplines (such as probability theory and statistics, measurement theory, or parts of cognitive science).

Among the *external* applications of philosophy of science to problems in a societal context, two in particular should be emphasized:

a   The *demarcation* problem is highly significant in society. In this context, it consists of the question of which of our ideas have a claim to the status of objective scientific knowledge that should be taught in public educational institutions, as opposed to subjective opinion, political values, ideologies, or religious convictions. This question became politically explosive in the controversy surrounding the creationism movement in the USA. For example, Judge W. R. Overton in 1981 (*McLean* vs. *Arkansas*), and Judge Jones in 2005 (*Kitzmiller* vs. *Dover*) based their decisions against the teaching of creationism in school on demarcation criteria between science and religious belief proposed by philosophers of science (cf. Bird 1998, 2–9; Branch 2011, 174). To tell the full truth, there were also philosophers of science, such as Laudan (1983), who argued against the possibility of demarcating science from pseudo-science, and they have frequently been quoted by creationists as support for their position (to the embarrassment of other philosophers; cf. Pennock 2011, 176ff).

b   Equally significant is the critical role of philosophy of science concerning the commercial and political utilization of science, which counteracts the danger of *abusing* science and its results. Politicians, the media and business leaders enjoy quoting expert opinions, which are presented all too often in a false or one-sided way in order to serve preordained purposes (sec. 2.10.1, 4.3.6–7, 4.4). But also applied scientists are often tempted to put subjective (e.g. financial) interests above objectivity. An example is the discovery of systematic biases in pharmaceutical research towards the financially supporting firms; philosophers of science have promoted scientific journal policies that may help to counteract such biases (Brown 2008).

1.2 On the Historical Development of Philosophy of Science

Although the term "philosophy of science" was only introduced in the 20th century, the philosophy of science is as old as science itself and had a parallel development (see Losee 2001). The history of the philosophy of science begins with *Aristotle* (384–322 BC), the ancient world's great systematizer of knowledge. Aristotle was much more oriented towards experience than was his teacher Plato. He was nevertheless, like most philosophers after him, a follower of the *foundationalist* epistemological program. In this epistemological program it is presumed that real knowledge is only possible if it stands on a foundation of certain and necessary principles, which are arrived at *not* through uncertain experience, but through rational intuition (cf. Triplett 1990, sec. I; Albert 1985, 18–28). Aristotle spoke in this context of "intuitive induction" (Losee 2001, sec. Ia). In current philosophy of science, by contrast, the *fallibilist* epistemological program has the upper hand, which concedes that our understanding of reality is basically *fallible*, and our scientific knowledge can be more or less well confirmed, but it cannot be guaranteed to be free of error.

Considerable advances in science and its philosophy had already been achieved by the late middle ages (Crombie 1959). Under the influence of philosophers such as *Roger Bacon* (1214–1292) or *William von Ockham* (1295–1349), the foundationalist program was gradually replaced by empirically oriented methodology. Of lasting importance is the principle of *Ockham's razor*, according to which one should reject all theoretical assumptions which are not needed to explain the observable. The decisive breakthrough, however, did not take place until the early modern period. Building on the great successes of scientific method in this historical period—thanks to pioneers such as *Galileo Galilei* (1564–1642), *Isaac Newton* (1642–1727) and (later) *Charles Darwin* (1809–1882)—the influential *empiricist* movement was established in the Philosophy, beginning with *Francis Bacon* (1561–1626) and *John Locke* (1632–1704) until *David Hume* (1711–1776) and *John Stuart Mill* (1806–1873). In the same period, the foundationalist epistemological program developed into the *rationalist* movement, prominently represented by *René Descartes* (1596–1650), *Gottfried W. Leibniz* (1646–1716) and *Immanuel Kant* (1724–1804).

The essential difference between the empiricist and rationalist philosophies can be characterized as follows. For the empiricists, sentences which may be justified *a priori*—that is, by pure reason and with rational certainty—are limited to so-called *analytical sentences*, i.e. sentences whose truth is based on logic and conceptual convention. Such sentences possess no realistic content, they say nothing about the real world—only *synthetic* sentences can do this, but they can only be justified *a posteriori*, that is, based on experience. For the rationalists, on the other hand, a-priori justifiable sentences with realistic content do exist, namely the so-called *synthetic a-priori* sentences. However, both Descartes' and Kant's attempts to justify synthetic a-priori principles of the sciences were unsuccessful and have been refuted by the further development of science. The development of the modern philosophy of science is closely bound with the insight that the foundationalist epistemological program was not tenable—at least not in its "strong" version as explained above.

For a long time, classical systems of philosophical empiricism too had reductionist and foundationalist tendencies. The skeptical consequences of empiricism, which called for epistemic humility, were first recognized and radically formulated by Hume. He showed that the two central tenets of scientific method, the *causality principle* and the *induction principle*, are neither logically nor empirically justifiable. The causality principle says that all regular successions between events are produced by cause–effect relations; but Hume objected that all that one can observe are the successions of the events, while the idea that the earlier event or "cause" produces the later event as its "effect" is metaphysical fiction (see sec. 6.7.2). The induction principle asserts that regular connections between events that have been observed in the past will also hold in the future; but Hume argued that this inference can be justified neither by logic nor by experience (see sec. 2.11). The problems involved in the justification of the principles of induction and causality have occupied philosophers up to the present day.

The apparent *insufficient justifiability* of empiricism put wind in the sails of subsequent rationalist movements, in which the foundationalist epistemological program, however, was gradually given up, or replaced by pragmatized or historicized "rationalisms" (see sec. 1.3.3–5). In the 20th century, *post-empiricist* and *post-rationalist* approaches have moved considerably closer to each other, and in the context of this tension, present-day philosophy of science has developed.

1.3 Philosophical Positions in Contemporary Philosophy of Science

1.3.1 Logical Empiricism

One of the most important origins of modern Philosophy of Science and Analytical Philosophy is logical empiricism, which was developed in particular by the Vienna circle, but also by others, for example by members of the Berlin circle around Hans Reichenbach (1891–1953). The *Vienna circle* was a group of philosophers and scientists in Vienna, whose core consisted of Moritz Schlick (1882–1936), Otto Neurath (1882–1945) and Rudolf Carnap (1891–1970). In the tradition of Ernst Mach (1838–1916), this group attempted to re-establish empiricism and scientific philosophy in general (cf. Stadler 2001). What was new about their situation was the development of *modern logic*, which had not been founded until the end of the 19th century. Modern logic made it possible to represent any language-based epistemological system with mathematical precision, and so the Vienna circle hoped they had found at last the methodological equipment for a philosophy which could progress in a scientific manner (cf. Schlick 1930/31, 155f). In the middle of the 1930s the Vienna circle, with political leanings from liberal to socialist, had to disband under pressure from the National Socialists. The majority of its members emigrated, some via other countries, to the USA, where the logical-empirical movement, uniting with related Anglo-American directions, developed into Analytical Philosophy, and gained a foothold in Europe in the post-war period.

What today's philosophy of science can learn from logical empiricism is not so much any particular thesis but, rather, the high standards of conceptual and argumentative precision. In the phase up to 1935, the philosophy of science of logical empiricism was restricted by *positivism* and *reductionism*. In the later phase, the logical empiricists gradually rejected their restricted positions and replaced them with theses, to which the designations "empiricism" or "positivism" in the usual sense *no longer apply*. In one regard, logical empiricism has parted company with its classical predecessors early on: with the refutation of the classical empiricist thesis that at least "direct" observation reports are infallible. In the so-called protocol sentence debate, Neurath and Carnap—but not Schlick—became convinced that even observation sentences such as "there is a table there" are, in principle, fallible. Empiricism, according to this new view, just meant that observation sentences have an epistemically favored role within the whole system of discovery (cf. Carnap 1932/33; Neurath 1934, 113).

Empirical *reductionism*, in contrast, was retained for quite some time. Classical empiricism advocated the following reductionist thesis: all "serious" scientific concepts must be translatable via a chain of definitions into observational concepts. This program of reduction was adopted by logical empiricism in its early phase (Carnap 1928a). Later, however, the view prevailed that *theoretical concepts* such as "power," "electrical field," or "human character" *cannot* be defined by observational concepts but, rather, go far beyond the immediately observable (Carnap 1956a; Hempel 1951). In the so-called *standard* philosophy of science of the 1960s, the classical empiricist epistemological model had already broken down. What remained was a *minimal empiricism*, which consisted of the requirement that scientific theories must have empirical consequences, by means of which they can be tested.

A similarly modest empiricism is defended by contemporary empiricists such as van Fraassen (1980, 2002). He does not only reject infallibilism and reductionism, but also the *linguistic* orientation of logical empiricism. Instead, he defends a semantic conception of theories, in which theories are regarded not as sets of sentences, but as sets of conceptual models, similar to a structuralistic philosophy of science (cf. sec. 3.1.2). Characteristic of van Fraassen's empiricism (1980, sec. 1) are two ingredients: First, a defense of the concept of theory-independent observation against Kuhn-followers (see sec. 1.3.3 below). Second, his rejection of scientific realism in favor of an instrumentalist position, according to which the theoretical (i.e. non-observable) part of a theory can only be reasonably said to be more or less *empirically adequate*, but not true or false. In this latter respect, van Fraassen is more restrictive than Carnap (e.g. 1928a) who always argued for ontological *pluralism*, according to which both realism and instrumentalism are possible practical attitudes towards scientific theories.

Two boundaries, which early logical empiricism had tried to maintain, became permeable in contemporary "minimal" empiricism. First, the boundary between *science* and *metaphysics* became porous: it turned out that principles which are of no empirical consequence *in isolation*, may give rise to new empirical consequences when joined with other theoretical sentences (see sec. 5.4.2; Hempel 1951, 115; Stegmüller 1969ff, vol. II.1, 293–5). In this way, the *post-positivist* philosophy of science gained new access to the discussion of metaphysical principles such as realism and causality. Second, the boundary between analytic and synthetic sentences became porous when it was recognized that the meaning of theoretical terms is not determined by isolated definitions, but by the respective background theory as a whole (Carnap 1956a, 1963). In parallel fashion, Quine (1951) argued that in *natural*, empirically present languages, no clear criterion exists by which one could undertake a demarcation between analytic and synthetic sentences.

As a consequence of this, analytical philosophy's *linguistic* orientation (e.g. Carnap 1950a) was gradually given up. Linguistically oriented philosophers try to answer all philosophical questions by means of semantical concept analysis. However, if a clear divide between (analytic) questions of meaning and (synthetic) questions of fact is missing, this exclusively linguistic orientation is no longer tenable. For this reason, Carnap (1956b, suppl. E) started to work on a system of pragmatics. Later on, Quine (1974) developed a *naturalistic* view, according to which science and philosophy form a continuum, the latter's theses also having to be corroborated by experience.

1.3.2 Critical Rationalism

Also associated with the Vienna circle was *Karl Popper* (1902–1994), the founder of so-called critical rationalism. From the beginning, Popper's theory of science displayed the very non-reductionist tendencies that logical empiricism had accepted only after years in transition. According to Popper, scientific theories may go any distance beyond our experience, as long as they are empirically testable. Popper's tests consist of *falsification attempts*, which should be as severe as possible. Popper supported his emphasis on falsification (instead of verification) by citing the *asymmetry* of *verification* and *falsification* of strictly universal hypotheses such as: "all metals conduct electricity." Such hypotheses cannot be verified by any finite number of observations, because they speak about a potentially infinite domain of instances—in our example, all metals in the past and in the future. However, these hypotheses can be falsified by a single observed exception (Popper 1935/2000, sec. I–IV).

For Popper, falsifiability was the decisive criterion of *demarcation* between science and speculation: scientific theories are not verifiable, but they must be falsifiable. Once falsified, they are *rejected* as false; but if they withstand many-fold falsification attempts, they are viewed as *corroborated*.

Popper's falsificationism was also subjected to diverse criticism in the discussion which followed. Lakatos (1970) pointed out that scientific theories are almost never rejected on the basis of one single counter-example, but may be immunized against conflicts with recalcitrant data by means of modifications that are usually more or less *ad hoc* (see sec. 5.6.1). Popper's *anti-inductionism*—i.e. his thesis that science could progress without making any use of induction—also came in for harsh criticism (see sec. 2.7.2).

Popper's critical rationalism is far removed from classical rationalism. Nowhere in Popper's philosophy is it claimed that real discoveries can be grounded in non-empirical a-priori intuition; on the contrary, Popper always rejected this. Thus, Popper's philosophy is *post-rationalist* just as that of the late logical empiricists is *post-positivist*. Popper stressed more strongly than late logical empiricism, however, that observation sentences are not only fallible, but also *theoretically biased*, so that the borderline between observational and theoretical terms cannot be sharply drawn (1935/2002, sec. V.30 addendum; new app. X). With this argumentation critical rationalism opened its doors to the attacks from historical relativism, to which we now turn.

1.3.3 The Historical Account and Relativism

At the end of the 1950s, the historian of science Thomas Kuhn (1962) rattled the scientific world by presenting a fundamental attack on the standard philosophy of science. Factual science, said Kuhn, behaves differently from the normative ideals "prescribed" by the philosophers of science. The alternative scientific model developed by Kuhn takes more of a historical-sociological than a logical-cognitive approach. According to Kuhn, scientific development takes place on the basis of so-called *paradigms*, such as the paradigm of classical (Newtonian) physics or (Darwin's) theory of evolution. A Kuhnian paradigm contains at least the following three components: (i) very general theoretical principles or models, (ii) typical examples of successful applications, and (iii) methodological-normative assumptions (cf. Kuhn 1977; Hoyningen-Huene 1993; Schurz 1998a). The sociological correlate of a paradigm is a *scientific community*, a community of experts in the given field, that sticks to a paradigm and works on its further development. According to Kuhn, a paradigm determines not only the fundamental principles, the major open problems and the *interpretation* of observed data—no, it even determines the observed data *themselves*, because according to this view, *all observation is theory-laden*, and hence theoretically biased. For Kuhn, there is no observation which is neutral of background theory or paradigm. Kuhn takes this strong thesis from Hanson (1958).

According to Kuhn, scientific development takes place in two successive phases, a *normal* and a *revolutionary* phase. Common acceptance of a paradigm makes the continuous growth of knowledge possible in the normal phase of a scientific discipline. When recalcitrant data, so-called *anomalies*, resist explanation by the given paradigm, the conflict is settled by more or less *ad-hoc* modifications of current versions of theories within the accepted paradigm. Should such anomalies become more frequent, however, younger scholars will begin to look for a *new* paradigm. As soon as one is found, scientific development enters a revolutionary phase for a certain time, in which two paradigms struggle for supremacy. Kuhn's examples (1962) include the transition from Ptolemaic to Copernican astronomy and from Newtonian to Einsteinian physics. Kuhn claims that there are no common standards of rationality during a paradigm change and all empirical data are seen by the new paradigm in a new way. For this reason the two competing paradigms are, according to Kuhn's "notorious" *incommensurability thesis*, rationally incomparable. So the struggle for supremacy does not take place in the form of a comparison of cognitive achievement, but rather in the form of a *power struggle*, in which supporters of the old paradigm eventually die out, as a result of which the new paradigm prevails, and a new normal scientific phase is heralded in.

Kuhn's alternative model of science was the subject of much controversial discussion in the decades that followed. As well as an opposition to Kuhn, both a moderate and a more radical branch of Kuhn-followers were formed (cf. Hoyningen-Huene 1993, 212f). A moderate Kuhn-follower, and a Popper-follower at the same time, is Lakatos and his conception of scientific research programs (see sec. 5.6.1). Another moderate Kuhn-follower is Laudan (1981/96) who challenged scientific realism: based on the history of science he gave various counterexamples to the view that the empirical success of theories is a reliable indicator of their approximate truth (see sec. 5.7.2). The more radical group gave relativism a strong impetus—most prominently in Feyerabend's "Anarchist Epistemology" (1975). Feyerabend, with his maxim "anything goes," argued against methodological rules that are guiding or should guide science.

The standard philosophy of science was unable to effectively counter the argument of the theory-dependence of scientific observations and its relativistic consequences. For all questions about the cognitive nature of observation had been banned by the narrowed perspective of the *logic* of science. For Popper, the question of what should be called an observation sentence was a question of pure convention (1935/2002, sec. V.30). The logical empiricists saw it in much the same way. It will be shown in sec. 2.9.2 that a different picture results as soon as we take on an *empirical-cognitive* perspective. After all: if there were no difference between what experience *shows*, and what theory leads us to *expect*, then empirical science would be an exercise in *permanent self-deception*. Any theory of the empirical sciences which cannot explain this central difference must be extremely unsatisfying.

1.3.4 Metaphysical and Scientific Realism

In reaction to the shortcomings of the logical-empirical model of science, many philosophers have suggested returning to the metaphysical approaches of realism and necessity, from which the philosophy of science in the early 20th century had tried to free itself. For example, it is a consequence of post-positivist philosophy of science that the term "mass" actually has different *meanings* in Newtonian and Einsteinian physics. This theory-dependence was also one of the main pillars of Kuhn's incommensurability thesis. The early Putnam (e.g. 1975b, 219ff, 229–235, 240f), together with Kripke (1972, 55–59), developed the following argumentation against this consequence: scientific progress in the sense of a movement towards objective truth is only possible if the *reference* of scientific terms, i.e. their relationship to reality, *is rigidly fixed* with metaphysical necessity, in the sense that this reference stays the same in all possible theories and across all possible worlds. Kripke and Putnam assumed the reference fixation to take place by acts of baptizing, together with a rigid sameness-relation between natural kinds, with the result that statements such as "water is H_2O" become true by "metaphysical necessity" (see also Shoemaker 1980).

We agree with Kripke and Putnam that the meaning of natural kind terms such as "water" cannot be learned by an empirical definition (as in Carnap's 1956b account), but by acts of ostension ("this is water") grasping the right sameness-in-kind relation between water-exemplars. But as a number of arguments have shown, scientific knowledge cannot rigidly determine sameness-in-kind relations and the reference of (theoretical) concepts.[1] Scientific classification systems, e.g. for chemical substances or biological species, are dependent on the scientific background knowledge which undergoes historical change (Hendry 2008). The idea that a necessary relationship between language and experience can be established independently of experience is, in the end, a regression towards a foundationalist epistemic model. In fact, the later Putnam (1977, 1982) relinquished his earlier metaphysical realism by arguing as follows: if neither our empirical nor our theoretical knowledge can determine the reference of our concepts in a unique way, then *nothing* can do this—the consequence is an unavoidable "indeterminacy of reference." The same indeterminacy of reference has been worked out by Quine, but while Quine remained a naturalistic realist, the late Putnam adopted a more or less idealistic position that he called "internal realism."

An account of necessity that is metaphysical in a weaker sense than the above ones is Armstrong (1983). According to him, laws of nature supervene on an assumed necessitation relation between "universals" (such as "water" and "H_2O"), which is, however, *contingent*—i.e. these necessities may be different in different possible worlds (sec. 6.6.6). A similar middle ground between metaphysics and empiricism is Lewis (1973a/1986, 1973b), who developed a possible worlds semantics for counterfactual and causal conditionals, but at the same time defends an elaborated Humean account to laws of nature, according to which laws supervene on empirical facts (sec. 6.6.5). More recently Mumford (1998) and Bird (2007) have developed an account of metaphysical necessity according to which laws of nature supervene on the dispositional properties of the objects to which they apply (sec. 3.10; for criticisms cf. Schrenk 2010).

In contrast to metaphysical realism, scientific realism argues for convergence of science towards truth, not by metaphysical assumptions but by empirical arguments from the history of science. According to Putnam's famous "no miracles" argument (1975a, 73), the empirical success of science would be a sheer miracle without the assumption that the more-and-more successful theories are converging to the objective truth. The no miracles argument has been criticized by Laudan (1981/96) and van Fraassen (1989, sec. 5–6, 2006, 296) among others, and defended by Boyd (1984) and Psillos (1999). This has initiated an enduring debate in philosophy of science, in which weaker forms of realism have been defended (see sec. 5.7.2–4).

1.3.5 Snapshots of Further Positions

1.3.5.1 Pragmatic Philosophy of Science

In the 1980s, several authors spoke of a *pragmatic turn* in Philosophy of Science (Stegmüller 1969ff, vol. I, sec. XI; Böhler et al. 1986; Bernstein 2010). Unfortunately, however, pragmatic philosophy and the use of the term "pragmatics" in general, falls into two *opposing* camps. While one camp (e.g. Peirce 1931ff; Rescher 1998, 2001; van Fraassen 1980; Schurz 1998b) understands pragmatics in the *epistemically internal* sense, the other camp (e.g. James 1907; Rorty 1982; Stich 1990; to some extent Putnam 1995; Bernstein 2010) sees pragmatics in an *epistemically external* sense.

For the epistemically external camp, the pragmatic components of discovery are essential, but have nothing to do with its truth. In contrast, for the epistemically internal camp, it is these very pragmatic components, which are supposed to establish an objective conception of truth in a non-circular sense. The epistemically external camp makes knowledge (or justified belief) dependent on *any* kind of interests, be it predictive accuracy, political control, or emotional well-being, and sees therein a compelling argument for the unavoidable subjectivity of knowledge. In this sense, Stich (1990, 131ff) has argued that there are as many different conceptions of truth as there are different cognition-guiding interests. In contrast, for the internal camp the reference to epistemically *internal* purposes is the very thing which makes possible a non-circular foundation of knowledge. For example, the reference to the cognitive purpose of maximizing true predictions enables a justification of induction that escapes Hume's skeptical challenge (sec. 2.11). In conclusion, the external and the internal camp *differ so greatly* in their understanding of pragmatics, that they should not be subsumed under a single term. For this reason, I have avoided using the term "pragmatic" of late, in contrast to earlier works (Schurz 1998b).

1.3.5.2 Structuralist Philosophy of Science

In search of a better defense against the Kuhnian offensive, Stegmüller (1976; 1977, vol. II., sec. 6; 1979b) suggested replacing the "statement view" of the standard philosophy of science with a so-called "non-statement view." Stegmüller's suggestion is based on the idea, traceable to Suppes (1999/1957, 246ff) and Sneed (1971), that it is better to reconstruct scientific theories as systems of set-theoretical models than as systems of statements in a formal language. Such systems of models are also called *structures*: hence the name "structuralist" philosophy of science. Stegmüller (1976, 105) envisions this step as a radical upheaval. Later he is more modest and argues for the transition from logical to set-theoretical formalization methods on "pragmatic and psychological reasons" concerning the simplicity of formal reconstructions (1979b, 65). However, since set-theoretical models are also characterized by statements, namely by statements in the language of set theory, there exist straightforward possibilities of *translation* between the theory representations in the "statement view" and the "non-statement view" (see sec. 3.1.2; Schurz 2013b).

While the statement-vs.-non-statement debate turned out to be a bit of a red herring, the structuralist philosophy of science can claim significant achievements in the *detailed reconstruction* of individual scientific theories and theory nets (cf. Balzer et al. 1987; Balzer/Moulines 1996). Moreover, the structuralist philosophy of science has received support from Anglo-Saxon philosophers such as van Fraassen (1980, sec. 2; 1989, sec. 9), who called this position the "semantic view of theories" and developed it in a less formal way. The semantic account was further developed (among others) by Giere (1988a) and Bueno et al. (2002) (cf. French 2008; for criticism see Chakravartty 2001).

1.3.5.3 Naturalism and the Cognitive Turn

For Quine, naturalized epistemology becomes an empirical discipline, which is "scientifically investigating man's acquisition of science" (Quine 1974, 3). The naturalistic program was emphatically taken up by a number of young epistemologists and philosophers of science (cf. Papineau 1993; Kornblith 1994). A first concretization of naturalism is *evolutionary epistemology* (e.g. Campbell 1984): many aspects of humans' cognitive capacities and achievements can be explained by facts of evolution. It has to be critically remarked, however, that naturalistic approaches themselves make certain epistemological assumptions that are in need of justification, for example concerning realism and induction, and so they cannot entirely replace classical epistemology. A second concretization of naturalism is the so-called *cognitive turn*. This turn resulted from the fact that meanwhile the cognitive sciences had attained the status of an interdisciplinary subject area in their own right, in which the basis of humans' cognitive and scientific capabilities is examined not only logically in philosophy, but also empirically in psychology or linguistics, and computationally in Artificial Intelligence research (cf. Thagard 1996; Anderson 2000). As a result, several philosophers have started efforts to bring the approaches of the cognitive sciences into philosophy of science, and vice versa (e.g. Bechtel 1988; Goldman 1986; Bishop/Trout 2005). The recent movement of "experimental philosophy" has even started to examine philosophical intuitions by empirical investigations instead of the traditional "armchair method," with interesting results concerning cultural differences (Weinberg et al. 2001; Machery et al. 2004).

1.3.5.4 Hermeneutics and Critical Theory

The *Philosophy of the Humanities*, which originated in the 19th century, goes back to Friedrich Schleiermacher (1768–1834), Wilhelm Dilthey (1833–1911) and Wilhelm Windelband (1848–1915). It started as a movement for the methodological demarcation of the humanities against the expanding natural sciences. Central to this philosophy is the use of *hermeneutics*, the study of interpersonal *understanding (Verstehen)*, for the purpose of such a methodological demarcation. The *methodological dualism* of the philosophers of the humanities has been brought to a head with the following thesis: in the natural sciences, we *explain*, but in the humanities, we *understand*. While scientific explanations are based on general law hypotheses, it was claimed that understanding in the humanities needs no recourse to such law hypotheses, because the human mind is not subject to strict law mechanisms, and *understanding* has direct access to the human mind.

Hermeneutics is part of a tradition from well before Schleiermacher, in which there is no mention of any rigid separation of the humanities from logic and natural sciences (see Scholz 2001, part I.B). The methodological dualism of the 19th century had a strong influence on methodology debates of the 20th century (cf. von Wright 1971; Manninen/Tuomela 1976; Apel 1984). The contemporary controversy in the humanities and social sciences about *quantitative* versus *qualitative* methods is partially a revivification of the old methodological dispute (cf. Lamnek 1988; Denzin/Lincoln 2000). In response, the analytical philosophy of science has produced a number of approaches, in which the unity of hermeneutics and empirical methods is worked out (see sec. 6.4; cf. Hirsch 1973; Follesdal 1979; Bühler 2003).

Critical theory was developed by the philosophers of the so-called "Frankfurt school," mainly Horkheimer, Adorno, Marcuse and Habermas. It combines the methodologically dualist version of hermeneutics with the doctrine of the unavoidable interest-dependence of discovery and knowledge (e.g. Habermas 1966; Apel 1984). This tenet stands in contradiction to the traditional requirement that science should be *value-neutral*, which is discussed in sec. 2.5 and 2.10.

1.4 Introductory Literature and Exercises

1.4.1 Introductory Literature

Ladyman (2002) offers a brief introduction into the philosophy of science that is focused on natural science. Rosenberg (2008) introduces the reader to the philosophy of social science. An excellent introduction to the history of the Philosophy of Science is offered by Losee (2001). Stadler (2001) presents an extensive study of the Vienna circle and its logical empiricism. For Popper's philosophy of science see Keuth (1998). Hoyningen-Huene (1993) offers an introduction to the philosophy of Kuhn. For a critical discussion of the metaphysics of science see Ladyman and Ross (2007). On evolutionary epistemology see Campbell (1984). The history and current situation of hermeneutics is dealt with by Bruns (1992).

1.4.2 Questions and Exercises

Sec. 1.1–2

1. What are the main questions in the general philosophy of science?
2. What is the main difference between the empiricist and rationalist ways of thinking in epistemology?

Sec. 1.3

1. What is understood by empirical reductionism?
2. What criterion of demarcation is suggested by critical rationalism?
3. What is a paradigm for Kuhn? Discuss Kuhn's incommensurability thesis.
4. Discuss the methodological dualism of the philosophers of the humanities.

Note

1. See sec. 5.7.1. Cf. Mellor (1980, 118f), Bird (1998, 108–120), Ladyman/Ross (2007, 290ff).

2
THE QUESTION OF UNITY: IN SEARCH OF COMMON FOUNDATIONS OF THE SCIENCES

2.1 Normative or Descriptive? The Method of Rational Reconstruction

Prima facie, we can identify two opposing views of the goals and methods of the philosophy of science:

1. According to the *normative* view, it is the goal of philosophy of science to say what science *should* be, and how it should be pursued. For this purpose, philosophy of science must determine in what scientific rationality consists, and on the basis of which criteria a scientific hypothesis may be justified.
2. According to the *descriptive* view, on the other hand, it is the task of philosophy of science to say what science de facto *is*, and how it proceeds. For this purpose, philosophy of science must describe and explain the existing sciences in terms of their historical development and their current structure.

The normative view is historically older, and currently still enjoys a wide following. Both logical empiricists and critical rationalists held this view. It was not until Kuhn (1962) set off the historical turn in philosophy of science, that the descriptive counterpart became popular. It can be found in the work of historically oriented philosophers of science (cf. McMullin 1970; Laudan 1977, 162), of structuralists (e.g. Stegmüller 1976, 267ff; Balzer et al. 1987, xvff), or of naturalists (cf. Giere 1999, 160–163; Ladyman 2002, 4). So which position is right?

The position of the normativists can be traced back to Hans Reichenbach's (1938, 6f) distinction between the *context of discovery* (i.e. the factual *genesis*) of scientific knowledge, and its *context of justification*. The plausible prima facie argumentation of the normativists can be broken down as follows (e.g. Popper 1935/2002, sec. 1.2):

(2.1–1) *Normativist argumentation:*

Premise 1: To assess the epistemic value of a hypothesis, *only* the question of rational justifiability of its truth claim is relevant.

Premise 2: Questions about the historical development of the hypothesis, the causes for its discovery, etc., are irrelevant to this purpose.

Conclusion: Therefore, the philosophy of science should only examine science's rational justification and not its context of genesis—the latter being the remit of the history, sociology or psychology of science, but having nothing to do with its philosophy.

Since Kuhn (1962), the argumentation of the normativists has been criticized in a very *sweeping* way. Here we will attempt to clarify what is correct and what is flawed in this line of argument. The argument is certainly logically correct—assuming we take it to be analytically true that the philosophy of science is concerned with the assessment of the epistemic value of hypotheses. That is to say, *if* the premises of the argument were really true, then the conclusion would also be true. There is also *no error* in premise (1)—this thesis also seems to be analytically true, to the extent that science is concerned with the discovery of truth, and nothing else. But premise (2) is already infected by the "germ" of the normativistic fallacy, because the historical genesis of a scientific hypothesis includes not only so-called "external" factors which are epistemically irrelevant, but also "internal" factors which are epistemically relevant: e.g., the experimental methods, which scientists de facto use, and the rational hypothesis evaluation, which they de facto apply.

The organic chemist Kekulé, for example, reported that his groundbreaking hypothesis of ring-shaped benzene molecules first appeared to him in a *dream* (see Hempel 1966, 16). This fact was, of course, epistemically irrelevant and played no role in the justification of the hypothesis. In contrast, the *Boyle-Mariotte law of gases* was discovered by means of the systematic extrapolation of data (Langley et al. 1987, 81)—and this fact played a decisive role in the justification of the hypothesis.

Philosophers should *learn* from the de facto methods and arguments of science as far as they are successful, and they can only do this by observing them. Instead of premise 2, all the normativists usually want to say, or at least all they should say, is the following *almost trivial* weakening:

(2.1–2) *Premise 2**: The epistemically *external* part of the history of the development of a hypothesis is irrelevant to the assessment of its epistemic value.

Of course, the conclusion of argument (2.1–1) no longer follows if premise 2 is replaced by the weaker premise 2*. And with this conclusion, the error of the normativist argumentation becomes *grave*. To realize this, we must simply ask the following question: how can philosophers of science *acquire* the appropriate rules and criteria for the scientific method? It would be naive to presume that these rules and criteria might be gained through pure logic or mere intuition; science is much too complex for that. That would be like somebody trying to write a bridge-building manual without having examined the de facto practice of bridge building and typical examples of existing bridges. The philosophy of science, then, *can* and *should* learn from the real examples provided by the history of science. This brings us to the following result: although it is the *primary* task of the philosophy of science to explain the methods and criteria of *rational* science, it can only fulfill this task by *also* studying the *factual sciences* in their historical development.

Kuhn's criticism crystallized into the insight that the scientific models provided by logical empiricism and critical rationalism were too *simplistic* to give a faithful picture of real science (cf. Stegmüller 1979b, 5; 1969ff, vol. II.3, 20). Reacting to this, young theorists proclaimed that the philosophy of science should even be restricted to the descriptive analysis of the sciences. But this position too is overstated. The question of the definition and criteria of scientific rationality must, of course, remain central to philosophy of science, as it is this question which defines philosophy of science as a discipline, and sets it apart from the history and sociology of science. In summary, the philosophy of science is a discipline, which contains both descriptive and normative elements—an insight that has been worked out by Stegmüller (1969ff, vol. IV.1, 9ff).

The philosophy of science's method may best be described as a *rational reconstruction*. My understanding of this method is different from Lakatos' understanding of it, which has been sharply criticized by Laudan (1977, 167–170). For Lakatos (1971, 119f), "history" as understood by rational reconstruction is not the *actual* history, but a projection of ideals of rationality into history, and a selection of those parts of history that conform to that ideal. In contrast, in my understanding, the actual history forms one pole of the method. More precisely, rational reconstruction moves between two poles: a (so-called) *descriptive corrective*, which should be adequately reconstructed, and a *normative corrective*, which contains rational norms. The descriptive corrective does not contain every piece of factual sciences. It contains only typical examples of de facto successful (i.e. unanimously and sustainably accepted) scientific discoveries. Moreover, it also contains typical "counter-examples," i.e. examples of de facto refuted scientific hypotheses. Philosophy of science bases its reconstructions on these consensually accepted examples of scientific success or failure, though only in a preliminary and defeasible way.

The normative corrective consists of certain epistemic intuitions that are normally assumed by scientists, in spite of their various cognitive differences. That such a common ground exists is the position that will be defended in this chapter. First of all the normative corrective contains one supreme *epistemically internal* norm, which may be explicated as follows (cf. Weingartner 1978, sec.3.2):

> (Prop. 2.1–1) The *supreme epistemic goal* (G) of science is to find *true* and *content-rich* statements, laws, or theories, relating to a given domain of phenomena.

A sentence is the more rich in content, the more *consequences* it has (see sec. 3.7). The restriction of the goal of science to true *and* content-rich statements is significant, because the probability and the content of hypotheses are often *inversely proportional*. We can maximize the truth chances of hypotheses by sticking to trivial tautologies like: "The Sun revolves around the Earth, unless it doesn't." Inversely, it is easy to present very substantial and impressive hypotheses if we disregard their truth value, e.g. "I have invented a perpetual motion machine." The true art of the scientist is to formulate hypotheses which have both empirical truth and substantial content and consequences.

In the above explication of the supreme goal of science, there appears the little word "truth." One might object that the goal of truth is not metaphysically neutral. However, we understand this concept in a liberal way, leaving room for different metaphysical interpretations (see sec. 2.8.1). On the other hand, we do not want to be too liberal about the meaning of "truth." For people have rather different ideas of what truth is. While one person seeks truth in the platonic heaven, another person may equate truth with empirical success, and for another truth is what makes herself happy.

To ensure that the goal of scientific discovery as explicated in prop. 2.1-1 is not entirely vague concerning the meaning of "truth," we need a *minimal* explication of what "search for content-rich truths" is intended to mean. This is provided by the second "normative" component that is normally assumed by scientists as well as by philosophers of science, namely a minimal common epistemological model of scientific discovery. In sec. 2.2, we will explain this minimal epistemological model of the sciences in detail. The key points are given here: it contains (1) a *minimal realism*, (2) *fallibilism* and critical attitude, (3) the struggle for *objectivity*, (4) a *minimal empiricism*, and (5) the struggle for *logical clarity*. Although this minimal epistemological model consists primarily not of normative, but of *descriptive* claims, we still regard it as part of the normative corrective of philosophy of science, as it gives clear meaning to the supreme goal of science, and is usually seen as a precondition of scientific discovery.

Given the above described normative and descriptive correctives, the method of rational reconstruction may be precisely characterized as follows:

> (Def. 2.1-1) *Method of rational reconstruction:* Develop generalized and logically precise *models* of scientific discovery, which on the one hand *fit the descriptive corrective*, i.e. provide optimal explanations for the success of the examples and the failure of the counter-examples from the history of science, and which on the other hand may be *justified according to the normative corrective*, as providing optimal *means* of reaching the general goal of scientific discovery, given the assumptions of the minimal epistemological model.

In short, the philosophy of science abstracts generalized models from the descriptive corrective, which at the same time are (or should be) in line with the normative corrective. This is summarized in the schematic diagram in fig. 2.1-1.

As long as both aspects of rational reconstruction—descriptive adequacy and normative justifiability—can be made to work in harmony with each other, the work of scientific reconstruction can be counted as successful and its results as *corroborated*. Of course, we cannot expect that everything we find in *factual* science will also be *rational* according

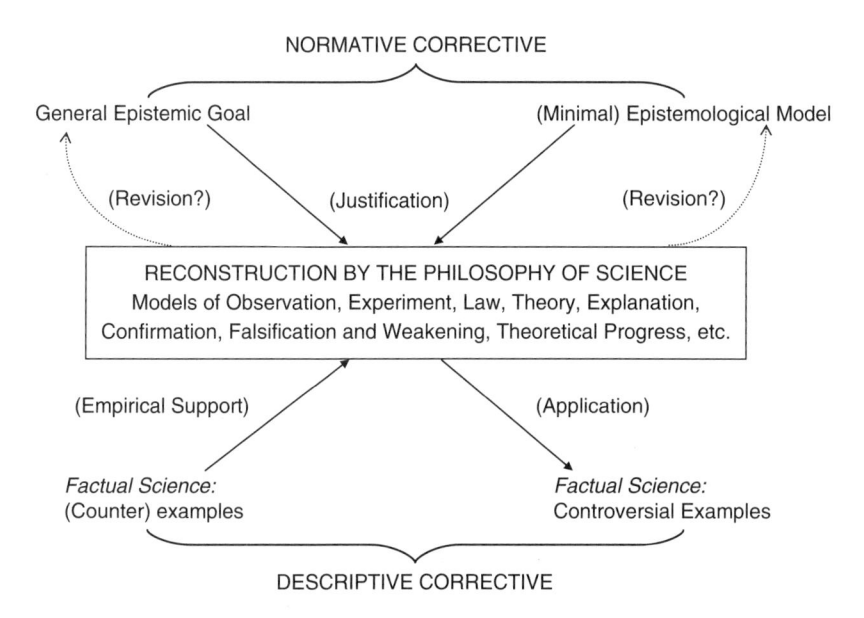

```
                        NORMATIVE CORRECTIVE
                     ⎧―――――――――――――――――――⎫
General Epistemic Goal                      (Minimal) Epistemological Model

     (Revision?)        (Justification)         (Revision?)

              ┌─────────────────────────────────────────┐
              │   RECONSTRUCTION BY THE PHILOSOPHY OF SCIENCE   │
              │  Models of Observation, Experiment, Law, Theory, Explanation,  │
              │  Confirmation, Falsification and Weakening, Theoretical Progress, etc. │
              └─────────────────────────────────────────┘

    (Empirical Support)                        (Application)

    Factual Science:                           Factual Science:
    (Counter) examples                         Controversial Examples
                     ⎩―――――――――――――――――――⎭
                        DESCRIPTIVE CORRECTIVE
```

Figure 2.1–1 The method of rational reconstruction

to the normative corrective. For this reason, the descriptive corrective of the philosophy of science contains only *accepted* (counter) examples. When models developed by the philosophy of science have been corroborated, we can take the next step of applying them to *controversial* areas of scientific disciplines, in which no consensus has been reached—be it the objectivity problem of quantum mechanics, the teleology problem in biology, or the explanation-understanding problem in the humanities. It is exactly here that philosophy of science can supply valuable decision-making aids to the individual sciences. So on one hand, the philosophy of science learns from the individual sciences and is corrected by them; on the other hand, its reconstruction work can be instructive to the individual sciences and thus help them solve specific problems.

The goal of rational reconstruction, though, bringing together descriptive analysis and normative justification, does not always have to succeed. This applies, for example, when philosophers of science proceed from unrealistically high or one-sided normative standards, which will persistently disallow them to reconcile their normative corrective with the descriptive analysis of science. In such cases, the philosophy of science must go on to *revise* its own normative corrective. When it does this—this has already happened several times in the history of the philosophy of science—then the philosophy of science, to borrow Kuhn's terminology, is no longer in a normal scientific phase, but in a revolutionary phase.

To conclude this section, we will compare the model of rational reconstruction with two similar characterizations of the method of philosophy of science. Carnap (1950b, sec. 2) described the procedure of the philosophy of science as *explication*. Here, a vague concept of everyday or scientific language (the explicandum), e.g. the idea of probability, is replaced by a precisely defined term (the explicatum), whereby the explicatum must differ from the explicandum insofar as it eliminates vagueness and ambiguity, but it should also remain as close to it as it can, and be as fruitful and simple as possible. Carnap does not explain, however, how exactly these partially contradictory demands should be combined. In comparison, the proposed model of rational reconstruction contains clear normative and descriptive guidelines; and by distinguishing normal and revolutionary phases in the philosophy of science, it takes into account the possibility that incoherencies can arise between the two. There are also significant differences between rational reconstruction and the method of reflective equilibrium according to Goodman (1955, 85–9) and Rawls (1971, 20f, 48–52). While the method of reflective equilibrium works purely coherentistically, aiming at the reciprocal adaptation of methodological *rules* and *intuition*, rational reconstruction is always *empirically grounded* by its descriptive corrective. Moreover, the normative corrective consists not of mere intuition, but of epistemological *hypotheses*, together with a supreme epistemological norm.

2.2 Common Epistemological Assumptions

The minimal epistemological model, common to more or less all scientific disciplines, contains five epistemological assumptions (E1–E5):

E1—Minimal Realism: According to this assumption, there is a reality, which exists independently of the (given) epistemological subject. It is not assumed that all properties of this reality are knowable. The possibility of fundamental limitations to scientific knowledge is left open and cannot be answered a priori, but only based on the factual epistemic success of science. Scientific disciplines aim to provide statements which are as true and as content-rich as possible about clearly defined areas of this reality. The term "truth" is used here in the sense of the *structural correspondence theory*, according to which the truth of a sentence consists in its structural agreement with the part of reality described by it. This notion of structural correspondence, which was first precisely defined by Alfred Tarski (1936a), does *not* imply any intrinsic relationship or mirroring between language and reality. It also allows that theories which are strictly speaking *false* may be true in an *approximative* sense, or *close* to the truth (sec. 5.6.2, 5.11.1).

E2—Fallibilism and Critical Attitude: There is no infallible "golden path" to the truth in the sense of the correspondence theory. According to the assumption of fallibilism, every scientific statement is more or less fallible; so we can never be *absolutely* sure of their truth, but we *can* consider their truth to be more or less probable. For this reason, everything depends on using empirical tests to find out more about the *probability* of a scientific hypothesis, in the sense of assumption E4 below. Fallibility goes hand in hand with a critical attitude, according to which no statement may ever be once and for all exempted from criticism.

E3—Objectivity and Intersubjectivity: According to this assumption, a statement's truth must hold objectively, i.e. independently of the beliefs and value-attitudes of the epistemological subject, because by assumption E1, reality has subject-independent existence, and truth is the correspondence between statement and reality. So the assumption of objectivity already follows from assumption E1. However, the characterization of objectivity as subject-independence does not help us in the practice of science, as only subjects make statements and formulate hypotheses. We have no direct access to objective truth, we can only approach it indirectly via—not certain, but probable—*criteria*.

The second part of assumption E3 says that a central criterion for objectivity and also for truth lies in the *intersubjectivity* of scientific statements. Intersubjectivity, correctly understood, is a plausible consequence as well as a plausible indicator of objectivity and truth. It is a plausible consequence because if a statement's truth can be established at all convincingly, then—at least in principle—it must be possible to convince any person of the statement's truth, provided the person is sufficiently cognitively *competent*. And it is a plausible indicator, because the agreement of many mutually *independent* and competent (i.e. fallible but truth-biased) researchers on the hypothesis provably increases its truth chances. This is an instance of the *Condorcet jury theorem* (cf. Bovens/Hartmann 2003, sec. 5.2).

E4—Minimal Empiricism: With the exception of formal sciences such as mathematics, which we will discuss later, the objects examined by any science must, in principle, be accessible to experience and observation. After all, reliable information about reality can only be gained through perceptual observation; for perception is our only form of direct informational contact with reality. Empirical observations, then, are a decisive referee in the scientific search for truth: scientific law hypotheses and theories must be *tested* in terms of them. This is the central statement of assumption E4. Observations are not infallible (that would contradict assumption E2), but they offer the easiest and fastest route to intersubjectivity and practical certainty. In other words, observations are "epistemically privileged." The empiricism contained in assumption E4 is *minimal,* because it is not claimed that all scientific statements must be traceable back to observations via a chain of definitions, or must be provable by observations. Scientific theories can and should contain theoretical concepts, by which they can talk about things that lie beyond what is observable to human senses. The decisive requirement of E4 is merely that statements about the unobservable must have observable consequences by which they may be tested.

E5—Logic in the wider sense: Using precise logical methods to introduce terms, to formulate sentences, and to construct correct arguments, is the most effective way to approach the goal of content-rich truth (according to assumptions E1–E4). For the meaning of a sentence cannot be established until the terms used in it have been clearly defined. And only sentences with a precisely formulated meaning may be examined for their logical consequences. Finally, only after the consequences of a hypothesis are known, may this hypothesis be precisely empirically tested in accordance with assumption E4. In conclusion, the procedure of empirical testing requires the use of exact logical methods at all times—in the wider sense of logic, not restricted to deductive logic.

Our minimal epistemological model makes as few assumptions as possible, but as many as necessary, in order to explain the possibility of objective science. Some of its assumptions are worthy of further explanation. We call the realism in assumption E1 "minimal," because it only asserts the objective *existence* of reality. Whether and to what extent reality is objectively discoverable cannot, according to assumption E2, be answered a priori, but only through the success of scientific discovery methods. This sets our minimal realism apart from metaphysical realism, in all its varieties. Moreover, we do not claim that science is impossible without the assumption of a subject-independent reality, but only that this assumption is *normally* made in scientific disciplines (see sec. 2.8.1).

To avoid misunderstandings, we should add that the correspondence theory of truth, while well suited as a *definition* of truth, does not offer any *criteria* to evaluate the truth of a sentence (cf. Rescher 1973, ch. 1; Kirkham 1992, 195). The path to such criteria is illuminated by assumptions E5 and E4: investigate the empirical consequences of your hypothesis and test them using empirical observations. For example, to find out the truth of the sentence "This flower is red," the correspondence-theoretical insight that this sentence is true if the flower is red will not get me anywhere; rather, I must be in a position to apprehend the object denoted by the ostensive individual term "this flower" and the perceptual quality expressed by the predicate "red" visually, in order to test the truth of the sentence by a simple act of perception.

In assumptions E4 and E5 we claim the existence of only two minimal levels, in which discovery finds its origin and its touchstone: observation, which allows us fragmentary but reliable and intersubjective access to reality, and logic in its wider sense, which provides a universal cognitive tool, but in itself says nothing about reality.

In assumption E3, we limited our characterization of *intersubjectivity* to "sufficiently competent" persons. This limitation is necessary, because persons who do not *understand* the content of a hypothesis, or who do not possess the relevant *evidence*, are unable to test a hypothesis for its truth. This difficulty shows us that intersubjectivity can on no account be used as a *definition* of objectivity or truth. The latter suggestion has been made in the constructivist "school" of Kamlah and Lorenzen (1984, 119), and one century earlier by the founder of the philosophical school of *pragmati(ci)sm*, Charles S. Peirce (1878b). But competence is an uncertain and gradual criterion, meaning that any number of persons judged to be competent may still err collectively. Peirce attempted to save his consensus definition by equating truth with the consensus that an *ideal* community of researchers with an infinite amount of time would approach in the limit. But even in this counterfactual version, an intersubjective consensus does not have to agree with the truth of correspondence theory. There are countless questions on whose true answer even an ideal community of researchers can never achieve consensus, because there is no evidential access to them, although there is no reason to assume that these propositions have an indefinite truth value—e.g., "How many microbes were located in Caesar's nose as he crossed the Rubicon?" In conclusion, intersubjectivity can, at best, be an uncertain criterion for objectivity.

2.3 Common Methodological Features

From the supreme epistemic goal (G) and the five epistemological assumptions (E1–5) there follow very plausibly four methodological features (M1–4), which are common to all empirical sciences in the broad sense. First, a word on terminology. By an *observation sentence*, we understand a sentence that expresses an *observable* state of affairs. We distinguish between *actual* and *potential* observation sentences. We call an observation sentence actual if the state of affairs expressed by it has indeed *been observed*. In contrast, an observation sentence is merely potential, if the state of affairs expressed by it has not been observed, but could be observed, e.g. at a later time or in a different place. Merely potential observation sentences express empirical *predictions*, e.g. "there will be a solar eclipse tomorrow." We can now formulate the four common methodological features as follows (similarly in Weingartner 1978, sec. 3.1–7).

M1: Science searches for hypotheses which are as general and as content-rich as possible, and recorded in a scientific language. In all disciplines, these hypotheses include *laws* and *theories*, and in some (e.g. the historical sciences) they also include *hypothetical singular sentences.*

M2: Science searches for *actual observation sentences*, as many as possible (and as relevant as possible), which reflect the results of observations, experiments or measurements.

M3: Science attempts, with the help of general and hypothetical sentences, to *explain* the currently known actual observation sentences, and to *predict* new, and as yet unknown *potential* observation sentences.

M4: Science attempts to *test empirically* its general and hypothetical sentences by comparing the predicted (potential) observation sentences with the currently known (actual) observation sentences. If the latter are in agreement with the former, the prediction was successful (it then becomes a successful explanation) and the hypothetical sentence (law or theory) is *confirmed* or *corroborated*. If there is a contradiction between the latter and the former, the prediction was without success and the law or theory is *falsified*, or in the case of a merely statistical prediction, *weakened*.

We only speak of an *explanation* if the state of affairs to be explained has already come to pass and is known, while in a *prediction* the predicted state of affairs is new and unknown. Viewed logically, both explanations and predictions take the form of deductive or probabilistic arguments (see sec. 6.1–4).

These four methodological features or modules are closely connected with the epistemological assumptions of science. Feature M1 results from the epistemic goal G, because laws and theories are the typical examples of general, content-rich sentences. M2 results from assumption E4 (sharpened by assumptions E2 and E3): to discover more about the conjectured truth of its hypotheses, science must collect empirical data. In order for general hypotheses to be tested on the basis of these data, the logical or probabilistic consequences of the hypotheses, in the form of predictions or potential explanations, must be investigated, and these consequences compared with the data—in this way, the methodological building blocks M3 and M4 are motivated by the assumptions E4 and E5.

Successful predictions and explanations not only have a bearing on the ultimate scientific goal of finding true and content-rich theories. They are also of crucial importance for human *planning behavior*, indeed to our survival. Predictions allow people to plan their future, by *adapting themselves* to the predicted sequence of events. Explanations are concerned with finding causes (sec. 6.2); they provide people with *knowledge of causes*. Causal knowledge gives people more power than merely predictive knowledge: it enables them to causally intervene in the course of events, and thereby *adapt* the world to suit *their own wishes*. The scientific sub-goals of prediction and causal control have been pursued by humanity since the Stone Age. Anyone who can *predict* that nourishing plants are growing in a given area can decide to migrate there and thereby ensure a high reproduction rate for their own tribal group. But those who know the *causes* of the growth of nourishing plants, who know how to plant and cultivate them, need no longer be gatherers, but can become farmers, and practice agriculture instead.

In advanced science, the scientific procedures of explanation and prediction operate not on two but on three levels: actual observation sentences at the lowest level, empirical law hypotheses at the middle level, and scientific theories at the upper level. Between the first and the second, and between the second and the third levels, the methodological procedures from M3 and M4 take place, as shown in fig. 2.3–1. This threefold division of scientific work is advantageous for many reasons; in all advanced scientific disciplines, a division of labor has arisen between practical experimenters (levels 1 and 2) and theoreticians (levels 2 and 3).

2.4 Scientific Disciplines and Their Classification

In this chapter, we will examine to what extent our epistemological assumptions E1–5 and the methodological features M1–4 match the existing scientific disciplines. To this end, we suggest the following division of scientific disciplines according to their area of enquiry (fig. 2.4–1). Our division is certainly imperfect and shall merely guide our

28 • Philosophy of Science

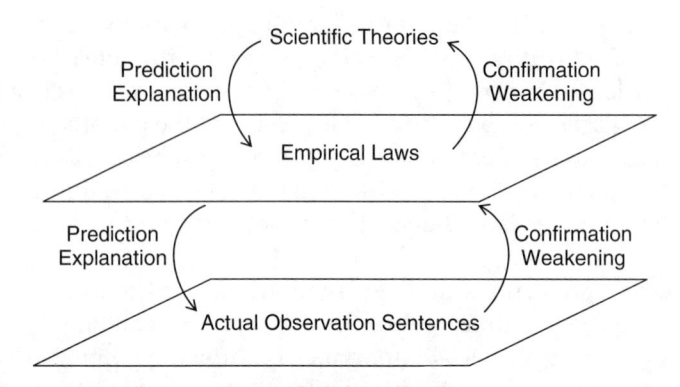

Figure 2.3–1 The three levels of the scientific method

investigation, but does not pretend to have a "final" status. Some disciplines are mixed disciplines, and are listed under "also." Not all disciplines can be listed here; several special disciplines are to be added.

Sciences...
1) ...*of nature:* physics, chemistry, biology, geology, medicine (astronomy, cosmology, geography, paleontology, history of biological evolution)
2) ...*of technology:* mechanical and electrical engineering ..., also: computer science
3) ...*of human beings:* psychology (also: education, medicine, cognitive science)
4) ...*of (human) society*: sociology, economics, political science (also: anthropology, ethnology, geography)
5) ...*of (human) history:* history (also: anthropology, ethnology, philosophy as history of ideas)
6) ...*of human cultural (mental, social) artifacts:* legal sciences, linguistics, literary science, sciences of fine arts and music, art history, media studies (also: education, religious studies)
7) ...*of formal structures (formal sciences):* mathematics (logic, statistics, theoretical computer science, system theory...), formal methodology and philosophy of science
8) ...*of the general foundations of human ideas:* philosophy (epistemology, philosophy of science and theoretical philosophy; ethics, aesthetics and practical philosophy)
9) ...*of God:* theology (also: religious studies)

Figure 2.4–1 Scientific disciplines, classified according to area of inquiry

Our classification has the advantage of not being tainted by partly value-based categories such as: (natural) *science, humanities,* or *real science* (etc.). If we try to apply these catch-all categories to our area-of-enquiry-based classification, we recognize that there is no clear consensus about what goes where, and that different systems of classification often have more to do with the politics than the philosophy of science. Group 1, for example, covers the core *natural sciences*. But mathematics, too, sees itself as a natural science, although it belongs to the category of *formal sciences*; moreover in the meantime mathematics is not only applied in natural sciences but also in economics and social sciences. Of late, also psychology sees itself predominantly as a natural science, although it could equally be assigned to the humanities or social sciences. The inclusion of mathematics and psychology in the natural sciences cannot be understood on systematic reasons alone; also the prestige of the natural sciences in our society, and the superior budgetary equipment that goes along with it, are a reason why these disciplines have recently moved to the natural sciences.

Groups 5 and 6 comprise the core of the traditional *humanities*. Philosophy, though, is just as close to the natural sciences as it is to the humanities, although in contemporary universities it is usually placed in the faculty of arts and humanities. In sec. 1.3.5.4 we explained that since the 19th century the traditional humanities were increasingly understood as a counterpart or even an opposition to the natural sciences. The term *humanities and social sciences* was coined in the 1960s and intended to serve as a modernized counterpart to the natural sciences. Whether this terminological group covers only groups 3 and 4, or also groups 5 and 6, was not fixed. In the last two decades, the new terminological group of the *cultural sciences* was formed, in part as a reaction to contemporary tendencies in psychology and social sciences to increasingly use methods of natural sciences. The term "cultural sciences" is predominantly used in continental Europe, and is understood in a broader sense than the Anglo-Saxon "cultural studies"; though its extension is not precisely defined.

The frequently supposed opposition between natural and cultural sciences is an instance of what Snow (1960) has called the two "cultures" in the current scientific age. In this book we intend to refute the view that there exists a principal methodological *gap* between the sciences of nature and culture; this gap, where it exists, is more a matter of different value-attitudes and world-views than a matter of unbridgeable differences in method.

In the term *factual sciences* (in German, *Realwissenschaft*), all sciences that have a part of the *real* world as area of enquiry are brought together; so, factual sciences include all groups apart from the formal sciences. Theology can only be seen as a factual science if we assume the reality of God; as this reality cannot be scientifically demonstrated, its inclusion here is questionable.

2.4.1 The Special Status of Mathematical Sciences

First we have to explain the special status of group 7, mathematics and formal sciences. In their totality, assumptions E1–5 and features M1–4 only make sense for the factual-empirical sciences. Mathematics and formal sciences do not have a domain of inquiry that consists of *concrete* and empirically accessible objects but, rather, deal with formal and *abstract* structures. Mathematics, then, has no empirical basis, and therefore assumption E4 and methodological features M2 and M4, which require an empirical basis, do not apply. This does not mean that mathematics is a speculative discipline that makes statements about reality with no empirical basis: pure mathematics makes no statements at all about (an empirically accessible) *reality*. All it does is develop formal structures and models, characterize them by using abstract axioms and definitions which are as general as possible, and derive logical consequences from them.

It would be nonsense, for example, to say that the axiomatic system of real numbers or of Euclidian geometry were per se "true" or "false." Such claims can only be made when mathematical terms are interpreted empirically, e.g. when real locations or time points are assigned to real numbers, or real forces to mathematical vectors. But then geometry is no longer a mathematical theory, but becomes a physical one. Einstein once formulated it like this: "As far as the theorems of mathematics relate to reality, they are not certain; and as far as they are certain, they do not relate to reality" (cf. Carnap 1967/1939, 56). So we can say: exactly *because* mathematics ignores the empirical interpretation of its models, it is the strictest of all sciences. To be sure, mathematics concerns itself primarily with those structural models that are applicable to certain areas of reality. Seen in this way, mathematical disciplines can be more or less *fruitful* for the real sciences, but they cannot be true or false in the sense of the factual sciences.

Assumptions E2, E3, E5 and the methodological feature M1 can be applied to mathematics without restriction (the assumption of fallibility E2 insofar as even mathematical proofs are not guaranteed to be error-free). Assumption E1 of minimal realism applies only in an indirect way, insofar as mathematical structures have the purpose of being applied to the real sciences. The methodological component M3 applies insofar as mathematicians are interested in the derivation of the various theorems, which express important properties of their models. Such derivations can be termed mathematical *explanations* (Weingartner 1978, 102), as long as it is clear that these are not causal explanations.

Let us not neglect the fact that the *philosophy of mathematics* includes opposing views on the nature of mathematical objects (cf. Hart 1996;

Shapiro 2000; Maddy 1997). According to the widespread view which is shared by us, mathematical objects are abstract *conceptual* objects, i.e. conceptual constructions. Real objects, e.g. five red roses, can *exemplify* mathematical objects, e.g. the number five, but can never be identical with them. This view, called *conceptual structuralism*, was worked out in detail by the group of mathematicians around Bourbaki (1961) and philosophers of mathematics such as Field (1980). The opposing standpoint in the philosophy of mathematics is *mathematical realism*, which assumes that mathematical objects exist per se. This position has been defended, for example, by Frege (1984, 43) and Gödel (1947, 271f). In this position, mathematical entities are also seen as abstract and *platonic* objects, not located in the reality of space and time, but in a "platonic world of mathematical ideas" which is accessible not empirically, but only through mathematical "intuition." An argument in favor of mathematical structuralism is Ockham's razor (cf. 5.9.2): structuralism explains mathematical phenomena just as well as realism, but without the assumption of strange platonic entities.

In summary, mathematics and the other formal sciences are a *specialization* within the whole system of science, dealing with formal models, algorithms and methods. This specialization has shown itself to be particularly *useful* in the history of science. Put in a nutshell, the information that the mathematician passes to the empirical scientist is this:

> *If* your empirical domain satisfies the axioms of this-and-this mathematical structure, *then* it must also satisfy these-and-these theorems about this structure that we have proved; *we* grant you the satisfaction of the theorems, provided *you* grant us the satisfaction of the axioms.

So we characterize the formal sciences as *prerequisite and auxiliary sciences*, which furnish the factual sciences with formal foundations and structural models with known properties.

2.4.2 Testing the Common Foundations of Science

Having clarified the special status of mathematics, let us now ask: with the *exception* of the formal sciences, to what degree do the assumptions E1–5 and the methodological features M1–4 comply with the listed groups of disciplines? Obviously, E1–5 and M1–4 fit all disciplines in groups 1–3 (natural sciences, technical disciplines, psychology). There is also no reason not to apply them to the social sciences and historical disciplines in groups 4 and 5. Minimal realism, fallibilism, objectivity and intersubjectivity (E1–3) and logical clarity (E5) are accepted standards in all these disciplines, and the same is true for the search for general hypotheses, explanations and predictions (M1, M3). In all these disciplines, empirical data are available, for example in the form of the results of psychological experiments, interview data, economic and demographic data, and in the historical sciences in the form of historical texts and source materials, etc. By this, assumption E4 and building blocks M2 and M4 are also fulfilled. Of course, it is significantly more difficult to find general law hypotheses in social science and history, because of the complexity of their area of enquiry—but all that is required for the applicability of the methodological building blocks to a given science is that the goals therein can reasonably be *sought after*, which does not necessarily mean that these goals are equally easy to attain in all different disciplines.

The same considerations apply to broad areas of the disciplines in group 6. Also here, the epistemological assumptions E1–3 and E5 are widely accepted standards. Moreover, these disciplines work with empirical data too; so assumption E4 and the methodological building block M2 apply. For example, linguistic texts comprise the data for linguistics, and works of art and music from various cultures or stylistic periods are the data of literary criticism, art history and music studies. Members of the hermeneutic school raise the objection at this point, that "data" in the social sciences and humanities, e.g. speech acts or texts, are always of an *interpretative* nature, so that understanding in the humanities is always subject to an unbreakable *hermeneutic circle* (cf. Gadamer 1975/2005, 235ff). But a number of philosophers of science have worked on the view that the testing of interpretative hypotheses concerning what an author intended to say proceeds in the same "holistic" manner as the testing of theories in the natural sciences (cf. Stegmüller 1979a, 27–86; Follesdal 1979; Rosenberg 2008, 43f). What hermeneutic philosophers rightly point out is that what one calls "data" in the humanities are usually not raw data, but semantically interpreted data in the form of meaningful linguistic or non-linguistic acts. However, also what physicists call data are usually theoretically interpreted measurement results, e.g., elementary particles observed in the cloud chamber. This does *not* mean that raw or uninterpreted data or stimuli do not exist at all: in our physical example, they exist as condensation droplets in the cloud chamber; and in the interpretation of linguistic acts, they exist in the form of sequences of sounds or letters. Although some advocates of hermeneutics doubt the existence of raw linguistic data, their existence can easily be verified: you just have to hear someone speaking in a completely foreign language; what you will then hear are exactly these raw linguistic data.

The school of *methodological dualism* mentioned in sec. 1.3.5.4 objects, once more, that there are no general law hypotheses in the humanities. If that were true, then the activities of these disciplines would have to be limited to methodological building block M2, that is to say, to the gathering of singular historical facts according to the "ideographic method." What is true is that in the humanities and the social sciences there are, as good as, no *strict* (or exceptionless) laws. But, as will be worked out later (see sec. 4.5, 6.4), there are *statistical* and, in particular, *normic* law hypotheses ("if A, then normally B"), which are indispensable for explanations and hypothesis testing in these disciplines. Therefore, the methodological components M1, M3 and M4 apply also to the historical sciences and humanities.

To avoid misunderstandings, when we say that the methodological components M1–M4 can be, and have been, successfully applied in the humanities, we do not imply that *all* representatives of this group of disciplines make use of these methods. Within the humanities and social sciences, there is still the opposition between proponents and opponents of empirical-analytic methods—we mentioned Snow's (1960) "two cultures," and Ross (1996) spoke even of "science wars" (see Godfrey-Smith 2003, sec. 9.3). Some scientists in the humanities and social sciences reject these methods simply *because* they are empirical and analytic. Nevertheless, what this book intends to show is that the methodological features M1–M4 are optimal means to pursue the supreme goal (G) of finding content-rich truths even in the human and social sciences.

There is, however, another phenomenon, found mainly in the humanities, that seems to stand in decisive opposition to the scientific method according to E1–5 and M1–4: namely, the phenomenon of *norms and value judgments*. We illustrate this problem at the hand of a subdiscipline of legal sciences: jurisprudence, i.e. the science of legal judgment. This discipline examines concrete actions and the facts of a case, to determine how they fit into the given legal system, and specifically whether they fall under a certain category of offense or crime (going along with a certain punishment). The philosophy of *legal positivism*, which goes back to Kelsen (1960/2002), held the view that jurisprudence is a value-free systematic-deductive procedure, based only on *positive* law, i.e. laws which have been passed by legislators. But Kelsen's thesis is controversial in the philosophy of law. For example, was the removal of private property from a grocer's shop *petty larceny* or *theft*? (an example from von Savigny 1976a, 101f). Or: does giving shelter to a criminal in one's own home amount to *complicity*? (an example from Kuhlen 2000, 37). In these and other cases, it does not follow from the stipulations of the law and empirical knowledge of the facts, how the deed of the accused should be classified; and the judges and other interpreters of the law now have the task of *interpreting* the underdefined stipulations of that law. In von Savigny (1976a, 106, 144ff) it is shown that these interpretations are often based on *value as*sumptions (or "assumptions of justness"), which cannot be found in legal texts but, rather, come from an "intuitive legal consciousness." Now a legal scientist can certainly show that *if* certain value assumptions are taken for granted, *then* a certain interpretation of the law is adequate. But how can she determine scientifically *which* value assumptions are justified? Can the legal scientist prove that a specified degree of misery of the accused person is sufficient for us to speak of "petty larceny" instead of "theft"? Can she scientifically decide whether a billboard advertising underwear is still in accord with "common decency" or is already an affront to the "dignity of women"? (see Hilgendorf 2000, 15, 24). So the question which arises *not only* in jurisprudence, but also in other disciplines relating to the human or social sciences, is this: can fundamental value assumptions be scientifically justified?

Without further ado the answer proposed by us is: *no*. This does not mean that value- and norm-related issues do not occur in science. For one thing, the de facto values of persons can be *empirically* investigated. Moreover, specific value sentences can be logically deduced from *assumed* fundamental value sentences (and further premises). But a fundamental scientific justification of values is impossible. Our view here is concordant with the general consensus of (empirical) science, and does not claim to be original; but our justification of this answer should contain some originality. For the value-neutrality requirement has been criticized so sharply by critics of positivism that it simply cannot nowadays be taken for granted, but needs to be worked through with great care. This task we will attend to in sec. 2.5.

2.4.3 Two Further Classifications of Sciences

The above subdivision of scientific disciplines was given according to area of enquiry. To end this section, we will explain two further possible systems of classification. One methodologically significant classification of the factual sciences follows the "invasiveness" of their empirical discovery methods. The classification is summarized in fig. 2.4–2.

1 *Empirical sciences* (in the sense of minimal empiricism): by this we understand all disciplines which refer in some way to empirical data, whether these data were obtained via free field observation, by study-

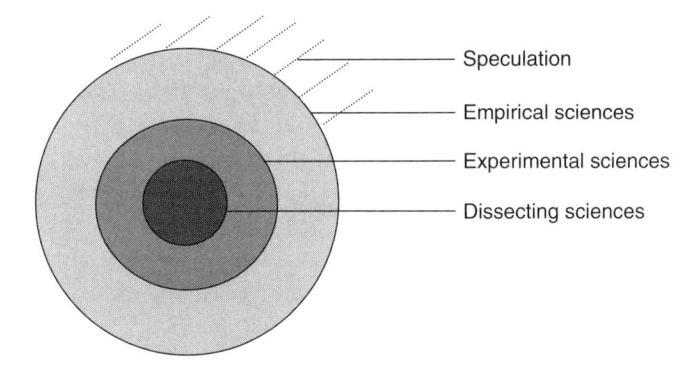

Figure 2.4–2 Classification of the factual sciences

ing historical records, or in laboratory experiments. To this most extensive group we assign all disciplines described by assumptions E1–5 and methodological building blocks M1–4, including the humanities. Only those disciplines whose theories are based on pure *speculation* are not in this group—as, for example, mysticism, esotericism, speculative metaphysics, or the dogmatic and creed-based components of theology. Based on our epistemological assumptions, it is doubtful whether these are factual sciences at all.

2 *Experimental sciences*: This *subgroup* of empirical disciplines obtains its data from *controlled experiments*. The significance of controlled experiments as opposed to free field observation is that in an experiment, certain sets of conditions can be deliberately created, which give us information about the causal relevance or irrelevance of factors (see sec. 4.2–4), while field observers might have to wait "forever" for a lucky coincidence to come up with the exact set of conditions required. For this reason, experimental sciences can explore their domain of enquiry much faster and more effectively than sciences which rely on mere observation or passive reception of historical data. The experimental criterion divides the disciplines in groups 1–3 at least tendentially from the ones in groups 4–6. For it is hardly possible, for both technical and ethical reasons, to perform experiments with large social groups, institutions, or legal systems. Of course, ethical concerns are already present in biological or psychological experiments, but here they are usually not strong enough to exclude them, only to restrict them.

3 *Dissecting sciences:* A significant subgroup of the experimental sciences are those which I will call—for want of a better word—the

"dissecting" sciences. By this I mean sciences which not only expose the objects to various experimental conditions in order to analyze them intellectually, but which also *materially analyze* their objects, i.e. take them apart or dissect them—perhaps in order to synthesize them afterwards, i.e. to put them back together again, provided this is still possible. I suggest that it is this dissecting character that constitutes the essential characteristic of *classical* natural sciences such as physics, chemistry, biology and medicine, in contrast, say, to experimental behavioral research or psychology.

Dissection of objects goes far beyond experimentation at the input-output level insofar it makes the objects' inner structure accessible to observation and experimentation. Chemistry and biochemistry have learned to break down items from our environment into their molecular and atomic constituents (analytical chemistry) and to put them back together again (synthetic chemistry). Nuclear physics has done the same at a *subatomic* level, here involving much greater amounts of energy. The analysis and synthesis of living creatures being worked on by science today—from genetic engineering and neuroengineering to artificial intelligence and robotics—could bring us to a point in the future where it is possible to genetically alter or even create a human or android being. Some people think these possibilities are terrifying; others that they are breathtaking. Here, as always, we should remember: scientific discoveries may be used for various purposes, both "good" and "evil." But certainly, the possible risks and dangers going along with these technological possibilities will get bigger and bigger. Therefore the *ethics of science*, whose purpose is to set limits to the technological realization of the scientifically possible, may become much more significant in the future than it is today.

Independently of this, scientific disciplines may also be divided up according to the degree to which their concepts and *methodologies* are quantitative and mathematical, as follows:

Graduated division of scientific methodologies by increasing degree (←) of logical-mathematical and quantitative precision

←───

Logical-mathematical language	Natural language
"Quantitative"	"Qualitative"
Logic	Hermeneutics
Statistics and measurement theory	Content analysis
Technology	Field research

Quantitative methods are on the left and *qualitative* methods on the right side of this spectrum. Note that on both sides we are looking at *scientific* methods—also qualitative hypotheses and methods can be pursued in a logically clean and empirically controlled way (cf. sec. 3.1.4; Denzin/Lincoln 2000). The ideological polarization between quantitative and qualitative methods that is held by some qualitative researchers (e.g. Lamnek 1988) appears unnecessary and exaggerated. Rather, qualitative and quantitative methods are *complementary*. The strength of qualitative methods (e.g. case studies, narrative interviews) lies in advance of quantitative methods—in the exploration of relevant parameters and the generation of promising hypotheses. But a qualitative exploration has to be followed up by a quantitative-statistical analysis, as this is the only reliable way to test the generality of one's hypothesis, especially in a situation in which one does not already possess pre-established background knowledge. That qualitative and quantitative methods are complementary in the explained sense is a widely held view among empirical researchers in the social sciences (cf. Lazarsfeld and Barton 1951; Giddens 1982, 328); however, this view is not uncontroversial (cf. Flyvbjerg 2006).

2.5 The Question of Value-Neutrality

2.5.1 *Max Weber's Value-Freedom Postulate and Its Critics*

The first detailed work on the value-neutrality requirement goes back to one of the main founders of sociology, namely *Max Weber* (1864–1920). Weber was involved in a controversy with Schmoller, who propagated the view that social science should work out moral value judgments relating to a desired social order. Weber spoke out strongly against the pseudo-objectivity of such "podium values," i.e. value judgments presented with "scientific" authority: Objectivity, said Weber, could only be reached in science if scientists limit themselves to factual, descriptive statements, and separate these clearly from their own values (Weber 1949, ch. II and X).

The main reason for the self-imposed limitation of science to descriptive judgments, recognized by Weber, can be summarized thus: *Values are not properties inherent to objects themselves, but rather are based on subjective interpretations by us humans. Norms* are also not objective facts, but *man-made* requirements, designed to aid the realization of certain values. In the case of testing value and norm sentences, there is nothing which corresponds to an *empirical foundation* according to assumption E4 and methodological building blocks M2 and M4.

At the same time, value and norm sentences are by no means purely formal claims, which might be justifiable by means of pure logic. There is, therefore, no objectivity in the sense of empirical science when it comes to norms and values. Ultimately, the decision for or against certain values or norms is a question of personal *freedom*.

This explanation of the value-freedom postulate is prima facie not only theoretically, but also practically plausible. Everyone knows from experience that finding a consensus on values between members of different cultures is much more difficult than finding a consensus on factual issues. Many strict Islamists would not take offence at western science; the western value system, however, seems twisted in their eyes. Nonetheless, the value-freedom requirement was massively criticized from the 1960s onwards, especially by neo-Marxist movements such as the *critical theory*, and in the German-speaking area the Weber–Schmoller controversy flared up once more as the "positivism dispute" (cf. Adorno et al. 1976; Frisby 1972; Dahms 1994) and the "value judgment dispute" (Albert/Topitsch 1971).

Proponents of critical theory raised the objection that a purely descriptive or "positivist" method in social science had the effect of simply theoretically reproducing the status quo of oppressive social structures and thereby implicitly sanctioning them, while *critical* science must concern itself with *changing* oppressive social conditions (Habermas 1966).

This accusation is based on a fatal *misunderstanding*: descriptive research, of course, also includes research into natural laws, and thereby research into that which is naturally, technically or practically *possible* and *impossible*. So in fact, empirical social science is the very thing which can show us how social conditions may be *changed*, thereby contributing to the emancipation demanded by representatives of critical theory. In fact, almost all the "neopositivists" of the Vienna circle had a de facto progressive political orientation, and saw much of their work as being connected with social progress (Stadler 2001; Dahms 1994, 125). The only difference is that critical-empirical social science, as defended by Popper and Albert against Horkheimer and Adorno in the "positivism debate," restricts itself to pointing out the *possibilities* for social change, and leaves normative decisions to the process of *democratic opinion-formation*, rather than wanting to justify these in a quasi-scientific way.

Even if the main accusation of critical theory was off the mark, the period that followed saw a number of legitimate objections being raised, which are in need of a more subtle discussion. Not only critical theorists (cf. Dahms 1994, 375), but also younger analytical philosophers warned that questions of values and norms should on no account be handed over to *irrationality*. Indeed, a rational treatment of value questions is both possible and exceedingly necessary in society, and science has an important role to play in this regard. In this regard too, it is advisable to turn to Max Weber, who made subtle refinements to the value-neutrality requirement, in the face of just such objections.

First, according to Weber, it is absolutely possible for a social scientist to do research on the factual presence of value and norm systems, *without* passing judgment himself (Weber 1949, 11f). To study polygamy in Islam, it is neither necessary to be an advocate nor to be an opponent of it. The statement that a person or a society *believes* in certain values is not in itself a value statement, but a *descriptive* claim, whose confirmation requires only empirical data.

Second, also according to Weber (1949, 21f), the scientist can identify *logical relationships* among value or norm sentences. Relevant to this task are the—meanwhile highly developed—disciplines of analytic ethics (e.g. Frankena 1963), deontic logic (e.g. Aqvist 1984) and decision theory (e.g. Raiffa 1968).

Third, with the help of *means-end-inferences* the scientist can infer from *given* norms and descriptive knowledge a series of derived norms and pass these on as recommendations of means to society and politics. This is the most important way in which sciences may become practically relevant, as we shall explain now.

2.5.2 Value-Neutrality and Means-End Inferences

Finding suitable means for given ends is an important task of descriptive science. It obeys the following logical form:

> (Def. 2.5–1) *The general scheme of means-end inferences:*
>
> *Descriptive means-end hypothesis:* M is in the given circumstances C a necessary—or alternatively an optimal—means for the realization of end E.
>
> *Thus: given* (fundamental norm:) end E is to be realized,
> *then* (derived norm:) means M should also be realized.

Means-end inferences are accepted by most ethical theories as analytically *valid* (Schurz 1997, sec. 11.4). Their practical significance lies in the fact that given a rich descriptive knowledge they make it possible to infer a *multitude* of derived norms from only a *few* fundamental norms. In this way, they transfer the justification load from the normative to the descriptive. All empirical disciplines can become practically relevant by applying means-end inferences, but they are especially frequent in disciplines that are related to a specific purpose of application, such as technical disciplines, medicine, education or legal sciences.

It is assumed in the means-end inference that M is either a *necessary* or an *optimal* means for E. If M, on the other hand, is a merely *sufficient* means for an end E, then the means-end inference is not valid, because one and the same end will, in general, have various different sufficient means of realization, and the harm caused by these sufficient means can often outweigh the benefit of achieving the end. For example, to achieve the end of letting fresh air into a room, smashing a hole through the wall is a sufficient but not recommendable means; in contrast, opening a window is an optimal means, and a necessary means is some sort of opening to the outdoors.

The fundamental norm of a means-end inference cannot be scientifically justified but is externally given. The scientist takes fundamental norms, for example from politicians or society, and uses her descriptive knowledge to give them back several derived norms. Thereby it is essential for the scientist to relativize her recommendations explicitly as being *derived* from the assumed fundamental norm in each given case. Therefore, the derived norm is called also a *hypothetical* norm ("*if* you want this, you should do that") and the fundamental norm a *categorial* norm ("you should do this"); a designation going back to Immanuel Kant.

Let us illustrate this by means of educational *teaching theories* (cf. Flanders 1970; Patry 1991). Let us take it that *cognitive success* (i.e. mastery of material to be learned) is the fundamental goal of teaching. Based on empirical research, an education scientist might reach the descriptive hypothesis that cognitive success can be maximized if between 70% and 80% of teaching time is teacher-guided. The education scientist passes on this conclusion to teachers as a *derived* value or norm sentence. This procedure is, however, only in accordance with the value-neutrality requirement if the means recommendation is formulated *hypothetically*: *if* your goal is to maximize cognitive success, then 70–80% of class time should be teacher-guided.

If the explicit reference to assumed values is neglected, ideologically worrying consequences can result. Assume that in our example the teachers have different fundamental goals from the scientists; they see *social learning* as an equally important goal to cognitive success. Let it be empirically shown, perhaps even by the same scientist, that the optimal means to reach this purpose is a maximum of just 60% of teacher-guided class time, alongside 40% of group activity. What if the scientist in our example, however, passes on her recommendation categorically rather than hypothetically, e.g. she asserts *80% of class time should be teacher-*

guided, and teachers believe her? Now the scientist is *manipulating* the teachers, because she is concealing the fact that her means recommendation is valid only for *her own* value assumptions. The teachers, who *do not* share these values, are being badly advised on how to reach their own chosen ends. The same is true of many other situations, from medicine (a doctor advises a patient) to law (a lawyer advises a married couple about how to get divorced). It is highly important in all such cases, that the scientific "expert" makes *explicit* the value assumptions that she assumes in her means recommendations, as this is the only way that the "customer" being advised can find out whether these correspond to his own values.

With these examples, we *emphatically* point out that the value-neutrality requirement does not have a dogmatic-scientific function, but rather a *critical* and *emancipatory* one. In section 2.10 we will defend this thesis in the context of contemporary debates on values and their role in science.

The conclusions of our considerations so far can be summarized as follows. The demand that science be completely free of value-based statements is too strong. Value- and norm-based statements can (and should) appear in the sciences in three ways without injuring the spirit of Weber's value-freedom postulate: Science can (1) empirically examine the occurrence of value systems, (2) examine the logical relationships between value or norm sentences, and (3) use means-end inferences to recommend derived values relative to given fundamental values. Only the *justification of fundamental values* is outside the area of descriptive science. From now on we will call this thesis the value-neutrality thesis, which is abbreviated as (V).

2.5.3 Explication of the Value-Neutrality Requirement

To reach the final formulation of our value-neutrality requirement, we need to take two further steps of clarification.

1 Many authors have argued that science cannot be value free in an absolute sense, because the whole enterprise of "science" itself rests on certain goals and values: the so-called *science-internal* or epistemic values (e.g. Schmidt 1959, 648ff; Doppelt 2007, 190ff). In sec. 2.1, we identified the search for general and content-rich truths as the supreme epistemic goal of all sciences. This fundamental science-internal value is implicitly assumed in scientific justifications and so is to be found in all sciences. The value-neutrality thesis must, therefore, be restricted to fundamental *science-external* or non-epistemic value assumptions. This does not imply that our thesis of the lack of empirical justifiability of

fundamental values should be restricted to science-external values, too. The supreme goal of science (G) (prop. 2.1–1) cannot be empirically justified either; it is much more by definition the fundamental goal of science. Of course, the goals of science can be ethically justified in many ways, for example by pointing out the value of knowledge for attaining one's non-epistemic goals, or the advantages of the critical method which, according to Popper (1994, 7), lets "theories die instead of persons." But this justificational enterprise belongs to ethics or meta-ethics rather than to philosophy of science.

2 Is the restriction to fundamental science-external values and norms enough to give us a sustainable version of the value-neutrality requirement? *No*—insofar as one views science not merely as a process of justification, but as a *social process*. Although values cannot be scientifically justified, value judgments are necessarily involved in several stages of the scientific discovery process, so that we must show at what stage of this process the value-neutrality requirement becomes relevant. Let us take the usual division of the process of scientific discovery into three phases, the *context of discovery* (CD), in which the scientifically relevant problems are first conceived or "constituted," the *context of justification* (CJ), in which data are gathered and systems of hypotheses generated and tested, and the *context of application* (CA), in which well tested discoveries are used for various different social purposes. In (CD), the objects of investigation are selected according to considerations of *relevancy*. This process is also dependent on science-external values: which problem is important is decided, among other things, by the interests of the client or financier of a scientific project, or by the subjective interests of the individual researcher. In (CA), there is a massive involvement of science-external values: Whether hypotheses in physics are used for peaceful means or for war, whether psychological discoveries are used to increase work efficiency or to promote family relationships, depends on who uses them or is allowed to use them because he has financed them. What the value-neutrality thesis demands relates exclusively to the *context of justification*. In (CJ), science-external values must not play any role. In conclusion, we can formulate and schematically represent the value-neutrality thesis as follows (see fig. 2.5–1).

(Prop. 2.5–1) *Value-neutrality requirement (V):* A specific realm of scientific activity, namely their context of justification, should be free from fundamental science-external value assumptions.

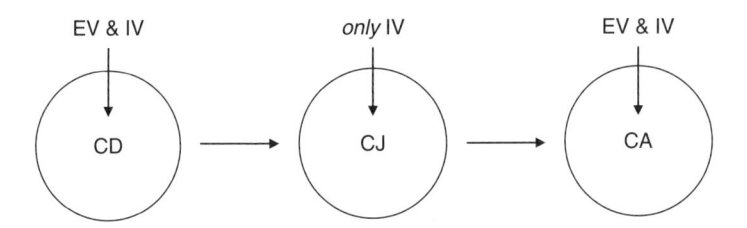

Figure 2.5–1 Schematic representation of the value-neutrality requirement

Legend: CD—context of discovery, CJ—context of justification, CA—context of application; IV—science-internal values, EV—science-external values.

An important consequence of this scheme of value-neutrality is the retro-corrective reference of the context of justification to the problem selection in the context of discovery. The selection of the investigated objects and parameters in (CD) is by no means *epistemologically neutral*, but has an effect on the context of justification in that it places limits on the possible results of the scientific investigation. In the course of research, it can emerge that in order to find the relevant causes it is necessary to take parameters into account which were already abstracted from in (CD). For this reason, the selection in (CD) can only be *preliminary*, and must be *accessible* to subsequent criticism and correction from discoveries in (CJ), *even when* this goes against the external goals of the research project. Otherwise we could not say that (CJ) is independent from external values. We will illustrate this with an example. For a long time, classical medicine had a purely biological and physiological orientation; to a certain extent this still applies today. Medicine of this kind already abstracts away from psychological parameters in the context of discovery. In the meantime, however, we know many organic diseases with psychological causes, and the significance of psychosomatic interaction cannot be dismissed out of hand. In order to be able to *examine* the question of psychosomatic connections, the restriction to biological and physiological factors in medical models must be given up, and the area of psychological phenomena included. In other words, the original and externally motivated restriction in (CD) must be dropped because of knowledge discovered in (CJ).

We finally emphasize that the value-neutrality requirement (V) should not be misunderstood as a descriptive claim about actual practice of (all or most) scientists. Rather, it is a normative recommendation. Not all scientists agree with it. As already mentioned, some scholars in the social and legal sciences argue that it is not possible in their discipline to separate descriptive from value judgments. In our above analysis of the means-end inference we have attempted to refute this view: with enough verbal care it is always possible to separate descriptive from normative claims. In the natural sciences the influence of external values is usually more hidden than in social and legal sciences, and has often to do with economical rather than ideological motives. An example is pharmaceutical research on drug effectiveness, which is usually financed by pharmaceutical firms. Meta-studies revealed a significant bias of pharmaceutical research in favor of its financial sponsors. These findings led pharmaceutical journals to adopt policies that can prevent such biases (cf. Brown 2008, 192f). In other words, an external influence by the sponsors of research is not inevitable, but can be inhibited by appropriate regulations.

In our modern value-pluralistic society, in which politicians need scientific legitimation, there is a permanent pressure, or at least temptation, for scientists to make external value-statements. In the long run, however, external biases—be it in the form of politically misused theories or of financially motivated bias—can only undermine the credibility of science. In conclusion, upholding the value-neutrality requirement is of undiminished importance also in the present situation of the sciences.

2.6 The Demarcation Problem and the Methodological Unity of Sciences

2.6.1 Demarcation

Using the value-neutrality requirement (prop. 2.5–1), we can now analyze all disciplines in order to characterize the boundaries of the scientific. As long as legal science, for example, analyzes empirically occurring legal systems, or establishes logical and means-end relationships between norms, it remains a descriptive science. The logical analysis of ethical statements is also carried out by analytical ethics, in particular the subdiscipline of *meta-ethics*, which also fits easily into the logical-descriptive scientific program. Literary and art theories, which deal with the aesthetic effects of various literary and artistic genres, fit into the framework of empirical-descriptive science, as long as aesthetic effect refers to a *factual* effect on people. Only absolute statements about aesthetic values, which are not relativized to a factually given artistic style, go beyond the scope of descriptive science. This criticism also applies to the tendencies within humanistic psychology and pedagogy which place values such as personal development and dignity above objective analysis (Bühler/Allen 1973). Religious studies, as long as they reconstruct factually occurring religious systems, belong to the descriptive scientific program, while theologies that dogmatically assume the truth of a certain religious "creed" are departing doubly from the realm of science: first by assuming the truth of speculations about the nature and existence of God, and second by making fundamental value assumptions.

In summary, we can demarcate the boundaries of science as follows: *Sciences in the sense used here are all empirical disciplines in the broad sense (according to (G), (E1–5), (M1–4) and (V)), together with their formal auxiliary sciences and their means-end based applied disciplines.*

This characterization of "science" gives us a demarcation between scientific and non-scientific disciplines and fields of mental activity. So it serves as a suggested solution of the *demarcation problem* (cf. sec. 1.1). We do not understand this demarcation problem, though, in the same way as logical positivism or critical rationalism did. First, we do not identify the non-scientific with the cognitively nonsensical (as e.g. Carnap 1928b). This identification is unacceptable, because empirically vacuous sentences such as "God exists," or fundamental norm sentences like "Help your neighbor" may nevertheless be *understood*, and so have a communicable *meaning*. Second, we do not devalue such sentences; we denote them as non-scientific, simply because there is no way to test them empirically. Third, we see the *practical* significance of the demarcation problem differently from Carnap. Our proposed solution of the demarcation problem does not serve the inner-philosophical purpose of eliminating a part of philosophy that is called "metaphysics." Rather, it serves the outer-philosophical or social purpose of delineating science from other intellectual activities in our society. This delineating is important in two respects.

One the one hand, the public debate on the question which kinds of information are sufficiently "objective" and "confirmed" to be taught in public schools, and which are not, demands demarcation criteria between science and religious ideology, and the satisfaction of this demand is, to a significant extent, the task of philosophy of science. As an example we mentioned in section 1.1 two famous cases in which judges based their decisions against the teaching of creationism in public schools on demarcation criteria developed by philosophers of science. We also mentioned that there is a controversy among philosophers of science themselves as to what the right demarcation criteria should be. Kitcher (2007, 11f) argued that because of the failures of the demarcation criteria proposed by logical positivists (see sec. 5.9.2), one should demarcate "intelligent design" not as a "pseudo"-science but as a "bad" or even "dead" science. Ladyman and Ross (2007, 30) prefer sociological over logical demarcation criteria. But sociological demarcation criteria are clearly insufficient. For example, Pennock (2011, 193ff) reports that Judge Jones suggested the application of peer-review methods as a social demarcation criterion. The reaction of Behe, a prominent defender of intelligent design, was to promote peer-reviews within the creationist camp. Behe pointed to a couple of creationist writers who, indeed, had been peer-reviewed—not by naturalistic scientists, but by other intellectual creationists. But the consent which a creationist writing earns from other creationists is clearly not an indication of its scientific character (cf. Schurz 2012).

On the other hand, demarcation criteria do not only have the task of delineation, but also of *explanation*. Looking back to the last one or two millennia of human development, science has made extremely rapid progress, compared to ethics, religion and arts which have developed slowly, at least in those domains where they have not been driven by external technological change. The factual differences in the level of *evolutionary impact* of the sciences in comparison to ethics, religion or art, and the degree in which they have changed our life, are so marked, that they positively beg to be explained. Anyone who wants to understand the powerful independent dynamics of science and technology has to find out what it is that separates science so strongly from non-scientific systems of ideas. In conclusion: any philosophy of science that wants to be of practical significance must face up to the demarcation problem.

2.6.2 Methodological Unity Instead of Physical Reductionism

Our demarcation account also contributes to the question of the *unity of science*. However, our understanding of the unity of sciences is not ontological, but methodological in nature, and therefore different from traditional accounts. The attempts in the 20th century to achieve a programmatic unification of the sciences were predominantly based on accounts of *reduction*, i.e. on attempts to provide an explanatory or ontological reduction from "higher-level" or "special" sciences to *physics*. There are, however, weaker and stronger sorts of reduction accounts. The career of 20th-century reduction accounts started with the program of *physicalism* of Otto Neurath, a prominent logical empiricist, who announced this program as a means to establish the unity of sciences. Neurath's physicalism was weaker than it sounds, insofar as it consisted only in the requirement that all scientific sentences should be translatable into statements about concrete spatiotemporal things and properties (Neurath 1934; Dahms 1994, 170).

A much stronger form of reductionism had been developed in the 1950s and 1960s: the program of *physical micro-reduction*, whose goal was a semantic or explanatory reduction of the laws of higher-level sciences to laws about underlying physical microstructure (see Oppenheim/Putnam 1958; Causey 1977). In spite of some positive examples (e.g., the micro-reduction of temperature to mean kinetic energy) this program was not especially successful, and does not describe the way according to which special sciences typically proceed. At every level of (at least moderately high) complexity, special sciences have discovered their own laws, which are called *system laws* in sec. 6.6.1. Examples are the chemical laws describing the behavior of molecules, biological laws about the functioning of organisms, psychological laws describing human behavior, etc.

There exist different concepts of reduction. In the standard account of Hempel (1969) and Nagel (1970, 125), a physical reduction of a law describing the behavior of a complex system consists in the derivation of this law, or an approximate version of it, from fundamental laws of physics together with contingent boundary conditions, and suitable correspondence principles that translate higher-level concepts into physical concepts. There exist three arguments, which show that the laws of special sciences are typically *not* reducible to physics in this sense, at least not fully (see also Cartwright 1983, 104f, 113f).

1 The argument from *hypercomplexity*: The fundamental physical law governing a specific physical system is expressed by its Schroedinger equation. However, already moderately complex systems such as a medium-sized molecule (as opposed to a simple atom) are far too complex to be solvable without radical simplification assumptions. These simplification assumptions do not come from fundamental physics but from empirical chemical knowledge. For this reason most chemists are convinced that chemistry will never be fully reducible to physics (cf. Hendry 2008, 525ff; Mortimer 1986). This is even more applicable for the laws that describe highly complex systems such as biological systems: here already the formulation of an approximately complete Schroedinger equation is impossible, and attempts to derive biological normal-case laws (sec. 4.5) from fundamental physics and factual descriptions of the physical microstructure of an organism are hopeless. Rather, biological laws are typically discovered by empirical-inductive means. This does not exclude the existence of *partial* reduction relations, e.g. between biochemistry and biology or neuroscience.

2 The argument from *multiple realizations*: Empirically identical macro-properties of a complex system, such as elasticity or intelligence, can be realized by very different physical microsystems (Fodor 1974). It is hard to find general principles that translate a given macro-property into an exhaustive disjunction of physical micro-properties.

3 The argument from the *systemic properties*: The parts of a complex system are systemic, which means that the properties of these parts in isolation or in a simpler system are different from the properties of the parts within the complex system. An example are the properties of the hydrogen atom H in water molecules H_2O (O for oxygen) which are different from the properties of the H atom in isolation, or in the H_2 molecule. This argument goes back to Broad (1925) and was elaborated by Hüttemann (2004, 42ff) and Ladyman/Ross (2007, sec. 1.6).

The argument from systemic properties only shows that a so-called "horizontal reduction" is usually impossible, i.e. the explanation of a complex system by the properties of its parts in isolation or in simpler systems. In contrast, "vertical reduction" means that the higher-level properties of a system are reducible to the lower-level properties of its parts *within* the system. Boogerd et al. (2005) argue with reference to biochemical networks that in spite of horizontal irreducibility, vertical reducibility is often possible, and is sufficient for explanations based on biochemical mechanisms. However, since the systemic properties of the parts are determined by the entire microstructure of the complex system, a full micro-reduction of the systemic properties of the parts is impossible for the same reasons that a micro-reduction of the entire system is impossible: for reasons of hypercomplexity.

These arguments show that hopes of a physical micro-reduction of the laws of complex systems are dim. On this reason, many philosophers of science have replaced the idea of explanatory reduction by the weaker requirement of *supervenience* (Hüttemann 2004). Supervenience requires not an explanatory reduction, but merely a "vertical" ontological determination: the physical microstructure of a system *determines* its higher-level properties (at the same given time point). As this determination relation may be infinitely complex, it does not imply the possibility of a reduction by human cognitive resources.

The opposite of supervenience is ontological *dualism*, according to which two physically identical systems can, nevertheless, differ in some higher-level non-physical properties, for example "having a mind" according to mind-body dualism. In fact, the supervenience position has been developed by Davidson (1970) as a naturalistic counter-position to Cartesian mind-body dualism. In the context of the reduction question for scientific theories, however, the supervenience position is fully compatible with the possibility, for which we have argued in this section, that an explanatory reduction of the sciences of complex systems to physics will not be possible in the foreseeable future.

In conclusion, the prospects of establishing the unity of sciences by methods of reduction to fundamental physics are not promising. What one finds along this route is not unity, but *ontological variety*. We suggest that the unity of the sciences should, rather, be sought by highlighting their epistemic-methodological common ground. The unity of the sciences, if it exists at all, does not exist at the ontological level, but in the form of their *methodological unity*. Of course, there are also important methodological differences between certain disciplines, which will be worked out in several chapters of this book (sec. 2.4.3, 3.1.4, 4.3.7, 4.5, 5.3.2, 6.4, 6.6.1). But our considerations so far have shown that there exist essential methodological features which are common to all empirical disciplines, despite their differences, and which delineate scientific from non-scientific intellectual activities: the ultimate epistemic goal (G), the epistemological assumptions (E1–5), the methodological building blocks (M1–4) and the value-neutrality requirement (V). In this methodological version, the idea of the unity of science can live on in a humbler, but more sustainable version.

2.7 Scientific Inference and Argumentation

In the methodological building blocks M3 and M4, scientific processes of argumentation and inference take place. Here we are dealing with very different processes of inference, which are explained in this section.

2.7.1 Deduction and Induction

When, in accordance with M3, we use a strict law hypothesis together with observation sentences to infer further observation sentences, then we are dealing with a logical-deductive inference. But when, in accordance with M4, we infer from the fact that a large number of actual observation sentences have so far confirmed a law hypothesis, that the law hypothesis is likely to be true, then we have made an inductive inference or, more accurately, an inductive generalization. Here are two examples:

(2.7–1)

Deductive inference (logic i.n.s.):	*Inductive generalization inference:*
All fish breathe using gills. This animal is a fish. Therefore this animal breathes using gills. *Certain*: truth transfer in all possible worlds.	All fish observed so far (no. 1, 2, … n) have breathed using gills. Therefore (probably) all fish breathe using gills. *Uncertain*: truth transfer only in sufficiently "uniform" possible worlds.

The decisive difference lies in the fact that only deductive inferences transfer the truth from the premises to the conclusion with *certainty*, that is, in all possible "worlds": *if* the premises (the sentences above the dividing line) are true, then the conclusion (the sentence beneath the dividing line) is also certainly true. Deductive inferences constitute the object of *logic in the narrow sense*. (Some authors place an inductive logic in opposition to deductive logic, e.g. Carnap 1950b, sec.43ff; this terminology is disputed however.)

In contrast, inductive generalizations are fundamentally uncertain— the double line in (2.7–1) indicates this uncertainty. This is because the premises of an inductive generalization tell us only about the cases observed *so far*, while the conclusion generalizes to *all* and, in particular, to all *future* cases. For this reason it is also said that inductive inferences are *content expanding*. Only in circumstances or worlds which are sufficiently uniform, whose future and past are sufficiently similar, can we reliably infer the truth of an inductive conclusion from the truth of the premises. Nothing can logically guarantee that the future course of events will be sufficiently similar to the course of events observed so far. An extinct fish without gills could, for example, be discovered tomorrow, or a new species of fish without gills could start to evolve through mutation.

This was (very roughly) the main argument of *David Hume*, who was the first philosopher to show that a justification of inductive inference is impossible by means of deductive logic. Hume went on, however, to cast doubt on the rational justifiability of induction as a whole, and even today more than a few philosophers think the problem of justifying induction is basically unsolvable. A closer look at the subtleties of this problem will be given in section 2.11. Before this, we introduce some refinements (this section), and explain the significance of inductive inferences in science (next section).

We have so far explained induction and deduction in the sense of the so-called *inductive-deductive scheme*. According to this scheme, which was already outlined by Aristotle, induction is a method of reasoning (or ascending) from the *particular* to the *general*, and deduction is a method of inferring (or descending) from the general back to the particular (see fig. 2.7–1).

Although this scheme includes some important methodological features of the sciences, it is oversimplified or even incorrect in several respects. For one thing, the binary division of types of inferences on which it rests is too narrow—there are far more types of inference, which we will briefly list here. Where the general is concerned, we must distinguish between *strict* (or deterministic) and *statistical* generalizations.

The *general* (laws and theories)

inductive ascent ⟶ ⟵ deductive descent

The *particular* (observations)

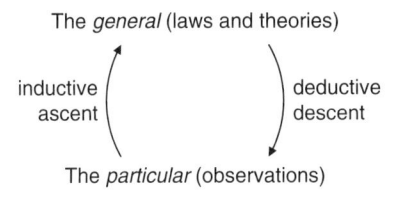

Figure 2.7–1 The inductive-deductive scheme

1 *Types of deductive inferences:*

   1.1 *From the (strictly) general to the particular*—e.g. All Fs are Gs, this is an F, therefore: this is a G.
   1.2 *From the general to the general*—e.g. All Fs are Gs, All Gs are Hs, therefore: all Fs are Hs.
   1.3 *From the particular to the particular*—e.g. This is an F or a G, this is not an F, therefore: this is a G.

In contrast, there are no deductive inferences from the particular to the (essentially) general.

2 *Types of inductive inferences* (see also Carnap 1950b, 207f):

   2.1 *From the particular to the general:*

      2.1.1 *The strict inductive generalization:* All Fs observed so far were G, therefore (probably) all Fs are Gs.
      2.1.2 *The inductive-statistical generalization*: r% of all Fs observed so far were G, therefore (probably) approximately r% of all Fs are Gs.

   2.2 *From the particular to the particular—the inductive prediction:* All Fs observed so far were G, therefore the *next* F will probably be a G too.
   2.3 *From the general to the particular—the inductive-statistical specialization:* r% of all Fs are Gs, this individual is an F, therefore we can be r% sure that this individual is a G.

Inductive specializations are also called "direct inference" (Levi 1977) and are related to the "statistical principal principle" (sec. 3.13.5). Two facts about them are remarkable: first, the strict variant of inductive specializations is deductively valid. Second, like inductive generalizations, inductive-statistical specializations assume uniformity: they are only reliable if our actual observation sample is representative for the total domain.

2.7.2 Popper and the Significance of Inductive Inference in the Sciences

The founder of critical rationalism, Karl Popper, advocated the thesis that the induction problem is, on the one hand, unsolvable, but, on the other hand, that empirical science can proceed without inductive inferences altogether (1935/2002, sec. I). In the following we want to demonstrate, based on a differentiation between *three kinds of induction*, that Popper's arguments bring to light important insights, but that his radical claim that empirical science could go without induction is not tenable (cf. Schurz 2002a).

1 *Methodological induction.* This view of induction connects directly with the inductive-deductive scheme explained in sec. 2.7.1. According to this view, induction is a method of inferring general laws and theories by inductive generalization from particular observations. Popper criticizes the view contained in methodological induction, that induction is the central method of discovering or generating law hypotheses and theories. The belief that such a discovery method is at all necessary in science rests, says Popper, on a confusion of the *context of discovery* and the *context of justification* (1935/2002, sec. I.1–2). How scientific hypotheses are generated, be it through induction, intuition, or trial and error, is completely irrelevant to the context of justification. Seen like this, methodological induction is dispensable in the context of justification of science.

By contrast, call to mind sec. 2.1: certain methods of generating hypotheses do not have to, but *can* give us a certain measure of justification as well. This is the case, for example, for the strictly and statistically inductive generalizations explained in sec. 2.7.1: these inductive inferences are methods of discovering empirical law hypotheses, which at the same time inductively justify these law hypotheses, i.e. preliminarily confirm them. More refined inductive discovery algorithms can be found in Langley et al. (1987) (see also sec. 4.2.2, 4.3.2). Hypothesis-generating procedures which, at the same time, give us a justification are of course cognitively much more efficient than blind trial and error procedures.

In two important points, however, Popper's criticism of methodological induction is right. (i) Hypotheses do not *have* to be produced by methodological induction—all methods of producing hypotheses are allowed and deserve critical assessment. (ii) Inductive generation methods exist for empirical law hypotheses, but for the construction of scientific theories, such generation methods do not exist—at least not in general. Even very simple theories—like for example the Galilean law of free fall, which posits the idealization of a friction-free fall—cannot be created by inductive generalization procedures alone, since they contain concepts that transcend the observable—so-called *theoretical concepts*, such as "friction-free movement," "mass," or "force." So Popper's criticism of the possibility to create scientific theories by methodological induction (see 1983, 118) is, to a large extent, legitimate.

2 *Logical induction.* This view of induction goes back to Carnap (1950b) and understands induction not as a method of discovery, but as one of justification of scientific hypotheses, that is, as a method of determining the *degree of confirmation* conferred on theories by given observational data. This should happen by the establishment of a system of logical probability, in which the inductive probability of a theory given a body of observational evidence may be determined in a rational way (see sec. 4.7.3). Instead of the inductive degree of confirmation, one can alternatively regard the degree of (epistemic) *truthlikeness* of a theory relative to a body of evidence as the central means of evaluating theories (see prop. 5.6–5).

Popper's criticism of the view of logical induction now says the following (1983, 19f, 23): while we are able to determine that relative to given observations a theory T_1 is *better* confirmed or corroborated than another theory T_2, or that T_1 is closer to the truth than T_2, we still cannot give an *absolute* value for the probability or truthlikeness of T_1 or T_2, as tomorrow a new superior theory T_3 may be developed, which completely overshadows both T_1 and T_2. Popper's argument represents a substantial insight into the limitations of logical induction. For in order to assign a non-arbitrary numeric value to the inductive probability or truthlikeness of a theory T given some evidence, one must have at one's disposal, among other things, a comprehensive list of all relevant alternative theories $\{T_1, T_2, ...\}$. However, to establish such a list in a non-arbitrary manner is, at least in the case of theories, impossible. For any given theory T, there are always indefinitely many alternative theories, as these might contain any number of new theoretical concepts. A measurable linguistic space containing all possible alternative theories simply does not exist (see Howson 2000, 46).

Again, in the case of *empirical* hypotheses the situation is different. Here it is possible to establish a finite list of all possible alternative hypotheses in a *limited* observational vocabulary. Let us consider, for example, the set of all interval hypotheses of the form H_n = "between n and n + 1% of all humans are brown-eyed," with $0 \leq n \leq 99$, and let us assume a uniform distribution of the prior probabilities of these hypotheses. Then the inductive probability of H_n, given a sample of m humans, including $k \leq m$ with brown eyes, can be calculated based on Kolmogorov's probability axioms and the statistical principal principle (sec. 4.7.2–3). In summary, Popper's criticism of logical induction for empirical law hypotheses is unjustified or at least exaggerated; but it is certainly justified in the case of scientific theories.

Based on Popper's criticism of logical induction, we can evaluate competing theories only *comparatively*, i.e. in relation to each other. Once we have carried out an empirical success comparison of currently available alternative theories, we will base our future predictions and actions on those theories which, up to now, have been most successful, in other words, on the ones which have been corroborated best. Popper, of course, also sees it this way (1983, 65; 1979, sec. I.9). It follows from this that Popper's "deductivist" program of corroboration, too, contains in its core a fundamental inductive step—a third kind of induction, which along with Musgrave (2002), I have called epistemic induction.

3 *Epistemic induction* (or *meta-induction*) says the following: If a theory T_1 has been more successful than T_2 *so far* (explanatory and prognostically), then it is probable, *relative* to the given state of evidence, that T_1 will also be more successful than T_2 *in future*. In other words, the success preferences established so far are projected inductively into the future. This induction principle is called "epistemic induction," or "meta-induction" in Schurz (2008b), because it is not object-level hypotheses (about ordinary events), but epistemic meta-hypotheses about the degree of corroboration of our object-hypotheses, which are being inductively projected. The epistemic induction principle is, indeed, indispensable for all empirical disciplines. Were this principle not to be accepted, there would not be any point in Popper's method of testing. Success so far would then simply be irrelevant to our future actions. Although, for example, the view that heavy bodies on Earth are disposed to fall to the ground and not to float freely has been better corroborated so far than the opposite view, this would not be a reason to make this view the basis of our future actions, since logically, all bodies might just as well start floating as of tomorrow. Unfortunately, Popper kept an exaggerated distance to logical empiricism throughout his life, and condemned any form of induction whatsoever. But his arguments on this topic in (1983, e.g. 66f) seem to rest more on mere terminologi-

cal maneuvers than on actual material reasons (see Schurz 2002a). Critical rationalists like Watkins (1984, 340f) and Musgrave (2002) have also accepted the epistemic induction principle.

Epistemic induction, let us remember, is always only *comparative*. An important consequence of this is the following: according to epistemic induction, the degree of confirmation of a theory is always *doubly* relative:

- relative to the given state of observational knowledge, and
- relative to the current state of alternative theories.

2.7.3 Abduction and Inference to the Best Explanation

Scientific theories differ from empirical law hypotheses in that they contain theoretical concepts which speak about unobservable entities or properties. Inductive generalization enables us to infer from particular observations to empirical law hypotheses, but not from empirical law hypotheses to scientific theories. This is because inductive inferences cannot introduce new (theoretical) concepts into the conclusion, which are not contained in the premises. There is, however, one further—but controversial—kind of inference, with which this is possible, namely abduction, or inference to the best explanation. Roughly expressed, this is an inference from an observed *effect* to a likely *cause*, e.g. from a curved trail in the sand to the recent passage of a sand viper.

Here we must warn against a terminological misunderstanding. A number of authors understand the concept of induction in a broad sense—they identify inductive inferences with *any* kind of content-expanding or non-deductive inferences, and so regard abduction as a form of induction (e.g. Earman 1992; Bird 1998, 13; Ladyman 1998, 28). In contrast, for the sake of a clear demarcation between distinct concepts, I understand induction always in the above outlined *Humean* sense, and see abduction as a second non-deductive or content-expanding kind of inference.

The abductive form of inference goes back to C. S. Peirce. In (1878a), Peirce explicated abductive inference formally as a retrodictive inference from "all Fs are Gs" and "this is a G" to "this is an F." While this characterization of abduction does dominate the computer science literature on abduction (see Flach/Kakas 2000), it is much too narrow to grasp what the late Peirce was trying to achieve. The essential thing for Peirce (1903, §170) was that abductive inference allows new theoretical concepts and models to be introduced in the sciences. Newton, for example, inferred abductively from the movement of the planets around the sun to the existence of a gravitational force. The epistemological inference from subject-internal perceptual experience to external empirical facts is also an abductive inference: the assumption that my visual experiences are being caused by objects existing independently of me is the best explanation for the constantly recurring regularities in my visual experiences (cf. Moser 1989, 91f). As is shown in Schurz (2008a), abduction comprises a whole family of kinds of inferences, which have the following pattern in common (cf. Peirce 1903, §189; Niiniluoto 1999):

> (Prop. 2.7-1) *General pattern of abduction*:
>
> *Premise 1:* A (singular or general) fact E, in need of explanation.
> *"Premise" 2:* A background knowledge K, which implies for a hypothesis H, that H is a possible and sufficiently plausible explanation for E.
>
> *Abductive conjecture:* H is true.

As Peirce himself emphasized, the trustworthiness of an abductively acquired hypothesis is rather preliminary: the abducted hypothesis must go on to be empirically tested by deduction and induction in order to acquire the character of a probable hypothesis (1903, §171). More importantly, the given background knowledge always contains *several* possible hypotheses, $H_1, \ldots, H_n$, which potentially explain the given evidence E; and the abductive inference selects the most plausible hypothesis among them. In this sense, Harman (1965) transformed Peirce's concept of abduction into the following inference to the best or best available explanation (IBE).

> (Prop. 2.7-2) *Inference to the best (available) explanation—IBE*:
> Infer abductively to the most plausible explanatory hypothesis among all explanatory hypotheses for the given explanandum E which are possible (or are available in the given background knowledge).

According to the understanding of Harman's (1965) and other representatives of IBE (Lipton 1991; Armstrong 1983), an IBE infers from the explanatory success of a theory to its *likely truth* in the realistic sense. Lipton (1991, 58) and van Fraassen (1989, 142ff) have pointed out that one can infer only to the best *available* explanation, because no one knows all possible explanations. In particular, some "explanations" may be "too bad" to be scientifically acceptable—for example, post-facto explanations of (otherwise unexplainable) phenomena by a "divine intervention" (see sec. 5.10.3). These facts cast doubt on the traditional view of IBEs as inferences to the probable truth of the best available explanation.

In this situation, Kuipers (2000, sec. 7.5.3) has made an interesting suggestion. He brings the same objection into play as Popper made against logical induction: de facto, we can only ever reach *comparative* judgments, according to which a theory is explanatorily more successful and, hence, likely to be closer to the truth than all alternative theories *known* to us. Since this "explanatory success" includes also "predictive success," Kuipers speaks more generally of "empirical success." Kuipers, therefore, suggests modifying the pattern of abduction in the following way: first, instead of speaking of an "inference to the best explanation," he speaks of an "inference to the best theory," and second, the premise that a theory T is empirically most adequate among all known alternative theories does not lead to the conclusion that T is likely to be true, but only that T is *closest to the truth* among all known alternative theories. The interaction of the epistemic inductive inference and the abductive inference to the best theory is shown in fig. 2.7-2.

In fig. 2.7-2 it becomes clear, how these two kinds of inference are connected with the positions of *instrumentalism* and *realism* in the philosophy of science. Instrumentalists, such as van Fraassen, accept the

(1) *Evidence:* T_k is among the alternative theories $T_1,...,T_n$ *so far* the empirically most successful.

| epistemic inductive inference
↓

(2) *Instrumentalist conclusion:* T_k is among $T_1,...,T_n$ the most empirically adequate (therefore also in future the most empirically successful)

| abductive inference to the best theory
↓

(3) *Realistic conclusion:* T_k is among $T_1,...,T_n$ the closest to the truth.

Figure 2.7–2 Interaction of epistemic induction and abduction

inference from (1) to (2), but reject the abductive inference from (2) to (3) because, according to them, theories can only be justified to be more or less empirically adequate, but not to be true or false in the realistic sense (van Fraassen 1980, 11f, 20; 1989, 142f). Realists in the philosophy of science believe, on the other hand, in the likely truth or truthlikeness of well-confirmed theories; for them it is that very inference from (2) to (3) which is essential.

Note that not all abductions infer theoretical hypotheses. Many abductions infer only empirical causes; their justification is usually reducible to induction (cf. Fumerton 1980, 592f). The justification of abductive inferences that introduce new theoretical laws, however, is even more difficult than the justification of induction; this problem is further discussed in sections 2.11 and 5.7.

2.7.4 Monotonic and Non-Monotonic Inferences

Because deductive inferences are certain, i.e. preserve truth (from premises to conclusion) in all possible worlds, they are monotonic in the following sense.

> (Def. 2.7–1) *Monotonicity:* A valid inference (from premises $P_1,...,P_n$ to a conclusion C) is called monotonic, iff it remains valid after the addition of arbitrary further premises.

In contrast, inductive or abductive inferences do not possess the monotonicity property, because they are uncertain, i.e. they do not transfer truth in all, but only in sufficiently "normal" worlds. We restrict the notion of *validity* to deductive inferences (indicated by a single forward slash "/"), while in the case of uncertain inferences we speak instead of their (non-deductive) *correctness* (indicated by a double forward slash "//"). With this notation, monotonicity means that if "$P_1,..., P_n$ / C" is valid, then "$P_1,..., P_n$, Q / C" is valid for every new premise Q.

The non-monotonicity of uncertain inferences makes it possible that "$P_1,..., P_n$ // C" is correct, but "Q, $P_1,..., P_n$ // C" is incorrect for some (true) premise Q, where Q typically expresses "exceptional information." For example, "1000 swans have been observed to be white // Therefore probably: All swans are white" is a correct inductive generalization, but the premise-expanded inference "1000 swans have been observed to be white and 10 to be black // Therefore probably: All swans are white" is inductively incorrect. The logical examination of *non-monotonic* inferences has become a significant area of enquiry since the 1980s (cf. Gabbay et al. 1994; Schurz 2004).

A non-monotonic inference with true premises has only *preliminary* value, and can be made worthless by new (true) information. The preliminary nature of non-monotonic inferences is expressed by the fact that they have a different *epistemic application rule* from monotonic inferences. Here, we take the *belief system* (or "knowledge" system) S of a person or group of persons to be the set of propositions which are justifiably accepted as true by these persons.

(Prop. 2.7–3) *Application rule for monotonic inferences:* If a deductive inference is valid, then you should add its conclusion to your belief system S, as long as S contains the premises.

(Prop. 2.7–4) *Application rule for non-monotonic inferences:* If an uncertain inference is correct, then you should add its conclusion to your belief system S, as long as S contains the premises, and these premises cover *all* propositions in S which are of relevance to the conclusion.

For inductive-probabilistic inferences, prop. 2.7–4 is equivalent to Reichenbach's rule of the narrowest reference class and Carnap's requirement of total evidence (see sec. 3.9.1, 3.13.5).

COMPLEMENTARY AND ADVANCED TOPICS

2.8 How Much Metaphysics is Presupposed by Science?

2.8.1 Truth, Idealism and Realism

It could be argued that our reconstruction of the supreme goal (G) of the sciences and the assumption (E1) of minimal realism assume too much of realism. Famous scientists and philosophers of science, such as George Berkeley (1685–1753), Ernst Mach (1836–1916), or the early Rudolf Carnap, were idealists or positivists, i.e. anti-realists. In their view, science is possible if it is merely based on human intersubjective experiences, *without* the presupposition of a subject-independent reality that transcends these experiences. We do not deny this possibility.

Admittedly, our assumption (E1) makes a (weak) realistic assumption, which is discussed below. Some philosophers argue that already our explication of (G), the discovery of content-rich truths, presupposes realism, insofar as truth means correspondence of statements with an assumed reality. But this is not the case, since (G) does not say that the domain of phenomena to which true statements correspond has to belong to an external and subject-independent reality, as claimed by realists. It may also consist of experiences, as assumed by idealists.

Following Dancy (1985, 136ff), the major epistemological positions can be summarized as follows: The domain of entities to which true statements correspond consists either of

a one's own subjective experiences (*subjective idealism* or solipsism),
b the experiences of all subjects (*intersubjective idealism*),
c the *possible* experiences of all subjects (*possibilistic idealism*), or
d a subject-independent reality that causes the experiences (*realism*).

Solipsism is a rather extreme position (most idealists have been possibilistic idealists). However that may be: the important point to observe here is that the concept of *truth* makes sense in *all* of these positions. Hence, truth in the sense of correspondence theory is not realistically biased but *metaphysically neutral* (cf. Kirkham 1992, sec. 6.5). So also our formulation of (G) is neutral. It does not entail that successful science presupposes the epistemology of realism. The goal of truth makes sense for *all* of the epistemological positions; only the *kinds* of truths that according to these positions are pursued by science are different (true descriptions of experiences versus true descriptions of subject-independent facts).

While (G) is metaphysically neutral, our epistemic assumption (E1) is not. It asserts that realism, in the explained weak version of it, is the *normal* epistemological assumption of science. I think this claim is defensible: more or less all empirical scientists assume the external reality of their objects of investigation; idealistic or anti-realistic world-views are the clear exception in normal science, although the realistic attitude of normal science can be rattled in scientific revolutions. Based on scientific revolutions even philosophy of science may be forced to revise its own normative corrective (recall sec. 2.1).

What distinguishes our minimal realism from all sorts of *metaphysical realism* is that neither the existence of a subject-independent reality, nor its knowability, is assumed to hold on a-priori reasons, or is a necessary presupposition of knowledge. In contrast, the minimal realism of assumption E1 is a *hypothetical-constructive* realism, insofar as we consider realism not as a presupposition, but as a hypothesis or model construction—in analogy to scientific hypotheses, but epistemologically more fundamental. Our realism is committed to *methodological naturalism*, as the hypothesis of realism must be corroborated by the *empirical success* of our cognitive belief system, as the *best explanation* of this success (cf. Schurz 2008a, sec. 7.4). In sec. 2.7.3 we have seen that this reasoning takes the form of an *abductive inference* from the empirical success of our theories to their (partial) correspondence with reality.

Because of its naturalistic tenets, hypothetical-constructive realism is compatible with legitimate doubts about a "full" realism found in the philosophical interpretations of *quantum mechanics*. In all of its interpretations, quantum mechanics assumes the existence of a microphysical reality that possesses some subject-independent and discoverable properties (so-called "observables"). Only certain properties of entangled (or superposition) states are not objectively discoverable, and in some interpretations, even subject-dependent, because it is a postulate of quantum mechanics that every measurement transforms an entangled state into a statistical ensemble of pure states (see Herbert 1985, sec. 8, 9; Penrose 2007, sec. 29).

Hypothetical-constructive realism is also compatible with *structural* realism. In its *epistemic* version structural realism says that only the structure, but not the intrinsic nature, of the entities making up reality are knowable (Worrall 1989/97; Psillos 1995; Votsis 2011). The *ontic* version of structural realism is motivated by quantum mechanics and claims that even the entities that make up reality are themselves not individuals but structures (Ladyman 1998; French/Ladyman 2003).

2.8.2 Constructive Realism versus Radical Constructivism

Hypothetical-constructive realism differs markedly from so-called radical *constructivism*. The latter position was developed by psychologists such as Glasersfeld (1995) or biologists like Maturana and Varela (1992). Historically speaking, radical constructivism is a modern variant of subjective idealism. The main argumentation of this philosophical position is based on the fact that our perceptions and concepts of reality are cognitive *constructions* of our mind or brain, respectively. Radical constructivists, however, infer from this hardly deniable premise that even "reality" is a construction—i.e. that a discoverable reality that is independent from our constructions does not exist. A similar argument has been put forward by social constructivists such as Latour and

Woolgar (1986), in regard to the "construction" of scientific facts by scientists.

In this subsection we want to show that the argument of radical constructivists is based on a *fallacy*. We reconstruct this argument as follows (e.g. Glasersfeld 1995, 40, 51; Kriz et al. 1990, 19f):

(2.8–1) *Premise of radical constructivism = epistemic constructivism:* Our perception and mental representation of reality is not something given, but the result of an active cognitive construction.

Conclusion of radical constructivism = ontological constructivism (idealism): Therefore reality, too, is not given "in itself," but "constructed" or "constituted" by us.

The crucial fallacy of this argument is the "magical transformation" of epistemic into ontological constructivism (cf. Sokal and Brickmont 1998, 102). Hypothetical-constructive realism shares the premise of (2.8–1) with radical constructivism, but it definitively rejects the conclusion. The *invalid* step from epistemic to ontological constructivism is frequently substantiated by constructivists with the help of the following "justification" (cf. Kriz et al. 1990, 20; Glasersfeld 1995, 51), which may be called the *Kantian fallacy*, because it corresponds to a popular interpretation of Kant's philosophy:

(2.8–2) *"Justification" of radical constructivism:* It is impossible to know something about reality *in itself*—independent of its epistemological construction. The only thing about which we can know something is the reality *constructed by us*.

The subtle error of this justification attempt is that the concept of "knowing" is understood in the *naive-realistic* sense of a kind of direct mirror-imaging. Then it is indeed impossible to know something about an object "independent of its epistemological construction"—which in this case means: "*not influenced* by this construction." Modern truth theory, though, understands the relationship between a true statement and its object not as a quasi-identical mirror-image, but as a *structural correspondence*, which *conveys certain information* and neither has to be complete nor unique. In this view, there is no incoherence in saying that *by means of* our epistemological constructions we know something about a reality which exists *independently* of our epistemological constructions, keeping in mind that our epistemological constructions are not a quasi-identical mirror-image of reality, but only an incomplete structural representation of it. An independently existing reality is not taken to be immediately given to our mind, as in metaphysical or "direct" realism, but is postulated as a system of hypothetical entities, whose existence can best explain the factual success of our knowledge. Giere (1999, 174ff) and Kuipers (2000, sec. 13) have called this position "constructive realism," and I call it hypothetico-constructive realism, in order to emphasize that realism too is ultimately a fallible hypothesis.

In conclusion, it is the very argumentation of radical constructivists which clings to naive realism, inasmuch as it uses a naive-realistic interpretation of the objects of our knowledge to prove that these objects are subjectively constructed; while from the hypothetical-realistic view, the statement (2.8–2) and so the whole argumentation of radical constructivists is untenable.

2.9 On the Theory (In)dependence of Observation

Classical empiricists argued that all scientific (or cognitively valuable) concepts are reducible to observational concepts. That this is not so was convincingly demonstrated by the recognition of *theoretical concepts* in the middle and later stages of logical empiricism (cf. Carnap 1936/37, 1956a). Theoretical concepts go beyond what is observable—this is a generally accepted insight in post-positivistic philosophy of science. Accordingly, the empiricism in our reconstruction of the common epistemological ground of science is reduced to a minimalistic version according to which theories, although going beyond what is observable, must at least have *some* observable consequences by which they are testable.

What minimalistic empiricism still assumes is the existence of at least *some* theory-independent observation concepts and sentences, which can be used to independently test competing theories. However, even this minimalistic empiricism came under attack in the post-positivistic philosophy of science. The thesis of the *theory-dependence* of all observation and experience has been made popular by Hanson (1958), Kuhn (1962), and Feyerabend (1975); with precursors in Wittgenstein (1945/2001, part 2, §xi) and Popper (1935/2002, new appendix X). Meanwhile this thesis seems to be accepted by the majority of philosophers of science. Closer inspection reveals, however, that what is accepted by the majority of philosophers is a cautious and loose version of this thesis, that leaves plenty of room for interpretations that are compatible with our epistemological assumptions (E3) of objectivity and intersubjectivity, and (E4) of minimal empiricism. For many philosophers of science, what is important in the theory-ladenness thesis is a critical attitude towards what is called "data" in science: these data are typically theory-laden interpretations of the scientist's perceptions, and the assumptions (e.g. concerning measurement devices) made in these interpretations are often enough concealed behind a veil of expertocraty. Nevertheless, I will try to show in this section that in all disciplines of empirical sciences one can find theory-neutral observation concepts and statements that scientists may draw on in cases of conflicts of opinion.

Before I start my enterprise, let me try to demonstrate the significance of this question for philosophy of science. A *complete* theory-dependence of observations, in the sense that *all* observations are theory-dependent, would turn empirical science into a circular affair without any hope of objectivity (cf. Nagel 1979, 79). For suppose that two adherents of rival theories T_1 and T_2 are observing the same area of space-time, and assume that their respective theories imply the contradictory predictions P_1 and P_2. If complete theory-dependence were given, then the observations of the theory-adherents would be determined by their theoretical *expectations*. The supporter of T_1 would then observe P_1 where the supporter of T_2 observes P_2. So each prediction would be a *self-fulfilling* prediction, and an independent empirical test of theories would be impossible.

In contrast, a *partial* theory-dependence, in the sense that there are at least some theory-neutral observations on which theory-dependent scientific data rest, is not a threat to the possibility of objective empirical tests. Adam (2004) and Brown (1993) have studied cases in which the recognition of a scientific datum D that falsifies a theory T, relies on the assumption that theory T is true. This sounds paradoxical, but in fact is not: the case is harmless, because the datum D was gained from a theory-neutral observation O using T. This means (in the simplest case) that T entails the implication *if O, then D*. Moreover, that T is falsified by D means that D entails not-T. Taken together this implies by simple logical means that O entails not-T, i.e. that the observation O falsifies T. Nothing paradoxical is involved in this situation.

In conclusion, for a defense of the objectivity of empirical science it is sufficient to refute the thesis of complete theory-dependence, i.e. to establish the existence of *some* theory-neutral observation concepts and statements in science. In the next subsection, I will suggest a disentanglement of different problems that fosters a reasonable evaluation of the theory-ladenness thesis. I will sketch eight central arguments in favor of different forms of theory-dependence as well as the corresponding counterarguments. I will try to show that although the pro arguments make correct points, they do not exclude the existence of theory-neutral observations in a certain sense.

2.9.1 Theory-Dependency of Observation—Pros and Cons

- *Pro-1: Observations are expressed as realistic statements.* Observation statements such as "this thing is green" are usually expressed in the realistic mode. So they imply the *hypothesis of realism*, i.e. the existence of subject-independently existing objects ("this thing") that cause our subjective perception (cf. Popper 1935/2002, sec. V, §25, for a version of this argument). Observation sentences in this realistic interpretation transcend the content of subjective experience. We can be in *error* about them, for example, because our sense experience might rest on a *hallucination*.
- *Contra-1:* This argument is true, but this is not what is meant with theory-dependency of observation. What is meant is that the *content* of one's observations depends on the *content* of one's background theory (expectation or world view). But the question whether one is an epistemological realist or phenomenalistic idealist does not affect the content of one's observations. It merely changes the interpretation of the term "thing": in the realistic interpretation, this term refers to assumed entities outside of one's experiences, and in the phenomenalistic interpretation it refers to entities within one's experiences. But whether one is realist or idealist does not turn a green-observation into a blue-observation (this argument can be found in Carnap 1928b).

- *Pro-2: Observations are theory-guided.* The selection of relevant problems and experiments is essential in all scientific research, for reasons of complexity alone. This selection is guided (among other things) by one's theory: which theory I support determines which observations I look for.[1]
- *Contra-2:* It is true that the selection of one's observations depends on one's theories and, more generally, on one's interests. But that observations are selected in a theory-dependent way does not imply that the observations *themselves* are theory-dependent, in the sense that supporters of different theories would observe different things when perceiving the same spatiotemporal region or measurement result. Supporters of theory T_2 *could* also make the observations made by supporters of theory T_1, and *would* then recognize their truth. More generally, the interest-drivenness of empirical research does not imply that certain observations *cannot* be made, but at most that these observations are not *wanted* to be made, or that they are *ignored*. An intersubjective test of the theories that select one's observations is not only possible, but is an important remedy against scientific dogmatism.

- *Pro-3: Perceptions are unconscious theoretical constructions.* That perceptions or observations in the *narrow* sense (i.n.s.) are unconscious theory-like constructions is an insight that goes back to Helmholtz

(1896/1910). The brain's visual regions use refined neural construction mechanisms to create a consciously experienced 3D image from the unconscious 2D retinal light-impressions. Normally this construction process generates a unique 3D image within milliseconds, so that its constructive character is *hidden* from the consciousness: you think you see "reality itself" (for this reason humans are intuitively naive realists). But in certain—typically in artificially engineered—situations, this visual construction process reveals its constructive character, because it leads to consciously experienced visual *ambiguities*, *illusions* or other strange effects. This has been impressively demonstrated by the findings of cognitive psychology (cf. Rock 1984). Simple examples of ambiguities are *tilting pictures* such as Jastrow's duck-rabbit, a picture that can be seen either as a duck or a rabbit (see fig. 2.9–1). The duck-rabbit has been used by Wittgenstein (1945/2001, part II, §xi), Hanson (1958, 12) and Kuhn (1962, 112ff) as evidence for the "theory-dependence" of perception, insofar as what we *expect* to see influences what we see.

An example of an *optical illusion* is the Mueller-Lyer illusion in fig. 2.9–2. The explanation of this illusion lies in mechanisms of 3D-vision: the arrows and inverted arrows produce the 3D-effect that the right stroke appears to be closer to the observer than the left stroke and, hence, appears to be shorter, although both strokes have equal length (see Rock 1984, 163, 167).

• *Contra-3*: Neither the logical empiricists nor Popper had good replies to the psychological arguments concerning the constructive character of perception, because according to their position of "logical purity," philosophy should be *independent* from psychology. What counts as an observation sentence was, logically speaking, a matter of "pure convention" (cf. Popper 1935/2002, sec. 5, §30; Neurath 1934). We now present some arguments against the theory-ladenness of perceptions that are themselves based on findings from cognitive psychology.

The findings about the constructive character of visual processes refute only *direct realism* (Dancy 1985, 144). According to this epistemological position we see things directly, as they are "in themselves,"

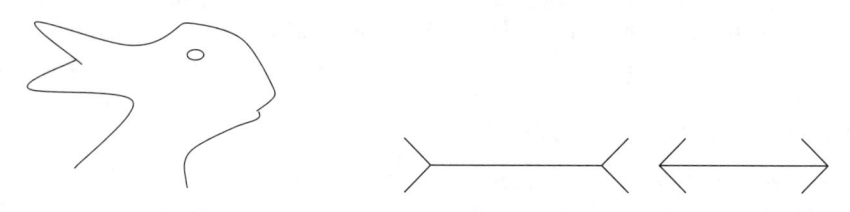

Figure 2.9–1 Duck-rabbit

Figure 2.9–2 Mueller-Lyer-illusion

without any mediating processes that construct intermediate images. In the light of contemporary knowledge about the complicated process leading from the reflection of light from an object via the stimulation of retina cells to successively refined neuronal images, direct realism seems to be an untenable position.

However, all findings of cognitive psychology also confirm that our visual perception processes and their results are quite stubbornly *independent* of our *learned* information. Everyone experiences the right stroke in fig. 2.9-2 as shorter than the left one, even if they have been informed that this visual experience is an illusion. These facts motivated Fodor's thesis of the modularity and impenetrability of vision (Fodor 1984, 34ff). Also the "Helmholtzian" constructivist Rock (1984, 228) acknowledges the independence of vision from acquired information.

In the tilting picture of fig. 2.9-1, everybody is able to perceive it either as duck or as rabbit and to switch back and forth between these two gestalts. Kuhn argued that a similar gestalt switch took place when astronomers saw Uranus before 1781 as a fixed star, but after 1781 as a moving planet (1962, 111, 121f). But it does not seem right to conceive the Uranus case as perceptual switch: The visual content of the Uranus-perception is always a bright spot in the sky, which is perceptively stable and does not switch; the question whether it represents a fixed star or a planet is not a question of perception but of theoretical interpretation.

The processes of human vision are based on innate mechanisms that have developed over millions of years of evolutionary history. Their selection history explains why the *same* mechanisms which under normal environmental conditions give a correct visual depiction of reality, can create optical illusions under certain non-normal conditions. Evolutionary considerations also explain why human perception, in order to be evolutionary successful, must be independent from expectations, for otherwise it could not correct *wrong* expectations. As an example, consider prehistoric men entering a cave which is inhabited by a cave bear that they did not expect: if their perception had not immediately corrected their wrong expectation, these prehistoric men would not have survived.

By "theory-dependence" of perception one could, at best, understand that perception is dependent not on learned information, but on "innate theories" which all humans share, because they are rigidly wired up in their visual cortex. However, we do not want to understand the concept of "theory" in such an overstretched way.[2] By the theory-dependence of perception we always only mean: the dependence of perception on *acquired* information, that may vary in different subjects, cultures, or scientific communities. It seems that visual perception in this sense is—at least to a large extent—theory-independent.

- *Pro-4: Sometimes visual perception depends on one's pre-expectations.* The last statement of Contra-3, that visual perception is independent from pre-expectation, is not generally true—it holds only for clearly presented visual stimuli. There exist some psychologically well-investigated experiments, to be discussed below, in which visual perception does indeed depend on pre-expectations.
- *Contra-4: This is only the case for the stimuli at the perceptibility threshold,* i.e. when the limits of perceptual recognition capacities are reached (cf. Brewer/Lambert 2001, S181). These limits are reached in three kinds of cases:

1 *Poorness* of the stimulus: For example, (1.1) in a dark forest at night anxious persons seem to see the contours of mysterious figures in the dark thicket, which disappear at daylight. Or (1.2), if the relevant stimulus is too small to be seen, e.g. when you ask which of two approximately equally long strokes is the longer one, the test persons' answers may become expectation-dependent. The perceptibility threshold is also reached when (1.3) the presentation time of the stimulus is very short, as in high-speed reading tasks (cf. Estany 2001, 208). Poorness of stimuli explains also certain expectation-dependent observations in astronomy (Forbes 1983).
2 *Ambiguity* of a stimulus that has no unique gestalt solution, such as the duck-rabbit in fig. 2.9–1: Also here, one's expectation about the gestalt influences which gestalt one sees.
3 A *high complexity* of the relevant stimuli pattern is a third reason, not for expectation-dependence, but for dependence on acquired knowledge. For here, visual *training* may be necessary to detect the relevant visual patterns. As an example, think of the radiologist who recognizes pneumonia in the X-ray image of your chest.

Because of these findings, some cognitive psychologists described human vision as a combination of bottom-up processes (information flow from the retina cells) and top-down processes (information flow from higher cognitive regions; cf. Estany 2001, sec. 4). Although this description is not false, it misses the important point of this combination, namely the *priority ordering* in favor of bottom-up information. Top-down information from expectation by memory can correct visual bottom-up information *only* if this bottom-up information is *too poor* to allow a clear gestalt interpretation. Otherwise bottom-up information *overrides* top-down expectations. This is illustrated, for example, by an experiment in which a test person looks through a peephole with one eye at two white balls of equal size and distance in an otherwise dark black box (cf. Rock 1984, 80f). In this experiment, all cues about the distance of the two balls coming from bottom-up information have been eliminated: there is no (a) binocular depth information nor (b) monocular depth vision (e.g. by motion parallax via eye movement). If one tells the test person that one is a tennis ball and the other a ping pong ball, the tennis ball is perceived as being further away. This illustrates the utilization of acquired information when bottom-up information is missing. However, as soon as cues of sort (a) or (b) are admitted, e.g. when the peephole is broadened and the person is allowed to move her eye or to look with two eyes, the illusion disappears and the person sees the two balls at equal distance and size.

• *Pro-5: Scientific data (or observations i.w.s.) are theory-dependent.* Scientists commonly use a *wider* concept of "observation" or "datum" than perception with the "naked eye." According to the scientific usage of this word, scientists observe galaxies, bacteria or electrons with suitable *instruments*. A number of authors, including Kuhn in many passages, relate their thesis of theory-dependence to this observation concept in the wide sense (i.w.s.).[3] Giere (1999, 12f, 80) and Kuipers (2000, sec. 13.3) argued that whenever a new measurement instrument is invented, a formerly theoretical concept is turned into an observational concept.

• *Contra-5:* Scientific data, or observations i.w.s., are theory-dependent *interpretations* of perceptions. The theories presupposed here are mainly theories about the way measurement instruments work, which are usually treated as an unproblematic part of the advanced knowledge of a scientist. This *pragmatically* extended observation concept i.w.s. is undoubtedly very important for the efficient progress of science, since one cannot always put everything simultaneously into question, and the investigation of scientific problems rests on large amounts of background knowledge that is highly corroborated and taken for granted. However, this fact does not imply what some philosophers of science wrongly infer from it, namely that there *are* no observations i.n.s. in science, i.e. direct *perceptions* (mainly visual perceptions). We claim theory independence only for this narrow concept of observation.

Most of the time scientists agree on their observations i.w.s., and there is no need for them to make their direct perceptions explicit. But when scientists disagree on what they have observed i.w.s., they will critically reflect their implicit theoretical assumptions that led them to infer different observations i.w.s. from their common perceptions. For example, a pulmonologist A may report to have seen pneumonia in the

X-ray image of a patient's chest. What he has directly seen was a certain blackening pattern that he interpreted as pneumonia. If another pulmonologist B doubts this diagnosis, then what B doubts are not the visual abilities of A. Rather, A and B will discuss whether the blackening pattern which they both see is indicative of pneumonia or not. In conclusion, the epistemological significance of observations i.n.s. lies not in being permanently verbally reflected, but in serving as a possible level of theory-neutral agreement to which scientists can step back in the case of disagreement about observations i.w.s.

- *Pro-6: There is a continuity between observational and theoretical concepts.* Maxwell (1962, 7), Carnap (1966, 255f) and Hempel (1966, 78–84) pointed out that there is a continuous transition from observability with the naked eye to intermediate stages such as observability with glasses or a magnifying glass, to observability with an optical telescope or microscope, an electron microscope or a radar screen. A number of authors inferred from this that any demarcation between perception and theory-dependent observation i.w.s. is arbitrary.
- *Contra-6:* That there exists a continuous transition in the extent to which concepts are theory-laden is true. But first, the fact that there exists a continuous transition between two features like, for example, black and white, does not by any means imply that there is no difference between black and white (cf. van Fraassen 1980, 214). So the distinction between observation in the narrow and in the wide sense is significant even if it is continuous. Second, there are marked jumps in this transition: while observation i.n.s. does not require any learned background knowledge, the required background knowledge increases successively for the usage of the above-named instruments. As an illustration of this point, imagine what a native tribesman would do with these instruments, without having received instructions. Presumably he would understand glasses, but optical microscopes and telescopes would hardly be understandable, let alone electronic microscopes or radar screens, as the tribesman has no clue about the background knowledge that is needed for an adequate handling of these instruments.
- *Pro-7: Observation concepts (as all other concepts) are language-dependent.* The thesis of the language dependence of experience was made popular by the philosopher Wilhelm von Humboldt and by the anthropological and ethnological research of Sapir and Whorf (see Kutschera 1976, sec. 4.1). Many native tribes, for example, have different and less differentiated concepts of color than members of western civilization (Berlin/Kay 1999). From this fact cultural anthropologists inferred that these natives really see the colors in their environment dif-

ferently from us. Conversely, Inuits (Eskimos) have, reportedly, many more concepts for sorts of snow than us (cf. Whorf 1956, 216; Kutschera 1976, 251f). Whorf derived from this his *linguistic relativity principle*, according to which we can only perceive what is describable, and in a sense also prescribed, by the concepts in our language.

- *Contra-7:* It must be admitted that different cultures, to a certain degree, develop different systems of concepts, in which they describe the perceptions of their different environments. But it does not follow from this that their sense experience itself is language-dependent. We could only conclude this if members of these cultures were also not able to *learn* the observation concepts of other cultures by *ostensive training*, i.e. by acts of pure ostension ("this is orange," "this is not orange"). This ostensive learning ability is present in all cases, however. The Zuni Indians are able to learn the concept "orange" for which they do not possess a word. In this way the Tiv and the Dani were able to learn many European color concepts for which there is no word in their mother tongue (Garnham/Oakhill 1994, 49–51; Berlin/Kay 1999, 24). Similarly, a European can learn the Inuit words for different kinds of snow ostensively.

It is essential for an *ostensive learning experiment* to work in a *nonverbal* way. This is because otherwise, the linguistic relativist could argue that the Zuni have learned to see the color "orange" only by learning the western color language. In the next section we present a definition of theory-neutral observation concepts as concepts that are ostensively learnable, independent from background knowledge. Also Quine says in several places that the characteristic property of observation sentences is their ostensive learnability, independently from acquired information (1960, 42; 1974, 37, 41f; 1992, 3f, 5f). But this thesis of Quine is in strong tension with his radical meaning holism, as will be seen in the next pro- and-contra. So, in spite of these similarities, Quine's theory of observation sentences is essentially different from our account.

- *Pro-8: Meaning holism makes observation concepts theory-dependent.* Quine (1951) doubted the traditional analytic-synthetic distinction (see sec. 3.11): he argued that the meaning of a concept cannot be distinguished from contingent or *synthetic* information about the concept's denotation. Quine's alternative semantic view was a radical meaning holism, according to which the meaning of a concept is determined by all that we know about it. If this were true, then theory-neutral observation concepts could not exist, because in scientific theories observation concepts get connected with theoretical concepts. According to meaning holism this would imply that their meaning becomes loaded with theoretical statements. In this sense, Chalmers (1986, 36) argued that "water" is a theory-laden concept, because chemical theory connects it with the molecular structure H_2O. This complies with a passage of Quine (1960, 37f, 43), where he points out that one cannot distinguish between the semantic part of the stimulus meaning (or observational meaning) and that part which is provided by acquired ("colateral") information.

- *Contra-8:* Radical meaning holism will be criticized in sec. 3.11 as more or less *untenable*. We will argue there that a moderate meaning holism applies to theoretical concepts, but it is clearly false for empirical concepts. Quine's inner conflict concerning observation concepts is revealed in (1992, 7f), where he attributes a "two-faced nature" to the sentence "this is water": "holophrastically," to Quine, the sentence is free of theory, but by its composite structure, the sentence contains theory. I am inclined to regard Quine's thesis about the "dual" nature of observation sentences as an ad-hoc maneuver to escape the untenable consequences of meaning holism. The meaning of observational concepts is fixed by processes of ostension or definition, and this meaning is *not* affected by theories which connect observational with theoretical concepts. If this were not so, then a layman and a physicist would mean essentially different things when saying "it is warm today." This consequence seems too strange to be true.

2.9.2 A Definition of Theory-Neutral Observation Concepts

Let us recapitulate three major insights about an adequate definition of (theory-neutral) observation concepts.

1. The defining criterion cannot come from logic, but must be an empirical-psychological one. Hence, the definition of "observation concept" will be relative to the sensorial capacities of humans. For example, magnetic field is non-observable for humans, but observable for animals with magnetic sense organs (cf. Carnap 1936/37, 454f; van Fraassen 1980, 56f).
2. The defining criterion should be empirically testable. Otherwise the radical theory-ladenness thesis would be irrefutable. Carnap (1936/37, 454f), for example, defined an observation concept as a concept whose denotation can be recognized by acts of pure perception. But the distinction between pure perception and theory-laden interpretation is not testable by introspective reports. Introspective reports of humans usually mix up perception and theory-dependent interpretation: esoteric healers say they perceive bad spirits, and

18th-century chemists reported to have observed phlogiston. To avoid this problem, we base our definition on ostensive learnability, which is an empirically testable criterion that circumvents the introspective reports of test persons, in short: *tps*.
3   If the criterion of observability were based on verbal behavior, it could be objected that the resulting concept of observation depends implicitly on the language that is used by the tps. An ostensive learning experiment, however, is based on nonverbal behavior, that involves only three communication acts that are culturally universal, namely acts of ostension ("this"), question-modes ("is this X?"), and words or gestures for "yes" or "no."

An ostensive learning experiment consists of a *training phase* and a *test phase*. In the training phase, the concept to be tested for observability is introduced to the tp with an *artificial word* "X" unknown to them, so that the tp does not associate *any* meaning with the artificial word. The concept referred to by "X" is illustrated to the tp with a set of positive and negative instances of the concept, and the information "this is an X" or "this is not an X" is given. The instances may be presented in the form of photos, movies, or real objects. They must be clearly visible to the tp; more precisely, the experiment takes place under "normal observation conditions" (see below).

The ostensive learning process to be achieved by the tp consists in the abstraction of the meaning of "X," i.e. the property cluster corresponding to X, from the examples presented. Whether the tp has succeeded in this is investigated in the *test phase* which follows, in which a series of *new* positive and negative instances of the concept are presented, and the question "is this an X?" is asked. The tps success frequency in correct answers in the test phase indicates whether the tp has successfully abstracted from the training instances the perceptual property cluster that corresponds to the concept "X."

If a concept can be learned from a small set of learning instances by (almost) all test persons, *independently* of their background culture and even if the tps possess no word for this concept in their spoken language(s), this is a more or less compelling reason to see this concept as a *theory-independent* observation concept. Without this assumption, the learning success would be a sheer miracle. If a Zuni Indian were unable to perceive the color feature "orange" because she has no concept of it, then she would not perceive the difference between the orange, red, and yellow pictures in the training phase, and it would be *inexplicable* how she could successfully pass the test phase. In conclusion, we propose the following definition of observation concept:

> (Def. 2.9–1) A concept is a *theory-neutral observation concept* (or an observation concept i.n.s.) iff almost all humans can acquire this concept in an ostensive learning experiment, under normal observation conditions, independently of their background information, language and culture.

Thereby, the *normal observation conditions* include: (i) the normal physical conditions (sufficient light, etc.), (ii) normal biological conditions (no biological deficiencies in the person's sensory organs and nervous system), and (iii) normal psychological conditions (the person is in a wakeful and mentally normal state, and her yes/no utterances are truthful). All three conditions can be experimentally tested.

Our definition of observation concepts does not imply that all cultures have the same system of observation concepts (this is de facto false, as we know). What the definition implies in this respect is the following: If O_1 and O_2 are systems of observation concepts of two different cultures C_1 and C_2, then there exists a superordinate system of observation concepts O_{12} that contains all concepts in O_1 and O_2 and can be acquired by the members of C_1 and C_2 by way of ostensive learning. This consequence accords with the facts mentioned in section 2.9.1 (contra-7), namely that native tribes can learn Europeans' color concepts, or that Europeans can learn the Inuit's concepts for kinds of snow (etc.).

It would be interesting to perform ostensive learning experiments of the described sort (according to my knowledge, this has not been done so far). Generally speaking, the number of instances that are necessary to grasp the perceptual property cluster that corresponds to the concept "X" will not only depend on the question whether the property is observable in principle or not, but also on the *complexity* of this property cluster. So the result of an ostensive learning experiment is expected to be a *gradual learning curve*. This turns the resulting notion of an observation concept into a *gradual* one: a concept may be more or less observational. Nevertheless we expect that there will be clear statistical divide between the following types of concepts:

1. For *simple* observation concepts (such as "red," "square" or "bird"), success frequencies will after a small number of instances climb towards values slightly smaller than 100% of tps.
2. For *complex* observation concepts (such as "either square and red, or circle and blue" or "hooded crow") the success rate will climb

slowly and will need many instances; often the success frequency will stagnate at lower levels, e.g. of 50%.
3   For genuinely *theoretical* concepts (such as "atom," "electric force" or "oxidation"), the learning curve will not climb at all, even after many instances.

These expectations (which deserve to be empirically tested) are illustrated in fig. 2.9–3.

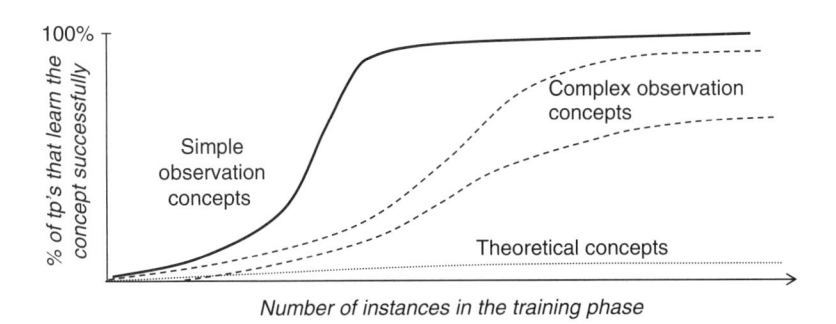

Figure 2.9–3 Expected learning curves in ostensive learning experiments

2.10 Value-Neutrality in the Context of Contemporary Debates

2.10.1 The Role of Values in Science

In sec. 2.5.2 we pointed out that the value-neutrality requirement (prop. 2.5–1) does not prevent scientists from drawing practically relevant conclusions, in the form of means-end inferences, in order to recommend derived values relative to some *assumed* fundamental values. Only the assumed fundamental values cannot be scientifically justified and have, therefore, to be separated from the statements of the scientist qua scientist.

Our view of the value-neutrality of sciences stands in contrast to the following influential division of epistemological paradigms according to their respective knowledge-guiding interests, which goes back to Habermas (1966, 241ff) (cf. Kriz et al. 1990, 151; Rosenberg 2008, 127ff):

1   Empirical-analytical paradigm: technical and instrumental knowledge-interests.
2   Hermeneutic paradigm: practical-normative knowledge-interests.
3   Critical-dialectical paradigm: emancipatory knowledge-interests.

According to our reconstruction of the role of values in scientific means-end inferences, these assignments are clearly incorrect. Science, being classified by Habermas as empirical-analytical, cannot be assigned to *any* specific interests that are external to science, but serves directly merely the science-internal epistemic goals, the search for content-rich truths. Scientific knowledge may be equally well used for technical purposes or for purposes of political reform. Adherence to value-neutrality certainly does not mean that a scientist must refrain from practical involvement in society, or remain unaware of her social *responsibility* (cf. Prim/Tilman 1979, 139t; Koertge 2000, S48). All that the value-neutrality requirement implies is that the scientist *separates* her scientific knowledge from fundamental value assumptions which she assumes in means-end inferences, and thereby *relativizes* her means-end inferences hypothetically to these value assumptions (recall the example in sec. 2.5.2).

The true difference between Habermas' three epistemological paradigms lies *not* in differing interests, but in the different treatment of the *value-neutrality question* (Schurz 1998a). Representatives of the empirical-analytical program are (unfortunately) the only ones striving for a clear division between description and value judgments. In hermeneutic approaches, in contrast, descriptive statements and value judgments are often deliberately not distinguished from each other (cf. Hilgendorf 2000, 39ff; Dupré 2007), and in critical-dialectical approaches, certain emancipatory norms are presented in a quasi-scientific make-up.

Our analysis has straightforward consequences on some more recent debates on the role of values in science in Britain and the USA (Kincaid et al. 2007; Carrier et al. 2008). While many of the contributors in this debate are in line with our analysis, others have criticized the thesis of value-free science. Their objections can be resolved by our analysis of means-end inference and the resulting requirement of separating empirically confirmed knowledge from value assumptions. Dupré (2007, 30–35), for example, argues that science needs to employ value-loaded terms in order to be practically relevant. Dupré is right insofar as the derived norms recommended by scientists employ value-loaded terms. But he seems to overlook that the scientist (qua scientist) recommends these derived norms only hypothetically and instrumentally, as means for certain fundamental norms that are given by society.

Another objection against value-neutrality is put forth by Douglas (2000). Referring to older papers of Rudner (1953) and Hempel (1965a), Douglas analyzes so-called *acceptance rules*, which concern the question how high the degree of confirmation of a scientific hypothesis must be in order to accept the hypothesis as true, or to publicly announce it as "established as true." The question which maximal risk of error is tolerable when one acts on the assumed truth of a hypothesis, turns out to depend on science-external values. As an example, consider the prediction: "There will be no earthquake of magnitude greater than 6.5 in the next few days." The maximally tolerable error probability of this no-earthquake prediction depends on the (science-external) weighting of the potential damage of an earthquake compared to the costs of an evacuation. A high potential damage might lead to the decision that even an error probability (i.e. a chance of an earthquake) of 5% is high enough to evacuate the region. But should one really infer from this—as Rudner and Douglas do—that therefore the scientific knowledge cannot be expressed in a value-neutral way? This seems to be wrong. What one should rather conclude from this problem are two requirements:

1. *Risk information:* When scientists declare an inductively established prediction or hypothesis as "firm," they should never forget to inform the public about the involved error possibilities (or the numerical error probability, if available). A decision to *accept* a hypothesis requires this information in order to count as objective (see sec. 5.10.8; cf. Jeffrey 1956).
2. *Hypothetical evaluation:* Scientists must be aware that the evaluation of the severity of the risk depends eventually on value-decisions of the *users* of their knowledge. If scientists deliver risk evaluations, they should always state them in the *hypothetical*, but never in the categorial mood. In our example, scientific recommendations should *not* have the categorial form "All-clear: no evacuation required," but for example, "No evacuation required *if* an earthquake chance of less than 5% is accepted as tolerable." This practice is not only fair to the users, but also relieves scientists from taking over unreasonable responsibilities.[4]

2.10.2 Value-Neutrality in the Context of Meta-Ethics

The value-neutrality requirement is based on the thesis that fundamental norm and value sentences are not capable of being justified by empirical science. In this subsection I discuss this thesis in the context of *meta-ethics*, which is that part of ethics that investigates the meaning and justifiability of ethical statements.

The standard meta-ethical justification of this thesis is Hume's *Is-Ought thesis* (cf. Pigden 2010), according to which ethical statements cannot be logically inferred from descriptive (i.e. non-ethical) premises (Hume 1739/40, 177f). Attempts to prove this prima facie highly plausible thesis by means of modern logic were confronted with unexpected problems, such as the paradox of Prior (1960) (cf. Stegmüller 1979a, 183–186). In the meantime, promising solutions of Prior's paradox have been developed, for example by Pigden (1989) or by Schurz (1991b; 1997). The latter proves a generalized version of Hume's thesis for all standard systems of alethic-deontic logic. He shows that it is only possible to derive non-trivial ethical statements from descriptive premises if one already presupposes Is-Ought bridge principles in one's ethical theory, such as the utilitarian principle, "Whatever is desired by the majority of humans, is ethically good, or ought to be realized." Is-Ought bridge principles are not analytically valid, but are synthetic assumptions which are part of one's ethical "theory." Therefore, norms or values cannot be justified by descriptive (non-ethical) premises without already assuming hidden ethical principles.

There exists a variety of different meta-ethical positions (e.g. utilitarianism, a-priorism, etc.), but none of them stands in a substantial conflict with Hume's Is-Ought thesis.[5] The only exception is the position of *value empiricism*. In this position one assumes a particular kind of "value experience." Although this value "experience" is different from ordinary sense experience, it serves in analogy with sense experience as a testing basis for empirical sciences. To some extent, this position goes back to Hume (1739/40, 177f). In 20th-century ethics, it was defended by Firth (1952) and Kutschera (1982, sec. 5.4), and in philosophy of science by Weingartner (1978, sec. 7.15ff; 1983). If intersubjective value "experiences" really exist, then there would be the hope that a "science of values" could be developed in analogy to the empirical sciences. In the next section I will argue that this hope is too good to be true.

2.10.3 On the Difference between Sense Experiences and Value "Experiences"

Value empiricism assumes the existence of value "experiences." Two arguments show that value "experiences" behave quite differently from real sense experiences: the *normal conditions argument* and the *independence argument*.

(A) The *normal conditions argument* says that intersubjectively deviating perceptual judgments can almost always be traced back to *defects* in the normal conditions of the observation. But this almost never applies to intersubjectively deviating value judgments. Let us consider, for example, the presumably true observation sentence: "There is a fire there." The thesis of the *intersubjectivity* of such an observation sentence implies that any or almost any person would agree with this sentence, insofar as the *normal conditions* of observation explained in sec. 2.9.2 are fulfilled. If a person within visual range of the fire really did persistently and repeatedly claim: "but I see no fire," then we would have every reason to presume that there is a defect in the person's normal conditions, and we would be able to find out this defect by independent tests. Such a person would most probably be blind or brain damaged, or could be in a state of extreme hallucination. For this reason, we would also be entitled to want to *cure* such a person of their observational defect.

But now let us assume that an adult person, under the same normal conditions of observation, systematically *disagrees* with a basic value sentence such as, "It is a good thing that *this* person is being saved from dying," although we assume that 99% of all persons do agree with it. Then we would *not be entitled* to assume that there is a defect in the "normal moral conditions" of this person, i.e. that this person is morally inferior, and should be cured, just like the blind should be cured of their blindness. Rather, we must *respect* this person's position *prima facie* as a deviating value position and also—as far as the rights of others are not thereby infringed—accept it. It is normal in Inuit society, for example, not to give food to a person who is so weak with age that they cannot feed themselves, but to let them die instead, because this is seen as a natural sign that their spirit wants to leave this world. Should we therefore declare the morals of the Inuits to be "morally defective," and try to "cure" them of their defects? If we treated basic value sentences exactly like observation sentences, we could find ourselves moving dangerously close to medieval religious moral practices.

I do not want to deny with this thesis that there are, indeed, cases of *psychopathological* blindness of conscience, which are in need of a psychological cure—but these cases are not the *rule*. So an extreme claim such as "I love killing other people" would rightly cause anybody to react by thinking "this person has a defect"—but this situation applies only to very few deviating basic value sentences, whereby the analogue situation in the case of deviating judgments of perception is the *rule*. In this vein, Prim and Tilman (1979, 93f) report an experiment on the objectivity of the observation sentence, "There is a piece of chalk in front of me," which they conducted on their students: the students reacted very indignantly, and declared that dissent in such questions was a problem for an *optician*, and not one of philosophy.

(B) The *independence argument* goes back to Toulmin (1950, 127) and runs as follows: our "value experiences" are *dependent* on our *moral background assumptions*. Our perceptual impressions, on the other hand, remain the same, even when our descriptive background assumptions change radically. For example, we see the sun make its way across the sky day in, day out. Let us assume that up to now we have held the geocentric view (the sun revolves around the stationary earth); but now, after detailed study of Kepler and Newton, we have changed to the heliocentric view (the earth revolves around the stationary sun). There has now been a radical change in our background theory—but as already explained in sec. 2.9.1 (contra-3), our visual experience is changed *in no way* by this fact: just as before, we see the sun "drawing" an arch across the sky every day. Our visual experience is independent of acquired background assumptions.

This is quite different in the case of value-based moral sentiments. If I see somebody donating a sum of money to the poor, I may spontaneously have the moral sentiment: *that was a good deed*. If I find out, however, that the donor is a politician about to stand for election, who has invested this donation as part of a calculated plan to win votes, but is otherwise more concerned about the well-being of the rich than of the poor, then a quite different moral sentiment will arise within me: I now see the politician as a *hypocrite*.

The normal conditions and independence arguments strengthen our thesis that value and norm-based judgments are not based on sensory experiences that are *imposed* on us by the facts of the world. Rather, they are subjective interpretations of experiences, which depend on cultural background values and emotional impressions arising in the context of the perceived situation. In conclusion, a fundamental justification of value or norm sentences by theory-neutral experiences in analogy to empirical science is hardly possible.

2.11 The Justification of Induction: An Unsolvable Problem?

How can inductive inferences be justified as epistemically reasonable in the sense of being truth-conducive? This is the problem of induction, or "Hume's problem." As explained in section 2.7.1, Hume made it clear to the philosophers of his time that, (*first*) inductive inferences cannot be justified by means of *logic*, because it is logically possible that the future (or the unobserved) is radically different from the past (or from the observed). However, Hume went much further: he cast doubt on the rational justifiability of induction as a whole (1748/2006, sec. 4). Second, induction also cannot be justified by observation, because in inductive inferences one infers that which has *not yet* been observed. And third, inductive inference also cannot be justified by induction, as this would lead us straight into a *circular argument*: if we think inductive inference is reasonable because it has been corroborated so far, then we are assuming that what has been corroborated so far will—by inductive inference—also be corroborated in future. In such a circular argument, we assume exactly the thing we want to show, and so we show nothing at all. Hume was also the first to show that, *fourth*, a reformulation of the induction problem using probability theory does not help (ibid., sect. 6): if we argue that inductive inferences do not always, but at least *with great probability* lead us from true premises to true conclusions, then we are assuming a probabilistic induction principle, according to which the *event frequencies* observed so far may be inductively transferred to the future or to non-observed cases. These were the reasons which led Hume to his deeply *skeptical* thesis, that inductive inference is not capable of being rationally justified, but is based merely on psychological *habit* (ibid., sect. 5).

Finding a satisfactory solution to Hume's induction problem would be of the greatest importance. And yet, this problem has remained largely unsolved up to today. We briefly discuss five solution attempts that have been suggested in the last few decades but could not find general acceptance:[6]

1 *Induction is not needed in science?* Popper's attempt to circumvent the induction program was to argue that scientific methodology does not need induction. In sec. 2.7.2 we have seen, however, that Popper's argument fails, because Popper's own methodology of "corroboration" contains in its heart the principle of epistemic induction.

2 *Induction as rational by definition?* Proponents of the "analytic" account (e.g. Strawson 1952, 257; Ayer 1956, 74f) have argued that induction is rational by the "definition" of rationality. Induction would share this feature with logical deduction. Recall, however, that by a rational justification we do not mean a mere "intuition of rationality" (which is then declared as being "true by definition"), but a demonstration that inductive inferences are truth-conducive, in the sense of optimizing our success in delivering true predictions. Of course, nothing of this sort can be shown by a mere "definition of rationality." Apart from that, Salmon (1974) has pointed towards a decisive difference between deductions and inductions: we hardly can imagine situations in which deductive logic fails, but we can easily imagine situations in which our inductive inferences fail. Moreover, millions of people *do* in fact believe in the superiority and even in the "higher rationality" of non-inductive to inductive-statistical methods of forecasting, be it clairvoyance, fortune-telling or

God-guided inner intuition. So, a satisfactory justification of induction would not only be of high philosophical, but also of high *cultural* importance, as part of the enterprise of explaining scientific rationality.

3 *Rule-circular "justification" of induction by induction?* Several philosophers have suggested that the circular "justification" of induction is not vicious but virtuous. This is so, it was argued, because the underlying kind of circularity is not premise-circularity but rule-circularity (Ladyman/Ross 2007, 75). This means that the conclusion (the reliability of induction) is not an element of the premise set, but is presupposed by the underlying inference rule (namely induction). That a rule-circular argument has epistemic value has been claimed, for example, by Braithwaite (1974), Black (1974), van Cleve (1984), Papineau (1993, sec. 5), Goldman (1999, 85) and Psillos (1999, 82). Unfortunately, simple counter-examples demonstrate convincingly that the hope of these philosophers is in vain: rule-circular arguments can also be used to justify obviously irrational rules. Enlightening is the following argument of Salmon (1957, 46), which shows that the same type of rule-circular argument that "justifies" the reliability of induction can be used to justify the rule of counter-induction, which says, roughly speaking, that one should predict the opposite of what one has observed:

(2.11–1)

Rule-circular justification of induction:

Premise: Past inductions have been successful
Therefore, by rule of induction:
Inductions will be successful in the future.

Rule-circular justification of counter-induction:

Premise: Past counterinductions have not been successful.
Therefore, by rule of counter-induction:
Counterinductions will be successful in the future.

That rule-circular arguments may also be practically dangerous can be shown with the following example of the rule-circular justification of the rule (IGV) (for "Imagination of God's voice"): "If you hear a voice in your mind saying p, and you believe it was God's voice, then infer that p is true." The "justification" of (IVG) has the true premise "I now hear a voice in my mind saying that rule (IGV) is reliable, and I believe it was God's voice," and infers from this by (IGV) that (IGV) is reliable. In conclusion, rule-circular arguments may infer from true premises rules with opposite conclusions, incorrect rules and practically dangerous rules. So, rule-circular arguments are definitely epistemically vicious, and this strategy of justifying induction does not work.

4 *Induction justified by uniformity of nature?* For John Stuart Mill, inductive inferences are justified by the assumption of the *uniformity* of nature (i.e. nature's future resembles her past). The well-known problem of Mill's account lies in the fact that the uniformity of nature can only be justified by an inductive inference. Therefore, the uniformity-justification of induction is *circular*. Note that as in (3) above one may give a corresponding circular justification of anti-induction by anti-uniformity: anti-induction is justified by anti-uniformity which is, in turn, justified by anti-induction from past observations. A "localized" version of the uniformity-account has been proposed by Norton (2003). For Norton, inductive reasoning is not governed by formal but by domain-specific or "local" inference rules such as "if some samples of bismuth melt at 271 °C, then all samples of bismuth will melt at this temperature." Local inductions, in turn, are justified by local uniformity assumptions, e.g. "samples of the same element agree in their physical properties." The fundamental problem of Norton's localized account is exactly the same as in Mill's account (cf. the criticism of Kelly 2010, 762): domain-specific uniformity assumptions are generalizations and must be justified by inductive inferences; so one ends up either in a circle or infinite regress.

5 *Induction justified by inference to the best explanation?* Several authors (Harman 1965; Armstrong 1983, sec. 6; Lipton 1991, 69) have argued that inductive inferences are justified because they are instances of inferences to the best explanation (IBEs). Recall from sec. 2.7.3 that an IBE infers from an observed phenomenon that the premises of its best (available) explanation are probably true. An inductive generalization—so the argument goes—is an instance of an IBE, because the best explanation of a regularity observed so far (e.g. "so far all observed ravens were black") is the corresponding lawlike generalization ("It is a law that all ravens are black").

Several special problems are involved in this argument. For example, the notion of "best" explanation is unclear and relative to an assumed storage of *available* explanations. The major problem of the IBE-account is, however, that the justification of IBEs is even more difficult than the justification of induction. This is so because IBEs admit many more uncertain inferences than inductive inferences (recall sec. 2.7.3). Analogous justification strategies to the ones discussed above for induction have been proposed for IBEs (cf. Bird 1998, 171). Armstrong (1983, 53), for example, has argued that IBE is rational "by definition." Lipton (1991,

167ff), Papineau (1993, sec. 5) and Psillos (1999, 82) suggested to justify IBE in a rule-circular way. But we have seen that both strategies are bound to failure. Moreover, it is unclear why one should regard the explanation of "All so-far observed Fs have been Gs" by "Because it is a law that all Fs are Gs" as a *best* explanation, if one does not accept the inductive premise that the world is uniform. If one assumes instead that from time to time the laws of nature undergo radical changes, the explanation "Because it was *so-far* a law that Fs are Gs" seems to be the better explanation.

In spite of so many failed attempts to solve Hume's problem, I do not conclude (as many contemporary philosophers do) that the induction problem is unsolvable. I agree with Hume's skeptical diagnosis that no non-circular argument can establish that induction is *reliable*, i.e. will be predictively highly successful, whatever the future looks like. However, an alternative justification strategy that is not blocked by Hume's argument is the attempt to show that induction is an epistemically *optimal* prediction method, in the sense that its predictive success is maximal among all prediction methods that are accessible to a given agent. Even in radically skeptical scenarios in which all methods of prediction are unreliable, induction can still be optimal in the sense of "being the best of a bad lot." Epistemic optimality arguments for induction have been developed by Schurz (2008b, 2009b; cf. Vickers 2010, sect. 6.3). They are game-theoretical generalizations of Reichenbach's best-alternative account (Reichenbach 1949, §91).

Unfortunately, Reichenbach did not succeed in establishing an optimality argument with respect to the goal of predictions. Nothing in Reichenbach's account excludes the possibility that a perfect future-teller may have perfect success in predicting random tossings of a coin, while the inductivist can only have a predictive success of 0.5 in this case (see Reichenbach 1949, 476f; Skyrms 1999, sec. III.4). Reichenbach's account suffered from the problem that it is impossible to demonstrate that *object-induction*, i.e. induction applied at the level of events, is an optimal prediction method. In contrast, the account of Schurz is based in the idea of *meta-induction*. The meta-inductivist applies the inductive method at the level of competing prediction methods. The simplest type of meta-inductivist predicts what the presently most successful prediction method predicts. A more refined meta-inductive strategy is weighted meta-induction, abbreviated as wMI, whose predictions for the next round are a weighted average of all players' predictions, where the weight of a player increases with its so-far success. Schurz proves that in prediction games with *arbitrary* event sequences and *finitely* many *accessible* players, wMI is a universally optimal prediction strategy (Schurz 2008a, 297, th. 4; 2009b, 214, th. 2). Even in "radically non-uniform" scenarios in which the success rates of the leading players permanently oscillate around each other, wMI's success rate converges to the maximal success rate, with a small short-run loss that converges to zero with increasing number of predictions.

This mathematical (or a-priori) justification of meta-induction establishes at the same time a non-circular a-posteriori justification of object-induction, by the following argument: we know by experience that, so far, object-inductive prediction methods have been more successful than non-inductive ones, hence it is meta-inductively justified to favor object-inductivistic methods also in the future.

Also the meta-induction account faces some problems, for example, the problem of infinitely many prediction methods (cf. Arnold 2010). Nevertheless, there are justified hopes that optimality-accounts open a perspective along which genuine solutions of the problem of induction can be found.

2.12 Introductory Literature and Exercises

2.12.1 Introductory Literature

On the method of rational reconstruction see Stegmüller (1969ff, vol. IV.1). A classic on the German value judgment debate is Albert/Topitsch (1971); for more recent debates see Kincaid et al. (2007) and Carrier et al. (2008). Psillos (1999) and van Fraassen (1980) discuss questions of scientific realism as opposed to empiricism. A recent collection on the question of the unity of sciences is Rahman et al. (2004). Rock (1984) introduces the cognitive psychology of perception. An excellent introduction into deductive logic is Klenk (1989). Swinburne (1974) and Vickers (2010) offer introductions into the problems of induction. Lipton (1991) is a classic on inference to the best explanation.

2.12.2 Questions and Exercises

Sec. 2.1

1 What is meant by "context of discovery" versus "context of justification"?
2 Explain the normativist argumentation and its criticism.
3 What is the supreme epistemic goal of science? Does it presuppose metaphysical realism?
4 Explain the method of rational reconstruction.

Sec. 2.2–4

1. Explain the five common epistemological assumptions of the sciences.
2. In which sense are minimal realism and minimal empiricism "minimal"?
3. What is the difference between falsifiability and fallibility?
4. Explain the common methodological features of sciences.
5. To what extent are the concepts of "natural sciences," "human and social sciences" and "humanities" ambiguous?

Sec. 2.5–6

1. Explain the means-end inference using examples from your area of study.
2. Explain the suggested formulation of the value-neutrality thesis and all concepts contained in it.
3. Discuss: How is the requirement of "value-neutrality" related to that of "political correctness"? Are the two in conflict?
4. Discuss physical reductionism and its criticism. What is "supervenience"?

Sec. 2.7

1. Which kind of inference (deductive, inductive or abductive) is being used in the following examples? (a) Most light switches are working. I am pressing the switch. Therefore the light will go on. (b) All humans are mortal. Aristotle is human. Therefore Aristotle too is mortal. (c) My refrigerator has always worked well up to now. Therefore I will be able to rely on it tomorrow. (d) Every time Gregor talks about his brother, his facial expression becomes strained. Therefore, he has a problem with his brother.
2. Explain the principles of methodological, logical and epistemic induction. What are the Popperian arguments against the first two kinds of induction?
3. Give an example of an inference to the best explanation.

Sec. 2.8–9

1. What is the difference between metaphysical and hypothetical-constructive realism?
2. Explain the argument of radical constructivism against realism and its criticism.

3   One person could fail to notice another because, (a) he is deliberately ignoring her, (b) he is blind, (c) he is asleep, or (d) it is pitch dark. Which normal condition of observation is infringed in each case?

Sec. 2.10–11

1   Explain Habermas' threefold division of scientific disciplines according to their respective interests. How is this view criticized?
2   Discuss the normal conditions and the independence argument.
3   Recapitulate David Hume's four arguments against the possibility of justifying induction.
4   Explain the symmetry between the inductive justification of induction and the anti-inductive justification of anti-induction.

Notes

1. For arguments in this direction cf. Chalmers (1986, sec. 3.4), van Fraassen (1980, 56ff), Albert (1985, sec. II.8), Brewer/Lambert (2001, S182f).
2. This does not mean that we do not consider as an important question to what extent our innate visual perception mechanisms construct an accurate image of the world.
3. E.g. Putnam (1962), Shapere (1982), Kuipers (2000), Giere (1999), Adam (2004).
4. This is relevant to the trials following the erroneous no-earthquake prediction 2009 in L'Aquilla.
5. Comprehensive classifications are found in Frankena (1963), Kutschera (1982, sec. 2), or Schurz (1997, sec. 11.3).
6. Cf. Stegmüller (1977, vol.II, ch. 4), Swinburne (1974), Rescher (1980), Howson (2000), Ladyman (2002, ch.1).

3
THE CONCEPTUAL TOOLKIT: LANGUAGE, LOGIC AND PROBABILITY

3.1 Kinds and Classification of Concepts

The basic logical building blocks of any language are its concepts. A concept is understood here as a linguistic expression *together* with its meaning. Grammatically, concepts are *beneath* the level of the sentence—they are *subsentential*. "Grass" and "green" are concepts; "grass is green" is a sentence. Though concepts signify something, they cannot in themselves be true or false; only sentences composed of concepts can. Concepts can be *atomic* or *complex*; e.g. "grass" is atomic, while "green grass" is complex. Sentences are composed of concepts, and the nature of a sentence depends on the nature of its concepts. So we will first deal with the various different kinds of scientific concepts, before dealing with the various different kinds of scientific sentences. Concepts can be classified in three respects: first according to their logical type, second according to their content type, and third according to their gradation (or scale) type.

3.1.1 The Logical Type of Concepts

Logical grammar classifies concepts according to their logical-semantic function. Fig. 3.1–1 presents an overview.

1   *Non-logical concepts* denote or signify *something in the world*. In contrast, logical concepts have a purely *structural* function.

1.1   *Singular concepts* or *terms* always designate a single *individual* (or spatiotemporal location). Singular terms subsume (a) *proper names* (e.g. "Saul Kripke," "Salzburg"), (b) *ostensive* or indexical *terms* (e.g.

```
                    ┌─ Singular concepts or terms
                    │                                    ┌─ Predicates
    Non-logical ────┼─ General concepts, 1st order ─────┼─ Relations
    Concepts        │                                    └─ Functions
        │           └─ General concepts, higher order
        │
        │           ┌─ Truth-functional sentence operators (propositional logic PropL)
        │           ├─ 1st order quantifiers and variables (1st order predicate logic PredL)
    Logical    ────┼─ Intensional sentence operators (modal logic ML)
    Concepts        ├─ Higher order quantifiers and variables (higher order PredL)
                    ├─ Element relationship (set theory)
                    └─ (Mathematical concepts)
```

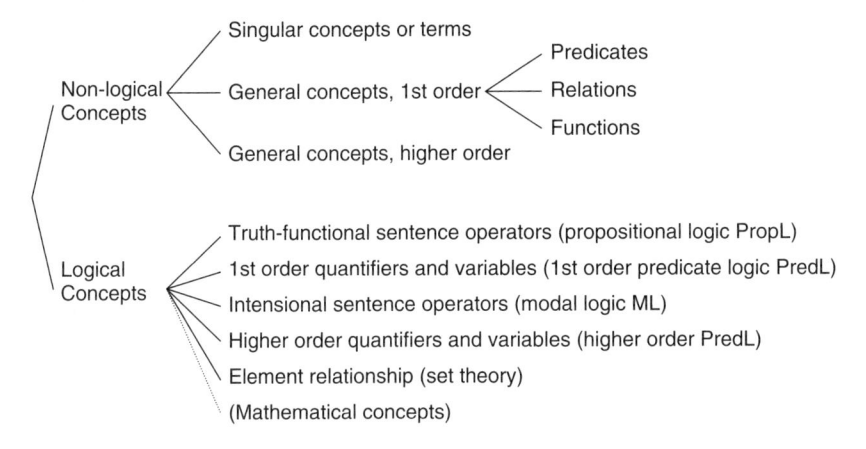

Figure 3.1–1 Division of concepts according to their logical type

"I," "now," "here," "that person there") and (c) *definite descriptions* ("that x which has characteristic property F"). *Formal notation:* atomic singular terms are called *individual constants* and are formalized by small letters $a_1, a_2,..., b, ...$ (specifically, t_i for time points and s_i for spatial locations).

1.2 *1st order general concepts* are applied to singular terms: this application is called *predication*, and through it, an *atomic sentence* is generated.

1.2.1 *1st order predicates* denote features that can be true of individuals or not. One may distinguish between *property concepts* such as "x is big," and *kind concepts* such as "x is a person." *Formal notation:* predicates are formalized using capital letters F, G, ... (or $F_1, F_2, ...$). Predicates are *one-place*, i.e. they have one argument *place*, which is written as a *variable* after the predicate letter: "Fx" for "x is an F." For example, if "Fx" stands for "x is slim," and "a" for "Peter," then "Fa" stands for the sentence "Peter is slim."

1.2.2 A (1st order) n-place relational sign denotes a relation between n given individuals. *Formal notation* is by upper-case letters R, Q, ... E.g. if "Rxy" stands for the two-placed relation "x is a brother of y," "a" for "Peter" and "b" for "Paul," then "Rab" stands for the sentence "Peter is a brother of Paul."

1.2.3 *Function signs:* A one-place (or n-place) function sign denotes a function which uniquely assigns to one (or n) individuals a further individual. *Formal notation* is usually by lower-case letters f, g,.... For example, if "f(x)" stands for "the mother of x" and "a" for "Peter," then "f(a)" is a singular term designating Peter's mother. In mathematics, functions play a fundamental role as operations on numbers; e.g. addition + is a two-place function, which assigns to the respective numbers x and y their sum + (x,y), usually written in infix notation "x + y." Moreover, all *quantitative* (e.g. physical) *properties* of individuals are functions: e.g. m(a) denotes the *mass* of the body a, and "m(a) = 5.6 kg" stands for "the mass of a is 5.6 kilograms."

1.3 *2nd (or higher) order predicates and functions* are applied to sentences or predicates and thereby generate sentences. An example of a higher-order predicate is the concept of *truth* which applies to sentences.

2 *Logical concepts:* There are different kinds of logical concepts, and their principles are explicated in corresponding kinds of logics.

2.1 *Truth-functional sentence operators—Propositional logic PropL* (where A, B, ... stand for arbitrary propositions):

- the negation $\neg$ (read: $\neg A$—*not A*),
- the conjunction $\wedge$ (read: $A \wedge B$—*A and B*),
- the disjunction (the *inclusive* or) $\vee$ (read: $A \vee B$—*A or B or both*),
- the so-called "material" implication $\rightarrow$ (read: $A \rightarrow B$—*if A, then B*),
- the "material" equivalence $\leftrightarrow$ (read: $A \leftrightarrow B$—*A if and only if (iff) B*).

Further sentence operators are thereby definable. For example, the exclusive *either-or* $\dot{\vee}$ is defined as $A \dot{\vee} B \leftrightarrow_{def} (A \vee B) \wedge \neg (A \wedge B)$ (A or B, but not both). The logical laws of these sentence operators are explicated by (non-modal) propositional logic.

A sentence operator, when applied to given sentences, generates a new, complex sentence. A sentence operator is called *truth-functional* (or *extensional*) iff the truth *value* of the complex sentence is uniquely determined by the truth values of its component sentences (arguments). The truth-functionality of the sentence operators of PropL is expressed by their "truth tables": every sentence A is either true or false; $\neg A$ is true iff A is false (else true); $A \wedge B$ is true iff both A and B are true (else false), etc. *Note:* the material implication $A \rightarrow B$ is defined as true iff A is false or B is true, i.e. $A \rightarrow B \leftrightarrow_{def} \neg A \vee B$ is valid. The material implication is *weaker* than the natural language if-then, because its truth does not presuppose any connection between the contents of A and B.

2.2 *1st order quantifiers and variables—predicate logic PredL*: 1st order *quantifiers* quantify over individuals with help of 1st order *individual variables* x, y,... (x_1, x_2,...). The two most important kinds of quantifiers are:

- the *universal quantifier* ∀x: read "∀xFx" as "For all x: Fx," and
- the *existential quantifier* ∃x: read "∃xFx" as "For at least one x: Fx."

The class of individuals to which a quantifier refers is called its (semantic) domain D. So ∀xFx says that all individuals in D have property F, and ∃xFx that some individuals in D have property F. When nothing further is stated, D is identified with the *universal* domain, i.e. the class of all individuals in the given scientific area.

We say that the individual variable "x" is *bound* by the quantifier "∀x" or "∃x." The sub-formula "Fx" in "∀xFx" is called the scope of the quantifier "∀x." Formulas in which all individual variables are *bound* are called *closed formulas* or *sentences*. The expression "Fx" (for "x is an F") is called an *open* formula, because the individual variable "x" is *free*, i.e. not bound by any quantifier. Open formulas such as "Fx∧Gx" express complex concepts.

A distinguished logical relation is *identity* "x = y," standing for "x is identical with y," i.e. "x" and "y" denote the same individual. The logic of sentences which are made up of singular terms, general 1st order concepts, extensional sentence operators and 1st order quantifiers, is called 1st order predicate logic PredL (for an introduction see Klenk 1989, Copi et al. 2010). 1st order PredL contains PropL as a fragment and is one of the most important formal frameworks of philosophy of science, among other reasons because type-free set theory, upon which all of classical mathematics builds, is expressible in this framework. Note: "$=_{def}$" and "$\leftrightarrow_{def}$" stand for "identical by definition" and "equivalent by definition", respectively.

2.3 *Intensional sentence operators* are not truth functional. An example is the necessity operator ("□A" for "A is necessary"): the truth value of "□A" is not determined by the truth value of A. For instance, if A and B stand for the sentences "I have brown hair" and "2 + 2 = 4," respectively, then both A and B are true, but only □B is true, while □A is false, as the fact that I have brown hair is not necessary. Other examples are *deontic* sentence operators ("□A is obligatory"), etc. The logic of intensional sentence operators is *generalized modal logic* (see Hughes/Cresswell 1996).

2.4 *2nd (or higher) order quantifiers* quantify over states of affairs or properties and are dealt within 2nd (or higher) order PredL. The logic of higher-order quantifiers is called logical *type theory*, which goes back to Russell (1903).

2.5 *Set-theoretical symbols:* Sets are aggregations of individuals into a complex individual called a "set." *Formal notation:*

- "x ∈ y" stands for "x is an element of the set y."
- {x: Fx} stands for the set of all individuals x which possess the property F.
- {$a_1,..., a_n$} stands for the set consisting of the individuals $a_1,..., a_n$.
- ($a_1,..., a_n$) by contrast, stands for the ordered sequence consisting of $a_1,..., a_n$.

Note: sets are *invariant* w.r.t. permutations or repetitions of their elements, hence {a,b} = {a,a,b} = {b,a} = {b,a,a,b} (etc.). In contrast, sequences or n-tuples consist in an ordering of individuals that allows for repetition: i.e. (a,b,b,c) ≠ (a,b,c) ≠ (b,a,c).

Set theory is a part of *informal* logic or metalogic, as "∈" too is a logical concept in a broader sense. The axioms of type-free set theory (after *Zermelo* and *Fraenkel*) are expressed in the language of 1st order PredL, but they go *beyond* purely logical principles (for an introduction see van Dalen et al. 1978; Hrbacek/Jech 1999). *Some formal notation:* x ⊆ y (x is an improper or proper subset of y), x ⊂ y (x is a proper subset of y); f: A→B (f is a function which assigns to every individual x in A exactly one individual y in B); further set-theoretical notions are explained in the text.

2.6 *Mathematical concepts,* as with logical concepts, characterize *abstract conceptual* objects or functions. They can be characterized either by internal axioms of mathematical theories or by set-theoretical definitions. Among the most important mathematical concepts are concepts for different kinds of numbers (e.g. ℕ for the set of natural and ℝ for the set of real numbers), and function concepts expressing operations on numbers (addition, multiplication, etc.).

3.1.2 Formalization: Syntax and Semantics, Statements and Models

Since Morris (1946) the dimensions of language are subdivided into *syntax, semantics* and *pragmatics.* Syntax deals with the grammatical form of linguistic expressions, semantics with the meanings of expressions, and pragmatics with those properties of expressions which are determined by their *context*. In this section we outline some foundations of syntax and semantics.

Terms and formulas of arbitrary high complexity can be constructed from atomic concepts. The translation of a natural language sentence into a logical sentence is called *formalization*. Here are some examples:

(3.1–1) *Examples of formalizations:*
Translations: a—this animal, Rx—this is a raven, Bx—x is black.
a This animal is a raven and it is black. Formalization: Ra∧Ba.
b All ravens are black. *Partial formalization:* For all x: if x is a raven, then x is black. *Formalization:* ∀x(Rx→Bx).
c Some ravens are not black. *Partial formalization:* There exists an x which is a raven and is not black. *Formalization:* ∃x(Rx∧¬Bx).

Sentences with the same natural language syntax can have a very different logical syntax. In particular, the natural language copula "is" serves the following three different logical functions:

(3.1–2)

Sentence	Formalization	
a Peter (a) is tall (T).	Ta	"is" as predication
b Peter is the father (f) of Paul (b).	a = f(b)	"is" as identity
c A raven (R) is a bird (B).	∀x(Rx→Bx)	"is" as inclusion of properties

In (3.1–2)(c), there is a *concealed* universal quantifier, which is revealed by formalization. The formalization of (3.1–3) reveals a *concealed* existential quantifier:

(3.1–3)
Peter (a) has a son. *Partial formalization:* There exists an x, such that x is the son (S) of Peter. *Formalization:* ∃xSax.

As these examples show, logical formalization is an important aid to the *advanced* philosophy of science, in order to uncover the logical structure of sentences and, building on this, to discover logical connections. Logical formalization is not an end in itself, but is justified by its cognitive *usefulness* compared to its effort. In this book we will rarely make use of formalizations—only when unavoidable.

In *semantics* one differentiates between two kinds of semantic denotation: every expression has, on the one hand, a *meaning*, and on the other an object *reference* (terminologies differ, however; cf. Kutschera 1976, ch. 2; Morris 2006). The meaning of a concept is that which must be known to a speaker in order to *understand* the concept properly. The meaning of an expression *together* with the *facts* of the world determine the expression's reference, i.e. the real entity denoted by the expression (if there is no such entity, the reference is empty). There are controversial views on the question of wherein *exactly* meaning exists (in the imagination, in thought, in the definition, in usage?). The reference of a singular term is uncontroversially an individual. The reference of predicates is also controversial: some authors (e.g. Carnap 1956b, ch. I) identify the reference of a predicate with its *extension*, i.e. the *set* of individuals which fall under the predicate; other authors (e.g. Fodor 1990, 93) identify the reference of a predicate with the *real property* or natural kind denoted by it.

The meaning of sentences is usually identified with the *proposition* expressed by the sentence. According to the traditional view, logically or analytically equivalent sentences express the *same* proposition. The reference of sentences is sometimes identified with truth values (e.g. in Frege 1948), but also with events or real states of affairs. The following definition of "state of affairs" and "fact" is uncontroversial: every descriptive sentence expresses a *state of affairs*; and if the sentence is true, the state of affairs really exists and is then a *fact*.

In *logical semantics*, which goes back to Alfred Tarski (1936a), one assigns to linguistic expressions formal object references, in the form of set-theoretical *interpretations*. Informal set-theory functions in this case as a *metalanguage*, in which the semantic relationship between the *object language* and a hypothetical object structure is modeled. The concrete definition is as follows: an extensional *interpretation* of a logical language $\mathcal{L}$ is a pair (D,I), consisting of a domain of individuals D and an interpretation function I, which assigns to every individual constant a and variable x from $\mathcal{L}$ an individual I(a) or I(x) in D, to every n-placed relation sign R in $\mathcal{L}$ a subset I(R) from D^n (where D^n is the set of all n-tuples of D-individuals), and to every n-placed function sign f in $\mathcal{L}$ a function I(f): $D^n \to D$.

An extensional interpretation (D,I) makes an atomic formula Fa true, in short (D,I) $\models$ Fa, iff I(a) $\in$ I(F). This basic truth definition is recursively extended to arbitrary formulas as follows: (D,I) $\models$ $Ra_1,\ldots,a_n$ iff $(I(a_1),\ldots, I(a_n)) \in$ I(R); (D,I) $\models \neg$A iff not (D,I) $\models$ A; (D,I) $\models$ A$\land$B/ A$\lor$B iff (D,I) $\models$ A and/or (D,I) $\models$ B; and (D,I) $\models \forall$xA(x)/$\exists$xA(x) iff for all/some *d* in D, (D,I[x:*d*]) satisfies A(x), where "I[x:*d*]" is like "I" except that it assigns "*d*" to "x" (for an introduction to mathematical logic see Machover 1996).

An extensional interpretation of an object language can also be seen as a *relationship of translation* between a logical and a set-theoretical language. This translation results, for example, in the following relationships:

(Prop. 3.1–1) *Translation (I) between logical and set-theoretical language*, where I(a) = a, I(F) = F, etc.:

Logical sentence	Set-theoretical sentence (translation)
Fa	$a \in F$
$\forall x(Fx \rightarrow Gx)$	$\forall x(x \in F \rightarrow x \in G)$, in short: $F \subseteq G$
$\psi(F)$	$F \in \psi$ (etc.)

In set-theoretical translations, then, individual constants and predicates or relation symbols are replaced by set terms which denote their extensions, and the element relationship $\in$ is inserted in between. This procedure is iterable for higher-order predications. Set-theoretical formalizations may be less intuitive than logical formalizations, but they have the advantage to be *type free*, i.e. they allow for the translation of all sentences of (higher-order) type theory into the language of 1st order PredL. For this reason, structuralistic philosophers of science have argued that set-theoretical formalizations are preferable to logical formalizations (cf. Stegmüller 1977, vol. II., ch. 6).

An extensional interpretation (D,I) of a language $\mathcal{L}$ is also called a *model* for $\mathcal{L}$. It plays the role of a "possible world" as expressible by means of $\mathcal{L}$. A model (D,I) which verifies a sentence A (i.e. makes A true) is called a model of A. Often the models (D,I) of a sentence are written in the form (D; $a_1,..., a_n$; $R_1,..., R_m$; $f_1,..., f_k$), in which instead of I, the designata of all individual constants, relational and function symbols assigned by I are listed. In this form, models are used by proponents of the (German) *structuralist* view and the (British/American) *semantic* view of theories (recall sec. 1.3.5.2). In the structuralist or semantic view, a theory T is represented by the set of its models, M(T)—a method that goes back to Suppes (1999/1957, 249). In contrast, in the traditional "statement" view, a theory T is represented by the set of its axioms, Ax(T), together with semantic characterizations of its concepts.

The (traditional) "statement view" and the (structuralistic) "non-statement view" have been set in opposition by Stegmüller (1976). This "opposition" is largely unjustified, for two reasons. First, the statement view is not (as is sometimes claimed) a purely syntactical, but also a semantical view, inasmuch as the statements of $\mathcal{L}$ are taken as semantically interpreted propositions (cf. French 2008, 272). Since his turn in 1947 (see 1956b), Carnap understood a linguistic framework always as a language $\mathcal{L}$ *together* with a semantic interpretation of $\mathcal{L}$. Second, model-theoretic theory reconstructions are not free from using statements (which is wrongly suggested by the name "non-statement view"). Rather, the class of models M(T) of a theory T is defined by nothing but the set of its linguistic axioms Ax(T), as follows: $M(T) =_{def} \{m \in M(\mathcal{L}): m \models Ax(T)\}$, where $M(\mathcal{L})$ is the set of models for the language $\mathcal{L}$ in which T is formulated (cf. Balzer et al. 1987, ch. 1). Therefore, there exist straightforward *translation relations* between linguistic and structuralistic theory representations. Here is a simple example:

(Prop. 3.1–2) *Linguistic and model-theoretic theory representation* (simplest case):

Linguistically by T's axioms:	Model-theoretically by T's models:
A_1: $\forall x(Fx \rightarrow Gx)\}$ ("factual" axiom of T)	Models: M(T) = the class of models (D,F,G) such that
A_2: $I(F) \subseteq D$, A_3: $I(G) \subseteq D$ ("semantic" axioms of T)	(D,F,G) $\models \{A_1, A_2, A_3\}$

Realistic examples of these translations relations are more complicated, since structuralist theories contain several ingredients; for details see Andreas (2010) and Schurz (2013b).

3.1.3 The Content Type of Concepts

This classification, which is particularly significant in the philosophy of science, applies only to *non-logical concepts*. Fig. 3.1–2 shows an overview.

First we have to distinguish between descriptive and prescriptive concepts. *Prescriptive* concepts consist of norm and value concepts (Hare 1952). There are only a few prescriptive concepts: the *normative* concepts of something being obligatory, forbidden, or permitted, and the qualitative, comparative and quantitative *value* concepts (X is ethically or aesthetically valuable, or more valuable than Y, or valuable to a certain degree). Philosophy of science deals primarily with *descriptive* concepts and sentences which describe the facts of the world. There

```
(logical concepts)
                                                         observation concepts
                              empirical concepts
                 descriptive                            empirical disposition
                 concepts     theoretical concepts      concepts
(non-logical
concepts)
                 prescriptive    norm concepts
                 concepts        value concepts
```

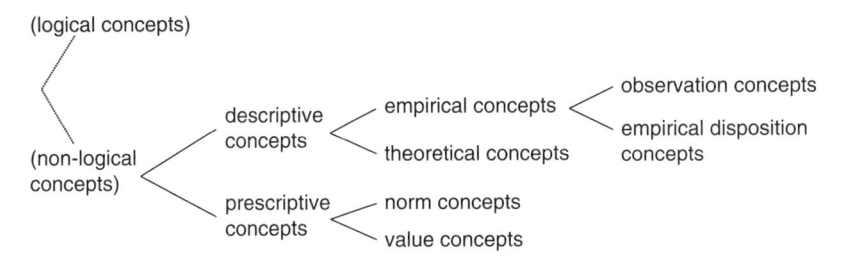

Figure 3.1–2 Classification of concepts according to their content type

is an enormous number of (singular and general) descriptive concepts of various types. The *most important* distinction within the descriptive concepts is the one between empirical and theoretical concepts and, within the empirical concepts, the one between observation concepts and empirical dispositional concepts.

1   A general observation concept expresses a property that is perceptible to the senses, or a complex of such properties. As we saw in sec. 2.9, a property perceptible to the senses is one which can be *ostensively learned* by humans, independently of their background knowledge. *Examples:* "x is red," "x is a raven," "x is longer than y," "the needle of the measuring instrument x is pointing to 5," etc. The classical and the early logical empiricists demanded that all descriptive concepts be observational concepts. In fact only a few concepts are genuine observation concepts in this narrow sense.

Note the following subtlety: strictly speaking, a property as such is not perceptible, but only a certain *instantiation* of a property (a so-called *trope*) in a perceptible individual. "Being red," for example, expresses an observational property as applied to visible objects; but in application to non-observable individuals such as microbes or molecules, the property of being red is not observable, as these individuals are too small to be visible. For this reason, Quine was right when he stressed that the primary level of "observability" is not that of concepts, but of "occasion sentences" like "this here is red" (1960, 35ff; 1992, 3). Putnam (1962, 242f) saw in this fact a fundamental obstacle to a clear definition of observation concepts. Our criterion of ostensive learnability, however, solves this problem as follows: a primitive property is ostensively learnable in the sense of def. 2.9-1 iff it possesses at least *some* perceptible instantiations in perceptible individuals which may serve as training instances.

2   An *empirical dispositional concept* expresses an empirical disposition. By this we understand the *lawlike regularity* of an individual in producing a certain observable *result* under certain empirical circumstances or *test* conditions. Example: the empirical dispositional concept "x is soluble in water" is, by definition, equivalent to the following lawlike hypothesis about "x" which generalizes over time points: "whenever x is or were placed in water, it will or would dissolve." Lawlikeness and counterfactual conditionals ("would") go beyond the observable and presuppose inductive projectibility (see sec. 3.6, 6.6.3). Nevertheless, dispositional concepts are *empirically operationalized* concepts, whose meaning is not dependent on a theory. Further examples: "x is hard," "x weighs 4 kg on a pair of scales," "person x is a German speaker," etc. Empirical dispositional concepts correspond to what the *operationalists* (e.g. Bridgeman 1936) demanded of *all* scientific concepts. In fact, though, theoretical concepts are not reducible to empirical dispositional concepts.

3   An *empirical concept i.n.s.* (in the narrow sense) is an observation concept or an empirical dispositional concept.

4   A *theoretical concept i.w.s.* (in the wide sense) is any descriptive concept which is not an empirical concept i.n.s., but still has a meaning. A theoretical concept i.w.s. does not have to be part of a scientific theory; it can also be based on speculation (e.g. "the prime cause of all being").

5   A *theoretical concept i.n.s.* is a theoretical concept i.w.s., whose meaning is *introduced* by a scientific theory. If we want to make explicit the reference to a specific theory T, we speak of a *T-theoretical* concept (Sneed 1971; refinements in sec. 5.9.1). *Examples:* physical force, kinds of molecules, biological genotype, psychological character, intention, social order, etc.

Convention: unless otherwise stated, we understand empirical concepts and theoretical concepts respectively in the *narrow* sense.

6   As discussed in sec. 2.9.1 (pro–5), a number of philosophers of science use the notion of an empirical concept *i.w.s.*, meaning any concept that expresses a *measurable property* or "datum." Empirical concepts i.w.s. are theory-dependent (they overlap with "theoretical i.n.s."): their meaning depends specifically on those theories that describe the functioning of the measuring instruments and are presupposed to be unproblematic. The border between empirical concepts i.w.s. and theoretical concepts i.n.s. can only be drawn *pragmatically* and in a *context-dependent* way. In contrast, there exists

an *objective* but gradual border between empirical concepts i.n.s. and theoretical concepts i.w.s.

3.1.4 The Gradation (Scale) Type of Concepts

Most properties in our world do not only occur or not occur; they come in certain *degrees*. The gradation or scale type of a concept reflects how finely the concept is graduated. Accordingly, scientific concepts may be classified as in the overview in fig. 3.1–3.

Qualitative concepts are not graduated, or more precisely, they are graduated only in the *yes-no* sense; comparative concepts are graduated in the sense of an *ordering*, and quantitative concepts are the most strongly graduated, i.e. in a *continuous* way. In science the graduation of a property is measured in terms of numbers, and we speak of the scale type of concepts (e.g. Krantz et al. 2006, ch. 1; Bortz 1985, 28–33). The *more finely* graduated a concept is, the *sharper* the information we express with it, and the *stricter* the tests to which the hypotheses using it can be subjected. The types of gradation will now be discussed.

```
                      ┌─ classificatory concepts
qualitative concepts ─┤  nominal (categorial) scales
                      │
                      └─ comparative concepts
                         ordinal (ranking) scales

                       ┌─ interval (difference) scales
quantitative concepts ─┤
                       └─ ratio scales
```

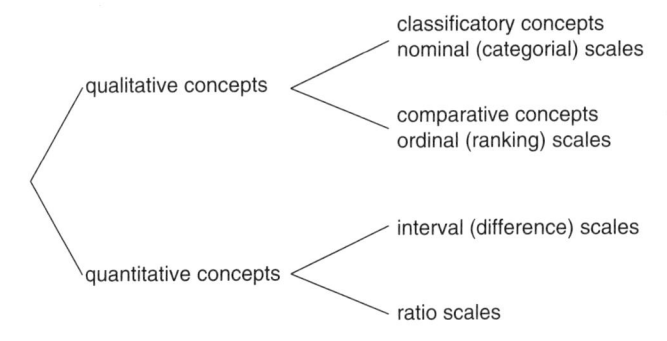

Figure 3.1–3 Classification of concepts according to their gradation type

3.1.4.1 Qualitative-Classificatory Concepts and Nominal Scales

With the help of qualitative or classificatory concepts we divide a domain D of objects into certain subgroups $D_1,..., D_n$, which are defined by their having certain properties or belonging to certain categories $C_1,..., C_n$. Here it is demanded that: (a) the classification is *disjoint*, i.e. the categories C_i must be mutually exclusive (the subgroups must not overlap), and (b) the classification is *exhaustive*, i.e. the union of the subgroups must contain all of D. A division $D_1,..., D_n$ of a domain D which satisfies conditions (a) and (b) is called a *partition* of D.

The set $F =_{def} \{C_1,..., C_n\}$ of the categories of a classification is called a (classificatory) *concept family* (Carnap 1971, 43ff). In the simplest case, an analytically independent concept Fx forms a two-valued or *binary* concept family {Fx, ¬Fx}: for example, x is either human or not. The conditions of disjunctivity and exhaustivity hold in this case purely logically. There are also concept families with more than two categories; e.g. the family of color concepts {red, yellow, green, blue, …}, or the family of social classes {lower class, middle class, upper class}. The conditions of disjunctivity and exhaustivity are, in these cases, based on analytical conventions.

Every concept family F corresponds to a family concept or *attribute* X_F. For example, the concept family {lower, middle, upper class} corresponds to the attribute "social class of x." Formally, X_F is a higher-order *function*, which assigns to every object in D its characteristic category, i.e. $X_F: D \rightarrow \{C_1, \ldots, C_n\}$. If we replace the categories C_i by *natural numbers* i, e.g. "lower, middle, upper class" by "1, 2, 3," then we obtain a nominal (or categorial) *scale*. For nominal scales, however, the use of numbering is inessential and arbitrary. In statistics, a function X which when applied to various objects can take on various *numerical values*, is also called a (random) *variable*. Simple binary properties (F) correspond to a *binary* variable X_F with values F and ¬F. Observe that statistical variables are functions; they should not be confused with variables in the logical sense.

3.1.4.2 Comparative Concepts and Ordinal Scales

With the help of comparative concepts, the objects of a domain D are *ordered* according to the grade of a given property, i.e. they are divided into *ranking groups* $D_1, \ldots, D_n$ (see fig. 3.1–4): D_1 contains all D-objects with the highest grade of the given property, D_2 all objects with the next highest grade, etc. The objects ("o") within a rank group have the same grade. If the rank groups D_i are assigned natural numbers i, we have an *ordinal* or *ranking scale*. The corresponding assignment function r: D→ {1,…, n} is an ordinally scaled variable, also called a ranking function.

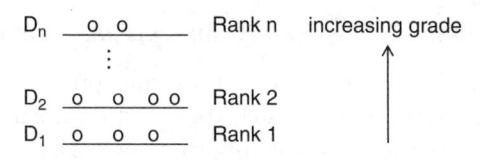

```
Dₙ    o  o           Rank n    increasing grade
       ⋮                            ↑
D₂    o  o  o o      Rank 2
D₁    o  o  o        Rank 1
```

Figure 3.1–4 Ordinal scale of D

The ranks of an ordinal scale give us only comparative information; quantitative differences between the ordinal ranks are unknown or undefined. In the Mohs scale for example, the hardness of minerals is determined by a reciprocal *scratch comparison*: if mineral A scratches mineral B, but not vice versa, then A has a higher degree of hardness.

Mohs used this method to devise a ten-point hardness scale: 1 (talcum), 2 (gypsum), 3 (calcium carbonate), up to 9 (corundum) and 10 (diamond). We must not conclude from this that the difference in hardness between talcum and gypsum is, for example, half as much as the difference in hardness between talcum and calcium carbonate, or a ninth as much as the difference between talcum and diamond. Similarly, the intensity of *psychological* attitudes can typically be measured only by an ordinal scale: for example, I can find one dish tastier than another without being able to say how much tastier it is.

An important method used in the empirical social sciences for *attitude surveys* consists in asking test persons (tps) to place their opinions on a given topic into a *pre-set* ordinal scale. A questionnaire on the attitudes of tps towards old age could, for example, contain the following question:

Please tick where appropriate: I believe that securing an old age pension is:

☐ very important ☐ quite important ☐ don't know
☐ not so important ☐ not important at all

The attitudes of the persons surveyed are thereby ordered into five ranking levels, from not important at all (1) up to very important (5).

The basic logical concept of ordinal scales is that of a *smaller-or-equal* relation $\leq_p$ in regard to the given property P: $x \leq_p y$ states that the P-grade of x is less than or equal to that of y. With help of "$\leq_p$," one *defines* the relation of *P-equality* as $x \equiv_p y \leftrightarrow_{def} x \leq_p y \wedge y \leq_p x$ (x's P-grade equals y's), and the *strictly-smaller* relation as $x <_p y : \leftrightarrow_{def} x \leq_p y \wedge \neg y \leq_p x$ (x's P-grade is smaller than y's). The concepts $\leq_p, \equiv_p, <_p$ are operationalized by *empirical* operations of comparison. In order to generate a *unique* ranking scale, these comparison operations must fulfill at least the axioms of a *quasi-order*: *reflexivity* ($\forall x: x \leq_p x$), *transitivity* ($\forall x,y,z: x \leq_p y \wedge y \leq_p z \rightarrow x \leq_p z$), and *connexivity* ($\forall x,y: x \leq_p y \vee y \leq_p x$), i.e. everything is comparable to everything else. Axioms and definitions entail the *anti-symmetry* of $\leq_p$ ($\forall x,y: x \leq_p y \wedge \neg x \equiv_p y \rightarrow \neg y \leq_p x$) and that $\equiv_p$ is an *equivalence relation*, i.e. fulfills the axioms of reflexivity, symmetry ($\forall x,y: x \equiv_p y \rightarrow y \equiv_p x$) and transitivity. (Note: an *order* in the mathematical sense arises from a quasi-order if no two D-objects occupy the same rank.)

The axioms of transitivity and connexivity are prerequisite for ordinal scaling. Whether they are at least nearly fulfilled is an *empirical* question (only reflexivity and anti-symmetry are fulfilled analytically). It is well known that the empirical preferences of tps are not always transitive (cf. Garnham/Oakhill 1994, 184ff). Additionally, all empirical *pair comparisons* have a certain *inaccuracy*. The relation of *approximate equality*, though, is no longer transitive when the grade differences between objects are very small. As an example assume that a is 0.6 mm taller than b, b is 0.6 mm taller than c, but that only height differences of more than 1 mm are observable. Then we observe that a is approximately equal to b, and b to c, but a is smaller than c. If we place objects of this sort in a *pre-set* ordinal scale, we make their rank relations artificially transitive: the result may then depend on the ordering in which the objects are considered by the tp.

3.1.4.3 Quantitative Concepts and Scales

These express the grade of a property P by means of a *numerical value*, along with a *unit of measurement*. Seen logically, a quantitative concept is a function $f: D \to \text{Num} \times \{u_f\}$, which assigns to every object x in domain D a numeric value $r \in \text{Num}$ along with a unit of measurement u_f; e.g. mass(x) = 5 kg, or temperature(x) = 20 °C. If f(x) is a *discrete* magnitude, then f assigns integers to the objects (Num=$\mathbb{I}$); if f(x) is a *continuous* magnitude, then f assigns real numbers to the objects (Num=$\mathbb{R}$). Almost all physical magnitudes are continuous (exceptions occur in quantum mechanics). Typical discrete magnitudes are counting numbers, e.g. population sizes.

At best, we can directly observe *comparative* magnitude relations: if we determine the length of a given distance by using a measuring tape, we can see whether this distance is longer, shorter, or approximately equal to certain scale divisions on the measuring tape. Converting a comparative concept into a quantitative concept by introducing an (empirical) measuring operation is called its *metrization*. In order to make a comparative property quantitatively measurable, certain preconditions must be satisfied, which are explicated axiomatically in *metrization theory* (see Krantz et al. 2006). On the other hand, any empirical measurement operation is based on certain *arbitrary conventions*, to which the results of respective measurements are relativized. Interval and ratio scales differ from each other in the amount of these arbitrary conventions. In an interval scale, both the *zero point* of the scale and the *unit of measurement* are set by convention. In a ratio scale, on the other hand, only the unit of measurement is conventional, while the zero point is empirically determined.

The empirical temperature scale, for example, is an interval scale. It is based on the fact that certain liquids, e.g. mercury in a glass column, expand uniformly as the temperature increases. But there is no zero point of warmth or coldness which might be discerned through mere observation. In the Celsius scale (°C), the freezing point of water is used as a conventional zero point, and the scale unit of 1 °C is conventionally defined as 1/100 of the length of expansion of mercury in a glass column as it rises from the freezing point to the boiling point of water. In the Fahrenheit scale (°F), the freezing point of water is set at 32 °F, and 1 °F corresponds to 5/9 °C. So physically, it makes no sense to say that a liquid at 20 °C is *twice as warm* as one at 10 °C. This relationship depends on the artificial choice of the zero point; in the Fahrenheit scale, the same relationship comes out as 68 °F to 50 °F. If, however, we have three liquids; a, b and c at 10 °C, 20 °C and 30 °C, respectively, then it certainly does make sense in physical terms to say that the *temperature difference* between b and a is exactly as great as the one between c and b, and half as great as the one between a and c, as this is valid *independently* of the choice of zero point: in the difference between two temperature values, the zero point is cancelled out. Because only statements about ratios of temperature intervals are objective, while statements about ratios of temperatures lack objective content, we talk of interval scales. Measurements of *position* and *time* also use interval scales, because the zero points of spatial and temporal coordinate systems are set by pure convention. We cannot say, for example, "the year 2000 is twice as late as the year 1000," as this is relative to the birth of Christ as the starting point of the calendar. If our calendar began in the Middle Stone Age, we would have instead the years 12000 and 11000.

In ratio scales, unlike interval scales, the absolute zero point is empirically determined. For example, mass, volume, length (as opposed to spatial position), and duration (as opposed to temporal position) are ratio scaled magnitudes. Physically, it makes sense to say that Peter, at 100 kg, weighs twice as much as his 50 kg little brother. Because such ratio statements have objective content, we speak of ratio scales. Similarly, quantitative magnitudes in economics, such as amounts of money or goods, are based on ratio scales.

These magnitudes are also called *extensive* magnitudes, because when joining or "concatenating" two objects (a, b) into a whole (a ∘ b), the resulting magnitude grows monotonically, i.e. it holds that f(a ∘ b) > f(a), f(b). (I prefer the monotonic definition of extensivity to its narrower *additive* definition, f(a ∘ b) = f(a) + f(b), because additivity is not always justified; see Krantz et al. 2006, sec. 3.6.1, 3.9.) Magnitudes such as temperature, for which this is not the case, are by contrast called *intensive* magnitudes—the temperature of say, water, is not increased if we increase the amount of water.

The metrization of extensive magnitudes leads to ratio scales. What is still arbitrary in ratio scales is the (conventional) choice of a *unit*. It makes no sense to say that the numerical value of Peter's weight is 100—this is only valid if the unit of mass is assumed to be the kilogram; if we chose the gram as unit instead, the numerical value of Peter's mass would be 100,000. One subtle problem is the justification of the assumption that the chosen unit remains *constant over time* (see on this Carnap 1966, ch. 8–9).

Only in simple *counting scales* is the unit naturally determined as one individual or item; such counting scales are also called *absolute scales*. The difference between various types of scales is mathematically described in terms of *admissible scale transformations*. The coarser a scale (the "lower" its level), the more scale transformations are admissible; for details see Krantz et al. 2006, 11.

In theories of metrization one proves, for example, the following: an extensive comparative magnitude relation $\leq_p$, e.g. "is longer than," over a domain of objects D is metrizable in the form of a ratio scale iff $\leq_p$ is a monotone quasi-order over D which satisfies the so-called *Archimedean* condition (see Krantz et al. 2006, 73). The latter condition demands that every object b, no matter how large, can be balanced out by a sufficient number of copies of an arbitrary object a, no matter how small a is. For social preference relations, the Archimedean condition is often not satisfied—for example, one would be reluctant to say that the value of a human life might be balanced out by a sufficient number of potatoes or Euro banknotes (cf. Schurz 1997, sec. 11.5.2).

Strictly speaking, the results of attitude measurements (e.g. 5 = very important, 3 = don't know, 1 = unimportant) only have the level of an ordinal scale, or they lie somewhere "between" ordinal and interval scale level. In spite of this, they are often evaluated using statistical tests which presuppose interval scales. To assess whether such an idealization is harmless in a given case, it is necessary to re-evaluate the results of interval scale-based tests by an ordinal scale-based (or "non-parametric") test (see Bortz 1985, 31f, 178f).

So far we have been concerned with *fundamental empirical* metrization. One speaks of *derived* metrization when the metrization of a concept is traced back to the metrization of other concepts, for example, density to the quotient of mass divided by volume, etc. One speaks, finally, of *theory-dependent* metrization, when the metrization is based on a certain theory, e.g. from physics (Balzer 1985b, 6). In theory-driven metrizations, a change in the scale level of an initially empirically defined metric may occur for theoretical reasons. An example of this is the *absolute* temperature scale after Kelvin (°K), which postulates the absolute zero point of temperature at –273.15 °C = 0 °K. This assumption resulted from the hypothesis of the *kinetic theory of gases*, according to which heat and temperature are to be attributed to the movement of molecules. In ideal gases the volume (V) increases in a *linear* way with rising temperature ($V = k \cdot T$). If one extrapolates this relationship in a T×V-coordinate system to the left into the region of negative °C-temperatures, one reaches a temperature of −273.15 °C, at which the volume of an ideal gas would have to be *zero*: here, the gas molecules would be crammed into an infinitely small space, and thus would be unable to move. Kelvin therefore identified this point as the absolute zero of temperature. His hypothesis that no cooling process could go below this absolute zero point has since been confirmed many times.

3.2 Classification of Sentences According to Their Content Type

Sentences can also be classified into several different dimensions. Most significant in philosophy of science is the classification of sentences according to their content type, which is treated here, and according to their degree of generality, which is dealt with in sec 3.5. Fig. 3.2–1 gives an overview.

```
              ┌─ logically determined
       analytic
      /       └─ determined by definition
     /
    /                           ┌─ observation sentences (…)
   /              empirical
  /              /              └─ general emp. sentences (…)
  \  descriptive
   \             \              ┌─ purely theoretical
    \             theoretical
     \                          └─ mixed-theoretical
      synthetic
                                ┌─ normative
                purely prescriptive
                                └─ evaluative
                mixed-prescriptive
```

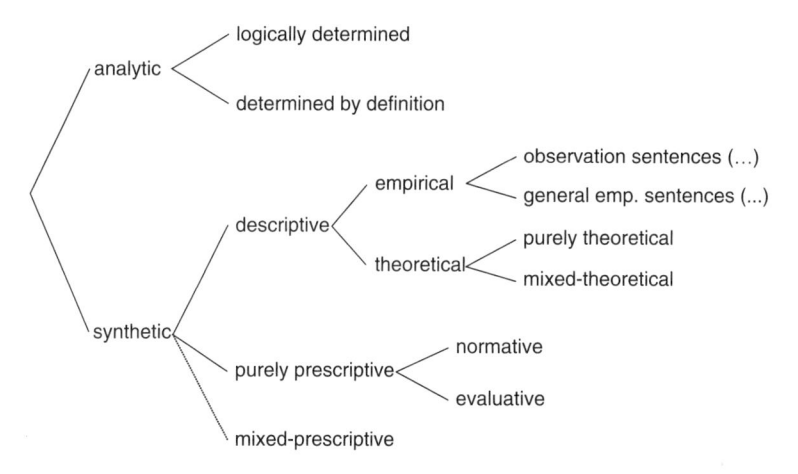

Figure 3.2–1 Classification of sentences according to their content type

Analytically true sentences are those whose truth is determined by the laws of logic or by extralogical conventions of linguistic meaning, independently of the factual constitution of the world. Analytically false sentences are, by analogy, those whose falsity is determined in this way, and *analytical sentences* are those whose truth value (true or false) is determined in this way. Analytical sentences can be broken down further into logically determined sentences (sec. 3.3) and sentences determined by definition or extralogical meaning convention (sec. 3.4).

In contrast, *synthetic* sentences are those sentences whose truth value is not analytically determined, but is dependent on the factual constitution of the world, or in the case of prescriptive-synthetic sentences, on our moral interpretation thereof. As with our content-based classification of concepts, we first divide synthetic sentences into descriptive and prescriptive ones; more precisely, into purely descriptive sentences, purely prescriptive sentences and mixed sentences with descriptive and prescriptive components. Descriptive sentences tell us something about the factual composition of the world; prescriptive sentences, on the other hand, express propositions about norms or values. In the following subsections we refine these distinctions.

3.2.1 Descriptive versus Prescriptive Sentences

Not every sentence containing a prescriptive concept is thereby prescriptive. Indeed, whenever a prescriptive concept lies within the *scope* of a *subjective attitude operator*—i.e. a sentence operator expressing a subjective attitude towards a state of affairs—the prescriptive concept loses its prescriptive force. So, for example, the sentences, "Peter believes that stealing is wrong," or "Peter believes that you shouldn't steal," are empirically descriptive, as they state something about Peter's factual attitude to values or norms. The same goes for all subjective attitude operators, such as: person X believes, thinks, feels, says, wishes, ... (etc.), that A. The significance of this fact for the value-neutrality thesis was worked out in sec. 2.5.1. We define:

(Def. 3.2–1)

a A sentence is *descriptive* iff every prescriptive symbol occurring in it lies within the scope of a subjective attitude operator.

b A sentence is *purely prescriptive* iff all of its descriptive components lie within the scope of a prescriptive operator.

c A sentence which is neither descriptive nor purely prescriptive is called *mixed-prescriptive.—Note:* Mixed-prescriptive sentences contain both descriptive components outside the scope of any prescriptive operator and purely prescriptive components outside the scope of any subjective attitude operator.

(3.2–1) *Examples of descriptive sentences* (logical structure at the right):

i Peter steals.—Steals(peter).
ii Peter believes that stealing is forbidden—Believes(peter, Forbidden(stealing)).

Examples of purely prescriptive sentences:
iii Stealing is forbidden.—Forbidden(stealing).
iv If an action is under all circumstances morally bad, then it is forbidden.—$\forall a,c(Bad(a,c) \rightarrow Forbidden(a))$.

Examples of mixed-prescriptive sentences:
v For persons suffering from hunger, stealing is allowed. —$\forall x(Suffering\text{-}hunger(x) \rightarrow Permitted(Steals(x)))$.

Two remarks: (a) Implicational connections between purely prescriptive sentences as in (iv) are, themselves, purely prescriptive. (b) Def. 3.2-1 is a *syntactic* definition; it can be refined by the method of *essential* sentence types in def. 3.5-1.

3.2.2 Observation and Basic Sentences, Empirical and Theoretical Sentences

Building on the content-based classification of concepts in sec. 3.1.3, we classify descriptive sentences according to their content type. Here, we have to address two subtleties which are rarely discussed in the literature. They have to do with the fact mentioned in sec. 3.1.3, that instantiations of observable properties are only observable if the individuals possessing them are also observable.

First subtlety: An *empirical* sentence is usually defined as a sentence which (apart from logical concepts) contains only empirical concepts (e.g. Tuomela 1973, 23f; Kutschera 1972, 260, 292). But this is insufficient. Consider a universal sentence "All Fs are Gs," which contains only the observation concepts F and G. This universal sentence can only be called empirical if it refers solely to perceptible individuals. Whether this is the case depends on the concept F: only if it follows from the meaning of F that F can be applied *only* to perceptible individuals is the universal sentence an empirical sentence. For example, "all ravens are black" is a universal empirical sentence, because it follows from the meaning of "raven" that only perceptible individuals can be ravens. However, "all loose objects on Earth fall downwards" is not a universal empirical sentence if by "objects" we are also talking about microscopically small particles. The same applies to existential sentences. Lewis (1970, 79) and van Fraassen (1980, 13f) conclude from this problem, that one cannot ascertain the empirical versus theoretical nature of a sentence from the meaning of its concepts. But as we will show now, this is indeed possible. For this purpose, we introduce the following *definition*: A quantifier in a given sentence has an *empirical range* iff this sentence is analytically equivalent with its quantificational restriction to observable individuals only. For a universal sentence

∀xA this restriction is defined as the sentence $\forall x(Ox \to A)$, and for an existential sentence ∃xA with $\exists x(Ox \wedge A)$, where "Ox" stands for "x is observable." Otherwise, the quantifier has a *theoretical* range.

Second subtlety: Observation sentences talk only of a finite or manageable number of individuals, because what humans can observe is of finite and limited complexity. It would be inadequate to limit observation sentences to *singular sentences* —i.e. sentences *without* quantifiers—which contain only observation concepts. *Localized existential sentences* of the form "at point k in space-time, there is such-and-such an observable thing" are also observation sentences; e.g. "in this basket (now) there is a red apple" (Popper 1935/2002, sec. V.28, speaks of "singular existential sentences"). This is the case because the existence quantifier in such a sentence has empirical range, and because the limited segment of space-time is small enough to afford us a visual overview. For similar reasons, even *localized universal sentences* have to be counted as observation sentences, which have the following form: "all (observable) individuals in this limited area of space-time have this or that observable property"; e.g. "All apples in this basket are red." Once again, the universal quantifier must have an empirical range; additionally it is important that the individuals satisfying the antecedent predicate have a perceptible spatial extension that does *not overlap* with other individuals. Given these conditions, it follows from the meaning of "apple" and "basket," that there is only room for a finite and manageable number of apples in the described basket, so that we can determine the truth value of the sentence by observation. This brings us to the following definition:

> (Def. 3.2–2) If S is a synthetic-descriptive sentence, the following holds:
>
> a S is an *observation sentence* iff apart from logical concepts, S contains only observation concepts, and S is either a singular sentence, or a *localized* existential or universal sentence, whose quantifiers possess empirical range.
> b S is an *empirical sentence* (i.n.s.) iff apart from logical-mathematical concepts, S contains only empirical concepts (i.n.s.), and its quantifiers possess empirical range.
> c S is a *theoretical sentence* (i.w.s.) iff S contains theoretical concepts i.w.s. *or* its quantifiers possess theoretical range.
> d S is a *T-theoretical* sentence (or theoretical i.n.s.) iff S is a theoretical sentence i.w.s. and the theoretical concepts of S are introduced by the scientific theory T (refinements in sec. 5.9.1).

In analogy to sec. 3.1.3, we speak of an empirical sentence in the *wide* sense if apart from logical-mathematical concepts, it contains only empirical concepts i.w.s. (and quantifiers with an empirical range i.w.s.). Empirical sentences i.w.s. are dependent on unproblematic pre-theories (sec. 5.9.1) and reflect what scientists pragmatically call "data." *Convention:* Unless otherwise stated, we understand observation, empirical and theoretical sentences in the narrow sense.

The class of empirical sentences is much more *comprehensive* than the class of observation sentences. Apart from observation sentences, it also comprises: (i) *universal* empirical sentences such as "all ravens are black," (ii) singular empirical *disposition* sentences such as "this is soluble in water," and (iii) general empirical disposition sentences such as "all sugar is soluble in water." An important subgroup of empirical disposition sentences are empirical *measurement* sentences such as "this tree is (rounded off) 10.52 meters high," or "fully grown fir trees are more than 10 meters high."

Theoretical hypotheses need not always be universal sentences. Singular or existence sentences can also be theoretical. For example, the singular sentence "this mineral is radioactive" expresses a theoretical hypothesis which can only be tested by means of theory-led measurements using complicated instruments. Finally, *theories* are *systems* of theoretical sentences (ch. 5). We stress here that *theories* or theoretical sentences may *also* contain empirical concepts, and even *must* do so in order to have empirical content, because some authors (e.g. Putnam 1962; Quine 1992, 6–8; Chalmers 1986, 36) give the misleading impression that a concept, once it occurs within a theory, becomes a theoretical concept. According to our definitions, this is clearly not the case (recall sec. 2.9.1, contra–8).

Narrower still than the category of observation sentences is the category of *basic sentences*: Basic sentences in the sense of Carnap (1950b, 67) and Hempel (1965b, 277) are empirical atomic sentences or their negations, e.g. this tree is (not) green. Basic sentences in the sense of Popper (1935/2002, ch. 5, sec. 28) are localized existential sentences, whose matrix is a conjunction of basic formulas, e.g. "there is a black raven there." All basic sentences are observation sentences, but not vice versa. In the Vienna circle, it was hoped that basic sentences would serve to demarcate the *immediately* observable from that which can only be observed in a *mediated* way, via deduction from that which is immediately observable. For example, disjunctions such as "there is a crow or a raven sitting there" are not immediately observable, but they can be deduced from immediate observation sentences. Closer analysis, however, shows that this demarcation is problematic.

3.3 Logical Truth and Deductive Logic

According to philosophical tradition, logical truths are understood to mean "necessities of thought." Both the history of philosophy and cognitive psychology show, however, that our *intuitive* ideas about necessities of thought are unreliable. Modern logic replaces the intuitive concept of necessity with exact concepts. The distinction introduced in sec. 3.1.1 between logical and non-logical concepts is of fundamental importance for the modern definition of logical truth. We will now present a general characterization of logical truth, which is applicable to any system of logic.

(3.3–1) *Logical truth—preliminary characterization:* A sentence is logically true iff its truth follows logically from its syntactic structure and the meaning of its logical concepts alone.

In an equivalent reformulation of this idea one can say: a sentence is logically true iff its truth follows from its *logical form* (this characterization goes back to Wittgenstein's *Tractatus* of 1921). We find the logical form of a (natural language) sentence by replacing all of its non-logical concepts with metalanguage *variables*. The logical form of a sentence, then, is exactly what we get after the *formalization* of the sentence (see sec. 3.1.2), but without any natural language interpretation of its non-logical terms.

The characterization (3.3–1) is only preliminary, as the words "follows logically" in the defining phrase make it circular. The essential thing about a logical sentence form is that its non-logical symbols may be *interpreted* in arbitrary ways. If every such interpretation makes the sentence true, then the sentence is logically true. We can, therefore, conclusively define the logical truth of a sentence, building on the idea in (3.3–1), as follows:

(Def. 3.3–1) A sentence is *logically true* (for short: *L-true*) iff its (logical) sentence form is true for every possible interpretation of its non-logical symbols. We then also call this sentence form logically true.

Definition (3.3–1) goes back to Tarski (1936b). It is easily applicable to specific systems of logic, by specifying the permissible interpretations. In PropL, these are the assignments of truth values to atomic sentences. In PredL, these are the extensional interpretations (D,I) explained in sec. 3.1.2. Note that in possible interpretations (D,I), not only the interpretation function I(φ) for non-logical symbols φ may vary, but also the individual domain D. Here are some examples:

(3.3–2) *Example of an L-true sentence:*

If everybody is mortal, then nobody is immortal.
Sentence form: If all Fs are Gs, then there exists no F which is not a G.
Formalization: $\forall x(Fx \rightarrow Gx) \rightarrow \neg \exists x(Fx \wedge \neg Gx)$

Further examples: $A \vee \neg A$, $A \rightarrow (A \vee B)$, $\forall xFx \rightarrow Fa$, $Fa \rightarrow \exists xFx$, etc.

The sentence form (3.3–2) is L-true, because it is true for every (extensional) interpretation of "F" and "G." In other words, it is true in every possible world, as extensional interpretations correspond to possible worlds.

In analogy to def. 3.3–1, one defines a sentence as *logically false* (L-false) iff its sentence form is false for every possible interpretation of its non-logical symbols. Examples of L-false sentence forms are $p \wedge \neg p$ (e.g. it will rain today and it will not rain), or $p \leftrightarrow \neg p$.

L-false sentences are also called *inconsistent*, or *contradictory*, because one may derive contradictions from them of the form "p and not-p." Finally, a sentence which is neither L-true nor L-false is called *contingent*. Examples of contingent sentences are Fa (e.g. Peter is ill) or $\forall x(Fx \rightarrow Gx)$ (e.g. all ravens are black), etc. Most sentences are contingent.

A sentence that is not L-false is called *consistent* (hence, a consistent sentence is either contingent or L-true). Consistency is also defined for *sets* of sentences: A sentence set is called consistent iff at least one interpretation verifies all sentences in the set; otherwise it is called inconsistent (or contradictory).

With the help of the same method, we define the logical *validity* of arguments or inferences. That the conclusion of an inference follows logically from its premises means that the *truth* is transferred from the premises to the conclusion with *certainty*, i.e. in all possible interpretations or "worlds":

> (Def. 3.3–2) An inference is *logically valid* (for short: valid) iff for the logical *form* of this inference the following holds: every possible interpretation which makes all premises true, also makes the conclusion true.—*Equivalently expressed:* … iff there is no interpretation which makes all the premises true, but the conclusion false.—If an inference is valid, then we say that its conclusion *follows* (logically) from its premises.

(3.3–3) *Example of a logically valid inference:*   Inference form:
Premise 1: All humans are mortal. $\forall x(Hx \rightarrow Mx)$
Premise 2: You are a human. Ha
Conclusion: Therefore you are mortal. Ma

As with logical truth, logical validity is a matter of *logical form*. This fact implies that the validity of an inference does *not* depend on the *truth* of its premises (a common misunderstanding). The fact that an inference is valid only means: *If* its premises *were true*, then its conclusion *would* also have to be true. An inference with false premises can also be valid, for example: "All humans are rich. You are a human. Therefore you are rich." This inference is logically valid, since in all possible worlds in which all humans were rich, you being a human would be rich, too. That in the actual world not all humans are rich is merely a contingent fact. Of course, in order to apply an inference for purposes of *justification* or *prediction*, one must have good reasons for believing that its premises are true. Valid inferences, however, may also be used for purposes of *falsification*: in such cases, one infers from the falsity of the conclusion that *at least one* of the premises must be false.

Def. 3.3–2 implies the following *test criterion* for L-validity: an inference is invalid iff there exists an inference of the same logical form with true premises and a false conclusion. Here is an example:

(3.3–4) *Example of a logically invalid inference*
Premise 1: All humans are mortal. $\forall x(Hx \rightarrow Mx)$
Premise 2: You are mortal. Ma
Conclusion: Therefore, you are a human. Ha

Application of the test criterion: there are inferences of the same logical form, which have true premises and a false conclusion—e.g. "All humans are mortal, this cat is mortal, so this cat is a human."

Semantic proofs of L-truth and validity in PredL are often complicated and abstract. For this reason, logic also uses another procedure: the method of *deductive proofs*. With this method, one assumes some fundamental L-truths as *axioms* and some L-valid inferences as *rules*, and aims to derive all other L-true sentences or valid inferences through the iterative application of axioms and rules in the form of "proofs" (see e.g. Copi et al. 2010). Here is an example:

(3.3–5) *Proof* of "∀x(Hx→Mx), Ha / Ma" by means of the rules "A, A→B / B" (Modus Ponens MP) and "∀xA(x) / A(a)" (Universal Instantiation UI):

1 ∀x(Hx→Mx)   Premise
2 Ha   Premise
3 Ha→Ma   UI (applied to) 1
4 Ma   MP (applied to) 2, 3

A full logical system consists of a language, a logical semantics and a deductive proof system (or calculus).

3.4 Conventions of Meaning and Definitional Truths

As with L-true sentences, definitions such as "A bachelor is a hitherto unmarried man" are *analytical* truths, i.e. their truth follows from the meaning of their concepts alone, independently of the factual constitution of the world. Differently from L-true sentences, however, the truth of definitions is determined not by the meaning of their logical concepts, but by conventions of meaning for their specific *non-logical* concepts, in our example "bachelor," "man" and "hitherto unmarried." The truth of sentences which are definitionally true is, therefore, *not* a matter of their logical form, but it is a matter of the conventions of meaning in the given language. So we define:

(Def. 3.4–1) (a) A sentence is *definitionally true* (or: *extralogically-analytically true*) iff its truth is based on certain *conventions of meaning* for its *non-logical* concepts.
In other words: A sentence is definitionally true iff it follows logically from the set of these conventions of meaning, without being itself logically true.
(b) *A sentence is analytically true* iff it is logically true or definitionally true.

(3.4–1) *Examples of definitionally true sentences:*

a   All bachelors are male. $\forall x(Bx \rightarrow Mx)$
b   The length of the standard measure in Paris is one meter. Length(a) = (1,m)

(3.4–2) *Examples of synthetically true sentences:*

a   All polar bears are white. $\forall x(Px \rightarrow Wx)$
b   The length of this rod is one meter. Length(b) = (1,m)

The difference between analytical and synthetic truths can be illustrated as follows: If a zoologist sees the truth of (3.4–2)(a) as empirically confirmed, then his justification makes sense. But if someone reported to us that, in spite of extensive empirical investigation, he has never met a female bachelor, then this person has clearly not understood the meaning of "bachelor": bachelors are by definition (unmarried) men; no empirical research is necessary to know this. The examples also make it clear that definitional truths cannot be distinguished from synthetic truths on the basis of logical form, as (3.4–1)(a) and (3.4–2)(a) or (3.4–1)(b) and (3.4–2)(b) have the same logical form, respectively.

Although definitions cannot be *empirically* true or false, they can be more or less *empirically adequate* (see also Hempel 1965b, sec. 6.5). Before Linnaeus, for example, animals and plants were classified by their phenomenological characteristics. Classification by common evolutionary descent, founded by Darwin a century later, turned out to be substantially more adequate, because it reflected a much larger number of common nomological characteristics. Nevertheless, nobody could be forbidden from defining "fish" as "water-dwelling vertebrates." The fact that dolphins, etc., would then also count as fish, although they descended from land-dwelling mammals, with whom they share many more common features than with the other (gill-breathing) fishes, does not disprove this definition—it does however highlight its empirical inadequacy.

Some authors call particularly natural or empirically adequate definitions "true" or "real definitions," as distinct from "nominal definitions" in the sense of linguistic conventions. This view goes back to Aristotle and presupposes an *essentialism*, according to which the world holds in itself a "true" partition into natural kinds, which are characterized by certain necessary or "essential" properties. What one counts as "essential" is, however, often unclear: there is ongoing debate about the optimal classification of biological taxa. For example, purely evolutionary classifications—though held as generally superior to Linnean classifications—would have to classify crocodiles not together with reptiles, but with birds, which is regarded as "unnatural" by most biological taxonomists (cf. Ridley 1993, 369). This shows that optimal definitions are not dictated by the facts of the world, but also depend on epistemic matters.

In conclusion, we do not adopt the notion of "real definitions," because we do not believe in essences (recall sec. 1.3.4). Moreover, the demarcation between definitions and synthetic sentences would thereby become *unclear*. By "definitions" we always understand more or less adequate semantic conventions.

There are three different kinds of sentences which are definitionally true, namely:

(D1) *Explicit definitions:* In these, a concept (the definiendum) is equated by convention with a complex of other concepts (the definiens). For general concepts, an explicit definition has the form of an *equivalence* (see Suppes 1999/1957, sec. 8.3):

(3.4–3)   (Definiendum)   (Definiens)

Example: $\forall x$:   x is a bachelor $\leftrightarrow_{def}$ x is a hitherto unmarried man
Logical form: $\forall x(Dx_1...x_n \leftrightarrow_{def} A)$, where in A only the individual variables $x_1 ... x_n$ are free.

For singular concepts and function concepts, explicit definitions have the form of an identity, e.g. $a =_{def} f(b_1,..., b_n)$, or $\forall x(g(x) =_{def} f(x_1,..., x_n))$.

(D2) *Meaning postulates* (also called "*implicit*" *definitions*): These are semantic conventions, which, like definitions, play the role of extralogical-analytic *axioms*, i.e. they are not arrived at by logical derivation. These meaning postulates, however, do not have the form of an explicit definition, but some other form, mostly that of an implication. *Examples:*

$\forall x(x$ is round $\rightarrow x$ has no corners),
$\forall x(x$ is red $\rightarrow x$ is colored).

Meaning postulates do *not* fully characterize a concept, and do not allow for its elimination. In other words, "implicit" definitions are *not* proper definitions.

(D3) *Derived definitorially true sentences:* These sentences are not logically true, but follow logically from sentences of type D1 or D2. *Examples:*

$\forall x(x$ is not male $\rightarrow x$ is not a bachelor),
$\forall x(x$ is colorless $\rightarrow x$ is not red) (etc.).

Proper definitions must fulfill the criterion of *eliminability* of defined concepts (cf. Suppes 1999/1957, 154). In order to satisfy this criterion, they have to satisfy the *non-circularity* requirement. For a single explicit definition this criterion demands that the definiendum concept must not occur in the definiens. If this is the case, then the definiendum of explicit definitions of the form (3.4–3) can be eliminated in every sentence S (or "context") in which it occurs, simply by replacing it by its definiens: the result is a sentence S* which is definitionally equivalent with S, i.e. the equivalence S↔S* follows from the given definition.[1]

For an entire *set* of definitions $\{D_1,\ldots, D_n\}$ it must be required that this set can be arranged in the form of a *non-circular chain* of definitions, which means that every definiens in this chain contains only concepts which are either undefined or are the definiendum of an *earlier* definition in the chain (cf. von Savigny 1976b, 116). An example of a non-circular chain of definitions is $Ax \leftrightarrow_{def} Bx \wedge \neg Cx$, $Bx \leftrightarrow_{def} Dx \wedge Ex$, $Dx \leftrightarrow_{def} \neg Fx$. If we carry out successive replacement in the definiens of Ax, we arrive at $Ax \leftrightarrow_{def} \neg Fx \wedge Ex \wedge \neg Cx$ as the basic definition of Ax, which contains only primitive (undefined) concepts in its definiens. An example of a circular chain of definitions is $Necessary(A) \leftrightarrow_{def} \neg Possible(\neg A)$, $Possible(A) \leftrightarrow_{def} \neg Necessary(\neg A)$, as after replacement, we arrive at the circular basic definition $Necessary(A) \leftrightarrow_{def} \neg\neg Necessary(\neg\neg A)$.

A further category of definition is *recursive* definitions. They play an important role in logic and computer science. Without going into details, we only mention that in spite of their iterative structure, recursive definitions also satisfy the non-circularity requirement, since they are provably equivalent with (quite complicated) explicit definitions (cf. Van Dalen et al. 1978, 157).

The central requirement for analytically true sentences is their empirical non-creativity, which is explicated as follows:

(Prop. 3.4–1) *Requirement of empirical non-creativity:* Analytically true sentences must neither have empirical content, nor create new empirical content in combination with the given system S of accepted background beliefs.

More precisely: A set of sentences Δ can *only* be analytically true *if* (a) the empirical content of Δ (the set of Δ's empirical consequences expressed without defined terms) is empty, and (b) the empirical content of S-united-with-Δ is the same as that of S.

Both requirements (a) and (b) must be fulfilled, in order to be able to say that the truth of such sentences is based on analytical convention. In

Suppes' criterion (1999/1957, 154) requirement (a) is missing, because he deals only with non-creativity *relative* to S.

Prop. 3.4–1 implies that *no concept may be defined twice* in different ways. It is well known that in the history of measurement, different conventions were suggested. Here are two examples:

1. 1 meter = the length of the platinum-iridium-bar in Paris.
2. 1 meter = the length of a pendulum at sea level with an oscillation frequency of one second.

(1) + (2) however, imply the following *empirical consequence*: the length of the platinum-iridium-bar in Paris equals the length of a pendulum at sea level with an oscillation frequency of one second. We cannot regard (1) and (2) *simultaneously* as the definition of one meter. If (1) is the accepted definition, then (2) is an empirical hypothesis, and vice versa. Many "definitions" to be found in textbooks, e.g. "Water = H_2O," or "Child = person less than 12 years old," do not fulfill the requirement of empirical non-creativity. This is because the concepts being defined ("water," "child") have already been analytically introduced to common-sense background knowledge in other ways, e.g. by ostensive characterizations. Such "definitions" should more rightly be called *explications* in the sense of Carnap (recall sec. 2.1) rather than definitions. Also so-called "definitions" of theoretical concepts, e.g. "force = mass times acceleration," generate new empirical content and, for this reason, are not proper definitions (see sec. 5.1).

As long as a concept in a system of knowledge is characterized only by *one* explicit definition, this definition is provably always empirically non-creative (see Shoenfield 1967, 57f). Also a *single* implicational meaning postulate for a new concept Fx such as $\forall x(Fx \rightarrow Ax)$, is not creative, because it is logically weaker than an explicit definition $\forall x(Fx \leftrightarrow Ax)$. Mostly though, an entire *system* of meaning postulates is introduced for one (or several) concepts; and for this there is no guarantee of non-creativity. The designation of systems of meaning postulates as "implicit definitions" (which goes back to Hilbert) is therefore easily misunderstood, because "implicit definitions" behave quite differently from proper definitions.

3.5 Classification of Sentences According to Their Generality

The overview is shown in fig. 3.5–1. The logical *strength* decreases successively with the transition from universal via singular to existential sentences: a universal sentence "Everything is an F" is logically stronger than its singular instance "This is an F" which is, in turn, logically stronger than the existential sentence "Something is an F."

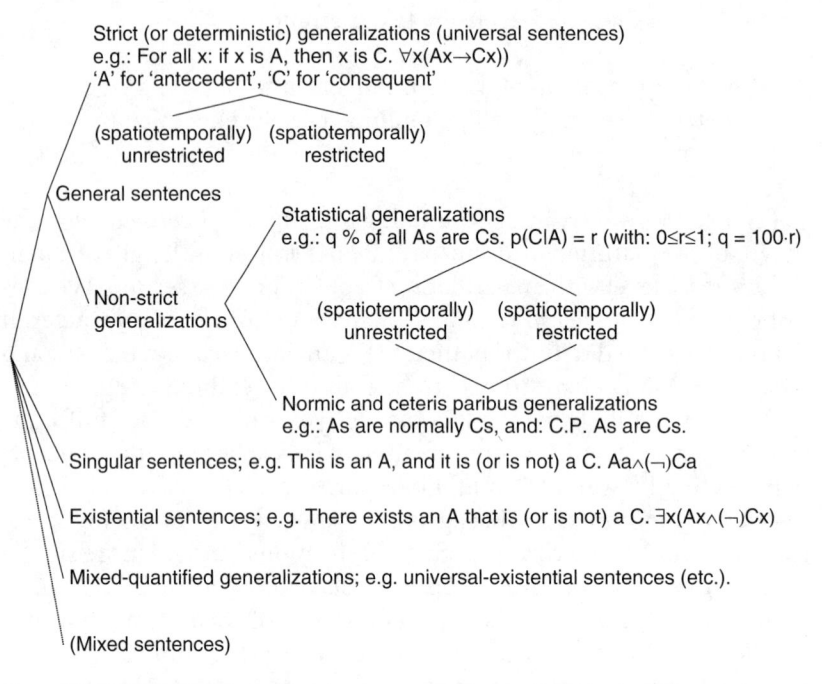

```
                Strict (or deterministic) generalizations (universal sentences)
                e.g.: For all x: if x is A, then x is C. ∀x(Ax→Cx))
               / 'A' for 'antecedent', 'C' for 'consequent'
              /
             /   (spatiotemporally)   (spatiotemporally)
            /      unrestricted           restricted
           General sentences
                       Statistical generalizations
                      / e.g.: q % of all As are Cs. p(C|A) = r (with: 0≤r≤1; q = 100·r)
            \ Non-strict
              generalizations   (spatiotemporally)   (spatiotemporally)
                                   unrestricted          restricted

                       Normic and ceteris paribus generalizations
                       e.g.: As are normally Cs, and: C.P. As are Cs.
           Singular sentences; e.g. This is an A, and it is (or is not) a C. Aa∧(¬)Ca

           Existential sentences; e.g. There exists an A that is (or is not) a C. ∃x(Ax∧(¬)Cx)

           Mixed-quantified generalizations; e.g. universal-existential sentences (etc.).

           (Mixed sentences)
```

Figure 3.5–1 Classification of sentences according to their generality

1 *Strict generalizations:* The *universal implication* "For all x: if Ax, then Cx" is the simplest form of a universal sentence. The if-component Ax is also called the *antecedent*, the then-component is called the *consequent*. In general, a *purely* universal sentence begins with one or more universal quantifiers, followed by a quantifier-free formula, which is called the *matrix* of the universal sentence and typically has the form of an implication, an equivalence, or a numerical identity. Universal sentences are also called *strict* or *deterministic* or *exceptionless* generalizations, since the truth of ∀x(Ax→Cx) implies for *every* individual a that if Aa obtains, the occurrence of Ca is inevitably determined.

2 *Non-strict generalizations:* In this category we include primarily *statistical* generalizations of the form "q% of all As are Cs." One calls this a statement of *conditional* probability, and writes it down as

p(Cx|Ax) = r, with r·100 = %. The probability "p" is understood statistically, as a frequency or frequency limit (sec. 3.9). Although statistical generalizations are general sentences, they are *not* universal sentences. The statistical generalization "q% of all As are Cs" says nothing about single individuals of type A, rather it only says something about the class of As, i.e. that q% of the individuals of the class of As are located in the class of Cs; see fig. 3.5–2. For this reason, there are no logical consequence relations, but only inductive-probabilistic relations between statistical generalizations and singular sentences, if the domain of individuals is unknown or potentially infinite.

A further kind of non-strict generalizations are *normic* generalizations or normal-case hypotheses of the form "As are *normally* Cs"—e.g., birds can normally fly (the term "normic" goes back to Scriven 1959a). For reasons explained in sec. 4.5.2 we can assume that a normic law *implies* a numerically unspecific statistical generalization of the form "*most* As are Cs." A third kind of non-strict generalizations are ceteris paribus generalizations, which say that Ax leads to Cx as long as other interfering factors are either held constant, or are absent (for details see sec. 4.5.1).

What statistical, normic and CP generalizations have in common, is that they allow for *exceptions*—these are instances which verify the antecedent and falsify the consequent predicate. Therefore, inferences from them are described by a non-monotonic consequence relation in the sense of sec. 2.7.4. Strict laws forbid such exceptions and are falsified by them.

Both strict and non-strict generalizations can be unrestricted or restricted in space and time. They are restricted if the antecedent predicate contains a restriction to a finite area of space and time—e.g. "All swans in *Europe* are white," as opposed to "All swans are white." Unrestricted universal sentences are also called *spatiotemporally universal* (sec. 6.6.4).

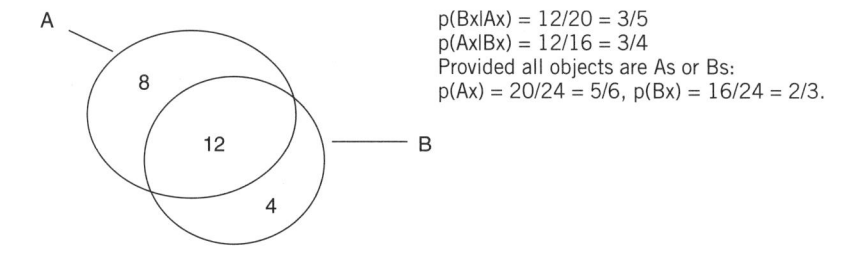

p(Bx|Ax) = 12/20 = 3/5
p(Ax|Bx) = 12/16 = 3/4
Provided all objects are As or Bs:
p(Ax) = 20/24 = 5/6, p(Bx) = 16/24 = 2/3.

Figure 3.5–2 Statistical generalizations

3 *Singular sentences* are all sentences which contain *no quantifiers*, and also no statistical probability function. Singular sentences are composed of atomic sentences using propositional operators (Fa, ¬Fa, Fa∧Rab, etc.). They always say something about one or more individual things.

4 *Existential sentences:* Pure existential sentences begin with one or more existential quantifiers, followed by a quantifier-free matrix formula. Usually, the matrix has the form of a conjunction ∃x(Ax∧(¬)Cx); e.g. "There is a black swan," etc. Such existential sentences may also be unrestricted or restricted, depending on whether Ax contains a restriction in space and time or not.

5 *Mixed-quantified generalizations* contain both universal and existential quantifiers. *Example:* Every action has a motive, formally ∀x∃y(Action(x) → Motive(y,x)). The meaning of generalizations with mixed quantifiers depends on the *order* of quantifiers: ∃x∀yRxy is a logically stronger statement than ∀y∃xRxy. *Example:* Let "Rxy" stand for "x is the cause of y." Then ∀y∃xRxy says that everything has some cause, but ∃x∀yRxy says that some x is the cause of everything, i.e. everything has the *same* cause, which is a much stronger statement. If the quantifiers are the same, though, their order is unimportant.

6 *Mixed sentences*, finally, are propositional combinations of the above sentence types, like for instance ∀x(Fx→Gx) ∨ Ha. They play a subordinate role.

Prop. 3.5-1 summarizes the most important logico-deductive relationships between the listed kinds of sentences.

(Prop. 3.5–1) *Notation:* "X ⊪— Y" stands for "Y follows logically from X," and "X —⫤ ⊪— Y" for "X and Y are logically equivalent."

1   Universal sentence ⊪— singular sentence
    All As are Cs ⊪— if a is A, then a is C
2   Universal sentence & singular sentence ⊪— singular sentence
    (*explanation scheme*) All As are Cs, and a is A ⊪— a is C
3   Singular sentence falsifies strictly universal sentence (*falsification scheme I*)

> Singular sentence ‖— negation of a universal sentence
> a is A and not-C ‖— not all As are Cs
> 4 Existential sentence falsifies strictly universal sentence (*falsification scheme II*)
> There is an A that is not a C ‖— not all As are Cs
> 5 Universal sentence is logically equivalent to the negation of an existential sentence.
> All As are Cs —‖ ‖— there is no A that is not a C
> 6 Singular sentence ‖— Existential sentence
> a is an A ‖— there is an x that is an A
> 7 There are no logical consequence relations between non-strict generalizations and singular sentences, only statistical or epistemic relations of probability.

The above characterizations of kinds of sentences are of a *syntactic* nature. Syntactic characterizations are not always invariant with respect to (w.r.t.) logically equivalent (L-equivalent) transformations. For instance, the singular sentence Fa is L-equivalent to the universal sentence $\forall x(x=a \to Fx)$ (all x which are identical with a have property F). This sentence, however, is not a universal sentence in the *semantic* sense, as it only says something about the individual a. If characterizations of sentences should express genuine properties of the *propositions* thereby expressed, they must be invariant w.r.t. L-equivalent sentence transformation, since L-equivalent sentences express the same proposition. A standard method of solving this problem is the method of *essential* sentence types (see Hempel/Oppenheim 1948, 271). Here, one regards a sentence as essentially universal (or existential) only if it is not L-equivalent to a singular sentence:

> (Def. 3.5–1) *Essential sentence types (according to their generality):*
> 1 A sentence S is an essentially universal/existential sentence iff S is a syntactically universal/existential sentence and not L-equivalent to a syntactically singular sentence.
> 2 In contrast, a sentence S is an *essentially* singular sentence iff S is L-equivalent to a syntactically singular sentence.

The division of kinds of sentences according to their generality is largely *independent* of the content-based classification of sentences given in sec. 3.2: the kinds of sentences listed above can be either empirical or theoretical sentences, depending on which non-logical concepts occur in these sentences, and which range their quantifiers possess. However, unrestricted universal or existential sentences, or those covering an immeasurably large area of space-time, can never be observation sentences.

A further distinction, which runs *crosswise* to our distinctions up to now, is the one between *evidences* and *hypotheses*. It relates to the *epistemic status* of our knowledge. Evidence statements are very well secured sentences—actual observation sentences are prototypical for this category. Hypotheses are less well secured sentences, which are in need of further testing—prototypical for this are general sentences, or potential observation sentences (i.e. observable predictions).

3.6 General Sentences, Lawlikeness, Determinism and Indeterminism

Unrestricted essentially universal sentences are prima facie candidates for laws of nature, i.e. *if* they were true, they would express a law of nature. In the philosophy of science, such sentences are called *lawlike* or *nomological*. Here are two *examples*:

(3.6–1) All bodies attract each other.
(3.6–2) All living creatures must die.

In the debate on lawlikeness it has become clear, however, that not every essentially universal sentence is also lawlike. This can be seen most quickly when we consider universal sentences which are essential in the logical sense, but spatiotemporally restricted.

Examples of restricted universal sentences with increasing restrictedness:

(3.6–3) All bodies close to the surface of the Earth fall downwards with a constant acceleration of 10 m/sec^2 (Galileo's law of gravity).

(3.6–4) All mammals in polar regions have a more rounded form than their conspecifics in warm countries (Bergmann's law).

(3.6–5) Until approximately 10,000 BC, all humans lived from hunting and gathering.

(3.6–6) In the middle ages, all agriculture was based on the feudal fief principle.

(3.6–7) All apples in this basket are red.

Whether or not we can speak here of a scientific law depends prima facie on the *size* of the spatiotemporal area to which the universal quantifier is applied. This becomes apparent from the hierarchy of the examples. (3.6–3) and (3.6–4) are regarded as scientific laws in physics and biology, respectively. For the historical universal sentences (3.6–5) and (3.6–6), the status as a law is debatable—many historians prefer to speak here of nomologically contingent facts. Finally, (3.6–7) is clearly not a lawlike universal sentence, but a *localized* universal sentence which is an observation sentence (recall sec. 3.2.2), although logically speaking (3.6–7) is also an essentially universal sentence. Universal sentences of this type (3.6–7) are also called *accidental* universal sentences (Chisholm 1946; Hempel 1965b, 266).

In this perspective the concept of the lawlikeness of universal sentences seems to be something *gradual*. A number of suggestions have been made in the philosophy of science concerning how to make the explication of lawlikeness more precise. Thereby, many unexpected difficulties have been encountered. Carnap (1947) and Hempel (1965b, 266) suggested avoiding the problem of the graduality of lawlikeness by distinguishing between *fundamental* and *derived* laws. They defined a derived law as a universal sentence that is derived from (other) fundamental laws in the given background knowledge, possibly together with singular boundary conditions, while a fundamental law is a universal sentence that is not derivable in this way, and which contains no individual constants. So Carnap and Hempel's suggestion was that fundamental laws must not refer to particular individual constants or space-time regions, while derived laws may refer to them. This seems to fit well for the above examples: Galileo's law of gravity (3.6–3) can be derived from Newtonian physics and the boundary condition of the Earth's mass, and Bergmann's law (3.6–4) is derivable from the general theory of evolution, together with the fact that a rounded body form stores body warmth better because of its smaller surface area in relation to volume. But Nagel (1961, 58) refuted Carnap and Hempel's suggestion. Nagel pointed out that clear examples of *accidental* universal sentences may also be derived, such as, "All the screws on Smith's car are rusty": this accidental universal sentence is, for instance, derivable from the boundary condition that Mr. Smith always parks his car outdoors, and lives in Scotland, where it rains a lot, along with the law of nature that iron rusts after frequent contact with water. Hempel (1977, 291ff) therefore abandoned his original characterization of lawlikeness for derived laws.

Goodman's criterion of lawlikeness also fails to avoid this problem. Goodman (1955, ch. 1) pointed out that an indicator for the lawlikeness of a general implication "All As are Cs" is the truth or acceptability of a corresponding *counterfactual* "If this were an A, it would be a C." However, the counterfactual implication is an *intensional* logical operation: its truth value is not determined by the truth values of antecedent and consequent. Rather, the truth conditions of counterfactuals depend themselves on the presupposed notion of lawlikeness (see sec. 6.6.3). For example, we regard the counterfactual "If this little comet were close to earth's surface, it would fall downwards" as true, because (3.6–3) is lawlike, and we regard "If this (green) apple were in this basket, it would be red" as false, because we consider (3.6–7) as accidental. But we are uncertain whether example (3.6–5) is lawlike or accidental, and therefore it is unclear for us whether we should regard the counterfactual "If I lived in 12,000 BC, I would feed from hunting and gathering" as true or false.

In conclusion: the lawlikeness of *restricted* universal sentences is a *gradual* matter. Metaphysically speaking, the gradual lawlikeness of restricted universal sentences results from the fact they depend on both physical necessities and contingencies. But even *spatiotemporally universal* sentences, which are not limited in space and time, are not always lawlike, as the following example, which goes back to Reichenbach, demonstrates (cf. van Fraassen 1989, 27):

(3.6–8) No lump of radioactive uranium has a diameter of more than one mile.

(3.6–9) No lump of gold has a diameter of more than one mile.

(3.6–8) is a law of nature, as any lump of radioactive uranium of this size would explode due to an atomic chain reaction. Probably (3.6–9) is true, too—but even if (3.6–9) were true, it would not be a law of nature, because a lump of gold of this size is physically possible. Further suggested solutions to the problems of explicating lawlikeness and physical necessity are found in sec. 6.6.

The question of lawlikeness also applies to statistical generalizations. Here again, are some examples:

(3.6–10) 50% of all cesium^{137} atoms (for any amount of the substance) will have decayed within 30 years.

(3.6-11) 80% of all lung cancer sufferers were heavy smokers.

(3.6-12) 70% of all bedwetting children have parents with a disturbed relationship.

(3.6-13) 80% of all Africans are dark-skinned.

(3.6-14) 60% of all apples in this basket are red.

(3.6-10, 11, 12) are unrestricted statistical generalizations, and (3.6-13, 14) are spatiotemporally restricted. In the case of restricted generalizations, we encounter the same *graduality* of lawlikeness as with restricted universal sentences. The radioactive decay law (3.6-10) is a paradigm case of a statistical law of nature (cesium^{137} is the main contamination set free in nuclear reactor explosions such as Tschernobyll 1986 and Fukushima 2011). (3.6-14) is the statistical counterpart of (3.6-7) above—a logically essential, but clearly accidental statistical generalization.

When judging the lawlike character of unrestricted statistical generalizations (3.6-10, 11, 12), the additional question of *determinism* versus *indeterminism* arises. According to the deterministic world view, as formulated by Laplace in the 19th century, the entire course of events in the world is completely determined and predictable by initial conditions and natural laws. A proponent of the deterministic physical world view could not accept the decay law (3.6-10) as a fundamental law of nature, but at best as a derived law. For if determinism is true and our knowledge about the initial conditions of each Cs^{137} atom were complete, we would have to be able to predict for every Cs^{137} atom when it will decay. Modern microphysics, however, teaches an objective indeterminism—according to quantum physics, there are *objective random processes* in nature. In this sense, (3.6-10) is an objectively indeterministic *fundamental law*: if and when one Cs^{137} atom will decay *cannot* be predicted by any knowledge of physics, no matter how complete. But the probability that a Cs^{137} atom will have decayed in 30 years is exactly 1/2; and so we are practically certain that in 30 years, 50% of a sample of Cs^{137} will have decayed.

We therefore distinguish between two kinds of indeterminism: *objective indeterminism*, according to which the statistical nature of generalizations is caused by objective properties of nature, versus *epistemic indeterminism*, according to which the statistical nature of generalizations results from the incompleteness of our knowledge. While (3.6-10) is an objectively indeterministic law, the generalizations (3.6-11, 12) are epistemically indeterministic generalizations. In the case of (3.6-11), this means: if we had exact knowledge of a person, then we could predict the occurrence or non-occurrence of lung cancer with a much higher probability, close to 1. The restricted generalizations (3.6–13, 14), of course, are also cases of epistemic indeterminism.

There is a difference, however, between (3.6–11) and (3.6–12): (3.6–11) is a clearly lawlike statistical generalization, as under (as good as) *all circumstances,* heavy smoking increases the probability of lung cancer. In (3.6–12), the lawlikeness is more debatable: there are many circumstances, under which disturbed parental relationships do *not* lead to bedwetting in children. So (3.6–12) has a high level of contingency.

The above examples have been *numerical*-statistical generalizations. There are also *qualitative* and *comparative* statistical generalizations:

(3.6–15) *Qualitative statistical generalization:*

Most bedwetting children have parents with a disturbed relationship
$p(DistParents(x) \mid Bedwetter(x)) = $ high.

(3.6–16) *Comparative statistical generalization:*

Bedwetting children are *more likely* to have parents with a disturbed relationship.
$p(DistParents(x) \mid Bedwetter(x)) > p(DistParents(x) \mid $ not $Bedwetter(x))$.

A comparative statistical generalization is very *weak,* as it tells us nothing about the *strength* of the statistical influence, but only that some, if only small, probability-increasing influence is present.

3.7 Content of Sentences and Kinds of Content

(Def. 3.7–1) Let S be a sentence or a set of sentences.[2]

1 The *logical content* of S (a "theory") is the set of the (logical) consequences of S. For this, we write C(S).

2 The *empirical content* of S is the set of all (logical) consequences of S, which are empirical sentences and not analytically true. Here we write E(S).

Narrower than the empirical content is the *observation content*, which we define as the set O(S) of observation sentences which follow from S. The concept of observation content, however, has only limited use— namely for purely universal hypotheses. No observation sentences follow from a *mixed-quantified* hypothesis such as (H:) $\forall x(Fx \rightarrow \exists y Gxy)$, even if it is an empirical hypothesis. Only $Fa \rightarrow \exists y Gay$ follows from H through universal instantiation, but this is not an observation sentence, because it (essentially) contains the unrestricted existential quantifier $\exists y$. For this reason, empirical hypotheses with mixed quantifiers are not only *unverifiable* by observation sentences, but also *unfalsifiable*. They may, however, be confirmed or disconfirmed by observation sentences.

Of further importance is the concept of *relevant* logical or empirical content, which is explained in sec. 3.12.

One content concept which has been neglected in the philosophy of science is the concept of *probabilistic content*. Let us assume that S is a set of statistical hypotheses. S does not imply any observation sentences O, but conveys to them at best a certain (epistemic) probability. The suggestion that we could define the probabilistic content of S as the set of all sentences whose conditional probability given S is sufficiently high, i.e. higher than a certain value r, does not work, for the following reason: the set of these sentences can be *inconsistent*, no matter how close r is to 1. Vivid illustrations of this problem are the *lottery* and the *preface paradox* (see sec. 5.10.8). We therefore make an alternative suggestion: we define the probabilistic content of a statistical hypothesis S as the set of all statistical *probability sentences* which follow from S according to the axioms of probability (sec. 3.9.1–2), together with all epistemic probability sentences that follow from the latter ones by the statistical principal principle (see sec. 3.13.5).

The above conceptions of content have been defined sententially. An alternative is the *model-theoretic* content M(S) of a sentence (set) S which was introduced in sec. 3.1.2, as the set of all models of the underlying language which verify S. Sentential and model-theoretic content are inversely correlated: it holds that $C(S_1) \subset C(S_2)$ iff $M(S_1) \supset M(S_2)$, or in informal words, S_1 is logically weaker than S_2 iff S_1 is verified by more models than S_2.

3.8 Verification, Falsification, Confirmation and Disconfirmation

(Def. 3.8–1)

1   A hypothesis H is *verifiable* iff there is a finite and consistent set B of observation sentences, from which H follows logically.
2   H is *falsifiable* iff there is a finite and consistent set B of observation sentences, from which the negation of H follows logically.
3   H is *confirmable* or *disconfirmable* iff there is a finite and consistent set B of observation sentences, which *raises* or *lowers* the probability or plausibility of H, respectively.

Let us not forget that verifiability or falsifiability only mean *possible* verification or falsification, and must therefore be sharply distinguished from actual verification or falsification. For example, the hypothesis "It will rain tomorrow" is verifiable and falsifiable today, but not until tomorrow can it actually be verified or falsified. The same is true for possible confirmation and disconfirmation.

If a hypothesis H is verified, then we can be *certain* of its truth, *given* that we are sure of the truth of the observation sentences B. Analogously, the same is true of falsification. Thus verification of H by B is the extreme case of confirmation of H by B with (epistemic) probability one ($P(H|B) = 1$), and falsification is the extreme case of disconfirmation with probability zero ($P(H|B) = 0$). As fig. 3.8–1 shows, only few kinds of hypotheses are falsifiable, and fewer still are verifiable. By contrast, all (consistent) hypotheses, so far as they possess only empirical content, can be confirmed and disconfirmed at least in principle. Also, observe that the following is valid for every hypothesis H: (a) H is verifiable iff ¬H is falsifiable; and (b) H can be confirmed iff ¬H can be disconfirmed.

Fig. 3.8–1 shows that Popper's famous *asymmetry thesis*, according to which scientific law hypotheses are not verifiable, but falsifiable, possesses only a very *limited* validity: it is limited to spatiotemporally unrestricted universal empirical hypotheses. Dually, unrestricted existential sentences such as, "There exists a white raven" are verifiable, but not falsifiable. Hypotheses which are limited in space and time are, in principle, both verifiable and falsifiable, by observing the finite number of empirical individuals in the relevant spatiotemporal domain. To be sure, in practice this is possible *only* if the relevant spatiotemporal domain is sufficiently *small*. On the other hand, mixed-quantified generalizations

		Empirical law hypotheses			Theories	
	Spatio-tempor. restricted	Spatiotemporally unrestricted			with empir. content	without empir. content
		Strict		Statistical (normic, c.p.)		
		Univ.	Univ.-existence			
Verifiable	+	−⎤	−	−	−	−
Falsifiable	+	+⎦	−	−	−	−
Confirmable	+	+	+	+	+	−
Disconfirmable	+	+	+	+	+	−

◂ Popper asymmetry

Figure 3.8–1 Testability of generalizations

(e.g. universal-existential, or existential-universal) are neither verifiable nor falsifiable (as explained in sec. 3.7), and the same holds for unrestricted statistical generalizations (recall sec. 3.5). Finally, theories are not only not verifiable (because their content goes beyond experience)—they are not even falsifiable, even when they are purely universal and have empirical consequences: this has to do with the *holism of theory testing*, which is explained in sec. 5.2–4.

3.9 Probability

3.9.1 Objective (Statistical) versus Epistemic (Subjective) Probability

The intuitive concept of probability involves an objective and a subjective or epistemic aspect (which is highlighted by the German "wahr-scheinlich," literally translated as "true-seeming"). The different nature of these two aspects of probability was not worked out until the 20th century. *Objective* probabilities (in our understanding of this term) express subject-independent properties of reality. Subjective or *epistemic* probabilities, on the other hand, express *degrees of belief* of one or several actual or hypothetical epistemic subjects. Although it would sound more natural to contrast "objective" with "subjective" conceptions of probability, we follow Gillies (2000, 2) and prefer the name "epistemic" for probability conceptions which equate probabilities with degrees of belief, because this family also includes the so-called "logical" or "objective Bayesian" conceptions of degrees of beliefs, which regard logical probabilities as "objective" in the sense of being *intersubjective*.

The most important kind of objective probabilities are *statistical* or *frequentistic* probabilities, and the most important kinds of epistemic probabilities are *subjective* ones, i.e. degrees of beliefs of a rational (actual or hypothetical) subject. Two further conceptions, namely objective propensities or logico-epistemic probabilities, are discussed in sec. 3.13.3–5. Statistical and subjective probabilities are defined as follows:

> (Def. 3.9–1) *Statistical (objective) probability:* The statistical probability of a type of event or state of affairs (e.g. Fx) is the relative frequency of its occurrence, or the limit of its relative frequency in the long run. *Formal notation:* p(–); e.g. p(Fx) (lower-case "p").
>
> *Subjective (epistemic) probability:* The subjective probability of a particular event or state of affairs (e.g. Fa) is the degree of belief, to which a given rational subject, or all subjects of a certain rationality type, believe in the occurrence of the event. *Formal notation:* P(–); e.g. P(Fa) (upper-case "P").

The *relative frequency* f(Fx) of a type of event Fx in a finite domain of individuals D is the number of all Fs in D divided by the number of Ds. If D is infinite, the relative frequency is undefined. Instead, we refer to a random ordering of the individuals in D in the form of a so-called *random sequence* $(d_1, d_2, \ldots)$, and define p(Fx) as the *limit* of the relative frequencies $f_n(Fx)$ of Fs in n-membered initial segments of this random sequence, as n goes towards infinity: $p(Fx) = \lim_{n\to\infty} f_n(Fx)$. The standard definition of "$\lim_{n\to\infty} f_n(Fx) = r$" is this: "for every arbitrarily small $\varepsilon > 0$ there exists a place number n such that for all $m \geq n$ the frequency $f_m(Fx)$ deviates from the limiting value r by less than ε." Frequency limits are theoretical idealizations whose treatment goes far beyond empirically observable frequencies; for this reason I prefer to speak of "statistical" instead of "frequentistic" probability conceptions (see sec. 3.13.3).

On one- and zero-probability events: For a finite domain of individuals D, "everything is an F" ($\forall x Fx$) and "the frequency of Fs is 1" (p(Fx)=1) mean the same. For infinite domains, however, this is no longer valid. Given an infinite random sequence $(d_1, d_2, \ldots)$ of individuals d_i and an event-type Fx, then p(Fx) = 0 does not imply that there is no individual in this sequence which has the property F, but only that the frequencies $f_n(Fx)$ converge towards *zero*. For example, the infinite sequence of natural numbers contains *infinitely* many numbers which are powers of two, namely all numbers of the form 2^k, but in spite of this it holds that $\lim_{k\to\infty} p(\text{"k is a power of 2"}) = \lim_{k\to\infty} k/2^k = 0$, i.e. $p(\text{"k is not a power of 2"}) = 1$. Therefore, the statistical hypothesis $p(Fx) = 1$ over an infinite domain is *weaker* than the universal quantification $\forall x Fx$, because it allows for exceptions with a frequency converging towards zero.

The probability of A under the *assumption* that B is called the *conditional* probability of A given B. For this, one writes $p(A|B)$ or $P(A|B)$, respectively, and this expression is defined as follows:

(Def. 3.9–2) *Conditional probability:* $p(A|B) = \dfrac{p(A \wedge B)}{p(B)}$, *provided* $p(B) > 0$.

In $p(A|B)$ or $P(A|B)$, B is called the *conditioning* event or antecedent, and A the *conditioned* event or consequent. Observe that $p(A|B)$ is undefined if the antecedent B has zero probability.[3] The statistical (conditional) probability $p(A|B)$ coincides with the relative frequency of As in the set of Bs if the latter set is finite (see fig. 3.5–2), or else with the frequency limit of As in an infinite random sequence of Bs. The subjective (conditional) probability $P(A|B)$ expresses the hypothetical degree of belief in A under the condition that B is believed with certainty.

Significant is the *non-monotonicity* of conditional probabilities: $p(A|B)$ = high in no way entails $p(A|B \wedge C)$ = high; in contrast, $p(A|B)$ = high is even compatible with $p(A|B \wedge C) = 0$. Fig. 3.9–1 shows an example of this situation.

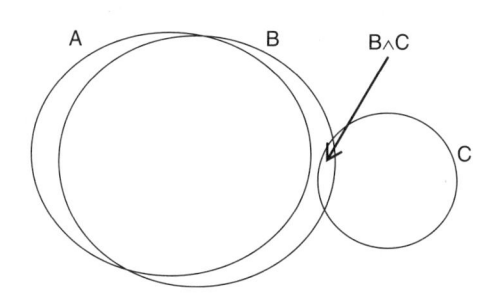

Figure 3.9–1 Non-monotonicity of conditional probabilities ($p(A|B)$ = high, but $p(A|B \wedge C) = 0$)

Statistical probabilities always refer to a *repeatable type* of event or state, i.e. a property that is expressed by a predicate, that is, logically speaking an *open* formula, whose variables are *bound* by the statistical probability operator. So p(Fx) = p({x: Fx}) = the frequency (limit) of Fs among all individuals in the (ordered) domain D. An example would be the limiting frequency of rainy days in London. Subjective probabilities on the other hand, always refer to a *particular* event, state of affairs or proposition as the object of a belief that is expressed by a *closed* formula, i.e. a sentence. For example, if someone has said that the probability of it raining *tomorrow* is 3/4, then prima facie this cannot be a statement about frequency—because there is only one tomorrow: either it will or it will not rain tomorrow. Probability assertions about "single cases" such as "tomorrow's weather" only make sense, at least prima facie, if they are understood as subjective probability statements concerning our degree of belief. Nonetheless, there are connections between the two concepts of probability. A well-known method of transferring statistical probabilities to single cases as their subjective probability is the following principle that goes back to Reichenbach (1949, §72):

> (Def. 3.9–3) *Principle of narrowest reference class:* The subjective probability P(Fa) of a single event Fa is determined as the (estimated) *conditional* statistical probability p(Fx|Rx) of the corresponding type of event Fx in the *narrowest* (nomological) reference class Rx, within which we know a lies (i.e. that Ra is true).

The principle of the narrowest class of reference is widely used both in everyday life and in the sciences. For instance, if we want to determine the subjective probability that a certain person will take a certain career path (Fa), then we rely on the characteristics of this person which are known to us as the narrowest reference class (Ra), and on the statistical probability that a person x with the characteristics Rx will take this career path (p(Fx|Rx)). The aforementioned weather forecast, "The probability that it will rain *tomorrow* is 3/4," has, according to Reichenbach's principle, the following interpretation: the statistical probability that it will rain on a day which is preceded by similar weather patterns as that preceding today is 3/4. This is what meteorologists mean when they make probabilistic weather forecasts: the development of weather patterns over the last few days functions as their narrowest reference class.

Technically, Reichenbach's principle combines the *inductive-statistical specialization* inference from sec. 2.7.1 with the application rule prop. 2.7–4 for non-monotonic inferences, which requires one to conditionalize Fa's subjective probability on all evidence that is relevant to the given single case (a); this is nothing but Reichenbach's narrowest reference class (Ra). Carnap (1950b, 211) had raised an analogous principle for the confirmation of hypotheses and called it the *principle of total evidence*: to determine our rational degree of belief in a hypothesis H, we must conditionalize its subjective probability on the total empirical evidence which is currently known to us. (The requirement of a "nomological" reference class is explained in sec. 3.13.5.)

Note that def. 3.9–3 determines only the subjective probability of *singular* sentences (i.e. sentences containing an individual constant), but not of quantified sentences. The probability of quantified sentences such as "All ravens are black" is a subjective probability, too, because there is only one actual world, which makes this sentence either true or false (for more on this see sec. 3.13.4 and 4.7.2).

The main founders of statistical probability theory include (pars pro toto) von Mises (1964), Reichenbach (1949) and Fisher (1956) (introductory literature, e.g. Hays/Winkler 1970; Field 2009). The main founders of the subjective theory are (among others) Bayes (1763), Ramsey (1926) and de Finetti (1974) (introductory literature, e.g. Earman 1992; Howson/Urbach 1996). Keynes (1921) and Carnap (1950b, 1971) founded the "logical" probability theory as an intersubjective variant of the epistemic theory which adds certain axioms that should fix the prior probabilities for all rational subjects in the same way; the "logico-analytical" character of these axioms, however, was exposed to strong criticism (sec. 4.7.3). For overviews of the different theories of probability, cf. Fine (1973), Howson/Urbach (1996) or Gillies (2000).

Present-day probability theory can be divided into the following four camps: (1) in the empirical sciences one speaks predominantly of *statistical* probability. (2) The group of *Bayesians* is highly influential in the philosophy of science and understands probability almost exclusively in the subjective sense. (3) The *mathematical* theoreticians of probability (e.g. Bauer 1996; Billingsley 1995) systematically *ignore* the interpretative conflict between (1) and (2). (4) The fourth group, to which I, myself, belong, are the *dualists* for which both probability conceptions are essential.

3.9.2 *Mathematical Laws of Probability*

The objective-statistical and the subjective-epistemic concept of probability obey the same fundamental mathematical laws which were first axiomatized by Kolmogorov (1933). In the following, A, B, ... stand for open formulas when probability is understood in the statistical sense, and for sentences when it is understood in the subjective sense. The fact that A and B are *disjoint* means in the statistical reading that the extension of A∧B is factually empty; and in the subjective reading, that A∧B is false in all admissible models of the language.

(Prop. 3.9–1) *Basic axioms of probability*—hold for "p" as well as for "P". For all A, B:

(A1) $p(A) \geq 0$ (non-negativity)
(A2) $p(A \vee \neg A) = 1$ (normalization to 1)
(A3) For *disjoint* A, B: $p(A \vee B) = p(A) + p(B)$ (finite additivity)

In words: probabilities are always greater than or equal to zero (A1); the probability of the total possibility space is 1 (A2), and the probabilities of disjoint (types of) events are additive (A3).

A number of well-known theorems can be derived from the basic axioms of probability, the most important of which are presented in the following. Formula A is called *exhaustive* in the statistical case iff all n-tuples of individuals (in D) have property A (where n is the number of A's free variables), and in the subjective case iff all possible models of the language verify A. A sequence of n pairwise disjoint A_i ($1 \leq i \leq n$) is called *partition* iff their disjunction $A_1 \vee ... \vee A_n$ is exhaustive.

(Prop. 3.9–2) *Theorems of unconditional probability*—hold for "p" as well as for "P":

(T1) $p(\neg A) = 1 - p(A)$ (complementary probability)
(T2) $\forall A: p(A) \leq 1$ (upper limit)
(T3) $p(A \wedge \neg A) = 0$ (contradiction)
(T4) For every partition $A_1, ..., A_n$: $\Sigma_{1 \leq i \leq n} p(A_i) = 1$, and $p(B) = \Sigma_{1 \leq i \leq n} p(B \wedge A_i)$.
(T5) $p(A_1 \vee A_2) = p(A_1) + p(A_2) - p(A_1 \wedge A_2)$ (general law of addition)
(T6) If $A_1 \rightarrow A_2$ is exhaustive, then $p(A_1) \leq p(A_2)$ (monotony)

> (Prop. 3.9–3) *Theorems of conditional probability* (for the formulas X in antecedent position "p(–|X)," we always assume p(X) > 0):
>
> (TC1) All laws of unconditional probability are valid for conditionalized probability functions $p_B(-)$, which are defined as $p_B(A) = p(A|B)$.
> (TC2) If B→A is exhaustive, then p(A|B) = 1. The reverse does not hold.
> (TC3) $p(A \wedge B) = p(A|B) \cdot p(B)$
> (TC4) For every partition $B_1, \ldots, B_n$: $p(A) = \Sigma_{1 \leq i \leq n}\, p(A|B_i) \cdot p(B_i)$ (general principle of multiplication).
>   —Specifically: $p(A) = p(A|B) \cdot p(B) + p(A|\neg B) \cdot (1 - p(B))$
> (TC5) $p(A|B) = p(B|A) \cdot p(A) / p(B)$ (Bayes' theorem, 1st version)
> (TC6) For every partition $A_1, \ldots, A_n$:
> $p(A_i|B) = p(B|A_i) \cdot p(A_i) / \Sigma_{1 \leq i \leq n}\, p(B|A_i) \cdot p(A_i)$ (Bayes' theorem, 2nd version)
> (TC7) Probabilistic independence:
> $p(A \wedge B) = p(A) \cdot p(B)$ iff $p(A|B) = p(A)$ or $p(B) = 0$
> (TC8) Symmetry of probabilistic dependence:
> $p(A|B) > p(A)$ iff $p(B|A) > p(B)$ iff $p(B|A) > p(B|\neg A)$ (analogously for $\geq$)

The significance of Bayes' theorem (TC5 and TC6) lies in those cases where one is interested primarily in $P(A_i|B)$, but only the inverse conditional probability $P(B|A_i)$ is accessible. This is the case for instance when the A_i are rival statistical hypotheses, and B is the result of experiments (sec. 4.7.2).

Two events A, B are said to be *probabilistically independent* of each other iff $p(A \wedge B) = p(A) \cdot p(B)$ holds. This is equivalent to $p(A|B) = p(A)$, provided p(B) > 0 (see TC7). In other words, two events are probabilistically dependent iff $p(A|B) \neq p(A)$ holds, i.e. if the presence of A *changes* the probability of B, as compared to B's unconditional probability. (TC8) informs us that probabilistic dependences (or "correlations") are symmetric.

COMPLEMENTARY AND ADVANCED TOPICS

3.10 Disposition Concepts

A disposition D of an object or system x consists in the nomological tendency of x to react in a characteristic way (R), whenever (or shortly after) x is exposed to certain triggering or test conditions (T). For example, the disposition of sugar to be *soluble* in water consists in its tendency to dissolve in water whenever it is put into water. The result R is also called the disposition's manifestation which is triggered by T. D is an empirical disposition iff T and R can be expressed by empirical concepts. Moreover, a disposition D of x is *strict* iff the result R obtains *always* when (or shortly after) T is realized; it is merely probabilistic if R follows T only with probability. In this section we focus on strict dispositions. A (strict) disposition D of an object x is called *permanent* if the object x has it for all times; it is called *temporal* if x has D only within a certain (short) time interval.

Carnap (1936/37, 440) was the first to recognize that it is impossible to define empirical dispositional concepts by observation concepts using only the implication of *extensional* logic, i.e. material implication →. To see this, assume that dispositional concepts were defined as follows:

> (3.10–1) For all objects x: x has disposition D *iff* for all times t: if x is exposed to conditions T at t, then x exhibits result R at t or soon after t.
> *Formally:* $\forall x(Dx \leftrightarrow \forall t(Txt \rightarrow Rx(t+\varepsilon)))$ (where ε is "small" or zero).
> *Example:* For all x: x is soluble in water *iff* every time x is placed in water, x will dissolve.

Recall from sec. 3.1.1 that a material implication is true if its antecedent is false or its consequent is true. So every object a which has *never* been exposed to the test condition ($\neg \exists t:Tat$) satisfies the general implication $\forall t(Tat \rightarrow Rat)$, so that by (3.10–1) we would have to say that the object a has the disposition D. But this result is intuitively unacceptable: nobody would say, for example, that the matchstick I burned yesterday is soluble in water, just because it was never placed in water in the entire duration of its existence. This problem is also called *Carnap's paradox* (Mumford 1998, 46).

For these reasons, Carnap (1936/37, 400) reached the conclusion that dispositional concepts are extensionally only *partially* or conditionally definable, in the form of a so-called *bilateral reduction sentence* (BR) (cf. Stegmüller 1969ff, vol. II.1, 227ff):

> (Def. 3.10–1) *Bilateral reduction sentence* (BR):
>
> For all objects x and times t: if x is exposed to conditions T at t, then: x has disposition D iff x exhibits reaction R at t + ε.
> *Formally:* $\forall x,t(Txt \rightarrow (Dx \leftrightarrow Rx(t+\varepsilon)))$
> *Example:* If x is placed in water at time t, then: x is soluble in water iff x starts to dissolve in water at t.

In a (BR) the definiendum Dx is set equivalent to an observable condition R only in contexts in which condition T is realized. For ¬Txt-contexts, the (BR) leaves the question open of whether Dx is the case or not. Thus, a (BR) does not satisfy the criterion of eliminability for proper definitions. Moreover, the (BR) in def. 3.10–1 is only justified for permanent dispositions, as it entails the *hypothesis of permanence* $\exists t(Txt \wedge Rxt) \rightarrow \forall t(Txt \rightarrow Rxt)$, saying that if x has *once* been placed into water and dissolved, then x will *always* dissolve when put into water. In other words, the (BR) is empirically creative. For merely temporal dispositions, the quantifier "for all times t" would have to be replaced by "for all times in a (short) time interval."

A full definition of dispositions is possible if one is willing to use the *intensional* concept of *nomological* (or lawlike) implication. Recall from sec. 3.6 that lawlike implications express regularities that have not arisen accidentally, e.g. not just because of the fact that the antecedent part of the implication was never realized. Lawlike implications are equivalent to *counterfactual* implications: if we *placed* the object into water, then it *would* dissolve. This characterization of solubility seems to be adequate, even if the object was never put into water. Therefore, the following definition of dispositional concepts has been accepted by a majority of philosophers since the 1960s:[4]

> (Def. 3.10–2) *Nomological definition of dispositions:*
>
> For all x: x possesses disposition D iff for all times t, x's being exposed to T at t nomologically implies x's exhibiting R at t, or shortly after t.
> *Formally:* $\forall x(Dx \leftrightarrow_{def} \forall t(Txt \rightarrow_n Rx(t+\varepsilon)))$, with "$\rightarrow_n$" for nomological implication.

The step towards def. 3.10–2 does not solve another host of problems connected with dispositional concepts, concerning their relation to theoretical concepts and their ontological nature. In (1936/37, 445), Carnap was of the opinion that all theoretical concepts of science should be treated as (empirical) disposition concepts. In (1956, §IX, X), Carnap changed his opinion and differentiated sharply between theoretical concepts and empirical disposition concepts, for the following reason. Dispositional concepts such as "solubility" are defined by a *single* lawlike temporal regularity (i.e. to dissolve when put into water). In contrast, theoretical concepts such as "molecular structure" imply *many* lawlike regularities or dispositions by which they can be empirically measured, *without* being semantically reducible to these dispositions (see sec. 5.1).

Carnap's observation is closely related to the more recent debate on the *ontological* nature of dispositions. According to the standard view (defended e.g. by Prior et al. 1982), dispositional concepts denote *functional if-then* properties which are not always manifest, but only when the triggering conditions are present. In contrast, theoretical concepts such as "molecular structure" express *structural* or *categorial* properties, which are "occurrent" or always manifest (cf. Earman 1986, 94; Bird 2007, ch. 1). This (somewhat nebulous) categorial-dispositional distinction gets more bite by connecting it with Carnap's observation that theoretical categorial structures are the causes of various dispositions, but they cannot be definitionally identical with them (this is proved in sec. 5.1). For instance, *polar chemical bonding* is the chemical structural feature which causes the solubility of a substance in water; at the same time, this structural feature is the cause of many further dispositions, for example electrolytic conductivity, increased melting point, etc. The structural properties which are causally responsible for dispositions are also called their (causal or categorial) *basis*. It follows that dispositions cannot be identical with their causal basis.

In spite of its plausibility, a number of philosophers have objected to the standard distinction between dispositions viewed as if-then properties and their underlying causal basis, for different reasons. Quine (1960, 223f; 1974, 10f) suggested that a disposition should be identified with the underlying structural property, because he rejected counterfactual implications, and hence def. 3.10–2 of dispositions. Armstrong et al. (1996) support this view on similar grounds. On the other side, Mumford (1998) and Bird (2007) argue for the identification of dispositions with the underlying structural properties because they defend the metaphysical view of *dispositional essentialism*, which says that all properties (including the purportedly categorial ones) are dispositional in nature.

According to the view of all of these authors, the disposition of solubility in water would be *identical* with having a certain chemical structure. This view seems to be refuted by the following two facts:

1 *Different* structural features can generate the *same* disposition. For example, the elasticity of a metallic spring is produced by a completely different molecular structure from the elasticity of a plastic spring. If we identified dispositional features with structural features, then we would have to say in these cases that a *different* disposition is present. The elasticity of a metallic spring would be a different elasticity from that of the plastic spring. But this is *counterintuitive* and misses the point of dispositional concepts: the fact that something is elastic says nothing less, but also *nothing more*, than that under the impact of a force it will bend.

Mumford (1998, 158) reacts to this objection with the suggestion to identify dispositions with structural bases not at the type level but at the token level. Not every instance of "elasticity" is identical with the same molecular structure, but every instance of elasticity is identical with *some* molecular structure. Mumford's suggestion, however, is nevertheless refuted by the second fact:

2 The *same* structural feature generates *different* dispositions. E.g. polar chemical structure causes not only solubility but also electric conductivity, etc. Therefore, dispositions cannot be identical with molecular structure, not even at the token level, for in that case different dispositions would be mutually identical, which is a contradiction.

Bird (2007, 149f) reacts to these objections with a weakening of dispositional essentialism: according to him, only physically *fundamental* properties, such as being electrically charged, or having a certain mass, are equivalent with certain dispositions. But even fundamental physical properties are frequently connected with several dispositions. For example, mass is connected with at least two dispositions: to retain constant velocity in a force-free state and to attract other masses. The overall conclusion, then, seems to be that the distinction between dispositional and structural (theoretical) properties is ontologically well-founded and in good fit with science.

Many further problems concerning dispositions that have been discussed can only be mentioned briefly.

a   Many philosophers (e.g. Armstrong et al. 1996; Lewis 1997) think that dispositions supervene on intrinsic properties (see Fara 2006). This view appears to contradict modern physics, as physics describes most fundamental dispositions in terms of interactions (Ladyman/Ross 2007, 19–21).
b   Often the nomological implications characterizing dispositions are subject to ceteris paribus conditions requiring that certain disturbing factors be absent (the problems of so-called "masks" and "antidotes"; see Fara 2006, sec. 2.2).

c   If a temporal disposition endures for a time interval that is shorter than the time delay between triggering conditions and reaction, then the disposition is undetectable (this is the problem of so-called "finkish" dispositions; cf. Martin 1994). Lewis (1997) proposed a solution which requires that the dispositional property must endure sufficiently long.

3.11 Challenges to the Logical-Definitional-Synthetic Distinction

The distinction drawn in sec. 3.3 between logical and extralogical-analytical truths is not observed by all analytic philosophers; Wittgenstein, Carnap and others have frequently mixed up the two kinds of analytic truths.[5] The distinction is, however, quite important, as logical truths have different properties from extralogical-analytic truths. For example, the former are closed under substitution of predicates; the latter are not.

The distinction between the two kinds of analytic truths (def. 3.3-1 and def. 3.4-1) is unproblematic as long as there is a clear demarcation between logical and non-logical concepts. In contrast, Etchemendy (1990) argued that this distinction is merely a matter of *pragmatic convention*: non-logical symbols are those whose (extensional) interpretation we allow to vary freely, while we fix the interpretation of logical symbols. For example, the non-logical definition "bachelors are unmarried men" comes out as logical truth if we decide to treat the predicates "bachelor," "men" and "married" as logical symbols; on the other hand, the tautology "p or not-p" comes out as non-logical truth if we decide to treat the conjunction as a non-logical symbol (ibid., 32f, 105f, 126–129). In order to counter Etchemendy's challenge, an objective and non-pragmatic distinction between logical and non-logical concepts is needed.

Already Tarski (1936b, 418) grasped this problem. In a paper published posthumously (Tarski 1986) he proposed distinguishing the two kinds of symbols by the so-called *invariance criterion*, which has been further elaborated by Sher (1991). According to this criterion, a symbol (φ) is logical iff its extensional interpretation, denoted by I(φ), is invariant under arbitrary permutations of the domain D. For example, the extension of a logically true predicate I(Fx$\vee\neg$Fx) remains the same, namely D, if some objects in D are permuted. In contrast, the extension of a non-logical predicate such as "is a lion" is changed if some lions are exchanged with non-lions. The idea is generalized by defining suitable extensions of propositional operators (truth functions) and quantifiers (domain-subdomain functions). The predicates and operations that come out as logical according to the Tarski–Sher criterion include tautological or inconsistent predicates, the identity and non-identity relation, truth-functional connectives and (generalized) quantifiers.

McCarthy (1981) has shown, however, that it is possible to define extensions with help of *empirical* predicates which nevertheless come out as logical according to the invariance criterion. One example is the property ψ defined as "x is ψ iff snow is white." The extension of ψ is the full domain if snow is white, or else the empty set. ψ's extension is therefore permutation invariant, although it depends on the contingent fact that snow is white. This shows that the Tarski–Sher criterion is not generally adequate.

A criterion for logicality that, in my view, is superior goes back to Carnap's "convention 2.1" (1956b, 10), which says the following: "A sentence is L-true in a semantical system S iff its truth can be established on the basis of the semantical rules of S alone, without any reference to [extra-linguistic] facts." Building on Carnap's conventions, Schurz (1999b, sec. 6) defines a symbol of an interpreted language as a *logical* symbol iff its extensional interpretation is fully determined by language-internal semantic rules, without reference to real facts. In this sense, the extension of sentence operators (truth functions) is language-internally defined with the help of truth tables which, in turn, determine the extension of logically determined predicates such as "Fx∨¬Fx." Extralogical conventions of meaning, on the other hand, do not fix the extension of a concept; they only imply cross-term restrictions (Etchemendy 1990, 71f). For example, the definition "Bachelors are so far unmarried men" merely demands that the extension of "bachelor" is identical with that of "so-far unmarried man," but *which* individuals are "so-far unmarried men" is not specified by the definition but depends on real facts. The Carnap–Schurz criterion implies the Tarski–Sher criterion because language-internal rules cannot discriminate between externally given objects; so their satisfaction remains invariant under arbitrary permutations of the domain. But the former criterion is stronger than the latter, inasmuch as it treats McCarthy-type examples as non-logical, because the extension of "being ψ iff snow is white" is not determined by language-internal rules.

More difficult than the challenge against the logical vs. extralogical-analytic distinction is Quine's challenge against the distinction between analytic and synthetic truths. Quine's criticism in (1951) says that in *natural*, empirically present languages, no clear criterion exists, by which one could undertake such demarcation. According to Quine's thesis of *semantic indeterminacy* (1960, §16), meaning is, in many cases, simply indeterminate. Carnap's logical semantics, though, was based on explicitly constructed *formal* languages (1972, 291). For these languages it is simply a *requirement* that all relationships of meaning be regulated explicitly by meaning postulates. Clusters of explicit definitions can also be found in the *nomenclatures* of *technical* and *scientific* languages. But they are only *seldom* to be found in natural languages: nobody has ever fixed a generally binding definition of concepts such as "table"—what counts as a table? How many legs does it have to have?, etc. *Herein* lies the difficulty that Quine pointed out.

All of Quine's critical examples concern *extralogical* analyticity, first in *natural languages,* and second concerning *theoretical* concepts of scientific theories. Carnap (1956b, app. D; 1956a) grants Quine these difficulties. The minimal consequence to be drawn from Quine's criticism, then, is that while the analytic-synthetic distinction *can* be drawn, it is only narrowly applicable to natural languages and theoretical concepts. Quine goes further, however: he dispenses with the distinction altogether, and instead develops the model of knowledge as a *layered preference system* —a "concentric force field," on which perceptual input takes its effect (1951, 47f). At the edge of this force field are those hypotheses that we are most easily prepared to abandon when our knowledge comes into conflict with experience, and at its center are the logical truths or meaning postulates with which we are least willing to part.

I think that this Quinean model adequately describes the *epistemic* situation. But it does not follow from this that we cannot make a distinction between analytic and synthetic truths. As explained in sec. 3.4, while definitions cannot be true or false, they can be more or less empirically adequate. New experiences can motivate us to *alter* or to abandon definitions. Even logical truths can be revised under certain circumstances, e.g. if a many-valued semantics with the truth values "true," "false" and "indeterminate" is used. So, the Quinean image of the layered order of preference is still correct, *even when* the logical-analytic-synthetic distinction is made.

If, like Quine, we dispense entirely with the analytic-synthetic distinction, we incur serious problems. For the relationship between language and world necessarily contains a *conventional* element. Only when the meaning of at least *some* expressions is fixed by convention can content-rich hypotheses be formulated: as long as it is not clear what "raven" means, there is no point in wanting to find out the truth value of "There is a raven there." The *analytical* is supposed to capture just this conventional moment in the use of concepts. If we say, however, that this conventional moment does not exist at all, how can we explain the fact that language users can *communicate* with each other in the first place, i.e. use their concepts in an *intersubjectively* agreeing way? One consequence which some authors have drawn from the Quinean criticism is *radical semantic holism*, according to which the meaning of a concept is determined by our entire web of beliefs about the extension of this concept. As Fodor (1984, 26f; 1990, xi) points out, the result of radical semantic holism would be that two speakers *could not have* different opinions about the same object. If, for example, Peter thinks that all swans are white, while Paul believes in the existence of black swans, then Peter and Paul would both mean something *different* by the word "swan." This consequence seems to be absurd. Obviously, people are well able to have differing opinions about something and still agree that they are talking about the same thing.

Any satisfactory theory of meaning must also include the conventional or normative moment of language, and this moment is contained in the concept of analyticity. The source of the Quinean problem is not that this conventional moment does not exist in natural languages but, rather, that this moment frequently works in an *ostensive* manner that cannot be captured by linguistic definitions. For example, when the concept "red" is acquired by a child, the child learns to associate the word "red" with a certain perceptual impression; in this way, primary conventions of meaning are generated within the child. *Ostensive conventions* such as "'red' means *this* color" are the *most basic* layer of analytical sentences. These sentences are *indexical* and cannot be clothed in a *purely* linguistic form. In scientific textbooks, illustrations or photographs are used for this purpose—e.g. the illustration of a kidney in a medical textbook. The upshot of our considerations is this: extralogical-analytic truths are also present in natural languages, but manifest themselves there mainly in the form of ostensive characterizations, and only seldom in context-free explicit definitions.

3.12 Relevance and Irrelevance in Logical Inferences

The classical definition of logically valid consequence includes, besides relevant consequences, so-called *irrelevant* consequences. The main type of irrelevant conclusions is *disjunctive weakening* (or addition):

(3.12–1) *Irrelevant conclusion (main type)—addition*:

(1) $\underline{H}$ e.g. The Earth is hollow   Likewise: (1*) $\underline{O}$

  $\underline{O} \vee H$ (Therefore:) Today it is $O \vee \underline{H}$
     raining or the Earth is hollow.

Time and again, irrelevant consequences have confronted the philosophy of science with seemingly *paradoxical* results (Weingartner/ Schurz 1986). For example, the widespread confirmation theory of *hypothetical deductivism* (sec. 5.10.1) claims that a (consistent) hypothesis

H is confirmed by its true observational consequences. If this thesis would apply also to *irrelevant* consequences as above, then according to (3.12–1), O∨H would confirm H, because H entails O∨H by (1), and O∨H is observational knowledge by (1*), as it follows from the (true) observation O. It sounds paradoxical, however, that the hypothesis that the Earth is hollow is confirmed by a logical consequence of our true observation "today it is raining" (see sec. 5.10.1).

Some philosophers concluded from such "paradoxes" that deductive logic is hopelessly inadequate for the reconstruction of science (e.g. Glymour 1980). Building on Körner (1947), however, Schurz and Weingartner have developed a way of solving the problem of irrelevant conclusions by logical means.[6] Fundamental to this is the observation that irrelevant conclusions always possess *inessential* sub-formulas—inessential insofar as the sub-formula in the conclusion may be replaced by *any* other formula *salva validitate*, i.e. this replacement preserves the validity of the inference. So in the conclusion of (1), the underlined sub-formula O may be replaced by any other formula, *salva validitate*: from H it follows that "X or H" for any X. Analogously in (1*), H is replaceable *salva validitate*.

While the type of inference (3.12–1) has to do with irrelevant conclusions, there are also inferences with *irrelevant premises*, which also lead to paradoxical results. The main type of premise-irrelevant inference is *conjunctive weakening* (or simplification) of the form H∧O ||— O, e.g. "the earth is hollow and it will rain today; therefore: it will rain today." Here too, "H" can be replaced by any X, *salva validitate*, but now in the premise (underlined). According to hypothetico-deductivism, O confirms H∧O. But it sounds paradoxical that every true observation O confirms a hypothesis (i.e. H∧O) which entails that the Earth is hollow (for more on this "tacking by conjunction" paradox see sec. 5.10.1).

Instead of replacing sub-formulas, it is simpler to replace predicates. Schurz (1991a, 409, 422) reaches the following definition:

(Def. 3.12–1) *Relevance in logical inferences:*

1. *C(onclusion)-relevance*: The conclusion C of a valid argument is relevant iff no predicate in C may be replaced in some of its occurrences (simultaneously) by any other predicate (with the same number of arguments), *salva validitate* of the inference.
2. *P(remise)-relevance*: The set of premises P of a valid argument is relevant iff no predicate in P may be replaced in a *single* occurrence by any other predicate (with the same number of arguments), *salva validitate* of the inference.

While in the definition of conclusion-relevance, multiple replacements of a predicate are considered, in the definition of premise-relevance only single replacements are allowed. This difference results from the following important asymmetry between the relevance of conclusions and premises: while the premises of relevant inferences can contain concepts that do not occur in the conclusion, the conclusions of relevant inferences can never contain concepts that do not occur in the premises. Here are some examples.

(3.12–2) *Examples* ("$\Vdash$" for "valid inference"; the underlined propositional variables or predicates are *salva validitate* replaceable):

P-relevant, C-irrelevant: $p \Vdash p \vee \underline{q}$; $p \Vdash \underline{q} \to p$; $p \Vdash p \wedge (\underline{q} \vee \neg \underline{q})$; $\forall x(Fx \to Gx) \Vdash \forall x(Fx \to Gx \vee \underline{H}x)$;

P-irrelevant, C-relevant: $p \wedge \underline{q} \Vdash p$; $\forall x(Fx \vee \underline{H}x \to Gx) \Vdash \forall x(Fx \to Gx)$;

P-relevant and C-relevant: $p \to q, p \Vdash q$; $p \to q \Vdash \neg q \to \neg p$; $\forall x(Fx \to Gx), Fa \Vdash Ga$; $\forall x Fx \Vdash Fa$; $Fa \Vdash \exists x Fx$;

P-irrelevant and C-irrelevant: $p \wedge \underline{q} \Vdash p \vee \underline{r}$; $\forall x(Fx \to Gx) \Vdash \forall x(Fx \wedge \underline{H}x \to Gx \vee \underline{Q}x)$ (etc.).

By incorporating the relevance requirement into the logical explication of scientific methods such as confirmation or explanation, a number of problems in the philosophy of science can be satisfactorily solved (sec. 5.10, 5.11, 6.2.4). A related approach was developed by Gemes (1993, 1994). According to the basic idea of these approaches, *applied* inferences in everyday life as well as science are always made up of *classical logic plus relevance*. This basic idea is also defended by Grice (1975) and Sperber/Wilson (1986), and is confirmed by studies in cognitive psychology (e.g. Rips 1994, 47ff). The logic-plus-relevance thesis says that the concept of validity in classical logic is just fine in itself, but does not *cover everything* that is important for applied inferences. The retention of the classical concept of validity distinguishes this approach from the program of *relevance logic*, which suggests replacing classical logic with a *non-classical relevance logic* (Anderson/Belnap 1975). However, the main types of irrelevant inference that were causing the paradoxes in philosophy of science are addition and simplification—and these inferences are also valid within relevance logic. For this reason, relevance logic is of no help in solving the paradoxes in the philosophy of science.

For many purposes it is necessary to decompose the relevant consequences of a theory or a belief system into its smallest relevant conjunctive parts—its so-called relevant consequence or content elements or, in short: *relevant elements*. The restriction of relevant consequences to relevant elements eliminates *logical redundancies*. For example, if A is a true consequence of a theory T, and B a false consequence of T, then the conjunction A∧B must not be counted as a *new* and third false consequence of T. Otherwise one produces the well-known paradoxes of Popper's notion of verisimilitude (sec. 5.11.1). The definition is based on the following pre-definitions: A *conjunctive normal form* (in short a CN-form) is a PropL-formula which is a conjunction of *clauses*, i.e. of disjunctions of literals (unnegated or negated atomic formulas). A *prenex* conjunctive normal form (a PCN-form) *of* a PredL-formula A is a formula which is L-equivalent to A and begins with a (possibly empty) sequence of quantifiers, followed by a quantifier-free formula (its "matrix") in CN-form. It is well known that any PredL-formula can be logically transformed into (at least) one PCN-form.

(Def. 3.12–2) *Relevant (consequence or content) elements:*[7]

1. A formula A is an *element* iff (i) A is in PCN-form, and (ii) A is not L-equivalent to a conjunction $A_1 \wedge \ldots \wedge A_n$ ($n \geq 1$) of PCN-formulas each of which is *shorter* than A.
2. A is a *relevant element* of a premise set P iff A is a relevant consequence of P which is an element.

(3.12–3) *Examples*   Relevant elements (of the sentence on the left)

¬(p∨q):   ¬p, ¬q
(p→q)∧ p: p, q
(p∧q)∨(p∧¬q):   p
∀x(Fx∨Gx → Hx∧Qx):   ∀x(Fx→Hx), ∀x(Gx→Hx), ∀x(Fx→Qx), ∀x(Gx→Qx), and all universal instantiations of these four sentences.

Because condition (1) of def. 3.12–2 is formulated for "$n \geq 1$," all logically redundant formula-parts (e.g. repetitions, eliminable literals, double negations) are eliminated in a relevant element. If we limit our notions of content to relevant elements, we get the following concepts of relevant content, which are highly useful in the philosophy of science:

(Def. 3.12–3)

a   The *relevant logical content* of a sentence or set of sentences S is the set of its relevant elements, abbreviated as $C_r(S)$.
b   The *relevant empirical* content of S is the set of its relevant elements which are empirical but not analytically true sentences, abbreviated as $E_r(S)$.

It is important that no classical information is lost through relevant representations of beliefs, i.e.:

(Prop. 3.12–1) Every sentence set S is L-equivalent to the set of its relevant elements:

$C(S) \dashv\vdash C_r(S)$, and $E(S) \dashv\vdash E_r(S)$.[8]

For many purposes (e.g. axiomatizations in sec. 5.3.1 or explanations in sec. 6.2.4) it is important to formulate a set of sentences S in an entirely non-redundant way. Such a formulation is called an *irreducible representation* of S and is defined as follows:

(Def. 3.12–4) An *irreducible representation* (IR) of a sentence (set) S is a non-redundant conjunction of relevant elements of S which is L-equivalent to S. (Non-redundancy means that no conjunctive part of the IR follows logically from the other parts of the IR.)

For sentences of propositional logic the definition reduces (provably) to the well-known notion of an irreducible CN-form, in short an ICN-form: this is a CN-form in which no elementary conjunct and no literal can be deleted without changing its logical content (cf. Stegmüller 1969ff, vol. I, 915). For example, $(\neg A \vee C) \wedge (\neg A \vee \neg C)$ is a CN-form but not an ICN-form of $A \rightarrow C \wedge \neg C$; only $\neg A$ is an ICN-form of $A \rightarrow C \wedge \neg C$.

3.13 More on Probability

3.13.1 Construction of Probability Models and Sigma-Additivity

There exist two possible constructions of probability models: the *mathematical* construction, which attaches probabilities to sets of an algebra and ignores different interpretations, and the *linguistic* construction, which attaches statistical probabilities to open formulas and epistemic probabilities to sentences. The linguistic construction can be developed in a *semantic* and in a purely *syntactic* manner. Here are the most important details:

1. *Mathematical* probability models are defined as *triples* (Ω, AL, p), where Ω is a non-empty set considered as *possibility* (or outcome) space, AL is an *algebra* of *subsets* of Ω, and p:AL→[0,1] is a probability function attaching to each element A∈AL a probability value p(A) in [0,1] (the interval of real numbers between 0 and 1). The possibility space Ω is understood as the set of all possible results of some given repeatable *random experiment*, such as throwing a die (Ω = {1, 2, 3, 4, 5, 6}) or the random selection of an individual from a domain of individuals or *population* D (Ω = D). The *algebra* AL is a set of Ω-subsets which is closed under formation of complements, finite unions and finite intersections. Depending on whether the elements of AL are interpreted as types of events or as individual events, probability in this setting can be understood statistically (p) or subjectively (P). In order to model independent repetitions of random experiments, one extends the probability function p, for each n, to the product algebra AL_n over the n-fold Cartesian product Ω^n (= $\Omega \times \ldots \times \Omega$, n times; see Jeffrey 1971b, 196; Bauer 1996, sec. 21).

2. *Linguistic-semantic* probability models are likewise algebraically defined, as triples (Ω, AL, p), only now Ω and AL are constructed via the models of a given language $\mathcal{L}$.

2.1 In the *statistical-semantical* setting (e.g. Bacchus 1990, ch. 3), one starts from a given interpretation (D,I) of $\mathcal{L}$ which supposedly reflects the real world. The domain of individuals D and its n-fold Cartesian products D^n function as the possibility space Ω for probability assignments to formulas in one free variable and in n free variables, respectively. As the algebra of sets AL_n over D^n one chooses the set of extensions $||A(x_1,\ldots,x_n)||$ of open formulas A of the given language in n free variables (the so-defined AL_n's are set-theoretic algebras). One assumes a probability measure over AL_n (for each n), p:AL_n→[0,1], which is transferred to arbitrary open formulas by defining p($A(x_1,\ldots,x_n)$) =$_{def}$ p($||A(x_1,\ldots, x_n)||$). To attach a statistical meaning to p, one equates p(A(x)) with the frequency limit of As in an infinite *random sequence* (d_1, d_2, …), i.e. an endless sequence of random draws from D such that every individual in D has the same statistical chance of being drawn.

2.2 In the *epistemic-semantical* setting (e.g. Carnap 1971) one chooses as the possibility space Ω the set M($\mathcal{L}$) of all epistemically possible models of the given language $\mathcal{L}$, and as the algebra AL the set of all model-classes M(S) of *sentences* S of the underlying language. Over AL one assumes an epistemic probability function P:AL→ [0,1] which is transferred to sentences of the language $\mathcal{L}$ by defining P(A) =$_{def}$ P(M(A)).

The logically important difference between statistical and epistemic probabilities is this: while statistical probabilities say something about the real world and thereby refer to *one* "actual" model (D,I), epistemic probabilities say something about our degrees of beliefs and thus refer to the range of all epistemically possible models M($\mathcal{L}$).

3 In the *epistemic-syntactic* setting (e.g. Carnap 1950b) the probability function P is directly defined over the sentences of the language and characterized axiomatically. Carnap (1971) preferred the semantic construction because of its greater expressiveness.

All of the mentioned kinds of probabilities satisfy Kolmogorov's basic axioms (prop. 3.9–1), from which the theorems in prop. 3.9–2 and 3.9–3 follow. A probability-statement A is said to be a *probability-theoretic consequence* of a set of probability statements Δ, abbreviated as Δ ||—$_P$ A, iff A follows logico-mathematically from Δ plus the basic Kolmogorov probability axioms.

An assumption for probability measures which goes beyond the basic Kolmogorov axioms is σ-*additivity*: p is called σ-additive (or countably additive) iff the probability of the union of a (countably) infinite number of pairwise disjoint events equals the infinite sum of their individual probabilities. Or formally, iff for every infinite sequence $(X_0, X_1, X_2,...)$ with $X_i \cap X_j = \emptyset$ for all $i \neq j \in \mathbb{N}$, it holds that $p(\bigcup_{i \in \mathbb{N}} X_i) = \Sigma_{i \in \mathbb{N}} p(X_i)$ (where $\mathbb{N}$ is the set of natural numbers and the infinite sum is defined as $\lim_{n \to \infty} \Sigma_{n \in \mathbb{N}} p(X_n)$). It is thereby assumed that the algebra AL is a σ-algebra, i.e. is closed under infinite unions and intersections.

The assumption of σ-additivity is important for the mathematical theory of probability *measures* over continuous possibility spaces (see sec. 4.6). It is questionable, however, whether it is a generally adequate requirement. It is well known that σ-additivity is not fulfilled by uniform probability distributions over countably infinite possibility spaces (cf. Howson/Urbach 1996, 326). De Finetti (1974, sec. III.11.6) concluded from this that one should not consider σ-additivity as a *general* probability axiom (cf. Gillies 2000, 77). Kelly (1996, 321) supported this view by pointing out that σ-additivity implies the *weak induction assumption* that $P(\forall xFx|Fd_1 \wedge \ldots \wedge Fd_n)$ converges to 1 for n → ∞, provided $P(\forall xFx) > 0$. However, for a Humean skeptic about induction, this consequence is unacceptable. She would object that for any number n of individuals d_i which have been observed to be F, there are still infinitely many unobserved individuals left, whence there is no reason that our degree of belief that $\forall xFx$ will be falsified in the future should sink with increasing n. In reply to these problems, Schurz/Leitgeb (2008) developed a frequentistic probability theory that allows a reasonable treatment of non-σ-additive probability functions over countable possibility spaces.

3.13.2 Binomial Distribution and Law of Large Numbers

Important in statistical probability theory are *independent repetitions* of the same (or "identical") random experiment. Here the same random experiment is carried out several times, each single time being physically and thus also probabilistically *independent* of the others. One example would be the results of n coin tosses $(e_1,\ldots, e_n)$ with $e_i \in$ {Heads, Tails}, linguistically depicted as $\pm Hx_1 \wedge \ldots \wedge \pm Hx_n$ ("±" for "unnegated" or "negated," "H/¬H" for "Heads/Tails"). I.e. different individual variables (x_i) in elementary conjuncts refer to different realizations (e_i) of the random experiment. The statistical probability of throwing heads does not depend on what was thrown in previous coin tosses; this is the reason for the *impossibility* of gambling systems in random games. From the assumption of independence follows the *product rule* for statistical probabilities: $p(Fx_1 \wedge Gx_2) = p(Fx) \cdot p(Gx)$, i.e. the probability of drawing, in two consecutive random drawings, first an F and then a G is equal to the product of the two probabilities p(F) and p(G). For example, the statistical chance that in two rolls of a dice the first result is 1 or 2, and the second is 6, is the product of these two chances, which is $(2/6) \cdot (1/6) = 1/18$.

Philosophically, independence means that a random experiment does not change its physical dispositions after it has been performed; this idealization is typically made for statistical probabilities.[9] In contrast, for subjective probabilities the product rule is usually *invalid*. As soon as our subjective measure of probability is *inductive*, our degree of belief that the next individual, a, is an F has to increase in line with the frequency of so-far observed individuals, b, which were F. So $P(Fa|Fb) > P(Fa)$ and thus $P(Fa \wedge Fb) > P(Fa) \cdot P(Fb)$ must hold, which contradicts the product rule. The difference can be explained as follows: in subjective probability theory, we presume that we *do not know* the true statistical probability value. For example, we do not know for sure if a given coin is symmetric (p = 1/2) or asymmetric with a bias, e.g. a magnetized coin with p = 1/3. In this case, it makes inductive sense to conclude from the more frequent occurrence of heads that the coin is more likely to show heads than tails. In statistical probability theory, we assume a *fixed* statistical distribution which satisfies statistical independence and hence the product rule. So if we know that the coin will land on heads with a relative frequency of r, we also know that when it is thrown twice, it will land on heads with a relative frequency of r^2 (etc.).

Derived from the statistical product rule is the well-known *binomial* (or *Bernoulli*) *law* for (independent) drawings of n-element *random samples*. Call $f_n(Fx)$ the (relative) frequency of a binary event Fx in an n-element random sample, then the following is valid:

(Prop. 3.13–1) *Binomial formula:* $p(f_n(Fx) = \frac{k}{n}) = \binom{n}{k} \cdot p^k \cdot (1-p)^{n-k}$
(where p = p(Fx)).
In words: the probability of n-element random samples with k Fs in them is n-choose-k times F's probability to the power of k times non-F's probability to the power of n-minus-k. Here,
$\binom{n}{k} =_{def} \frac{n \cdot (n-1) \ldots (n-k+1)}{k!}$ is the number of possibilities of choosing k from n individuals (and $k! =_{def} 1 \cdot 2 \cdot \ldots \cdot (k-1) \cdot k$).
Example: The probability of obtaining in ten rolls of a dice three 6s is $(10 \cdot 9 \cdot 8 / 1 \cdot 2 \cdot 3) \cdot (1/6)^3 \cdot (5/6)^7 = 0.155$.

The binomial distribution is shown in fig. 3.13–1 over the unit interval [0,1] for three sample sizes (it takes non-disappearing values only for numbers r = k/n). For increasing sample sizes (n) the distribution becomes steeper, and the binomial distribution moves asymptotically towards a continuous normal (or Gauss) *distribution*. For n→∞, $p(f_n)$ approximates 0 at $f_n \neq p(Fx)$ and has an infinitely steep peak at $f_n = p(Fx)$ (see sec. 4.6). Derivable from this are the weak and strong laws of *large numbers*:[10]

- The *weak* law of large numbers says that for every arbitrarily small ε>0, the probability that $f_n(F)$ deviates from p(F) by less than ε goes to 1 for n→∞ ($\forall \varepsilon > 0: \lim_{n \to \infty} p(|f_n(F) - p(F)| < \varepsilon) = 1$).

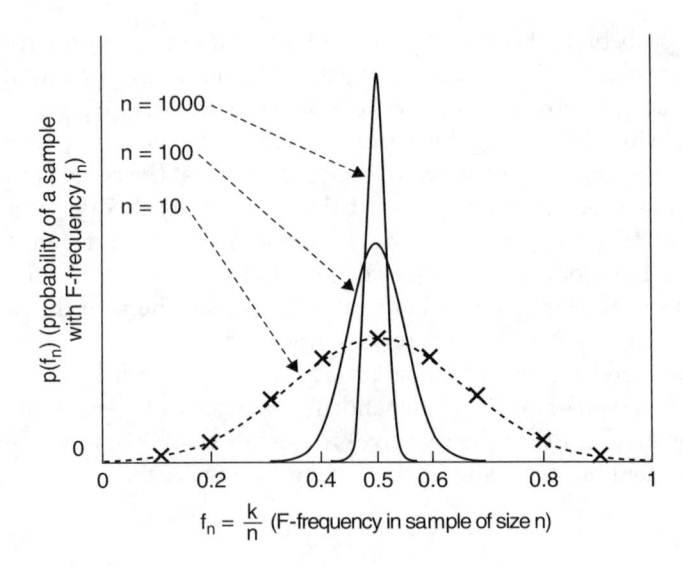

[Figure: Binomial distributions with curves for n = 10, n = 100, n = 1000, x-axis $f_n = k/n$ from 0 to 1, peaked at 0.5]

Figure 3.13–1 Binomial distributions $p(f_n = \frac{k}{n})$ for $p = 1/2$ (approximated by normal distribution, i.e. area under curve is normalized to 1)

- According to the *strong* law of large numbers, the probability that the limiting frequency of Fs in an infinite random sequence equals p(F) is 1. The strong law presupposes the assumption of σ-additivity (recall sec. 3.13.1).

3.13.3 Problems of Objective-Statistical Probability Concepts

Both the objective-statistical and the subjective interpretation of probability harbor *problems* which to this day have not been fully solved. With the statistical concept of probability, these are, above all, problems of *definition*. In the case of the subjective concept the problems are mainly of *justification*. In this section we focus on problems of the statistical probability concept including generic propensities, with a brief look at single case propensities.

The *justification* of the basic axioms A1–3 (prop. 3.9–1) is unproblematic for statistical probabilities: these axioms *follow* from the definition of statistical probability as a frequency limit (cf. Gillies 2000, 109). The epistemic *significance* of the statistical concept of probability is also obvious: information about statistical frequencies of alternative kinds of events (e.g. {Fx, ¬Fx}) makes it possible for us to predict what event will occur with highest frequency, and this strategy maximizes provably our long-run success in true predictions (sec. 3.13.5). The difficulty lies in the adequate *definition* of statistical probability.

First of all, the notion of an "endless" repetition of a random experiment is a theoretical idealization. Second, by endless repetitions of a random experiment, potentially infinitely *many* infinitely increasing sequences of outcomes $(d_1, d_2,...) \in D^\infty$ can be produced—why should they all have the *same* frequency limit p(Fx), and why should they all have a frequency limit *at all*? The problem is that frequency limits are *order-sensitive*: from a given sequence of results one can always construct a sequence with an *alternative* frequency limit, either with help of permutations (re-orderings), or with place selections (selection of results). Take an arbitrary infinite sequence of 0s and 1s with p({1}) = 1/2. Then we can rearrange the sequence, so that we take the first two 1s, then the first 0, then the next two 1s, the next 0, etc., ad infinitum. The original sequence has only been permutated, and yet the frequency limit of 1s in the permutated sequence is now 2/3. By suitable permutations we can also rearrange the sequence into one which has *no* frequency limit at all, for example by letting the frequency of 1s oscillate eternally between 2/3 and 1/3. In a more simple way, "weird" sequences like these can be generated with the help of place selection instead of permutations: e.g. we choose from a given random sequence only the positions with the result 1 and get a sequence with p({1}) = 1.

Of course, sequences generated by *outcome-dependent* transformations—whose application presupposes that we already know which outcome was produced—cannot be regarded as *random* sequences. But is it not also possible that weird sequences like these could be produced as an astronomically improbable coincidence, using a regular coin toss? This is a controversial question. What I call the *naive* statistical theory reacts to this question with the (strong) law of large numbers and argues as follows: the claim "p(Fx) = r" does not mean that the frequency limit of Fx is r in *all* random sequences, but rather that there is a *probability of 1* that it is r. However, as critics have objected correctly, this attempt of defining statistical probability is *circular*: in the definiens of the expression "the probability of Fx is r," the phrase "with a probability of 1" occurs once again. Probabilities, then, are not traced back to frequency limits, but rather back to probabilities themselves.[11]

More generally speaking, the law of large numbers is a *mathematical* truth which makes sense in any interpretation of probabilities. For subjective probabilities this law says that if a probabilistically coherent person has a degree of belief $P(Fe_i) = r$ for every member e_i of an infinite event-sequence $(e_1, e_2, ...)$, and believes that the Fe_i-events are mutually independent, then this person is certain that the limiting frequency of Fs in the sequence is r.

A way out of the circularity problem is offered by the account of von Mises (1964). Von Mises assumes that there is an (idealized) *ground sequence* $s = (e_1, e_2, \ldots)$ of all realizations of an experiment of a given kind—for instance, the results of all throws with dice of the same physical type arranged in chronological order and hypothetically extended into the indefinite future. Von Mises calls this total sequence a *statistical collective*. More specific random sequences are characterized by von Mises using the concept of *admissible* place selection. Admissible place selections are *outcome-independent*. Von Mises (1964, ch. 1) makes two basic assumptions (or "axioms") about a ground sequence s with possibility space Ω:

1. *assumption of convergence:* every possible outcome Fx in Ω possesses a frequency limit in s, which is identified with Fx's probability, and
2. *assumption of randomness:* this frequency limit is *insensitive* to admissible place selections, i.e. in all subsequences s' of s generated by admissible place selections, outcome Fx has the same frequency limit as in s.

Von Mises understands the two conditions not as a-priori truths, but as empirical statements about the real *dispositions* of the underlying random experiment. In continuation of von Mises' work, Church (1940) defined an admissible place selection as a *computable* function π which specifies for every position n of a sequence $s = (e_1, e_2, \ldots)$ whether it is selected or not, possibly in dependence on the preceding outcome sequence $(e_1, \ldots, e_{n-1})$ but *not* dependent on e_n.[12]

Von Mises' randomness assumption defines the concept of a random sequence in a natural way. Moreover, it guarantees the condition of statistical *independence*. The proof is simple: $p(Fx_1 \wedge Gx_2)$ is defined as the frequency limit of pairs (Fe_i, Ge_{i+1}) in the ground sequence $s = (e_1, e_2, \ldots)$. This is identical with the frequency limit of Fs in s, times the frequency limit of Gs in the subsequence s* of s-members which are preceded by an F. But since s* is an admissible place selection, p(G-in-s*) = p(G), and so $p(Fx_1 \wedge Gx_2) = p(Fx) \cdot p(Gx)$. By analogous considerations, the ground sequence s contains the infinite sequence of all finite n-membered sequences $((e_k, \ldots, e_{k+n-1}): k \in \mathbb{N})$, which permits the derivation of the binomial distribution within von Mises' account. The ground sequence even contains the infinite sequence of all infinite sequences $((e_{k+i}: i \in \mathbb{N}): k \in \mathbb{N})$, which allows us to derive the law of large numbers within von Mises' account.[13]

Von Mises' definition of randomness is an *internal* randomness, because place selections depend only on properties of preceding members of the collective. Reichenbach (1949, sec. 32) and Salmon (1984, 61f) have extended the definition of place selection such that it also depends on *external* events at preceding time points. This can be formalized by assuming an extended possibility space Ω^* whose possibilities are combinations of Ω-outcomes with possible external events at the *same* time point. Let s* be the corresponding sequence of complex events, ordered in discrete time. If all external events that are predictively relevant to Ω-outcomes are included in Ω^*, and s* is random in regard all admissible place selections, then s is called *objectively* random. For example, *throwing* of a coin is an objective random process, while *laying down* a coin is not objectively random, because the results can be predicted by the will of the person that lays down the coin, though also a sequence of coins that have been laid down might satisfy von Mises' internal randomness conditions. Note that objective randomness does not presuppose quantum-mechanical indeterminism; it is also compatible with the situation of deterministic instability explained in sec. 6.2.3 (cf. Strevens 2008, ch. 10).

The statistical concept of probability, explained in this way, is a *dispositional* concept. Along with Popper (1959) we understand the statistical probability of Fx as the generic *propensity* of the underlying random experiment to produce the result Fx with limiting frequency p(Fx). We agree with Howson/Urbach (1996, 338) that this dispositional perspective was already present in von Mises' theory. Propensities in the sense of the early Popper (1959) are *generic* propensities, i.e. dispositions of a *type* of random experiment, as opposed to single case propensities, which were developed by the later Popper (1990) and are discussed below.

The suggested elaboration of von Mises' account in terms of generic propensities solves most objections against frequentistic probabilities that have been raised in the literature. Hájek (1999) compiles 15 objections of this sort. His objections 10–15 concern side-problems (e.g. violations of σ-additivity; recall sec. 3.13.1). Objections 4–9 are based on the fact that by non-admissible place selections one may construct event sequences with "weird" frequency limits; these objections are rebutted by von Mises' theory of random sequences.

Hájek's objections 1–3 are more serious. Objection 1 asserts that the explication of a frequency limit as a *counterfactual* disposition abandons empiricism. This is more a true insight than an objection, inasmuch as we have seen in sec. 3.6 and 3.10 that the notions of lawlike and counterfactual implication are not empirically definable, but presume the notion of physical possibility. Hájek's objection 2 argues that limiting frequencies are defined with respect to infinite repetitions of random experiments, but infinite sequences are not even physically possible. I am not sure whether this is true. But even if it were true, one could construct infinite sequences from random combinations of finite sequences from countably many physically possible worlds.

In my view, the only really troublesome objection of Hájek (1999) is objection number 3, which has been raised by many authors: it points out that, contrary to von Mises' account, there is not just only *one* physically possible infinite random sequence; there are *many*, indeed uncountably many. It seems arbitrary to pick out one of them and declare it to be the "ground sequence." In response to this objection I see two methods that work:

- *Method 1:* One assumes that in strictly *all* physically possible continuations of actual random sequences the frequencies converge to the *same* limit. This assumption would mean that our notion of "physical possibility" excludes worlds with probability zero, i.e. entails a very weak inductive assumption, because random sequences with deviating frequency limits are not strictly impossible but merely have probability zero by the law of large numbers.
- *Method 2:* One admits random sequences with probability zero and explicates probabilities as the frequency limits that random sequences possess "with probability 1." As explained above, this move makes the explication of statistical probability circular (or produces an infinite regress). So a further step is needed, which has been suggested by Kolmogorov (1933, 4), Cramér (1946), and Gillies (2000, 161): to interpret the 2nd order assertion "with probability 1" not as a statistical probability, but as an *epistemic* probability assertion, i.e. as "with certainty."

Method 1 (which is in the spirit of von Mises) has the prima facie advantage that it leads to a self-sustained explication of statistical probabilities. Method 2, in contrast, leads to a *dualistic* account, inasmuch as the explication of statistical probabilities employs subjective probabilities in its definiens. However, the advantage of method 1 is only superficial. As soon as one turns to the problem of the empirical content of statistical probability assertions, one is forced to make inductive assumptions, and thus to employ subjective probabilities, at least implicitly.

The *problem of empirical content* consists in the fact that hypotheses about frequency limits do not logically imply any empirical content: The fact that a random sequence possesses a frequency limit of r is logically compatible with any frequency $f_n \neq r$ reached so far, for any n no matter how large. Many authors (e.g. Howson/Urbach 1996, 331) have formulated this as an objection against statistical probabilities. However, it expresses only the well-known fact that no observation sentences follow *logically* from statistical hypotheses. Neither von Mises nor Reichenbach have tackled the problem of empirical content; they content themselves with the mathematical definition of convergence (cf. von Mises 1964, 59, 91; Reichenbach 1949, ch. 11).

The only way to obtain (probable) observation consequences from statistical hypotheses is by way of *inductive* specialization inferences (sec. 2.7.1), in which the statistical probability of a type of event is inductively transferred to a single case as its inductively inferred degree of belief. Hence, the empirical content of statistical hypotheses is not deductive, but *inductive* in nature: it consists of statements about the subjective degree of belief of observations. This inductive content is also fundamental to the theory of *statistical testing* which rests on the idea that a statistical hypotheses H is rejected by an observed sample frequency f_n if the probability of f_n given H is smaller than a pragmatically chosen "acceptance threshold"; for details see sec. 4.3.1.

Important in the present context is the following: regardless of whether method 1 or 2 is employed in defining statistical probabilities, the inductive-empirical content of a statistical hypothesis is exactly the *same*, because possibilities with subjective probability zero play no role in inductive consequences. The overall conclusion seems to be that an adequate explication of statistical probabilities requires the use of subjective probabilities. In the next two sections we will see that the converse is also true.

Some authors have tried to obtain *objective single case probabilities* without the complicated detour to frequency limits of random experiments and their inductive consequences. According to the reconstruction of Popper (1990) by Miller (1994, 182–186), single case propensities are causal tendencies of particular events to produce particular effects, without necessary connections to frequencies. An example is the tendency of *this* plane in *this* flight to crash. Causal tendencies of this sort are conditional to the entire state of the universe, which exists only once. In the same way, objective single case propensities have been explicated by Lewis (1980), but with two refinements: (i) For Lewis, the objective chance that an event e_t happens at time t is relative to a given time point t* which figures as the "present." (ii) While the chance of possible "future" events (t* < t) is equal to the world's causal tendency at t* to produce the event, the chance of past events (t* ≥ t) is either 1 or 0, depending on whether the event did occur or not.

The major criticism of single case propensities is that single cases are not assumed to be instantiations of repeatable random experiments. So their assumed propensities have no consequences concerning frequency tendencies, not even inductively. Nothing seems to block irrational single case propensity assertions such as, "In *this* throw Judy the mentalist caused the coin to land heads by means of her mind with propensity 1, but she succeeds only in 50% of the cases." In conclusion, single case propensities seem to be metaphysical speculations that are *empirically untestable* and thus, scientifically useless. A couple of more special objections against single case propensities have been raised, such as the reference class problem or Humphrey's paradox, which will not be covered here (see Eagle 2004; Gillies 2000, 126–136).

3.13.4 Problems of Subjective-Epistemic Probability Concepts

In the case of the subjective concept of probability, it is not the definition problem which causes difficulties: subjective probabilities are simply *defined* as epistemic degrees of belief which fulfill the Kolmogorov axioms of probability A1–3 (prop. 3.9–1). The main problem of the subjective theory of probability is the *justification problem*: for what reasons *should* our degrees of belief fulfill the basic axioms A1–3? Why is this *rational* in relation to the epistemic goal of finding content-rich truths?

The best-known justification of the axioms A1–3 for subjective probabilities goes back to Ramsey (1926) and de Finetti (1937). It consists in explicating subjective degrees of belief in terms of the betting behavior of rational persons, as *fair betting quotients*. Here is a rough description of this idea.[14] A bet on a proposition A is represented as the triple $\mathcal{B} =_{def} (A, g, c)$, where g and c are real numbers standing for "gain" and "cost," respectively. The person who bets on A (the "bettor") wins the amount of g (in money units) if A obtains and loses the amount of c if ¬A obtains. The quotient $q =_{def} c/(g+c)$ is called the betting quotient of bet $\mathcal{B}$. Defining $S =_{def} g+c$ as the total stake of the bet, one may represent $\mathcal{B}$ as the triple $(A, (1-q) \cdot S, q \cdot S)$. The bet $\mathcal{B}^c =_{def} (\neg A, c, g)$ is called the *counter-bet* of bet $\mathcal{B}$; whenever a person X bets with person Y the bet $\mathcal{B}$ on A, Y bets with X the counter-bet $\mathcal{B}^c$ on ¬A. A bet $\mathcal{B}$ and its betting quotient q is called *fair* in the view of the bettor X iff $\mathcal{B}$'s cost and gain are adjusted in a way that X has no preference between $\mathcal{B}$ and the counter-bet $\mathcal{B}^c$, given that X would be forced to choose one of the two bets.

The basic assumption of the betting approach is now that the true degree of belief which a person X has in A can be empirically measured by A's fair betting quotient. The central result of this approach is the following:[15]

> (Prop. 3.13–2) *Subjective probabilities as coherent fair betting quotients:*
>
> The fair betting quotients of a bettor fulfill the basic axioms A1–3 (prop. 3.9–1) iff they are *coherent* in the following sense: there is no finite class of fair bets which under all possible circumstances will lead to a total loss for the bettor (i.e. the sum of the money outcomes of all bets in the class is necessarily negative).

According to proposition (3.13–2), it is a kind of *logical* rationality requirement that fair betting quotients behave like probabilities: it would be similarly irrational to accept an incoherent system of bets which leads to a *sure loss* of money whatever happens, as it would be irrational to assert an inconsistent prediction that leads to a *sure failure* whatever happens. A system of bets which brings the bettor a sure loss is called a *Dutch book*. For example, I accept a Dutch book if I bet with betting quotient 1/2 on event A, but at the same time with betting quotient 3/4 on the negation of event A. Then (where S is the stake) I get $0.5 \cdot S - 0.75 \cdot S = -0.25 \cdot S$ if A occurs, and $-0.5 \cdot S + 0.25 \cdot S = -0.25 \cdot S$ if ¬A occurs; which means that whatever happens I lose $0.25 \cdot S$ money units.

The betting quotient approach was subjected to many criticisms, concerning for example the problem of *non-linear dependence* between money-outcome and utility, or the problem of betting on *non-verifiable propositions* (see e.g. Earman 1992, 41ff). There are ways to handle these objections, though at the cost of complications and idealizations (Howson/Urbach 1996, ch. 5; Gillies 2000, ch. 4). A more troublesome objection was made by Ryder (1981). According to the subjective approach, different persons may of course have *different* degrees of belief: as long as their beliefs are coherent, they are nevertheless "rational." Ryder, however, pointed out that whenever two (or several) persons have different fair betting quotients, a Dutch book can be made against them as a group, i.e. there exists a system of fair bets such that the sum of the earnings of all persons is necessarily negative. For example, if person X1's fair betting quotient on A is 1/2, and X2's fair quotient on A is 3/4, then I bet with X1 for A and with X2 against A, and I will earn $0.25 \cdot S$ whether A obtains or not. Ryder argues that a rule for rational betting behavior which when carried out by two persons leads to a necessary loss of the two persons' joint income can hardly be called rational. Gillies (2000, 170ff) concludes from this that persons should have an interest in reaching a consensual degree of belief (at least if they have shared interests). But how could they reach a consensus in a *non-arbitrary* manner, if *all* that they have are their *subjective* degrees of belief?

This last question brings us to the most *fundamental* objection against subjective probabilities: coherent and fair betting quotients are a far cry from being rational in the sense of *truth-oriented*. The definition of coherent and fair betting quotients refers only to the subjective degrees of beliefs and preferences of the betting persons, but *nowhere* does it refer to the true frequencies of the bet-on events. Take, for example, a subjectivist who offers odds of 1:1 that he will roll a six with a normal die, and considers the bet fair, i.e. he is willing to accept the opposite bet at 1:1 that he will not roll a six. Our subjectivist remains coherent even after he has lost his entire fortune, and he will not be able to spot any mistake in his betting behavior. He will, of course, be puzzled that while everybody has readily accepted his bet, nobody has accepted the counter-bet, although in his view both bets are equally fair. But he cannot explain to himself why he of all people has lost everything while others have made their fortune, *as long as* he does not consider the frequentistic chances of the type of event he has been betting on. This shows that the axioms A1–3 at best provide a *minimal condition* for rational degrees of belief, which is, however, too weak to exclude *irrational* betting behavior from an objective point of view.

The greatest weakness of the subjective betting approach, then, consists in the fact that it has no intrinsic relationship with statistical probabilities. As soon as one accepts such a relationship, one encounters a way to justify the basic probability axioms A1–3 which is, in my view, superior: namely, the stipulation that rational subjective degrees of belief are *intended* to reflect the real statistical probabilities. They can only do this if they fulfill the basic axioms A1–3. I call this the *frequency-intended* justification of the subjective probability axioms (for similar arguments cf. Carnap 1950b, 167ff; Earman 1992, 46). That subjective-epistemic probabilities reflect statistical probabilities is, of course, only possible if certain connections between subjective and statistical probabilities are established. We have met one such connection in def. 3.9-3: the principle of narrowest reference class. The next section contains a more thorough investigation of subjective-objective connection principles. They are usually explicated in the form of *additional* axioms for epistemic probabilities and gradually transform subjective probability concepts into intersubjective or "logical" conceptions of epistemic probability.

3.13.5 Connections between Objective and Epistemic Probabilities: A Dualist Account

The most elementary connection between epistemic and objective probabilities is established by the so-called *principal principle*. According to this principle, subjective probabilities of singular propositions should coincide with objective probabilities when the objective probabilities are known. This principle comes in two versions, which are of very different natures. The *single case* principal principle, going back to Lewis (1980), is held by subjective probability theorists who intend to connect subjective probabilities with single case propensities. Lewis calls single case propensities "chances." Let "chance$_t$(Fa$_i$)" be the single case propensity at time t, that a possible event Fa$_i$ happens at some other time point t$_i$ (think of "a$_i$" as a sequence of individual constants that includes t$_j$). If t$_i$ > t this is the chance of a future event, and if t > t$_i$ it is the chance of a past event. Recall from sec. 3.13.3 that past chances are either 1 or 0. Let "E$_{\leq t}$" be a so-called "admissible proposition," which is a proposition that speaks only about events *before* t. Then Lewis' principle says the following (see Lewis 1980, 87ff; Earman 1992, 52f):

(Prop. 3.13–3) *Single case principal principle:* P(Fa$_i$|chance$_t$(Fx)=r ∧ E$_{\leq t}$) = r.

In words: the degree of belief that a certain event occurs at a time t$_i$ conditional on this event's chance at time t and on propositions about events before time t, is identical with the event's chance at time t.

Degrees of belief in Fa$_i$ must not be conditionalized on evidence about events later than the chance-time t; otherwise one may obtain incoherent probability assignments (e.g. with t < t', the assertion P(Ft'| chance$_t$(Ft')=0.5∧Ft') = 0.5 is incoherent, because by the Kolmogorov axioms this probability must be 1).

As explained in sec. 3.13.3, single case propensities are empirically inaccessible, and so we cannot go along with them. Important for applications to empirical sciences is the *statistical* version of the principal principle, abbreviated as (StPP). It goes (indirectly) back to de Finetti and is defended by subjectivists who recognize the statistical concept of probability (e.g. Kutschera 1972, 82; Howson/Urbach 1996, 345;

Williamson 2010, 40). (StPP) is condensed in prop. 3.13–4. The application to random samples is an easy consequence of the first version; here $f(F|\{a_1,..., a_n\})$ denotes the frequency of Fs in the particular sample consisting of individuals $a_1,..., a_n$.

(Prop. 3.13–4)

Statistical principal principle (StPP):
$P(Ga_i | p(Gx|Fx) = r \land Fa_i \land E(b_1,..., b_n)) = r$.
Special case: $P(Ga_i | p(Gx)=r) = r$ (obtained when Fa_i is a tautology).
Extension: For "$p(Gx|Fx)=r$" one may substitute a statistical hypothesis that probabilistically entails "$p(Gx|Fx)=r$."
StPP for random samples:
$P(f(F|\{a_1,..., a_n\}) = k/n | p(Fx)=r) = \binom{n}{k} r^k \cdot (1-r)^{n-k}$.

(StPP) is of particular importance for proponents of Bayesian statistics. Subjectivists are called "Bayesians" because they use Bayes' theorem (prop. 3.9–3) to compute the subjective probability $P(H|E)$ of a (statistical) hypothesis H given an evidence E. They thereby use the inverse probability $P(E|H)$ of E conditional on H, the so-called *likelihood*. For Bayesians it is essential that likelihoods are *objective*, i.e. are equated with the corresponding statistical probabilities according to H, because only then will subjective probabilities of hypotheses converge to intersubjective (or objective) probabilities with accumulating evidence (more on this in sec. 4.7.4). This fact is emphasized by Hawthorne (2005, 286) and Strevens (2004), who calls (StPP) the "probability coordination principle."

The "extension" of (StPP) is important for application to combined outcomes, e.g. $P(Fa \land Gb | p(Fx)=r \land p(Gx)=q) = P(Fa \land Gb | p(Fx_1 \land Gx_2) = r \cdot q) = r \cdot q$. Note that in (StPP) "$a_i$" and "x" are abbreviated notations: when F is a relation, a_i and x stand for a sequences $a_{i_1},..., a_{i_n}$ and $x_1,..., x_n$, respectively. Fa_i may also have the form "$Ff(a_i)$" where $f(a_i)$ designates individuals at time points other than t_i. Different from single case chances, the statistical probability of the event-type Gx that is transferred to the single case Ga_i must explicitly be conditionalized to that reference class Fx, whose instantiation Fa_i expresses the evidence about

a_i on which P is conditionalized. Conditionalization on additional evidence $E(b_1,\ldots, b_n)$ is only allowed if this evidence does not speak about the single case a_i ($b_j \neq a_i$ for $1 \leq j \leq n$). Without this restriction, the principle could lead to incoherences: for example, with $H = (p(Fx|Gx) = 0.5)$ $\wedge$ $(p(Fx|Qx) = 0.8)$ we would obtain $P(Fa_i|Ga_i \wedge Qa_i \wedge H) = 0.5$ and at the same time $P(Fa_i|Ga_i \wedge Qa_i \wedge H) = 0.8$.

It is important to note that the statistical principal principle is reasonable without restrictions only for subjective "a-priori" probabilities: these are hypothetical degrees of belief of a rational subject who has not yet had certain experiences. This notion of "a priori" is not a Kantian one: it does not imply that a-priori probabilities are necessary or intersubjective, nor that they may not be conditionalized to hypothetical experiences; it only means that they must *not* depend on actual experiences. For *actual* or personalized degrees of belief, (StPP) is not generally valid. For example, if we know from observation that the coin has fallen on heads (= Fa), then our *actual* degree of belief in Fa is 1, $P(Fa) = 1$, even if we know that $p(Fx) = 1/2$; i.e. $P(Fa \mid p(Fx)=1/2) = 1$ will hold, which contradicts (StPP). Carnap (1971, 21–23) called an a-priori probability function P a "credibility function Cred" (in distinction to the actual belief function which he called a "credence function C"). Another way of expressing P's a-priori nature is Pearl's *all-I-know* interpretation (1988, 475): $P(A|B)$ expresses my counterfactual degree of belief in A if all I knew were B. In particular, $P(A)$ is my degree of belief in A if I knew nothing.

(StPP) determines only the subjective a-priori probability of singular sentences, i.e. sentences containing individual constants that can be replaced by individual variables, but not of quantified sentences without individual constants (such as "all Fs are Gs" or "90% of all Fs are Gs"). The subjective a-priori probability of quantified sentences or hypotheses (H_i) is assumed to be "given somehow" within the Bayesian framework. The posterior probability of a hypothesis H_i given empirical evidence is computed from these a-priori probabilities with the help of the Bayesian formula $P(H_i|E) = P(E|H_i) \cdot P(H_i) / \Sigma_{1 \leq i \leq n} P(E|H_i) \cdot P(H_i)$ (recall TC6 of prop. 3.9-3), where the "likelihood" $P(E|H_i)$ is determined by the (StPP) for random samples.

Moreover, (StPP) determines the subjective probability only for *those* singular sentences whose statistical probability is *known*. However, if one assumes an a-priori distribution P over all possible statistical hypotheses ($H_1, H_2, \ldots$), then by (StPP) the a-priori probability of each singular sentence is determined as the subjective expectation value of corresponding statistical probabilities, as follows:

(3.13-1) *Subjective probabilities as expectations of statistical probabilities:*

$P(Ga_i) = \Sigma_{1 \leq j \leq n} P(Ga_i|H_j) \cdot P(H_j) = \Sigma_{1 \leq j \leq n} r_j \cdot P(H_j)$ (by StPP), where H_j asserts "$p(Gx) = r_j$," and $\{H_1, ..., H_n\}$ is the set of all possible statistical hypotheses of this form whose disjunction has subjective probability 1.

$P(Ga_i|Fa_i)$ is determined by applying equation (3.13-1) to the numerator and denominator of $P(Ga_i \wedge Fa_i)/P(Fa_i)$ (cf. Bacchus 1990, 189). In the case of an uncountably infinite partition (H_r: $r \in [0,1]$) the sum has to be replaced by an integral ($\int_r r \cdot dP(r)$).

(3.13-1) shows that subjective a-priori probabilities, although independent from evidences, may depend on theoretical assumptions or "prejudices," expressed in the form of an a-priori P-distribution over hypotheses. Hawthorne (2005) calls epistemic probabilities as determined in (3.13-1) *support functions* and argues that they should be used in Bayesian confirmation theory. Contemporary Bayesians do not like "a-priori" probabilities; they prefer to use *prior* probabilities, which are prior to some but not all evidence. This is possible only under the following restriction: if P depends on actual evidences $E_1(a_i)$, then (StPP) may only be applied to predictions $E_2(b_i)$ about *new* individuals b_i different from the a_i that have been observed; otherwise (StPP) could produce contradictions.

A-priori probabilities that are defined according to (3.13-1) have a fundamental property that was first formulated by de Finetti: they satisfy the axiom of *exchangeability*, or the equivalent axiom of *symmetry* (as Carnap 1971, 117f, called it). An exchangeable belief function P is, by definition, one which is *invariant* w.r.t. arbitrary permutations of the (countably many) individual constants $\{a_i : i \in \mathbb{N}\}$ of the language, i.e. it holds that $P(A(a_1, ..., a_n)) = P(A(a_{\pi(1)}, ..., a_{\pi(n)}))$ for every permutation function $\pi: \mathbb{N} \to \mathbb{N}$ over the natural numbers $\mathbb{N}$ (see Earman 1992, 89; Gillies 2000, 71). Exchangeability is an obvious consequence of equation (3.13-1), which implies $P(Ga_i) = P(Ga_j)$ for arbitrary $i, j \in \mathbb{N}$, because the definiens $\Sigma_{1 \leq j \leq n} r_j \cdot P(H_j)$ does not depend on the individual constants a_i. De Finetti (1937) proved a famous *representation theorem*, according to which every exchangeable subjective probability function is identical to a probabilistic mixture of (independent) statistical probability distributions in the sense of equation (3.13-1). Moreover, equation (3.13-1) is equivalent to (StPP) together with the assumption that with subjective probability 1, the property Gx possess a frequency limit.[16] We summarize these facts as follows:

> (Prop. 3.13–5) *Exchangeable probability functions:*
>
> The following conditions are equivalent:
> 1. P is exchangeable.
> 2. P is representable as P-expectation value of statistical probability functions as in (3.13–1).
> 3. With P = 1 every event Fx in the underlying algebra has a frequency limit p(Fx), and P satisfies (StPP).

The most important fact about all these (equivalent) conditions is their nature as (weak) probabilistic *assumptions of induction*. The (StPP) transfers frequency tendencies in the long run, under the assumption that they are known, to arbitrary given observation samples as their subjective expectation values. This is only reasonable under the inductive assumption that any particular situation (sample or time span) is more or less *representative* for the whole domain or world; i.e. our world is uniform. Likewise, exchangeability rests on the assumption that prior to particular experience the subjective-probabilistic tendencies are the same for all individuals a_i. Thinking of the a_i as events in space, ordered in time, this is the assumption that the fundamental dispositions to generate events conditional on other events are the same for all space and time points; i.e. our world is inductively uniform. It can be proved that exchangeability together with the condition of "non-dogmaticity" entail uniform inductive learning, also called "instantial relevance":[17]

> (Prop. 3.13–6) *Uniform inductive learning:*
>
> If P is exchangeable and "non-dogmatic" in the sense that $P(Fa_i) \neq 0, 1$, then the degree of inductive support increases with the number of confirming instances.
>
> *Formally*: $P(Fa_{n+1}|Fa_1 \wedge \ldots \wedge Fa_n) > P(Fa_{n+1}| Fa_1 \wedge \ldots \wedge Fa_{n-k})$ (for $0 < k < n$).

The inductive nature of exchangeability is stressed, for example, by Kutschera (1972, 74f), Earman (1992, 108) and Gillies (2000, 73). This is important insofar as some authors have argued that exchangeability is an a-priori or logical property (e.g. van Fraassen 1989, ch. 7; de Finetti 1937; Carnap 1971). However, situations are easily imaginable in which it is reasonable to give up exchangeability: for example, when we recognize that after some time t, the frequency tendencies of a random experiment have significantly changed; then t is a non-uniform "subversion" point and events-indices before and after time t are no longer exchangeable (for further counter-examples see Gillies 2000, 69–83).

Exchangeability is not strong enough to determine a unique a-priori belief function, because it does not fix the a-priori probabilities $P(H_i)$ of possible hypotheses (or states of the world). Therefore, proponents of intersubjective probabilities have suggested even stronger conditions that fix this prior distribution $P(H_i)$. The most important suggestion of this kind is the *indifference* principle, which asserts that in the absence of experience one should assign the *same* prior probability to every possible hypothesis. However, we will see in sec. 4.7.3 that "indifference" is dependent on linguistic formulations and, thus, cannot have the status of an "a-priori" principle. The Laplace-Carnapean idea that "logic" can determine probability values seems to be untenable. "Logical" probabilities should not be regarded as a third kind of probabilities, but as epistemic probabilities that intend to be intersubjective by obeying additional conditions.

Let us finally explain the connection between evidence-independent a-priori probabilities and *actual* degrees of belief that are evidence-dependent. This connection is established by the principle of *conditionalization* (see Carnap 1971, 18; Earman 1992, 34; Howson/Urbach 1996, 102f).

> (Prop. 3.13–7) *Rule of strict conditionalization:* Let P_0 be the a-priori probability at a starting point in time t_0, let P_t be the actual probability at time t, and let K_{0-t} be total (singular and statistical) knowledge acquired between time points t_0 and t. Then it holds for every proposition S that: $P_t(S) = P_0(S| K_{0-t})$.

Strict conditionalization also works stepwise, i.e. $P_t(S) = P_{t-1}(S|K_t)$ where P_{t-1} is the actual probability function at time $t-1$ and K_t the new knowledge acquired at time t. A generalization of strict conditionalization is Jeffrey-conditionalization, which conditionalizes on uncertain evidence. If $\{E_1,..., E_k\}$ is a partition of uncertain evidence-possibilities acquired at time t with probabilities $P_t(E_i)$, then according to Jeffrey-conditionalization, $P_t(S) = \Sigma_{1 \leq i \leq k} P_{t-1}(S|E_i) \cdot P_t(E_i)$.

The principle of narrowest reference class which was explained in sec. 3.9.1 can be derived from the conjunction of the (StPP) and the rule of strict conditionalization as follows: Assume that Ra is our entire knowledge of the individual a, $E(b_1,\ldots, b_n)$ our knowledge of other individuals, and we know that $p(Fx|Rx) = r$. By (StPP) this implies that (*) $P_0(Fa|Ra \wedge p(Fx|Rx) = r \wedge E(b_1,\ldots, b_n)) = r$. By strict conditionalization, (*) implies for the actual belief function that $P_t(Fa) = r$ (since K_{0-t} = Ra $\wedge\ p(Fx|Rx)=r \wedge E(b_1,\ldots, b_n)$)—which is the statement of the principle of the narrowest reference class.

Why should we conditionalize our predictions on narrowest reference classes? For a given event Fa, the individual a can belong to many different classes of reference, which assign different conditional probabilities to Fx. Let "a" for instance be a person who lives in Calcutta and is a millionaire heiress, and assume the following statistical probabilities: p(Wealthy | Heir-to-millionaires) = 0.95, and p(Wealthy | Lives-in-Calcutta) = 0.001. If we related subjective single case probabilities to different classes of reference, then we would reach contradictory probabilistic predictions: P(Wealthy(a)) = 0.95 versus = 0.001. Hempel (1965b, sec. 3.4) called this the *ambiguity* of statistical inferences. Only through selection of a *distinguished* class of reference can incoherent degrees of belief and contradictory single case predictions be avoided.

In order to avoid contradictions we should conditionalize our beliefs on one *unique* reference—but why should this distinguished reference class be the *narrowest* reference class? This question is answered by a *decision-theoretic* justification that was first given by Good (1983, 178ff). If we are confronted with a partition of possible actions $A_1,\ldots, A_m$, then according to the standard decision rule we choose that action with highest expected utility. The expected utility of action A_k is given as $E(A_k)$ = $\Sigma_{1 \leq i \leq n} u(A_k|C_i) \cdot P(C_i)$, where $C_1,\ldots, C_n$ is a partition of possible circumstances, $u(A_k|C_i)$ is the utility of action A_k in circumstance C_i and $P(C_i)$ is the probability of circumstance C_i. Good proved that conditionalizing the probabilities $P(C_i)$ on narrowest references classes R, i.e. basing our decisions on the probabilities $P(C_i|R)$, can only improve our expected utility. Specifically, when the actions are predictions, Good's theorem implies that conditionalizing on narrowest reference classes maximizes our expected predictive success.

The principle of the narrowest reference class involves the following further subtleties:

a Reference classes must be determined by *qualitative* or so-called *nomological* attributes (see sec. 6.3.2), and not by purely *extensionally* defined attributes. Otherwise, the narrowest reference class of an individual a would always be the class {a} or the attribute x = a, which would lead to the nonsensical result that P(Fa) = p(Fx| x = a) can only take the values 1 or 0.

b Above, we have defined the concept of the narrowest reference class *epistemically*, in agreement with Reichenbach, Carnap and Hempel, as the narrowest reference class Rx for which we *know* or think to know (in our epistemic background system) that a lies in it. Salmon (1984, 37), on the other hand, used an *objective* concept of the narrowest reference class: the objectively narrowest reference class of an event Gat at time t is the conjunction of *all* nomological properties $F_i at'$ at earlier time points $t' < t$ that are statistically relevant for Gat (sec. 6.3.3).

c A practically important simplification is afforded by the use of narrowest *relevant* reference classes: these do not necessarily have to comprise all known information about the given individual a, rather only that information, on which Fx is probabilistically *dependent*. The replacement of narrowest by narrowest relevant reference classes is harmless since it does not change the resulting subjective probability P(Fa). Suggestions in this direction are Hempel's *maximally specific* reference class (1965b, 397) and Salmon's *broadest* homogeneous reference class (1984, 37).

The overall conclusion of our treatise on probability theory speaks in favor of a *dualistic* account to probability. Both the statistical and the subjective probability accounts have problems, but these problems are in a sense complementary. In Kantian terms, statistical probabilities without a connection to subjective probabilities are *empty* (have no observable implications), and subjective probabilities without a connection to statistical probabilities are *blind* (have no relation to reality).

3.14 Introductory Literature and Exercises

3.14.1 Introductory Literature

A compact introduction into the philosophy of language is given by Kutschera (1976) or Morris (2006). Klenk (1989) and Copi et al. (2010) are excellent introductions to logic. Advanced students may read e.g. Hrbacek/Jech (1999) on set theory, Machover (1996) or Mendelson (2009) on logic, and Krantz et al. (2006/1971) on the theory of measurement. Suppes' introduction to logic (1999/1957) contains important chapters on the theory of definitions. Popper (1935/2002), Carnap (1966) and Hempel (1965b, 1966) are classics of analytic philosophy of science. Parts of Stegmüller's monumental introduction to the analytical philosophy of science (1969ff) are translated in his English collection (1977, Vol. II). An excellent introduction to probability theory is offered by Gillies (2000). Carnap (1936/37) is a classic on disposition concepts; a contemporary introduction is Mumford (1998). Sher (1991) introduces the problems of separating logical from non-logical concepts. Classics on analytic-synthetic questions are Carnap (1956b) and Quine (1960). Howson/Urbach (1996) offer an advanced treatment of probability theory from a Bayesian viewpoint.

3.14.2 Questions and Exercises

Sec. 3.1

1 Which kind of logical concept (term) is expressed in the following examples? (a) "Peter the Great," (b) "the left foot of ...," (c) "The left foot of Peter the Great," (d) "... is in love with ...," (e) "... is logically impossible," (f) "neither ..., nor ...," (g) "there is no ..., which ... ."
2 Classify the following concepts according to their content type: (a) "x is reprehensible," (b) "x is a red square," (c) "x exerts a force on y," (d) "x is fragile," (e) "x understands what y means," (f) "x is a carnivore," (g) "x is politically correct," (h) "x is the owner of y."
3 What is the scale type of the following concepts: (a) gender, (b) population number, (c) membership of a biological species, (d) physical attractiveness, (e) point in time, (f) intelligence quotient, (g) energy.

Sec. 3.2

1 Which of the following sentences is prescriptive, descriptive, or mixed? (a) "Economic growth is good," claims the business newspaper. (b) If economy growth goes on, capitalism is good. (c) Susie has a bad character. (d) Susie is ill.
2 What is the content type of the following descriptive sentences? (a) Sociology is being discussed in the next room. (b) The window is open in the next room. (c) My skin is sensitive to sunlight. (d) There is a table in Maria's garden. (e) Dogs bark. (f) Magnetic fields have a curative effect.

Sec. 3.3–6

1 Which of the following sentences is logically true, definitionally true, or synthetically true? (a) No unsplittable object can be split. (b) Every unsplittable object is atomic. (c) Every atom consists of protons,

neutrons and electrons. (d) Stable democracies are not vulnerable to crises. (e) Democracies can be vulnerable to crises or not. (f) Democracies can only be stable when they possess a stable economy.

2 Classify the following sentences according to their degree of generality: (a) 70% of all students in Munich have problems with their flats. (b) There is no perpetual motion machine. (c) Peter finished his PhD yesterday. (d) Most people believe in God. (e) Everyone living in this house is a musician. (f) There are white ravens in Australia. (g) All acids are proton donors.

3 Which of the general sentences in (2) is lawlike?

Sec. 3.7–9

1 Which hypotheses are verifiable and/or falsifiable? (a) 70–80% of all birds can fly. (b) 70–80% of all Germans earn more than 2,000 euros per month. (c) Force = mass times acceleration. (d) All swans are white. (e) That swan there is white.

2 Analyze the following statements according to the principle of the narrowest class of reference: (a) With the small amount of sleep you have had today, you will probably be tired tomorrow. (b) You will probably catch flu from him. (c) It probably won't be a clear day up in the mountains tomorrow.

3 The frequency of unmarried (U) vs. married (V) women (F) and men (M) in a seminar are distributed as follows: $U \wedge F$ 20%, $U \wedge M$ 30%, $V \wedge F$ 27%. Visualize this using Venn diagrams. What are the frequencies of: $V \wedge M$, V, U, M, F, $U \vee M$, $V \vee F$, $M \vee F$, $V \wedge U$? Compute the following conditional frequencies: V given M, V given F, M given U, F given U, M given $V \vee F$, $V \vee M$ given M.

Sec. 3.10–13

1 Characterize the following dispositions using a bilateral reduction sentence: (a) x is elastic, (b) x is helpful.

2 Try to define the following concepts: (a) table, (b) stone, (c) traffic light, (d) sky, (e) energy. Are your attempted definitions analytical?

3 Which of the following consequences are valid consequences and which are relevant (valid) consequences of the set of premises "All humans are social beings, (and) no social being wants to be alone"? (a) All female humans are social beings. (b) No human wants to be alone. (c) No human who is a social being wants to be alone. (d) Only humans are social beings. (e) Every human either wants to be alone or does not.

4   What is the probability of getting at least five heads with ten tosses of a normal coin?

Notes

1   This becomes different when individual or function concepts are defined via predicates, as in $\forall x(a=x \leftrightarrow_{def} Fx)$. This definition presupposes the *uniqueness* condition "there exists exactly one F." Its definiendum is only eliminable *relative* to a background knowledge which contains this uniqueness condition (cf. Suppes 1999, 158–160).
2   The definition of "logical content" is found in Popper (1935/2002, sec. 35) and Carnap (1937, 120), and that of "empirical content" in Hempel (1958, 211) and Kutschera (1972, 298).
3   This is a disadvantage of the standard definition. Popper (1935/2002, new append. ch. II*) and Carnap (1971, 38f) have suggested independent axiomatizations of conditional probabilities which allow p(B|A) to have non-trivial values even when p(A) is zero (except when A is a contradiction).
4   E.g. Goodman (1955), sec. 2.3, Pap (1978, 44), Armstrong et al. (1996), Bird (2007, 43f); Mumford (1998, 66) speaks of the "accepted view."
5   Cf. Wittgenstein (1921), sec. 5.134, 2.061 versus sec. 2.013, 6.3751; Carnap (1956b, 15); a more recent example is Bergmann et al. (1998, 11).
6   See Schurz (1991a, 1994), Schurz/Weingartner (1987, 2010).
7   This is an improved version of Schurz (1991a, 423); cf. Schurz/Weingartner (2010, def. 4).
8   A proof for PropL is found in Schurz/Weingartner (1987, 58, prop. 6); a general proof for PredL has so far only been possible if 2nd order quantifiers are allowed.
9   Independence is violated in experiments whose outcome probabilities depend on the results of previous performances; their outcome sequences are called "Markov chains."
10 See Hays/Winkler (1970, 222f, 609f), Bauer (1996, sec. 36–38), Howson/Urbach (1996, 47f).
11 Cf. Eagle (2004, 396f), Hájek (1999, 223), Kutschera (1972, 104), Stegmüller (1969ff, vol. IV.2, 37).
12 See von Mises (1964, sec. 1A), Gillies (2000, 105–109), Salmon (1984, 55ff).
13 Von Mises rejects the strong law of large numbers because of his "verificationist" philosophy (cf. sec. II.B; 240, fn. 7); but there is no need to limit von Mises' account in this way.
14 More details in Carnap (1971, ch. 8), Skyrms (1999, ch. 6), Howson/Urbach (1996, ch. 5), Gillies (2000), ch. 4.
15 A proof is found in each of the references in note 14. Various variants of prop. 3.13–1 exist in the literature.
16 This holds, since the assumption is equivalent to $P(H_1 \vee \ldots \vee H_n) = 1$, which together with (StPP) yields (3.13–1). Similarly, (3.13–1) implies (StPP) and the assumption.
17 This follows from the Cauchy-Schwartz inequality; see Earman (1992, 107, 198) and Humburg (1971, 233, th.5).

4
A QUESTION OF FIT: LAW HYPOTHESES AND THEIR EMPIRICAL TESTING

In the following sections, we deal with *qualitative* law hypotheses. In most practically significant cases, these have the following form: a conjunction of several antecedent factors A_1x, A_2x (…) implies a certain consequent property Cx—either strictly, or with a certain conditional probability. The conjunction of all antecedent factors makes up the complex antecedent predicate A, i.e. $Ax =_{def} A_1x \wedge A_2x (\wedge \ldots)$. Here A_ix and Cx stand for literals, i.e. unnegated or negated atomic formulas, whose predicates express qualitative (or nomological) properties. Generalizations of this form will be mentioned briefly. In sec. 4.6 and 5.10.5 we will consider quantitative law hypotheses.

Formal refinement: Instead of the individual variable x we can have an n-tuple of variables, e.g. objects, places and points in time x,s,t. The argument places in "A_ix" may also be functional terms "$f(x)$," which is for example needed to formalize *succession laws* $A(x,t) \rightarrow C(x,t+\varepsilon)$.

Which conditions must a universal sentence or its statistical counterpart fulfill, in order to be acceptable as a scientific law or generalization? Above all two: (1) most obviously, the *truth condition*: false law hypotheses deliver false predictions and can thereby lead to harmful planning errors. Of course, we can never be sure of the truth of a universal law, but can only confirm it to a greater or lesser extent—therefore we speak of "true or confirmed." There is, however, a second, often overlooked, condition for scientifically acceptable law hypotheses, i.e. (2) *the condition of relevance*, which we will now discuss.

4.1 The Condition of Relevance

4.1.1 Relevance of Strict Laws

Consider the following two strict generalizations of the form $\forall x(A_1x \wedge A_2x \rightarrow Cx)$:

(4.1–1)
1. All men (A_1) who take contraceptive pills (A_2) do not get pregnant (C).
2. Deadly nightshade (A_1), picked at midnight by the full moon (A_2), has hallucinogenic effects (C).

In both cases, we are dealing with universally *true* law hypotheses. Nonetheless, there is something wrong with these examples: one element of the conjunction of each law's antecedent is *irrelevant*, i.e. it is not necessary in order for the consequent of the law to occur. In case 1, it is already a biological fact that men never get pregnant—even if they do *not* take contraceptive pills (this example is taken from Salmon 1971, 34). In case 2, deadly nightshade always causes hallucinations, even when not picked by the full moon at midnight. This second example is based on medieval accounts of witches' ointments (cf. Dürr 1985, 3) and highlights something that is characteristic of many mystical traditions: the addition of scientifically irrelevant mystical content to otherwise empirically correct statements.

Based on this analysis, we can formulate the condition of relevance for strict law hypotheses as follows:

(Def. 4.1–1) *Condition of relevance for strict law hypotheses:*

A true or confirmed implication law of the form $\forall x(A_1x \wedge \ldots \wedge A_nx \rightarrow Cx)$ is *relevant* (in regard to its antecedent predicate) iff no conjunctive antecedent component A_ix is superfluous, in the sense that it may be deleted from the law *salva veritate*, i.e. the law remains true or confirmed after its deletion.

Explanatory example: The result of removing A_2x in (1): $\forall x(A_1x \wedge A_2x \wedge A_3x \rightarrow Cx)$ is (2): $\forall x(A_1x \wedge A_3x \rightarrow Cx)$. A_2 is only relevant in (1) if (2) is false.—*Special case:* The result of removing Ax in $\forall x(Ax \rightarrow Cx)$ is $\forall xCx$.

An irrelevant antecedent factor of a law hypothesis is neither *prognostically* nor *causally relevant* for the consequent. It is not prognostically relevant, because its verification is unnecessary for the prediction of the consequent. It cannot be considered as a causal factor, because causal factors must be partly responsible for the occurrence of the effect. We can reformulate the condition of "relevance" in terms of "dependency": if the antecedent factor A_i is relevant for consequent C, then the occurrence of C *depends* on A_i. However, we should note that while the relevance of an antecedent factor in the defined sense is equivalent to its prognostic relevance, it is, by contrast, only necessary but *not sufficient* for its causal relevance. In order to be acceptable as a *causal* law, a relevant and true law of the form $\forall x(A_1x \wedge A_2x \to Cx)$ must satisfy further conditions which are discussed in sec. 4.4 and 6.7.

The condition of relevance is closely related to the INUS-theory of strict causal hypotheses, going back to Mackie (1980). Two concepts are fundamental to Mackie's analysis: Ax is called a (nomologically) *sufficient* condition for Bx iff $\forall x(Ax \to Bx)$ is a true, lawlike sentence; and Ax is called a (nomologically) *necessary* condition for Bx iff $\forall x(Bx \to Ax)$ is a true, lawlike sentence. Mackie asks: What do we mean by "cause" in an everyday causal claim such as "The cause of the fire at the hay barn was a burning cigarette"? The burning cigarette alone is not a sufficient condition, as further conditions have to be fulfilled in order for a hay barn to catch fire, for example that enough oxygen was present and that the hay was dry. Neither does the burning cigarette constitute a necessary condition, as the fire at the hay barn could also have been started by another cause, e.g. by a burning match or a bolt of lightning. According to Mackie (1980, 62), a cause is an *i*nsufficient but *n*ecessary conjunctive part of an *u*nnecessary but *s*ufficient condition for the effect—in short, an INUS-condition. Building on Mackie, we can reformulate our condition thus: for the acceptability of $\forall x(A_1x \wedge A_2x \to Cx)$ as a true relevant law, it is not only required that the entire antecedent predicate $A_1x \wedge A_2x$ is a *sufficient* condition for Cx; additionally, every antecedent component A_ix must be a *necessary part* of this sufficient condition.

Mackie was aware that the criterion of the INUS-condition alone is not enough to characterize causal relationships. He also emphasizes that in everyday causal claims, the sufficient conditions are often incompletely known to us, so that we formulate 2nd order existence claims of the form "there are remaining conditions φx, so that Ax∧φx is sufficient for Cx, but neither Ax alone nor φx alone" (1980, 70f). This is nothing but an exclusive ceteris paribus law in the sense of sec. 4.5.1.

We briefly show how this condition of relevance can be abstractly generalized to qualitative laws of arbitrary form. We define a true mixed-quantified law L as relevant iff it has an *irreducible representation* IR(L) in the sense of def. 3.12–4, whose conjunctive elements E are relevant in the following sense: no literal in the matrix of E can be eliminated *salva veritate*. Recall that each E is a PCN-form and E's matrix is a conjunction of disjunctions of literals: since each implication can be rewritten as a disjunction, relevance for purely universal implications according to def. 4.1–1 is a special case of this more general criterion.

The condition of relevance is closely related to the definition of relevant consequences from sec. 3.12. It is easy to see that a true law L is irrelevant (in the above sense) exactly if there exists a true law L* (obtained from L by eliminating an irrelevant component), which entails L as an *irrelevant consequence*. For example, if "$A_1 x$" is irrelevant in $\forall x(A_1 x \wedge A_2 x \rightarrow Cx)$, then $\forall x(A_2 x \rightarrow Cx)$ is true and $\forall x(A_2 x \rightarrow Cx) \;||\!\!-\!\!-\; \forall x(\underline{A_1 x} \wedge A_2 x \rightarrow Cx)$ is a conclusion-irrelevant inference (the underlined sub-formula is replaceable *salva validitate*).

We finally mention the problem of logical *invariance*. Since L-equivalent sentences express the same proposition, the application of a relevance criterion should be logically invariant, i.e. should lead to the same result for all L-equivalent transformations of a sentence. However, without certain "safeguard" operations, this is not the case. The standard safeguard method to guarantee logical invariance is to require that a sentence be transformed into a suitable normal form *before* the relevance criterion is applied to it. In this sense, def. 4.1–1 applies the relevance criterion only to laws with a restricted form, and our generalized definition requires the existence of an irreducible representation which satisfies the relevance criterion. Resulting from this representation method, the generalized relevance criterion is logically invariant.

However, if one were to (naively) apply the idea of relevance as non-eliminability to antecedent conjuncts of *arbitrary* form (instead of applying it only to literals in normal forms), then invariance w.r.t. L-equivalent formulations would no longer be satisfied. Due to this problem, Hempel (1977, 109) rejected Salmon's condition of relevance for the law premises of explanations. Salmon had characterized the condition of relevance in terms of the *extensions* of the predicates Ax and Cx in the law $\forall x(Ax \rightarrow Cx)$, and thereby (falsely) presupposed that any L-equivalent reformulations of these predicates was allowed. Based on this (false) presupposition, Hempel raised the following objection. Consider the following three law hypotheses:

(4.1–2) *Example of non-invariance:*

L_1 Sugar is soluble in water. $\forall x(SUx \rightarrow Wx)$
L_2 Salt is soluble in water. $\forall x(SAx \rightarrow Wx)$
L Sugar or salt is soluble in water. $\forall x((SUx \vee Sax) \rightarrow Wx)$

Problem: L_1 is L-equivalent with:

L_1^*: $\forall x((SUx \vee SAx) \wedge (\underline{SUx \vee \neg SAx}) \rightarrow Wx)$

According to Salmon, the two law hypotheses L_1 and L_2 cannot figure as relevant (explanatory) laws, but rather only the law hypothesis L.[1] For SUx is L-equivalent to $(SUx \vee SAx) \wedge (SUx \vee \neg SAx)$. But in the L-equivalent version L_1^* of L_1, the underlined antecedent conjunct is irrelevant for Wx. Hempel concludes from this that Salmon's relevance criterion is inadequate. He assumes thereby that whether the antecedent of a law can be weakened *salva veritate* by *eliminating* a conjunct of it, or by *adding* a disjunct to it, makes no difference to its relevance. But this difference is decisive according to our view of relevance.

4.1.2 Relevance of Statistical Laws

An analogous condition of relevance is valid for statistical laws. Once more, it was Salmon who drew our attention to it (1971; 1989, 58ff). Consider the following example of a statistical generalization with only one antecedent factor, $p(Cx|Ax) = r$.

(4.1–3) 95% of all persons having a cold, who regularly take high doses of Vitamin C (A), make a full recovery within a week (C).

As domain of individuals or *population* D we choose here the set of all persons who have a cold. *Note* that if there is no danger of confusion, we leave out the individual variable "x," and write "$p(C|A)$" instead of "$p(Cx|Ax)$," etc.

The statistical generalization (4.1–3) has been well confirmed by empirical findings. Further studies, however, found that quite independently from the intake of high doses of Vitamin C, 95% of all persons with a cold recovered fully within one week (see Salmon 1971, 83, fn. 20). The factor A is therefore *statistically irrelevant* for C, because it is already true that

$p(C) = p(C|A) = p(C|\neg A) = 0.95$.

The statistical condition of relevance, therefore, says the following: the presence of a *high conditional probability* $p(C|A)$ of the consequent property given the antecedent property (which is the statistical counterpart of the truth condition) is *not* enough for a relevant statistical correlation. In addition, the presence of the antecedent must raise (or at least change) the conditional probability of the consequent, p(C|A), compared to its *prior probability* p(C). In other words, there must be a probabilistic *dependence* between C and A (recall sec. 3.9.2). Antecedent features which raise probability of the consequent are called *positively* relevant; those which lower its probability are called *negatively* relevant. Of course, only positively relevant features count as prognostically relevant for C; negatively relevant features are prognostically relevant for not-C. As in the strict case, positive statistical relevance is only necessary but not sufficient for causal relevance.

The tricks of many mentalists or magicians are based on *unrecognized* irrelevancies. One example was Uri Geller's supposed art of long-distance repair in the 1980s: Uri Geller claimed to be able to use telekinesis through the television screen to restart his viewers' broken watches. After his request to viewers to get their old watches out of their boxes and see if they were working again, several hundred people indeed rang up and declared: "It's true, my watch is working!" The probability, however, that out of a million old watches which have been put away, some hundred will start going again when somebody fiddles around with them, is given, with or without Geller's telekinetic repair.

Recognized irrelevancies, on the other hand, often form the basis of *jokes*—an example is the title page of Salmon (1971) shown in fig. 4.1-1:

Figure 4.1–1 Irrelevance and joke (title page of Salmon 1971; drawing by Richter ©)

A relevant statistical relationship between two features A and C is also called a *correlation*. The simplest measure of correlation for binary properties is the probability difference p(C|A)—p(C). We summarize this as follows:

(Prop. 4.1–1) *Statistical relevance and correlation for binary properties:*

A is (statistically) *relevant* for C   *iff*   p(C|A) ≠ p(C).
A is *irrelevant* for C   *iff*   p(C|A) = p(C).
A is *positively relevant* for C   *iff*   A raises C's probability, p(C|A) > p(C).
A is *negatively relevant* for C   *iff*   A lowers C's probability, p(C|A) < p(C).

Simple correlation measure for binary properties:
corr(A,C) =$_{def}$ p(C|A) − p(C).
corr(A,C) is always situated between the values +1 and −1.

A is $\begin{cases} \text{positively relevant for C} \\ \text{negatively relevant for C} \\ \text{irrelevant for C} \end{cases}$ *iff* corr(A,C) = $\begin{cases} \text{positive} \\ \text{negative} \\ \text{zero} \end{cases}$

In practical applications the non-identity condition "≠" in prop. 4.1–1 has to be understood as "significantly different." Note the fundamental parallelism between strict and statistical relevance: A is strictly relevant for C if ∀x(Ax→Cx) is true, but not ∀xCx; A is positively statistically relevant for C if p(Cx|Ax) is high, but not p(Cx).

Our correlation measure corr(A,C) is also called the *difference* measure. There are a number of related correlation measures, which we mention briefly.

1 The definition of probability change can also be formulated conjunctively as p(A∧B) ≠ p(A)·p(B), by prop. 3.9–3 (TC7). The quantitative correlation measure which corresponds to the conjunctive definition of correlation is the so-called *covariance* between properties:

cov(C,A) = p(C∧A) − p(C)·p(A).

The covariance measure has the advantage that it is *numerically* symmetric, i.e. cov(A,C) = cov(C,A). In contrast, the difference measure is only qualitatively symmetric in the sense that corr(C,A) > (<) 0 iff corr(A,C) > (<) 0. But corr(C,A) and corr(A,C) are not always numerically identical. "Cov" and "corr" are numerically related as follows:

$$cov(A,C) = cov(C,A) = p(A) \cdot corr(A,C) = p(C) \cdot corr(C,A).$$

2 In statistics, particular features such as C are treated as *values* of nominally scaled feature variables X_C (recapitulate sec. 3.1.4: the values of the binary variable X_C are C, ¬C). The antecedent variable X_A is also called the *predictor* variable and the consequent variable X_C the *criterion* variable. Traditional statistical correlation measures are defined not for particular values of variables, but for variables in general. A correlation measure for variables, corr(X_A,X_C), is obtained by *adding up* and subsequently normalizing the correlations between all values of the variables, $\Sigma_{i,j}$corr(X_A=A_i,X_C=C_j). Since the correlation between positive and negative values of the variables would add up to zero, one adds up the *squares* of the correlations between the values (see sec. 4.6). A so-defined correlation measure for nominally scaled variables is the chi-square coefficient and for quantitative variables the product-moment correlation (Howson/Urbach 1996, 183ff; Hays/Winkler 1970, 174). Note, however, that in these "averaging" correlation measures, information about particular dependencies between the values of the variables may get lost.

3 A statistical correlation measure of preference in recent times is the *effect strength*. It presupposes a binary antecedent variable A, ¬A and a consequent feature C scaled in *any* way, and is defined as the difference between the C-average in the A-population and in the entire population, divided by the standard deviation of C (sec. 4.6). For binary consequent features, the effect strength is directly proportional to the difference measure corr(A,C) = p(C|A) − p(C). Because of its scaling-independence, effect strength is popularly used in *meta-analyses*, in which the results of different empirical studies are brought together (Hunter/Schmidt 1990).

Correlations are not always *transitive*: it may happen that Corr(A,B) > 0, Corr(B,C) > 0, but Corr(A,C) < 0. For example, Corr(Living-in-Munich, Living-in-Germany) > 0, Corr(Living-in-Germany, Living-in-nonBavarian-Germany) > 0, but Corr(Living-in-Munich, Living-in-nonBavarian-Germany) < 0. It can be proved that positive correlations are transitive when conditioning on A does not lower the conditional probability of C given B, i.e. when p(C|B∧A) ≥ p(C|B).

The generalization of the condition of statistical relevance for laws with several conjunctive antecedent components is obvious:

> (Def. 4.1-2) *Statistical relevance for conjunctive antecedents:* A true or confirmed statistical generalization $p(C|A_1 \wedge \ldots \wedge A_n) = r$ is relevant (with respect to its antecedent predicate) iff no conjunctive antecedent component A_i can be deleted *salva probabilitate*, i.e. with the probability value remaining the same.

Example: The factor A_1 is statistically relevant in the true law $p(C|A_1 \wedge A_2 \wedge A_3) = r$ iff $p(C|A_2 \wedge A_3) = r$ is false. The true law $p(C|A_1 \wedge A_2 \wedge A_3) = r$ is statistically relevant if all of its three antecedent factors are statistically relevant in this sense.

The measure of relevance of a single antecedent factor is expressed with help of so-called *conditional correlations:* $\text{corr}(C,A_i|Q_j) =_{\text{def}} p(Cx|A_i \wedge Q_j) - p(C|Q_j)$ is the conditional correlation between C and A_i, given a conjunction Q_j of the $n-1$ remaining antecedent factors $A_1 \wedge \ldots \wedge A_{i-1} \wedge A_{i+1} \wedge \ldots \wedge A_n$. Conditional correlations are essential for *causal analysis* (sec. 4.4).

The condition of statistical relevance can be generalized to statistical laws with disjunctive consequents of the form $p(C_1 \vee \ldots \vee C_m | A_1 \wedge \ldots \wedge A_n) = r$: here the condition demands that neither the antecedent conjuncts nor the consequent disjuncts can be deleted *salva probabilitate*.

In spite of the parallelism to the strict case, we finally mention a marked difference, which has to do with the fact that conditional probability $p(C|A)$ is *non-monotonic*. While in the strict case, the irrelevant universal sentence $\forall x(Ax \wedge \underline{Bx} \rightarrow Cx)$ has no additional information value over the relevant universal sentence $\forall x(Ax \rightarrow Cx)$, but rather follows logically from it, the irrelevant generalization in the probabilistic case, $p(Cx|Ax \wedge Bx) = r$, possesses *additional information value* over $p(Cx|Ax) = r$, because it does not follow from it, but expresses an independent fact. The irrelevant generalization does not give us any information about a new correlation, but rather information about the statistical *irrelevance* of a property B in regard to the given correlation between A and C. This information is always necessary, when we want to predict Ca for an individual a, for which both Aa and Ba are known—because according to the principle of the narrowest reference class (sec. 3.9.1), we must make sure for this purpose that conditionalization on B does not change the probability $p(C|A)$, i.e. that $p(C|A \wedge B) = p(C|A)$ holds. Of course, for any empirical prediction there are always a huge number of irrelevant features, and it makes no cognitive sense to *explicitly store* all irrelevance claims of this kind. Rather, such assumptions of irrelevance are generated *by default*, i.e. we make them as long as nothing speaks against the assumption of irrelevance. Non-monotonic probabilistic logic rests on this basic principle (see Goldszmidt/Pearl 1996; Schurz 2005a; Schurz/Thorn 2012). For example, in our basic biological knowledge of birds, apart from the normic law: "most birds can fly," we do not store an assumption of irrelevance for every irrelevant feature (large birds, small birds, male birds, female birds, etc.); rather, we store only a list of significant exception predicates, such as penguins, birds with broken wings, etc.

4.2 Testing of Strict Law Hypotheses for Truth and Relevance

In this and the next section we will deal with the question of how to test a law hypothesis for its possible truth and relevance. We assume that the size (N) of the respective domain of individuals is *large*, i.e. either potentially infinite, or larger by powers of ten than the limited size (n) of our empirical sample (N >> n). The test methods explained in sections 4.2 and 4.3 apply to unrestricted as well as spatiotemporally restricted generalizations, provided nothing is known about the domain that would undermine the application of induction (e.g. that the domain is too small or inhomogeneous). In addition, we assume that we are dealing with *empirical* law hypotheses, at least in the broader sense of empirical: so the truth of the law's antecedent and consequent predicates for empirically accessible individuals can be investigated *independently* of the law, for example by observation or measurement. Of particular importance to us is the fundamental *parallelism* of the testing procedure for the strict and the statistical case, which does exist, despite all the complications of the statistical case. There is hardly any literature in which hypothetico-deductive and statistical testing methods are explained in parallel; this is what we shall do in the next sections.

4.2.1 *The Method of Agreement and Difference*

The testing of a strict law hypothesis comprises two activities, which are called the method of agreement and difference, after the logician and philosopher John Stuart Mill (1865, vol. II, book III; Losee 2001, ch. X(a)). The method of agreement serves to test for truth or falseness, and so leads to the result of a falsification or confirmation of the strict law. The method of difference serves to test for relevance or irrelevance. Here, we test first for possible truth or falseness, and only when the hypothesis is confirmed, do we take the *second* step of testing for relevance. For in the strict case, only true law hypotheses can be relevant (see def. 4.1-1), while the question of relevance is superfluous for false law hypotheses. Let us consider an implicational law with two or more antecedent factors, e.g.:

(4.2-1) L: All solids (A_1) expand when heated (A_2).
Formally: $\forall x(A_1x \land A_2x \to Cx)$.

For the conjunction of both antecedent factors, we write Ax (= $A_1x \land A_2x$).

4.2.1.1 Method of Agreement

In order to find out whether the law hypothesis L is true or false, we examine a series of individuals $a_1,\ldots, a_n$ which verify the entire law antecedent A, so Aa_i is true for all a_i. A set of such individuals is called an *A-sample* (in statistics we speak of an "experimental" or "treatment group"). In our example, we are looking at a number of solid substances, which we heat up. We now examine for all individuals of the A-sample, whether they also possess the consequent property C of the law; in our example, whether the solid substances expand when heated. If they all do this, i.e. if our empirical examination verifies the sentence $Aa_i \land Ca_i$ for every examined individual a_i from the A-sample, then the law hypothesis has been *confirmed* by the A-sample. However, if even just one individual a_k exists in the A-sample which did not expand on being warmed, i.e. for which our observation led to the observation sentence $Aa_k \land \neg Ca_k$, then the law has been *strictly falsified*, because $Aa_k \land \neg Ca_k$ entails the negation of the law hypothesis, $\neg \forall x(Ax \to Cx)$. For strict law hypotheses then, the Popperian asymmetry of verification and falsification applies.

If the law hypothesis L is confirmed by the A-sample, we see L as provisionally *confirmed*, i.e. confirmed as long as no new falsifying evidence or samples become known. *Confirmed* then, always means *probably true given the current state of evidence*. Hence, statements of confirmation are always conditional (or two-placed): "L is confirmed by sample or evidence E." If we make an unconditional (one-placed) statement of confirmation "L is confirmed," we have to refer to the entire current observational knowledge—in other words, we apply Carnap's principle of the *total evidence* (see sec. 3.9.1).

Question: why do we use the A-sample method at all, and not instead use an arbitrary sample S ⊆ D and test whether all individuals a in S fulfill the material implication Aa → Ca? *Answer:* such a sample will as a rule consist predominantly of individuals a to which A does not apply (¬Aa): such individuals verify the implication Aa→Ca for *trivial* reasons and do not represent any genuine confirmation of the hypothesis. We would not say that the hypothesis "All ravens are black" is confirmed by a set of non-ravens, such as flowers or gorillas. Only A-samples yield *severe* tests in the sense of Popper (1935/2002, sec. X.82).

4.2.1.2 Method of Difference

Assume that the law hypothesis L is provisionally confirmed. In order to test whether it is also relevant, we arrange a so-called A_i-*control sample* for every antecedent factor A_i. This is a sample of individuals, to whom all antecedent factors *apart from* A_i apply (in statistics we speak of a "control group"). We test whether the individuals in this A_i-control sample still display the consequent feature C. If they *all* do, then the irrelevance of the antecedent factor A_i, and so the irrelevance of the law hypothesis, is provisionally confirmed. If, however, there is at least one individual in the A_i-control sample which does not display property C, then the relevance of the antecedent factor A_i is verified, *provided* the law hypothesis is true. In our example, in order to test the relevance of the antecedent factor "solid substance" (A_1), an A_1-control sample of non-solid substances, e.g. of liquids or gases must be examined, to determine whether they also expand when heated. If they all do this, then we may suppose that the factor "solid" is irrelevant for the heating-expansion hypothesis, i.e. that the heating-expansion hypothesis L holds for substances of any aggregate condition. To test the relevance of the second antecedent factor of heating (A_2), we have to check whether substances can expand "by themselves" without being heated; this is falsified by simple everyday knowledge, for which reason the relevance of the second antecedent factor is guaranteed. Note that an irrelevance claim for a strict law L is equivalent with the assertion of the truth of another (logically stronger) law L* and can therefore only be provisionally confirmed, while a relevance claim asserts the falseness of L* and is therefore verifiable, though only conditional on the assumption that L is true.

4.2.1.3 The representativity requirement in the strict case

The A-sample should "represent" the set of all A-individuals in the population D as well as possible. In the strict case, this representativity demand means the following: it is not so important to examine as *many* A-individuals as possible, but above all to examine A-individuals under as *strongly varying* circumstances as possible. This follows from the following line of thought: if there are indeed individuals which falsify the hypothesis $\forall x(Ax \to Cx)$, then these must differ from those individuals which verify the hypothesis in some *qualitative property*, which is the *reason* for this difference and has not yet been considered in the examination, but belongs to the "circumstances." So, if we vary the circumstances of our A-sample as strongly as possible, then we maximize our chance of finding falsifying individuals in the A-sample, should there be any. This thought makes use of the heuristic principle of *sufficient reason*. Leibniz viewed this principle as a metaphysical necessity. However, it is only generally valid in deterministic universes. In indeterministic universes, there are exceptions without any special reason. Nevertheless Leibniz's principle is very useful heuristically, as it helps us to proceed to causally relevant factors as quickly as possible.

The representativity requirement is another instance of what Popper meant by his demand for *severe* tests (Popper 1935/2002, sec. X.82). It would not be a severe test, if we only examined metals when testing our solid substance expansion hypothesis. As the hypothesis applies to any solid substance, we must test it for as many different kinds of solid substance as possible: e.g. also for crystalline, amorphous, or organic solids. Indeed, organic chemistry has discovered synthetic rubbery solids which contract when heated. In other words, the above law hypothesis has, strictly speaking, been falsified; it only applies to *most* solids. It also applies only to *most* liquids: here the famous exception is the so-called anomaly of water, which contracts slightly when heated from 0 to 4 °C. Only to *gases* does the hypothesis apply without exception, i.e. strictly. A *chemist* must therefore formulate the hypothesis as follows: most solid substances, all liquids apart from water, and all gases expand when heated.

This example makes it clear that after the falsification of a strict hypothesis, scientists do not reject this hypothesis without offering a replacement (cf. Lakatos 1970). Instead, scientists *replace* L with a minimal weakening of it, L*, which is *consistent* with the L-falsifying instances. This hypothesis is often generated by the following principle: if an instance of falsification of $\forall x(Ax \to Cx)$ with the additional property B has been found, then we suppose that the next best hypothesis is $\forall x(Ax \land \neg Bx \to Cx)$; thus we exclude the observed exceptions in the antecedent of the law. Prop. 4.2–1 summarizes our discussion.

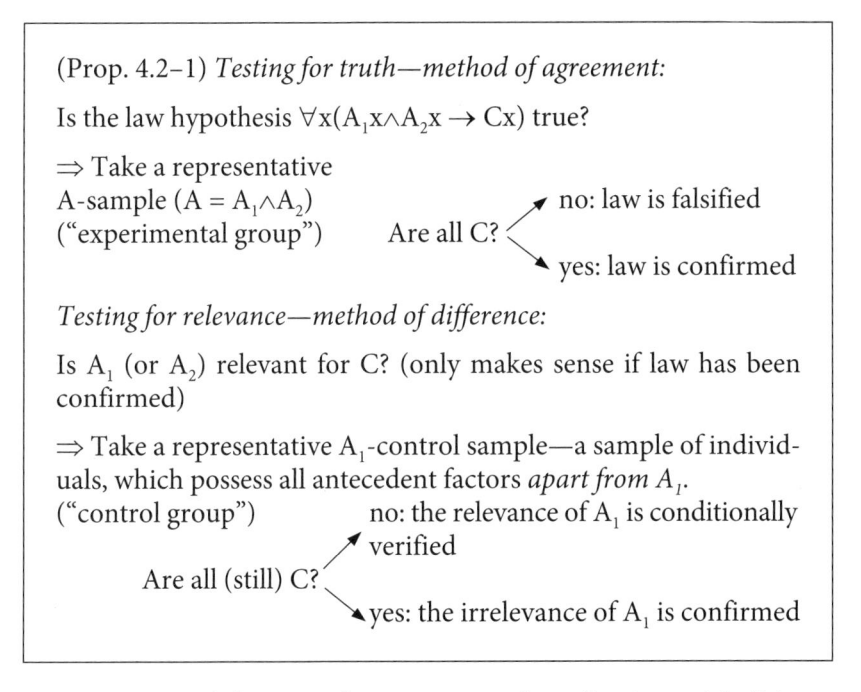

> (Prop. 4.2-1) *Testing for truth—method of agreement:*
>
> Is the law hypothesis $\forall x(A_1x \land A_2x \to Cx)$ true?
>
> $\Rightarrow$ Take a representative
> A-sample ($A = A_1 \land A_2$)
> ("experimental group")   Are all C?
>   no: law is falsified
>   yes: law is confirmed
>
> *Testing for relevance—method of difference:*
>
> Is A_1 (or A_2) relevant for C? (only makes sense if law has been confirmed)
>
> $\Rightarrow$ Take a representative A_1-control sample—a sample of individuals, which possess all antecedent factors *apart from A_1*.
> ("control group")   Are all (still) C?
>   no: the relevance of A_1 is conditionally verified
>   yes: the irrelevance of A_1 is confirmed

We can extend this procedure to universal implications with *disjunctive consequents*, for example $\forall x(Ax \to C_1x \lor C_2x)$, as follows: to test the relevance of the disjunctive component C_1 of $C_1 \lor C_2$, we examine whether all individuals from the A-sample also possess the stronger property C_2. If they do this, the irrelevance of C_1 is confirmed; if they do not, the relevance of C_1 is conditionally verified.

4.2.2 Methodical Induction: How to Discover Strict Law Hypotheses

If we test a *given* strict hypothesis, we *first* test its supposed truth and *then* its relevance. The situation is different when we *search* for an as yet unknown cause or law hypothesis for a known effect: in this case, both procedures take place *simultaneously*. A good example for the simultaneous application of the methods of agreement and difference is the discovery of the cause of puerperal fever by Semmelweiß (cf. Hempel 1966, ch. 1).

The situation: The number of mothers suffering from puerperal fever in the first delivery ward of the hospital where Semmelweiß was working in the year 1845 was unusually high. What was the cause of this alarming effect?

First set of hypotheses: At first it was asked whether poor standards of care, shortages of beds or meteorological influences could be the cause for the puerperal fever. But all these ideas could be refuted by Semmelweiß by drawing a comparison with the second delivery ward of his hospital—for here, there was virtually no puerperal fever, although the factors mentioned were also present. These hypotheses, then, were refuted by the method of agreement: the supposed causes were also present in the second delivery ward, but the puerperal fever did not occur there.

Second set of hypotheses: In the second delivery ward, in which there was no elevated occurrence of puerperal fever, Semmelweiß had his control group. Semmelweiß now began using the method of difference to look *systematically* for a causal factor which was present in the first ward but not in the second. Several factors were taken into consideration; for example, (a) in the first ward, women mainly gave birth in supine position, in the second mainly on their sides; and (b) in the first ward, the priest usually arrived later than in the second. Semmelweiß now ordered that everything be done in exactly the same way in the first ward as in the second, with the negative result that the puerperal fever in the first ward stayed just as high as before. These possible causes (delivery in supine position, late arrival of priest) were eliminated as irrelevant using the method of difference: the effect remained even when these factors were removed.

Third hypothesis, which was successful: In the first ward, medical students took part in the deliveries, who had previously been in the autopsy room and still had material from the corpses on their hands. This was not the case in the second ward. Was this the reason? Semmelweiß's instruction to the medicine students to wash their hands in chlorinated lime resulted in an immediate decrease in the rate of puerperal fever in the first ward down to normal levels. So this causal hypothesis was confirmed as *relevant* by the method of difference (as the removal of the cause made the effect disappear), and at the same time it was confirmed as *true* based on the fact that puerperal fever occurred, as long as the students in the first ward helped with deliveries after coming from the autopsy room without chemical hand-cleaning. The discovery of this empirical causal law by Semmelweiß was connected with an important innovation: the theory of the origination of illnesses via infectious substances, e.g. material from a corpse. This contributed significantly to the development of disinfectants and, in general, to the progress of bacteriological medicine.

We can summarize the method of discovering law hypotheses by the simultaneous application of the methods of agreement and difference as follows. Assume we observe an effect C with unknown causes in certain notable circumstances:

Step 1	Circumstances	Causes	Effect
Case group 1	A, B	???	C

Then we first look for a control group of cases, in which the effect C has not been observed, and list the notable circumstances:

Step 2	Circumstances	Causes	Effect
Case group 2 (control group)	A, ¬B	???	¬C

We now use the method of difference to suppose that those factors, in which the circumstances of the two case groups differ, are causes:

Step 3	Circumstances	Causes	Effect
First hypothesis	A	B	C

We now test the hypothesis by bringing in new B-cases (method of agreement). As long as no falsification results, the hypothesis is provisionally confirmed. If the hypothesis is falsified, we search for further antecedent factors which exclude the falsifying cases:

Step 4	Circumstances	Causes	Effect
Case group 3	A, D	B	¬C

Step 5	Circumstances	Causes	Effect
Second hypothesis	A	B∧¬D	C

This portrayal clearly shows the advantage of controlled experiments over mere observation as explained in sec. 2.4.3: the systematic search for relevant causes requires the *specific* variation of factors. If Semmelweiß had only ever observed what was happening in his hospital, instead of issuing instructions for hands to be washed in chlorinated lime, he might never have found the right factor. It is for this reason that it is so difficult to find the relevant factors in disciplines with little or no scope for experimentation, such as history, sociology and economics. So-called *paradigms* in these disciplines are often characterized by the fact that they regard some factors as relevant and exclude others as irrelevant in a theoretically prejudiced way. The Marxist paradigm, for example, told us that all fundamental causes of social conditions are economic ones. Such paradigms of relevance are necessary to initiate and focus the research in a given area, but as long as they are not subjected to any *critical test*, the paradigm must be viewed as ideologically laden.

4.3 Testing Statistical Laws

In the statistical case, we proceed analogously. Compared to the strict case, however, there are four differences: First, there is no strict falsification in the statistical case, rather only gradual weakening. Second, the question of where the boundary between confirmation or preliminary acceptance on the one hand, and disconfirmation or preliminary rejection on the other lies, depends on quantitative probability considerations. Third, the relevance test is no longer bound to the presence of a true population hypothesis, as here it is only being tested whether $p(C|A) \neq p(C)$ is true, independently of the knowledge of the true value of $p(C|A)$. *Fourth* and finally, the representativity of random samples is characterized differently.

Consider a simple statistical generalization with only one antecedent factor:

(4.3–1) L: 80% of all trees beside motorways (A) are sick (C).
$p(Cx|Ax) = 0.8$

We assume that the domain of individuals to which this law refers—the so-called *population*—is the set of all trees in Central Europe between 2005 and 2010, and moreover, that the predicates "beside motorways" and "sick" are operationalized in sufficiently precise manner. Here too, the test has two steps: testing for (likely) truth, and testing for relevance.

4.3.1 Testing for Likely Truth and Acceptance Intervals

Analogously to the method of agreement in the strict case, we test the law hypothesis $p(C|A) = 80\%$, by choosing a representative sample of A-individuals (the A-sample), and examining how many of these individuals possess the consequent feature C. So we choose, let us say, 100 trees from beside randomly selected stretches of motorway, and investigate whether they display symptoms of sickness. Suppose that 75 out of 100 trees in our sample are sick: is this a confirmation or a disconfirmation of our law hypothesis of 80%? More generally put: how do we infer from the measured sample frequency $f_n(C|A)$ to the plausibility of the hypothesis about the frequency in the population $p(C|A)$? *Notation*: from now on, $f_n(C)$ and $f_n(C|A)$ denote the *relative* frequency of property C in an n-element random sample, and in an n-element random sample of A-individuals, respectively.

It is not to be expected that frequencies in a sample and in the population will correspond *exactly* to each other—this is extremely improbable, due to the random variation of samples. Therefore, there is no strict falsification in the statistical case. The question of whether a hypothesis is being confirmed or disconfirmed cannot now be resolved qualitatively, but requires a quantitative calculation. The standard statistical procedure for this is the method of *acceptance and rejection intervals*, which goes back to Fisher (1956).[2] It is possible to calculate the statistical probability that the frequency $f_n(C|A)$ of an n-element random sample lies within a certain interval of values (e.g. between 78% and 82%), *given* that the hypothesis $p(C|A) = 80\%$ is true in the given population. This calculation is based on the binomial distribution in the discrete case and on the Gaussian distribution in the continuous case (sec. 4.6). In our example we calculate: provided that 80% of all A's in the population are C's, there is a 95% probability of the absolute frequency of C in a 100-element A-sample being situated in the interval between 72 and 88. The pragmatically selected probability value of 95% is called the *acceptance coefficient*, and its complementary value of 5% the significance coefficient. The interval between 72 and 88 of 100 is called the *acceptance interval* for the given hypothesis with an acceptance coefficient of 95% (or significance coefficient of 5%).

Fig. 4.3–1 schematically depicts the probability distribution of the frequencies of 100-element A-samples from a population of A-individuals with $p(C|A) = 0.8$ and with the acceptance interval marked.

The most probable sample frequency coincides, as we can see, with the population frequency. Left and right of this, the expected probability

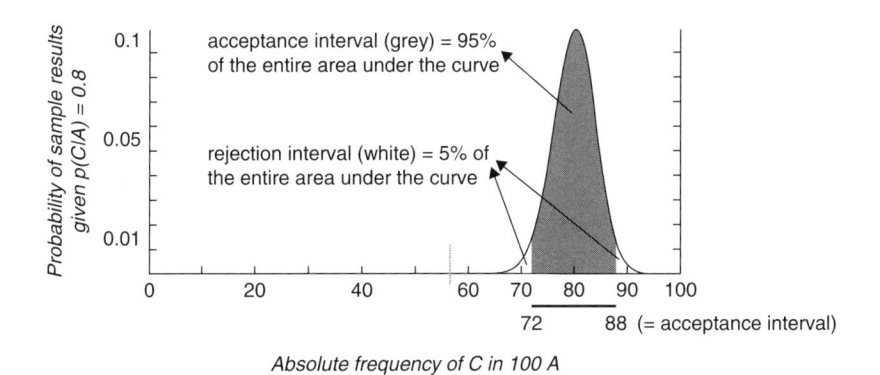

Figure 4.3–1 Acceptance interval for $p(C|A) = 0.8$ (computed with MatLab)

sinks almost symmetrically. (*Note:* exact symmetry would only occur at a population frequency of 50%.) If we approximate the discrete possible frequency values 0, 1/100,..., 99/100, 1 using a continuous variable, then the size of the area in a particular interval under the curve corresponds to the probability of finding the sample frequency within this interval. Thus, the entire area under the distribution curve is 1, and the gray area beneath the curve in the acceptance interval between 72 and 88 takes up exactly 95% of the total area. To either side of the acceptance interval lies the *rejection interval*, with 5% of total area. If the sample frequency lies within the acceptance interval of the hypothesis, then the hypothesis is seen as *weakly confirmed*, and is *retained*. On the other hand, if the sample frequency is outside the acceptance interval, i.e. in the rejection interval, then the hypothesis is *strongly disconfirmed* or is *rejected*. Our sample result of 75 out of 100 is within the acceptance interval; so we conclude: the hypothesis $p(C|A) = 0.8$ is accepted on the basis of the sample result $f_{100}(C|A) = 75/100$ with an acceptance coefficient of 95%. If the result had been 70 out of 100, then we would have rejected the hypothesis with a significance coefficient of 5%. A rejection with a significance coefficient of 5% is called "significant" and of 1% as "highly significant." The general definition of acceptance interval is as follows:

(Def. 4.3–1) *Acceptance interval* = the (symmetrical) interval of the most probable sample frequencies in which the sample frequency is located with a probability equal to the acceptance coefficient, given that the law hypothesis being tested is true.

It should be stressed that the acceptance coefficient of 95% is chosen pragmatically, but not at random. If we choose a coefficient which is too large, e.g. 99.5%, then the acceptance interval becomes too wide, and too few hypotheses are rejected. If it is too small, e.g. 50%, then the rejection interval will become too wide, and the disconfirmation in the negative case is not strong enough. If we approximate the binomial distribution through the normal distribution (which is legitimate for sample sizes > 30), then the acceptance intervals are given by the formulas in (4.3–2) below. Here, "p±r" stands for the interval "[p–r, p+r]," and $\sigma_s = \frac{\sigma}{\sqrt{n}}$ (with $\sigma =_{def} \sqrt{p \cdot (1-p)}$) is the *standard deviation* of the sample frequencies; this is, roughly speaking, the average difference between the frequencies in random samples and the true population probability (see sec. 4.6):

(4.3–2)
Acceptance coeff.   Acceptance interval   Example for p = 0.8, n = 100:

99.5%:	$p \pm 2.8 \cdot \sigma_s$	[0.69, 0.91]
95%:	$p \pm 1.96 \cdot \sigma_s$	[0.72, 0.88]
70%:	$p \pm 1.03 \cdot \sigma_s$	[0.76, 0.84]

As can be seen from the formulas, for fixed acceptance coefficients the width of acceptance intervals is determined as a certain multiple of σ_s, which is in turn inversely proportional to the square root of the size of the sample. So the acceptance interval grows ever *narrower* as samples get larger: the larger the samples, the *sharper* our 95%-probable predictions for the expected sample value. At the same time the σ_s-formula implies a tendency of *falling yields*: a quadrupling of the sample will lead only to a halving of the acceptance interval, etc. Here are some 95% acceptance intervals for various sample sizes n:

(4.3–3)
Acceptance intervals for p = 0.8 (acceptance coeff. = 0.95) for varying n:

n =   1: [0, 1]   n =   50: [0.69, 0.91]   n = 1,600: [0.78, 0.82]
n = 10: [0.56, 1]   n = 100: [0.72, 0.88]   n = 10,000: [0.79, 0.81]
n = 20: [0.63, 0.97] n = 400: [0.76, 0.84]

In the case of one-layered investigations, in which the sample does not need to be subdivided, sample sizes of larger than 50 are usually regarded as large; samples should not be smaller than 15 or 20. Moreover, when the hypothetical population probability is close to 0 or 1, the sample sizes chosen must be large enough that the acceptance interval limits come to lie properly between 0 and 1 (in the above example, this becomes the case only if $n \geq 20$). Note that the size of the total population is by itself of no importance for questions of sample size; the only requirement is that it be substantially (at least 100 times) larger than the sample size (Bortz 1985, 112).

4.3.2 Discovery of Statistical Hypotheses and Confidence Intervals

The hypothesis $p(C|A) = 0.8$ is only *weakly* confirmed by the sample result $f_{100}(C|A) = 0.75$. This is the case because all alternative statistical hypotheses that assert the probability value $p(C|A)$ to lie somewhere in the interval 0.75 ± 0.08 would also be weakly confirmed and retained with a sample result of f_{100} (C|A) = 0.75, if they were due for testing. For all these hypotheses the sample result lies within their 95%-acceptance interval. The interval of all hypothetical population probabilities, for which the given sample result lies within their 95% acceptance interval, is known as the *confidence interval* of the hypothetical population probability; instead of an acceptance coefficient, we now speak of a *confidence coefficient* of 95%.

The method of *confidence intervals* goes back to Fisher and Neyman (Neyman 1937; Bortz 1985, 132; Hays/Winkler 1970, 328f). If f is the sample frequency, and r the hypothetical population probability, then we have the following mathematical relationship between acceptance intervals (drawn around r) and confidence intervals (drawn around f):

$$f \in [r-a, r+a] \quad \text{iff} \quad r \in [f-a, f+a].$$

So, we get the confidence interval by placing the acceptance interval ±a symmetrically around f (instead of around r). Fig. 4.3–2 makes this relationship clear. The confidence interval corresponds to the statistical interval hypothesis p(C|A) ∈ [f–a, f+a], which states in our example: *between 67 and 83% of all trees beside motorways are sick*. It is this *confidence interval hypothesis* which is *strongly confirmed* by the sample result f_{100}(C|A) = 75% (with a confidence coefficient of 95%). If we are interested in predicting narrow confidence intervals, then the sample chosen must be correspondingly large.

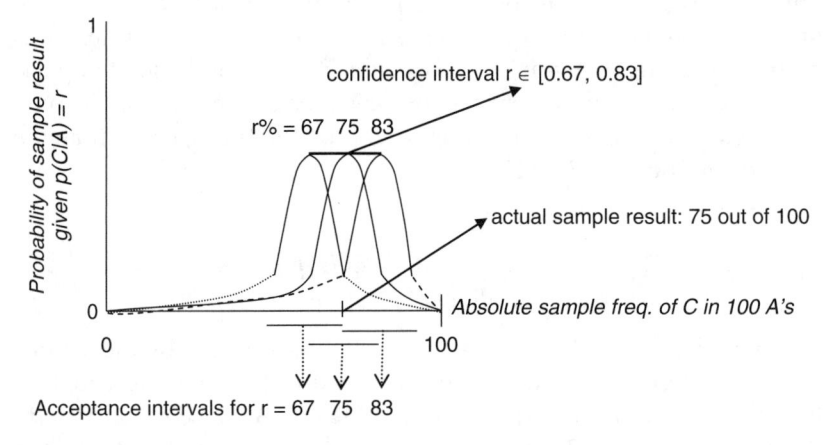

Figure 4.3–2 Relationship between acceptance and confidence interval

4.3.3 Testing for Relevance and Significant Differences

In order to test whether the property A is relevant for C, we compare—analogously to the method of difference in the strict case—the frequency of C in an A-sample with the frequency of C in an A-control sample. The A-control sample consists of a set of individuals which do *not* possess property A (alternatively it could also consist of a random sample of D-individuals with random proportions of A- and ¬A-individuals). In our example, 75 out of 100 trees beside motorways were sick. Suppose we now take an A-control sample of 100 trees, from wooded areas *not* located anywhere near a motorway, and find that in it, only 60 trees are sick. Does this mean that the proximity to motorways raises the probability of trees becoming sick, or could the discrepancy between the A-sample and the A-control sample, which is 15 out of 100, just have been coincidental? Once again, this is a *quantitative* question and, as above, we use an interval method. One can calculate the probability that the discrepancy between the A-sample and the A-control sample was purely coincidental—i.e. that this sample-discrepancy occurred although there is no statistical correlation in the population between A and C: $p(C|A) = p(C|\neg A)$. This irrelevance hypothesis is also called the *null* hypothesis. The *alternative hypothesis* to it is the relevance hypothesis, which states that there is a statistical relationship in the population between A and C: $p(C|A) \neq p(C|\neg A)$.

The probability distribution of the frequency *differences* of two samples with sizes n_1, n_2 from the *same* population takes the form of a binomial distribution with the mean value 0 and the standard deviation $\sigma \cdot \sqrt{\frac{1}{n_1} + \frac{1}{n_2}}$ (Bortz 1985, 166f). Using this information we can calculate the symmetrical 95%-interval of the most probable positive or negative sample differences. This 95%-interval figures as the acceptance interval for the irrelevance hypothesis (null hypothesis), and the two-sided extreme 5%-interval of the least probable sample differences serves as the acceptance interval of the relevance hypothesis (alternative hypothesis). The absolute amount of the maximum frequency difference that lies within the 95% acceptance interval is called the *significant difference*, and the coefficient of 5% is called the *significance coefficient*. See Fig. 4.3-3.

If the sample difference actually found is higher than the significant difference, then the irrelevance (or null) hypothesis is rejected and the relevance hypothesis is accepted. In this case, the probability of finding a sample difference as large as the one actually found, assuming

194 • Philosophy of Science

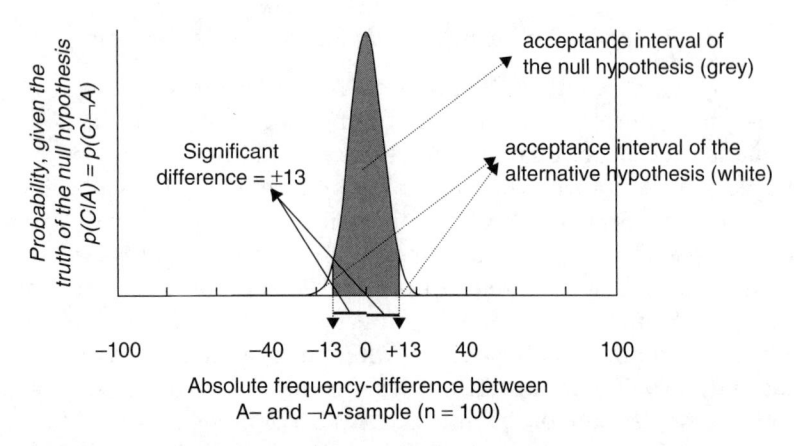

Figure 4.3–3 Probability distribution of sample differences and significant difference

> (Def. 4.3–2) *Significant difference* = the threshold which is exceeded by the difference between the A-sample frequency and A-control sample frequency of C with a probability that is equal to the significance coefficient, under the assumption that the null hypothesis is true (i.e. there is no statistical relationship between A and C in the population).

the irrelevance hypothesis is true, is smaller than the significance coefficient of 5%; so the irrelevance hypothesis is *strongly disconfirmed* and the relevance hypothesis is *strongly confirmed*. We say in this case that there is a *significant* correlation between A and C. If the sample difference is positive, i.e. if A leads to a raised frequency of C, then the significant correlation is positive; if the sample difference is negative, then the correlation is negative. If the sample difference found, however, is smaller than the significant difference, then the irrelevance hypothesis continues to be accepted. In our example (assuming an approximately normal distribution) we calculate a significant difference of 13 out of 100; hence the difference found, 15 out of 100, is significant.

The same procedure can also be applied to differently chosen significance coefficients. A 1% significant difference is called "highly significant." One often mentions the significance coefficient at which the measured difference is *just about* significant. In our example, the measured difference of 0.13 is just about significant at a coefficient of 2.5%, which means that the probability of finding a sample difference of ≥ 15, given the null hypothesis is true, is 2.5%.

(Prop. 4.3–1) summarizes the test methods for statistical laws.

(Prop. 4.3–1) *Testing the statistical law hypothesis p(C|A) = 80%*

Testing for Truth—Method of Acceptance and Confidence Intervals:
⇒ Take an A-sample: e.g. 100 As. Found: e.g. 75 Cs.
⇒ Choose the acceptance coefficient: e.g. 95%.
From sample size (n=100) and acceptance coefficient (95%) calculate the
⇒ acceptance interval: in our case: 72 – 88 Cs out of 100 As.

Is the A-sample frequency of C within the acceptance interval?
- No: law is strongly disconfirmed
- Yes: law is weakly confirmed

⇒ What has been strongly confirmed is the (weaker) confidence interval law, which for the given sample result is: 67% ≤ p(C|A) ≤ 83%.

Testing for Relevance—Method of Significant Difference:
⇒ Take an A-control sample: e.g. 100 ¬As. Found: e.g. 60 Cs.
⇒ Choose the significance coefficient: e.g. 5%.
From the sample size (n=100) and significance coefficient (5%) calculate the
⇒ significant difference: in our case 13 out of 100.

Is the actual difference between the A-sample frequency of C and the A-control sample frequency of C larger than the significant difference?
- No: Relevance of A for C is strongly disconfirmed
- Yes: Relevance of A for C is strongly confirmed: ⇒ *significant correlation*
  - positive difference: correlation positive
  - negative difference: correlation negative

In a relevance test, the alternative hypothesis is the negation of the null hypothesis. Therefore, the former is strongly confirmed exactly when the latter is strongly disconfirmed. This is different from truth testing, where the given hypothesis p(C|A)=r has a potentially infinite number of alternative hypotheses of the form p(C|A)=r* ≠ r. The above relevance test is also called a *two-sided* test, because positive and negative differences are taken into account. If one knows from the beginning that factor A can only have a one-sided effect (if any) on C's frequency, then one applies a *one-sided* test, in which the one-sided extreme 5%-interval is chosen as a rejection interval.

Once again, the *relative* significant difference (in our example 0.13) decreases in proportionality with the square root of the sample size. Any relative sample difference, no matter how small, becomes significant when the sample size chosen is sufficiently large. The claim that a significant correlation has been found between two features A and C is therefore a very *weak* claim, as long as we have no information about the sample size. It tells us only that *some*, possibly very small correlation exists between A and C. In particular, a highly significant correlation does not necessarily mean that the correlation itself is very high, but only that there is a very *high probability* of a statistical connection between A and C, no matter how small it may be. This is often confused in popular accounts of statistical results. If it is reported, let us say, that medical scientists have observed a significant connection between eating *sausage* and *cancer*—to name but one of many possible examples—then this will be taken to be a sensational result, regardless of the fact that the connection might well be negligibly small. It is therefore very important when providing information about the existence of a significant correlation to inform the audience also about the presumable strength of the correlation. A suitable measure of correlation strength is the expected frequency difference in the population, which we estimate using the observed sample difference. If we divide this frequency difference by σ, we get the *effect strength* as mentioned in sec. 4.1.2.

The test of statistical relevance is generalized to law hypotheses with several conjunctive antecedent factors $p(C|A_1 \wedge \ldots \wedge A_n)$ by applying the procedure to every antecedent conjunct A_i: one prepares an A_i-control sample and tests the frequency difference between the A-sample and the A_i-control sample for significant difference.

4.3.4 Statistical Representativity

In the statistical case, the representativity requirement demands not only that the individuals examined be as varied as possible, as in the strict case.

It states more specifically that all other factors which are relevant for the consequent predicate C, apart from A, must have an approximately *equal* frequency distribution in the sample as in the population as a whole. In our example, this would include other factors apart from car exhaust which make trees sick, e.g. industrial pollution or attacks by parasites.

It is usually said that the representativity of a sample is a *prerequisite* for an inductive generalization from the sample to the population. In this respect, however, it is essential to distinguish between the *definition* and the (uncertain) *criteria* of statistical representativity. According to the standard definition, a sample is representative if all relevant properties are distributed in it as they are distributed in the population (Bortz 1985, 113). The assumption that a sample is representative in this sense is based on an inductive inference and therefore *cannot* be required as a prerequisite of an inductive inference, because that would be circular. Rather, the decisive role is played by the criteria for representativity whose satisfaction can be guaranteed by sampling methods independently of inductive assumptions: only these criteria can be required as a prerequisite for inductive inferences (cf. Campbell/Franklin 2004, 84).

The criteria for representativity describe *methods* for generating representative samples. The most important method is *random sampling*—this method can be recommended when little or nothing is known about the distribution of the other properties in the population. A sample is random *in the narrow sense (i.n.s.)* when a random selection procedure is being used, which gives every individual in the population the same chance of being selected into the sample. Of course, random samples might differ *at random* from the population as a whole, but the probability distribution of their random variation is statistically calculable—a fact that forms the basis of the statistical methods explained above.

A random selection procedure i.n.s. requires that all individuals in the population are accessible and have been recorded in some way—e.g. using card files or lists of names, from which blind samples are then taken at random. This definition is both *unnecessarily* narrow and *too* narrow. Too narrow, because it is usually not realizable. In our example, we would have trouble numbering every Central European tree near a motorway, then pulling 100 numbers out of a huge drum. Unnecessarily narrow, because it is sufficient to apply an equal-chance sampling procedure to a manageable *subpopulation* of individuals which, according to our knowledge, deviates from the population only in regard to *irrelevant* properties: if this is the case, then we speak of a random sample i.w.s. (in the wide sense). In other words, it is only necessary that the selection procedure does not skew the distribution of *relevant* properties (see Mayntz et al. 1976, 67f).

The notion of a random sample i.w.s. is also useful in another respect. It rebuts an occasionally heard argument against the testing of statistical hypotheses about *infinite* populations: i.e. that it is impossible to take random samples from countably infinite populations, because any selection operation must be limited to a finite part of the population (Spielman 1977). This argument is not applicable to the broad definition of a random sample. Consider a coin-tossing experiment with the hypothesis p = 1/2. If I test this hypothesis *today*, then only the coin tosses of the present day have a chance of being included in my sample, but not the coin tosses in the more distant future. But we can justifiably assume that the mere *point in time* of the coin toss is a statistically irrelevant property, and therefore our finite sample is still random i.w.s.

If the distribution of the relevant properties in the population is known, then instead of a random sample, we can also take a so-called *stratified* sample, in order to reach representativity. For example, if we want to assess the consumption habits of the average German citizen, then we can assume that factors such as the urban–rural divide, age, family size, and gender will influence consumer behavior, and we are well advised to take a *proportionally stratified* sample: for each relevant property F we put as many randomly drawn F-individuals into the sample as are needed for the F-sample-frequency to match the F-population frequency (see Mayntz et al. 1976, 84ff; Howson/Urbach 1996, 247–252).

4.3.5 Test Statistics and Inference Statistics

Acceptance (or rejection) intervals are *sample intervals*; confidence intervals on the other hand are *hypothesis intervals* (see Hays/Winkler 1970, 383). Acceptance intervals are part of so-called *test statistics*, which is concerned with testing *given* hypotheses that already have some plausibility. Confidence intervals, on the other hand, are part of what is called *inference statistics*, which is concerned with finding the most plausible hypotheses based on a given sample result. In the practice of statistics, these two types of problems are often not sharply distinguishable from each other: even if we already possess certain hypotheses, which we subject to an acceptance interval test, we are still interested in hypotheses that are as well confirmed as possible, and so we are also interested in their confidence intervals.

Inductive inferences are used in the procedures of both inference statistics and test statistics. According to the distinction made in sec. 2.7.2, however, the difference is as follows: in pure test statistics, only the *epistemic* induction principle is used, in the sense that so-far successful hypotheses are retained, and only unsuccessful hypotheses rejected. In inference statistics, on the other hand, we use a *methodological* induction procedure, which uses sample findings to give us the 95%-interval of all the most plausible hypotheses.

Fisher's test theory is sometimes called *quasi-falsificationist*, because it gives us methodological rules, which tell us whether to reject or retain a given hypothesis, based on observed sample results (Howson/Urbach 1996, 174). The difference between this and a *real* falsification is, of course, that the rejection of the hypothesis as assumedly false is only valid with a certain probability, and therefore always *preliminary* in nature; and likewise preliminary is its acceptance as "assumedly true." Popper (1935/2002, ch. II, 68) and Gillies (2002, 148f) regard Fisher's rejection as a "methodological falsification rule," and Popper suggested embedding statistical test theory into his falsificationist account by regarding extremely improbable results as practically impossible or "prohibited." But as Howson and Urbach point out, this way of speaking is not really justified, as improbable events occur all the time (e.g. the exact distribution of alleles in a newborn baby).

Some authors (e.g. Stegmüller 1969ff, vol. IV.2, 142f; Howson/Urbach 1996, 203) criticize the statistical test theory because it limits one's epistemic decisions to acceptance versus rejection. This criticism applies to some but not to all interpretations of statistical test theory. For example, Hays/Winkler (1970, 399f) include the option of *suspending judgment* in their test theory alongside the options of acceptance and rejection—e.g. by using the central 66%-interval as the acceptance interval, the extreme 5%-interval as the rejection interval, and the interval in between as the abstaining interval.

It is important to remain aware that the concept of statistical probability can only be used to calculate the probability of sample results given certain population hypotheses, but never the probability of the population hypotheses themselves. Statistical probabilities are based on repeatable random experiments, and taking samples from a population is a repeatable random experiment. In contrast, the entire population or "actual world" exists only *once*: it possesses no statistical probability, because there are no random sequences of "possible worlds" (see also Hays/Winkler 1970, 328; Howson/Urbach 1996, 239f). The probabilities of population hypotheses are of an epistemic or subjective nature, and so belong in the area of *epistemic* probability theory. For this reason, it would be a confusion to read the result of the confidence interval method as follows: there is a 95% probability of the population frequency being within the given confidence interval. In fact, what the confidence interval method says is: for all hypotheses in the confidence interval, the actual sample result is within their 95% acceptance interval.

In all statistical test and inference procedures then, the following is happening: the strength of the statistical probability of the sample result E given a statistical hypothesis H, p(E|H), is used as an indicator for the plausibility or epistemic probability of the hypothesis H given the sample result E, P(H|E). In sec. 4.7 I call this approach the *likelihood-intuition*, because the statistical probability p(E|H) is called the *likelihood* of the hypothesis (given E). In this advanced section several objections against standard methods of test and inference statistics that have been raised by Bayesians will be discussed. In accordance with my dualistic probability account I will try to show that these methods are well justified, but for a full justification of them one needs epistemic probabilities.

4.3.6 Sources of Error in Statistical Methods

Statistical methods should be applied *sensitively*. They contain many sources of error. These can be divided into two main groups: (1) sources of errors in *testing*, and (2) sources of errors in *interpreting* statistical hypotheses. Sources of errors in interpretation are, above all, of two kinds: statistical hypotheses are often applied too hastily to *individual cases*, and they are often interpreted too hastily as *causal*; and both of these are, however, only legitimate under specific circumstances. We will deal with these sources of error in interpretation in sec. 4.3.7 and 4.4. In this section we will look at sources of error in testing statistical hypotheses.

The testing of a statistical hypothesis of the form $p(C|A) = r \neq p(C|\neg A)$ is based on three preconditions: (1) the A-sample should be as representative as possible, (2) there must exist an A-control sample, and this too should be as representative as possible, and (3) A-sample and A-control sample should be similar with respect to all C-relevant features that are not effects of A.

Examples of error sources of representativity:

a   An impromptu survey on a political topic is conducted by telephone, using only land lines. This way, however, we do not reach those members of the younger generation who only use mobile phones. The sample is not representative.
b   A psychologist does an experiment on forms of partnerships. She places an advertisement in the newspaper. Test persons make contact. But what kind of person responds to such an ad? If the payment of the test persons is not very good (which is mostly the case), then the sample will contain only those who are interested in psy-

chological reflections and engagement. The sample is not likely to be representative.

c A sociologist sends out a questionnaire to discover more about how much housework is done by women. Twenty percent of questionnaires are returned. Which women fill out the questionnaire and send it back? Possibly those with a higher standard of education or an interest in political matters—and certainly the ones who have less housework to do. The sample is not representative.

d *Omission of negative cases:* a very drastic error of representativity occurs when the cases which go contrary to one's own theory are simply left out. This error is to be found not only in ideological writings, but also in cases where scientific test results are deliberately manipulated, e.g. under financial pressure or for career reasons.

e *Publication bias:* Ioannidis (2005) found that failures of representativity occur frequently in contemporary empirical studies in medicine, even if they are rigorously designed. The reason for this fact lies in two *publication biases* which the scientific "career" system brings with it: (1) the *positivity* bias: null results rarely get published in journals; (2) the *sensation* bias: new effects have the highest chance of being published, but most new effects are weak and the risk of confounding random effects with significant results is high. The good news of Ioannidis' study is that every time a research result is replicated, the probability of error drops. The general conclusion is that scientists are better off if they cooperate, i.e. try to replicate each other's experiments, instead of only "hunting for sensations."

Examples of error sources in the control group:

f *Control group missing:* A frequent error in non-scientific interpretations of experience is that a comparison with a control group is completely absent. For example, most reports about the success of esoteric healers lack tests based on control groups. If some people's health improves noticeably after the use of a "healing pendulum," this tells us very little, as we do not know (i) whether the improvement in health would have happened *without* the pendulum, as a result of normal healing processes, (ii) whether a *placebo* effect was at play (strong faith in the power of healing can at times lead to an accelerated improvement in health), or (iii) whether the healer has given the person other instructions, for example to live a more healthy lifestyle, which he did not mention in his report ("hidden variables"), but which were really the effective factors. All of these possibilities can only be excluded by means of control groups.

There have been similar examples in science. Huff (1954, 40) reported the following example: a polio vaccine was tested on 100 children in one village, in which the polio virus occurred shortly after the vaccinations. Not a single child became ill, and this was interpreted as a spectacular success. In fact, the children who had not been vaccinated also did not become ill—since polio rarely leads to diagnosable symptoms. Today, advanced control group comparisons are common practice in testing the effects of pharmaceutical medicines. So-called *double blind tests* are carried out, in which one randomly chosen half of the test persons (tps) are given real medicine, while the other half is given fake pills, and neither the patients nor the persons carrying out the tests know which pills are real and which ones are placebos. All known forms of comparative distortion of experimental and control group are thereby excluded, modulo random errors.

g *Lack of similarity:* The similarity between a (random) A-sample and an A-control sample—their comparison is called a *quasi-experiment*—can only be guaranteed in respect to those factors which are *statistically independent* of A. This fact forms the basis of non-causal correlations which are discussed in the next section. As we shall see there, the similarity of the two samples with respect to all features that are *not effects* of A can only be reached by a *randomized experiment*. But even in that case, *hidden variables* could find their way into the A-sample and lead to a distortion of comparability. An example: a new teaching method is to be compared with a traditional method, by comparing the results attained by two groups of pupils, of which one is taught with the new method, and the other with the traditional one. But were the teachers in each group equally good? Also: could it be that the teachers using the new method were more motivated to teach well than their colleagues using the old method? And: did the pupils know about the experiment and, given this knowledge, were they better motivated as a result? All these possible factors could lead to distortions of comparability, and to *false* hypotheses about the success of the new teaching method.

h Also the problem of possible *interactions* between experimenter and tp falls into the category of hidden variables. As Huff (1954, 22f) reports, a survey on the political rights of black people turned up very different results, depending on whether a black or white person was the interviewer. Another well-known distortion effect is the so-called *Rosenthal effect*, in which the evaluation of the result of an experiment depends on the preconceptions of the experimenter.

Rosenthal and Jacobson (1968) had students evaluate a group of pupils regarding their achievements in a test as successful or not successful. Some of the students were told beforehand that they were highly gifted pupils, whereas others were told that they were particularly weak pupils. In fact, as had been ascertained in a preliminary exam, the pupils in both groups had the same level of giftedness. The experimenters who had been given the information "highly gifted" evaluated the pupils significantly more positively than the ones who had been given the information "particularly weak."

There are always methods of neutralizing these sources of error as effectively as possible—one must simply make the *effort* to apply these methods. Interactions between experimenters and tps can be prevented by means of anonymous surveys. The most generally effective method, as mentioned, is the *double blind experiment*, in which neither experimenter nor tp knows who belongs to the experimental group and who to the control group.

4.3.7 *Applying Statistical Hypotheses to Individual Cases*

The non-monotonicity of conditional probabilities (fig. 3.9–1) results, in comparison to strict hypotheses, in a decisive difference concerning the application of statistical hypotheses for the purpose of predicting or explaining individual cases. The conclusion Ca of a deductive inference with true premises $\forall x(Ax \rightarrow Cx)$ and Aa may be *detached* from its premises, in the sense that we can reason from the truth of the premises to the truth of the conclusion, without having to consider what *else* true. However, given the premises $p(Cx|Ax) = 90\%$ and Aa of an inductive-statistical specialization inference, we may only infer to Ca with a belief probability of 0.9 if the condition of the *narrowest reference class* (sec. 3.9.1) is guaranteed: i.e. the antecedent information Aa encompasses all statistically relevant information for Ca about the individual a in question. Because even if $p(Cx|Ax)$ is high, $p(Cx|Ax \wedge A^*x)$ could be low, and if both A and A^* are applicable to the individual a in question, then only the narrower predicate $A \wedge A^*$ may be used as an antecedent predicate for a prognosis about the individual a. For example, penicillin (A) will cure a heavy cold in most people (C), but for people who are allergic to antibiotics (A^*), the use of penicillin is fatal.

This context has drastic consequences for *practical applications* of statistical information (see Schurz 2004, sec. 2). For example, if statistical studies show that a given teaching method is advantageous in 80% of all cases, and we then apply this knowledge to pupil Peter, we must first check whether more specific information is available which might undermine the probability value of the statistical law. For example, it could be that the new teaching method is only advantageous for those pupils with a visual learning style, who constitute 80% of all pupils, but that Peter happens to have an auditory learning style, making him part of the remaining 20%. The application of the law to Peter would then not only be illegitimate; it would damage, rather than help his education. With this in mind, let anybody *applying* statistical theories be warned against using them too hastily in individual cases, without first having thoroughly checked whether these individual cases display further relevant characteristics which change the probability and give us a quite different picture. If a statistical study shows, for example, that children growing up in the country are happier overall than those in cities, and are less likely to be emotionally disturbed, this still does not mean that we should advise Mr. and Mrs. Jones to move with their children out to the country, even if they can afford to do so, without first checking which further consequences such a move might have in the specific case of their children. It could be, for instance, that the long-term damage to their children's friendships and social lives is so grave that moving to the country does them more harm than good, no matter how idyllic their surroundings. In particular, let politicians be warned against the over-hasty conversion of statistical findings about the majority of the population into laws which are binding for all.

4.4 Correlation and Causality

Let us assume that two properties, A and B, share a significant and a sufficiently high correlation. Such a correlation may be used to make probabilistic predictions. We cannot directly conclude from this, however, that there is also a *causal relationship* between A and B, for two reasons: first, because the correlation may have arisen because of hidden variables, and second, because correlations are symmetric and do not inform us about the direction of a causal relationship. We will base our following consideration on a weak probabilistic understanding of a "cause": we call an event A a cause of another event B, if A is *some* causally contributing factor which raises the probability B, but A need not be the total cause of B, i.e. the set of all factors causally relevant to B.

4.4.1 Hidden Variables

A high positive correlation corr(A,B) may be a so-called "spurious" correlation: in such cases, there is no causal relationship at all between A and B, but rather both properties are the result of a hidden *common cause* C, and the correlation between A and B arises only as a result of the causal relationships C→B and C→A. Rather than speak of a "spurious correlation" (which is a frequently used name; cf. Simon 1954), we prefer to call this situation a *spurious causality*, as the correlation does really exist in this case, and the only spurious thing is the posited causal relationship between A and B. The situation is graphically depicted in fig. 4.4–1. Observe that causal relationships (→) are *directional*, going from cause to effect; while mere correlations (- - -) are without direction, i.e. symmetric.

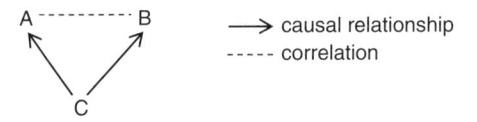

Figure 4.4–1 C is a common cause of A and B

The existence of a correlation between A and B can be explained as follows: because correlations are symmetric, the occurrence of effect A also raises the probability that its cause C has occurred. At the same time C raises the probability of its effect B (and A is irrelevant for this, hence the correlations are transitive). So, the presence of A increases the probability of B. Here are some *examples:*

(4.4–1) There is a high correlation between an abrupt drop in barometer readings (A) and an approaching storm (B) (Grünbaum 1963, 309f).

As the brewing storm occurs *after* the drop in the barometer, one could think the drop was itself the cause of the approaching storm. This is, of course, nonsense: actually, both events are caused by a third event C, i.e. an abrupt drop in atmospheric pressure.

(4.4–2) A high positive correlation was measured between the mental health of workers (A) and their positive attitudes to the employer (B).

Does this mean that those workers who constantly moan about their company do so because they have psychological problems which they project on to the company, while the company is quite innocent? Statistical analysis of hidden variables showed a different picture. It turned out that both properties were the joint effect of a hidden common cause:

stress in the workplace (C). Workers with worse conditions complained more about the company, and at the same time, their mental health suffered as they were subjected to ongoing stress at work. This example comes from Lazarsfeld (see Mayntz et al. 1976, 193f) and refers to a study carried out in the 1950s.

A well-known statistics joke is the myth of the stork that brings children. There is indeed a positive correlation between the frequency of storks and newborn humans. This non-causal correlation has its common cause in the variable *rural versus urban area*: more children are born in the country, and there are more storks there too.

There is a well-known statistical method for uncovering non-causal correlations, which goes back to Reichenbach (1956, 159) (cf. Salmon 1984, 159f; Hitchcock 2010, sec. 2.3). If the correlation between A and B is resulting from a common cause C, then this correlation disappears when the values of the variable C are *fixed*: so in the case of binary variables, if we take only individuals which possess the property C, then the additional presence of B no longer increases the probability of A; and analogously so when we take only individuals which do not possess the property C. In our example (4.4–2): if we study only those employees working under good conditions, then the correlation between their attitude to the company and their mental health should disappear; and the same should happen when we study only those working under poor conditions. This prognosis was indeed confirmed.

Reichenbach made the following suggestion on how to characterize common causes using purely statistical conditions, which he called the condition of *screening-off* (i.e. the variable ±C screens off A from the probabilistic influence of B):

(Prop. 4.4–1) *Reichenbach conditions for screening-off (indicating common causes)*

1   $p(A|B \wedge C) = p(A|C)$ }   C and ¬C screen A off from B
2   $p(A|B \wedge \neg C) = p(A|\neg C)$ }   or: A is screened off from B by ±C

3   $p(A|C) > p(A)$ }   C is positively relevant for both
4   $p(B|C) > p(B)$ }   A and B

From (1)–(4) follows (5): $p(A|B) > p(A)$, i.e. B correlates positively with A (the proof was explained above; see Reichenbach 1956, 160).

Reichenbach chose the conjunctive formulation: (1') p(A∧B|C) = p(A|C)·p(B|C), (2') p(A∧B|¬C) = p(A|¬C)·p(B|¬C), (3') p(A∧C) > p(A)·p(C), (4') p(B∧C) > p(B)·(C), which under the assumption p(B∧¬C), p(B∧C) > 0 is equivalent to the conditions in prop. 4.4–1. The conjunctive formulation makes it clear that screening-off is symmetrical, in the sense that ±C screens A off from B iff ±C screens B off from A.

One problem with Reichenbach's conditions for screening-off lies in the fact that they cannot be used to distinguish between a common cause and an *intermediate* cause—in either case, all criteria of prop. 4.4–1 are met (see fig. 4.4–2). In the latter case, C functions as a mediating cause between A and B: C is the direct effect of A and direct cause of B. Intermediate causes are also called "intervening variables" (cf. Lazarsfeld 1955); we prefer the name "intermediate" because "intervening" is ambiguous.

```
A----------B              A----------B
 ↖        ↗                 ↘        ↗
   ↘    ↙                      ↘   ↙
      C                           ↓
                                  C
(common cause)            (intermediate cause)
```

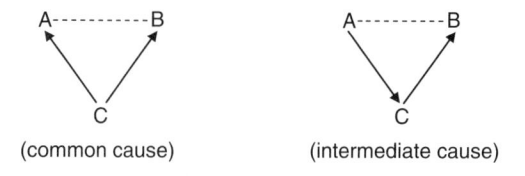

Figure 4.4–2 Common cause vs. intermediate cause

Direct causes screen off their effects from indirect causes in the sense of Reichenbach. Therefore, the two cases are probabilistically *indistinguishable*, although they are causally different: when C is an intermediate cause, A is an *indirect* cause of B, but not so when C is a common cause. Which of the two cases is present can only be determined using supplementary causal information, e.g. via an *experiment* (see below), or by using background knowledge about the *causal direction*, which in the common cause case goes from C to A, but in the intermediate cause case goes from A to C. An *example*:

(4.4–3) A high correlation was measured between the marital status of professional women (A = married) and the frequency of their absence from work (B).

So, are married women lazier? Not at all: as it turns out the mediating variable here is the amount of extra housework to be done (C). A leads to a high level of C = extra housework, and therefore, married women are more frequently absent from work (high B). This insight changes our interpretation of the example in one fell swoop: married women are not more frequently absent from work because they work less, but because they work more (the example comes from Zeisel; see Mayntz et al. 1976, 196f).

Reichenbach's conditions of common cause are enormously useful in statistical practice, since they can confirm or falsify causal hypotheses. This is illustrated by the following example from Cartwright (1979; see Eells 1991, 62f). In an American university, it was observed that the proportion of female applicants (= F) accepted to the university (= A) was lower than for male students (based on an entrance exam). The following causal hypotheses were posited, and falsified by examining background variables:

- *1st hypothesis:* Women are less intelligent and therefore less likely to pass the entrance exam. For this hypothesis to be true, the correlations would have to disappear when IQ scores are kept constant. In other words, were we to compare women and men of equal intelligence, then we must observe no further difference between the two in terms of university places offered. In fact, however, corr(A,F| IQ=constant) was once again negative. The intelligence quotient was thus eliminated as an intermediate cause.
- *2nd hypothesis:* The university system prefers male applicants. This is a typical case of a macrosociological hypothesis which is difficult to examine, as the variable of the "patriarchal" preference structure of the university can hardly be experimentally varied. Nevertheless, a further piece of statistical information showed that this variable was also not the cause of the correlation, because:
- *3rd hypothesis:* It was observed that women, compared to men, tended to apply for places in more popular subjects (e.g. psychology or languages), i.e. those subjects in which a higher demand leads to stricter entrance exams and lower acceptance rates. When the variable of course of studies was kept constant, the correlation between gender and successful applications disappeared completely—i.e. in each individual course of study, there was no longer any difference between the proportion of successful male and female applicants. So, the choice of *course of studies* turned out to be the intermediate variable, and the case was cleared up: women more frequently tend to apply for oversubscribed courses, which is the cause for the lower number of successful applications.

In spite of their practical usefulness, Reichenbach's conditions have a number of problems. Apart from the statistical indistinguishability between common and intermediate causes, these are the following:

a   Reichenbach's screening-off conditions do not exclude the possibility that the correlations between C and B or between C and A are themselves of a *pseudocausal* nature, i.e. come into being through a further common cause D or E. To exclude this possibility, one must either examine all further relevant background parameters (which requires a high amount of background knowledge), or one introduces the putative cause in a randomized experiment (see beow) and sees whether the putative effect still follows.
b   In *deterministic* situations, where all conditional and inversely conditional probabilities are 1 or close to 1, Reichenbach's conditions provide inadequate results (cf. Otte's 1981 criticism of Suppes 1970): here Reichenbach's conditions would lead to the false conclusion that not only ±C screens off A from B, but also ±B screens off C from A, and ±A screens off C from B.

It is a deep question in the philosophy of science, whether and to what extent causal relationships can be reduced to empirically testable relationships such as statistical correlations. It might be asked why one would want to attempt this. These attempts are inspired by the great challenge of David Hume (1748/2006, 82ff): Hume argued that behind our claims of causality there is nothing more than the observation of regularities, i.e. regularly repeated successions of events (recall sec. 1.2). Any claim of causality which goes beyond this, according to Hume, is metaphysical ballast without empirical content. Today there is broad agreement among philosophers of science that claims of causality are not simply reducible to strict or statistical correlations (as Hume's analysis implies)—they are *more* than this. The problem for philosophers of science is to describe this *more* in terms of scientific criteria, without becoming embroiled in metaphysical speculations. Reichenbach's criterion of screening-off is *one* suggestion in this direction. More in sec. 6.7.

We will now explain why *randomized experiments* can exclude spurious causality claims modulo random errors. In this kind of experiment, a sample of individuals is *divided at random* into two samples, and not until after this division is one group (the experimental group) exposed to factor A by way of an active manipulation, while factor A does not occur in the other group, the control group (or if it does, then only with random frequency). After this, the frequency of B in the experiment group, $f_e(B) =_{def} f_e(B|A)$, is compared with the conditional frequency $f_c(B)$ in the control group. All remaining factors (C, D, …), which are not causal effects of A, are now statistically *evenly* distributed in the experiment and control groups apart from random errors, since the groups were divided up at random. The manipulation which brings about A is also called an *intervention* (see sec. 6.7.6; Pearl 2009, 23; Woodward 2003, 98).

Should the correlation between A and B in the population be the result of some (possibly unknown) common cause C, then a random experiment cannot lead to a correlation between A and B. Based on the Reichenbach conditions (prop. 4.4–1) (3,4), it must then hold that:

i $f_e(B|C) \approx f_c(B|C)$ and $f_e(B|\neg C) \approx f_c(B|\neg C)$,
since A has no causal influence on B when the value of C is kept constant (here $\approx$ stands for "approximately the same, modulo random errors"). Moreover, since C is not an effect of A (only the other way around), C must be equally frequent in the experiment and the control group, modulo random errors, i.e. it must hold:
ii $f_e(C) \approx f_c(C)$ and $f_e(\neg C) \approx f_c(\neg C)$.
By the law of multiplication (TC4 of prop. 3.9–3), we have:
iii $f_e(B) = f_e(B|C) \cdot f_e(C) + f_e(B|\neg C) \cdot f_e(\neg C)$
iv $f_c(B) = f_c(B|C) \cdot f_c(C) + f_c(B|\neg C) \cdot f_c(\neg C)$

By substituting the approximate equivalences i and ii in the equations iii and iv, we obtain the proclaimed result $f_e(B) \approx f_c(B)$.

In conclusion, a randomized experiment is causally much more conclusive than a statistical survey (a quasi-experiment), because it can empirically demonstrate, modulo random errors, that there exists a causal relationship that leads from A to B. This does not yet show whether this causal relationship is direct or indirect. Also, the "infiltration" of variables which are unknown effects of the intervention can only be excluded given sufficient background knowledge about the experimental setup.

We finally mention that, beyond spurious causality, there is also the case of *spurious causal independence* and of *spurious negative causality*: here, we first measure a zero correlation or a negative correlation between A and B, but when we conditionalize on fixed values of a background variable ±C, then both in the case of C and of ¬C we measure a positive correlation between A and B. This prima facie "paradoxical" situation has the following qualitative explanation, illustrated in fig. 4.4–3:

Figure 4.4–3 Spurious causal independence: corr(A,B) = 0, but corr(A,B|±C) > 0

A has a *direct* positive causal influence on B, but an *indirect* negative causal influence on B, since A simultaneously activates the factor C, which is a counter cause of B. In the case of a spurious causal independence, these probabilistic effects *compensate* for each other, producing a result of exactly *zero*. However, if we conditionalize on C or ¬C, the causal arrow from A to C becomes ineffective, and the positive causal arrow from A to B leads to a positive correlation; i.e. we have p(B|A∧C) > p(B|C) and p(B|A∧¬C) > p(B|¬C), although p(B|A) = p(B).

(4.4–4) *Example of spurious causal independence* (after van Fraassen 1980, 149): in a group of middle-aged men one cannot find a correlation between smokers (S) and cardiovascular illnesses (C), because smokers, to compensate for their habit, take much more exercise (E) than non-smokers. If one studies only those people who take plenty of exercise, or only those who do not, then both subgroups turn up a positive correlation between S and C.

If the indirect negative effect of A on B is stronger than the direct positive effect, then p(B|A) < p(B) and simultaneously p(B|A∧C) > p(B|C) and p(B|A∧¬C) > p(B|¬C) are the case. I call this *spurious negative causality*. Cases of spurious causal independence and negative causality are summarized under the term *Simpson-Paradox* (Cartwright 1983, 24; Hitchcock 2010, sec. 2.5).

4.4.2 Causal Direction

Even in the (rather unrealistic) situation in which we know that apart from A and B, there are *no* further hidden variables at play, we cannot derive a causal hypothesis directly from the presence of a high correlation between A and B, as the correlation does not yet inform us about the causal *direction*—it is not yet determined what is the cause and what the effect. The reason for this is that correlations are symmetrical. So, if there is a positive correlation between two characteristics A and B, without this being attributable to common causes, then there are two simple and one complex causal possibility: either A is a cause of B, or B is a cause of A, or A and B are affecting each other in the form of causal feedback (see fig. 4.4–4). We should note that in cases of causal circularity, the causal relationship does not become symmetrical, but retains its direction: the causal process leading from A to B is, in such cases, *different* from the one leading from B to A.[3]

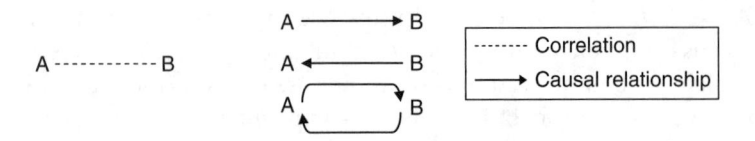

Figure 4.4–4 What is the direction of causality?

Here are some examples taken from actual studies:

(4.4–5) High IQ and high social status correlate positively.

The decisive question is: what is the cause here, and what is the effect? Is IQ a product of upbringing and education, which depends on one's social status? Or does the person who discovered the correlation have a genetic elite in mind? Or is there a causal feedback between IQ and social status? Obviously, this correlation's relevance to our world view depends on the hypothesis of causal direction, which can by no means be gleaned from the correlation alone.

(4.4–6) Aggressive people like watching violent films.

This result is well known. The important question is, though: do people become aggressive and tendentially violent as a result of watching violent films? Or do aggressive people enjoy watching violent films because it acts as a form of compensatory psychological mechanism? Again, the normative political relevance depends on our understanding of the causal direction: in the former case, watching violent films should be prevented; in the latter case, it should be tolerated, or even encouraged.

On encountering such examples, we quickly tend to spot in the correlation a causal direction which corresponds to *our own* way of seeing things. A real scientific position can only consist in reserved judgment about the causal direction, unless we are able to offer additional reasons for the causal direction. Such reasons can, for example, result from scientific background knowledge about causal *mechanisms*. In the case of relationships between temporally distinct events, the earlier event must be the cause of the later one, since causal relationships are temporally *forward*-directed. This gets more difficult when we look at temporally coexistent dispositional features without a specific chronological location, such as in the examples (4.4–5) and (4.4–6). In such cases, we have to find out which is the *independent* and which the *dependent* variable, or whether any feedback exists. In some cases the direction of causation between coexistent dispositional features is clear because of background knowledge, e.g.:

(4.4–7) Gender correlates with certain gender-specific features.

(4.4–8) Air pollution correlates with the frequency of respiratory illnesses.

In example (4.4–7) the gender must be the cause and not vice versa, because it is biologically determined. In example (4.4–8), it is known that the causal process can only move from air pollution to respiratory illness, not the other way around. In examples (4.4–5) and (4.4–6), however, the causal direction is quite unclear, assuming there is any causal relationship at all, and the correlation does not result from a common cause. As a final example of a false interpretation of the causal direction, we mention the case of the banker John Law, who concluded from the correlation between the amount of paper money in circulation and the wealth of France, that the wealth of France could be raised by introducing large amounts of unsecured paper money into circulation. This led to the collapse of the French financial system in 1720.

Especially in the (mass) media it frequently happens that statistical correlations are interpreted all too quickly as causal findings, often with "sensational" value. Here are some *examples:*

1   A long period of breastfeeding lowers the risk of breast cancer in women (from the Austrian newspaper "Österreichische Krone," 23.7.2002). Is there a causal connection? Or is it simply the case that some women, for genetic reasons, are both able to breastfeed for longer and have a lower risk of breast cancer?

2   It was reported a few years ago that having frequent skin contact (with other people) correlates with a stronger immune system. This leads to the question: is there a direct causal connection, or is it just that healthier people with strong immune systems have a stronger sex drive and so tend to be more focused on physical contact?

3   Women who jog a lot have a lower bone density (from the Austrian newspaper "Salzburger Nachrichten," 3.2.2003). Are we really to believe that frequent jogging reduces bone density? Or could it just be that people whose bones are less dense for genetic reasons are usually also better at running, and so go running more often?

4   Men who eat a lot of chocolate are gentler and have better social skills (Bavarian television 27.2.2003). Is there really a causal connection here, and if so, in which direction? Or is there not a

common cause, perhaps a genetically determined character trait, which is responsible for both gentleness and the drive to eat sweet things? Are we to be so stupid as to derive from this correlation that men should eat more chocolate?—this would just raise their cholesterol and lower their life expectancy.

The list could go on. Of course, causal interpretations of correlations are not always subjective; they may be well justified. There are laborious methods of testing more closely whether, and in which direction there is a causal connection—for example, by randomized experiments, and in particular by means of *longitudinal studies*. Most studies, however, are *cross-sectional* studies based on information collected at one point in time, and often enough unjustified conclusions about causal relationships are drawn, which motivate politicians to take measures that have an effect quite different from the one intended.

COMPLEMENTARY AND ADVANCED TOPICS

4.5 Ceteris Paribus Laws and Normic Laws

4.5.1 Comparative versus Exclusive CP Laws

Philosophers of science have repeatedly pointed out that most law statements, especially those in the non-physical sciences, do not express strict exceptionless laws. Rather, they express so-called ceteris paribus laws, in short CP laws.[4] The scientific "dignity" of CP laws, however, is controversial: they have been accused of being trivial, immune to testing, or accidental (cf. Earman et al. 2002; Reutlinger et al. 2011).

Schurz (2002b) argues that in regard to their status as genuine laws, one has to distinguish between *comparative* ceteris paribus laws (cCP for short) and *exclusive* ceteris paribus laws (eCP for short). A cCP clause understands "ceteris paribus" in the *literal* sense of *all others being equal*:

(Prop. 4.5–1) *A comparative CP law "cCP A leads to C" means:*

A leads to C when all *other* (relevant) factors which are not effects of A—*whatever* these factors are—remain *unchanged* in two compared situations S_1 and S_2. Thereby "A" and "C" assert that two corresponding variables X_A and X_C have increased (or decreased) their value in S_2 compared to S_1.

Examples:

(4.5–1) cCp an increase of the total force leads to proportionally increased acceleration.

(4.5–2) cCp more rain leads to better growth of green plants.

The phrase "whatever these factors are" is an implicit 2nd order *universal* quantification over possible remaining factors. The phrase "remain unchanged" makes clear that cCP laws are always comparative, i.e. refer to two compared situations. In the philosophical debate, however, CP laws have more often been understood in the exclusive sense. An eCP clause understands "ceteris paribus" as *all others being right* (see Cartwright 1983, 45), or equivalently as *no wrong (disturbing) factors are present* (cf. Pietroski/Rey 1995, or Joseph 1980, who speaks of "ceteris absentibus" clauses). The second formulation underlies the name "exclusive" CP clauses in Schurz (2002b). More precisely:

> (Prop. 4.5–2) *An exclusive CP assertion ("law") "eCP A leads to B" means:*
>
> A leads to B when all *other* factors which are not effects of A are *right*, i.e. there *exists* a range of admissible factor-constellations to which they belong.

Examples:

(4.5–3) eCP if a match is struck it will light.

(4.5–4) eCP a bird can fly.

In distinction to a cCP law, an eCP "law" contains a 2nd order *existential* quantification. As we shall see, it is therefore dubious whether eCP assertions can be regarded as lawlike: on this reason I prefer to speak of eCP assertions.

In some cases the range of admissible factors for an eCP assertion can be fully specified and the existential clause replaced by an explicit description of them, *salva veritate*. Such eCP clauses are called "lazy" by Earman/Roberts (1999) and "definite" by Schurz (2002b, sec. 3). Lazy eCP laws are philosophically harmless: I do not count them as proper eCP assertions, because they are equivalent to ordinary laws. In the example (4.5-3) from physics, it may be possible (though quite complicated) to replace the eCP clause by definite conditions (concerning the match's chemical composition, its temperature, etc.). In the example (4.5-4) from biology, however, a specification of all factors which must be present and absent to enable the bird's flying, seems to be altogether impossible. So (4.5-4) is a proper eCP assertion.

cCP laws may also be constrained by added conditions. While (4.5-1) is an example of an unrestricted cCP law, example (4.5-2) holds only under the restriction that the amount of rain per day does not exceed a certain threshold. A restricted cCP law still counts as a cCP law, as long as its restriction is *definite*. Sometimes cCP clauses are in the range of an *indefinite* restriction, as in the following example:

(4.5-5) eCP (i.e. if disturbing factors are excluded), an increase in demand leads cCP to an increase in price.

In (4.5-5) the cCP clause lies in the scope of an eCP clause. Therefore we count (4.5-5) not as a restricted cCP law, but as an eCP assertion.

Schurz (2013c) reconstructs cCP and eCP assertions by means of (statistical) *variables* (recall sec. 3.1.4). In what follows, X is the antecedent, Y the consequent variable, and boldface **Z** denotes the set of *remainder* variables which are *not effects* of X, with lower-case letters **z** ranging over sequences of *values* of **Z**-variables.

(Prop. 4.5-3)

a   A cCP law asserts that *for all* **Z**-values **z** (possibly subject to a definite restriction): an X-increase leads to a (probable) Y-increase, *provided* the **Z**-variables stay at value **z**.

b   An eCP "law" asserts that *for some* **Z**-value **z** (possibly subject to a definite restriction): a particular X-value x [or an X-increase] leads (probably) to a particular Y-value y [or to a Y-increase, respectively], *provided* the **Z**-variables stay at value **z**.

The square brackets in b make clear that eCP assertions can have either a non-comparative or a comparative form.

According to Cartwright (1989, 145f), Strevens (2013) and Schurz (2013c), the importance of CP laws lies in providing *causal* information. Both cCP and eCP assertions express the existence of a correlation, *conditional* on *fixed* values of the remainder variables. We know from the analysis of screening-off in sec. 4.4.1, that such conditionalization excludes non-causal correlations between X and Y which result from a common cause Z. The exclusion of X-effects from the Z-variables is necessary, because X-effects which mediate between X and Y would screen off X from Y; but mediating variables must be admitted. That CP laws make a causal assertion is indicated by the word "leads" in prop. 4.5–3.[5]

(Prop. 4.5–3) makes the universal nature of cCP laws and the existential nature of eCP assertions plain. Following from this logical difference, the *content* of a cCP law is *strong*, while that of an eCP assertion is *weak*. An eCP assertion entails a causal *relevance* claim, since prop. (4.5–3b) entails that under some circumstances **z**, the Y-value is an effect of the given X-value *and* **z**, but not of **z** alone. This relevance condition corresponds to Fodor's *completer* account of eCP assertions (1991, 23). Schurz (2002b, 361) shows that if eCP assertions are formulated without such a relevance condition, they are vacuous.

The logical difference between cCP and eCP laws has significant consequences for their *testability*. Following from their universal nature, it is hard to confirm and easy to disconfirm cCP laws, and following from their existential nature, it is easy to confirm and hard to disconfirm eCP assertions. The standard method of testing a cCP law is a *randomized experiment* as explained in sec. 4.4.1: one splits a sample of individuals (satisfying given restrictions) randomly into two samples s_1 and s_2. Then one increases by intervention the X-value of all s_1-members, and compares Y's mean value (μ) in s_1 with that in s_2. If $\mu_{s_1}(Y)$ is *not* increased compared to $\mu_{s_2}(Y)$, the cCP law is disconfirmed. On the other hand, if $\mu_{s_1}(Y)$ *is* increased, the cCP law is still not fully confirmed. What has been confirmed in this case is that an X-increase leads to a Y-increase *when* the Z-values in the two compared samples are similarly distributed as in the population from which the samples were taken. I call such a cCP law a *population-restricted* cCP law.

A population-restricted cCP law is weaker than an unrestricted cCP law. Population-restricted cCP laws are confirmable without causal background knowledge. This is different for non-population-restricted cCP laws. In order to confirm them, one has to perform a random experiment for a representative class of possible variations of X- and Z-values. This presupposes at least some background knowledge about the remainder variables in **Z**.

eCP assertions can also be tested by a random experiment. For comparative eCP assertions (square brackets in prop. 4.5–3b), the experiment is exactly as above. For non-comparative eCP assertions, s_1 is a sample of individuals whose X-value is x, s_2 a sample with X-values different from x, and a positive outcome is an increased probability of Y=y in s_1

compared to s_2. Because of the switch of the universal with an existential quantifier, we have a dual situation. A positive outcome of the random experiment confirms the eCP assertion, since in that case there is *some* (unknown) value-constellation **z** under which X had a positive influence on Y. This confirmation does not presuppose any causal background knowledge about **Z**. On the other hand, if the outcome is negative, *nothing* can be inferred about the probable falsehood of the eCP assertion, since the **Z**-values in the domain from which samples s have been drawn might not have been the "right" one. Only if causal background knowledge provides procedures by which one can vary the **Z**-values in a representative way, can one refute the eCP assertion, by obtaining a negative outcome in all of the variations of X- and **Z**-values.

I finally turn to the question whether eCP assertions can be regarded as "laws." The problem with this view is that one can easily find eCP "laws" with the same antecedent but opposite consequents. Here is an example:

(4.5–6) *True eCP "laws" with opposite consequents:*

a   eCP if I look to the right I see a kangaroo.
Here the admissible constellations of remainder factors require that there is a kangaroo to my right side.

b   eCP if I look to the right I do not see a kangaroo.
Here the admissible constellations of remainder factors require that there is no kangaroo to my right side.

I do not see how one can escape the conclusion that both eCP "laws" are true. In both cases we have the same causal mechanism of "seeing," and the result of this mechanism (variable Y) depends on the direction of my gaze (variable X) as well as on the light-reflecting objects in the direction of my gaze (variable Z). Depending on the fixed value of Z, I either see a kangaroo or not. If these eCP "laws" do not count, then eCP laws such as (4.5–3) "eCP if the match is struck it will light" also do not count.

I think this result clearly shows that eCP "laws" cannot be conceived as lawlike, in the wide sense of supporting counterfactuals (recall sec. 3.6). The two counterfactuals "this would be a C, if it were an A" and "this would not be a C, if it were an A" cannot possibly be simultaneously true. This points to the second deficiency of eCP "laws": they may express completely accidental coincidences, such as "eCP if I look to the right, I see a kangaroo." Third, if A can lead both to C and to non-C, then these eCP "laws" cannot be used to make predictions.

4.5.2 Normic Laws and Their Evolution-Theoretic Foundation

A possible way out of the problem of accidentality is to interpret an eCP "law" as saying that A leads to C if the remainder variables are in a value-range which is *normal* in respect to the antecedent property A. Schurz (2002b) calls this the *normic* interpretation of eCP assertions:

(Prop. 4.5–4) *Normic interpretation of eCP laws:*

eCP A *leads to* C means: *Normally* A *leads to* C.
More precisely: A leads to C for constellations of remainder variables **Z** which lie in their *normal* range in regard to A.

Examples:
(4.5–7) *Normally* birds can fly.

(4.5–8) *Normally* electric installations work.

According to prop. 4.5–4, normic eCP laws assert a *universal* quantification over the normal **Z**-values. So normic eCP laws—in short: *normic* laws—are more similar to ordinary laws. The decisive question for the normic account is: how can one discriminate the normal from the non-normal constellations of the remainder factors? A proposal which gives normic laws statistically testable content is to assume that normality implies *high statistical majority*. This account has been defended by Earman and Roberts (1999), and in an evolution-theoretic version by Schurz (2001; 2002b, 365f). On this interpretation, normic laws entail ordinary statistical laws of the form $p(C|A) \geq t$, where t is a context-dependent "statistical normality" threshold greater than 0.5.

Normic law hypotheses were discovered in the 1950s, when philosophers of science investigated the applicability of the deductive-nomological model of explanation to the social sciences and the humanities (see sec. 6.4; the name "normic" was introduced by Scriven 1959a). At that time, the dominant strand of opinion was that normic generalizations were without empirical content, because they could not be falsified by counter-examples (see Dray 1957, 132; Scriven 1959a). This (Popperian) view was given up when philosophers of science looked more closely at the nature of statistical hypotheses. They are also not falsifiable by individual counter-examples, but nevertheless have empirical content, as they may be *gradually disconfirmed* by significantly divergent statistical samples. Similarly, normic generalizations can be gradually disconfirmed when exceptions gain the upper hand.

Hüttemann/Reutlinger (2013, sec. 5) have argued against the statistical majority account by pointing to an objection of Cartwright (1983, 45): in many cases of eCP "laws" in physics, the supposedly "normal" case describes an especially simple situation which is the statistical *minority*. They consider the following example:

(4.5-9) eCP a physical body continues its state of uniform motion.

In this example, the eCP clause refers to a situation in which the total force exerted on the physical body is zero. In the real world this is a minority case. Indeed, a statistical reading of (4.5-9) would be misconceived. But obviously, this eCP clause is a lazy one: it can be replaced by a definite theoretical description, saying that the sum of all forces acting on the given body is zero (relative to an assumedly complete classification of forces).

Schurz (2002b, sec. 6.2) argues that in almost all cases of eCP "laws" of physics, the eCP clause is replaceable by a definite theoretical description. However, the situation is radically different in the *special* sciences which deal with "living" or evolutionary systems: here it is usually impossible to turn the eCP clause into a definite description of admissible factor-constellations.

But here, a crucial feature of evolutionary systems comes to the rescue: they are known to exhibit a certain *normal* behavior. The *evolutionary normal* range of states and traits of evolutionary systems is that range which has been continuously selected in the evolution of these systems and their ancestors. According to the basic argument of Schurz (2001), the reason that these evolutionary normal traits are also *statistically normal*, at least in most phases of evolution, is that their maintenance is necessary for the *survival* and *reproductive success* of the individuals of the given species or evolutionary system. It is necessary for these systems to be in their normal states in the high majority of cases and times, for otherwise they could not have survived in evolution and would have become extinct.

In conclusion, Schurz (2002b) argues that as a rule, the interpretation of eCP laws as normic laws is *inadequate* for idealized systems of physical sciences, but *adequate* for evolutionary systems of the special sciences.

Note that what we have presented here was just an oversimplified sketch of the evolution-theoretic account of normic laws. For example,

Schurz (2001) does not claim that all, but only that *many*, properties of evolutionary systems are "normic" in the sense of being the result of a sustainable selection in one direction. Typically the normic properties of evolutionary species are not actual states but *capacities*: for example, almost all organisms have the capacity to reproduce, but they perform this capacity only a few times in their life (cf. Millikan 1984, 4f). Moreover, Schurz (2001) bases his account on the *generalized* theory of evolution, according to which the transmission of cultural traits (so-called "memes") forms a second level of evolution, superposed on the evolution of genes (cf. Mesoudi et al. 2006). This allows him to apply the account also to normic laws in non-biological disciplines such as in example (4.5-8).

4.6 Probability Distributions for Continuous Variables

Mathematically, a probability function p is constituted by a probability *distribution* function p: $V \rightarrow [0,1]$ over a subset $V \subseteq \mathbb{R}$ of the real numbers, which figures as possibility space Ω. Thereby, V is the set of *values* of a (statistical) variable X: $D \rightarrow V$, which assigns to each individual x in the domain D its value $X(x) \in V$. X is called a *random variable* (Bauer 1996, sec. 9, 27; Hays/Winkler 1970, 103ff). An example of X would be the *weight* of persons in a population D. If the variable X(x) can take only finite or countably many values in $\mathbb{R}$ (e.g. weight in pounds *rounded*), then one calls p a *discrete* probability distribution. If X(x) can take all values of some interval $[a,b] = \{r \in \mathbb{R}: a \leq r \leq b\}$ of real numbers, then p is a *continuous* probability distribution—a so-called *probability density* distribution d(x) (see below). In what follows we use "p(r)" as an abbreviation of "p(X(x)=r)," i.e. the probability that variable X takes value r in population D, and "p([a,b])" as an abbreviation of "$p(X(x) \in [a,b])$," i.e. the probability that X's value lies between a and b.

In sec. 3.13.2 we introduced the most fundamental discrete distribution of statistics: the binomial distribution. Now we consider the most fundamental continuous probability distribution, the normal (or Gaussian) distribution p(r) or d(r), displayed in fig. 4.6-1.

Continuous distributions have the following peculiarity in comparison to discrete distributions: the probability that a quantitative variable takes exactly one of uncountably many real values (i.e. a real value with infinite precision) is typically *zero*. What is practically interesting is the probability of non-vanishing intervals $[r_1,r_2] \subseteq \mathbb{R}$ (e.g. p(140±0.5 pounds); these interval probabilities are typically positive. Therefore one cannot represent a continuous distribution by the probabilities p(r) of real numbers, for this would yield a trivial zero line. What one uses

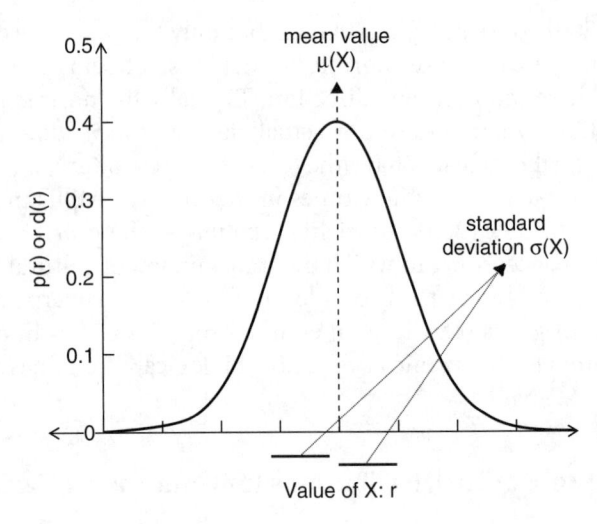

Figure 4.6–1 Normal distribution

instead is the so-called probability *density*. The probability to find the X-value in an interval [a,b] is defined by the *integral* of the probability density d(r) over this interval, written as in (4.6–1b):

(4.6–1)
(a) *Discrete case:* (b) *Continuous case:*

$$p([a,b]) = \Sigma_{a \leq x \leq b}\, p(x) \qquad p([a,b]) = \int_a^b d(r)\, dr$$

In the discrete case the integral is replaced by the sum-operation (4.6–1a). So the integral generalizes the sum-operation to the continuous case. *Graphically*, the integral in (4.6–1b) corresponds to the *area* under the d(r)-curve for X-values from a to b. Thereby total area under the d(r)-curve, from $-\infty$ to $+\infty$, is normalized to 1 = p(V).

By means of equations (4.6–1) one extends the distribution function over V to a probability *measure* p: AL→[0,1] over a suitable algebra AL over V, which in the discrete case is typically identified with V's powerset, and in the continuous case with the *Borel-algebra* over $\mathbb{R}$.[6]

The explained facts do not only hold for normal distributions as in fig. 4.6–1, but for *arbitrary* distributions—for example, *uniform* (or flat) distributions, *asymmetric* (skewed) distributions, or *multimodal* distributions (with several peaks). The most important statistical parameters of a probability distribution over X are the arithmetic *mean* (or expectation) value μ(X) and the standard deviation σ(X). These parameters are defined for arbitrary distributions; for the normal distribution they are marked in fig. 4.6–1. The mean value μ(X) is the *average* value of X among individuals of the population D. For symmetric and monomodal (one-peak) distributions the mean value coincides with the most frequent value, the so-called *modal* value. The standard deviation σ(X) informs about the average distance of the individual X-values of D-members from the mean value. Because the directed distances from the mean, $\pm(r_i-\mu(X))$, would compensate each other to a zero-sum, one adds up the *squares* of these distances, whose sum is the so-called *variance* v(X), and defines the standard deviation as the square root of the variance. The mathematical definitions are as follows:

(Def. 4.6–1)

Discrete case: $X(x) \in \{r_1,\ldots,r_n\}$ *Continuous case:* $X(x) \in \mathbb{R}$

Mean value: $\mu(X) = \sum_{i=1}^{n} r_i \cdot p(r_i)$ $\mu(X) = \int_{-\infty}^{+\infty} r \cdot d(r)\, dr$

Variance: $v(X) = \sum_{i=1}^{n} (r_i - \mu(X))^2 \cdot p(r_i)$ $v(X) = \int_{-\infty}^{+\infty} (r_i - \mu(X))^2 \cdot d(r)\, dr$

Standard deviation: Square root of variance: $\sigma(X) = \sqrt{v(X)}$

The definition of the mean value subsumes binary attributes $X_{\pm F}$ if the value Fx is coded by 1 and ¬Fx by 0. This implies that $\mu(X_F) = p(Fx)$ and $\sigma(X_F) = \sqrt{p(Fx) \cdot (1 - p(Fx))}$.

A normal distribution is completely determined by its mean value μ and its standard deviation σ: μ determines the location of its center on the X-axis, and σ its flatness. Sixty-six percent of the total probability area under the curve lies within the so-called 1σ-interval from μ–σ to μ+σ; and 95.5% of the probability lies within the 2σ-interval [μ–2σ, μ+2σ)]—this is the usual acceptance interval. If one sets μ = 0 and σ = 1, then one obtains the so-called *normalized* normal distribution, which has the mathematical form $g(z) = (1/\sqrt{2 \cdot \pi}) \cdot e^{-(z^2/2)}$. One transforms an arbitrary normal distribution over X into a normalized distribution over the transformed variable Z_X by subtracting from the X-values their mean and dividing by the standard deviation:

(4.6-2) *z-transformation*: $z = \frac{r - \mu}{\sigma}$

(i.e. $\forall x \in D: Z_X(x) = (X(x) - \mu(X)) / \sigma(X)$).

The integrals of g(z) are not analytically computable, but are looked up in integral tables (e.g. Hays/Winkler 1970, 601ff). With the help of these tables one calculates the acceptance intervals and significant differences of sec. 4.3 (since binomial distributions are usually approximated by normal distributions for sample sizes ≥ 30).

Often one considers the *joint* probability distribution d(r,q) of two random variables X: D→ℝ and Y: D→ℝ over the same population D. Two random variables are called probabilistically *independent* iff for all intervals A, B ⊂ ℝ the following holds: $p(A,B) = p(A) \cdot p(B)$, where p(A,B) abbreviates $p(X(x) \in A \wedge Y(x) \in B)$ (Bauer 1996, sec. 31). Thus, two probabilistically independent variables are uncorrelated for *all* of their possible values. On the other hand, two variables X and Y are called (simply) *uncorrelated* iff their so-called *covariance* is zero, which is defined as $\text{cov}(X,Y) =_{\text{def}} \mu(X \cdot Y) - \mu(X) \cdot \mu(Y)$. The covariance measures the *joint* deviation of the two variables X and Y from their mean (its restriction to binary values was introduced in sec. 4.1.2). For variables with more than two values, probabilistic uncorrelatedness is *weaker* than probabilistic independence, because the covariance averages over the correlations for particular values (cf. Bauer 1996, def. 32.2).

For the description of an *individual* n-element sample $s_n = \{a_1, \ldots, a_n\}$, one defines the mean value μ_{s_n} and the standard deviation σ_{s_n} of a random variable X in s_n just as in the discrete case of (4.6-1), except that instead of the $p(r_i)$'s one uses the relative frequencies $f_n(r_i)$ of the value r_i in the given sample s_n. In inference and test statistics one is especially interested in the probability distributions of the statistical parameters of *arbitrary* random samples—in particular, the distribution of the *sample means*. For the probability distribution of the n-element sample means, $\mu_{s_n}(X)$, one computes the following mean value $\mu(\mu_{s_n}(X))$ and variance $v(\mu_{s_n}(X))$ (Hays/Winkler 1970, sec. 5.21):

(Prop. 4.6-1) *Mean value and standard deviation of the distribution of sample means:*

$\mu(\mu_{s_n}(X)) = \mu(X)$ $v(\mu_{s_n}(X)) = v(X)/n$ $\sigma(\mu_{s_n}(X)) = \sigma(X)/\sqrt{n}$

The mean (or expectation) value of the sample means is identical with the population mean; it is a so-called *unbiased* estimator (Hays/Winkler

1970, 308). The standard deviation of the sample mean shrinks with increasing sample size n, proportionally to the square root of n, and converges to zero for n→∞. This fact implies the *laws of large numbers* for continuous variables (which were explained for binary variables in sec. 3.13.2). Equally important is the *central limit theorem*, according to which for every arbitrarily distributed variable, the *form* of the distribution of its sample means converges with increasing sample size n to a normal distribution with mean value $\mu(X)$ and standard deviation $\sigma(X)/\sqrt{n}$ (Bauer 1996, sec. 51). The central limit theorem justifies the approximation of the distribution of the sample means of an arbitrarily distributed variable by a normal distribution, provided the sample size is sufficiently large (n ≥ 30). This explains the importance of the normal distribution for the methods of test and inference statistics: it turns out to be the general form of a distribution of *random errors* around a central parameter value.

Statisticians also compute the distribution of *sample variances*. Following from the squaring operation, this distribution is not symmetrical, but left-skewed (a so-called χ^2-distribution; see Hays/Winkler 1970, 310). Therefore, the sample variance is not an unbiased estimator of the population variance. But the so-called *corrected* sample variance $\sigma_{s_n}^{corr}(X) = \sigma_{s_n}(X) \cdot \sqrt{n/(n-1)}$ is an unbiased estimator, which is used to estimate the population variance.

Based on these facts we now know how to compute the acceptance intervals and significant differences that were introduced in sec. 4.3. Here is an example. Assume the variable X measures the age of the first love affair of girls; our hypothesis H asserts that the mean of X, $\mu(X)$, is 15 years. We draw a 25-element random sample of girls with a corrected sample variance of $\sigma_{s_n}^{corr} = 2.5$. We thus estimate the population variance as 2.5. We look up the boundaries of the symmetric 95% interval in the integral table of the z-distribution; they are z = ±1.96. Based on the z-transformation we now calculate the 95% acceptance interval for X as follows:

$$\mu(X) \pm 1.96 \cdot \sigma_{s_n}^{corr}/\sqrt{n} = 15 \pm 1.96 \cdot 2.5/\sqrt{25} = 15 \pm 1.$$

So our hypothesis that the mean age of the first love affairs among girls is 15 years is accepted when the observed sample mean is between 14 and 16 years, and rejected otherwise. To check for significant differences between girls and boys we use the so-called *t-test* for independent samples. The probability distribution of the difference $\Delta = \mu_{s_n} - \mu_{s_m}$ between the means of two (n- and m-sized) random samples taken from the same population converges to a normal distribution with mean value 0 and variance $v(\Delta) = v \cdot (1/n + 1/m)$, where v is estimated from the corrected variances of both samples as $v = (n-1) \cdot v_{s_n}^{corr} + (m-1) \cdot v_{s_n}^{corr}/(n+m-2)$ (Bortz 1985, 166f). With help of $\sigma(\Delta) = \sqrt{v(\Delta)}$ we compute the significant difference Δ_{sig} from the boundaries of the 95% acceptance interval ($z = \pm 1.96$). Assume we have drawn a random sample of 30 boys with a corrected sample standard deviation of 3. For the corrected variance of the union of both samples we compute $v = (24 \cdot 6.5 + 29 \cdot 9)/53 = 7.86$. This gives us

$$\Delta_{sig} = 1.96 \cdot \sqrt{7.86 \cdot (1/25 + 1/30)} \approx 1.5.$$

Thus an observed difference in the mean age of the first love affair between girls and boys that exceeds 1.5 years would be significant at the 95% level.

4.7 Bayesian Statistics

4.7.1 The Likelihood-Intuition: Objections and Replies

Only the probabilities of experiences, i.e. sample results E, *given* that certain statistical hypotheses H about the population are true, are statistically defined. We write $p_H(E)$ for these statistical probabilities.[7] In contrast, the probabilities of hypotheses H *given* our evidences E are always of a subjective-epistemic nature (recall sec. 4.3.5). The methods of test and inference statistics rely on the following basic intuition, which I call the statistical *likelihood-intuition* (which is more general than the likelihood "method"; see below). According to this intuition, the statistical probability $p_H(E)$ is the *basic criterion* for the plausibility or degree of confirmation of H given E, and for the choice of one among several competing hypotheses in the face of E.

The probability of E given H, $p_H(E)$ is called the *likelihood* of H given E. So likelihoods are *inverse* probabilities (however, terminologies are not uniform[8]). Also note that $p_H(E)$ is the statistical likelihood, to be distinguished from the epistemic likelihood $P(E|H)$ introduced in the next section.

There exist two different versions of the likelihood-intuition in test and inference statistics:

1. *Method of likelihood-maximization:* According to this method (which goes back to Fisher 1956 and Hacking 1965) the support of a hypothesis H concerning a probability distribution p_H by a sample result E is *higher*, the higher H's likelihood $p_H(E)$. So if one has to

choose among competing hypotheses in the light of evidence E, one chooses a hypothesis with maximal likelihood. In the situation of inference statistics, where one has sample result E(θ_s) concerning an observed sample parameter θ_s (usually the sample mean μ_s), one conjectures that hypothesis H as the most plausible one, for which the sample result θ_s coincides with the *modal* value of θ given H, i.e. that value of θ which has *highest* probability in the distribution $p_H(\theta)$ (cf. Hays/Winkler 1970, 318).

2 *Method of likelihood-expectation:* This method conceives the support of a hypothesis H concerning p_H by a sample result E as higher, the *closer* the observed sample parameter θ_s expressed by E comes to the *mean* or expectation value of θ given H. This method is based on the likelihood-intuition, too, inasmuch as the mean value of θ is based on the likelihoods of all possible θ-values given H,

$$\mu(\theta) = \int_{-\infty}^{+\infty} \theta \cdot d_H(\theta) \, d\theta.$$ In the situation of inference statistics, one conjectures that hypothesis H as the most plausible, for which the sample result θ_s coincides with the *mean* value of θ in the distribution $p_H(\theta)$.

The two statistical inference methods are sometimes set in mutual opposition. In contrast to this viewpoint, we want to emphasize that both methods are based on the likelihood-intuition. What is more important, both methods *coincide* for symmetric one-peak probability distributions $p_H(\theta)$, and in particular for all normal distributions, because for these distributions modal and mean value of θ are identical. For these distributions both methods coincide with the inductive-statistical generalization inference (see sec. 2.7.1), which inductively transfers the observed sample mean (in the binary case the observed sample frequency) to the population. In other words, the likelihood-intuition contains the basic *induction* principle of inference and test statistics.

The two methods diverge for asymmetric distributions, such as the left-skewed χ^2-distribution of sample variances whose modal value is located at the left of its mean value. In this case, the question of whether the observed sample value θ_s should be transferred to the population as its modal or as its mean value has no unique answer. But let me emphasize that even for asymmetric distributions this problem arises only for inferences to *point hypotheses* (they infer a particular value of the population parameter), but not for the method of *confidence intervals*, which infers intervals of hypotheses and is the more appropriate method of inference statistics. Confidence intervals are uniquely determined even for asymmetric distributions. Recall from sec. 4.3.2 that they are defined as the interval of those point hypotheses H_r such that for each point hypothesis H_r in this interval, the observed sample parameter θ_s lies in the acceptance interval of H_r. This acceptance interval is defined as the interval of the 95% *most probable* sample results, given H_r is true—i.e. the interval of those 95% of possible sample results θ_s that yield the highest average likelihood $p_H(\theta_s)$ (Jaynes 1976, 197). This also shows that the method of acceptance intervals is based on the likelihood-intuition; except that here one does not look for a hypothesis with maximal likelihood, but accepts all the disjunction of all hypotheses whose likelihood belongs to the 95% highest likelihoods. What is important is that acceptance intervals are *uniquely* defined, even for skewed distributions; so the confidence intervals are also uniquely defined.

That acceptance intervals are uniquely defined for all one-peaked distributions can be seen from fig. 4.7–1. Each of the three areas below the two curves (left: symmetric; right: asymmetric) make up 70% of the total area (we consider 70% instead of 95% areas because their complements are more visible). The average height of these areas is computed by dividing the area by the length of the area. So the 70%-area with a maximal average height is simply the 70%-interval with *shortest* length: it is this interval which is selected by the maximal average likelihood criterion. This interval is uniquely defined for symmetric and asymmetric distributions: if one shifts this interval to the left or right, its mean height decreases and its length increases.[9]

Fisher's interval methods are statistical standard practice. Bayesians have raised several objections against these methods. There are, however, convincing responses to most of these objections.

For example, it has been argued that there exist many different 95% intervals, and it is arbitrary which of these one chooses as the acceptance interval (Howson/Urbach 1996, 201). But this is incorrect: as we have just seen, one chooses that 95% interval of sample results which yields the highest average likelihood for the hypothesis, and this is exactly the

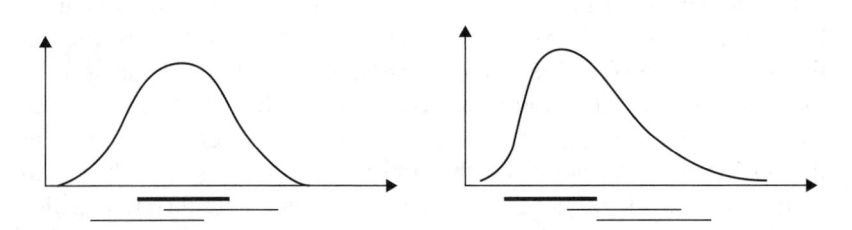

Figure 4.7–1 Shortest 70% interval (bold) and two longer 70% intervals (non-bold) in a symmetric (left) and asymmetric (right) probability distribution

shortest 95% interval. The criterion of choosing *shortest* acceptance intervals is widely used in statistics (Hays/Winkler 1970, 330). Unfortunately, the justification of this criterion given by statisticians is often unclear. Howson and Urbach doubt whether this criterion has a non-arbitrary justification at all. But, to repeat: the shortest interval criterion has the *best* justification one can think of, namely a justification in terms of maximal average likelihood.

A well-known extension of Fisher's test method is the test method of Neyman and Pearson, which assumes that besides the "null" hypothesis, e.g. $\mu = 0.8$, there exists an "alternative" hypothesis, e.g. $\mu = 0.7$ (see Hays/Winkler 1970, 401ff). The possible error of rejecting the null hypothesis although it is true is called the α-error; the possible error of accepting the null hypothesis although it is false is the β-error. Observe that Fisher's rejection coefficient of 5% is the probability of an α-error. Neyman and Pearson suggested that one should choose that rejection interval that minimizes the β-error, among all rejection intervals with same α-error probability of 5%. The problem of Neyman and Pearson's method is that it works only if null and alternative hypotheses are both point hypotheses, which is rarely the case. For alternative hypotheses that are interval hypotheses, there exists an extension of the Neyman-Pearson method, in the form of so-called UMPU tests (Howson/Urbach 1996, 216). An UMPU test requires that one choose a 95% acceptance interval for a "null" hypothesis which minimizes the β-error of *all* alternative point hypotheses: this is provably the case for the shortest 95% acceptance interval. Hence, the application of Neyman-Pearson's method to interval hypotheses leads back to Fisher's methods.

4.7.2 The Bayesian Justification of the Likelihood-Intuition

The philosophical problem of statistical test and inference methods is deeper: these methods are well justified—*but only*, if we accept the likelihood-intuition. But what justifies the likelihood-intuition? Why should the *inverse* statistical probability $p_H(E)$ of the evidence given the hypothesis be considered as a plausibility measure of the *hypothesis* given the evidence? Within the framework of statistics, there is no answer to this question, because the probability $P(H|E)$ of a hypothesis H given an evidence E is a *subjective-epistemic* probability, about which the statistical theory does not say anything.

The theory of epistemic probability possesses an answer to our question. The answer is based on Bayes' theorem (sec. 3.9.2) and the statistical principal principle (StPP) (prop. 3.13–4), which identifies the epistemic probability P(E|H) of a particular evidence E given H with the statistical likelihood, i.e. P(E|H) = p_H(E). (StPP) plus Bayes' rule give us the following:

(Prop. 4.7–1) *Principle of Bayes statistics:*

$$P(H|E) = P(E|H) \cdot P(H)/P(E) \quad \text{(by Bayes' rule)}$$
$$= p_H(E) \cdot P(H)/P(E) \quad \text{(by the StPP)}.$$

In words: The epistemic probability of hypothesis H given sample result E equals the statistical probability of E given H, multiplied by the ratio of the epistemic prior probability of H and that of E.

Strictly speaking we have to write p_H(Ex) in the statistical case (where Ex ranges over *all* samples of the type E) and P(Ea|H) in the epistemic case (where Ea refers to a *particular* sample a of type E). We call "p_H(E)" the statistical and "P(E|H)" the epistemic likelihood of H given E.

It is a characteristic of Bayesian statistics that one has to assume prior probabilities of hypotheses, so-called *priors*. These priors are *irreducible* and therefore of an unavoidably *subjective* nature: they reflect one's degree of belief in hypotheses in an epistemic state of evidential ignorance. The formula in prop. 4.7–1 also contains the prior probability of the evidence, P(E): this prior, however, is eliminable. The simplest way to eliminate P(E) is to restrict oneself to *comparative* evaluations of hypotheses. If H_1, H_2 are two competing statistical hypotheses, then the ratio of their epistemic posterior probabilities is computable as the product of the ratios of their likelihoods and their priors as follows:

$$(4.7\text{–}1) \quad \frac{P(H_1|E)}{P(H_2|E)} = \frac{PE|H_1)}{PE|H_2)} \cdot \frac{P(H_1)}{P(H_2)}.$$

Equation (4.7–1) implies that a maximal likelihood P(E|H_i) among a given set of alternative hypotheses is an indicator of the most probable hypothesis H_i (conditional on E) exactly if the priors of the compared hypotheses are *equal*, i.e. if in our example if P(H_1) = P(H_2) holds. The assumption that the prior probabilities of competing hypotheses are equal is called the *principle of indifference*. It says that *in the absence* of further information, competing possibilities are assumed to be equally probable. Equation (4.7–1) together with the principle of indifference gives us the basic form of the Bayesian justification of the likelihood-intuition, which is summarized as follows:

> (Prop. 4.7–2) *Bayesian justification of the likelihood-intuition:* The likelihood of H conditional on E is an indicator of the epistemic probability of H given E under the assumption of the principle of indifference.

If we want a quantitative calculation of the probability of hypotheses, then we can eliminate the prior probability of E by laying down a *partition* of alternative statistical hypotheses. If we are concerned with the statistical probability of a binary property F, this partition could consist of all uncountably many hypotheses of the form H_r: $p(F) = r$, for $r \in [0,1]$. In this case one assumes a subjective prior probability density function $D(H_r)$ over all hypotheses H_r's. Alternatively one could assume a discrete partition of alternative hypotheses $\{H_1, \ldots, H_n\}$ based on background knowledge. One computes the prior probability of E and, based on this, the posterior probability (density) of a particular hypothesis H_r as follows (see Hays/Winkler 1970, 233ff, 461):

(4.7–2) $P(E) = \int_0^1 p_{H_x}(E) \cdot D(H_x)\, dx$

Discrete case: $P(E) = \sum_{i=1}^{n} p_{H_i}(E) \cdot P(H_i)$

By prop. 4.7–1, this implies:

> (Prop. 4.7–3) *Posterior probability (density):*
>
> $D(H_r|E) = p_{H_r}(E) \cdot D(H_r) \Big/ \int_0^1 p_{H_x}(E) \cdot D(H_x)\, dx$ $\qquad (r \in [0,1])$
>
> Discrete case: $P(H_r|E) = p_{H_r}(E) \cdot P(H_r) \Big/ \sum_{i=1}^{n} p_{H_i}(E) \cdot P(H_i)$ $\quad (1 \le r \le n)$

It is essential for the program of Bayesian statistics that the epistemic likelihoods $P(E|H)$ are assumed to be "objective" in the sense of *intersubjective*, i.e. are identified with the statistical likelihoods $p_H(E)$. Recall from sec. 3.13.5 that in the statistical principal principle, the epistemic probability P does not stand for the *actual* degree of belief of a given rational agent A at a given time t, which we denote by $P_{A,t}$, but, rather, for an evidence-independent prior probability. The surplus of P(H|E) over P(H) is a measure of the *degree of confirmation* of hypothesis H by evidence E (see sec. 5.10.2).

As explained in sec. 3.13.5, intersubjective confirmation values would be impossible if the likelihoods were dependent on actual evidences. Related to this point is the so-called *problem of old evidence* (see Earman 1992, ch. 5): if at time t a given agent is in an epistemic state in which he already has the evidence E, i.e. $P_{A,t}(E) = 1$, then $P_{A,t}(E) = P_{A,t}(E|H))$ and thus $P_{A,t}(H|E) = P_{A,t}(H)$ follows (by prop. 4.7–1). So if one were to express degrees of confirmation in terms of actual degrees of belief, one would obtain the strange result that evidence that is believed with certainty can no longer increase H's probability, i.e. confirm H. If $P_{A,t}(E) \neq 1$, one would still obtain the unreasonable result that the degree of confirmation of H by E depends on *how certain* we are about E. If the difference P(H|E) − P(H) is intended to express the change of H's probability *due to E*, then P should not already presuppose the evidence by making it certain or highly probable. Moreover P should *not* depend on other evidences E' in favor of H which are "hidden" in P. For these reasons, P should not be the actual degree of belief function, but an evidence-independent *prior probability*.

4.7.3 Objective Bayesianism and the Principle of Indifference

Objective Bayesianism differs from subjective Bayesianism inasmuch as it strives for intersubjective ("objective") prior probabilities of hypotheses by assuming the principle of indifference.[10] Let us assume the prior density $D(H_r)$ is a *uniform* (or flat) distribution, which implies (by normalization) that $D(H_x) = 1$ for all $x \in [0,1]$. From this and prop. 4.7–3 we infer immediately that the posterior density of H_r has its maximum at that r-value which maximizes the likelihood $p_{H_r}(E)$ (since $D(H_r)$ and the integral are independent from the choice of r). More importantly, we can now compute the *numerical* values of the posterior probabilities. Consider again all possible hypotheses about the statistical probability of property F: $H_r =_{def}$ "p(F)=r" (for $r \in [0,1]$). Let $s_i(F: k/n)$ (for $k \leq n$) denote a complete n-sample description that asserts that k *particular* individuals out of n given individuals have property F, and the others do not. Assuming statistical independence, the statistical probability of each $s_i(F: k/n)$ is given as $p(s_i(F: k/n)) = x^k \cdot (1-x)^{(n-k)}$, where $x = p(F)$ is the unknown statistical probability value of F. Integrating this value with a uniform prior distribution $D(x) = 1$ over x, one obtains (by standard integration techniques):[11]

(Prop. 4.7–4) *Probabilities obtained from indifference:*

a $P(s_i(F: k/n)) = \dfrac{1}{\binom{n}{k} \cdot (n+1)}$

b $P\!\left(f_n(F) = \dfrac{k}{n}\right) = \dfrac{1}{n+1}$

c $P\!\left(Fa_{n+1} \mid f_n(F) = \dfrac{k}{n}\right) = \dfrac{k+1}{n+1}$ (Laplace's rule of succession)

(b) asserts that the prior distribution over all possible sample frequency hypotheses is flat. (c) is Laplace's famous rule, which is a strong form of an induction principle that is valid in Carnap's preferred c*-system of inductive "logic" (1950b, 568).

Unfortunately, the indifference principle stands on *weak legs*. It turns out to be strongly language-dependent (Gillies 2000, 37–48). For example, assume a uniform prior probability distribution for the unknown frequency (μ) of a particular kind of electromagnetic radiation (e.g. the light emitted by sodium). The wavelength (λ) of a radiation is given as the light velocity c divided by its frequency, i.e. $\lambda = c/\mu$. If one transforms the uniform distribution for μ into a distribution for λ, one obtains a non-uniform (exponentially decreasing) distribution. See fig 4.7–2.

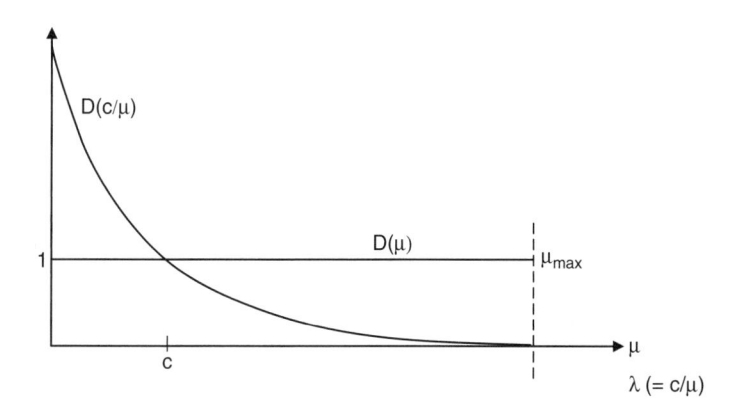

Figure 4.7–2 A uniform density over μ (frequency) leads to a non-uniform density for λ (wavelength)

234 • Philosophy of Science

Similar "paradoxes" of the indifference principle have already been reported by Keynes (1921, ch. 4). Keynes was an advocate of the indifference principle; he proposed an improvement of this principle which, however, does not work for the above counter-example (Gillies 2000, 43f; Howson/Urbach 1996, 61). The broadly accepted consequence of this problem is the following: *no prior probability distribution is unbiased, or void of information*, not even the uniform prior distribution. This conclusion receives additional support from the following two arguments.

1 A description which fixes the truth value of each atomic sentence of the language is called a *state description* after Carnap (1950b, 71). If the probability distribution P is uniform over all state descriptions (instead of over all statistical hypotheses), then inductive learning from experience becomes *impossible*: for then one obtains the result that $P(Fa_{n+1}|s_n(F)) = 1/2$, for every possible complete sample description $s_n(F)$ of n individuals, $s_n(F) =_{def} \pm Fa_1 \wedge \ldots \wedge \pm Fa_n$.[12] One could reply that complete sample descriptions are irrelevant for inductive estimations of frequency limits. This reply is true, but it shows at the same time that a uniform prior distribution over possible frequency limits is not free of presuppositions, but makes a strong inductive assumption (stronger than the inductive assumption involved in exchangeability).

2 Assume that for a given binary property, the prior density distribution over all statistical *point* hypotheses is uniform, i.e. $D(H_r) = 1$ for all $r \in [0,1]$. Then the epistemic probability of each point hypothesis is *zero*, since the integral over a single point is non-zero only if this point has an infinite density. Therefore, the prior probability of a strict universal hypothesis $\forall x Fx$ is also zero. This implies an extreme *bias* since it means that strict universal laws are conceived as impossible. For note that prior probabilities of 0 or 1 make learning from experience impossible, i.e. if $P(H) = 0$ (or 1), then $P(H|E) = 0$ (or 1) for every possible experience E. On the other hand, if P assigns to a universal hypothesis a prior greater than zero, then the corresponding density D must be infinitely high at the point $r = 1$, which means that now D is not uniform but extremely biased in regard to H_1 (cf. Earman 1992, 87–94). The unavoidable conclusion of this is that no prior probability distribution can be unbiased in all respects.

The problem of zero-priors of universal hypotheses has been discovered by Carnap and Popper. While Carnap (1950b, 571f) circumvented this problem by his method of "instance confirmation," Popper (1935/2002, new appendix vii*) inferred from it (wrongly) that inductive probabilities are impossible. Earman (1992, 91f) showed (building on R. Jeffrey (1983, 194) and H. Jeffrey (1973)) that $P(\forall xFx) > 0$ is only possible under the following condition:

(4.7–3) $P(\forall xFx) > 0$ implies that for $n \to \infty$ the conditional probabilities $P(Fa_{n+1}|Fa_1 \wedge \ldots \wedge Fa_n)$ converge "rapidly"[13] to 1.

(4.7–3) is a *strong* induction assumption, even stronger than Laplace's (prop. 4.7–4c). Hintikka (1966) extended Carnap's (1950b) system to allow for inductive learning of universal hypotheses.

4.7.4 Subjective Bayesianism and Convergence of Opinions

Because of the explained problems, most contemporary Bayesians do not assume the indifference principle as sacrosanct. Rather, they adhere to the view of subjective Bayesianism, which argues that there are no objective rules for choosing priors; one may start from any prior distribution one wants. What subjective Bayesians attempt to show is that certain results of empirical learning hold *independently* of one's prior distribution. These results, however, are quite weak, because they hold only *in the limit*, i.e. when the number of observed individuals approaches infinity.

Assume again a given prior density distribution $D(H_r)$ over the possible statistical probabilities $r \in [0,1]$ of a binary property, and a particular sample evidence E. Then Bayesians compute the posterior density distribution $D(H_r|E)$ according to prop. 4.7–3. This procedure is called Bayesian *updating* of probability distributions. It works in a particularly simple way for so-called β-distributions (Hays/Winkler 1970, 461f), but is also possible for other distributions, e.g. normal ones (Howson/Urbach 1996, 354ff). One can prove, independently from the particular form of the prior distribution, that the conditionalization of this distribution on evidence reporting a particular sample frequency r_E always produces a shift of the mass of this distribution towards r_E. With increasing sample size the resulting posterior distribution gets successively steepened with an increasing amount of the probability mass located over the reported sample frequency. The only presupposition is that the prior distribution P is *undogmatic* in regard to the true population frequency r_{Pop}, which means (by definition) that it assigns a positive density to every arbitrarily small ε–interval around r_{Pop} (de Finetti 1974, sec. XI.4.5).

The explained fact is a so-called *convergence* result, i.e. a limiting result for the posterior probabilities independently from the prior distributions one starts with. Convergence results are also called the "washing-out of priors" (Earman 1992, 141ff). They are central to subjective Bayesianism, since they establish a form of intersubjectivity (or objectivity) independently from the subjective choice of prior distributions. In the rest of this section we explain some further important convergence results and their presuppositions, thereby assuming a denumerably infinite domain with standard names $a_1, a_2,\ldots$.

Recall from prop. 3.13–6 that exchangeability plus undogmaticity imply uniform learning, or in other words, *continuous* convergence:

(Prop. 4.7–5) *Continuous convergence for predictions*: Here "$f_n(F) = k/n$" asserts that the F-frequency in a given sample of size n is k; and [r] is the integer-rounding of a real number r. *Assumption*: P is exchangeable.

a $P(Fa_{n+1}|\, f_n(F)=(k+1)/n) > P(Fa_{n+1}|f_n(F) = k/n)$. *Proviso*: P is not dogmatic w.r.t. any $r \in [0,1]$.

b $\lim_{n \to \infty} P(Fa_{n+1}|\, f_n(F)=[r\cdot n]/n) = r$. *Proviso*: P is not dogmatic w.r.t. r.[14]

Exchangeability is needed for continuous convergence. Prop. 4.7–6 lists some important simple convergence results. They are not continuous, but admit that the convergence starts after an arbitrarily *late* position or "time point" a_k in the sequence of observed individuals ($a_1, a_2,\ldots$). Convergence result (a) of prop. 4.7–6 was proved by Gaifman/Snir (1982). Thereby $H(\mathcal{L})$ consists of all hypotheses expressible in a language $\mathcal{L}$ containing arithmetics, which is able to express statistical frequency limits. $\mathcal{L}$ contains names a_i for all individuals in $D = \{d_i: i \in \mathbb{N}\}$, and the sequence $(\pm_w A_i: i \in \mathbb{N})$ consists of all unnegated or negated atomic statements that are true in possible world w.

Gaifman and Snir's result a is powerful. But it has two severe restrictions: (1) It does *not* hold when the data stream does not determine the extension of H's concept, which is the case when H contains *theoretical* concepts (or latent variables) which are not part of the data. (2) Theorem a holds only for a subset of possible worlds with probability 1. Hence the truth-convergence for belief function P is certain only

(Prop. 4.7-6) *Simple convergence results*:

a   Gaifman/Snir-convergence: For all $H \in H(\mathcal{L})$, the set of possible worlds (or $\mathcal{L}$-models) w for which $\lim_{n \to \infty} P(H | \pm_w A_1 \wedge \ldots \wedge \pm_w A_n)$ equals H's truth value in w has probability $P = 1$.
In words: With P-certainty, the probability of a hypothesis H converges to H's truth value in a given world w, conditional on an increasing data stream about w which converges to the complete information about w.[15]

b   Special case of a: $\lim_{n \to \infty} P(H_r | f_n(F)) = [r \cdot n]/n) = 1$.
Proviso for a and b: σ-additivity of P.

c   Convergence for strict predictions:
$\lim_{n \to \infty} P(Fa_{n+1} | Fa_1 \wedge \ldots \wedge Fa_n) = 1$.
Proviso: $P(\forall x Fx) > 0$.

d   Convergence for strict generalizations:
$\lim_{n \to \infty} P(\forall x Fx | Fa_1 \wedge \ldots \wedge Fa_n) = 1$.
Proviso: $P(\forall x Fx) > 0$ and σ-additivity of P.

from the viewpoint of P—Earman (1992, 148) calls this the "self-gratulatory success of the Bayesian method."

Result b is a consequence of a. Both results presuppose σ-additivity, which involves a weak inductive assumption, as explained in sec. 3.13.1. The convergence results c and d for strict inductions require the assumption $P(\forall x Fx) > 0$, which—as explained below (4.7-3)—is a much stronger inductive assumption. Result d requires, in addition, σ-additivity.

The explained convergence results have a significant *disadvantage*: they hold only in the infinite limit, but may fail for any finite stage of evidence accumulation. The following is easily provable:

(Prop. 4.7-7) *Biased priors*: Assume H is a *true* hypothesis over an infinite domain $D = \{a_i: i \in \mathbb{N}\}$, then for every arbitrarily long conjunction of evidence statements $Ea_1 \wedge \ldots \wedge Ea_n$ entailed by H, there exists a non-dogmatic but sufficiently biased prior probability distribution P ($P(H) \neq 0,1$) such that $P(\neg H | Ea_1 \wedge \ldots \wedge Ea_n) > P(H | Ea_1 \wedge \ldots \wedge Ea_n)$.[16]

Thus, subjective-Bayesian convergence results are unable to prevent irrationality for arbitrarily long but finite time spans. They do not guarantee the washing-out of priors for finite beings.

The preceding considerations have shown that all inductive inferences which were qualitatively described in sec. 2.7.1 have precise probabilistic explications in the form of convergence results that follow from weaker or stronger inductive probability assumptions. By assuming in addition the indifference principle, one can compute even *numeric* inductive probabilities as explained in sec. 4.7.3.

We finally point out that *without* inductive assumptions, epistemic probability theory *cannot* justify inductive inferences. This sounds unsurprising, but is nevertheless important, since some Bayesians promulgated the wrong impression that already the basic (Kolmogorov) probability axioms have inductive consequences. Howson (1997, 279), for example, argued that probabilism implies a weak inductive logic, because it follows from the basic axioms that if a hypothesis H entails an evidence E, and $0 < P(E), P(H) < 1$, then H's probability is raised conditional on E, i.e. $P(H|E) > P(H)$. However, we shall see in sec. 5.10.3 that the consequence $P(H|E) > P(H)$ is based on mere *content-cutting*, which means that E increases H's probability only because E is a content part of H and increases its own probability to 1 ($P(E|E) = 1$), while E does not increase the probability of any content part of H that goes logically beyond E. In conclusion, probabilism merely based on the basic probability axioms cannot justify induction—a conclusion which was later drawn by Howson himself (2000, 133).

4.8 Introductory Literature and Exercises

4.8.1 Introductory Literature

A nice introduction to probability theory and inductive methods is Skyrms (1999). Also Hempel (1966) contains a lot about this subject. A classical introduction to methods of statistics including Bayes statistics is Hays/Winkler (1970). Also Howson/Urbach (1996) contains informative chapters on this topic from a Bayesian viewpoint. Earman (1992) discusses the pros and cons of Bayesianism. More on the relation between correlation and causality is found in Suppes (1970) and Cartwright (2007). On ceteris paribus laws see Earman et al. (2002).

4.8.2 Questions and Exercises

Sec. 4.1

1. A domain of individuals with properties F, G and H contains the following kinds of individuals: F∧G∧H, F∧G∧¬H, ¬F∧G∧¬H, ¬F∧¬G∧¬H. List all strict universal implications of the form $\pm A \rightarrow \pm C$ or $\pm A_1 \wedge \pm A_2 \rightarrow \pm C$ which are true in this domain.
2. Which of the true implications in (1) are relevant? Among the irrelevant ones, which antecedent conjuncts are irrelevant?
3. Refer to question (3) for sec. 3.7–9: Compute the correlations between sex and marital status according to the difference measure.

Sec. 4.2

1. Consider the following strict law hypotheses:

   (L1) All male tribe members are tattooed.
   (L2) All male tribe members over 40 years are tattooed.
   (L3) All tribe members over 40 years are tattooed.

   Three samples have been investigated with the following results (+/− means that *all/no* individual in the sample satisfied the antecedent property:

	male	over 40	result:
1st sample:	+	+	all tattooed
2nd sample:	+	−	all tattooed
3rd sample:	−	+	not all tattooed

   (a) Which of the three law hypotheses are confirmed according to the method of agreement, and by which sample?
   (b) Tell for each antecedent conjunct of each confirmed law hypothesis whether it is relevant or irrelevant. Justify your claim by the method of difference.

2. You are a commuter and have two nice residences, but at one of them you always get an allergic sniffle. How can you find its cause by methodological induction?

Sec. 4.3

1. Your hypothesis states: 60% of all beer drinkers are smokers. For a sample of 500 beer drinkers you compute a 95%-acceptance interval

of 282–318. Which sample result would strongly disconfirm your hypothesis, and which would weakly confirm it?

2   Continuation of 1: Assume you found 315 smokers in your sample. What is the resulting confidence interval for the frequency of smokers among beer drinkers in the population?

3   Consider a sample of 100 coffee drinkers with 48 smokers and a control group of 100 non-coffee drinkers with 32 smokers. For which values of the significant difference does the observed difference count as significant?

4   By which factor does the acceptance interval and significant difference shrink, when the sample size is multiplied by 10?

5   Give examples of error sources in statistical methods from your own subject of study.

Sec. 4.4

1   Assume two properties F and G are not causally connected (i.e. neither is F a cause of G nor vice versa). Under which condition it is nevertheless possible that F and G are positively correlated? Give an example.

2   Assume F and G are positively correlated, and no third hidden variable has a causal influence on the two properties. Why is it still not possible to infer the unique causal relation between F and G from this correlation? Give an example.

3   Consider the following statistical findings: (a) People eating more meat are more aggressive. (b) Healthier people have more money. (c) People that go more frequently to the cinema have more car accidents. For each example discuss all plausible causal interpretations of these correlations.

Sec. 4.5

1   Discuss the following ceteris paribus (CP) assertions: (i) CP wood floats on water. (ii) CP nuclear reactors are safe. (iii) CP women are more peaceful than men. (iv) CP corpulent people are less healthy.

(a) Which are comparative and which are exclusive CP assertions?
(b) In the exclusive cases, can you give a reasonable interpretation of the CP clause which makes the assertions true?

2   Your hypothesis H asserts that the mean weight of (adult) male German people is 80 kg. You draw a 30-element sample of male Germans and observe a sample mean of 76 kg. The corrected standard

deviation estimated from your sample is 12 kg. Compute the 95% acceptance interval for your hypothesis ($z_{95\%} = \pm 1.96$). Can H be retained?
3 Continuation of (2): Now you draw a 34-element sample of Japanese men. Their mean weight is 70 kg. The corrected standard deviation estimated from both samples is 7 kg. Compute the significant difference at a significance level of 5%. Is the difference significant? How high is the effect strength?
4 What is the likelihood-intuition? Explain its justification within subjective-epistemic probability theory.

Notes

1. Hempel gave his example in probabilistic form: $p(G|F)=0.95$, $p(G|H)=0.95$ and $p(G|F \lor H)= 0.95$.
2. See Hays/Winkler (1970, 380ff), Bortz (1985, 141ff), Howson/Urbach (1996, 171ff).
3. Moreover, the variables must describe temporally coexistent features (see below).
4. E.g., Lakatos (1970, 17f), Cartwright (1983), Joseph (1980), Hempel (1988), Fodor (1991), Pietroski/Rey (1995), Kincaid (1996).
5. That the causal direction goes from X to Y and not vice versa does not follow from the CP correlation, but must be given by temporal or intervention assumptions (see sec. 6.7).
6. p: AL→[0,1] can be retrieved from a given distribution over an algebra over D provided X: D→V is measurable. For details cf. Bauer (1996, sec. 4–8), Jeffrey (1971b), Billingsley (1995, ch. 2–4).
7. Strictly speaking, "p(E|H)" would be incorrect because H is not an element of the algebra over the sample space.
8. Our terminology follows, e.g. Forster/Sober (1994, 31) and Howson/Urbach (1996, 28). Other authors (e.g. Hays/Winkler 1970, 316; Earman 1992, 34) call $p_H(E)$ the likelihood of E given H—in their terminology likelihoods are not inverted but ordinary probabilities.
9. Many multiple-peak distributions also have unique shortest acceptance intervals. Flat distributions or distributions with peripherical peaks may have non-unique acceptance intervals.
10. Cf. Williamson (2010, 16, 28f), who calls it the principle of "equivocation."
11. Cf. Jeffrey (1971b, 219), Gillies (2000, 72ff), Howson/Urbach (1996, 55ff), Billingsley (1995, 279).
12. Proof: There are twice as many state descriptions verifying $s_n(F)$ than verifying $Fa_{n+1} \land s_n(F)$.
13. There must exist $k \in \mathbb{N}$ and $c \in (0,1)$ s.t. $\forall n \geq k$: $x_{n+1}/x_n \leq c$, where $x_n =_{def} P(\neg Fa_{n+1}|Fa_1 \land \ldots \land Fa_n)$.
14. Proof of (a) see fn. 17 in Chapter 3. A proof of (b) is found in Kutschera (1972, 85f).
15. This is a reformulation of Gaifman and Snir's requirement that the sentences $\{\pm_w A_i : i \in \mathbb{N}\}$ must "separate" the set of $\mathcal{L}$-models (D,v) over $\mathcal{L}$.
16. Proof: Choose P such that $P(Ea_1 \land \ldots \land Ea_n | \neg H) > 0$ and $P(H)$ is sufficiently low and apply Bayes' rule.

5
GOING BEYOND EXPERIENCE: THEORIES AND THEIR EMPIRICAL EVALUATION

5.1 Theoretical Concepts and Multiple Laws of Correspondence

Theoretical concepts refer to things or characteristics which we humans are unable to perceive with the senses. Theoretical singular terms of the natural sciences, for example, denote individuals that are too small to be seen, from bacteria to molecules, atoms, and subatomic particles. Theoretical general concepts of the natural sciences denote properties or kinds of effects, for the perception of which there is no sense organ at our disposal, for instance electrical or magnetic fields; or they denote *inner* (chemical, biological, neural) *structures* of a system, of which we are only able to observe the external *input–output* relations. In the human and social sciences, singular theoretical terms can stand for complex social structures, e.g. the national state called Germany. Theoretical predicates of these sciences denote for example mental or emotional states of people, or complex conditions of societies.

We have seen in sec. 2.9.1 that it is difficult to draw a strict borderline between empirical and theoretical concepts. We characterized concepts as empirical i.n.s. if they can be learned by pure ostension. We also mentioned that scientists often use a pragmatic notion of empirical i.w.s., designating concepts that are measurable on the basis of unproblematic pre-theories. Our following considerations do *not* depend on exactly how one draws the borderline between empirical (or non-theoretical) and theoretical concepts. The only important presupposition of Chapter 5 is that the values of *some* concepts or variables are directly measured, i.e. *contained* in the evidence, while the value of other (theoretical) concepts or variables can only indirectly be inferred, in a theory-dependent way, from the values of the directly measured variables. In statistics, the former variables are called the *manifest* and the latter ones the *latent* variables. This distinction is not only unproblematic, but at the same *crucial* for an adequate understanding of scientific theories, their merits and the specific problems involved in their testing.

As mentioned in sec. 3.10, the following relationship exists between theoretical concepts and empirical disposition concepts. Empirical dispositions are *functional* features, and their meaning is characterized *analytically*, qua meaning postulate, by a single bilateral reduction sentence or a single nomological implication (def. 3.10–1, 2). Theoretical concepts, on the other hand, denote *structural features*, which are the *causes* of various empirical dispositions, but are not analytically equivalent to these. Theoretical concepts are therefore always characterized by several bilateral reduction sentences, or more generally, by several laws of correspondence, the list of which is *open* and potentially infinite. Thereby a *law of correspondence* for a theoretical (or disposition) concept $\tau(x)$ correlates the property $\tau(x)$ under certain conditions with a corresponding empirical indicator property. (Our understanding of "laws of correspondence" is different from that of Carnap, as explained below.)

We can explain this situation using the example from sec. 3.10, the empirical disposition of *solubility in water*. The cause of solubility in water of all known kinds of chemical molecules is their *dipolar structure*, i.e. the molecules have a positively and a negatively charged end. Since water molecules also possess such a dipolar structure, the latter may insert themselves easily between the molecules of the given substance, the plus-pole pointing towards the minus-pole and vice versa, and so the substance gets distributed at the molecular level, i.e. dissolves in water. This dipolar structure, however, is not only the cause of the solubility, but also of many other empirical dispositions, which are summarized in fig. 5.1–1 (cf. Mortimer 1986, ch. 12).

The fact that theoretical properties figure typically as common causes of correlated empirical dispositions explains a central method by which new theoretical properties are discovered in science. This is the method of *common cause abduction*: whenever two or several (singular or general) empirical phenomena are inductively discovered to be *correlated*, and it can be excluded that these phenomena stand to each other in a cause–effect relationship, then (by the causality principles in sec. 6.7.8) they must have had an unobserved common cause. Reichenbach (1956, 157f) described this method in application to simultaneously correlated

Theoretical characteristic τ(x)	Empirical Dispositions D_i	Correspondence laws for D_i
	(Specifically:) x is soluble in water (D_1)	$T_1xt \rightarrow (D_1x \leftrightarrow R_1xt)$
	(Specifically:) x is not soluble in oil (D_2)	$T_2xt \rightarrow (D_2x \leftrightarrow R_2xt)$
	(Generally:) x is soluble in all polar solvents (Water, Ammonia, ...) (D_3)	$T_3xt \rightarrow (D_3x \leftrightarrow R_3xt)$
Molecules of substance x have dipolar structure	(Generally:) x is not soluble in all non-polar solvents (Oil, Benzene,...) (D_4)	$T_4xt \rightarrow (D_4x \leftrightarrow R_4xt)$
	x has a high melting point (D_5)	$T_5xt \rightarrow (D_5x \leftrightarrow R_5xt)$
	x-solutions conduct electricity (D_6)	$T_6xt \rightarrow (D_6x \leftrightarrow R_6xt)$
	x absorbs and emits electromagnetic radiation of certain wavelengths (D_7)	$T_7xt \rightarrow (D_7x \leftrightarrow R_7xt)$
	etc...	etc...

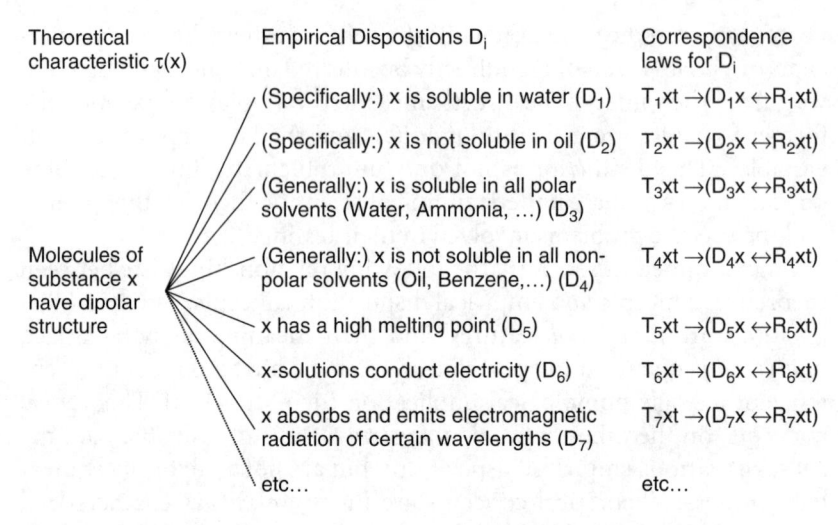

Figure 5.1–1 One theoretical feature causes many empirical dispositions

events; and Salmon (1984, 213ff) and Schurz (2008a) in application to correlated empirical dispositions, as in fig. 5.1–1.

Let us record the logical relations between theoretical concepts, empirical dispositions and regularities, in the case where the involved regularities are strict ones. The given background theory T entails that the theoretical characteristic τ(x) can be identified empirically by a series of permanent disposition properties D_ix:[1]

(5.1–1) For all objects x, and $i \in \{1,...,n\}$: x has τ iff x has D_i.

Formally: $\forall x(\tau(x) \leftrightarrow D_ix)$.

Every dispositional feature D_i is partially *defined* by a law of *correspondence* $C(D_i)$, which has the form of a bilateral reduction sentence:

(5.1–2) C-for-D_i: For all objects x, times t, and $i \in \{1,...,n\}$: If T_i applies to x at t, then x has D_i iff x exhibits R_i at t.

Formally: $C(D_i): \forall x \forall t(T_ixt \rightarrow (D_ix \leftrightarrow R_ixt))$.

Here, T_i is the empirical test condition and R_i the empirical reaction. E.g. if x is placed in water at time t (T_ixt), then x is soluble in water (D_ix) iff x dissolves in water shortly after t (R_ixt). This law of correspondence defines the very meaning of "solubility in water." As explained in sec. 3.10, we may also define dispositions using a nomological implication, but here we prefer their characterization by laws of correspondence, since only these laws provide us with the conditions of empirical identification or measurement, which can then be transferred to the theoretical concept.

The n theoretical laws in (5.1-1) together with the n meaning postulates in (5.1-2) logically imply the following n laws of a correspondence $C_i(\tau)$ for *one and the same* theoretical characteristic $\tau(x)$:

(5.1-3) C_i-for-τ: For all objects x, times t: If T_i applies to x at t, then x has τ iff x exhibits R_i at t (for all $i \in \{1, ...,n\}$).

Formally: $C_i(\tau)$: $\forall x \forall t(T_i xt \to (\tau(x) \leftrightarrow R_i xt))$.

Example: if x is placed in water at t, then the molecules of x possess dipolar structure iff x dissolves in water shortly after t.

Although the laws of correspondence for theoretical concepts (5.1-3) have the logical form of bilateral reduction sentences, they should *not* be called "reduction" sentences, because they *cannot* be seen as analytically true, i.e. as partial definitions of the theoretical concept. This is impossible because two (or several) laws of correspondence taken together possess *empirical content*, as the following argument shows:

(5.1-4)

C_1 If a substance x (at time t) is placed in water, then x's molecules possess dipolar structure iff x dissolves in the water. ($T_1 xt \to (\tau(x) \leftrightarrow R_1 xt)$.)

C_2 If a substance x (at time t) is placed in oil, then x's molecules possess dipolar structure iff x remains undissolved in the oil. ($T_2 xt \to (\tau(x) \leftrightarrow R_2 xt)$.)

Therefore: If a substance x has been dissolved in water (at some time), then the (retrieved) substance will never be dissolvable in oil. ($\exists t(T_1 xt \wedge R_1 xt) \to \forall t(T_2 xt \to R_2 xt)$.)

Therefore, several laws of correspondence for the same theoretical concept τ cannot be understood to be analytically true, since two taken together already have empirical content. We could award the status of being analytically true to *at most* one law of correspondence for τ, assuming T's hypothesis of permanence for τ as given (recall def. 3.10-1 and below). But to pick out one of many laws of correspondence for τ and declare it as analytically true would be completely arbitrary. Why should we regard "solubility in water" as an analytical truth for molecular dipolar structure, and why exactly this and not some other empirical correlate of "dipolar structure"? The only effect of this step would be that this law of correspondence becomes *immune* to possible empirical corrections, and this would be clearly inadequate. This brings us to the following conclusion:

> (Prop. 5.1–1) *Laws of correspondence* for theoretical concepts are of a *synthetic nature*—they are components of the respective background theory, which, like all other components, are of a hypothetical nature, and can thereby be confirmed or revised.

The empirical consequences which may be derived from several laws of correspondence for the same theoretical concept illustrate at the same time two central *virtues of scientific theories* which make them superior to mere empirical generalizations:

1. their ability to entail *novel predictions*, that is, predictions of qualitatively new (empirical) phenomena which one cannot infer by means of simple inductive generalizations over empirically given kinds, and
2. their capacity of *unification*, i.e. their ability to explain many empirical regularities by means of a few theoretical laws.

To explain these two points, observe that the n laws of correspondence of the form (5.1–3) logically imply the following empirical consequences (P_{ij}):

(5.1–5)

$P_{ij}: \exists t(T_i xt \wedge R_i xt) \rightarrow \forall t(T_j xt \rightarrow R_j xt)$, for $1 \leq i, j \leq n$.

In words: if a substance (or system) x exhibited reaction R_i under test condition T_i, it will always respond with reaction R_j under test condition T_j.

Since i and j vary independently between 1 and n, there are exactly n·n = n^2 consequences P_{ij}. In the case of i=j, the consequence P_{ii} expresses that the disposition D_i is of a permanent nature. For $i \neq j$ (which is the important case), the consequence P_{ij} expresses a *cross-sectoral* prediction, which allows us to infer from the observed behavior R_i of substance x under conditions T_i the behavior R_j of x under possibly completely *different* circumstances T$_j$, without having ever observed entities of the same kind as x under conditions T$_j$. To give an example, assume we find a new kind of crystal C, and it turns out that substances of kind C dissolve in water. Then we can infer from the correspondence laws in fig. 5.1-1 that this new substance has dipolar structure, from which we can predict that it cannot be dissolved in oil (etc.). This is a *qualitatively* new prediction, because we have never put this new kind of substance into oil before. Qualitatively new predictions cannot be inferred from past observations by induction, as induction can only generalize over kinds of phenomena that *have* already been observed. For the prediction of qualitatively new phenomena one needs *theories* that stipulate a theoretical common cause of qualitatively different phenomena. We shall see later (sec. 5.10.3) that a theory's ability to entail cross-sectoral predictions is an essential condition for its non-speculative character and independent testability.

Intimately connected with the cross-sectoral predictions P$_{ij}$ is the theory's unification power. By the introduction of the theoretical property $\tau(x)$ as the common cause of n dispositions D$_i$ =$_{def}$ $\forall x \forall t(T_i xt \rightarrow R_i xt)$, n^2 empirical laws are traced back to only n theoretical laws of correspondence, which is a polynomial reduction of the number of elementary laws (cf. Schurz/Lambert 1994, sec. 2.3; Schurz 2008a, sec. 7.2).

Back to the question of *meaning*: if laws of correspondence do not define the meaning of theoretical concepts, how can the latter's meaning be determined at all? A widely accepted answer in contemporary philosophy of science states: by the net of background *theories* which are responsible for this concept (or at least by their theory *cores*; see below). We are well advised, however, to differentiate further at this point. For the more special theoretical concepts such as "dipolar structure," the empirical laws of correspondence do *not* come from the *same* theory as those laws with the help of which we would characterize the meaning of this concept. The empirical indicator laws for dipolar structure (concerning the solubility behavior) come from qualitative inorganic chemistry. For an explication of the meaning of the concept "dipolar structure," though, we would use the chemical theory of atoms and molecules, and the theory of electrostatics. In doing so, we trace the meaning of more special theoretical concepts such as *dipolar structure* back to the meaning of more general theoretical concepts—in our example, *electron*, *bonding*, and *electric charge*.

By this step, the question of meaning has only been deferred, as we have to keep asking: how is the meaning of the most *fundamental* theoretical concepts characterized, such as *mass* and *force* in mechanics, or *charge* in electrostatics, etc.? Again, the answer is: by the respective background theory which is responsible for the concepts—for mass and force, this background theory is mechanics. In this case, we can see that the empirical laws of correspondence for mass and force originate from the *same* theory which characterizes the meaning of these concepts overall. We will now illustrate this situation with the concept of *mass*—for the sake of simplicity, we will restrict ourselves to *classical* (Newtonian) physics. According to the standard view, the kinematical concepts of mechanics (time, position in space, velocity and acceleration) are the non-theoretical or empirical ones, while mass and force are the theoretical concepts.

Put pre-theoretically, *mass* is the *quantity* of material of a substance. It is the cause of various empirical dispositions of material objects, associated with laws of correspondence by which the concept of mass can be empirically *measured*. In everyday life, masses can be measured with the help of either a beam balance (as in C_1) or a spring scale (as in C_2):

(5.1–6) *Two mass measurements:*   (For all x, t:)

C_1 $T_1xt \longrightarrow$ $(Mx \longleftrightarrow R_1xt)$

Object x (at time t)   Mass of x = k   x is balanced out (at t) by
is placed on beam   k units of mass (e.g. gram)

C_2 $T_2xt \longrightarrow$ $(Mx \longleftrightarrow R_2xt)$

Object x (at time t) is   Mass of x = k   Spring is stretched or
placed on spring scale   compressed (at t) by k
                                          units of length

C_1 and C_2 are *laws of measurement*. One usually writes measurement laws in the compact functional form.

(5.1–7) For all x, t: If T_1xt, then m(x) equals $r_1(x,t)$
$\forall x,t: T_1xt \to (m(x)=r_1(x,t))$,

where "m" is the theoretical *mass function* and "r_1" denotes the empirical function which assigns to the object x the number of units of mass which balance x. A functional law of the form (5.1–7) is however logically equivalent to the following bilateral reduction sentence, where "k" is a variable over rational numbers:

(5.1–8) For all x, t and k: $T_1xt \to (m(x)=k \leftrightarrow r_1(x,t)=k)$.

Going Beyond Experience • 249

If we take "Mx" for the formula "m(x)=k" and "R_1xt" for the formula "$r_1(x,t)=k$," this is the logical form of the above law of correspondence C_1. This shows that bilateral reduction sentences comprise a *very broad* class of laws of correspondence: all empirical indicator laws and measurement laws for theoretical terms.

Measurements using beam balances and spring scales are based on different physical mechanisms. The result of a measurement using a beam balance does not change when gravity changes; the result of the spring scale measurement, however, does. Balance in beam balances occurs because the *same* gravity is at work on the left and on the right side; the stretching or compression of the spring, on the other hand, depends on the *strength* of gravity. Beam balances would produce correct measurements on the Moon or on Jupiter, but spring scales would not (see fig. 5.1–2).

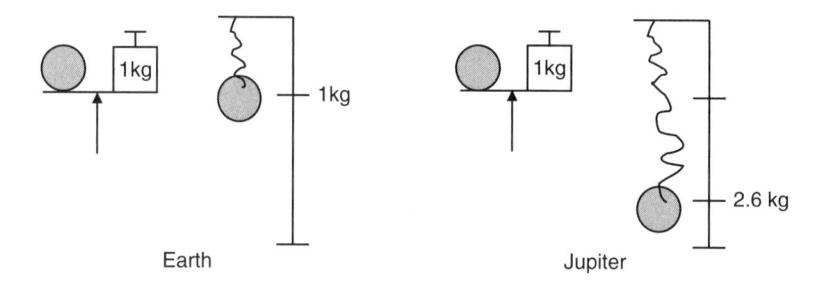

Figure 5.1–2 Beam balances and spring scales on Earth and Jupiter

Both beam balances and spring scales are based on the *weight effect* of mass, i.e. on the existence of a gravitational force affecting the object—therefore, we also speak of "heavy" mass. This means that the area in which the laws of correspondence C_1 and C_2 can be applied is limited: where there is no gravitational force, such as the weightless areas of outer space, neither law of correspondence is applicable. If we wish to measure mass under conditions of weightlessness, e.g. in an orbiting space-shuttle, then we must make use of another effect of mass, i.e. its *inertia* in situations in which the mass is *accelerated*, as for example in collisions. A *collision* experiment can be used to determine an object's mass even in the absence of gravitation. In a so-called *inelastic* collision experiment, the colliding masses remain in contact with each other after the collision. With the help of the law of the conservation of momentum one obtains the following relation between the colliding masses and their velocities, which can be used as a law of correspondence for masses in the absence of gravitation:

(5.1-9)

C$_3$ If x collides inelastically with a resting unit mass of 1 gram at speed v, then x's mass (measured in gram) equals v*/(v–v*), where v* is the joint speed of x with the unit mass after the collision.

It can be said that C$_3$ measures the "inertial" mass. The discussion in physics as to whether heavy and inertial mass really are identical comes from an *operationalist* perspective, which attempts to identify theoretical concepts with empirical dispositions. We have seen that this perspective is inadequate. In the context of the theory of mechanics, the answer to the question concerning the identity of heavy and inertial mass is "yes," simply because this theory speaks only of *one* theoretical characteristic named "mass," and all three laws of correspondence C$_1$–C$_3$ follow from this background theory. Note finally that there are numerous further laws of correspondence for measuring masses that are needed in *specific* contexts, for example for bodies which are too large (e.g. the earth) or too small (e.g. an electron) to be put on a beam balance. For example, the mass of large bodies can be determined by their volume and their density; Newton estimated the mass of the Earth in this way.

Again, we see that laws of correspondence, taken together, possess empirical content. The empirical prediction $\exists t(T_1xt \wedge R_1xt) \rightarrow \forall t(T_2xt \rightarrow R_2xt)$, which is implied by C$_1$ and C$_2$ for the measurement of mass, can be expressed in words as follows: *if an object on a beam balance has balanced out k units of mass, then this object will extend or compress a spring scale by k units of length.* Hence, none of these laws of correspondence can be seen as an analytical definition of mass. Once more, we are compelled to note: the concept of mass is determined by the background theory in which this concept occurs. As we will show in the next section, all the basic axioms of mechanics are needed in order to derive the above mentioned laws of correspondence. It follows from this that a *change* in the background theory also changes the meaning of the theoretical concept. Mass in classical mechanics has a different *meaning* from mass in the special theory of relativity. This insight caused much excitement in the course of the Kuhn controversy, but the excitement was in part exaggerated. Although the Einsteinian mass depends on the velocity of the object while the Newtonian mass does not, they still have a significant part of their meaning in common: both concepts of mass satisfy the above laws of correspondence C$_1$–C$_3$, provided the measurements are made in reference systems which are at rest in relation to the body being measured.

The insight that it is not possible to draw a *local* analytic-synthetic distinction within scientific theories at the level of their individual axioms or consequences gave rise to a revolution in the philosophy of logical empiricism, which only *slowly* came to be accepted. In (1936/37, vol. 3, 451), Carnap had already recognized that several bilateral reduction sentences characterizing the same theoretical concept generate empirical content, but with the concept of a "reduction sentence," he remained nevertheless loyal to the program of semantic reduction (see sec. 1.3.1). In (1939), Carnap replaced the concept of "reduction sentence" with that of an "interpretative sentence," but (like Hempel in 1958, 208ff) he *separated* the *interpretative* system J from the theory T, though without regarding J as being analytically true. The same is still true of Carnap (1956a), where laws of correspondence are called "rules of correspondence" (C). As late as (1963, 961), Carnap separates the theoretical axioms T from the correspondence rules C and speaks of "T∧C" as the "total theory." In contrast, we work out in sections 5.1–2 that laws of correspondence are just *ordinary* synthetic consequences of a theory which provide possibilities for the empirical measurement of theoretical concepts, and which follow from the composite influence of *all* axioms of the theory T. In (1963, 964) Carnap confesses that he has so far searched *in vain* for a functioning concept of analyticity for scientific theories. As a solution, he suggests for the first time the *global* division of a total theory into a synthetic "Ramsey"-sentence and an analytical "Carnap"-sentence, which will be explained in sec. 5.8. This suggestion, however, does not affect the insight that an analytical-synthetic distinction among the individual axioms or consequences of a theory is impossible. The same insight had been reached by Nagel (1961) and Stegmüller (1969ff, vol. II.1, ch. 2).

In a *direct* law of correspondence, test condition T and reaction R denote empirical characteristics. It is often the case that T or R themselves contain theoretical conditions—in this case, we speak of an *conditional* law of correspondence: such a law acts as a correspondence law for a theoretical concept $\tau_1(x)$, on condition that the value of a second theoretical concept $\tau_2(x)$ has already been determined. Carnap spoke here of *chains of reduction* (1936/37, 434–436), and Balzer (1985b, ch. IV) of *chains of measurement*. Every non-circular chain of correspondence laws for a theoretical term τ entails a direct correspondence law for τ. Here is an example:

(5.1–10)

Direct C-Law for τ_1: $T_1 x \to (\tau_1(x) \leftrightarrow R_1 x)$
Conditional C-Law for τ_2: $T_2 x \wedge \tau_1(x) \to (\tau_2(x) \leftrightarrow R_2 x)$

Implied: Direct C-Law for τ_2: $T_1 x \wedge R_1 x \wedge T_2 x \to (\tau_2(x) \leftrightarrow R_2 x)$

One historically significant example is the Thomson-Millikan chain of measurement used to determine the mass and the charge of electrons (Mortimer 1986, 29f). In 1897, Thomson succeeded in using a cathode ray experiment to determine the ratio of charge to mass of the electron (e/m). In 1909, Millikan used an experiment involving droplets of oil to successfully determine the charge of an electron. Fom this, finally, the mass of an electron was determined to be 9.11×10^{-28} g.

In the human and social sciences, too, many concepts are of a theoretical nature. The laws of correspondence linking these theoretical concepts with empirical concepts are known in these disciplines as *indicator* laws (or as *operationalizations*). They are likewise hypothetical components of the respective theory, and in no way true per definition.

(5.1–11) *Examples of C-laws from psychology and social sciences:*

Theoretical concepts:	Indicators:
People's attitudes	Answers to certain interview questions; or behavior in experimental situations
Level of cognitive development of a child	Result in tests of cognitive competences
Character traits of persons, e.g. aggression, emotional instability	Behavior in certain experimental situations; or results of personality tests
Political attitudes of a social class	Their average voting behavior, or results of opinion polls

The indicators on the right are empirical dispositions, whose semantic characterizations produce indicator or correspondence laws for the theoretical concepts on the left. The form of such indicator laws in the human and social sciences is, however, rarely of a strict nature. A person with mainly conservative political tendencies need not answer all questions about politics in a conservative way but, rather, will have a high probabilistic tendency to do so. A highly intelligent person does not have to produce good results in every intelligence test, rather only when she is in good mental form, etc. The correspondence laws for theoretical concepts in these disciplines are, as a rule, of a normic or probabilistic nature. In simple cases they can be stated as follows:

(5.1-12) *Form of normic-probabilistic correspondence laws:*
$T_ixt \Rightarrow (\tau(x) \leftrightarrow R_ixt)$, where "A $\Rightarrow$ B" means "Normally if A then B" and entails "p(B|A) is high."[2]

The consequences of normic correspondence laws follow from the probability axioms (prop. 3.9-1), together with probabilistic *irrelevance* assumptions which are generated *per default*. For example, to infer from two normic C-laws (C_1) $T_1 \Rightarrow (\tau \leftrightarrow R_1)$ and (C_2) $T_2 \Rightarrow (\tau \leftrightarrow R_2)$ the empirical prediction $T_1 \wedge R_1 \wedge T_2 \Rightarrow R_2$ in a probabilistically valid way, one needs the irrelevance assumptions (I_1): $p(\tau \leftrightarrow R_1 | T_1) = p(\tau \leftrightarrow R_1 | T_1 \wedge R_1 \wedge T_2)$ and (I_2): $p(\tau \leftrightarrow R_2 | T_2) = p(\tau \leftrightarrow R_2 | T_1 \wedge R_1 \wedge T_2)$.[3]

In contrast to the natural sciences, indicator relationships in human or social sciences are determined to a lesser extent by theory. Sometimes they result from more or less arbitrary decisions. This gives rise to specific problems which we discuss now. For theoretical concepts in the human and social sciences, there are, prima facie, always *many* more or less plausible indicators. The crucial question is, however, whether these indicators in fact measure a *homogeneous* theoretical characteristic. For example, we could test for the conservative character of test persons (tp) by using questions about their ideological attitude, such as (a) "Are Christian values important to you?," or by using questions about practical attitudes such as (b) "Do you avoid frequent changes in your life?" If studies showed that many tps answer questions of type (a) positively, but those of type (b) negatively, or vice versa, then we would have to conclude that these questions do not measure any theoretically homogeneous characteristic.

The property of an indicator to measure that theoretical characteristic which it is supposed to measure is also called its *construct validity*. As theoretical characteristics cannot be measured directly, judgments about the construct validity of an indicator are only indirectly possible. We can measure, for example, how strongly a whole group of indicators for a theoretical concept correlate among each other. If the correlation is sufficiently strong, then we conclude from this that all indicators measure the same homogeneous theoretical feature. A refined procedure of this type is the Likert scale, which works as follows (Mayntz et al. 1976, 53f): Assume that for some theoretical characteristic, e.g. the degree to which a tp has a pacifistic attitude, various prima facie plausible test questions exist, to which answers are placed on a scale of 0 to 4, where 4 corresponds to a maximum of pacifistic attitude. Using these questions, one determines in a pre-test the 25%-group of tps with the highest average values for *all* questions, and the 25%-group with the lowest average values for all questions—call these two groups of T^{high}

and T^{low}. Then, for every individual question, the difference between the average value in the T^{high}-group and the T^{low}-group is tested for significance using a t-test. Only those questions are chosen for the subsequent main test whose average difference between T^{high} and T^{low} is highly significant: the answers to these questions correlate most strongly among each other, from which one concludes that they are the best measure of pacifistic attitude. Note, however, that although this conclusion is plausible, it is not guaranteed to be true. The internal correlation of a bundle of empirical indicators makes it probable that these indicators measure *some* homogeneous theoretical characteristic, but whether this characteristic is indeed that one which the researchers originally had in mind is another question, which can be answered only within the context of the given background knowledge.

The result of the study of a theoretical property τ depends to a high degree on the chosen empirical indicators for τ. Often the indicators for a theoretical characteristic are selected simply at the researcher's own discretion—in these cases there is a danger of two different kinds of *indicator distortions*:

1 *Biased indicators due to one-sidedness:* An example are Piaget's tests of cognitive competence described more closely in sec. 5.5. To estimate the cognitive development in children, which Piaget describes in highly theoretical language, many *different* indicators might be considered. It was shown that quite different results are reached when indicators differing from those of Piaget are chosen. To avoid one-sided indicators, the following rule should therefore be observed:

> (Prop. 5.1–2) *A theoretical hypothesis should be tested based not only on one, but on as many plausible indicators as possible.*

Due to the mentioned indeterminateness of indicators in the human and social sciences, empirically robust theories can only be achieved in these disciplines by following this rule.

2 *Biased indicators due to hidden variables:* Occasionally by realizing the test conditions of the chosen indicators, unintended hidden variables are smuggled in which *distort* the resulting indicator of the theoretical concept to be measured. An example is given when the tps' answers to questions about their attitudes, for example towards the importance of environmental protection, is taken as an indicator of their attitudes.

The only thing being directly measured in an interview is the *self-assessment* of one's own attitude, which may be biased insofar as psychological studies confirm that most tps tend towards an exaggeratedly positive self-assessment (Krebs 1998). So, answers indicating a high self-estimation of ecological awareness need not correspond with the actually quite low ecological awareness as expressed in the practical behavior of people. The hidden variable here then is the degree of truth of people's assessment of themselves. This insight leads us to a second methodological rule:

> (Prop. 5.1–3) *For every chosen indicator one should test whether, and if so which, hidden variables may be introduced through it.*

5.2 The Example of Newtonian Physics

Newtonian Physics is a *prime example* of a (good) scientific theory. In this section, we shall use this example to shed light on three typical features of scientific theories:

1. the *system character* of scientific theories and the *holism* of their *testing*,
2. the distinction between the *axioms* of a theory and the *consequences* derived from them, and
3. within a theory's axioms, the gradual distinction between the *core* of a theory and its *periphery*.

While the theory's core comprises those laws which are of decisive significance for the theory and define its *identity*, the periphery contains specific hypotheses of lesser significance, which may be changed or abandoned without endangering the identity of the theory.

The fundamental empirical or, better, *pre-theoretical* (non-logical) concepts of classical physics are the singular terms for physical bodies (x) and points in time (t) as *independent* variables, and position (s), velocity (v) and acceleration (a) as *dependent* variables, i.e. as *functions* of objects and time. Hereby, velocity and acceleration are defined as the first and second derivative of position with respect to time. The fundamental theoretical concepts of classical physics are the mass and force functions (m and f). A plenitude of further concepts, e.g. momentum, work and energy, are defined with the help of these concepts. The first core axiom of Newtonian mechanics is the following:

(5.2–1) *(N1) Total force = mass times acceleration.*

More precisely: The sum of all forces acting on a body x at a time t is equal to the product of the mass of x and the acceleration of x at t.

Formally: $\forall x \in D, t \in T: \Sigma_{i \in I} f_i(x,t) = m(x) \cdot a(x,t)$; with $a(x,t) = d^2s(x,t)/dt^2$.

Notation: D is the set of physical objects x; T the set of points in time t, equated with the set of real numbers $\mathbb{R}$; m(x) is the time-independent mass of x (m: $D \to \mathbb{R}_+$); s(x,t) and a(x,t) are the time-dependent position and acceleration vectors of x (s: $D \times T \to \mathbb{R}^3$), and $f_i(x,t)$ is the force vector of type i exerted on x at t (f: $D \times T \times I \to \mathbb{R}^3$). $I \subseteq \mathbb{N}$ is a *variable* index set for kinds of forces (not fixed by (N1)) which covers *all* forces acting on x. All physical magnitudes are associated with *units* (see sec. 3.1.4.3) which are omitted for sake of simplicity.

(N1) is the second axiom of Newton's *Principia*. Its first axiom "Every body persists in its state of rest, or moves uniformly straight forward" is a consequence of (N1), since from $a(x,t) = 0$ follows $\Sigma_{i \in I} f_i(x,t) = 0$. Note that (N1) states *two* things at once. First, that the total force is simply the *sum* of all individual forces (the principle of vector addition). This means that forces when working together do not interact. Second, that the total force is equal to the product of mass and acceleration.

Axiom (N1) is a mixed axiom, since it contains both theoretical and non-theoretical concepts. (N1) alone, however, does *not* yet deliver any law of correspondence for mass or total force. Only the quotient between the two is empirically determined by (N1) as equal to the acceleration. For the same reason, axiom (N1) alone has *no* empirical content, i.e. no empirical predictions about the movement of bodies are derivable from (N1) alone. These and similar facts have been demonstrated by Sneed (1971, 118, 127). Sneed makes use of model theory (see sec. 3.1.2): the fact that (N1) viewed in isolation is empirically empty means in model-theoretic terms that for every partial non-theoretical model (D,T,s) one can find mass and force functions m and $F(x,t) =_{def} \Sigma_{i \in I} f_i(x,t)$ that extend (D,T,s) into a full theoretical model (D,T,s,m,F) which satisfies axiom (N1). To obtain these functions one simply has to choose F(x,t) and m(x) in such a way that their quotient coincides with the acceleration a(x,t).

The second core axiom (N2) of Newton's theory is the principle of "actio equals reactio" (the third axiom of the *Principia*). As opposed to (N1), which speaks of total force, (N2) makes a statement about individual forces:

(5.2-2) *(N2) Force = counterforce.* More precisely: If two bodies x and y exert a force on each other, then the force of x working on y is of equal amount and opposite direction as the counterforce of y working on x.—*More generally:* the sum of all forces that are acting within a closed system is zero.

(N2) contains only theoretical concepts, and so is a purely theoretical law. It is also a core law, like (N1) (cf. Balzer et al. 1987, 182).

If we combine (N1) with (N2), then according to the interpretation of Sneed (1971, 129ff), we already have empirical content. Sneed's interpretation is, however, not fully accurate: such empirical content follows only when additional peripheral conditions are taken on, which I call *system conditions*: they state that *only* such-and-such forces are present (i.e. they specify the set of relevant forces $\{f_i: i \in I\}$). From (N1) and (N2), the definitions of "energy" and "momentum," and the system condition that no external forces are influencing the given system of physical bodies, one can derive the mechanical *conservation laws* for energy and momentum (cf. e.g. Young/Freedman 1996, sec. 7.3, 8.3). In application to colliding particles one obtains therefrom the laws describing inelastic and elastic collisions, which entail the correspondence law in (5.1-9) for mass measurements in the absence of gravitational fields. Furthermore, together with the definition of torque one obtains from (N1+N2) the law of levers (force × lever arm = weight × load arm) and so the correspondence law (5.1-6) (C_1) for mass measurement on a beam balance (Sneed 1971, 131ff)—but only under the system condition that the same downward force is acting on either side of the beam.

(N1+N2) plus system conditions deliver correspondence laws for mass measurement, but they entail *nothing* about the nature of individual kinds of forces at work. In the derivations of the measurement laws for mass from (N1+N2) and system conditions, the forces at work cancel each other out with the help of the action–reaction principle (N2). For this reason, the empirical content of (N1+N2) plus system conditions is still comparatively low. A veritable *explosion* of the empirical content is generated when the core laws (N1+N2) are supplemented with *special force laws* describing individual kinds of force, most importantly the law of gravitation that had already been discovered by Newton:

(5.2-3) *(N3)* The gravitational force $f_g(x,y,t)$ exerted by a body x on a body y at a given time t is proportional to the product of both masses, divided by the square of their distance at time t, and aligned from y to x, i.e. x draws y towards itself in a straight line.

(N1)–(N3) give us various *differential equations* of classical gravitational mechanics, whose exact or approximate solution makes it possible to predict the movements of arbitrary masses in gravitational fields, depending on the *system conditions*, which specify which particles exert a non-negligible gravitational force in the considered system, and on the *initial conditions*, which specify the positions and velocities of the particles in the considered system at an arbitrarily chosen "initial" time point t_0. System conditions give us a *theoretical model* of the system, and initial conditions provide an empirical snapshot of the system at a given starting point. A large number of qualitatively different phenomena thereby become predictable or explainable. For instance:

1   the movements of rigid bodies on Earth, such as free fall, trajectory of projectiles, movement on inclined planes, gravitational pendulum, rotational movements around axes, levers, spinning tops, etc.;
2   the movements of celestial bodies in the gravitational fields of outer space, e.g. the orbits of planets around the Sun, the Earth's rotation, the Moon's orbit around the Earth; in connection with this the changing of the seasons, day and night, the movements of tides; and more recently, the paths of comets and trajectories of spaceships;
3   the mechanical laws of solids, liquids and gases describing the phenomena of friction, currents, heat and pressure, which are obtained by the application of Newtonian physics to matter understood as composed of molecules, held together by intermolecular forces in solids and fluids, and moving freely in gases.

Numerous regularities which had heretofore been known only through empirical-inductive generalization could now be explained in a theoretically unified way: Archimedes' law of levers, Descartes' laws of impact, Galileo's law of falling bodies, Kepler's law of the planets, etc. And this is by no means all, as we have so far looked only at *one* special force law, the law of gravitation. There are a number of further special force laws describing other kinds of forces, for example, Hooke's elastic force or the force of friction; these force laws make it possible to explain periodic motion of pendulums and waves in elastic mechanical media. Finally, by adding electric or magnetic forces, electrodynamically caused forms of motions become explainable, from electric circuits to Bohr's model of the atom. Let it not go unmentioned that ultimately the combination of classical mechanics and electrodynamics gave rise to several incoherences. The attempts to solve them led to the development of relativity theory and quantum mechanics in the early 20th century. The former corrected classical mechanics in regard to extremely fast particles, and the latter in regard to extremely small ones. But in application to objects of ordinary sizes and velocities, classical physics is an approximately true and enormously successful theory program whose application to complex systems is still *progressing*. An overview of the manifold empirical applications of classical mechanics is shown in fig. 5.2–1.

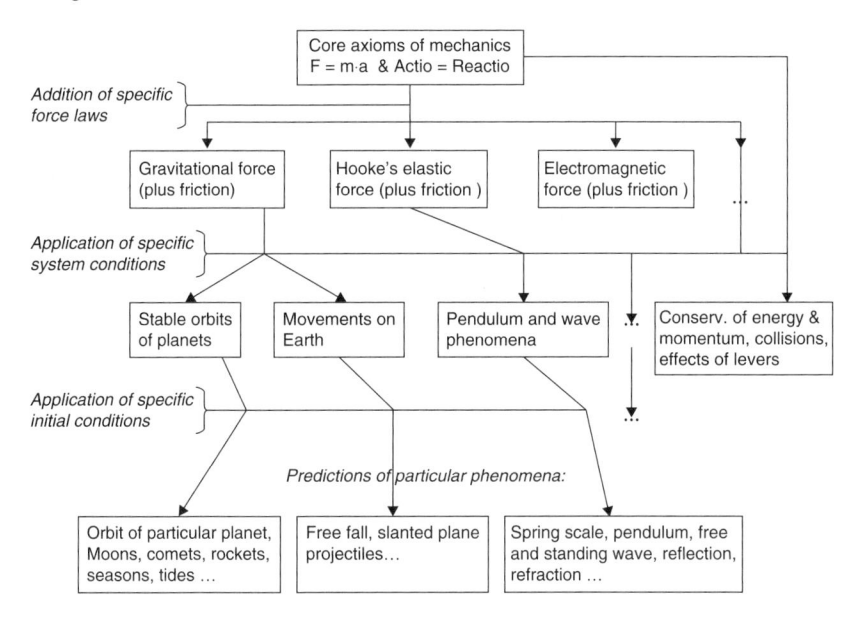

```
                    ┌─────────────────────────┐
                    │ Core axioms of mechanics │
                    │ F = m·a & Actio = Reactio│
                    └─────────────────────────┘
Addition of specific
force laws
       ┌────────────────┬────────────────┬────────────────┐
       ▼                ▼                ▼
┌───────────────┐ ┌───────────────┐ ┌───────────────┐
│Gravitational  │ │Hooke's elastic│ │Electromagnetic│  ...
│force          │ │force          │ │force          │
│(plus friction)│ │(plus friction)│ │(plus friction)│
└───────────────┘ └───────────────┘ └───────────────┘
Application of specific
system conditions
     ┌─────────┬─────────────┬──────────────────┐
     ▼         ▼             ▼                  ▼
┌─────────┐ ┌─────────┐ ┌──────────────┐ ┌──────────────────┐
│Stable   │ │Movements│ │Pendulum and  │ │Conserv. of energy│
│orbits of│ │on Earth │ │wave phenomena│ │& momentum,       │
│planets  │ │         │ │              │ │collisions,       │
│         │ │         │ │              │ │effects of levers │
└─────────┘ └─────────┘ └──────────────┘ └──────────────────┘
Application of specific
initial conditions
              Predictions of particular phenomena:
     ▼              ▼                  ▼
┌──────────────┐ ┌──────────────┐ ┌──────────────────┐
│Orbit of      │ │Free fall,    │ │Spring scale,     │
│particular    │ │slanted plane │ │pendulum, free    │
│planet, Moons,│ │projectiles...│ │and standing wave,│
│comets,       │ │              │ │reflection,       │
│rockets,      │ │              │ │refraction ...    │
│seasons,      │ │              │ │                  │
│tides ...     │ │              │ │                  │
└──────────────┘ └──────────────┘ └──────────────────┘
```

Figure 5.2–1 Theory lattice in classical mechanics and its manifold applications

Fig. 5.2–1 makes it clear that theories in physics (as well as in other sciences) are organized in the form of hierarchical *theory lattices*. At the apex, we find general *core* laws, which one level lower get enriched by special force laws, which in application to specific system conditions yield theoretical models of special kinds of physical systems. As in structuralist philosophy of science we shall call the units of such theory lattices *theory elements*; the vertical relationship between these elements from top to bottom is the relationship of *specialization*. (Note that our "theory lattices" are called "theory nets" by the structuralists, while we will reserve the term "theory net" for what the structuralists call a "theory holon"; see sec. 5.3.2.)

The example of Newton's theory has shown us three important properties of good scientific theories. These are: (i) their *system character*, i.e. the empirical content results from the *combination* of individual axioms, which are without content in isolation, (ii) in relation to this, the *empirical creativity* of such theories, and (iii) their *globality* and *unification power*, i.e. qualitatively quite different phenomena are explained through the same theoretical mechanisms. In particular, Newtonian physics succeeded in subsuming the physics of earthly and heavenly bodies, which had been separate in the Aristotelian world view, under one common theory.

Property (iii) is related to (iv) the ability to predict *qualitatively new* kinds of phenomena, of which no individual instance has yet been observed. Recall from sec. 5.1 that qualitatively new predictions cannot be obtained from empirical inductions; one needs theories to get them. *Pars pro toto* we mention the Newtonian prediction that the gravitational force should also be at work between all ordinary earthly bodies. As no such thing can be observed in everyday life, this prediction seemed so unbelievable that most of Newton's contemporaries doubted it. Not until Henry Cavendish demonstrated the attraction between the masses of two steel balls using his torsion scales in 1798, could common sense be convinced of the universal validity of Newton's law of gravity.

Based on its exalted successes, Newtonian physics grew in the 18th and 19th centuries to become a universal explanatory paradigm. This paradigm was associated with the explanatory *promise*, that all natural phenomena could eventually be explained by Newtonian physics, if one finds out the specific force laws responsible for the different kinds of phenomena (Kitcher 1981, 513f). The Newtonian programmatic is a typical example of what Lakatos described with his concept of a *research program* (sec. 5.6.1).

Through Newtonian physics we can also recognize two important *special* features of *physical* theories (which are uncommon but not completely absent in non-physical disciplines). First, the fundamental laws of physical theories have the form of *differential equations*. A differential equation expresses a lawlike functional relationship between the *variable* state s(t) of the observed system at a given time point t and the rate of *change* of s(t), as described by the 1st or the 2nd derivative of s(t). In classical mechanics s(t) is the position function. For example, the differential equation that describes a planet orbiting around a resting star is obtained by replacing the "sum of all forces" in (N1) by the gravitational force between star and planet according to (N3). *Solving* a differential equation means finding the class of state functions s(t) which satisfy the equation. Every differential equation possesses a whole set of possible *solutions*, which describe all possible *trajectories*, i.e. time-dependent state developments of the given system, depending on the variable initial conditions. By inserting particular initial conditions one obtains a unique solution function—in our example a planet trajectory.

Differential equations possess an even *higher unifying power* than the qualitative (non-numerical) theories discussed in sec. 5.1, because quantitative variations of their system- or initial conditions (e.g. initial velocities) can lead to qualitatively different behavior, e.g. a planet in a stable orbit versus its collapse into the Sun.

The *second* special feature of physical theories is the aforementioned interaction of fundamental laws of nature, such as (N1–3) and system conditions. System conditions are typical *auxiliary hypotheses* in the sense of Lakatos (1970), which are located at the periphery of the theory: they list all non-negligible forces, and therefore involve an exclusive ceteris paribus (eCP) clause, which states that apart from the forces mentioned, *no* others are present. In our view (unlike Hempel's diagnosis in 1988), this eCP clause is *definite* in the sense of sec. 4.5.1, because the "sum of all forces" in axiom (N1) does not refer to "arbitrary forces," but only to *physical* forces according to the accepted physical background theory: at present, these are the four fundamental interaction forces (gravitation, electromagnetic force, strong and weak nuclear force) and the forces of inertia occurring through collisions.

The system conditions describing a physical system involve always a certain amount of *idealization* (Nowak 1980). It is impossible on grounds of overcomplexity to consider strictly *all* forces that are acting in a real system. One neglects all small forces as "disturbances" and considers only those forces which are relevant and computationally tractable—in our example, only the gravitational influence of the Sun on the planet, and maybe that of other planets which come close to it, but not the influence of far distant stars or tiny interstellar particles, etc. One should not draw from this the radical consequence of Cartwright (1983), for whom "all physical theories lie." What follows from it is the well-known fact that the quantitative predictions of physical theories are never strictly, but always only *approximately* true—the closer the predicted curves come to the true data, the better the approximation (cf. sec. 5.10.5).

We finally turn to the *holism of theory testing*, which is the methodologically most important consequence of the system character of scientific theories. To understand what it means, consider the argument schema (5.2-4) which depicts qualitatively how a *full* Newtonian theory element (core + periphery) entails an empirical prediction:

(5.2-4) Schematic derivation of a prediction from Newtonian mechanics:

Core axiom N1 (Total force = mass times acceleration)
Core axiom N2 (Force = counterforce)
Specific law of gravitational force (semi-core)
Auxiliary hypothesis (system condition): only the gravitational force of the Sun is acting on planet p

---

Prediction: Path of planet p is such-and-such function of time and initial conditions

Prediction is correct: Total system is corroborated!

Prediction is incorrect: holism of testing—where is the error? Ad-hoc core protection: in the auxiliary hypotheses!

If the prediction is correct, then the total system of premises has been corroborated. We call this total system of all premises used for various empirical prognoses, the *current version* of a theory. However, if the prediction is incorrect, i.e. our observations of the planet reveal a significant discrepancy from the predicted path, then we can only conclude that *at least one* of the premises of the current theory version must be false, but we do not know *which* premise contains the error. This indeterminacy is meant by the "holism of theory testing," or "holism of falsification."

Lakatos (1970, 16ff) demonstrated convincingly that when the current version of a theory conflicts with experience, proponents of this theory will at first not call the theory's core into question but, rather, will protect the core from falsification, by giving up or altering the auxiliary hypotheses at the periphery of the theory. This means that yet unobserved *disturbing* factors are postulated, which have not yet been taken into account in the system conditions, and which are expected to explain the observed divergences from the theoretical predictions. This sounds like a very ad-hoc maneuver, but when examined more closely turns out to be a prima facie plausible step to take, which can only be criticized as an ad-hoc maneuver if the postulated unknown disturbing factor cannot be *independently confirmed*. Here are two examples from the history of science (Grünbaum 1976, 332–335, 358):

1 In 1846, when J. Adams and U. Le Verrier discovered a considerable discrepancy between the predicted and the actually observed orbit of the planet *Uranus*, they postulated the existence of an as yet undiscovered planet, *Neptune*, whose gravitational effect on Uranus was said to be responsible for its divergence from the predicted orbital path. On the

basis of the observed divergence in the orbit of Uranus, they predicted the approximate size and orbit of this new planet, and explained the fact that nobody had ever seen it by arguing that it was too small and far away to be seen with the telescopes of the day. Indeed, the planet Neptune was observed a short time later with stronger telescopes, and this was regarded as a great success for Newtonian physics.

2 In contrast to this, Le Verrier also observed a divergence of the planet *Mercury* from its predicted orbit and, around 1856, he postulated the existence of a yet smaller planet named *Vulcan*. Despite tenacious attempts, this planet could not be found using telescopes. Not until much later could Mercury's divergence from its predicted orbit be successfully explained—not by a new auxiliary hypothesis, but the replacement of Newtonian theory by a new theory core: Einstein's theory of relativity.

The question of the right definition of the ad-hoc character of scientific hypotheses gave rise to wide-ranging controversy (e.g. Popper 1935/2000, 51f; Hempel 1966, 28–30; Grünbaum 1976; Lakatos 1970, 39f, 88). All these authors agree that ad-hoc character is a *contextual* feature. We call a hypothesis H *ad hoc* in relation to an epistemic background system S at a given point in time t, if H has only been introduced to reconcile a core theory in S with a specific empirical observation O in S. So, at time t, H does not have any independent confirmation within S. The two examples above show that the current ad-hoc status of a hypothesis must not be understood to be a permanent verdict for the future. Everything depends on future developments—in particular on two questions: (1) does the hypothesis H in the context of the background knowledge of S produce new empirical content, on the basis of which it might be tested?, and (2) does such testing, if it is possible, lead to a confirmation of H? Should (1) be the case, the hypothesis will be either empirically corroborated or, in the case of a negative test result, empirically falsified or weakened; in either case, H loses its ad-hoc character. Only when case (1) never happens, i.e. when H never produces any new empirical content, does the ad-hoc character of H become permanent and turn into a negative verdict concerning H. In such a case, even the core of a theory, though prima facie exempt from empirical criticism, becomes subject to empirical criticism and revision.

5.3 Theory Statics: The Structure of Scientific Theories

5.3.1 Components of Scientific Theories

Based on the previous results we can divide scientific theories T into component parts in four ways (see fig. 5.3-1 below).

1 With regard to the *concepts* of a theory T, we distinguished in sec. 3.1.3 between (a) the *empirical* concepts of T i.n.s., (b) the non-empirical concepts of T, which we called "theoretical i.w.s.," and (c) as a subset of (b), the theoretical concepts of T i.n.s., or *T-theoretical* concepts, whose meaning is explained within theory T by means of correspondence laws. A further subset of (b) is (d) T's *pre-theoretical* concepts: these are T-concepts whose meaning is explained within *pre-theories* of T, which are theories T' containing *fewer* non-empirical concepts than T. For example, the position function is a pre-theoretical concept of mechanics, because its meaning is explained in kinematics, which is a pre-theory of mechanics containing only the concepts of position, time, velocity and acceleration. Precise definitions of these notions, together with a discussion of different accounts of T-theoreticity, are provided in sec. 5.9.1.

With regard to the *language* of the theory, we distinguish between the *total* (theoretical) language $\mathcal{L}(T)$ of T, which contains all (logico-mathematical, empirical, pre-theoretical or theoretical) terms of T and all expressions composable from them; and the *empirical* (or *pre-theoretical*) sublanguage $\mathcal{L}_e(T)$ of T, which contains, apart from logico-mathematical terms, only empirical (or pre-theoretical) terms of T and expressions composed from them.

2 With regard to the *logical nature* of the sentences of T, we distinguish between the *axioms* of T and the logical (or probabilistic) *consequences* of T. We identify T with the set of its axioms, $T = Ax(T)$, while we summarize the consequences in the logical (or probabilistic) content $C(T)$ of T, or in the relevant content $C_r(T)$ according to sec. 3.12.

Theories can be axiomatized in different, but logically equivalent ways. We demand from an axiomatization $Ax(T)$ of T that it is *natural*, and we understand by this that $Ax(T)$ is an *irreducible representation* of T in the sense of def. 3.10–5. Natural axiomatizations exclude logically irrelevant components in the axioms, and guarantee that axioms are "smallest," i.e. conjunctively *indivisible* content parts, which is central for questions of confirmation, verisimilitude or unification (sec. 5.10–11). Usually the natural axiomatization of a set of sentences is unique. If several natural axiomatizations are possible, these do not express mere logical trivialities, but interesting structural rearrangements. For Newtonian particle mechanics, two alternative axiomatizations were developed: *Lagrangean* and *Hamiltonian* mechanics.

3 With regard to the *conceptual* nature of the sentences (axioms or consequences) of T: here, we differentiate between *purely theoretical* laws of

T, which, apart from logico-mathematical terms, contain only theoretical terms; *mixed sentences* of T, which contain both empirical (pre-theoretical) and theoretical terms; and *empirical* or *pre-theoretical* sentences of T, which contain, besides logico-mathematical terms, only empirical (pre-theoretical) terms. An important subset of the mixed laws of T are the *correspondence laws* of T. In normal cases, the axioms of T contain only purely theoretical laws or correspondence laws, while the empirical or pre-theoretical sentences result as consequences.

4 With regard to the *epistemic status of the axioms* of T: here, we distinguish gradually between the *core* and the *periphery* of Ax(T). Core axioms of T define the *historical identity* of a theory—if core axioms are changed, then we are dealing with a *different* theory. Peripheral hypotheses of T characterize only the *current version* of a theory at a certain time or in certain applications—if they are changed, then the current version of the theory is changed, but not the theory itself. In between, we find special laws of T which can be closer to or further from the core. Note that peripheral hypotheses too have, logically speaking, the status of "axioms," as they cannot be derived from other axioms of T. The distinction between core and periphery only makes clear sense for the

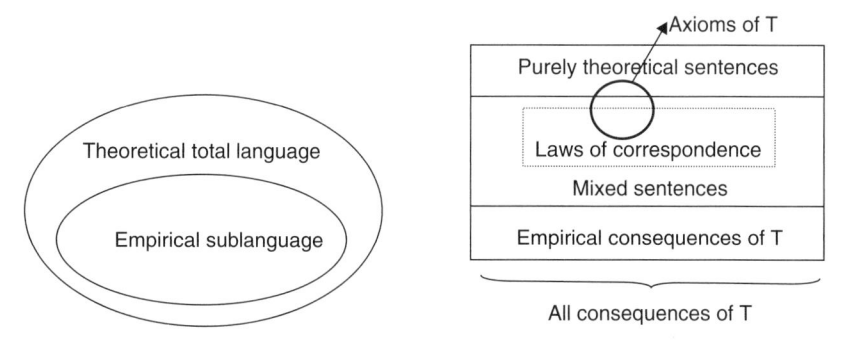

Figure 5.3–1 Subdivision of T according to T's language

Figure 5.3–2 Subdivision of T according to the logical and the conceptual nature of T's sentences

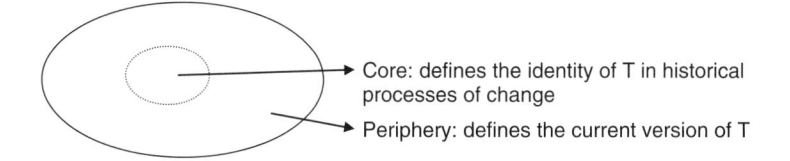

Figure 5.3–3 Subdivision of the axioms of T according to their epistemic status

axioms of T. Dividing the consequences of T into those which are closer to or further from the core is problematic, because it will often occur that a consequence S follows from a core axiom together with a peripheral auxiliary hypothesis, and then it is arbitrary whether S is considered as core or peripheral.

5.3.2 Theory Nets and Intertheoretical Relations

Recall the notion of a theory *lattice* (fig. 5.2–1). A *theory net* consists of different theory elements or theory lattices. There are at least three kinds of relationships between the theory elements of a theory net (see also Balzer et al. 1987):

1. Through the relation of *specialization* as explained in sec. 5.2 hierarchical theory lattices come into being.
2. The relation of *pre-theoreticity* explained in sec. 5.3.1 can exist both within and between theory lattices.

The relations of specialization and pre-theoreticity may connect only theoretically *homogeneous* theory elements. If T_1 is a specialization of T_2, then T_2 is logically entailed by T_1, and if T_2 is a pre-theory of T_1, then T_1's language is a sublanguage of T_2. Theory elements connected in this way can never contradict each other or compete with each other. This is different for the third category of intertheoretical relationships:

3. Between different theory lattices, there exist *intertheoretical relations* (structuralists call them "links"). A first and trivial case are relations of *identity*: for example, if Coulomb forces are used in a mechanical model, then the concept of Coulomb force is borrowed from the theory lattice of electrostatics. Relations of *correspondence* are a second important kind of intertheoretical relations. The prototypical example is the correspondence relation between thermodynamics and statistical mechanics, according to which the absolute temperature of a substance is proportional to the average kinetic energy of its molecules. A third kind of intertheoretical relation is strict or approximate *theory reduction*.

We have seen in sec. 2.6.2 that laws of special sciences are usually not fully reducible to theories of fundamental physics. However, many interesting reduction relations exist between physical or chemical theories. For example, classical mechanics follows approximately from the special theory of relativity when the particle speeds are very small in relation to the speed of light. Or, the phenomenological gas law (pressure × volume is proportional to absolute temperature) follows from the statistical mechanics of a swarm of gas molecules when absolute temperature is interpreted as the mean kinetic energy of the molecules. According to the classical accounts of Nagel (1970) and Hempel (1969), a theory T_1 is *strictly* reducible to a theory T_2 if there is a set C of correspondence principles which characterize T_1-concepts with the help of T_2-concepts, as well as a set L of limiting conditions under which the reduction is possible, so that T_1 may be derived from T_2, C and L. Such a reduction is called *approximate*, if not T_1 itself, but rather an approximation T_1^* of T_1, can be derived from T_2, C and L—i.e. the empirical predictions of T_1^* come quantitatively very close to the predictions of T_1 (Nagel 1970, 121, 125; Hempel 1969, 193). In the case of the reduction of classical mechanics to special relativity theory, C asserts that classical mass equals relativistic rest mass, and L that the particle speeds are small compared to light velocity. The Hempel-Nagelian concept of reduction can still be seen as well corroborated.

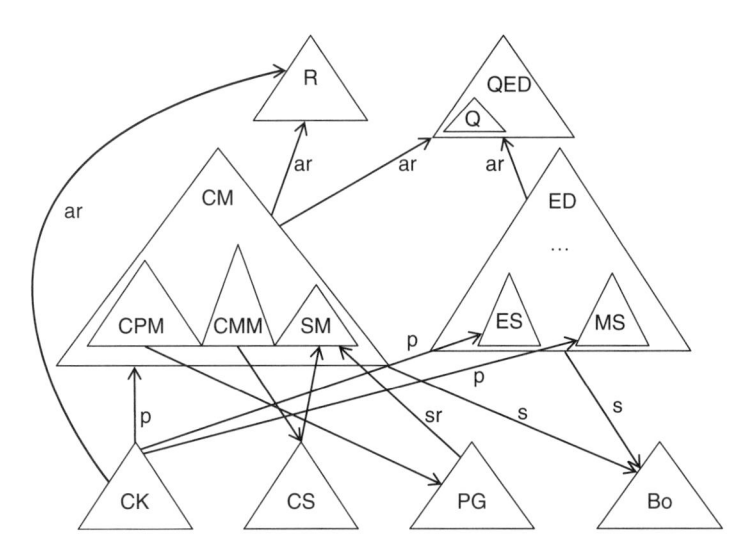

Figure 5.3–4 Part of the theory net of physical and chemical theories. Triangles represent theory lattices ordered by the relation of specialization. *Abbreviations:* "x→y" for "x exports some of its concepts identically to y," "x →^{s}y" for "x is a specialization of y," "x →^{p}y" for "x is pre-theory of y," "x→^{sr}y [x→^{ar}y]" for "x is strictly [approximately] reducible to y." CK for classical kinematics, CM classical mechanics, CPM classical particle mechanics, CMM classical mechanics of matter (hydro- and aerodynamics), PG phenomenological gas theory, SM statistical mechanics, CS chemical stoichiometry, B Bohr's atomic model, ED electrodynamics, ES electrostatics, MS magnetostatics, R relativity theory, Q quantum mechanics, QED quantum electrodynamics.

Figure 5.3–4 illustrates a part of the theory net of physics and chemistry.

The theories of physics and chemistry are connected in a dense theory net. Even parts of biology and psychology (e.g. biochemistry and neuropsychology) can easily be assigned a place in this net. If we switch to evolutionary biology, then we have a relatively autonomous theory net, which does not import many concepts from the net of physical and chemical theories, but does in its turn export central concepts to psychology, human and social sciences. In these "higher-level" disciplines, we find instead of unifying fundamental theories an increasing competition between theoretical *approaches* in loose combination with factual knowledge (Schurz/Weingartner 1998). This difference has, presumably, much to do with the highly complex nature of the objects of these disciplines. In spite of this difference we will see in the next sections that the same insights that have been illustrated so far with examples from natural sciences apply also to human and social sciences.

5.4 Methodological Features of (Good) Scientific Theories

5.4.1 System Character: Holism of Meaning, Content, and Theory Testing (Duhem's Thesis)

By the *system character* of theories, we mean the fact that we cannot understand a theory if we view its individual axioms or hypotheses in isolation, but only when we observe the interaction of its axioms. While a single axiom does not, as a rule, possess any empirical content, diverse empirical content is generated by the conjunction of several axioms. Three kinds of holism follow from the system character of theories:

1 The *holism of meaning* of theoretical concepts is the fact (explained in sec. 5.1) that the meaning of theoretical concepts is determined by the relevant background theories for this concept. It is not possible to distinguish among the theoretical axioms or consequences of a scientific theory between analytic and synthetic statements. In application to theoretical statements, then, Quine's thesis (1951) of the indistinguishability of the analytic-synthetic is confirmed.

2 By *holism of empirical content* we understand the related fact that we can only confront an entire *system* of theoretical hypotheses with experience, as it is only such a system which generates empirical content.

3   What follows directly from the holism of empirical content is the *holism of theory testing*, which was illustrated at the end of sec. 5.2: if the empirical prediction P follows from a system of theoretical hypotheses T = {$H_1,...,H_n$}, and P conflicts with an experience E, i.e. E ||⎯⎯ ¬P, then we know that the system T must contain *somewhere* a false hypothesis. It is, however, logically *undetermined*, which of the hypotheses H_i is false or should be discarded. The first to point this out was Duhem (1908/1991), who coined the famous formula: there is no *experimentum crucis* for a theory, i.e. the result of an experiment can never conclusively force us to give up the core of the theory or other *individual* components of the given theory version. The same fact was later worked out by Neurath (1916). Quine (1951, 47) worked out the *empirical underdetermination* of theories, which follows from their system character: with regard to conflicting experience, different but empirically equivalent changes to a theoretical system are always possible. The holism of theory testing operates within the framework of deductive logic:

(Prop. 5.4–1) *Logical background of the holism of testing:* If the set of premises {$H_1,...,H_n$} logically implies the prediction P, then the negation of the prediction, ¬P, logically implies (per Modus Tollens) the negation of the conjunction of all premises, ¬($H_1 \wedge ... \wedge H_n$). The latter is logically equivalent with the disjunction of all negated premises, $\neg H_1 \vee ... \vee \neg H_n$, which expresses that *at least one* of the premises H_i is false.

If the prediction P is a *probabilistic* or *non-monotonic* consequence of a system of hypotheses T = {$H_1,...,H_n$} (see sec. 2.7.4), this makes the following important difference for the holism of theory testing (cf. Schurz 2004, sec. 3): in order to avoid the consequence P, it is then no longer necessary to *remove* some hypothesis H_i in T, as is the case with deductive-monotonic consequences. It would also suffice simply to *add* a new auxiliary hypothesis H* which prevents the derivability of P.

All different forms of holism explained here are kinds of a *moderate* holism: we neither claim (as in "radical holism") that everything is connected with *everything* else, nor that the meaning of *all* concepts is determined by background theory.

5.4.2 Empirical Creativity, Global Unification, and Novel Predictions: Answers to Hempel's Dilemma

Intimately connected with the system character and holism of scientific theories are three essential virtues of theories:

1 The *empirical creativity* of scientific theories expresses the fact that the conjunction of two or more theoretical hypotheses may generate *new* empirical content, which *exceeds* what is entailed by the *combination* of the empirical content of the individual hypotheses (see Kutschera 1972, 304f). Recall def. 3.7–1 of the logical content C(S) and empirical content E(S) of a sentence S.

> (Prop. 5.4–2) *Empirical creativity:* The conjunction of two theoretical hypotheses H_1 and H_2 may generate new empirical content that is not entailed by the union of the empirical contents of the individual hypotheses, i.e. formally:
> $E(H_1 \wedge H_2) \supset C(E(H_1) \cup E(H_2))$ (where "$\supset$" means "proper superset").

Example: Assume $H_1 = \forall x(Fx \rightarrow \tau(x))$ and $H_2 = \forall x(Gx \rightarrow \tau(x)) \wedge \forall x(\tau(x) \rightarrow Hx)$, where F, G, H are empirical predicates. Then $E(H_1) = \emptyset$, $E(H_2) = C(\forall x(Gx \rightarrow Hx))$, so $C(E(H_1) \cup E(H_2)) = E(H_2) = C(\forall x(Gx \rightarrow Hx))$. But $E(H_1 \wedge H_2)$ contains the new empirical consequence $\forall x(Fx \rightarrow Hx)$, i.e. $E(H_1 \wedge H_2) = C(\forall x(Fx \rightarrow Hx) \wedge \forall x(Gx \rightarrow Hx))$.

Prop. 5.4–2 explains how it is possible that a theoretical speculation H possessing no empirical content can generate new empirical content in the context of a theory T developed later. For although E(H) is empty, $E(T \wedge H)$ can be substantially larger than E(T). This is an important insight concerning the possible empirical *fruitfulness of metaphysical speculations* for later developments in science.

2 Connected with (1) is the feature of *global unification power*. By globality of a theory we mean that it can explain qualitatively different empirical phenomena, and by unification power that it explains these phenomena in a unified manner, and thereby traces a large number of empirical hypotheses back to a few theoretical principles. We have illustrated both features in sec. 5.1 and 5.2 (there will be more about unification in sec. 5.11.2 and sec. 6.5).

3 As explained below prop. (5.1–1), the ability of a theory to generate *potentially novel predictions*, which make the theory independently testable by *use-novel evidence*, goes hand in hand with (2) (see also sec. 5.10.3).

The three virtues of theories explained above go essentially *beyond* what can be achieved by mere empirical generalizations. So they give an answer to an old question: i.e. in what does the *positive* function of theoretical concepts consist, provided it exists at all? This question has an interesting history. In a paper which has been called "Putnam's challenge," Putnam (1962) argued that logical empiricists had only given a negative characterization of theoretical terms, as being "not empirically definable," but their positive scientific role is not understood. Putnam argued that this positive function is encapsulated in the function of theoretical terms to *refer* to unobservable entities. However, this characterization was unsatisfying insofar as it left unclear how a "reference to something unobservable" is epistemically accessible at all. What philosophers of science were after was an explication of theoreticity which is not based on free-floating metaphysical reference assumptions, but on the *positive role* which theoretical concepts play in a given theory. Surely this role should somehow go *beyond* the role of empirical concepts, for otherwise theoretical concepts would be superfluous. But how *can* the role of theoretical concepts go beyond the empirical, if the ultimate evaluation measure of theories is empirical success? Hempel (1958, 186) sharpened this problem into a famous dilemma, the *theoretician's dilemma* (see Tuomela 1973, 3): (a) either theoretical concepts *do not* fulfill an empirical role, in which case they are not needed in science, or (b) they do fulfill an empirical role, in which case they are also not needed, because then it is sufficient to assert solely their empirical consequences without mentioning the theoretical concepts. If this were true, then by *Ockham's razor*, theoretical concepts should be abandoned.

Hempel's dilemma seemed to imply that theoretical concepts are superfluous in any case. This was water on the mills of the empirical operationalists, who wanted to eliminate theoretical concepts from science. But this was not the conclusion reached by Hempel, who was well aware that successful theories *do* contain theoretical concepts. So Hempel (1958) looked for positive properties of theories by which they go beyond empirical generalizations. He discusses a theorem of Craig (1953) which intended to show the opposite. Craig showed that one can always construct a recursive set of axioms $Ax(E(T))$ which is free of theoretical concepts and logically equivalent with T's empirical content. This was taken to show that theoretical concepts are dispensable without losing empirical content. Craig's axiom set, however, is highly artificial: It is countably *infinite* and contains for every empirical consequence of T exactly one axiom. So it cannot produce any empirical unification. This fact was already acknowledged by Hempel (cf. 1958, 212f; Tuomela 1973, 28ff).

Our list of virtues above gives a solution to Hempel's dilemma which goes beyond this insight. If we were to replace a finitely axiomatized theory T by Craig's infinite axiom set Ax(E(T)), then we would lose *every* one of these virtues. Not only will Ax(E(T)) have no unification power, it will also not be empirically creative. Therefore, although T and Ax(E(T)) are empirically equivalent, they will not necessarily be empirically equivalent in the context of a background knowledge B which contains some of T's theoretical concepts (i.e. $E(B \wedge T) \supset E(B \wedge Ax(E(T)))$ may hold). Moreover, since Ax(E(T)) is infinite, only a finite part $Ax_{fin}(E(T))$ can be constructed, which means that some part of T's empirical content and novel predictions will get lost. Finally, the construction of $Ax_{fin}(E(T))$ is possible only *post-facto*, based on a pre-selected set of empirical consequences of T; but to produce this consequences one *needs* the theory T.

A final warning: that a theory possesses the explained virtues does not guarantee that *every* one of its theoretical concepts is empirically significant, i.e. plays an essential role for these virtues. This question is treated in sec. 5.9.2.

5.5 The Example of Piaget's Theory of Cognitive Development

The central core thesis of Piaget's theory of cognitive development states that the development of intelligence in children is based on the *step-like formation* of general *logical-structural abilities* (Brainerd 1978, 33; Schurz 1985, 342). Once these cognitive abilities have been formed, they can then be applied everywhere within a short time. Before this, the relevant cognitive tasks can simply not be grasped by the child. A further core thesis states that the so-called *concrete-operational stage* is reached by the child at six to seven years of age. Apart from this, there is also the *sensomotoric* stage, which is reached at two, and the *formal-operational* stage, which is reached at 13–14 years of age. Here, we will concentrate on the concrete-operational stage.

The concrete-operational stage is characterized by the development of the following abilities: (1) *Change of perspective*, i.e. the ability to distinguish one's own visual perspective from that of other persons. In connection with this, the transition from egocentric to sociocentric thinking. (2) *Recognition of reversibility*, i.e. the ability to recognize that operations which change the visual appearance or geometrical shape of certain things can also be reversed. Connected with this second insight, a third, even more important insight emerges: (3) *Recognition of invariance*, i.e. certain essential properties of things are *not changed* by operations which merely change their visual appearance. Piaget examined the recognition of reversibility and invariance mainly in two areas: first, the invariance in the *number* of objects when placed in various different orders; and second, invariance of the *quantity* of a substance when this substance takes on different shapes or changes its geometrical form.

Piaget checked these abilities of children with the help of certain *tests*, which provided empirical laws of correspondence for his highly theoretical theses. The ability to change perspective was tested by Piaget using a three-dimensional model of *mountains*: the children were first allowed to walk around the model and look at it. Then they sat down to one side and said, based on pictures shown to them, how the mountains looked from various different perspectives. The ability to recognize the invariance of number was investigated by Piaget's team with the help of a number test, in which a given number of coins were shown on two pictures, in one far apart, in another close to each other. The children were then asked: "are there more, the same number, or fewer coins in this picture than in that one?" Finally, the invariance in the amount of a substance was tested using Piaget's famous clay ball experiment, in which a clay ball was pulled into the shape of a long sausage, and the children asked: "Is there more clay now, or less, or the same amount as before?"

The result of all of these tests showed that the abilities in question were, in a high percentage of cases, absent in children under six years of age, and present in children of seven and over. Piaget interpreted these results as a strong confirmation of his theory of cognitive development. We summarize the briefly described cognitive development theory and its central empirical prediction in (5.5–1).

C1–4 are core laws, Piaget's theory stands and falls with them. They are highly theoretical laws; the only empirical concept used in them is the age of the child. S1–4 are special laws, which also have a central status: they exemplify the highly abstract abilities in C2–4 with concrete cognitive abilities. Nevertheless, S2–4 are still theoretical law hypotheses, which lack exact empirical laws of correspondence. These are added to by the indicator laws I1–3, which introduce for each of the three abilities an empirical test developed by Piaget. The indicator laws I1–3 are located furthest out in the periphery of Piaget's theory.

(5.5–1) *Piaget's theory of cognitive development:*

C1　　The development of intelligence in children rests (primarily) on the step-like formation of generally applicable *logical-structural* abilities.

C2–4　The concrete-operational stage is characterized by the formation of the following competences: (C2) change of perspective, (C3) recognition of the reversibility of operations and (C4) recognition of invariance.

S1　　At the age of 6–7 years, nearly all children have reached the concrete-operational stage.

S2–4　Typical examples of the abilities named in C2–4 are: For the change in perspective (C2): the ability to coordinate different visual perspectives. For reversibility and invariance (C3–4): first the ability to recognize the invariance of number with respect to different orderings, and second the ability to recognize invariance in the amount of a substance with respect to changes in shape.

I1–3　Selective tests (indicators) for the abilities in (S2–4) are: (I1) for visual changes in perspective, Piaget's mountain test; (I2) for invariance of number, Piaget's number test; and (I3) for invariance in the amount of a substance, Piaget's clay ball test.

P:　　Empirical prediction: Nearly all children fail Piaget's tests before reaching their sixth year, but successfully complete Piaget's tests upon reaching their seventh year.

C1–4, S1–4 and I1–3 imply logically the prediction P. The core law C1 is not directly necessary for this implication. Its content (which goes beyond C2–4 and S1) is nevertheless important for the right interpretation of the special laws S2–4. Let C_1, C_2 and C_3 stand for the three abstract competences mentioned in C2–4, and A_1, A_2, A_3 for the three corresponding concrete abilities mentioned in S2–4. Then core law C1 entails that core laws C2–4 as well as the special laws S2–4 are not to be understood as (one-sided) implications, but as (two-sided) equivalences of the following form, where the individual variable x varies over children:

C2–4　$\forall x(CSx \leftrightarrow C_i x)$, for i=1,2,3. In words: Whenever a child x has reached the concrete-operational stage (= CSx), and only then, it has the abstract competences C_1, C_2 and C_3.

S2-4 $\forall x(C_i x \leftrightarrow A_i x)$, for i = 1,2,3. In words, a child has the abstract competence C_i exactly if it has the concrete ability A_i

Only with this reconstruction can one infer the first part of the prediction, that before the age of six years children fail Piaget's tests.

The indicator laws (I1–3) have the form of correspondence laws:

I1-3 $\forall x(T_i x \rightarrow (A_i x \leftrightarrow MT_i x))$, for i=1,2,3. In words: Whenever a child x performs Piaget's test T_i, then it has the concrete ability A_i if and only if it masters this test (MT_i).

The special law (S1) cannot be reconstructed as a strict implication, because of the existence of *exceptional* children. It has to be reconstructed as a normic generalization:

S1 Under_6_years $\Rightarrow \neg CS$, and: Over_7_years $\Rightarrow CS$,

where "A$\Rightarrow$B" expresses that the conditional probability p(B|A) is high (recall sec. 4.5.2). C2-4, S2-4 and I1-3 deductively imply the intermediate conclusions $\forall x(CSx \rightarrow (T_i x \rightarrow MT_i x))$ and $\forall x(\neg CSx \rightarrow (T_i x \rightarrow \neg MT_i x))$ (for i=1,2,3). These intermediate conclusions plus S1 imply by probability theory the empirical prediction:

P Under_6_years $\Rightarrow (T_i x \rightarrow \neg MT_i x)$, and:
Over_7_years $\Rightarrow (T_i x \rightarrow MT_i x)$, for i=1,2,3.

The studies relating to Piaget's theory of cognitive development have been replicated numerous times during the 1960s and 70s. These replication studies are well suited for demonstrating the holism of theory testing which we have already observed in physical theories. A central premise of Piaget's theory is that the used tests measure the respective cognitive abilities adequately. This has been questioned by a number of authors. Applying the methodological rule in Prop. 5.1–2, Piaget's theory should hold for other indicators of the children's cognitive abilities that are equally plausible. For instance, it should not matter whether the visual test for switching perspectives uses one specific three-dimensional figure or another one. Following this line of reasoning, Piaget's visual test trial has been replicated using a box with differently colored surfaces on all four sides, a figure much simpler than the original three-dimensional mountains model. After having the children walk around the box one or several times and sitting down facing one particular side, they were asked again: "Which color is the box when seen from this or that direction?"

Surprisingly the modified test trial resulted in children mastering this easier visual task as early as four years of age (Brainerd 1978, 103–106).

When facing these problematic results, developmental psychologists acted according to Lakatos' principle: they did not want to give up the core of Piaget's theory. Instead they concluded that Piaget's visual mountain test was not truly selective in measuring the ability to switch perspectives, but involved additional hidden variables which increased the task difficulty (Brainerd 1978, 80; Schurz 1985, 352). In this task children had to rotate a group of mountains in their mind's eye in order to reidentify the rotated mountains on the pictures shown to them. Arguably this goes beyond the basic ability of distinguishing and coordinating one's own and others' visual perspectives. It has thus been suggested that only two *peripheral* laws in Piaget's theory ought to be corrected, namely special law S1 and indicator law I1. The revision of S1 involved the belief that children master the stage of concrete operations 1–2 years *earlier* than originally proposed by Piaget. The new indicator law used the colored box test instead of the mountains test.

A similar line of reasoning was applied to Piaget's test for the invariance of number. The hidden variable which increased the task difficulty in this case was conjectured to be the child's mastery of its native language. Had the children grasped the exact meaning of "more coins," namely more in the sense of an increased *number* of coins as opposed to the coins covering a *larger* surface? Based on this argument the test for conservation of number was replicated in the form of a nonverbal learning experiment. Children were rewarded for correctly matching pictures with the same number of coins in them. And indeed, after some amount of training children aged 4–5 could already master the test for the invariance of number (Siegel 1978, 56f). For a period of time, these findings gave a boost to those psychologists who intended to only correct the periphery of Piaget's theory. The findings were seen as further evidence for the need to change the special law S1 into S1*, saying that children reached the concrete-operational stage at the age of 4 or 5 years, combined with a modification of the indicator law I2 in terms of nonverbal learning experiments. Also Piaget's third conservation experiment, the task in which a ball of clay is stretched, was replicated by means of nonverbal learning experiments—but in this case, the test modification led to an advancement of test mastership of less than one year, so that the confirmation of revised special law S1* was not as great as one hoped (Siegel 1978, 59f).

Other authors, however, brought forth findings and experiments that could not be reconciled by a mere modification of the theory's periphery. One example of this is the case of *propositional logic*. Following Piaget, the laws for correct inference in propositional logic should be mastered at the age of 13 or 14, when the formal-operational stage is reached. In fact some laws of propositional logic, e.g. *Modus Ponens*, are mastered as early as the age of three, whereas other laws such as *Modus Tollens* are never fully mastered by a considerable number of people, not even in the adult stage (cf. Brainerd 1978, 248f; Evans 1982, ch. 8–9). According to Piaget's model, however, *Modus Ponens* and *Modus Tollens* are affiliated with the same abstract structural ability. This discrepancy can definitely not be amended by only modifying an indicator law or a special law. It directly attacks the very *core* of Piaget's theory.

An analogous difficulty was found for the so-called *conservation of the object*. This cognitive principle says that visible objects which, by some transformation, become invisible do not pop out of existence, but continue to exist (though in an invisible way). A simple variant of this principle is already mastered by children at the end of the sensomotoric stage: if 1–2-year-old children see a ball, and then the ball is hidden behind a screen, they will *search* for it (Brainerd 1978, 46–70). However, another variant of the principle of object conservation, namely its application to the dissolution of sugar in water, is not even mastered by children at the age of six years. If children of this age observe the dissolution of sugar in water, and after all the tiny crumbs of sugar in the water have disappeared one asks the children "what has happened now to the sugar—is it no longer there?," then the majority of them answer that the sugar is no longer there (Piaget 1974, ch. 4; Schurz 1985, 352).

Empirical findings of this sort led several developmental psychologists to give up Piaget's theory, i.e. its core law C1. An alternative theory was suggested according to which the development of intelligence does not proceed by the formation of logically general and abstract cognitive competences, but via the generation of content-specific and content-bound abilities, which are first mastered only within a specific domain of application, and are then successively transferred to further domains of application by the operations of differentiation and generalization (Ausubel et al. 1978; Novak 1980, 20; Schurz 1985, sec.6.1). In other words, these authors suggested a replacement of Piaget's theory core C1 with the following alternative theory core C1*:

C1* The development of intelligence in children rests (primarily) on the formation of *content-specific* abilities, which get successively differentiated and generalized.

With this turn an alternative paradigm and research program for the psychology of cognitive development has been created.

5.6 Theory Dynamics

5.6.1 Lakatos' Model of Theory Revision

The methodology of scientific research programs developed by Lakatos (1970, 47f) is based on the following two assumptions:

L1 In case a conflict with experience occurs, it is always possible to save the core of a theory by adjusting the periphery (see also Rott 1994, 38). We refer to L1 as the *Lakatosian immunization thesis* (beware: the thesis is not as strong as it seems).

L2 To make an empirical prediction, every (physical) theory is in need of specific auxiliary hypotheses which involve exclusive ceteris paribus (eCP) hypotheses (recall sec. 4.5.1). These serve as a *protective belt* in the outer periphery around the middle and the core of the theory (1970, 18). In case of a conflict with experience, it is always possible to solve the conflict by dropping an eCP hypothesis or replacing it. We refer to L2 as the *Lakatosian ceteris-paribus-thesis*.

Lakatos was uncertain concerning the nature of eCP hypotheses (cf. his fn. 3 on p. 98 with his p. 26). Our concept of *system conditions* explained in sec. 5.2 offers a solution: it is the system conditions which always implicate the following eCP assumption: such-and-such a force affects the system and *no other*.

Obviously, L2 strongly supports L1. Lakatos refers to an empirical datum which contradicts the theoretical system as an *anomaly* (1970, 26). An anomaly can falsify a non-peripheral part of the theory only if the eCP hypothesis contained in the system condition is adhered to. As a rule, however, the advocate of a theory drops the original eCP hypothesis and assumes more complicated system conditions instead: conditions which postulate unknown *disturbing factors*. Postulates of this kind are typical *ad-hoc hypotheses* in the sense explained in sec. 5.2.

An ad-hoc hypothesis postulating unknown interfering factors only removes the contradiction between the irregular datum E and the given theory version T. But it does not *explain* the recalcitrant datum. This is why, even *after* this ad-hoc adjustment is made, the recalcitrant datum *stays* an anomaly, or, as we will call it in the next section, a *failure* of the theory. Furthermore, such an ad-hoc adjustment is, according to Lakatos, only acceptable if it is scientifically progressive. At this point, Lakatos refers to Popper (1935/2000, sec. 20), and he proposes the following conditions for *progressiveness*. A transition from one theory version, T_1, to another, T_2, which was made in order to remove an anomaly, is called *theoretically progressive* in case T_2 contains all of the confirmed parts of T_1's empirical content, and additionally contains some empirical excess content which is not contained in T_1 and need not be confirmed yet. Moreover, such a transition is called *empirically progressive* by Lakatos if the empirical excess content of T_2 is at least partly confirmed (1970, 33f). The transition is called *progressive*, if it is at least theoretically progressive. Otherwise it is called *regressive*.

Lakatos' approach examines, instead of single theory versions T_i, complete historical *sequences* (T_1, T_2 ...) of theory versions, which follow from each other as a result of theory changes due to recalcitrant data. Thereby one shall think of a single theory version T_i not as a single theory element but as a theory lattice in the sense of sec. 5.2. If the theory versions of such a sequence have a common *theory core*, the sequence represents a historical development of a theory *paradigm* in the sense of Kuhn, or a *research program* in the sense of Lakatos. Lakatos' (so-called) *refined falsificationism* consists of two basic thoughts:

RF1 In view of recalcitrant data (failures), a theory version T_i is only said to have failed and is rejected, if a *better* theory version T_{i+1} was developed, i.e. a version, which is progressive compared to T_i (1970, 35). According to Lakatos, there is no *immediate rationality* in science: the success of a theory core or research program can only be assessed based on the historical theory-development under the pressure of a permanent input of novel data (ibid., 57).

RF2 Developing a theory core in terms of a sequence of theory versions is only rationally acceptable as long as it is not *degenerative*, i.e. as long as ad-hoc adjustments create new empirical content (1970, 34)—whereas Lakatos adds at a later stage that the empirical excess content produced by a progressive sequence of theories has to be confirmed empirically betimes (ibid. 49).

By a *research program*, Lakatos understands a hard theory core together with negative and positive heuristics (1970, 49). The *negative heuristics* states that theory adjustments should not be made to the core but to the protective belt of the periphery. Lakatos limits this claim, however, by stating that in case of a degenerative development the *Modus Tollens* inferences from recalcitrant data may be directed against the core as well. The *positive heuristics* outlines a program by which the theory core could cope with recalcitrant data making use of increasingly complex theoretical models, and corresponding system conditions. Newton himself serves as an example here, as he knew in which way his initial idealizations would have to be replaced by more realistic system conditions: in a first step, Newton treated planets and the Sun not as mass points anymore, but as mass spheres, then he took account also of the rotation of the planet spheres, and finally, he developed first steps towards a disturbance theory in which interplanetary gravitation effects were considered (ibid. 50).

Lakatos' two maxims can also come into mutual conflict. This happens when the transition from a theory version T_i to T_{i+1} is degenerative, but a better theory version T_{i+2} is not in sight. Then according to maxim RF2, T_{i+1} is not acceptable, but according to maxim RF1, T_{i+1} should not be rejected, because a better alternative theory is not available. In conclusion, Lakatos' maxim RF2 cannot always be realized: a short-term degeneration of the actual theory version can be tolerated as long as a better theory is not in sight—an example was the development of Bohr's atomic model with its ad-hoc postulate of stable electron orbits with an angular momentum being a multiple of Planck's quantum (Schurz/Lambert 1994, sec. 4.3). In scientific practice, problems of this sort are usually resolved as follows: the more degenerative a theory version becomes, the more young scientists begin to look for alternative theory cores and try to develop alternative research programs. This is the situation in which the respective discipline enters a revolutionary phase in Kuhn's sense. In most revolutionary phases in the history of natural sciences, at least so far, superior alternative theories have been found: in the case of Bohr's atomic model this alternative theory was quantum mechanics. In the human and social sciences, a different picture emerges: in many of these disciplines one finds, instead of one dominating paradigm, a sustainable *coexistence* of rival paradigms none of which is predominant (Schurz/Weingartner 1998). In other words, the state which Kuhn calls "revolutionary" is the normal state in these disciplines.

Lakatos' methodology is also applicable to sequences of theory versions in which a "revolution," i.e. a change of the theory core, takes place. His criteria of theoretical and empirical progressivity can also be applied to theories with different cores, as long as one can assume that the rival theories share a common empirical or pre-theoretical language. Lakatos illustrates his model of science with historical examples from physics. Section 5.5 has shown, however, that Lakatos' maxims apply equally also to theories from non-physical sciences.

5.6.2 Theory Evaluation and Theory Progress

In what follows by a theory version we mean always a theory core together with all of its (actually accepted) periphery, and we write C_iV_j—short for "the jth version of the ith theory core." A theory version contains all premises which are necessary to derive empirical predictions. Like Lakatos we consider *historical sequences* of theory versions. Through its development a theory can run through many versions: its periphery can be expanded, modified or contracted. As long as only the periphery is changed we are still dealing with changes of the *same* theory. In contrast, an alteration of the theory core leads to a *new* theory and is the start of a new research program. The possible theory dynamics are schematically displayed in fig. 5.6–1.

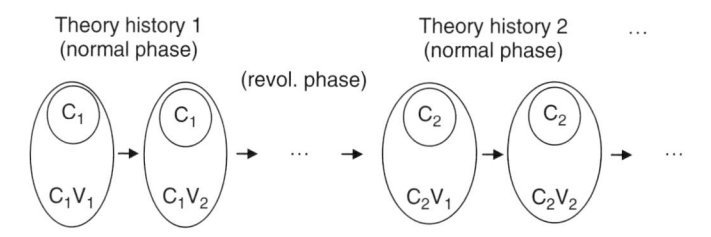

Figure 5.6–1 Historical theory sequence

It is also possible that the history of a scientific discipline contains more than one theory sequence of this sort, i.e. paradigms which are developing in parallel and mutual competition.

According to the three levels model of science in sec. 2.3, theories are usually tested through their *general* empirical consequences, which are in turn tested based on singular observation statements by the methods of Chapter 4 which are tacitly presupposed here as given. In some disciplines there exist theories which directly speak about particular individuals and, thus, imply only singular empirical consequences, e.g. astronomical theories about the history of a certain solar system or galaxy. In what follows, a *confirmed* general or singular empirical fact which lies in the intended domain of a theory is called an (empirical) *phenomenon*. When we say that certain phenomena *follow* from a theory, we mean that the corresponding statements expressing these phenomena follow from it. The underlying inference relation is often of a *deductive* nature, but may also be of a probabilistic or normic nature.

Within the described framework we now develop our central concepts of theory evaluation, in the first step for theory versions, and in the second step for theory cores.

> (Prop. 5.6–1) A *theory version* C_iV_j is *falsified* iff it logically entails some empirical consequences which have been falsified by actually observed phenomena. *Normally* this leads to the construction of a successor theory version C_iV_{j+1} with the same theory core.

So theory *versions* with deductive consequences are still falsifiable. Only theory versions with probabilistic consequences or theories understood as theory cores are unfalsifiable (recall sec. 3.8). Next we define the notions of success and failure.

> (Prop. 5.6–2) A *success* of a theory version C_iV_j is an empirical phenomenon which is correctly explained or predicted by C_iV_j.

Thereby, successful predictions have more confirmation value than successful ex-post explanations (see sec. 5.10.3–4).

> (Prop. 5.6–3) A *failure* of a theory version C_iV_j is a recalcitrant phenomenon, i.e. an empirically well-established phenomenon P which has one of the following two properties:
>
> a *P contradicts C_iV_j*, either in the logical sense (C_iV_j entails not-P) or in the probabilistic sense (C_iV_j makes not-P highly probable), or
> b P has contradicted the predecessor version C_iV_{j-1} of C_iV_j, and C_iV_j resulted from C_iV_{j-1} through adjustment by means of an auxiliary hypothesis H which served to prevent the falsification of C_iV_j by P, and which is ad hoc in the historical stage C_iV_j in the following sense: apart from avoiding the consequence *not-P*, H does *not* produce new empirically confirmed content in C_iV_j (which neither excludes nor implies that H produces excess content in C_iV_j that has so far not been empirically tested).

To avoid logical irrelevancies and redundancies we assume that successes are represented by relevant consequence elements in the sense of def. 3.12–2, and failures by negations of relevant consequence elements. It is important that our notion of failure covers not only logically or probabilistically contradicting phenomena, but also those phenomena which contradicted earlier theory versions and were converted into non-contradicting phenomena by ad-hoc adjustments of the theory. Phenomena of the latter kind *break* the explanatory promise given by the theory or the underlying research program. Also note that if a theory (version) T is associated with an eCP clause saying that *all* non-negligible causes have been taken into account, then every *unexplainable* phenomenon P in T's domain counts as a failure of T.

The degree of confirmation or disconfirmation of a theory version is assessed on the basis of the sets of its successes and failures. Thereby we restrict ourselves to unfalsified theory versions.

> (Prop. 5.6–4) An *unfalsified theory version* C_iV_j is the more *confirmed*, the more successes and the fewer failures it has.

Two clarifications are important. First: the "more" and "fewer" are meant in the sense of a *set-inclusion* and not in the sense of counting (see below). Second: the successes and failures of a theory version C_iV_j are always *relative* to the set S of accepted background beliefs of a given scientific community at a given time. This implicit relativization holds for all further notions of theory evaluation that are developed in this section. One may refine the explications (prop. 5.6–1–5.6–4) by explicitly relativizing the notions of deductive or probabilistic consequence to S, via replacing "A ∥— B" by "S,A ∥— B" and P(B|A) by P(B|A∧S) (cf. Glymour 1981, 35).

The restriction of prop. 5.6–4 to unfalsified theory versions has the following reason: a theory (version) T can only be said to be confirmed relative to an evidence E, if E increases the probability of T, but if E falsifies T then P(T|E) = 0, which is the strongest possible disconfirmation of T by E. This probabilistic viewpoint has been criticized, however, by proponents of the concept of *truthlikeness* or verisimilitude. According to the basic idea of Popper (1963, 233f), a theory (version) T_1 is closer to the truth, the more true and the fewer false consequences it possesses, where the "more" and "fewer" are again understood in the sense of set-inclusion, as above (for details on truthlikeness see sec. 5.11.1). This is a purely *semantic* definition of truthlikeness. To obtain an *epistemic* definition of truthlikeness, relative to a given *evidence* E, one has to take "empirically confirmed" instead of "true," and "empirically disconfirmed" instead of "false" consequences.

Proponents of truthlikeness argue as follows: even if theories entail consequences that are known to be false, they need not be dismissed as long as they are sufficiently close to the truth, or at least closer to the truth than all known alternative theories. This criticism is valid against the naive falsificationism with its "immediate rationality." Kuipers (2000, sec. 6.2.1) argues that the truthlikeness standpoint has significant advantages compared to Lakatos' refined falsificationism. But I do not see crucial differences between the two. Both standpoints agree that a theory should not be given up when facing recalcitrant data. A theory proponent who detects a conflicting datum will (at least usually) try to make adjustments at the theory's periphery which avoid this conflict. If this attempt succeeds, then it will simultaneously increase the theory's epistemic truthlikeness *and* its confirmation value. So the strategies of refined falsificationism and truthlikeness-maximization are not in opposition but in harmony.

Our explication of theory confirmation in terms of successes and failures has an important advantage compared to the account of truthlikeness: this advantage lies in our notion of failure which does not designate a false (or disconfirmed) consequence of the theory, as in truthlikeness accounts, but a true (or confirmed) phenomenon that is in *conflict* with the theory. This notion of failure is needed to cover also failures of type (b) in prop. 5.6–3, because the negations of such failures are not implied by the actual version of the theory. One may, however, develop a modified conception of truthlikeness, which is directly explicated in terms of successes and failures in the sense of prop. 5.6–2 and 5.6–3. I call this concept *dynamical truthlikeness*, because it refers to historical predecessors of the current theory version:

> (Prop. 5.6–5) The *dynamical truthlikeness* of a theory version $C_i V_j$ is higher, the more successes and the fewer failures it has.

Prop. 5.6–5 differs from prop. 5.6–4 *only* in that it is also applicable to falsified theory versions.

Propositions 5.6–4 and 5.6–5 open up the possibility of *intertheoretical* theory comparisons. The compared theory versions may possess different theory cores, as long as they share a common empirical or pre-theoretical language in which phenomena are formulated. Our criterion of theory comparison is stated in prop. 5.6–6 and illustrated in fig. 5.6–2:

> (Prop. 5.6–6) *Intertheoretical theory comparison and theory progress:*
>
> Theory version C_1V_1 is *empirically more successful* than C_2V_2 iff
>
> a either C_1V_1 has more successes than C_2V_2 without producing new failures, or
> b it has fewer failures than C_2V_2 without losing some successes, (or both), where the "more" and "fewer" are understood in the sense of set-inclusion, i.e.
>
> (a) $Suc_1 \supset Suc_2 \land Fail_1 \subseteq Fail_2$ or (b) $Suc_1 \supseteq Suc_2 \land Fail_1 \subset Fail_2$.
>
> The transition from C_1V_1 to C_2V_2 is an empirical *theory progress*, iff C_1V_1 is empirically more successful than C_2V_2.

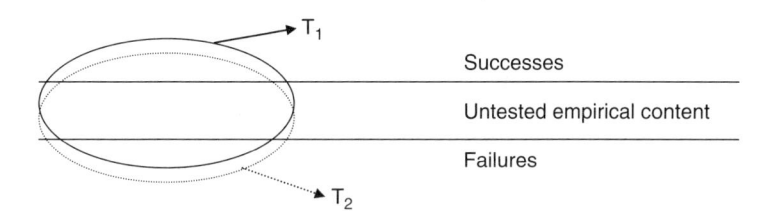

Figure 5.6–2 T_1 is empirically more successful than T_2

It would be problematic to compare theories by *counting* the number of their successes and failures, because reasonable "units" of "one" success or failure are difficult to define. Therefore the interpretation of "more" or "fewer" successes as a set-inclusion is more adequate. However, the inclusion-interpretation has the consequence that the relation of being empirically more successful yields only a *partial* ordering relation among theory versions. Whenever one theory has both successes and failures which the other theory does not have, the two theories are *incomparable* by the relation of empirical success, and no success preference is possible between them.

This brings us to a further important relation between theories in regard to their empirical success: that of empirical complementarity. Two theory versions T_1 and T_2 are *empirically complementary* iff both possess significant successes in regions of phenomena in which the other theory possesses failures. In addition the two theories may have some successes and failures in common. See fig. 5.6–3.

Notation as in fig. 5.6-2:

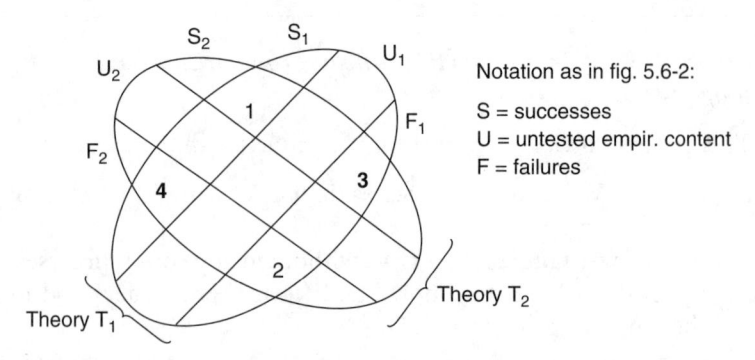

S = successes
U = untested empir. content
F = failures

Figure 5.6–3 Empirically complementary theories (versions) T_1 and T_2

Region 1: joint successes of T_1 and T_2; region 2: joint failures; region 3: T_2-successes which are T_1-failures; region 4: T_1-successes which are T_2-failures. The regions of complementarity 3 and 4 are occupied by more (or more significant) phenomena than the regions of agreement 1 and 2.

An example of empirically complementary theories are psychological theories of *aggression* (cf. Schurz 1998a, 33): in this area, the *frustration* theory, the *learning* theory and the *drive* theory are well-established paradigms, none of which is able to replace the other two. For each of the three theories there exist empirical examples of aggression that fit with this theory but are not explainable by the other two theories: there exist cases of aggression caused by frustration where learning or drive play no causal role; other cases of aggression result through learning from "role models" (e.g. computer games) without any frustrating stimulus being detected; finally, examples of spontaneous aggressive behavior in children in the absence of any frustration stimuli or learning history speak in favor of the drive model.

Our explication of empirical theory preference in prop. 5.6–6 can be refined in several ways. For example, one can attach *weights* of epistemic importance to successes and failures (positive for successes and negative for failures); by adding up these weights one obtains a *quantitative* measure of the empirical success of a theory. In addition one can use super-empirical criteria of theory comparison such as *simplicity*. The criterion of simplicity, though, is exposed to two problems: (1) the explication of simplicity is ambiguous, and (2) it is questionable why an *esthetical* criterion such as simplicity should play any role at all in rational theory choice (more on this in sec. 5.11.2).

Our model of theory evaluation is supported by the practice of science: when scientists evaluate competing theories they are oriented on successes and failures in the sense of prop. 5.6–2 and 5.6–3. As an

Empirical Phenomena ↓ \ Theories of Light →	Ray optics (HERO from Alexandria)	Hydrodynamic aether theory (DESCARTES)	Corpuscular theory (NEWTON)	Longitudinal wave theory (HUYGENS)	Transversal wave theory (FRESNEL; CAUCHY; GREEN)	Electromagnetic theory (MAXWELL)	Electromagnetic theory without aether	Electromagnetic theory with curved space	Electromagnetic theory and electron theory	Quantum electrodynamics and nonrelativistic Q.M.	Quantum electrodynamics and relativistic Q.M.
1. Rectilinear propagation	+	+	+	+	+	+	+	+	+	+	+
2. Reflection	+	+	+	+	+	+	+	+	+	+	+
3. Refraction	+	+	+	+	+	+	+	+	+	+	+
4. Extremal travel time	+	+	+	+	+	+	+	+	+	+	+
5. Dispersion	+	+	+	+	+	+	+	+	+	+	+
6. Superposition				+	+	+	+	+	+	+	+
7. Double refraction				+	+	+	+	+	+	+	+
8. Decrease of speed in transparent media				+	+	+	+	+	+	+	+
9. Diffraction				+	+	+	+	+	+	+	+
10. Interference				+	+	+	+	+	+	+	+
11. Doppler effect				+	+	+	+	+	+	+	+
12. Polarization					+	+	+	+	+	+	+
13. Radiation pressure			+			+	+	+	+	+	+
14. Anomalous dispersion									+	+	+
15. Invariant speed light							+	+			+
16. Change of frequency in gravitational field								+			
17. Light scattering									+	+	+
18. Blackbody spectrum										+	+
19. Photoelectric effect										+	+
20. Compton effect										+	+

Figure 5.6–4 Theories of optics; "+" for "success," empty space for "failure" (after Bunge 1967, 47)

example consider fig. 5.6–4, which summarizes the major explanatory successes ("+") and failures (no symbol) of theories of *optics* as one finds them in standard textbooks in physics (after Bunge 1967, vol. II, 47). Unexplainable phenomena are counted as failures even if they were not known at the time of the theory's reign.

We now turn to the question of when a theory version is (still) rationally acceptable by the scientific community, and when it would be better to reject it. This does not only depend on its empirical success record, but also on the alternative theories that are available at the given time:

> (Prop. 5.6–7)
>
> 1 A *theory version* is *rationally acceptable* as long as it is sufficiently empirically confirmed, and no alternative theory version is available whose empirical success is significantly higher.
> 2 A *theory version* is to be *rationally rejected* iff it is either strongly disconfirmed or a theory version with significantly higher empirical success is available.

Intentionally, (2) is *not* the negation of (1), as "strongly disconfirmed" is logically stronger than "not sufficiently confirmed." So our explication admits the case that a theory version stays in an *intermediate* state between rational acceptance and rejection. This happens when a theory version is neither strongly disconfirmed nor sufficiently confirmed, but a better alternative theory is not in sight: theories of this sort have to be tolerated without sufficient reasons of acceptance or rejection. Our explication admits also the situation of empirical underdetermination in the sense of Quine (1951), in which more than one theory versions are rationally acceptable, because all of them are empirically confirmed and none of them is significantly better than the others. Since such equally successful theories may even contradict each other, we say that they are accept*able*, but not that all of them should be simultaneously accepted, for that would mean accepting a contradiction.

In the above case of empirical underdetermination the two rival theories need not be empirically equivalent (i.e. have the same empirical content); they need only be equally empirically successful. As indicated in fig. 5.6–2, the empirical content of a theory also contains the so-far untested part, which might be different in two so-far equally successful theories. According to Lakatos' notion of theoretical progress in the previous section, possessing a larger untested empirical content is a ceteris paribus preference criterion between rival theories. This is nothing but the virtue of *boldness* in the sense of Popper (1935/2002, 225f, 373). Caution is demanded, however, in the application of this criterion: not every untested content-increase produces real theoretical progress. Lakatos himself mentions the *tacking paradox*, which consists in the possibility to increase a theory's untested content by "tacking" to the theory an arbitrary empirically untested assertion via conjunction (1970, 46). For example, if one adds to the established theory version of quantum mechanics the statement that the idea of God originated in our ancestor's brain through a quantum fluctuation, then this should not be considered as theoretical progress but just as muckraking. Lakatos requires that the connection between an auxiliary hypothesis that produces new untested content and the accepted theory should be "more intimately connected" than a mere conjunction, but he does not explain exactly what he means by this.

The tacking paradox has been intensively discussed in the context of theories of confirmation (sec. 5.10.1–3). A solution of the tacking paradox in regard to the question of content-increase can be achieved by demanding that the compared theories must be empirically homogeneous in the following sense: it is not possible to *factorize* the natural axiomatization Ax of T (sec. 5.3.1) into two disjoint subsets Ax_1 and Ax_2 such that $E(Ax) = C(E(Ax_1) \cup E(Ax_2))$, i.e. T's empirical content is the L-closed union of Ax_1's and of Ax_2's empirical content. If, on the other hand, such a factorization of T is possible, T is called an empirically heterogeneous theory. Every theory T∧H obtained from an irrelevant strengthening of T by H is factorizable in the explained sense, because T and H do not have theoretical concepts in common, and therefore do not theoretically interact. This means in the terminology of sec. 5.4.2 that the conjunction of T and H is not empirically creative.

Lakatos' preference criterion of empirical excess content can now be given a reasonable explication, by restricting its application to empirically homogeneous theories.

(Prop. 5.6–8) *Untested empirical excess content:*

If C_1V_1 and C_2V_2 are two empirically homogeneous and equally empirically successful theory versions, then C_1V_1 is rationally preferable over C_2V_2 iff C_1V_1 possesses more untested empirical content than C_2V_2 ("more" in the sense of set-inclusion).

Having developed the criteria of confirmation and rational acceptance for theory versions, we finally extend these criteria to theory cores. The confirmation of a theory core does not only depend on the success of its actual theory version but also on the *history* of its previous versions. Our confidence in a theory core becomes diminished if many theory versions based on this core have already been falsified in the past.

> (Prop. 5.6–9) A *theory core* is the more confirmed:
>
> i the more confirmed its actual version is (in the sense of Prop. 5.6–4),
> ii the more empirical content the actual version has, provided it is empirically homogeneous, and
> iii the less its earlier versions have been falsified.

We understand the three criteria in prop. 5.6–9 as hierarchically ordered: (i) dominates (ii) dominates (iii). This leads to the following criterion of rational preference between rival theory cores:

> (Prop. 5.6–10) A *theory core* C_1 is to be *rationally preferred* to a theory core C_2 iff:
>
> i either the actual version of C_1 is empirically more successful than the actual version of C_2, or
> ii C_1 and C_2 are equal in regard to i, but the actual version of C_1 is empirically homogeneous and has more untested empirical content than the actual version of C_2, or
> iii C_1 and C_2 are equal in regard to i and ii, but the history of C_1 contains fewer falsified predecessor versions than the history of C_2.

The question whether a theory core and its corresponding research program is (still) rationally acceptable depends, as in the case of theory versions, on the context of available alternative theory cores.

> (Prop. 5.6–11)
>
> 1 A *theory core* is *rationally acceptable* as long as it is sufficiently confirmed and no rationally preferable alternative theory core is available.
> 2 A *theory core* is to be *rationally rejected* iff it is either strongly disconfirmed or a rationally preferable theory core is available.

Observe again that 2 is not the negation of 1: like theory versions, theory cores can remain in an *intermediate* state between rational acceptance and rejection. Moreover, prop. 5.6–11 admits the situation of a rationally justified pluralism of paradigms, in which several competing theory cores are rationally acceptable at the same time.

COMPLEMENTARY AND ADVANCED TOPICS

5.7 Instrumentalism and Realism: The Ontology of Scientific Theories

The preceding chapters have highlighted characteristic features of scientific theories and their surplus value compared to mere empirical generalizations. But what does this mean for the realistic impact of theories, their reference and truth? This is the question of this section.

5.7.1 Versions of Instrumentalism and Realism

Scientific realism assumes that the theoretical concepts of scientific theories refer. For example, the term "electron" denotes really existing though inconceivably tiny entities, which can only be measured very indirectly. Or "electric force" designates a real causally effective interaction which attracts particles of opposite charge. In contrast, scientific instrumentalism doubts that theoretical entities of this sort literally exist, or at least that we can ever know their existence. Rather we are only justified in assuming the existence of *observable* entities or properties. Theoretical concepts possess only an instrumental function for the purpose of a "most economical representation" of empirical knowledge, as Ernst Mach put it (1883, 586f). In this sense, the assumption of "electrons" as the negatively charged constituents of the shell of atoms allows a unified explanation of phenomena such as polarization, ionization, electric current and electrolysis. And the quantity called "electric force" helps to predict the trajectories of electrically charged particles in a unified way.

The controversy between scientific instrumentalism and realism has a long tradition which goes back to antiquity (Losee 2001, sec. IIc). In contemporary philosophy of science, instrumentalist positions have been supported by logical positivists who were influential in the 1950s and 1960s (e.g. Carnap 1956a; Hempel 1958; Sneed 1971). Beginning in the 1960s the pendulum swung and realistic positions gained ground (e.g. Putnam 1962; Maxwell 1962; Boyd 1984, Leplin 1984). The debate is still ongoing: a recent defense of instrumentalism is found in van Fraassen's empiricism (1980, 2002, 2006), and a balanced defense of scientific realism is given by Psillos (1999).

There are *different versions* of instrumentalism (see Psillos 1999, 17f). The strong instrumentalist claims that theoretical sentences *cannot* be "literally" true. A weak instrumentalist such as van Fraassen (1980) admits that theories can be literally true, but argues that one can never be *justified* in believing this. What we can justifiably assert is only that a theory is more or less empirically adequate. A still different position is the *metaphysical pluralism* of Carnap. For him, the realist, the instrumentalist and the fully idealist interpretation of a theory are all legitimate ways of speaking (Carnap 1956a, 45; Psillos 1999, ch. 3). Van Fraassen delineates his position sharply from positivism. He criticizes Carnap for not taking the ontological questions "literal[ly]" (1980, 10). But this criticism is inappropriate. Rather, the two understand the notion of "truth" differently. Van Fraassen understands "truth" in the realistic sense. In contrast, for Carnap "truth" is metaphysically neutral in the sense explained in sec. 2.8.1: the referents of a theory which is accepted as "true" can not only be interpreted realistically, but also idealistically as cognitive constructions. Carnap (1966, 256) argues that under certain provisos, both ways of speaking are *practically* equivalent (see Psillos 1999, 59). In what follows, however, I will follow common usage and understand the word "truth" in the realistic sense.

There are two more general epistemological differentiations which cut across the instrumental-realism distinction and should not be confused with it:

1   *Epistemological idealism vs. realism*: While realism assumes that our concepts refer to a subject-independent reality, idealistic positions do not make this assumption at all, neither for observable nor for theoretical phenomena. In the context of this distinction, scientific instrumentalism is *half way* between idealism and realism, insofar as it attributes reality to the observable phenomena *but not* to the unobservable ones.
2   *Property nominalism vs. realism: Nominalism* is an ontological position which asserts that only *individuals* can have real existence, but not generic entities such as properties or relations, the so-called "universals." The reason is that properties (such as "redness"), in contrast to individuals (such as "this red thing"), do not possess concrete spatiotemporal existence, but are abstract conceptual entities. In contrast, for the position of *universals realism*, not only individuals but also generic properties and relations can have real existence. The dispute between the two positions has its origin in scholastic philosophy.

The position of *property nominalism* reduces the existence of properties to the existence of *classes*, i.e. property *extensions*. This position has the problem that most possible classes of individuals are artificial and do not correspond to natural or physical properties. For universals realism, on the other hand, only *some* possible classes of individuals correspond to really existing properties. A version of nominalism which can account for the reality of properties is *trope* nominalism: this position attributes real existence not to the generic properties, but to the particular (spatiotemporally located) *instances* of generic properties, such as "this redness," "that redness," which are called tropes (see Loux 1998, ch. 1–2; Armstrong 1989). Trope nominalism is *coherent* with property realism, if one assumes a relation of strict trope equality, so that properties are definable as equality classes of tropes. In what follows we define *property realism*—in opposition to property nominalism—as an ontological position that admits the real existence of properties or relations, either in the framework of universals realism or trope nominalism.

The nominalism–realism question for properties is crucial for a better understanding of certain problems in philosophy of science, in particular for the interpretation of the Ramsey sentence which is treated in the next section. For example, van Fraassen (1980, 13ff) and Bueno (1997) assume a property nominalist and instrumentalist position, insofar as they introduce the observable/non-observable distinction only for individuals, but not for properties. Cartwright (1983) accepts the reality of theoretical individuals, but not of properties; so she seems to be a property nominalist, too. Other philosophers of science, including the structuralists, introduce the observable/non-observable distinction primarily for properties (e.g. Ramsey 1929, 120f; Sneed 1971; Balzer et al. 1987; Ketland 2004). They are not property nominalists, but they attribute physical reality only to observable properties and let theoretical predicates refer to arbitrary set-theoretic extensions. Finally, Lewis (1970) is a realist with respect to individuals and properties.

Like instrumentalism, there exist different forms of scientific realism (cf. Kuipers 2000, sec. 1.2). Of fundamental importance is the distinction between *metaphysical* realism versus *hypothetical* realism. For metaphysical realism—a particularly strong form of realism—the assumption that theoretical concepts have real references is a *necessary* precondition of theoretical science (e.g. Putnam 1978, 110ff; Bunge 1974, 45; Harré 1986). From a scientific viewpoint this position seems to be untenable, as there are many examples of theories in the history of science which were empirically successful at their time, although they assumed the existence of theoretical entities which, according to present knowledge, do not exist (examples are given in the next subsection). In contrast, for the *hypothetical-constructive* realism which was defended in sec. 2.8.2, theoretical concepts are conceptual constructs, and whether they correspond to real entities or properties is a contingent *hypothesis* which must be justified based on the empirical success of the scientific theories. On this perspective, the problems of assessing empirical success and of justifying a realistic theory-interpretation are two sides of the *same coin*. The problem of justifying scientific realism is treated in the next two subsections.

5.7.2 *No Miracles Argument versus Pessimistic Meta-Induction*

The best-known argument which supports the inference from the empirical success to the approximate truth of a theory is the *no miracles* argument, or *NMA* for short. The NMA goes back to Putnam (1975a, 73) and has predecessors in Smart (1963, 39) and Maxwell (1962, 18) (see Psillos 1999, ch. 4). It says, roughly, that without the assumption of scientific realism the empirical success of science would be a sheer miracle. More precisely, the NMA is an instance of an abduction or inference to the best explanation (IBE) (recall sec. 2.7.3). It argues that the *best* if not the only reasonable explanation of the continuous empirical success of scientific theories is the assumption that their theoretical part or "superstructure" is approximately true and, hence, that their theoretical terms refer to real constituents of the world.

However, as explained in sec. 2.11, the justification of IBEs is an open problem. What justifies the assumption that IBEs of this sort are reliable? A plausible answer to this question seems to be the NMA, as it would be a "sheer miracle" if the best explanation of something were not true (cf. Psillos 1999, 81ff). At this point, however, the justification of the NMA becomes entirely *circular*: the justification of IBE assumes the reliability of NMA which is, in turn, an instance of an IBE. In section 2.11 we have seen that these kind of rule-circular arguments are *without any* justificatory value. Psillos (ibid.) defends the NMA by arguing that the NMA is not "inherently circular" insofar as one *need* not justify it by the assumption that IBEs are generally reliable. But then the obvious question is: which *other* reasons do we have for putting trust into the NMA?

The major argument against the (unrestricted) reliability of the NMA is the *pessimistic meta-induction* argument (PMA), which goes back to Laudan (1981/96). The PMA points to the fact that in the history of scientific theories one can recognize radical changes at the level of theoretical superstructures (or "ontologies"), although there was continuous progress at the level of empirical success. On simple inductive grounds, one should expect therefore that the theoretical superstructures (or ontologies) of our presently accepted theories will also be overthrown in the future, and hence can in no way be expected to be approximately true.

One of Laudan's examples is the transition from the phlogiston theory to the oxygen theory of combustion. According to the phlogiston theory (developed in the late 17th and early 18th centuries), every material which is capable of being burned or calcinated contains *phlogiston*—a substance different from ordinary matter which was thought to be the bearer of combustibility. When combustion or calcination takes place, the burned or calcinated substance delivers its phlogiston, usually in the form of a hot flame, and a dephlogisticated substance-specific residual remains. In the 1780s, Lavoisier introduced his alternative *oxygen* theory according to which combustion and calcination consists in the oxidation of the substance being burned or calcinated, i.e. in the formation of a chemical bond of its molecules with oxygen. The "hot flame" was identified as light-emitting carbon-dioxide gas, and the assumption of phlogiston as the bearer of combustibility became superfluous. In modern chemistry, Lavoisier's theory is accepted in a generalized and corrected form, in which the oxidizing substance need not be oxygen, but can be any electronegative substance.

According to contemporary chemistry, the theoretical superstructure of phlogiston theory is false, because it assumes the existence of phlogiston which *does not exist*. Nevertheless, phlogiston theory was remarkably *successful* in explaining the chemical reactions of combustion, calcination (roasting) of metals, and salt-formation through the solution of metals in acids, as well as the inversion of these reactions.

5.7.3 *Empirical Underdetermination and Use-Novel Evidence*

The PMA is an *empirical* argument against the NMA. It receives additional support by a theoretical argument: the *empirical underdetermination* argument (EUA), which goes back to Quine. Quine has repeatedly demonstrated that given an empirically successful theory T, one can usually construct an empirically equivalent theory T* which has a different and even incompatible theoretical superstructure (see 1960, 141ff; 1992, §41). The EUA implies that the NMA cannot be generally reliable, since the two empirically equivalent theories T and T* share their empirical success, but *at most one* of them can have a true theoretical part.

A subtle counterargument to the EUA points out that all of Quine's constructions of empirically equivalent theories T* are post-facto

(Carrier 2003). By suitable adjustments of "hidden" (theoretical) variables, it is always possible to construct a theory post-facto so as to fit the given empirical data which were already known *beforehand*. What really counts for the empirical success are either (i) *novel predictions* of the theory, i.e. correctly predicted phenomena which were unknown at the time of the theory construction, or at least (ii) *use-novel* evidence in the sense of Worrall (2006), i.e. confirmed empirical consequences which—though they may have been known beforehand—have not been used in the construction of the theory. Use-novel consequences are *potentially* novel predictions, because they *could* have been unknown while the theory was constructed. They play an important role in the theory of confirmation, since they make the theory *independently* testable (see sec. 5.10.4).

Based on these considerations Psillos (1999, 76) and others suggested restricting the applicability of the NMA to the inference from use-novel empirical success (Ladyman/Ross 2007, sec. 2.1.3). However, Carrier (2003, sec. 7–8) gave two examples of theories which make false theoretical claims but were even capable of generating true novel predictions: the theory of phlogiston mentioned above, and the theory of caloric (see Schurz 2009a, sec. 2). So even this restricted version of the NMA—restricted to use-novel empirical success—is not generally tenable.

5.7.4 Intertheoretical Correspondence, Structural Realism and the Justification of Abduction

With *strong success* we mean success by use-novel evidence. If even strongly successful theories can be theoretically false, how can the inference from strong success to theoretical truth be justified at all? A possible solution to this problem is to argue that in spite of their false ontologies, strongly empirical successful theories contain at least *something true* in their theoretical superstructure, where this "something" is picked out by means of *relations of correspondence* between outdated and contemporary (assumedly true) theories.

Boyd (1984) has pointed towards the existence of *correspondence* relations between successive scientific theories. A well-known example is the correspondence between the velocity of the ether molecules in Fresnel's theory of light and the oscillation strength of the electromagnetic field in Maxwell's electromagnetic theory (cf. Worrall 1989/97; Psillos 1999, ch. 6). The two theoretical concepts are "in correspondence" because they are related to the same empirical phenomena in precisely the same way. Boyd argues that those theoretical content parts which are preserved through correspondence relations have a justified realist interpretation. For Worrall (1989/97) these correspondence relations are the major support for his *structural realism*, i.e. his proposal that what is theoretically knowable is the relational structure, but not the "intrinsic" nature of the unobservable constituents of the world.

Laudan replies that these "nice" cases of correspondences mentioned by Boyd and Worrall are mere *exceptions*. Laudan (1981/96, 121) gives a much-debated list of examples of scientific theories which were strongly successful in their time, but have assumed an ontology which is *incompatible* with contemporary theories. He mentions the succession from the phlogiston to the oxygen theory as an example of this sort, and argues that if two consecutive theories have incompatible ontologies (as in this case), then it is *impossible* that there exist relations of correspondence between their theoretical superstructures.

Schurz (2009a), however, develops an argument to the contrary: even if an outdated theory T and a presently accepted theory T* have incompatible ontologies, there may exist relations of correspondence between them. He shows that under natural assumptions such relations of correspondence *must* hold on logical reasons, provided there is cumulative success at the empirical level:

(Prop. 5.7–1) *Correspondence theorem* (Schurz 2009a, sec. 4): Assume:

  i   T and T* are both consistent and causally normal theories,
 ii   T contains a T-theoretical expression $\tau(x)$ which yields strong potential success, and
iii   T* is a successor theory of T with an arbitrarily different theoretical superstructure which entails T's strong potential success in a T*-dependent way.

Then T* contains a theoretical expression $\tau^*(x)$ such that T and T* together imply a *correspondence relation* of the form

(C): $\forall x: Ax \rightarrow (\tau(x) \leftrightarrow \tau^*(x))$

in words: if a physical system x satisfies the conditions A (which define the range of T and T*'s shared empirical success), then x satisfies the T-theoretical description τ iff x satisfies the T*-theoretical description τ^*.

Corollary: $C(T,\tau) \cup T^*$ is consistent, and (C) follows already from $C(T,\tau) \cup T^*$, where $C(T,\tau)$ is the set of T's laws of correspondence for τ.

Prop. 5.7–1 makes three "natural" assumptions (i), (ii) and (iii), whose technical definitions cannot be explained here; the reader is referred to Schurz (2009a, sec. 4).

If T and T* are theoretically inconsistent (as in the phlogiston–oxygen case), it would be a trivial assertion that the union of T and T* entails the correspondence relation (C), because in this case this union entails everything. Here the corollary becomes significant, which tells us that (C) follows in a non-trivial way from a certain part of T, namely C(T,τ), which is consistent with T*. Only this part of T, and not the whole of T, is *preserved* by the correspondence to T*.

Based on the correspondence relation (C) one can say that $\tau(x)$ *refers indirectly* to the theoretical state of affairs described by $\tau^*(x)$, provided $\tau^*(x)$ refers at all. In other words, (C) entails the possibility of a *reference shift* which makes T partially true, provided T* is true. A deeper justification of this reference shift is provided by the *Ramsey sentence* of a theory which is explained in the next section.

Schurz (2009a) applies the correspondence theorem to the historical phlogiston–oxygen example and arrives at the following result: the theoretical concept which yielded phlogiston theory's strong success was not "phlogiston" itself—this term was empirically underdetermined—but, rather, the complex concept of *dephlogistication = release of phlogiston*. For this concept, Schurz (2009a) derives the following correspondence relation:

(5.7–1) *Correspondence relation between phlogiston and oxidation theory:*

Dephlogistication of a substance corresponds (and indirectly refers) to the *donation of electrons* of the substance's atoms to their electronegative bonding partner.

Of course, these correspondences do *not* preserve *all* of the meaning of "dephlogistication." It cannot be regarded as an *analytic* truth but is, rather, a *synthetic* statement which is true in the domain of applications in which phlogiston theory was empirically successful. It is important, thereby, that the expression τ which yielded T's strong success was not a primitive term but a *composite* expression. For although dephlogistication (τ) corresponds to electron donation (τ^*), phlogiston theory (T) makes theoretical assumptions about τ's *inner composition* (i.e. the release of a substance called phlogiston) which from the viewpoint of T* are false. Hence, τ does only *partially* refer to the "reality" as described by T*.

Schurz (2009a, sec. 7.3) argues that, together with a further assumption, the correspondence theorem may provide a justification of a weak form of realism. The correspondence theorem *alone* justifies only a conditional realism: *if* one assumes the truth of the presently accepted theory T*, then also outdated theories T satisfying the assumptions of prop. 5.7–1 are partially true. To obtain an unconditional justification of realism, Schurz suggests applying the correspondence theorem not to the relation between earlier and presently accepted theories, but between arbitrary theories and an *unknown ideal* theory T⁺. This ideal theory is assumed to provide an approximately true description of the structure of reality which satisfies the conditions of prop. 5.7–1. Schurz (2009a) calls this the assumption of *minimal realism* (MR). He argues that under the assumption of MR, the correspondence theorem *entails* that the inference from the strong success of a theory to its partial realistic truth is justified. By this line of argumentation, the *abductive* inference from strong success to partial truth is replaced by the *analytic* inference from MR plus strong success to partial truth. In this way the correspondence theorem provides an *independent* justification of the NMA and IBE.

5.8 The Ramsey Sentence of a Theory: (Non-)Eliminability of Theoretical Concepts

5.8.1 Ramsey Sentence and Carnap Sentence

Recall from sec. 5.4.2 that positivists searched for methods to eliminate a theory's theoretical concepts without losing its empirical content. Craig's method turned out to be inadequate. More promising for this purpose seemed to be a method that was introduced by Ramsey (1931, 212–215), disseminated by Braithwaite (1953, ch. 3), and independently rediscovered by Carnap (1958/75) (see Psillos 1999, 148–151). Ramsey's method, however, does *not completely* eliminate a theory's theoretical terms—it *existentially quantifies* over them. Assume a theory $T(\tau_1,\ldots \tau_n,\varepsilon_1,\ldots,\varepsilon_m)$, with theoretical terms $\tau_1,\ldots,\tau_n$ and empirical (or non-theoretical) terms $\varepsilon_1,\ldots,\varepsilon_m$, where T stands for the conjunction of the theory's axioms. Then the Ramsey sentence of T is defined as follows:

> (Def. 5.8–1) The *Ramsey sentence R(T)* of a theory $T = T(\tau_1,\ldots\tau_n,\varepsilon_1,\ldots,\varepsilon_m)$:
> $\exists X_1,\ldots,\exists X_n: T(X_1,\ldots X_n,\varepsilon_1,\ldots,\varepsilon_m)$, or in words: there exist theoretical entities $X_1,\ldots,X_n$, which satisfy all assertions of the theory T.

Some authors (e.g. Ramsey 1931; Carnap 1966, ch. 26) introduce the empirical-theoretical distinction only at the level of predicates and function symbols; so for them all of theoretical variables "X_i" are 2nd order. Other authors (e.g. van Fraassen 1980, 13ff) introduce this distinction only at the 1st order level of individual terms. But clearly, one should admit both cases. So we allow that the theoretical terms may be individual constants, predicates or function symbols, and the variables $X_1,\ldots,X_n$ may be of 1st *or* 2nd order.

Under the assumption that all we know about T's theoretical concepts is given solely by the theory T, it is reasonable to identify the full *synthetic content* of the theory T with its Ramsey sentence R(T). (Otherwise the Ramsey sentence must quantify over the conjunction of all theory elements that characterize the theoretical concepts of T.) This consideration led Carnap to the idea that the *global analytic meaning postulate* of T can be represented by the following implication, which I call the Carnap sentence C(T) of T:

(Def. 5.8–2) The *Carnap sentence* C(T) of theory T: R(T)→T.

In words: the n-tuple of T-terms $(\tau_1,\ldots,\tau_n)$ designates some n-tuple of entities $(X_1,\ldots,X_n)$ (of the corresponding type) which satisfies the theory's claim $T(X_1,\ldots,X_n)$, *provided* there exists such an n-tuple.

Obviously the conjunction of R(T) and C(T) is L(ogically)-equivalent with T itself:

(5.8–1)   R(T)∧C(T) ↔ T.

Moreover, it is easy to prove that C(T) does not imply any contingent empirical sentence (Tuomela 1973, 59):

(5.8–2)   E(C(T)) = E(∅)   ("∅" for "empty set").

Carnap takes these facts as justification to regard C(T) as analytically true. In this way, Carnap succeeded in carrying out a *global* separation of T's content into a synthetic and an analytic content part. At the level of particular axioms and consequences of T, the analytic–synthetic distinction is still impossible (as explained in sec. 5.1). It is also important to note that C(T) gives us merely a *partial* semantic characterization of T's theoretical terms, because the truth of R(T) will not always uniquely fix the entities or properties designated by T's theoretical terms (see sec. 5.8.4).

Although it is reasonable to assume that R(T) represents the total synthetic content of T, there exists a reason why in scientific practice theories can hardly be replaced by their Ramsey sentence. This reason has to do with the empirical creativity of theories (recall sec. 5.4.2): if two theories $T_1(\tau_k)$ and $T_2(\tau_k)$ share a theoretical concept τ_k, then the Ramsey sentence of their conjunction $R(T_1 \wedge T_2)$ may be logically and even empirically stronger than the conjunction of the two Ramsey sentences $R(T_1) \wedge R(T_2)$. The truth of latter conjunction does not guarantee that the existential quantifiers $\exists X_k$ in the two conjuncts refer to the same entity. For example if $T_1 = \forall x(Fx \rightarrow \tau_1 x)$ and $T_2 = \forall x(\tau_1 x \rightarrow Gx)$, then $R(T_1 \wedge T_2)$ entails the empirical content $\forall x(Fx \rightarrow Gx)$, which is not implied by $R(T_1) \wedge R(T_2)$. Kutschera (1972, 304) calls this fact the "cross-theoretical significance" of theoretical terms. In conclusion, the replacement of theories by their Ramsey sentence works only globally, i.e. if applied to the conjunction of *all* theories which are relevant to a given set of theoretical terms $\tau_1,\ldots,\tau_n$. This is possible in principle, but cumbersome in practice.

5.8.2 The Instrumentalist Interpretation of the Ramsey Sentence

It is easy to prove that an empirical sentence follows from T exactly if it follows from its Ramsey sentence (Tuomela 1973, 57; Ketland 2004, 293, th. 3). So we have

(5.8-3) $E(R(T)) = E(T)$,

i.e. a theory and its Ramsey sentence have the same empirical consequences. Since R(T) does not contain theoretical terms, but only bound "theoretical variables," several authors have regarded the Ramsey sentence to be an empirical or non-theoretical sentence—including for example Ramsey, partly Carnap (1966, ch. 26), the structuralists (Stegmüller 1969ff, vol. II.3, 46), or Ketland (2004, 294f). For these authors, the goal of finding a compact empirically equivalent formulation of a theory without theoretical terms is achieved with the Ramsey sentence.

But as pointed out by Maxwell (1962, 17) and Hempel (1958, 216), this view is problematic, for the obvious reason that the Ramsey sentence still asserts the *existence* of entities X_i that we regard as "theoretical." A non-theoretical interpretation of the Ramsey sentence is only justified if its existential quantifiers are assumed to be *without* realist *ontological import*, i.e. if they range over purely conceptual (mathematical) entities, as opposed to real physical entities. I call this the *instrumentalist* interpretation of the Ramsey sentence, as opposed to its realist interpretation (explained below).

In the instrumentalist interpretation of R(T), the total domain $D = D_e \cup D_m$ of individuals is regarded as the union of an empirical (or non-theoretical) domain D_e and a conceptual domain of mathematical entities (usually real numbers) D_m.[4] The 1st order variables X_i range over objects in D_m, and the 2nd order variables range over *arbitrary extensions* of the appropriate set-theoretic type, constructed from objects in D but not from D_e alone. These extensions need not correspond to any real (physical) properties or relations, so the existential quantifiers of R(T) are understood in a nominalist sense.

The instrumentalistically interpreted Ramsey sentence is a sentence of a logico-mathematically enriched empirical (non-theoretical) language; its existential quantifiers range over empirical or mathematical entities. Possible models for R(T) have the form $(D_e; D_m; e_1, \ldots, e_m)$, where the "$e_i$" are the extensions of the empirical concepts $\varepsilon_1, \ldots, \varepsilon_m$ (e.g. $\varepsilon_1 \subseteq D_e$, ε_2: $D_e \to \mathbb{R}$, etc.). Recall that a possible model M is called a *model of T* iff it verifies T. The following is easily provable (Ketland 2004, 293, th. 4):

(Prop. 5.8–1) (*Newman's problem:*) R(T) is true in an empirical model $M_e =_{def} (D_e; D_m; e_1, \ldots, e_m)$ iff M_e is a *partial* model of T—which means (by definition) that M_e can be extended to a *full* model $M =_{def} (D_e; D_m; e_1, \ldots, e_m, t_1, \ldots, t_n)$ of T, where the "t_i" are suitably chosen extensions of T's theoretical terms τ_i over $D_e \cup D_m$.

The notion of "partial models" has been introduced by structuralists (Balzer et al. 1987, 57). Ketland (2004) calls a theory T *strongly empirically adequate* iff the *actual* (or *intended*) empirical model $M_e^* =_{def} (D_e^*; D_m; e_1^*, \ldots, e_m^*)$ is a partial model of T. What prop. 5.8–1 expresses is that the truth of a theory's Ramsey sentence R(T) (in M_e^*) coincides with T's strong empirical adequacy. On the other hand, we have seen in sec. 5.8.1 that R(T) expresses the full synthetic content of T. So prop. 5.8–1 gives us the result that the synthetic content of a theory coincides with its "strong" empirical adequacy.

The result of prop. 5.8–1 is an unsurprising consequence of the instrumentalist interpretation of the Ramsey sentence. But it has been regarded as a problem that goes back to Newman (1928) and has been reformulated by Demopoulos/Friedman (1985). The "Newman problem" is usually expressed by saying that the truth of R(T) requires no more than the strong empirical adequacy of T, since the additional theoretical structure required by T can always be constructed over the mathematically extended domain $D = D_e \cup D_m$, provided D has the right *cardinality*.[5]

But note that the *strong* empirical adequacy of T, which is equivalent with the truth of R(T), may be stronger than the truth of T's empirical content E(T). For R(T) is a *2nd order* quantification which may be logically stronger than the set of T's empirical *1st order* consequences. So R(T)'s empirical models may be a proper subclass of E(T)'s models. The additional structure which R(T) implies for D may impose cardinality constraints on the extensions of T's empirical concepts, which are not expressible in T's empirical sublanguage, if T admits infinite domains. This insight goes back to Sneed (1971, 54f): He gives a nice counter-example, in which the existence claim for a bijective theoretical function entails that two empirical concepts F, G of T have an equal but infinite cardinality; this is not expressible by an empirical 1st order sentence. Examples of this sort show that *even if* theoretical terms are interpreted instrumentalistically, a 2nd order quantification over these terms might be necessary to express structural properties of the "empirical phenomena" which would otherwise be inexpressible (Ketland 2004, 296f). For many theories, however, R(T) is indeed equivalent with E(T) (Craig and Vaught 1951). If R(T) is logically equivalent with E(T), then T's theoretical concepts are called *Ramsey-eliminable*.[6]

5.8.3 The Realist Interpretation of the Ramsey Sentence

Newman's "problem" arises only for the instrumentalistically interpreted Ramsey sentence. In its *realistic* interpretation, which one finds in Lewis (1970) or Papineau (1996a), the existentially quantified variables X_i are assumed to range over *real* entities. The non-empirical domain of the realist R(T) consists of the union of the mathematical domain D_m with a theoretical domain D_t of unobservable *physical* individuals. The 1st order variables among the X_i range over individuals in D_t, or over individuals D_m if they are meant to refer to mathematical entities (this distinction can be expressed by assuming domain predicates). More importantly, the 2nd order variables among the X_i do not now range over arbitrary extensions constructible from D, but only over those extensions which are assumed to reflect real physical properties or relations. Hence, a realistic interpretation of R(T) presupposes that one is a *property realist* in the sense explained in 5.7.1.

There are two ways of semantically modeling the 2nd order existence claim of a realistically interpreted Ramsey sentence. The first way is to assume that the existential quantifiers $\exists X_i$ have *realistic import*: here one assumes for each n a *proper subset* $\mathcal{R}^n$ of Pow(D^n), which contains the extensions of those n-ary relations which are assumed to have real existence, i.e. physical meaning. The 2nd order existential quantifiers range over the subsets in $\mathcal{R}^n$ (for higher-order relations one needs higher set-theory types; cf. Balzer et al. 1987, 8f). Of course, the extensions of these "really existing" physical relations are largely unknown, but their assumption is necessary to avoid Newman's problem. For prop. 5.8–1 says only that if R(T) is strongly empirically adequate, there exists a full model of T which assigns to T's n-ary theoretical terms extensions in Pow(D^n), but not necessarily one that assigns to these terms extensions in $\mathcal{R}^n$.

A second semantic modeling of the realistically interpreted Ramsey sentence is possible by employing only a conceptual 2nd order existential quantifier "Σ" which ranges over arbitrary extensions in Pow(D^n), and by using an *existence predicate* "E" instead of the realist quantifier "$\exists$." "E" designates "real existence" and applies to individuals as a 1st order predicate Ea and to n-ary relations as a 2nd order predicate E(R). The existential-import quantifier "$\exists$" is definable in this framework as "$\exists xFx \leftrightarrow_{def} \Sigma x(Ex \wedge Fx)$." Both ways of modeling existence are well known from *free-logic* which allows for languages with non-referring terms: For "Σ" the classical rule of existential quantification Fa/ΣxFx is valid; for "$\exists$" it is invalid and has to be replaced by the free quantification rule Fa/Ea→$\exists$xFx (cf. Garson 2001, 269f; Schurz 1997, 201). I prefer this second modeling because the language with "Σ" and "E" has more expressive power: it allows for theories which assert real existence only for *some* but not for other terms.

A third kind of modeling has been employed by Lewis (1970, 80). He represents all properties and relations R by corresponding "special" individuals c_R which are related to ordinary individuals a by the relation of "possessing" (P): so Fa is reconstructed by him as P(a,c_F), Qab as P(a,b,c_Q), etc. In this way Lewis avoids 2nd order quantification completely. Lewis' reconstruction may have advantages, but it is unusual and hardly explored. So I follow Papineau (1996a) in reconstructing Lewis' realistic theory-interpretation by means of a realistically interpreted 2nd order quantification.

In the light of the preceding analysis we can discuss an objection against the realistic Ramsey sentence that has been raised by Psillos (1999, 65–67) and others in the context of structural realism. For structural realists, R(T) is exactly the right way of expressing the synthetic content of the theory T. But if structural realism can rightly be called a "realism" as opposed to an "instrumentalism," R(T) must be interpreted realistically. For Psillos and other authors (e.g. Melia/Saatsi 2006) this means that R(T) must be enriched by *special* (2nd order) predicates which distinguish merely conceptual from real properties, such as the *naturalness* of theoretical kinds, or the *causal* nature of force functions, etc. (cf. Ladyman/Ross 2007, 126–128). This presupposes that these *special* predicates must be exempted from Ramsey's existential quantification, i.e. their knowledge is no longer regarded as purely structural. Psillos concludes that Ramsey-style structural realists are caught in a *dilemma*: either they insist on a full structuralism (all theoretical relations are Ramsey-quantified), in which case they give up theoretical realism; or they insist on full realism, in which case they must assume that some knowable theoretical relations are non-structural.

In my view, the "naturalness" of kinds and "causal" character of forces should *not* be taken as "primitive," but should be explicated within the framework of (higher-level) theories. Therefore one should Ramsey-quantify over "naturalness" or "causality," too. Nevertheless Psillos' point that the realist Ramsey sentence assumes at least one non-structural "reality" predicate remains valid: in our second modeling of the realistic R(T), this is the existence predicate "E" which discriminates the "real" from the "non-real" properties or relations, and in our first modeling of the realist R(T), this role is taken over by the realist quantifier "∃." We arrive at the following *conclusion*: if one adheres to a *realist* interpretation of theories, then one has to accept at least one theoretical concept that is not characterizable in a Ramsified way, and this is the very concept of *real existence*.

5.8.4 Lewis Definitions

We know that theoretical concepts are not empirically definable. There remains the question whether they could not be at least *theoretically definable*. Such an attempt has been undertaken by Lewis (1970). He suggests strengthening Carnap's account by the assumption that the theory would implicitly postulate that in the actual world the reference of its theoretical terms are uniquely determined (ibid., 83–85). Thus for Lewis, a scientific theory implicitly asserts what I call the Ramsey-Lewis sentence RL(T) (with "∃!" for "there exists exactly one"):

(Def. 5.8–3) The *Ramsey-Lewis sentence* RL(T) of T:
$\exists! X_1, \ldots \exists! X_n \, T(X_1, \ldots, X_n)$

As Lewis (1970, 87f) observes, under the assumption of RL(T) the analytic content of T can be represented by the conjunction of the following *local* "definitions" with the help of *definite descriptions* of T's theoretical concepts τ_i:

(5.8–4) *Lewis definition of term* τ_i, Def(τ_i):

$\tau_i =_{def}$ (that X_i)$\exists!X_1\ldots\exists!X_{i-1}\exists!X_{i+1}\ldots\exists!X_n$: $T(X_1,\ldots,X_n)$

In words: τ_i's designation is that entity which is the ith member of the unique n-tuple of entities $X_1,\ldots,X_n$ which satisfies T's claim.

Expressions of the form "(that x)Ax" are called "definite descriptions" of the entity x. The unique object which is A's extension is assigned to the definite description "(that x)Ax" in all possible worlds in which the unique existence claim $\exists!Ax$ is true. But in all worlds in which this claim is false, the definite description is denotation-less, and statements of the form B((that x)Ax) are then either regarded as false (as suggested by Russell 1905), or as lacking truth value. So Lewis definitions Def(τ_i) come out as false or as truth-value-less in every possible world in which the Ramsey-Lewis sentence RL(T) is false. This shows that the Lewis definitions are merely *partial* definitions, because they fix the designation of theoretical terms not in all possible worlds but only in those which verify RL(T). To circumvent the partiality of his definitions, Lewis assumes that in all worlds in which RL(T)'s unique existence assumption is violated, an "empty" designation δ is assigned to the definite descriptions "that X_i" (Lewis 1970, 80f). But this is just a "formal trick" which cannot avoid the result that Lewis definitions are merely partial and do not determine the real reference of theoretical terms in worlds in which RL(T) is false.

Also Lewis' thesis that scientific theories make implicit unique existence claims for the designations of their theoretical concepts is problematic. First of all, this thesis only makes sense if the existential quantifiers are interpreted realistically (cf. Papineau 1996a, 6, fn. 5). For an instrumentalistically interpreted Ramsey sentence there exist by logical necessity different possible extensions of T's theoretical concepts which satisfy T, provided R(T) is strongly empirically adequate, e.g. by construction of isomorphic models (Winnie 1967). But the Ramsey-Lewis sentence is even doubtful if its existential quantifiers are interpreted realistically, which is assumed by Lewis. For many theoretical concepts in science the question of their real reference is highly controversial among scientists, although these theories are empirically successful. An example is time in classical physics; another example is wave functions in quantum mechanics.

5.9 Criteria for Theoreticity and Empirical Significance

5.9.1 Pre-Theoretical and Theoretical Concepts

In sec. 5.3.1 we distinguished between the following concepts (or terms) of a theory T: (a) T's *empirical* concepts i.n.s., (b) T's non-empirical concepts, which are theoretical i.w.s., (c) T's *T-theoretical* and (d) T's *pre-theoretical* concepts, where (c) and (d) are subsets of (b). In this subsection we give precise definitions of these notions.

By a theory we understand a theory element or a theory lattice in the sense explained earlier in fig. 5.2–1.[7] In def. 5.9–1(i) and (ii) below we explicate the relation of *pre-theoreticity* (building upon an idea of Balzer/Mühlhölzer 1982, 32). We thereby refer to a given *theory net N*, consisting of a set of theories together with intertheoretical relations, as explained in sec. 5.3.2. Def. 5.9–1(iii) explicates the notion of T-theoreticity, based on the idea that a concept τ is T-theoretical if T entails at least one (and typically several) law(s) of correspondence for τ. Recall from sections 5.1 and 5.2 that each correspondence law provides a T-dependent *measurement method* for τ.

(Def. 5.9–1)

i T_1 is a *pre-theory* of T_2 in a given theory net N (abbreviated as $T_1 \to_{pre} T_2$) iff T_1's non-empirical concepts are a proper subset of T_2's non-empirical concepts.

ii τ is a *pre-theoretical concept* of T in N iff τ is a non-empirical concept of T which is T*-theoretical for some pre-theory T* of T in N.

iii τ is a *T-theoretical* concept (of T) in N iff τ is a non-empirical and not pre-theoretical concept of T (in N), and at least one *law of correspondence* for τ follows from T, i.e. a lawlike (synthetic) sentence of the form $\forall x \forall t(A_i xt \to (\tau(x) \leftrightarrow R_i xt))$, where $A_i xt$, $R_i xt$ are empirical or pre-theoretical expressions of T in N.[8]

Our definitions guarantee that "empirical," "pre-theoretical" and "T-theoretical" are *disjoint* properties. So a concept τ for which T entails a correspondence law is only T-theoretical if τ is neither empirical nor pre-theoretical.

The relation of pre-theory according to i is transitive. Since we assume that every theory in N contains only finitely many theoretical concepts i.w.s., every descending chain of pre-theories of a given theory

T_1 is *well-ordered*, i.e. has an initial pre-theory T_n which has no further pre-theory in N ($T_n \to_{pre} T_{n-1} \to_{pre} \ldots \to_{pre} T_1$). We call T_n an *initial theory* of the theory net N. It follows that definitions ii and iii, which mutually refer to each other, are not circular but *recursive* (iterative): to check whether a term, say µ, of T_1 is pre-theoretical, we have to determine whether one of the finitely many pre-theories of T_1 in N entails a correspondence law $A_i \to (\mu \leftrightarrow R_i)$ for µ. If such a theory, say T_2, is found, we have to check whether the expressions A_i, R_i are pre-theoretical in T_2, and so on, until we arrive at a theory T_n which has no further pre-theories, and the chain of checks comes to an end. The important feature of this recursive definition of pre-theoreticity is that it allows for *chains of measurement* in the sense of (5.1–10).

A law of correspondence $T_i \to (\tau \leftrightarrow R_i)$ for τ is called *direct* if its test condition T_i and indicator property R_i are empirical. Due to the recursive nature of def. (5.9–1) the following can be proved:

> (Prop. 5.9–1): If φ is T_1-theoretical in theory net N, then there exists a descending chain of pre-theories $T_n \to_{pre} T_{n-1} \to_{pre} \ldots \to_{pre} T_1$ in N such that T_n is an initial theory of N and the union of theories $T_1, \ldots, T_n$ entails a direct law of correspondence for φ.

As a further complication, we often find theoretical concepts within theories, whose meaning and empirical significance is explained by *superordinate* theories, which are not pre-theories of T. For example, the chemical theory of the atom contains the concept of "electrical charge," which is explained in the theory lattice of electrodynamics. We call such concepts "externally theoretical" and define them with help of the concept of an "interpretative theory" as follows:

> (Def. 5.9–2)
>
> i T_1 is an *interpretative theory* for T_2 in a theory net N (abbreviated as $T_1 \to_{int} T_2$) iff T_2 contains some non-empirical and non-T_2-theoretical concepts that are T_1-theoretical, although T_1 is neither a pre-theory nor a specialization of T_2.
>
> ii φ is an *external theoretical* concept of T iff φ is T*-theoretical for some interpretative theory T* for T in N.

Summarizing, the (non-logical) concepts of a theory T in a theory net N fall into the following disjoint categories:

a   the *empirical* concepts of T, including observational concepts and empirical dispositions concepts (sec. 3.2.2),
b   the *pre-theoretical* concepts of T in N (def. 5.9–1(ii)), and
c   the *theoretical* concepts of T in the *narrow* sense (i.n.s.), which subsume

   c.1 the *T-theoretical* concepts and
   c.2 the *external theoretical* concepts of T, and finally

d   the *speculative* concepts of T, which are all (non-logical) concepts of T which are neither empirical nor pre-theoretical nor theoretical i.n.s. These concepts are *empirically insignificant* in the sense of (5.9–2) below.

Categories b, c and d together define the theoretical concepts i.w.s., which coincide with the non-empirical concepts.

We call a theory (element) T of a theory net N a *basal* theory of N if T does not possess either a pre-theory or an interpretative theory in N. A theory net N is *empirically well-founded* iff it does not possess any *speculative* concepts. It is easy to see that the basal theories of empirically well-founded theory nets must satisfy the following property:

> (Prop. 5.9–2) If a theory net N is empirically well-founded and T is a basal theory of N, then every non-empirical concept of T is T-theoretical.

We regard empirical well-foundedness as an ideal adequacy requirement for scientific theory nets.

Finally, let us compare our definitions of theoreticity with the accounts of theoreticity in structuralist philosophy of science. According to Sneed (1971, 33), a concept ψ of a theory T is *T-theoretical* iff in the given state of knowledge, *every* measurement of $\psi(a)$ in some application a of T *presupposes* the truth of theory T for this or some other application (see Stegmüller 1976, 45f). This is close to our def. (5.9–1)(iii), if we assume that the linguistic reconstruction of a Sneedian measurement method for ψ is a law of correspondence $C(\psi)$ for ψ. For if $C(\psi)$ is entailed by T, then using $C(\psi)$ for measuring ψ "presupposes T" insofar as it is reasonable to use the method $C(\psi)$ only if one assumes that T is true. Sneed's requirement that *every* measurement method of ψ presupposes T excludes that ψ can be measured already empirically or within pre-theories of T. So our requirement in def. 5.9–1(iii) that a

T-theoretical concept must be neither empirical nor pre-theoretical is implicitly contained in Sneed's definition, too.

There is only one point in which our definition differs substantially from Sneed's definition: def. 5.9–1(iii) does not exclude that a T-theoretical term ψ can at the same time be T*-theoretical for some interpretative theory T* of N in the sense of def. 5.9–2. Sneed's definition excludes this possibility, since if ψ is T*-theoretical, then it is T*-dependently measurable without the need to presuppose T. The exclusion of this possibility by Sneed's definition has been criticized by Balzer/Moulines (1980, sec. iv) as being too strong, since it often happens in science that a T-theoretical term ψ can be simultaneously measured within *another* theory T* which is not a pre-theory of T. If we *improve* Sneed's definition by allowing this possibility, then this improved Sneed definition *converges* with our def. 5.9–1(iii).

Recall that this convergence holds only under the assumption that a T-dependent measurement method for a term ψ is understood as a T-entailed law of correspondence for ψ. It is unclear whether Sneed understood T-dependent measurement methods in this way. The Munich structuralists have explicated this notion in a much more liberal way, as the determination of ψ's extension in a measurement model by the extension of the *other* relations of T, independent of whether these relations are empirical, pre-T-theoretical or T-theoretical. Recall from sec. 3.1.2 (prop. 3.1–2) that structuralists represent theories not by sets of axioms Ax(T), but by corresponding sets of models M(T) $=_{\text{def}}$ {m∈M($\mathcal{L}$): m $\models$ Ax(T)} (actually structuralist theories are more complicated, but for our purpose this is sufficient). Let "$r_k(m)$" be the extension of the kth relation term ψ_k of T in model m. Then Balzer (1985a) defines a *T-dependent measurement method for relation term* ψ_k of theory M(T) as a specialization $M_1(T) \subset M(T)$ for which there exists a function f such that for every model m in $M_1(T)$, $r_k(m)$ is an f-function of the other relations in m, i.e. $r_k(m) = f((r_i(m): 1 \leq i \leq n, i \neq k)$. Thereby, T_1 must be "r_s-T-invariant," which means linguistically that the additional axioms characterizing $M_1(T)$ do not contain the relation term "ψ_k" (see Schurz 2013b, th. 8).

Sneed's criterion is difficult to test, because it refers to *all* measurement methods for a given concept. Therefore, Gähde (1983) and Balzer (1985a,b) have developed a new criterion of theoreticity, in which the universal quantifier over measurement methods is replaced by an existential quantifier. Stegmüller (1969ff, vol. II.3, ch. 6) was emphatic about this new criterion, hence I call it the *Munich* criterion. Balzer's version of this criterion is especially simple: he defines a non-logical relation term ψ of T as *T-theoretical* iff there exists a T-dependent measurement for ψ in the explained sense.

The Munich criterion of T-theoreticity is purely *theory-internal*, insofar as it does not refer to any independent notion of empiricity or pre-theoreticity, not even indirectly, as in Sneed's definition. This is seen as an advantage by structuralists. However, this theory-internal character brings with it *two problems*:

First: The Munich criterion no longer excludes a T-theoretical concept ψ from being empirical. For if a theory T entails an equivalence between a theoretical and an empirical relation under certain measurement conditions, this does not only allow one to determine the theoretical from the empirical relation, but also the other way round, to determine the empirical relation from the theoretical one. That such situations do occur has been shown in Schurz (1990) by way of counterexamples. For example, the acceleration a(x,t) of a particle x at a given time t is intuitively an empirical or pre-theoretical concept of CPM. Nevertheless acceleration comes out as CPM-theoretical according to the Munich criterion, because CPM allows us to determine the acceleration as a(x,t) = F(x,t)/m(x), where F(x,t) is the total force acting on x at time t, and m(x) is x's mass.

Second: the Munich criterion allows *circular determination chains*. Assume for example that a theory T entails a bifunctional dependence ∀x(φ(x) =c/ψ(x)) of two concepts which are unrelated to any other measureable concepts. T may, for example, say that every object x is under the influence of two powers, called "Good" and "Evil," and the strength of Good (φ(x)) is inversely proportional to the strength of Evil (ψ(x)). Then φ and ψ are T-theoretical according to the Munich criterion, because the extension of one concept is determined by the extension of the other, but neither of the two concepts can really be measured, because they are related in a circular way. Circular relations of this sort are carefully avoided in our definition 5.9–1 of pre-T-theoreticity.

5.9.2 Empirical Significance

According to the principle of *Ockham's razor*, the introduction of a new theoretical concept is only justified if this concept plays an essential role for the empirical success of the respective theory. We call such a theoretical concept *empirically significant*. For example, if T is Newtonian physics, and S(τ) is the speculative hypothesis "The universe was created by God," then T∧S(τ) has the same empirical success as T, but obviously, S(τ) and its new "theoretical" term "God" (τ) are without any empirical significance in T∧S(τ). The positivist philosophy of science spoke here of *cognitive significance* (Hempel 1951). But the identification of cognitive with empirical significance seems to be too narrow, as theoretical concepts which do not (yet) possess empirical significance can nevertheless be cognitively meaningful (recall sec. 2.6). It is therefore better to speak of "empirical significance."

Philosophers of science attempted to provide criteria for discriminating between theoretical concepts which are empirically significant and those which are superfluous (cf. Hempel 1951; Carnap 1956a, 51ff; Stegmüller 1969ff, vol. II.1, ch. V). This enterprise suffered many setbacks, which had to do with the problem of irrelevant conclusions explained in sec. 3.12. For example, Stegmüller (ibid., 348) discusses the following logical problem raised by Achinstein (1968): Assume an axiomatized theory T^* contains an empirically redundant conjunct $S(\tau)$, as in the example of $T^* = T \wedge S(\tau)$ given above, i.e. $E(T \wedge S(\tau))=E(T)$. One could try to capture this kind of insignificance by defining a concept τ of a theory T^* as empirically significant if it occurs in an empirically non-redundant conjunct $S(\tau)$ of T^*. But this definition is inadequate, since $T \wedge S(\tau)$ is logically equivalent with $S(\tau) \wedge (S(\tau) \rightarrow T)$, and in $S(\tau) \wedge (S(\tau) \rightarrow T)$ the conjunct $S(\tau)$ is not redundant. But obviously, $S(\tau) \rightarrow T$ is an *irrelevant* consequence of T in the sense of def. 3.12-1.

This and similar problems can be solved by applying the concept of a *natural axiomatization* (i.e. irreducible representation) of T (recall sec. 5.3.1 and def. 3.12-4). With help of this notion we formulate the following necessary condition for empirical significance:

(5.9-1) A theoretical concept τ (i.w.s.) is *empirically significant* in a theory T *only if* there exists no natural axiomatization $Ax(T)$ of T which has an empirically equivalent subset $\Delta \subset Ax(T)$ (i.e. $E(Ax(T))=E(\Delta)$) in which τ no longer occurs.

Criterion (5.9-1) has been proposed in Schurz (1991a, §5.1.4) and, using a different definition of "natural axiomatization," by Gemes (1998, 15).

An equally plausible and simpler condition for the empirical significance of a theoretical term τ is the following:

(5.9-2) A theoretical concept τ (i.w.s.) is *empirically significant* in T *only if* T entails a law of correspondence for τ (in the sense of def. 5.9-1(iii)).

The two criteria (5.9-1) and (5.9-2) are mutually independent. To see that (5.9-2) does not imply (5.9-1), assume a theory T which consists only of correspondence laws and contains the same correspondence laws $(A_j x \rightarrow (\tau_1(x) \leftrightarrow R_j x))$ and $(A_j x \rightarrow (\tau_2(x) \leftrightarrow R_j x))$ for two distinct theoretical terms τ_1 and τ_2. Then (5.9-2) is satisfied, but the empirical content is not diminished if the correspondence laws for one of the two theoretical terms are eliminated in T's natural axiomatization; so (5.9–1) is violated. On the other hand, consider the theory naturally axiomatized as $\{\forall x(Fx\rightarrow\tau_1(x)\wedge\tau_2(x)), \forall x(\tau_1(x)\wedge\tau_2(x)\rightarrow Gx)\}$, which has the empirical consequence $\forall x(Fx\rightarrow Gx)$. Then criterion (5.9–1) is satisfied for τ_1 and τ_2, but T does not entail a correspondence law for τ_1 and for τ_2; only one for the complex term "$\tau_1(x)\wedge\tau_2(x)$." An example is the phlogiston theory mentioned in sec. 5.7.4 which contains a correspondence law for "release of phlogiston," but not for "phlogiston."

Both criteria of empirical significance are only *necessary*, but not *sufficient* conditions. They are not strong enough to discriminate scientific theories from pseudo-science. A further requirement is that scientific theories must not consist entirely of post-facto explanations, but have to entail some *use-novel* consequences by which they can be independently tested. This is explained in sec. 5.10.4.

5.10 General Accounts of Confirmation

In Chapters 4 and 5 we developed *specific* methods for the testing and confirmation of specific kinds of hypotheses: strict empirical laws, statistical hypotheses, theory versions and theory cores. In philosophy of science there have also been developed *general* theories of confirmation which are intended to apply to hypotheses of *all* kinds. The problem of these accounts is, usually, that they are too unspecific to capture all relevant aspects of confirmation. Viewed as necessary conditions, however, these accounts are quite useful.

In this section, H, H_1, H_2 … will always stand for hypotheses (which may be theories, empirical laws, or singular predictions), E, E_1, E_2,…,for evidences (typically observations or empirical data), and B, B_1, B_2,…,for conjunctions of accepted background beliefs. We assume that evidence statements E are either true (*semantic* version) or at least highly probable (*epistemic* version).

In regard to the gradation type, three kinds of confirmation relations can be distinguished: (1) *qualitative* confirmation (E confirms H), (2) *comparative* (E confirms H_1 more than H_2) and (3) *quantitative* confirmation (E confirms H to such-and-such a degree). While hypothetico-deductive confirmation relations (sec. 5.10.1) are typically qualitative, probabilistic confirmation relations (sec. 5.10.2) can be qualitative, comparative or quantitative. Depending on whether the confirmation relation is relativized to accepted background beliefs B, one distinguishes between two-placed confirmation relations (E confirms H) and three-placed ones (E confirms H relative to background beliefs B).

5.10.1 Hypothetico-Deductive Confirmation

According to the basic idea of hypothetico-deductive (HD) confirmation, hypotheses are confirmed by their true or actually observed empirical consequences. Thereby the notion of "consequence" is understood in the logico-deductive sense. Observe that the relation of HD-confirmation is the *converse* of the consequence relation; so, viewed as "inference rules," HD-confirmations are highly uncertain.

The HD-account of confirmation was qualitatively described in sec. 2.3. It was introduced by Whewell (1837) and has been defended by Popper (1935/2000), who spoke of "corroboration" (see sec. 2.7.2). The HD-account can only be applied to strict but not to probabilistic hypotheses, because the latter do not deductively entail their empirical consequences, but make them only inductively probable.

Beginning with Hempel (1945), the seemingly innocent idea of HD-confirmation has been put under logical scrutiny by different authors, with surprising results. Consider the following definition:

(Def. 5.10–1) *Classical definition of HD-confirmation:*

a   Evidence E confirms hypothesis H given background beliefs B iff: (i) H and B entail E (H∧B ||— E), (ii) H is consistent with B ({H,B} ||–/– ⊥), and (iii) E has content given B (B ||–/– E).
Example: Ga confirms the hypothesis ∀x(Fx→Gx) given Qa and ∀x(Qx→Fx).

b   The unconditional confirmation relation "E confirms H" is obtained from (a) by letting B be a logical truth.
Example: Fa→Ga confirms ∀x(Fx→Gx) (unconditionally).

Explication a is found, e.g., in Glymour (1981, 35), Christensen (1990) or Kuipers (2000, §2.1.1); explication b in Hesse (1970, 50) or Lenzen (1974, 25–30). As the follow-up discussion has shown, the classical HD-account of confirmation leads to various "paradoxical" results. They emerged in the context of four proposed "adequacy conditions" for confirmation concepts:

(5.10–1) *Proposed "adequacy" conditions for confirmation concepts:*

Assume E confirms H given B according to def. 5.10–1a.

1 *Weakening of H* (essential for "full confirmation"): If H ||— H*, then E confirms also H* given B.

2 *Strengthening of H* (follows from def. 5.10–1): If H* ||— H, and H* is consistent with B, then E confirms also H* given B.
3 *Weakening of E* (follows from def. 5.10–1): If E ||— E*, and E* has content given B, then also E* confirms H given B.
4 *Strengthening of E* (essential for "data collection"): If E* ||— E, and E* does not confirm ¬H given B, then also E* confirms H given B.

Conditions 1 and 2 are mentioned in Hempel (1945, 31), who calls 1 the "special consequence condition" and 2 the "converse consequence condition." Conditions 3 and 4 are dual counterparts of 2 and 1, respectively. Further "adequacy conditions" are discussed in Hempel (1945), Lenzen (1974, 30–45) and Huber (2008). While conditions 2 and 3 are necessary consequences of def. 5.10–1, 1 and 4 are additional conditions.

Condition 4 is intuitively evident in application to data *collections*: if E* is a large *conjunction* of data that contains a particular evidence E which confirms hypothesis H, and nothing else in E* speaks against H, then one would certainly say that also the more comprehensive set E* confirms H. Condition 1, on the other hand, is a necessary condition for the notion of *full* as opposed to merely *partial* confirmation. We say that E confirms H fully (vs. partially), iff E confirms every (vs. at least one) relevant conjunctive part of H (see below). Full confirmation is essential for *applications* of confirmation results, since to *trust* a hypothesis because it is sufficiently confirmed means that we trust the consequences of this hypothesis; but this is only reasonable if condition 1 holds.

In conjunction with condition 1, classical HD-confirmation produces the following "paradoxical" result:

(5.10–2) *Tacking by conjunction paradox:* Def. 5.10–1 and cond. (5.10–1)1 imply: Every contingent evidence E confirms every hypothesis H which is consistent with E (relative to an empty B).

Proof: (i) E confirms the hypothesis "H∧E" (according to def. 5.10–1), because H∧E ||— E and by assumption, ||–/– E and {E,H} is consistent. Moreover (ii) H∧E ||— H, which implies by condition 1 that E confirms H.

The name "tacking by conjunction" was introduced by Lakatos (1970, 46) and Glymour (1981, 67). Result (5.10–2) is quite fatal for the classical HD-account. Defenders of this account suggested that one could escape this paradox by giving up adequacy condition 1 (e.g. Kuipers 2000, sec. 2.1.2). But to abandon condition 1 is tantamount to giving up the goal of explicating the concept of *full* HD-confirmation in the explained sense. Moreover, even without condition 1 the classical HD-account implies the counterintuitive consequence that whenever an evidence E confirms a hypothesis H, then E also confirms the conjunction H∧X for arbitrary H-consistent X.

Even if one confines oneself with an account of *partial* HD-confirmation, this does not avoid a second kind of "paradoxical" result, which arises from conjoining def. 5.10–1 with adequacy condition 4 and has been called the paradox of "tacking by disjunction" (Grimes 1990, 520; Gemes 1993, 485; Schurz 2005b, sec. 3):

(5.10–2) *Tacking by disjunction paradox:* Def. 5.10–1 and cond. (5.10–1)4 imply: Every contingent evidence E confirms every hypothesis H which is logically independent from ¬E (relative to an empty B).

Proof: (i) H∨E confirms H (according to def. 5.10–1) because H ||— H∨E and ||–/– H∨E (since ¬E and H are L-independent). Moreover (ii) E ||— E∨H, and E does not confirm ¬H (since ¬E and H are L-independent); so by condition 4, E confirms H.

This result is devastating for the classical HD-account, since the adequacy condition 4 seems to be innocent. Even if one gives up condition 4, one still has the strange consequence that E∨X confirms X for every arbitrary ¬E-independent X. Glymour (1980) concluded from these results that the HD concept of confirmation is completely "hopeless." Glymour (1981, 51ff, 130f) developed an alternative "bootstrap" account of confirmation, which is also defined via deductive inference relations, but Christensen (1990) showed that Glymour's bootstrap account is exposed to similar paradoxical results.

Both paradoxes (5.10–1) and (5.10–2) result from *irrelevant* deductive inferences in the sense of def. 3.12–1. The tacking by conjunction paradox relies on the inference (5.10–1)(i) H∧E ||— E with an irrelevant premise-conjunct (underlined), and the tacking by disjunction paradox on the inference (5.10–2)(i) H ||— H∨E with an irrelevant conclusion-disjunct (underlined). Schurz (1991a, 1994) shows how these (and more complex) problems of the classical account to HD-confirmation can be solved by applying the requirement of relevant premises and conclusion to def. 5.10–1. To grant the invariance of the confirmation relation with respect to L-equivalent transformations of premises and conclusion, we must require that premises and conclusion are transformed into an irreducible representation of them in the sense of def. 3.12–4:

> (Def. 5.10–2) *Relevant HD-confirmation:*
>
> a Evidence E confirms relevantly hypothesis H given background belief B iff there exist irreducible representations I(H), I(B) and I(E) of H, B and E, respectively, such that I(H), I(B) ||— I(E) is a deductive inference whose conclusion and premises are relevant (def. 3.12–1).
> b The unconditional relevant HD-confirmation concept is obtained from a by omitting B and I(B).
>
> *Examples*: Ga confirms relevantly ∀x(Fx→Gx), given Fa; and Fa confirms relevantly ∀xFx. But Ga∨Ha does not confirm relevantly ∀x(Fx→Gx), given Fa; and Ga does not confirm relevantly ∀x(Fx→Gx)∧∀x(Hx→Qx), given Fa.

The conditions (ii, iii) of def. 5.10–1—that H∧B is consistent and E has content given B—are guaranteed by the requirement that I(H), I(B) ||— I(E) is a premise- and conclusion-relevant inference. The two "adequacy" conditions 2 (strengthening of H) and 3 (weakening of E), which are the culprits of the tacking paradoxes of HD-confirmation, are no longer valid for relevant HD-confirmation. So the paradoxes of classical HD-confirmation no longer arise.

A similar account has been developed by Gemes (1993, 1994, 1998), who employs his notion of "content part" instead of our notion of "relevant element"; a comparison is found in Schurz (1994) and (2005b, sec. 6). We finally emphasize that although def. 5.10–2 is a reasonable *necessary* condition for confirmation based on hypothetico-deductive inference, it is questionable whether it can be regarded as a *sufficient* condition, because it does not capture the condition of sufficient *inductive* strength. According to def. 5.10–2 both a single instance Fa and a representative sample of instances $Fa_1 \wedge \ldots \wedge Fa_n$ confirm the hypothesis ∀xGx, although intuitively many people would speak of confirmation only in the second case. This difference cannot be captured by a deductivistic, but only by a probabilistic account of confirmation, which is the topic of the next subsections.

5.10.2 Bayesian Probabilistic Confirmation

The Bayesian confirmation concept is based on the epistemic probability of the hypothesis given the evidence, P(H|E), which was explained in sec. 4.7.2 in application to statistical hypotheses. Bayesians generalize this account to hypotheses of all sorts. There exist two kinds of Bayesian confirmation concepts: *incremental* and *absolute* confirmation. Incremental confirmation means that conditionalization on E *raises* H's probability, though not necessarily to a high value, while absolute confirmation means that H's probability conditional on E has a *sufficiently high* value:[9]

(Def. 5.10–3) *Incremental and absolute Bayesian confirmation:*

a   *E confirms H incrementally* given background beliefs B iff P(H|E∧B) > P(H|B) (where in practical applications ">" should be understood as "significantly higher than").

b   *H is absolutely confirmed given E* and background beliefs B iff P(H|E∧B) is "sufficiently high," i.e. is greater than a contextually determined acceptability threshold α which must be at least greater than 0.5 (so that P(H|E∧B) > P(¬H|E∧B) holds).

c   The corresponding unconditional confirmation concepts are obtained from a and b by identifying B with a logical truth.

Absolute confirmation does not include a condition of probability increase, which is a deficiency of this concept. On the other hand, the standard rule of *rational acceptance* (sec. 5.10.8), according to which one should prefer that hypothesis which is best confirmed by the total evidence, only makes sense for the absolute, but not for the incremental confirmation concept. For example, if P(H) = 0.95 and P(H|E) = 0.9, then ¬H is incrementally confirmed by E (since P(¬H|E) = 0.1 > P(¬H) = 0.05), but H is absolutely confirmed given E (assuming α ≤ 0.9) and should be preferred to ¬H, if E is the total evidence. One may also conjoin both conditions into a concept of *relevant absolute confirmation* of H by E, being defined as P(H|E) > α and P(H|E) > P(H).

Contemporary Bayesians prefer the *incremental* concept. We follow this trend and focus on the incremental confirmation concept, too: when we say that E *Bayes-confirms* H we mean from now on that E incrementally confirms H. Bayes-confirmation has two important properties. First, prop. 3.9–3(TC8) implies that Bayes-confirmation of H by E coincides with the increase of H's likelihood P(E|H):

(5.10-3) $P(H|E \wedge B) > P(H|B)$ iff $P(E|H \wedge B) > P(E|B)$.

Second, classical HD-confirmation is a special case of Bayes-confirmation for all *non-dogmatic* probability functions P given B, which means that $P(S|B) \neq 0,1$ for every contingent S.

> (Prop. 5.10-1) *HD-confirmation implies Bayes-confirmation:*
>
> If E HD-confirms H given B (def. 5.10-1), then E Bayes-confirms H given B, for every probability function P which is non-dogmatic w.r.t. H and E given B.

Proof: If E HD-confirms H, then H is B-consistent and E has content given B, so $P(H|B) > 0$ and $P(E|H) < 1$, whence $P(E|H \wedge B) = 1 > P(E|B)$: so by (5.10-3), E Bayes-confirms H given B.

Bayes-confirmation is a qualitative confirmation concept. Different *quantitative* refinements of incremental confirmation have been developed, for example (a) the difference measure $P(H|E \wedge B) - P(H|B)$, (b) the ratio measure $P(H|E \wedge B)/P(H|B) - 1$, (c) the modified difference measure $P(H|E \wedge B) - P(H|\neg E \wedge B)$, or (d) the product measure $P(H \wedge E|B) - P(H|B) \cdot P(E|B)$ (cf. the overviews in Fitelson 1999 or Crupi/Trentori 2010). These measures have different numerical properties, but all of them are ordinally equivalent with incremental Bayes-confirmation, in the sense that their degree of confirmation of H by E is greater than zero iff E Bayes-confirms H.

The concept of Bayes-confirmation has the following shortcomings:

1 *The problem of old evidence:* This problem has already been discussed in sec. 4.7.2. It has the consequence that the concept of Bayes-confirmation can work properly only if the probability function "P" does not reflect the subject's actual degree of beliefs, but her epistemic a-priori probability which is independent of her actual state of evidence.

2 *The arbitrariness of likelihoods:* Recall from sec. 3.13.5 that it is important for Bayesians that the likelihoods are determined in an objective or at least intersubjective way. There are, however, only two cases in which the likelihoods $P(E|H \wedge B)$ are objectively determined. First, the case in which H is a *statistical* hypothesis and $P(E|H)$ is identified with the statistical likelihood $p_H(E)$ (recall prop. 4.7-1). Second, the case in which H entails E; this case coincides with classical HD-confirmation (prop. 5.10-1). In other cases the determination of the likelihood is

scientifically undetermined: for example, what is the likelihood that general relativity theory is true given the current evidence?

3 *Paradoxes of irrelevance:* The fact that classical HD-confirmation is a special case of Bayes-confirmation has been celebrated as a success of Bayesian confirmation theorists (Earman 1992, 54; Howson/Urbach 1996, 119ff). In view of the *paradoxes* of HD-confirmation discussed in sec. 5.10.1 this "success" is questionable: for it implies that the tacking by conjunction and disjunction paradoxes apply likewise to Bayes-confirmation. This is more a disaster than a success.

Bayesian confirmation theorists have made some proposals to handle the tacking by conjunction paradox. Based on the difference measure of confirmation, Hawthorne/Fitelson (2004) have argued that if E Bayes-confirms H, and X is irrelevant to E given H in the sense that $P(E|H \wedge X) = P(E|H)$, then E Bayes-confirms also the conjunction $H \wedge X$, but demonstrably to a lesser degree, i.e. $P(H|E) - P(H) > P(H \wedge X|E) - P(H \wedge X)$. So the hypothesis H is confirmationally preferred over $H \wedge X$ in the light of E. However, if arbitrary conjunctive representations are allowed, then the Hawthorne-Fitelson strategy would fall prey to the following argument of Popper and Miller (1983): H is logically equivalent to $(E \vee H) \wedge (\neg E \vee H)$, and while the first conjunct is entailed by E, the second conjunct is provably disconfirmed by E. If this decomposition of H were allowed, then Hawthorne/Fitelson (2004) would have to confirmationally prefer $E \vee H$ over H, which is not what they want. But of course, this decomposition of H is *irrelevant*; only conjunctive decompositions of H into relevant elements are allowed. We shall see below that a satisfying solution to the tacking paradoxes requires the application of the method of relevant elements.

4 *Bayesian pseudo-confirmation.* The Bayesian confirmation concept is too weak to distinguish genuine scientific confirmation from pseudo-confirmation. This major problem is treated in the next subsections.

5.10.3 Bayesian Pseudo-Confirmation through Content-Cutting

That Bayesian confirmation cannot discriminate genuine from pseudo-confirmation is most easily seen in the case when H entails E: the required probability increase $P(H|E) > P(H)$ arises solely because H contains E as a content part, independently from those content parts of H which go beyond E. This problem is a simple consequence of proposition (5.10–1) and can be formulated as follows:

> (Prop. 5.10–2) *Bayesian pseudo-confirmation:* Every hypothesis H with non-zero prior probability (however weird) is confirmed by every non-certain evidence E, if H only entails this evidence.

In other words, E does not need to raise the probability of the E-transcending content parts of H, in order to Bayes-confirm H. Gemes and Earman (see Earman 1992, 98, 242, fn. 5) have called this type of non-genuine confirmation "confirmation by mere *content-cutting*": we cut-off ¬E's possibility space from the total possibility space and thereby increase H's share of the possibility space. In what follows we will say that E *genuinely* confirms H only if (informally speaking) E also Bayes-confirms the E-transcending content parts of H. The fact that Bayes-confirmation admits cases of non-genuine confirmation is responsible for three problems:

a tacking by conjunction,
b missing inductive character, and
c pseudo-confirmation of post-facto speculations (next subsection).

The most basic case of a is given when the conjunct is "tacked" directly to the evidence. For example, "grass is green" (E) Bayes-confirms the conjunction of the doctrine of Jehova's witnesses (X) with "grass is green." This is not genuine confirmation, since the only relevant content part of X∧E which goes beyond E is X, and E is probabilistically irrelevant to X, i.e. $P(X|E) = P(X)$. In other cases (as discussed before) the irrelevant conjunct X is tacked to a hypothesis H which is confirmed by E.

As explained above, not every conjunctive decomposition of the hypothesis H into conjuncts is admissible, but only its decomposition into relevant content elements, or in short: *content elements* (def. 3.12–2). In what follows, by (relevant) *content part* we mean always a *conjunction* of content elements. Note that when H relevantly entails E, there does not always exist a content part H* of H such that H is L-equivalent with H*∧E. But by prop. 3.12–1 there exist always some content elements of H that go beyond E (provided H is not entailed by E), and genuine confirmation requires that these E-transcending content elements of H are Bayes-confirmed by E. In sec. 5.10.6 we make this idea logically precise. Before this we discuss further important applications of the notion of genuine confirmation.

A first application concerns inductive generalizations. The weakness of Bayesian content-cutting manifests itself in the fact that it applies to inductive as well as anti-inductive generalizations. The evidence E that all emeralds observed so far are green Bayes-confirms the inductive generalization H_1: "all emeralds are green" as well as the anti-inductive generalization H_2 "all observed emeralds are green, and all non-observed ones are not green," since both hypotheses entail E. This problem is related to Goodman's paradox which is treated in sec. 5.10.7. It shows that Bayes-confirmation works without any inductive assumptions. Let Obs be the set of so-far observed individuals; and E the formula $\forall x \in \text{Obs}(Ex \rightarrow Gx)$. We conjunctively decompose the generalizations H_1 and H_2 into the conjunctions

(5.10–5) $H_1 = E \wedge H_1^*$, with $H_1^* = \forall x \notin \text{Obs}(Ex \rightarrow Gx)$,
$H_2 = E \wedge H_2^*$, with $H_2^* = \forall x \notin \text{Obs}(Ex \rightarrow \neg Gx)$.

The content part of H_i that goes beyond E is in both cases H_i^* (i = 1,2). Only H_1^* and not H_2^* is *inductively* confirmed by E. So only H_1 and not H_2 is genuinely confirmed by E. Of course, that E inductively confirms H_1^* but not H_2^* does *not* follow from the basic (Kolmogorovian) probability axioms alone—in distinction to Bayesian content-cutting, which follows from these axioms alone. In saying that E genuinely confirms H_1 but not H_2, we make the assumption that the probability measure P is *inductive*, i.e. satisfies some of the additional inductive principles explained in sec. 4.7.4, such as exchangeability of P or the stronger principle of indifference. Without any inductive assumptions, content-transcending confirmation is impossible.

5.10.4 Latent Variables, Parameter Fitting and Use-Novel Evidence

Confirmation by content-cutting becomes especially problematic when evidences are used to confirm hypotheses that contain *theoretical* concepts, or more generally *latent* variables which are not present in the evidence. In this context the weakness of Bayesian confirmation which is expressed in prop. 5.10–2 can be exploited by proponents of all sorts of rational speculation (cf. Schurz 2008a, sec. 7.1; 2013a, sec. 1). For example, the fact that grass is green Bayes-confirms the hypothesis H that God wanted this and made it that grass is green, because H entails E. Of course, the fact that grass is green "confirms" not only the God-hypothesis, but also the competing hypothesis of the "church of the flying spaghetti monster,"[10] and all other sorts of strange hypotheses, as long as they entail that grass is green, including the scientific explanation of the green color of grass in terms of chlorophyll. All these hypotheses H_i are Bayes-confirmed by E. If they have different posterior probabilities $P(H_i|E)$, then this can only be because they have different prior probabilities, since $P(E|H_i) = 1$ implies (by Bayes' rule) that $P(H_i|E) = P(H_i)/P(E)$.

Based on these facts neo-creationists have applied Bayesian confirmation methods to confirm refined versions of *creationism*: Swinburne (1979, ch. 13) argues that certain experiences *increase* the probability of God's existence, and Unwin (2003) calculated the posterior probability of God's existence as 67%.

Bayesian philosophers of science are aware of this problematic result. Their standard reply is to argue that scientific hypotheses are preferable to religious speculations because they have a significantly higher prior probability than religious speculations (Howson/Urbach 1996, 141f; Sober 1993, 31f). This reply is questionable, since prior probabilities are subjective: from the religious point of view, creationism has a higher prior probability than evolution theory. Moreover, it seems that the hypothesis that a benevolent God (or a spaghetti monster) made it that plants are green is not just "a little bit less" confirmed compared to the scientific chlorophyll hypothesis, but is not confirmed *at all*. In conclusion, the Bayesian confirmation concept is too weak to demarcate genuine science from pseudo-science.

Let me add two important points: First, the discussed inadequacy results do not only undermine Bayesian confirmation, but also the classical HD concept of confirmation (recall prop. 5.10–1). Second, pseudo-confirmation of speculations is also a problem when H does not entail E, but makes E highly probably. For example, the fact that grass is green Bayes-confirms probabilistic weakenings of the above pseudo-explanation, such as "a spaghetti monster whose wishes become reality in 99% of all cases has wanted the grass to be green."

The characteristic property of these pseudo-explanations is that they are entirely *post-facto*. They result from fitting the values of the latent variable of "God's wishes" to already known data, but can never figure as predictions. Many philosophers of science have suggested regarding the failure of delivering *novel predictions* as the discrimination mark between pseudo-confirmation versus genuine confirmation.[11] However, the novel prediction criterion faces the objection that the mere *point in time* at which an empirical evidence has first been recognized is per se irrelevant for its confirmational value. All that matters is whether the evidence has been *used* in the *construction* of the hypothesis or not. There exist indubitable examples of confirmations of scientific theories by facts which the inventors of the theory did not use (and often did not know) when constructing their theory, although these facts were known long before the theory's construction. One such example is the confirmation of general relativity theory by Mercury's abnormal orbit (Musgrave 1974, 11f).

Therefore, Worrall (2006) has suggested the criterion of *use-novelty*, in short the UN-criterion, as an improvement of the novel prediction criterion (the idea goes back to Zahar 1973). According to the UN-criterion an evidence E can only confirm a hypothesis H if E has not been used in the construction of H. Recall from sec. 5.7.3 that "use-novel evidence" is just another word for "*independent* evidence" and is equivalent with "potential predictiveness," i.e. E *could* have been unknown while H was constructed.

Worrall's UN-criterion is beset by some serious objections, too. Howson (1990) pointed out that the UN-criterion is violated by hypotheses arising from inductive generalizations: here the frequency hypothesis about the population is obtained by adjusting the unknown population frequency parameter to the observed sample frequency. This is a perfect example of ex-post fitting, and yet the general hypothesis is doubtlessly confirmed by the sample frequency (provided one assumes an inductive probability measure). Worrall (2006, 69f) replied to this counter-example that it does not constitute a proper case of confirmation. I do not find this reply satisfactory: why should an inductive generalization of an evidence E not be genuinely confirmed by E?

A more adequate handling of Howson's counter-example is provided by the following *probabilistic* analysis of theory construction by data-driven *parameter fitting*. (This topic is also part of Worrall's account, but in "deductive clothing"; for detailed comparisons see Schurz 2013a, sec. 3). The intended application of the UN-criterion of confirmation is general background hypotheses which contain one or several freely variable parameters, i.e. latent variables, whose values can be adjusted ex-post towards given evidence E, in such a way that E is made highly probable or even follows from the parameter-adjusted hypothesis. In what follows I let $\exists x Hx$ stand for the *general* hypothesis with variable parameters x, E for the evidence, and Hc for a parameter-adjusted *specialization* of Hx with constant parameters c. So "$\exists x Hx$" says that there exists *some* value of the variable x such that Hx holds where "H" asserts something in regard to the evidence (see examples below), while Hc asserts that the value of x is c. To indicate that Hc was obtained from fitting Hx to E we also write c_E for c and Hc_E for Hc.

Two technical points are important: (1) "Hx" is an abbreviation: Hx may contain *several* parameters, i.e. x stands for an *n-tuple of variables* $x_1,...,x_n$, and, likewise, c for $c_1,...,c_n$, where these variables may be of first or second order. (2) $\exists x Hx$ follows from Hc and is typically a *content element* of Hc (if not, then it is L-equivalent with a conjunction of content elements of Hc). As our examples will show, ∃xHx is usually the most important, if not the only, *E-transcending* content part of Hc_E.

We illustrate these notions with the example of post-facto creationism. Here the general hypothesis ∃xHx asserts (in its simplest version) that God created the world with some variable (unknown) facts X: "∃X(God created X)." The parameter-adjusted hypothesis Hc_E says that God created the world with the specific (known) facts E: "God created E."

When we say that "∃xHx can be fitted to an evidence E," we mean precisely this: there exists a parameter-adjustment Hc_E of Hx which increases Hc_E's likelihood, i.e. $P(E|Hc_E) > P(E)$). This fitting is "optimal" if c_E is chosen such that Hc_E's likelihood is maximal among all possible parameter adjustments, i.e. $P(E|Hc_E) \geq P(E|Hc)$ for all $c \neq c_E$. In this sense, the general hypothesis "God created some unknown facts X" can be fitted towards evidence E because the fitting result "God created fact E" analytically entails E (i.e. $P(E|Hc_E) = 1 > P(E)$), and this fitting result is optimal because $p(E|Hc_E)$ is maximal.

Consider now the posterior probability of Hc_E's evidence-transcending content part ∃xHx. Obviously ∃xHx can be "fitted" to every possible fact E_i whatsoever, out of a partition of possible evidences or experimental outcomes $E_1,\ldots,E_n$ (with $0 < P(E_i) < 1$ for all i). Therefore, ∃xHx does not increase the probability of *any* of these possible outcomes, i.e. $P(E_i|\exists xHx) = P(E_i)$ holds. This implies by probability theory that no such E_i increases ∃xHx's probability, i.e. $P(\exists xHx|E_i) = P(\exists xHx)$ must hold for all E_i ($1 \leq i \leq n$). So no such E_i can Bayes-confirm ∃xHx and, thus, can genuinely confirm Hc_E.

Turning back to Howson's example, the parameter-adjusted hypothesis Hc_E asserts that the frequency(-limit) of some property F is such-and-such, resulting from an inductive generalization of the sample frequency (E). The general hypothesis ∃xHx states in this case that "there exists a frequency(-limit) of property F." If the underlying domain is finite, then ∃xHx is a logical truth which is not a content part of Hc_E (by def. 3.13–2 of relevant elements). So the problem disappears and we have genuine confirmation of Hc_E by E. If the domain is infinite, ∃xHx asserts the existence of a frequency limit (in random sequences of the domain). This is no longer a logical truth, but a weak inductive assumption, which indeed cannot be confirmed by inductive frequency estimations, but is a presupposition of inductive sampling methods (recall prop. 3.13–5(3)). So also in this case we do not have a counter-example.

We do not say that *every* time when Hc_E resulted from a parameter-adjustment of ∃xHx to E, ∃xHx is not Bayes-confirmed by E, but *only* that this holds if ∃xHx can be fitted to *all* possible evidences. If ∃xHx can be fitted only to some but not all possible evidences (e.g. if ∃xHx asserts that F's frequency lies between 0.3 and 0.7), then an actual evidence to which ∃xHx can be fitted will increase ∃xHx's probability. In other words, not every violation of the UN-criterion leads to a pseudo-confirmation, but only those violations in which ∃xHx can be fitted towards *every* possible evidence. This is a significant difference between the account of genuine confirmation and the unrestricted UN-criterion (Schurz 2013a, sec. 3.3).

On the other hand, if ∃xHx is strong enough to be independently testable, then the adjustment Hc_{E1} to evidence E_1 implies use-novel predictions E_2 which can be tested in an independent test procedure. If Hc_{E1} does also fit with the outcome E_2 of this independent test procedure, then Hc_{E1}'s content part ∃xHx is confirmed by E_2, and so Hc_{E1} is genuinely confirmed by E_2, since Hc_{E1} has no further free variables to be adjusted towards E_2. For example, the chlorophyll explanation of the color of grass is strong enough to imply independent chemical identification methods for chlorophyll, by which the chlorophyll explanation can be independently tested. No such independent test method exists for our *post-facto* version of creationism. (Of course one may enrich creationistic hypotheses with independently testable content, but this is not our problem.) In the next subsection we apply our probabilistic account of genuine confirmation to the problem of *curve fitting*.

5.10.5 Curve Fitting

In probabilistic curve fitting it is assumed that two (or several) real-valued variables X and Y are related by some general function f, together with a random error dispersion d around this function. For example, in an electric circuit the current (Y) is a linear function of the voltage (X), but because of measurement mistakes and irregularities in the wire the measured dependence is not exact but modulated by a random error dispersion (d) around the ideal linear curve. Hence $Y = f(X) + g(d)$, where g(d) is a Gaussian distribution with mean zero and standard deviation d. Recall from sec. 3.1.4.3 that the (random) variables X and Y are themselves functions (e.g. physical magnitudes) over the individuals d_i in a given domain D; so the formula "$Y = f(X)$" is a shorthand for "$\forall d \in D: Y(d) = f(X(d))$." The evidence is a set of m measured data points in the X-Y-coordinate system, i.e. $E = \{(X_1,Y_1),\ldots,(X_m,Y_m)\}$. The general hypothesis ∃xHx asserts a certain *type* of functional dependence between X and Y, e.g. that f is linear or quadratic, etc.

Curve fitting is usually done with polynomial functions, because they can approximate other functions with arbitrary precision. A polynomial function of *degree n* in two variables X,Y has the form $Y = c_0 + c_1 \cdot X + \ldots + c_n \cdot X^n$. For n = 1 the polynomial is linear, for n = 2 quadratic, etc. In this context, the general hypotheses $\exists x H_n x$ have the form $\exists p_0, \ldots, p_n, \delta \in \mathbb{R}_+: Y = p_0 + p_1 \cdot X^1 + \ldots + p_n \cdot X^n + g(\delta)$, where the $p_0, \ldots, p_n, \delta$ are the (n + 2) free parameters of $\exists x H_n x$ which range over positive reals. So $\exists x H_n x$ asserts a polynomial dependence of Y on X of degree n, with unknown (existentially quantified) coefficients $p_0, \ldots, p_n$ and standard deviation δ (so "x" abbreviates the parameter-sequence "$<p_0, \ldots, p_n, \delta>$"). The parameter-adjusted hypothesis $H_n c_E$ is that particular curve of the curve *type* $\exists x H_n x$ that fits x optimally to the given set of data points E.

The standard statistical method to find the optimally E-fitted curve of a given type is *SSD-minimization*. This method finds that curve among all curves of type $\exists x H_n x$ for which the sum of squared deviations of the data points from the predicted curve, $SSD = \Sigma_{i=1}^{m}(Y-f(X_i))^2$, is minimal (Bortz 1985, 219–241). So $H_n c_E$ is obtained from $\exists x H_n x$ by replacing the free parameters $p_0, \ldots, p_n$ by the coefficients $c_0, \ldots, c_n$ of the optimally fitted nth degree polynomial, and δ by the corrected standard deviation $d = \frac{\sqrt{SSD}}{m-1}$, which was obtained from this fitting procedure.

However, the method of SDD-minimization does not tell us which is the right *type* (i.e. degree) of polynomial curve that we should inductively infer from the data in E. Finding the right type of curve constitutes the essential problem of curve fitting (cf. Glymour 1981, ch. VIII). The problem is that *every set of m data points can be approximated by every polynomial function* up to variable remainder dispersion d. This remainder dispersion is the smaller, the higher the degree of the polynomial, and becomes zero if $n - 1 \geq m$, i.e. if the polynomial has at least as many freely variable coefficients as there are data points. As an example, consider the set of *white* data points on the two curves in fig. 5.10–1, and forget for a moment the gray data points. Both curves result from fitting the free parameters of a linear versus a high-degree polynomial curve, H_{lin} versus H_{pol}, optimally to the white data points. Of course, H_{pol} approximates the data better than H_{lin}, because it has more free parameters to be adjusted—but is H_{pol} therefore better confirmed by E than H_{lin}? No, because H_{pol} may have *overfitted* the data, that is, it may have fitted on *random accidentalities* of the sample instead of the systematic dependency between X and Y (cf. Hitchcock and Sober 2004).

If applied in a post-facto fashion, the method of SSD-minimization cannot tell us which is the right type of curve—at least not without independent information about the true dispersion, which is *not available* in our setting. So, how can we rationally choose between $H_{lin} x$ or $H_{pol} x$?

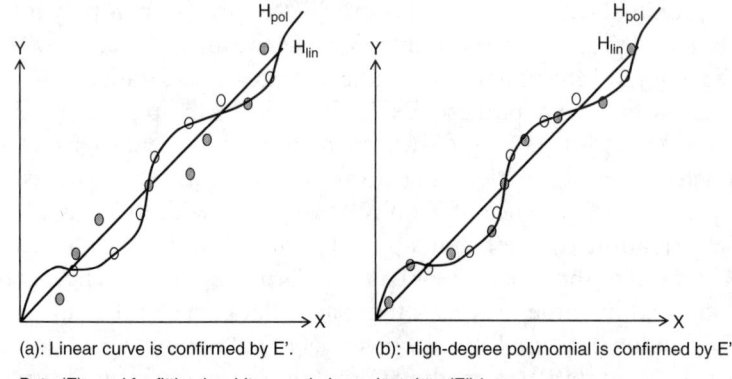

Figure 5.10–1 (a): Linear curve is confirmed by E'. (b): High-degree polynomial is confirmed by E'. Data (E) used for fitting in white, new independent data (E') in grey.

Figure 5.10–1 Curve fitting and independent evidence

A traditional answer to this question recommends always giving preference to the *simpler* curve, i.e. the curve with the fewer number of free parameters (Schlesinger 1974). But this answer is questionable, because simplicity per se is a subjective criterion: why should the objective laws in our world always be most simple?

What we want is an objective criterion, and we find it in the requirement of use-novel evidence. Confirmation of the general hypotheses $\exists x H_{lin} x$ or $\exists x H_{pol} x$ can only be achieved by use-novel evidence, i.e. evidence that is made probable by Hc_E but was *not used* for parameter-adjustment. Such independent evidence can easily be obtained in the case of curve fitting by testing the fitted curves by means of a *new* data set E' that was not used for parameter-adjustment. Should the curve (Hc_E) which resulted from fitting towards E also fit with the new data set E', this constitutes a genuine confirmation not only of Hc_E but also of the underlying general hypothesis about the right type of curve. This is shown in fig. 5.10–1, where the new data points are drawn in gray. In the left case (a), the new data constitute independent confirmation of the linear curve, because they lie far off the wriggly line of the polynomial curve, but are within the standard deviation expected by H_{lin}. In the right case (b), the new data lie quite tightly on this wriggly line and, hence, provide independent support for the polynomial curve H_{pol}.

Observe that the roles of the two data sets E and E' may be switched. So the confirmation of $\exists x Hx$ depends not only on the *content* of the evidence E, but also on its *procedural role*: whether it was used in the parameter-adjustment of $\exists x Hx$ to Hc or not. We have included this procedural information in our notion "Hc_E," meaning that Hc_E resulted from $\exists x Hx$ by parameter-adjustment towards evidence E (see Schurz 2013a, §4.5).

In statistics, the selection of general hypotheses with different numbers of free parameters is also called *model selection*. A well-known method of model selection that corresponds nicely to the use-novel criterion is *cross-validation*. Here one starts with just one (big) data set E = {e_i:1 ≤ i ≤ m} (each e_i being a data item), splits E randomly into two (disjoint) data sets E_1 and E_2, then fits the general hypothesis towards E_1 and tests the fitting result with E_2. For each competing general hypothesis, one repeats this procedure several times and calculates the average likelihood ($\overline{P(E_2|Hc_{E1})}$) of the second independent set. The result is a highly reliable confirmation score. Two related methods of model selection are the BIC (Bayes information criterion) and the AIC (Akaike information criterion). These methods are based on the probabilistic *expectation value* of the likelihood of a polynomial curve that is optimally fitted towards some set E_1, in regard to another independently chosen data set E_2 (Hitchcock and Sober 2004). According to a mathematical theorem (Shao 1997), the outcome of m-out-of-n cross-validation converges to the BIC-score when the number of data items n gets very large (similarly, 1-out-of-n cross-validation converges to the AIC-score). Paulßen (2012, ch. 8), however, has demonstrated by computer simulations that for small samples the results of cross-validation are far more accurate then the results of BIC and AIC, thus supporting the adequacy of the use-novelty criterion in the context of curve fitting.

5.10.6 *Genuine Probabilistic Confirmation*

Genuine confirmation means that the probability increase of H by E *spreads* to the E-transcending content parts of H (a loose version of this idea is found in Earman 1992, 106). The idea leaves us with a choice: if we require that *all* E-transcending content elements of H must be Bayes-confirmed by E, then we speak of *full* genuine confirmation, which is a rather strong notion. Or we may only require that *some* E-transcending content elements C of H are confirmed by E—then we speak of *partial* genuine confirmation. In the partial case it is important to insist that H's content element C is fully genuinely confirmed by E, i.e. C must not entail a weaker content element whose probability is not raised by E. Otherwise the notion of partially genuine confirmation would (provably) collapse into ordinary Bayes-confirmation. Moreover, if the hypothesis H is not a mere inductive generalization of E, but contains latent variables, then at least some of the latent variables in H should occur in C, i.e. should play a role in making E highly probable (more on this point in Schurz 2013a, sec. 4.8). We thus arrive at the following definition:

> (Def. 5.10-4)
>
> a H is *fully genuinely confirmed* by E according to a given probability function P iff the probability of every content element C of H is increased by E, $P(C|E) > P(C)$.
> b H is *partially genuinely confirmed* by E according to a given probability function P iff (i) *some* content element C of H that is not logically entailed by E is genuinely confirmed by E, where (ii) if H contains latent parameters, C contains some of them.

How is the spread of probability increase rationally determined? An orthodox Bayesian would answer that this spread is determined by the prior probabilities of the content parts of H and the likelihoods of these content parts in regard to E. For us, this answer is insufficient, because both the priors of the content elements of scientific hypotheses as well as their likelihoods are usually not objectively determined. What we need in order to overcome this indeterminacy are rational criteria for the spread of probability increase to H's E-transcending content parts. The question whether the probability of a content part C of H is raised by E should be answered by the role and weight which the content part C plays in the increase of the probability of E by H. This weight is partly dependent on the concrete nature of H and the given background knowledge. So we cannot state *sufficient* general criteria for our problem. But our previous considerations have established the following *necessary* general criteria for spread of probability increase:

> (Prop. 5.10-3) *Necessary criteria for spread of probability increase:* If H increases E's probability, the probability increase of H by E spreads from H to an E-transcending content part C of H ($P(C|E) > P(C)$) *only if:*
>
> 1 C is necessary within H to make E highly probable, i.e. there exists no conjunction H* of content elements of H that makes E at least equally probable ($P(E|H^*) \geq P(E|H)$) but does not entail C, and
> 2 it is not the case that C has the form $C = \exists xHx$ and H resulted from a parameter-adjustment of $\exists xHx$ towards E, i.e. $H = Hc_E$, and such a fitting of $\exists xHx$ would have been equally possible for every possible evidence (or experimental outcome) E_i.

We summarize the advantages of the proposed account of genuine confirmation as follows: (a) it offers a uniform solution of the tacking problems and the parameter-adjustment problem, (b) it is uniformly applicable to inductive generalizations and hypotheses with latent variables, and (c) it offers a probabilistic justification of prima facie non-probabilistic confirmation ideas such as use-novel evidence or cross-validation.

5.10.7 Goodman's Paradox

Goodman (1946) confronted the community of philosophers with a new "riddle" of induction that is equally troublesome as Hume's old riddle. He showed that even if one considers inductive inferences to be justified in principle, one cannot apply induction to *all* predicates, primitive as well as defined ones, without producing logical contradictions. Consider Goodman's famous definition of the predicate "grue," abbreviated as G^*x (1955, sec. 3.4):

> (Def. 5.10–5) *Goodman's grue predicate:* An object x is called "grue" (G^*x) iff x has been observed before some future time point t_k (Oxt_k) and is green (Gx), or it has not been observed before the time t_k and is blue (Bx).
> *In formulas:* $\forall x \forall t (G^*x \leftrightarrow_{def} (Oxt_k \wedge Gx) \vee (\neg Oxt_k \wedge Bx))$.

Given a sample of green emeralds (E) that have been observed before the future time t_k, then all these emeralds are, by definition, grue. More precisely, the assertions $Ex \wedge Oxt_k \wedge Gx$ and $Ex \wedge Oxt_k \wedge G^*x$ are, by def. 5.10–5, analytically equivalent. If we apply the inference of inductive generalization to "green" as well as to "grue," we infer from our sample the two strictly general hypotheses (H) $=_{def}$ "All emeralds are green" and (H*) $=_{def}$ "All emeralds are grue." But H and H* entail for all emeralds which have not been observed before time t_k the contradicting predictions that they are green versus blue.

There exist several alternative ways of formulating Goodman's paradox. One alternative formulation comes from Hempel (1965b, 70), who assumes the color state to be time-dependent. Let "Gxt" stands for "x is green at time t." Then Hempel defines: $G^*xt \leftrightarrow_{def} ((t \leq t_k \wedge Gxt) \vee (t > t_k \wedge Bxt))$, i.e. an emerald which is grue for all times changes its color at time point t_k from green to blue. Priest (1976) has demonstrated that Goodman's paradox can also be formulated in the context of curve fitting.

Goodman's predicate "grue" has been called a *pathological* predicate, because applying *inductive* generalization over instances of "grue" means to apply *anti-inductive* generalization over instances of the ordinary predicate "green." We have seen in example (5.10–5) (sec. 5.10.3) that Goodman's paradox arises also for the concepts of Bayes-confirmation and of classical HD-confirmation, because both hypotheses "all emeralds are green" and "all emeralds are grue" entail the evidence "all emeralds observed so far were green."

For probabilistic induction principles, Goodman's paradox implies that one cannot apply these principles to both "green" and "grue" without producing a contradiction. Recall from prop. 3.13–6 that probabilistic exchangeability and non-dogmaticity of P for the predicate G entails the inductive principle (I-G): $P(Gb|Ga_1 \wedge \ldots \wedge Ga_n) > P(Gb)$ (for all $n \geq 1$). Assume $a_1,\ldots,a_n$ are the emeralds observed before t_k and b is an emerald not observed before t_k (and we assume these facts are known, i.e. their probability is 1). Then the exchangeability and non-dogmaticity of P for the predicate G* implies the inductive principle (I-G*): $P(G^*b|G^*a_1 \wedge \ldots \wedge G^*a_n) > P(G^*b)$. But G*b is analytically equivalent with $\neg Gb$, and G^*a_i with Ga_i (for $1 \leq i \leq n$). So (G-I*) is analytically equivalent with $P(\neg Gb|Ga_1 \wedge \ldots \wedge Ga_n) > P(\neg Gb)$, which contradicts (I-G). This result has been worked out by Kutschera (1972, 144), who draws the conclusion that an inductive *logic* in the sense of a system of analytical axioms that hold for *all* predicates—which was the hope of Carnap (1950b)—is impossible.

For a solution of Goodman's problem one needs *rational reasons* for regarding certain "ordinary" (non-pathological) predicates as *inductively projectible*. Many criteria for inductive projectibility have been suggested, but turned out to be inadequate (cf. Stalker 1994). For example, it would be too narrow to regard only primitive (undefined) predicates as inductively projectible, because most ordinary predicates which we inductively project are complex or defined (e.g. "body on our earth," "emerald," etc.). Carnap (1947, 146; 1966, 211) has made the highly plausible proposal that inductively projectible predicates must be *qualitative*, which means that they are either primitive, or their definition does not essentially contain individual constants referring to particular individuals or space-time points. Predicates whose definitions contain such a reference are called *positional* predicates.

The reason why we *should* inductively project only qualitative and not grue-like properties is simple: induction consists in transferring the *same* property-patterns from the observed to the unobserved. To formulate rules of induction we must know what has remained *invariant* in our observations and what has *changed*. This depends on the qualitative and, eventually, on the primitive qualitative predicates, because we assume that instances of primitive qualitative predicates (at different locations) refer ontologically to the *same* ontological property. In this perspective, positional properties such as grue are *pseudo*-properties, because when we project "grue" from instances observed before t_k to instances not observed before t_k, then we have not performed an inductive but an *anti-inductive* inference with respect to the ontologically "real" properties "green" and "blue."

Carnap's criterion of qualitativity eliminates successfully Goodman-type predicates because (in every version of them) they are defined with reference to particular individuals or time points. However, Carnap's suggestion works fine only relative to a given linguistic framework with a given set of primitive predicates which are assumed to represent qualitative properties. Goodman (1955) has set up a powerful objection against Carnap's criterion: the problem of *language dependence*. This problem arose also in other areas of philosophy of science and will be treated in sec. 5.11.3.

5.10.8 Confirmation and Acceptance

What is the relation between the degree of confirmation of a hypothesis H and its rational acceptance, or acceptance as true? Recall the two concepts of incremental and absolute confirmation from def. 5.10–3. Incremental confirmation of H by an evidence E is not enough to accept the hypothesis, because it only means that H's probability has been raised by E. What is important for acceptance is the absolute confirmation of H by E, i.e. a sufficiently *high* conditional probability $P(H|E)$. A further obvious requirement is Carnap's principle of *total evidence* (1950b, 211): our rational degree of belief in a hypothesis H should be ascertained conditional on the total evidence which is currently known to us (recall sec. 3.9.1). If this degree of belief is "high enough," it is rational to accept the hypothesis. Putting all this together, one can postulate the following connection between rational degrees of belief and acceptance:

(5.10–5): *Locke's acceptance rule*: It is rational to accept a hypothesis H relative to a given rational belief function P and a body of total evidence E, iff $P(H|E) \geq \alpha$, where $\alpha > 0.5$ is a contextually determined acceptability threshold.

Rule (5.10–5) has been proposed by John Locke (Foley 1992). Behind this innocent looking rule a nest of deep problems is lurking. Let us first ask: *how high* should the acceptability threshold α be, and *which context* is responsible for it? We distinguish between two different kinds of contexts, along with two different meanings of "acceptance":

i   *Practical context:* Here "to accept a proposition H" means to *rely* on the assumption that H is true in *practical* actions.
ii *Epistemic context:* Here "to accept H" means to *believe that H is true* (if $P(H) < 1$ in a revisable way), as a part of our cognitive model of the world.

In the practical context, the acceptability threshold α for a hypothesis H depends on the relation between the *practical utilities* of our actions under the two assumptions that H is true versus false. We have discussed this in sec. 2.10.1 in relation to the prediction H: "there will be *no* earthquake of magnitude > 6.5." If H is accepted, the concerned people stay in their houses as usual, which brings them a relative gain of zero if H is true, but high (possibly fatal) costs c_{high} if H is false, i.e. an earthquake takes place. If ¬H is accepted, this brings them comparatively low costs of evacuation c_{low}, whether H is true or false. The *expected utilities* (EU) are computed by the famous formula of *decision theory*, EU(action A) = Sum-over-all-C's: (Utility of A in circumstance C)·(Probability of C):

(5.10–6) *Computation of acceptance threshold:*

Utility matrix: Possible actions:	Possible circumstances: H (no earthquake)	not-H (earthquake)
Act-on-H (do not evacuate)	0	$-c_{high}$
Act-on-not-H (evacuate)	$-c_{low}$	$-c_{low}$

Expected utilities: $EU(\text{Act-on-H}) = P(H) \cdot 0 - (1-P(H)) \cdot c_{high}$
$= -c_{high} + P(H) \cdot c_{high}$
$EU(\text{Act-on-not-H}) = -P(H) \cdot c_{low} - (1-P(H)) \cdot c_{low} = -c_{low}.$

Evaluation: Acting-on-H is reasonable iff EU(Act-on-H) > EU(Act-on-not-H).
This holds iff $P(H) > (c_{high} - c_{low})/c_{high} =_{def} \alpha$. This is the *practical acceptance* threshold for acting-on-H, i.e. for accepting the hypothesis "no earthquake."
Example: If $c_{high} = 100 \cdot c_{low}$, then $\alpha = 99\%$.

The example shows that practical acceptance thresholds can be very high if the costs of an erroneous acceptance of the hypothesis are very high.

In the epistemic context, our decision concerning the acceptance threshold for believing in the truth of an uncertain hypothesis depends on our *epistemic utilities* (cf. Levi 1967). Wilholt (2009) shows, however, that these epistemic utilities are not objectively fixed but dependent on context and conventions. So the fixation of "epistemic" acceptance thresholds involves a certain amount of arbitrariness.

Even if we assume that the acceptance threshold is reasonably fixed (either practically or epistemically), Locke's acceptance rule leads into problems. It clashes with the following logical rationality principle:

(5.10-7) *Rule of conjunction:* Rational acceptance should be closed under conjunction, i.e. if a rational agent accepts propositions $P_1, \ldots, P_n$, that agent should also accept $P_1 \wedge \ldots \wedge P_n$.

The clash is illustrated by two famous "paradoxes," the *lottery paradox* of Kyburg (1961) and the *preface paradox* of Makinson (1965).

In the lottery paradox one assumes a fair lottery with n tickets $1, \ldots, n$ and considers for each ticket i the probability of its *not* winning: $P(\neg W_i) = (n-1)/n$. The number n is sufficiently high so that $P(\neg W_i)$ passes the acceptability threshold α. So according to Locke's rule we should accept for each ticket i the prediction $\neg W_i$, that it will not win. By the rule of conjunction we should therefore accept the conjunction of these statements, (1) $\neg W_1 \wedge \ldots \wedge \neg W_n$, which says that no ticket will win. But we assume it as certain that the lottery takes place and is fair; so we accept the belief that at least one ticket will win, i.e. (2) $W_1 \vee \ldots \vee W_n$, which is in direct contradiction with (1). So rules (5.10-5) and (5.10-7) taken together lead to inconsistent sets of accepted beliefs.

In the preface paradox we do not have the background knowledge $W_1 \vee \ldots \vee W_n$, as in the lottery paradox. We merely have a large set of (n) highly probable but uncertain propositions, $S = \{A_1, \ldots, A_n\}$, all of which pass the acceptability threshold α and are not mutually positively dependent, i.e. $P(A_i|S^*) \leq P(A_i)$ for every subset $S^* \subseteq S - \{A_i\}$. Under this condition the probability of larger and larger conjunctions becomes smaller and smaller, because the error possibilities are adding up. In Makinson's preface example, A_i is the proposition that page number i of a carefully written scientific textbook is free of errors. Although the author, after many proof readings, believes for each page that it is error-free, she nevertheless states in her preface that with high probability there will still be some undetected errors lurking somewhere in the book. Formally speaking, although (1) $P(A_i) > \alpha$ holds for each i, we obtain (2) $P(A_1 \wedge \ldots \wedge A_n) \leq \alpha^n$, where $\alpha^n < (1-\alpha)$ iff $n > |\log(1-\alpha)|/|\log \alpha|$, which is what we assume. So by Locke's rule and the rule of conjunction, we accept $A_1 \wedge \ldots \wedge A_n$ because of (1) and we accept $\neg(A_1 \wedge \ldots \wedge A_n)$ because of (2), which yields a contradiction. If $\alpha = 0.95$, for example, then n must be at least 59 to produce this contradiction; and if $\alpha = 0.99$, then n must be at least 299.

Earlier authors (including Kyburg and Makinson) have concluded from these paradoxes that the rule of conjunction does not hold for rational acceptance. Later, authors such as Lehrer (1975, 303) or Douven (2002, 396) tried to save the conjunction rule by strengthening Locke's rule by conditions that prohibit lottery situations. These later proposals suggest reasoning *skeptically*, i.e. to refrain from accepting any one of the lottery propositions "ticket i will not win," because these propositions are mutually self-undermining. Without being able to go into detail, let me point out the common deficiency of these skeptical proposals: by ruling out lottery situations they simultaneously rule out preface-situations, and thereby undermine the very possibility of large bodies of conjectural knowledge.

While in the lottery paradox it is debatable whether one should accept the proposition "ticket i does not win," in the preface paradox the rejection of the highly probable propositions would be clearly *unreasonable*, both in the practical and in the epistemic context. For practical contexts consider *insurance practices*: I believe that I will not have a car accident this day, or next day, etc., and act each day on the basis of these beliefs, but I certainly *do not act on the conjunction* of all of these beliefs, i.e. I do not believe that I will never have a car accident in my life and therefore do not need car insurance. This shows that in practical contexts we are inclined to keep Locke's acceptance rule and give up the rule of conjunction.

In epistemic contexts, the situation seems to be similar. Makinson's example of a scientific textbook is the best example to demonstrate this: we accept all propositions in the book and "hold" their conjunction before our mind, yet we are quite sure that there are some undetected falsehoods in it, i.e. we do not believe in the truth of this conjunction. Summarizing, reasonable acceptance rules are a quite subtle and context-sensitive affair.

5.11 Non-Confirmational Accounts of Theory Evaluation

5.11.1 Truthlikeness

Most scientific theories involve idealizations and approximations which neglect small deviations from reality. So these theories are, strictly speaking, false. Moreover, these deviations are usually empirically observable. So these theories should be rejected by confirmation accounts. This has been considered as a disadvantage of confirmation accounts. Therefore, Popper has developed the account of *truthlikeness*, as an alternative non-confirmational account of theory evaluation which has already been mentioned in sec. 5.6.2. Popper started from the idea that although most scientific theories are, strictly speaking, false, some of them are *closer to the truth* than others, so that we can understand objective theory progress as progress in truthlikeness. He defines truthlikeness—or verisimilitude, as he called it—as follows (1963, 233f, 393f; 1979, ch. 9):

(Def. 5.11–1) *Popper-truthlikeness:* Theory T_1 is *closer to the truth* than theory T_2, abbreviated as $T_1 >_P T_2$ ("P" for "Popper-truthlikeness") iff

a T_2's true consequences are a subset of T_1's true consequences,
b T_1's false consequences are a subset of T_2's false consequences, and
c at least one of the two subset-relations a and b is proper, i.e. either T_1 has true consequences which T_2 does not have, or T_2 has false consequences which T_1 does not have.

If a and b hold but not c, then T_1 is *at least as truthlike* as T_2, $T_1 \geq_P T_2$.

Let T denote the set of all true and F the set of all false sentences of the underlying language $\mathcal{L}$ (relative to a given truth-evaluation), and $C_t(T) =_{def} C(T) \cap T$ and $C_f(T) =_{def} C(T) \cap F$ the sets of true and false consequences of theory T, respectively, where $C(T)$ = the set of T's logical consequences (recall def. 3.7–1). Then Popper's definition can be reformulated as follows:

(Def. 5.11–2) *Formal Popper-truthlikeness:*

i $T_1 \geq_P T_2$ iff (a) $C_t(T_2) \subseteq C_t(T_1)$ and (b) $C_f(T_1) \subseteq C_f(T_2)$.
ii "$T_1 >_P T_2$" is defined as: $T_1 >_P T_2$ iff $T_1 \geq_P T_2$ and not $T_2 \geq_P T_1$.

Tichý (1974) and Miller (1974) have demonstrated that Popper's definition of truthlikeness fails: Popper's definition has the unintended consequence that a false theory can impossibly have more verisimilitude than any other theory. This implies the breakdown of Popper's definition, since the possibility of a false theory being more truthlike than another theory was its major intended application.

The proof of Tichý's and Miller's breakdown result goes as follows: Let theory T_1 be false, thus $C_f(T_1)$ contains some false consequence which we call f. Now assume that T_1 would be closer to the truth than T_2, which means by definition that (a) $C_t(T_2) \subseteq C_t(T_1)$, (b) $C_f(T_1) \subseteq C_f(T_2)$, and one of the two following cases must hold:

- *Case 1:* $C_t(T_1)$ contains a true consequence, t, which is not contained in $C_t(T_2)$. But then, $C_f(T_1)$ would contain the false consequence t∧f which is *not* contained in $C_f(T_2)$. So condition (b) above is violated and $T_1 >_P T_2$ cannot hold.
- *Case 2:* $C_f(T_2)$ contains a false consequence f* which is not contained in $C_f(T_1)$. But then $C_t(T_2)$ would also contain the true consequence f*∨¬f, which cannot be contained in $C_t(T_1)$ (since f∈$C(T_1)$, but f* ∉ $C(T_1)$). So condition (a) above is violated and, again, $T_1 >_P T_2$ cannot hold.

So it is impossible that $T_1 >_P T_2$ when T_1 is false.

In a series of papers,[12] Schurz and Weingartner have argued that the philosophical intuitions of Popper's truthlikeness definition are fine, and the reasons for its breakdown are not wrong intuitions, but Popper's failure to exclude logically redundant and irrelevant consequences in his notions of true and false content. To recognize this point, inspect once more the two cases of the Tichý-Miller proof. In case 1, t∧f is obviously not a "new" false consequence or content part of T_1, beyond the true content part t and the false content part f. It is simply a redundant repetition of these two content parts. In case 2, the disjunctive weakening f*∨¬f of f*∈$C(T_2)$ is obviously not a *relevant* consequence of T_2, because the disjunctive component "¬f" is replaceable *salva validitate* by any formula whatsoever. In conclusion, irrelevant and redundant consequences must be eliminated from the content parts of theories before evaluating their truthlikeness.

Based on these insights, Schurz and Weingartner have repaired the shortcomings of Popper's notion of verisimilitude by restricting the true and false consequences of theories to the sets of their true and false *relevant* (consequence) *elements* as defined in def. 3.12-2. With $C_r(T)$ for the set of T's relevant elements (recall def. 3.12–3), and $C_{tr} =_{def} C_r(T) \cap T$ and $C_{fr} =_{def} C_r(T) \cap F$ for the set of T's true and false relevant elements, respectively, their revised definition of truthlikeness is this (Schurz/Weingartner 2010, sec. 4):

(Def. 5.11–3) *Schurz/Weingartner-truthlikeness:*
Theory T_1 is at least as close to the truth as theory T_2, abbreviated as $T_1 \geq_{SW} T_2$ ("SW" for "Schurz-Weingartner") iff (a) $C_{tr}(T_1)$ $\| \!\!-\!\! C_{tr}(T_2)$ and (b) $C_{fr}(T_2) \| \!\!-\!\! C_{fr}(T_1)$, where "$C(T) \| \!\!-\!\! C(T^*)$" is defined as "$\forall S \in C(T^*): C(T) \| \!\!-\!\! S$."
"$T_1 >_{SW} T_2$" is defined from "$\geq_{SW}$" as usual (def. 5.11–2ii).

Since the set $C_r(T)$ is no longer closed under all logical consequences, the subset condition "$C(T_1) \subseteq C(T_2)$" of Popper's definition has been replaced by the entailment condition $C_r(T_2) \| \!\!-\!\! C_r(T_1)$ in def. 5.11-3. It is easily verified that SW-truthlikeness avoids the breakdown results of Tichý and Miller. Moreover it fulfills the following intuitions which are satisfied by almost all accounts of truthlikeness:[13]

(5.11–1): *Intuitions about truthlikeness* (where $p_1, p_2, \ldots$ are true atomic statements):

1 Among true theories, truthlikeness (>) increases with their logical strength. For example, $p_1 \wedge p_2 > p_1 > p_1 \vee p_2$.
2 For partially false theories, it holds: $\neg p_1 \wedge p_2 > \neg p_1 > \neg p_1 \wedge \neg p_2$.
3 Truthlikeness is logically invariant, i.e. if T_1 is L-equivalent with T_1^*, and T_2 with T_2^*, then $T_1 \geq T_2$ iff $T_1^* \geq T_2^*$.
4 Contradictions are worse in truthlikeness.

Schurz/Weingartner (2010, sec. 5) extend def. 5.11–3 to a numerical measure of truthlikeness which is ordinally equivalent with $\leq_{SW}$.

Popper's and Schurz-Weingartner's truthlikeness are instances of consequence-based accounts, which evaluate truthlikeness by comparing true and false consequences. An alternative approach to truthlikeness is possible world-based accounts. The major difference between these two accounts consists in how they *represent* theories:

1 Consequence-based accounts are *conjunction-of-parts accounts*. They represent theories as conjunctions of the content parts of the theory. These content parts are either identified with arbitrary consequences (as in Popper's account, which does not work), or with relevant elements (as in the Schurz-Weingartner account), or with Gemes' (2007) content parts, or with literals as in the account of Cevolani et al. (2011), which is restricted to theories without disjunctions or implications.

2   *Disjunction-of-possibilities accounts* represent theories either as disjunctions of *possible words* (Hilpinen 1976), or syntactically as disjunctions of *constituents* (Tichý 1974; Niiniluoto 1987). The dominating subfamily of disjunction-of-possibility approaches are *similarity*-based approaches. They define a numerical notion of truthlikeness tr(T) of a theory T, either as the maximum or the average similarity of T's possible worlds with the complete truth (for details see Niiniluoto 1987, ch. 7).

A discussion of the advantages and disadvantages of these two kinds of accounts is found in Schurz/Weingartner (2010, sec. 3) and Oddie (2011).

The concepts of truthlikeness introduced so far have been purely *semantic*: they were explicated relative to the unknown "set of all truths." In epistemic practice, though, we evaluate the truthlikeness of a theory in regard to our known or accepted *evidences* E. This brings us to the concept of *evidential* truthlikeness, relative to a body of evidences E. In conjunction-of-parts accounts, this concept is simply obtained by replacing the true and false relevant elements of T in def. 5.11-3 by T's empirically confirmed versus disconfirmed relevant elements. Note that in evidential truthlikeness, we have not a twofold but a *threefold* division of the relevant content of a theory into its empirically confirmed content, disconfirmed content and its empirical *excess* content in the sense of sec. 5.6.1, i.e. the set of T's elements which so far have not been put under empirical test.

5.11.2 Unification, Coherence and Simplicity

In sections 5.1-4 it was pointed out that a characteristic property of good scientific theories is their *unification power*, i.e. their ability to explain a variety of empirical phenomena in terms of a small number of basic principles. The idea that *unification* is the main goal of scientific theories and explanations has been articulated by prominent philosophers such as Mach (1883/2009, 586f), Whewell (1837) and Feigl (1970, 12).

The ideal of unification is related to, but not identical with the ideal of *coherence* (Lehrer 1974, ch. 7; Shogenji 2005; Bovens/Hartmann 2003, ch. 2). The coherence of a belief system requires that the believed propositions mutually *support* each other, without discriminating non-circular from circular support relations. This is problematic, insofar as purely speculative beliefs can be in mutual support, too. In contrast, unification consists in the coherence of a few hypothetical beliefs with a variety of *observational* beliefs. According to Schurz and Lambert (1994,

72), this means that circular coherence is discounted in unification, and empirical coherence is rewarded more than theoretical coherence.

It is difficult to *define* the degree of unification of a belief system in a generally satisfying way. So far, only a few philosophers of science have tried to do this: Friedman (1974), Kitcher (1981), and Schurz/Lambert (1994). For this purpose one needs a *representation* of a given (scientific) belief system S which tells us what counts as "one" (elementary) belief or statement, and what as a conjunction of two or more beliefs. A solution of this problem is needed to solve Hempel's *conjunction problem* (1965b, 273, fn. 33): Hempel asked why we do not simply "explain" and "unify" a set of accepted laws $\{L_1,...,L_n\}$ by their conjunction $L_1 \wedge ... \wedge L_n$? If this were allowed, it would undermine any reasonable account of unification. Schurz/Lambert (1994) avoid Hempel's conjunction problem by representing a given cognitive system S by the set of its relevant elements S_r (def. 3.12–4).

For sake of space we cannot present here a discussion of Friedman's and Kitcher's accounts. We only explain the problem of *spurious unification* which besets Kitcher's approach. Spurious unifications are post-facto explanations such as "P has happened because God wanted P and whatever God wants, happens." Kitcher (1981, 527f) argues that argument patterns of this sort would not be "stringent enough" in order to be unificatory (ibid., 527f). But we can make the argument pattern more stringent by adding details such as "God has white hairs" (etc.). Nothing in Kitcher's account prevents pseudo-unifications of this sort.

Schurz and Lambert avoid spurious unifications by assigning different costs and gains to observations and hypotheses. In their basic account (1994, sec. 2.2) they define a unification classification of S_r as a partition $\{B,U\}$ of S_r such that all elements of U, the subset of "unified elements," are conclusions of known (deductive or probabilistic) inferences having their premises in B, the subset of "basic elements." *The unification classification $\{B_S, U_S\}$ is a classification which maximizes the unification of S_r* according to the following criteria (Ci):

C1 Every content element P is associated with a certain *weight* w(P), which reflects its cognitive *complexity*. The complexity of general or theoretical propositions is greater than that of singular empirical propositions.

C2 If a hypothesis H is newly added to B, its weight is paid as a unificatory *cost* –w(H), while if a new observation O is added to B, this costs nothing.

C3 If a hypothesis H is inferred and hence added to U, this costs nothing, while if an observation O is inferred and added to U, then its weight is added as a unificatory *gain* +w(O).

Schurz and Lambert (1994, 86) apply their account to a variety of cognitive belief changes including examples from science. A critical discussion of Kitcher's and Schurz and Lambert's unification accounts is found in Gijsbers (2007). He argues that Schurz and Lambert's account works fine as a unification account, because it successfully avoids spurious unifications. He doubts, however, that unification is an essential feature of good explanations; this objection will be discussed in sec. 6.5.

The complexity-component of Schurz and Lambert's unification account expresses a demand for *simplicity*: simpler explanations are preferred, both in terms of *fewer* and of *simpler* premises. In philosophy of science, the epistemic *surplus value* of the virtue of unification and simplicity has been called into question (recall sec. 5.10.5). In what could epistemic surplus value of unification over and above empirical adequacy consist? One such surplus value could consist in the fact that unification includes not only "confirmation from below" (by the facts), but also "confirmation from above" (by higher-order theories). Moreover, we have seen in sec. 5.4.2 that unification goes hand in hand with a theory's ability to generate novel predictions, which is important for its independent testability and genuine confirmation. *Simplicity per se*, on the other hand, is a virtue whose truth-conducive nature is doubtful. We agree with Humphreys (1993) that the simplest theory need not always be the most truthlike theory. Nevertheless, simplicity is an epistemic ceteris paribus advantage in terms of greater *cognitive economy* (cf. Goldman 1986, sec. 6).

5.11.3 The Problem of Language Dependence

This problem has been studied in different areas of philosophy of science. An especially severe version of it arises when two (or more) linguistic systems $\mathcal{L}_1$ and $\mathcal{L}_2$ are *analytically equivalent* in the following sense: there exist explicit definitions of $\mathcal{L}_1$'s primitive predicates in terms of $\mathcal{L}_2$-expressions, and vice versa. In this case one would expect that it makes no difference whether one's beliefs are expressed in terms of one or the other language. So all epistemic evaluation criteria—such as confirmation, truthlikeness, etc.—are expected to be *invariant* in regard to translations between analytically equivalent languages. For example, if E confirms H in language $\mathcal{L}_1$, the translation of E into language $\mathcal{L}_2$ should confirm the translation of H into $\mathcal{L}_2$. To the amazement of analytic philosophers, several counter-examples to this expectation have been discovered.

A first example is connected with Goodman's paradox in sec. 5.10.7. Goodman (1955, sec. 3.4) showed that one can construct back-and-forth translations by which one can shift from our ordinary language ($\mathcal{L}$) to a Goodmanian language ($\mathcal{L}^*$) which has the same expressive power as $\mathcal{L}$, but uses "grue" (G*) and "bleen" (B*) as primitive predicates. Goodman's language translation can be reconstructed as follows:

(5.11–2) *Language dependence of inductive confirmation* (Goodman's paradox):
G for "green," B "blue," G* "grue," B* "bleen," "F" for "emerald" and Tx for "x is temporally located before (future) time t_k":

Languages

$\mathcal{L}$ (T, F, G, B) $\qquad\qquad\qquad$ $\mathcal{L}^*$ (T, F, G*, B*)

Analytic definitions

G*x $\leftrightarrow_{def}$ (Tx∧Gx)∨(¬Tx∧Bx) $\qquad$ Gx $\leftrightarrow_{def}$ (Tx∧G*x)∨(¬Tx∧B*x)
B*x $\leftrightarrow_{def}$ (Tx∧Bx)∨(¬Tx∧Gx) $\qquad$ Bx $\leftrightarrow_{def}$ (Tx∧B*x)∨(¬Tx∧G*x)

Evidences

E = {Fa$_i$∧Ga$_i$∧Ta$_i$:1≤i≤n} $\qquad$ E* = {Fa$_i$∧G*a$_i$∧Ta$_i$:1≤i≤n}

Hypotheses

H$_1$ = ∀x(Fx→Gx) $\qquad\qquad$ H$_1$* = ∀x(Fx→ ((Tx∧G*x)∨(¬Tx∧B*x)))
H$_2$ = ∀x(Fx→ ((Tx∧Gx)∨(¬Tx∧Bx))) $\qquad$ H$_2$* = ∀x(Fx→G*x)

Inverted results on inductive confirmation

E confirms H$_1$ and disconfirms H$_2$ $\qquad$ E* disconfirms H$_1$* and confirms H$_2$*

We obtain the shocking result that perhaps the most important epistemic criterion for probable truth, namely inductive confirmation, turns out to be language-dependent. Many authors have drawn radically skeptical conclusions from this problem. Goodman even went so far as to claim "Choosing 'green' rather than 'grue' as inductively projectible … may seem like raindancing" (1978, 138).

Recall Carnap's proposal from sec. 5.10.7 that inductive confirmation relations should be restricted to *qualitative* predicates. But the "qualitativity" of a predicate is language-dependent: in the language system $\mathcal{L}$, G and B are qualitative and G* and B* positional predicates, and in $\mathcal{L}^*$ it is the other way round. However, for observation predicates there exists a possibility to circumvent the problem of language dependence that has already been applied in sec. 2.9.2: the inspection of the process of *ostensive learning* of a primitive property. The ostensive learning of a qualitative (e.g. color) property from a couple of positive and negative instances does not require any positional information, e.g. about the time point of the learning exemplars. In contrast, a positional property such as "grue" can only be learned by ostension (if it can be learned at all) under two conditions: (a) the training instance (pictures of grue emeralds) must contain information about the actual time point, for example by means of a calendar, and (b) they have to include instances before *and* after the future "subversion" time t_k. We have thus found a language-independent and empirically testable demarcation criterion between qualitative and positional properties, namely the independence of their ostensive learning process from positional information about individuals or space-time points.

For the notion of truthlikeness the problem of language dependence has been discovered by Miller (1974, 176; 1978, 201ff; 1994, 201). His example involves only translations between qualitative properties:

(5.11–3) *Language dependence of truthlikeness* (Miller's paradox):

W for "the weather in a certain region is windy," "H" for "the weather is hot," "A" for "the weather is "Arizonan," i.e. "hot iff windy":

Propositional languages

$\mathcal{L}$ (W, H) $\qquad\qquad\qquad\qquad$ $\mathcal{L}^*$ (W, A)

Analytic definitions

$A \leftrightarrow_{def} (W \wedge H) \vee (\neg W \wedge \neg H)$ $\qquad$ $H \leftrightarrow_{def} (W \wedge A) \vee (\neg W \wedge \neg A)$

Truth

$W \wedge H$ $\qquad\qquad\qquad\qquad\qquad$ $W \wedge A$

Hypotheses

$H_1 = \neg W \wedge H$ $\qquad\qquad\qquad$ $H_1^* = \neg W \wedge \neg A$
$H_2 = \neg W \wedge \neg H$ $\qquad\qquad$ $H_2^* = \neg W \wedge A$

Inverted results on truthlikeness

H_1 is more truthlike than H_2 $\qquad$ H_1^* is less truthlike than H_2^*

It follows that the truthlikeness-ordering of hypotheses may be inverted by translating them from one into another analytically equivalent language. At least, this holds for all truthlikeness accounts which satisfy the minimal intuitions (5.11–1)(2). Like Niiniluoto (1998, 16f) we infer from this result that truthlikeness-comparisons have to be performed in certain "privileged" language systems.

But how can we rationally discriminate between the two analytically equivalent languages of example (5.11–3)? Again we can find a solution by inspecting the ostensive learning process of the properties corresponding to the primitive predicates of the two languages. We suggest that one should choose those predicates as analytically independent primitives whose corresponding properties can be *independently learned* by ostension. More precisely, if F and G are primitive observational predicates, then it should be possible to ostensively learn the property F *independently* from acquiring information about G. In Miller's counter-example, this condition is satisfied for the pairs of properties "windy" and "hot," but not for the pairs "windy" and "Arizonan," or "hot" and "Arizonan." The property "Arizonan" can only be ostensively learned by presenting training examples which contain information about the presence of "windy" and "hot." This gives us a language-independent criterion for our choice of primitive observation predicates: we prefer a system of primitive predicates whose ostensive learning process is mutually independent.

Note that our preference criterion can only be applied to observational but not to theoretical properties. But once we have established a preference criterion for the empirical sublanguage, we can easily formulate preference criteria for our choice of theoretical predicates, for example in terms of the unification power of the resulting theoretical laws.

5.12 Introductory Literature and Exercises

5.12.1 Introductory Literature

Basic information on the structure of scientific theories is found in Hempel (1966), Bunge (1967), Stegmüller (1976) and Ladyman (2002). Psillos (1999) provides an introduction into scientific theories and the quest of realism. Comprehensive collections of essays are Curd/Cover (eds., 1998) and Psillos/Curd (eds., 2008). A classic on the dynamics and evaluation of theories is Lakatos (1970). Important collections of essays on scientific realism are Leplin (ed., 1984), Papineau (ed., 1996b) and Schurz/Votsis (2011). Information on the Ramsey sentence and Carnap sentence is found in Carnap (1966) and Tuomela (1973). Basics about confirmation theories are found in Hempel (1945), Glymour (1981), Earman (1992) and Howson/Urbach (1996). Goodman presents his paradox in (1955). Collections of essays on truthlikeness are Kuipers (ed., 1987) and Kuipers/Schurz (2011).

5.12.2 Questions and Exercises

Sec. 5.1–2

1 Give two correspondence laws for each of the following theoretical concepts: (a) "person x is anxious," (b) "substance x is metallic." What is the empirical prediction implied by them?

2. Continuation of 1: Why can theoretical concepts not be empirically defined by laws of correspondence?
3. What is an ad-hoc hypothesis and on which things does a future assessment of it depend? Give an example.

Sec. 5.3–4

1. What is the core and periphery of a scientific theory? Explain this using Newtonian physics or Piaget's cognitive psychology.
2. Explain the most important intertheoretical relations in theory nets.
3. What are the methodological properties of good scientific theories? Give examples.

Sec. 5.5–6

1. Explain the holism of theory testing using Piaget's theory of cognitive development.
2. Continuation of (1): Invent an ad-hoc hypothesis which could save the core of Piaget's theory in regard to the Modus Tollens anomaly.
3. Under which condition is the introduction of an ad-hoc hypothesis rationally acceptable according to Lakatos?
4. What counts as a failure of a theory version? Explain different kinds of failures.
5. A theory version/core is the more confirmed … Please complete.

Sec. 5.7–9

1. Explain Putnam's no miracles argument.
2. Continuation of (1): Is Putnam's argument refuted by Laudan's pessimistic meta-induction and Quine's underdetermination arguments? Discuss possible weakenings of Putnam's argument which may withstand this challenge.
3. Why may the Ramsey sentence of a theory T be identified with T's full synthetic content, and T's Carnap sentence with T's total analytic content?
4. When is a non-empirical concept of a theory (a) T-theoretical and (b) pre-theoretical? Explain this using concepts from Piaget's theory of cognitive development.

Sec. 5.10–11:

1. Illustrate the two tacking paradoxes of the classical concept of HD-confirmation by means of examples.
2. What is the difference between incremental and absolute (Bayesian) confirmation?
3. Someone thinks she can outwit chance laws. She draws the results of 100 roulette spinnings in a diagram and finds a curve with interesting regularities. Discuss the problem of overfitting and the significance of the use-novelty criterion using this example.
4. By means of the law hypothesis "all ravens are black," define the Goodman-predicates "blite" and "whack." Explain why all so-far observed ravens are blite.
5. Someone has thrown a 6 on a dice five times in a row and argues that this fact confirms her magic powers. Analyze this argument in the light of Carnap's requirement of total evidence.

Notes

1. Instead of "x" we may have a sequence of variables denoting all components of a physical system.
2. If τ, R_i and A_i are mathematical variables, probabilistic correspondence laws have the form of p-distributions $p(\tau, R_i | A_i)$.
3. A simple way to obtain these consequences is the system P of conditional probability logic supplied with irrelevance assumptions (Adams 1975; Schurz 2005a; Leitgeb 2004; Schurz/Thorn 2012, sec. 2.4).
4. There exist variations of this setting which we cannot discuss here; see Carnap (1966), Ketland (2004), Balzer et al. (1987).
5. See Psillos (1999, 61–67) and Ketland (2004, 298), who speaks of "cardinality-correctness."
6. Cf. Tuomela (1973, 60), Pearce/Rantala (1985, 163), Sneed (1971, 57).
7. The axiom set of a theory lattice is defined as the union of the axiom sets of its elements.
8. τ may be time-dependent; then we write "$\tau(x,t)$" instead of "$\tau(x)$." We also admit probabilistic correspondence laws (see 5.1–12).
9. Carnap (1950b, xvi) differentiates between the two concepts, and more recently Huber (2008, 184). For incremental confirmation see Howson/Urbach (1996, 117ff), Kuipers (2000, sec. 2.1.2).
10. This "church" was founded by a physicist who intended to turn creationist teaching requirements into absurdity. See www.venganza.org/aboutr/open-letter.
11. Cf. Musgrave (1974), who cites Descartes, Leibniz, Whewell, and Duhem; more recently Watkins (1964), Lakatos (1977), and Ladyman and Ross (2007, sec.2.1.3).
12. Cf. Schurz/Weingartner (1987, 2011), Schurz (1991a, sec.5.1.2), Weingartner (2000).
13. These intuitions fit with Niiniluoto's adequacy conditions in (1987, 232f). Niiniluoto mentions exceptions to these intuitions.

6

IN SEARCH OF CAUSES: EXPLANATION AND ALL THAT GOES WITH IT

6.1 The Deductive-Nomological Model of Explanation

As stated in sec. 2.3, empirical facts are explained or predicted by being derived from general laws together with antecedent conditions. This idea of explanation has a long philosophical tradition which goes back to Aristotle (Losee 2001, 18). Hempel tried to make this idea logically precise. His endeavor was exposed to a host of difficulties which caused a broad debate in philosophy of science (for overviews see Salmon 1989; Stegmüller 1969ff vol I; Schurz 1996a).

Hempel (1942) and Hempel/Oppenheim (1948) developed the following model of the deductive-nomological explanation:

(Prop. 6.1–1) A *deductive-nomological* (DN) *explanation* of an *event* or a *singular fact* E consists of a deductive argument of the form "$L_1,\ldots,L_n, A_1,\ldots,A_m / E$" with $m, n \geq 1$ such that:

1 *Form condition*: (i) $L_1,\ldots,L_n$ are strictly general statements ("laws"), (ii) $A_1,\ldots,A_m$ (the *antecedent*) are singular sentences, and (iii) E is a singular sentence. The total set of premises is called the *explanans* ("that which explains") and the conclusion E the *explanandum* ("that which is to be explained").
2 *Consequence condition*: E is a logical consequence of $L_1,\ldots,L_n, A_1,\ldots,A_m$.

> 3a *Truth condition—semantic version*: The explanans premises and (hence) the explanandum are true. Then the explanation is called *true*.
>
> 3b *Acceptance condition—epistemic version*: The explanans premises are empirically confirmed within the given *epistemic background system* S, and the explanandum is verified by the evidence in S, independent of the explanans. The explanation is then called *well confirmed*.

A simple example:

L:	All metals conduct electricity	$\forall x(Mx \rightarrow Ex)$
A:	This vase is metallic	Ma
E:	Therefore it conducts electricity	Ea

In the semantic model version of the DN-model, the truth of the explanans premises is required. Of course, the explaining law premises are never definitely verifiable. Therefore the epistemic model version of the DN-model is more important in practice. It refers to an epistemic background system (or background "knowledge") S by which we understand all sentences or propositions rationally accepted by a given person or scientific community at a given time.[1] Both the explanans and the explanandum of a well-confirmed DN-explanation must be included in S.

Besides the semantic and epistemic concept of explanation, Hempel (1965b, 273, 338) introduced the concept of *potential* explanation: here the mere logical consistency of the explanans premises is required, instead of conditions 3a or 3b. The concept of potential explanation is needed for the notion of an *inference to the best explanation* (sec. 2.7.3): in this notion one infers from the explanatory power of a so-far unconfirmed hypothesis its degree of confirmation; this could not work if explanatory power already presupposed the confirmedness of the explanans premises.

The simplest example of a DN-explanation has the form "All As are Es, this is an A / so this is an E." Because antecedent and explanandum are here implicatively connected by a single law, Dray (1957) labeled this model the *covering law* model of explanation—an expression that became established later on. Hempel (1965b, 355) rejected Dray's label because his DN-model also includes more complex explanations in which the explanans does not contain Dray's covering law, but merely implies it in a complicated way. One example is the DN-explanation of the trajectory of a planet from system conditions and the laws of Newtonian mechanics as outlined in (5.2–4).

Hempel stresses that in everyday explanations such as "this is an E *because* it is an A," the law premises are often omitted and have to be implicitly assumed. As the title "The Function of General Laws in History" reveals, Hempel (1942) wants to show, contrary to the program of methodological dualism (sec. 1.3.5.4), that even the historical and social sciences are reliant on law hypotheses whenever they try to explain something. To support his thesis Hempel (1942, 235f) gave several examples of DN-explanations in history and the social sciences. Hempel also conceded the point that many critics would later make, namely that there are scarcely any *strict* laws to be found in these disciplines (1942, 237). Instead of them, one finds "soft" laws in these disciplines which, according to Hempel, one could understand as *statistical* hypotheses. The probabilistic counterpart of his strict-deductive explanation model, however, was not developed by Hempel until 20 years later (sec. 6.3).

It is philosophically important that the DN-model does not set *description* and *explanation* in mutual opposition. Idealist philosophers (such as Hegel) regarded explanation as something that in principle exceeds description, as a kind of intuition of "essences" which are concealed behind the facts. Such metaphysical ideas of explanation made Duhem (1908, 20f), Wittgenstein (1921, 6.371) and others claim that science is only concerned with facts and hence can provide only descriptions but not explanations. In this situation Hempel's anti-metaphysical model functioned as a kind of liberation for explanation theorists, because in Hempel's model explanations do not transcend descriptions in any principled sense. Not only the explanandum and antecedent, but even the laws of explanations are *descriptions* according to the DN-model— the latter are just *general* descriptions. The only way that DN-explanations transcend descriptions is that they establish a *logical connection* between explanans and explanandum.

For the same reason there are no *ultimate explanations* in science: every explanation must presuppose something which is *unexplained*. No matter how long a chain of explanations is, it must always have a beginning in which some unexplained premises are simply assumed— as for instance the law of gravitation in physics or the existence of a "big bang" in cosmology. This thesis can also be expressed as follows: *Self-explanations* as they supposedly exist in theology or metaphysics— such as: "God has his cause in himself"—are scientifically unacceptable *pseudo-explanations* which do not explain anything.

Scientifically, the explanation of general laws by higher-level theories, in the sense of fig. 2.3–1, is perhaps even more important than the explanations of events or particular facts in terms of prop. 6.1–1.[2] Hempel *intended* to take DN-explanations of laws into account and the only reason why he did not do so was the "conjunction problem" explained in sec. 5.11.2 (Hempel 1965b, 273, fn. 33). We reconstruct the DN-model of explanation of laws as intended by Hempel as follows:

(Prop. 6.1–2) A DN-explanation of a *law* L consists of a deductive argument of the form "T∪A / L" such that:

1   *Form condition*: (i) T is a non-empty set of laws or axioms of theories which are all essentially quantified and some of which are essentially general; (ii) A (the *antecedent*) is a *possibly empty* set of singular or localized existential sentences, and (iii) L is an essentially general sentence.
2   *Consequence condition*, (3a) *truth condition* and (3b) *acceptance condition* are as in the model of the DN-explanation of events (prop. 6.1–1).

Examples: the theoretical explanation of the planetary orbit in (5.2–4), or the theoretical explanation of Piaget's law of cognitive development in (5.5–1).

The explanation debate that started in the 1950s led to several different problem areas which are briefly presented in the next sections.

6.2 Explanation versus Prediction and Justification

Generally speaking an explanation is an *answer* to a *why*-question (Hempel 1965b, 354; Bromberger 1965; van Fraassen 1980, 134). Hempel (1965b, 354f) saw clearly that two kinds of why-questions have to be distinguished—he referred to them as explanation-seeking versus reason-seeking why-questions. The former inquire about the causes, or *reasons for being*, which led to the occurrence of the explanandum event. In contrast, the latter request *reasons for belief*, i.e. they ask why it is justified to believe that the explanandum event occurred or will occur. Reasons for being are *causes* in a broad sense, whereas reasons for belief are justificatory. The division is by no means disjoint: on the contrary, in most cases knowledge of the causes of an event provides us at the same time with the reasons for belief, and vice versa. But is this *always* the case? This was in fact Hempel's view in his early and middle stages when he defended the thesis of the *structural equality of prediction and explanation* (Hempel 1942, 234f; 1965b, 367; Stegmüller 1969ff, vol. I, ch. II). Popper held the same thesis of structural equality in his motto "*causality = deduction of predictions*" (1935/2002, sec. III.12).

According to the thesis of structural equality, explanation and prediction only differ regarding the *pragmatic* circumstances of the *time* when premises and conclusion *become known*. We speak of an *explanation* if the explanandum was observed or became known *first* and the explanans premises were obtained *afterwards*. We speak of a *prediction* in the *epistemic* sense if initially *only* the explanans premises were known and the explanandum was deductively inferred from them. Note that predictions in the epistemic sense need not be predictions of *future* events—so-called *retrodictions*, i.e. hypothetical inferences to historically *past* events, are also predictions in the epistemic sense.

Stegmüller (1977, vol. I, 55–60; 1969ff, vol. I, ch. II) developed an elaborate terminology which we adopt here. A DN-argument whose antecedent provides reasons for believing an explanandum is called a DN-*justification*. If the premises of the DN-argument are known first and the conclusion is derived afterwards, we speak of an *ex-ante* (DN) justification. An ex-ante justification is a *prediction* in the *temporal* sense if the antecedent event occurs *before* the explanandum event; it is a *retrodiction*, if the antecedent event occurs *afterwards*. If, on the other hand, the conclusion of the argument was already known before the justified premises were found, then we speak of an *ex-post* justification. If, finally, a DN-argument has an ex-post character and its antecedent provides reasons for being for the explanandum, we speak of a DN-*explanation*. The thesis of structural equality obviously applies to the relation between ex-ante and ex-post justification. Hempel, however, claimed the structural equality between ex-ante justification and explanation. Is this thesis true?

Hempel (1965b, 367) divided his thesis into two sub-theses:

Sub-thesis 1: Every prediction (ex-ante justification) is a potential explanation.
Sub-thesis 2: Every explanation is a potential prediction (ex-ante justification).

Extensive debate has shown that both sub-theses are untenable.

6.2.1 Predictions without Explanatory Function: Objections to Sub-thesis 1

Non-causal regularities are predictive but not explanatory. According to sec. 4.4, there are two types of them:

1 *Pseudo-causality through common causes.* In temporal laws of succession the antecedent event A temporally precedes the consequent event E. This does not yet guarantee that A is a cause of E—A and E can also be joint effects of a common cause. In this case A is merely a DN-*indicator* but not a DN-cause of E. *Example*: A sudden drop of the barometer reading is a sure reason for the prediction of an approaching storm, but it is not its causal explanation—rather, both are joint effects of an abrupt drop in atmospheric pressure (Grünbaum 1963, 309; Hempel 1965b, 374f).

2 *Directedness of the cause-effect relation.* A temporal *law of succession* "if A then E *will* obtain" is L-equivalent with its contraposition "if not-E, then not-A *was* the case." But not-E cannot be a cause of not-A, because causal-effect relations between temporally separated events are *forward-directed* in time. *Example*: The fact that Mr. Corsi (on whose life an attempt is planned by the mafia) is standing in front of a kiosk today constitutes a reason for believing that he was not shot yesterday, but is not a cause of what happened yesterday.

In temporal *laws of coexistence* of the form $\forall x,t(Axt \leftrightarrow Bxt)$, the state of two variables (A, B) is correlated at the same point in time t. Here, too, cause-effect relations are present, though not in a temporal but in a more general sense (sec. 6.7.2). *Example*: Given a constant angle of sunlight, the height of a flagpole is proportional to the length of its shadow (Bromberger 1966, 92). But the height of the pole is the cause of the length of its shadow, and not the reverse. Therefore, only one direction of the two-sided implication can be used for an explanation, from the pole's height to its shadow's length, while the other direction, from the shadow's length to height, can only be used for a prediction of the height of the pole.

6.2.2 Causality and Lawlikeness

In order to delimit DN-explanations from mere DN-justifications, a theory of *causality* is required. Such a theory has to include a theory of *lawlikeness*—as a necessary but not sufficient component. This is so because one can only speak of a causal explanation if the antecedent and the explanandum event are *nomologically* connected (Hempel/Oppenheim 1948, 66). Thus the following DN-argument: "All apples in this bag are red (L), this apple was taken out of this bag (A) / Therefore this apple is red (E)" would not be considered as an explanation for why this apple is red. L is here an accidental regularity in the sense of sec. 3.6—that this apple is in this bag is accidental and does not cause the apple's color. On the other hand, the lawlikeness requirement is not necessary for predictions or justifications: in order to predict that an apple taken out of this bag will be red, it entirely suffices that the general sentence "All apples in this basket are red" is inductively confirmed.

Lawlikeness and causality are difficult philosophical problems. The majority of the explanation models in the early phase of the debate tried to avoid these problems and to explicate the concept of explanation *independently* from questions of causality. Bromberger (1965, 73) and other authors, therefore, critically noted that these putative models of explanation were not actually explicating the concept of explanation, but rather something else. Like Hempel in later years (1977) we adhere to the idea that providing causes belongs to the *core* meaning of the concept of the explanation of *events*.

In contrast, causality requirements are not (or at most indirectly) applicable to the explanations of *laws* by higher-level theories. A law is not a spatiotemporal localized state of affairs and therefore it cannot be the direct object of a causal relation. It would also go too far to demand that every explanation of laws must provide a causal *mechanism*: many explanations of laws by theories in "higher-level" sciences do not provide causal mechanisms, as, for instance, evolutionary explanations, or Piaget's explanation of cognitive development. Van Fraassen (1980, 124–127) stresses that in the field of physics there are also numerous explanations that are not of a causal nature, for instance explanations with help of symmetry principles, or explanations in quantum mechanics.

Van Fraassen (ibid.) argues that our understanding of causal processes is *theory-dependent*. We concur with that. In Schurz (1996a, sec. 4.1) it is suggested that we explicate the conditions of causality by referring to the *maximal complete causal model* about the relation between the antecedent event A and the explanandum event E that is available in the epistemic background system S. This causal model, which we abbreviate as CM(A,E|S), consists of three classes of statements: first, a list of all known possibly causally relevant events in the spatial environment and the prehistory of A and E; second, all available information about the strict or statistical nomological connections among these events and between them and A and E, and third, all accepted theoretical principles about the nature of causal processes. CM(A,E|S) must imply or at least make it probable that A caused E. For this it is necessary that CM(A,E|S) does not imply that A and E had a common cause, and that the assumption of a causal process leading from A to E is compatible with the causality principles in CM(A,E|S) such as temporal forward-directedness or locality; for details see sec. 6.7.

We summarize the requirements of lawlikeness and causality as follows:

> (Prop. 6.2–1) In a DN-explanation of events (i) the general premises have to be *lawlike* and (ii) the maximally complete causal model CM(A,E|S) in the accepted epistemic background system S makes it probable that the antecedent is a *cause* of the explanandum.

6.2.3 Explanations without Predictive Function: Objections to Sub-thesis 2

Most explanation theorists reject sub-thesis 2 for probabilistic explanations, on reasons explained in sec. 6.3. But even for DN-explanations, Scriven (1959a, 468–469) raised a formidable objection to the thesis that they are always potentially predictive: it often happens that we explain an effect E with a cause A, but our only reason for believing in the occurrence of the cause A is that we have observed the effect E. In such a situation A can never serve as a justificatory reason for predicting or believing E. Hempel (1965b, 372) called such explanations *self-evidencing explanations*. To give an example: we explain the *red shift* in the spectrum of the stars (E) with the help of the expansion of the universe (A), but the only reason why we consider the hypothesis of the expansion of the universe to be confirmed is the spectroscopic observation of the red shift.

Self-evidencing arguments are acceptable as explanations, but not as justifications, because they involve *circles of justification*. In order to avoid such circles the following adequacy condition for DN-justifications is required (Schurz 1982, 328f):

> (Prop. 6.2–2) A DN-justification must have a *predictive function* within the given background system S, which means that there has to be evidence in S which confirms A without entailing E.

In the red shift example, the requirement that DN-justifications have a predictive function is violated, since here the only evidence which confirms A is the observed explanandum E, which trivially entails E. Yet this argument is acceptable as a DN-explanation, because for explanations it is enough to require that A outlines causes for E, independent of how our knowledge about A was acquired.

DN-explanations without predictive functions are common in the field of the explanation of *unstable* or *chaotic* systems (see Weingartner/Schurz 1996). These systems are governed by deterministic laws. The systematic reason of their unpredictability is the extreme *sensitivity* of their trajectories (temporal developments) on immeasurably small variations of their initial conditions. As an example, think of a perfectly round ball sitting on the top of a round hemisphere. Smallest fluctuations in the position of the ball determine whether and on which side the ball will roll down. One calls this a *bifurcation* point; chaotic systems have infinitely many of them. Although the behavior at a bifurcation point is unpredictable, it is easily post-facto explainable, for if the system's final state has been observed, one can compute the initial state from the final state with high accuracy, and thus ex-post explain the final state on the basis of the initial state (Suppes 1985; Schurz 1996b).

6.2.4 Logical Problems of Irrelevance and Redundancy

In (Hempel/Oppenheim 1948, 273ff) Hempel realized that the consequence condition of his DN-model (prop. 6.1-1(2)) was too weak to exclude certain trivial or absurd DN-arguments, so-called pseudo-explanations. In the ensuing debate a variety of examples of pseudo-explanations and pseudo-justifications were discovered, and attempts were made to handle them with the help of stronger conditions (overviews see Stegmüller 1969ff, vol. I, ch. X; Schurz 1982). Not all, but many of these examples were concerned with irrelevant logical inference in the sense of sec. 3.12. The basic cases of logically irrelevant DN-arguments discussed in the DN-explanation debate were these:

1 *Complete self-explanations*, e.g. "$\forall x(Fx \rightarrow Gx), Ha/Ha$," where E follows already from A alone and L is deductively superfluous.
2 *Partial self-explanations*, e.g. "$\forall x(Fx \rightarrow Gx), Fa \wedge Ha/Ga \wedge Ha$," where one conjunctive component of E follows from A alone.
3 *Complete (or partial) theoretical explanations*, where E (or a conjunctive component of E) follows already from L alone, and A is deductively superfluous, as e.g. in "$\forall x(Fx \rightarrow Gx), Ha/\neg Fa \vee Ga$."
4 *Irrelevant explanandum-weakenings*, as in "$\forall x(Fx \rightarrow Gx), Fa/Ga \vee Ha$."
5 *Redundant explanations*, which have a sound explanans core but contain additional superfluous premises, like "$\forall x(Fx \rightarrow Gx), \forall x(Hx \rightarrow Qx), Fa, Ra/Ga$."

Pseudo-explanations (1)–(3) were mentioned first by Hempel/Oppenheim (1948, p. 275), (4) by Gärdenfors (1976, 425) and in combination with other cases by Kim (1963), and (5) is found in Schurz (1982). Gärdenfors' explanation model eliminates pseudo-explanations (1)–(3), and the models of Tuomela (1976) and Schurz (1982) eliminate

(1)–(5). By applying the notions of relevant premises, conclusion and irreducible representation (def. 3.12–1, 4), pseudo-explanations due to logical irrelevance or redundancy can be eliminated by the following adequacy condition (see Schurz 1982):

> (Prop. 6.2–3) A DN-explanation or DN-justification (of events or of laws) is logically adequate *only if* there exist irreducible representations IP and IC of its premises and conclusion, respectively, such that for every elementary conjunct IC_i of IC, the DN-argument "IP/IC_i" has relevant premises and a relevant conclusion. Moreover, no law premise of the argument is an irrelevant consequence of a stronger law accepted in the epistemic background system S (recall sec. 4.1.1).

The conditions of prop. 6.2–3 apply to DN-explanations as well as DN-justifications. Salmon (1984, 92f) has called attention to the fact that relevance conditions have a different status for explanations versus justifications. A redundant antecedent premise makes a DN-justification cognitively inefficient, but not "false." In contrast, a redundant antecedent premise produces a *false* DN-explanation, because a DN-explanation must list the *causes* of the explanandum, but a logically redundant antecedent conjunct cannot possess any causal relevance.

Summarizing the contents of sec. 6.2, we have suggested the following conditions for the DN-models of the justification of events (DNJE), justification of laws (DNJL), explanation of events (DNEE) and explanation of laws (DNEL):

Model:	Characterized by conditions:
(DNJE):	Prop. 6.1–1(1–3), Prop. 6.2–3, prop. 6.2–2.
(DNEE):	prop. 6.1–1(1–3), prop. 6.2–3, prop. 6.2–1(i+ii).
(DNJL):	prop. 6.1–2(1–3), prop. 6.2–3, prop. 6.2–2.
(DNEL):	prop. 6.1–2(1–3), prop. 6.2–3, prop. 6.2–1(i).

6.3 Probabilistic Explanation Models

6.3.1 Inductive-Statistical Explanation

The inductive-statistical (IS) model of explanation was developed by Hempel in (1965b, 381ff), improved in (1968) and generalized by Niiniluoto in (1981, 441f) as follows:

> (Prop. 6.3–1) An *inductive-statistical* (IS) *explanation* is a *quasi-argument* of the form "$L_1,\ldots,L_n$, Aa $//_r$ Ea" for which it holds that:
>
> 1. *Form condition*: $L_1,\ldots,L_n$ are lawlike statistical sentences, and Aa and Ea singular sentences containing the individual constant(s) a.[3]
> 2. *Consequence condition*: $\{L_1,\ldots,L_n\}$ entails (by probability theory) a "minimal" statistical law of the form $p(Ex|Ax) = r$, so that r is *close to 1*.
>   Note: 2 implies the *inductive support* condition: for all epistemic probability functions P that fulfill the statistical principal principle (prop. 3.13–4), the explanandum probability given the explanans is r, or formally: $P(Ea|Aa \wedge L_1 \wedge \ldots \wedge L_n) = r$. This is indicated by the double stroke "$//_r$."
> 3. *Acceptance condition*: The explanans premises are empirically confirmed within the given *epistemic background system* S, and the explanandum is verified by the evidence in S, independent of the explanans.
> 4. *Maximal specificity*: The antecedent A is maximally specific for E in the epistemic background system S.

A simple example (Hempel 1968, 177):

L: 95% of people infected with *Plasmodium vivax* get malaria.
A: Jones has become infected with Plasmodium Vivax.   [95%]
―――
E: Jones fell ill with malaria.

While in Hempel's original IS-model the laws of an IS-explanation are limited to the minimal law $p(Ex|Ax) = r$, Niiniluoto generalized Hempel's model by requiring only the derivability of a minimal law from the law premises, as in 2. Moreover, Hempel formulated the inductive support condition as an independent requirement; but this condition holds for every epistemic probability measure which satisfies the statistical principal principle and is therefore considered here merely as a derived property of an IS-explanation. Form condition 1, consequence condition 2 and acceptance condition 3 are the corresponding counterparts of the DN-model of explanation (prop. 6.1–1). In contrast, condition 4 concerning the maximal specificity is completely *new*: it is connected with the non-monotonicity of IS-arguments and is the reason why IS-explanations are actually only *quasi*-arguments in the sense explained in the next section (when we speak of "IS-arguments" we always mean such "quasi-arguments"). Note that the consequence relation in 2 is monotonic; only the IS-support relation "$L_1,\ldots,L_n, A //_r E$" is non-monotonic.

The distinction between explanations and predictions or ex-post justifications, which we have explained for DN-arguments, is equally valid for IS-arguments. In analogy to prop. 6.2–1 an IS-argument can be an IS-explanation *only if* according to the complete causal model CM(A,E|S) in S, A can be regarded as a *causal factor* for E. Since Hempel requires that the probability value r must be close to 1, IS-explanations are also possible predictions or ex-post justifications, but only if the justification has a predictive function, according to prop. 6.2–2. Moreover, a logical *relevance* condition is needed for the consequence relation in prop. 6.3–1(2), analogous to the one of prop. 6.2–3; this condition must also include a (positive) statistical relevance condition for the minimal law of the IS-argument, i.e. $p(Ex|Ax) > p(Ex)$. In the following we assume that the concepts of IS-explanation and IS-justification have been *improved* in these respects. In the next two sections we turn to those questions that are *specific* for probabilistic explanations: (i) the condition of maximal specificity and (ii) the question of the required height of the probability of the explanandum.

6.3.2 Maximal Specificity

In an IS-argument the *statistical* probability of the minimal law $p(Ex|Ax)$ is transferred to the *individual case* of the explanandum (a), in the form of an epistemic probability P. According to sec. 3.9.1 Reichenbach's condition of the narrowest reference class has to be fulfilled. Hempel's (1968) condition of maximal specificity is a weakly relevance-constrained version of this condition which can be equivalently rephrased as follows:

(Prop. 6.3–2) A description Aa of the individual a is *maximally specific* for Ea in the epistemic background system S iff

(MS1): there is a statistical law $p(Ex|Ax) = r$ in S such that for every description A*a in S for which (i) $\forall x(A^*x \rightarrow Ax)$ is in S (i.e. A*x is in S at least as specific as Ax) and for which (ii) an alternative statistical law $p(Ex|A^*x) = r^*$ is in S, it holds that $r = r^*$; and

(MS2): for every description A**x in S which is also maximally specific for Ea in S according to condition (MS1), S entails that $p(Ex|A^*x) = p(Ex|A^{**}x)$.

Condition (MS1) implies that the sentence Aa contains *all* the information about the individual a that is available in S and statistically relevant for Ea (recall the examples in sec. 4.3.7). This condition corresponds to the application rule (prop. 2.7–4) for non-monotonic inferences. In practical applications, "=" should be understood as "approximately equal." Salmon (1989, §3.6) calls IS-arguments *quasi-arguments*, because due to their non-monotonic character one is not generally allowed to *detach* their conclusion from their premises, but only if the antecedent condition Aa is maximally specific. We illustrate condition (MS1) by the *example* below prop. 6.3–1: the IS-explanation according to which Jones fell ill with malaria (Ma) because he was infected with *Plasmodium vivax* (Va) and 95% of all people infected this way fall ill with malaria ($p(Mx|Vx) = 95\%$). This explanation is no longer acceptable if we learn that Jones also has a genetic constellation (Ia) which makes him immune to malaria in 95% of all cases ($p(Mx|Vx \wedge Ix)=5\%$). The antecedent A*a = Va∧Ia is *more specific* than Aa = Va. Instead of possessing a causal explanation we now have to say that Jones' malarial disease is due to a tragic *coincidence*—he fell ill with malaria, even though he had the gene constellation Ia.

The requirement in prop. 6.3–2(MS1) that $p(Ea|Aa) = r$ is a statistical *law* is meant to entail that "$p(Ex|Ax) = r$" is contingently true and that Ax is a *nomological* predicate; and the same holds for the predicate A*x mentioned in (MS1). Extending Hempel's suggestion (1968, 124, 127) we understand a nomological predicate as a *spatiotemporally universal* predicate in the sense of def. 6.6–1. The nomologicity condition handles an objection of Wójcicki, who showed that condition (MS1) would be trivially violated by extensionally defined predicates such as A'x $\leftrightarrow_{def}$ Ax ∨ x=a; but these predicates are not nomological.

Condition (MS2) implies that in those cases where two competing maximally specified antecedents exist for the same explanandum without a *specificity preference* between them, one should react in a *skeptical* way and not accept either of the two IS-arguments as an explanation or prediction. An *example*: Suppose Mary lives in England (Ea), making it quite probable that Mary is Protestant (Pa), at the same time her father is Italian (Ia), making it probable that Mary is Catholic (Ca). We do not know anything about the statistical probability of Cx given Ex∧Ix. (MS2) tells us that in such a case we should refrain from making an explanation or prediction.

The IS-model of explanation is *epistemically relative* to the accepted background system S. Recall that the epistemic version of Hempel's DN-model of explanation was also epistemically relative: the requirement (3b) of prop. 6.1–1, that the explanans premises are well confirmed, was relative to a given background system S. Coffa (1974) has called this background dependency of Hempel's DN-model as epistemic relativity in the *confirmation sense*. He argued that this kind of epistemic relativity is harmless, since one can easily transform the epistemic model into a semantic model by substituting the confirmation condition by the truth condition.

The epistemic relativity of the maximal specificity condition is, however, no longer harmless in this sense, because it is potentially related to *all* sentences accepted in S. Coffa (1974, 151–153) argued that even in the case of the strong epistemic relativity that is present in the (MS) condition, one is able to transform the epistemic version of the model into a semantic version, by replacing the background system S with the *class of all true sentences*, in an ideal language capable of expressing all facts of the world.

6.3.3 Probabilistic and Causal Relevance Models

Salmon (1984) took up Coffa's suggestion in his "objective" model of probabilistic explanation, although he avoids explicit reference to a language and speaks of *classes* or attributes instead of predicates (etc.). Moreover, for Salmon the condition of *causality* is essential. If, within the IS-explanation model improved by the causality and relevance condition (see last paragraph of sec. 6.3.1), we replace the background system S by the set of all true sentences in an ideal language, then we obtain an *approximation* to Salmon's "objective" explanation model—following Coffa we can speak here of a *true* statistical explanation.

The counterpart of Hempel's maximal specificity requirement is Salmon's condition that the antecedent has to be *objectively homogeneous* for the explanandum. If we translate Salmon's condition into the linguistic way of speech, then it says the following: there must not exist a true causally relevant antecedent description A*a which is at least as specific as Ax such that $p(Ex|A^*x) = r^* \neq p(Ex|Ax)$ is a true statistical law. Note that Salmon's objective homogeneity condition implies that Aa provides *complete* information about all relevant causes for Ea. Schurz (1996a, sec. 6.2) shows that Hempel's maximal specificity condition, strengthened by the requirement of "causal relevance," coincides with Salmon's objective homogeneity condition if one identifies S with the set of all true sentences. Furthermore, Salmon requires that Aa has to be the *broadest* objective homogeneous reference class for Ea—in other words, Aa is not only allowed to omit irrelevant information about a (as in Hempel's IS-model), but A is required to omit all irrelevant information about a.

Coffa (1974) recognizes the following fact: if the world were *deterministic*, then the only true IS-explanations would be those which have a statistical probability of 1. For in a deterministic world every causally complete antecedent condition would *determine* the resulting conclusion. As Coffa rightly concludes, genuinely true IS-explanations can only exist in an objectively indeterministic world.

If Aa is objectively homogeneous for Ea then one may consider the probability p(Ex|Ax) as a kind of *ersatz* single case propensity of Ea, insofar as the causally complete reference class Aa for Ea is then uniquely determined.[4] This is the basic idea of the *deductive-nomological-probabilistic* (DNP) explanation model of Railton (1978) which is closely related to Salmon's model (see Salmon 1989, sec. 4.6). Railton replaces the statistical law p(Ex|Ax)=r by the implication $\forall x(Ax \rightarrow p(Ex)=r)$, thus Railton's DNP-explanations have the form "$\forall x(Ax \rightarrow p(Ex)=r)$, Aa/p(Ea)=r," in which the single case propensity claim p(Ea) = r is *detachable*. To give an example, Ea could assert the decay of an atom a, and Aa the fact that a was a radium atom; the accepted physical theories imply that radioactive decay is objectively indeterministic, i.e. there exists no further cause which affects the decay probability of this atom beyond the fact that it is a radium atom; so Aa is objectively homogeneous for Ea.

Outside the domain of microphysics, objectively homogeneous explanations are extremely rare, since typically there exist many factors with a small causal influence which are neglected in explanations. So in scientific practice, Hempel's epistemic concept of a maximally specific explanation is more important than the Salmon–Railton concept of a causally complete explanation. Railton (1978) and Salmon (1984; 1998, ch. 20) also emphasize that in an *ideal* explanation the minimal law should be derivable from a scientific *theory* which provides a *causal mechanism* (cf. sec. 6.7.5). This idea—which is independent from the requirement of objective homogeneity—received support from a number of philosophers of science (Darden/Craver 2000; Glennan 2002; Bechtel/Abrahamsen 2005).

6.3.4 Conflicting Intuitions about the Height of Explanatory Probabilities

Even if there is agreement that the positive relevance condition p(Ex|Ax) > p(Ex) has to be added to the IS-explanation model, the question remains: *how high* does the probability value p(Ex|Ax) have to be? In (1965b) Hempel claims that this value should be close to 1—but why? Tuomela (1981, 276) and Stegmüller (1969ff, vol. I, 972) argued that the probability value of p(Ex|Ax) should only satisfy the *minimal* condition of being greater than 1/2 (the so-called "Leibniz-condition"), because only then is p(Ex|Ax) greater than p(¬Ex|Ax), and only in this case can it be reasonable to predict Ea instead of ¬Ea. The Leibniz-condition is doubtlessly necessary for probabilistic justifications and predictions, but does it also apply to explanations?

This is not the case, if one regards the nature of a probabilistic explanations in citing *positively relevant* causal factors, that need not necessarily constitute predictive reasons. We illustrate this point using an example from Scriven (1959b): only 10% of all people with untreated syphilis (Sx) contract progressive paralysis (Px). But syphilis is the only known positive causal factor for progressive paralysis: it holds that p(Px) = 0.01 < 0.1 = p(Px|Sx), i.e. untreated syphilis leads to a tenfold increase in the chance of contracting progressive paralysis. If someone who has untreated syphilis develops progressive paralysis, we will therefore explain his illness by the fact that he had untreated syphilis. This is the way that Gärdenfors (1980, 413) motivates the central condition of his probabilistic explanation model, which requires merely that the probability of the explanandum, given the explanans, be *increased*, compared with the prior probability: p(Ex|Ax) > p(Ex). Related to Gärdenfors' condition of probability increase is the explanation model of van Fraassen (1980, 141ff), which requires that the antecedent probabilistically *favor* the explanandum E, within a given *contract class* $\{E_1,...,E_n\}$ of possible alternative events which contain the explanandum $E = E_k$.

The deepest conflict of intuitions occurs when we compare the probability conditions of the previous explanation models, which all entail a sufficiently high or at least an increased probability of the explanandum given the antecedent, with the probability condition in Salmon's causal explanation model. For Salmon (1971, 63; 1984) an antecedent Aa is an explanation for Ea if Aa lists all causally relevant factors for Ea (present in situation a), independent of whether they will increase or decrease the probability of the explanandum. In order to make this condition plausible Salmon (1984, 109) discusses the example of an experiment of cross-breeding pea plants with white and red flowers. Our causal knowledge (A) implies that the genes responsible for the red flowers are dominant over the genes responsible for the white flowers. So according to Mendel's laws, the crossed pea plants will consist of 75% pea plants with red flowers (genotypes RR, RW, WR) and 25% pea plants with white flowers (genotype WW). The prior probability for red or white colored flowers is 50%. Salmon now argues that our causal understanding in the case of a crossed pea plant with red flowers is exactly the same as in the case of a crossed pea plant with white flowers—there is nothing that we understand when the crossing experiment produces a pea plant with red flowers and that we do not understand when it produces a pea plant with white flowers. Therefore, if we consider the IS-argument "$p(\text{Red}(x)|Ax) = 0.75$, Aa $//_{0.75}$ Red(a)" as an explanation of a's having red flowers, then we also have to regard "$p(\text{White}(x)|Ax) = 0.25$, Ab $//_{0.25}$White(b)" as an explanation of b's having white flowers, even though the antecedent of the latter argument lowers the probability of the explanandum. Therefore, Salmon requires in his so-called *statistical relevance* (SR) model of explanation that the antecedent Ax has merely to *change* the probability of Ex, either positively or negatively.

Salmon's argument that an explanation (in the narrow sense) has to list all relevant causal factors is plausible; the later Hempel (1977, 99f) was also convinced of this. But it seems to be counterintuitive to say that an explanandum has occurred *because* a factor was present that made its occurrence improbable (see Cartwright 1979). This argument has been strengthened by Strevens (2000, 373ff), who calls the Salmon–Railton type of explanation accounts *egalitarian* accounts, because they treat probability-increasing and probability-decreasing arguments as explanatorily equal. Strevens argues that egalitarian accounts can make no sense of probabilistic explanations in *statistical mechanics* (SM). For example, the fact that heat flows from the hotter to the colder body and not in the other direction, which is an instance of the law of entropy, is explained by SM with an extremely high probability which is still not 1. According to egalitarian accounts, however, we would have to say that SM could equally explain the inverse process, if it would occur. But no physicist would say this; she would rather insist that the explanatory success of SM lies in the fact that SM can explain why heat flows from the hotter to the colder body and *not* in the other direction.

Because of these difficulties of egalitarian explanation accounts, we support Humphreys' suggestion (1989, 117) that one should not refer to negatively relevant antecedent factors as causes but as *counter-causes*. With this terminology the explanation of Ex by a negatively relevant antecedent Ax would have to say that Ex occurred (not because, but) *although* Ax occurred. We suggest that in a complete explanation about an event E all of its causes *and* counter-causes should be listed. We attribute explanatory power only to the causes of E, but their explanatory power depends on which coutercauses are present. For further discussions see Stegmüller (1969ff, vol. IV.2, 281ff), van Fraassen (1985) and Strevens (2008, sec. 9.5).

6.4 Normic Explanations and the Explanation of Human Actions

The school of methodological dualism (see sec. 1.3.5.4) criticized Hempel's DN-explanation model by arguing that explanations in the historical sciences and humanities are based on the *understanding* of the individual case which does not involve covering laws. William Dray, a philosopher of the historical sciences, argued for this point by means of a plethora of examples. His best-known example concerns *Ludwig XIV* (1957, 33): Historians explain the unpopularity of Ludwig XIV by arguing that he often involved his country in wars and loaded heavy burdens onto his people. According to the DN-explanation model these historians would have to adopt for this purpose the following strictly general law:

(6.4–1) All sovereigns who involve their country in wars and load heavy burdens on their peoples will become unpopular.

But every historian knows that such a law can never be valid without exception—not even if one strengthens its antecedent by further conjunctive conditions, such as "and discriminate against minorities" (etc.). Exceptions to (6.4–1) are (unfortunately) well known.

Hempel's *covering law* thesis can generally be justified thus: whenever historians use the word *because* in historical narratives (and they often do), they implicitly appeal to *general* regularities. These general regularities, however, are not of a strict but of an *uncertain* nature: they admit exceptions of various sorts. Can they alternatively be described by numeric-statistical laws, as Hempel (1965b) has suggested in his IS-explanation model? Applying this view to our example of Ludwig XIV, historians would then explain with help of laws of the following sort:

(6.4–2) The probability that a sovereign who involves his country in wars becomes unpopular is 84%.

This suggestion is also hardly tenable, because numeric probabilities of historical events are usually *unknown* in the historical sciences (cf. Dray 1957, 51ff), for the reason that one cannot make statistical experiments with history, and observations of similar historical situations differing from each other in just one or a few known factors are very rare. Rather, what historians have in mind in their explanation of Ludwig XIV's unpopularity is, according to Dray (1957, 31ff), the following *normic* hypothesis in the sense of sec. 4.5.2:

(6.4–3) Sovereigns who fulfill such-and-such conditions *normally* (or: usually, mostly) become unpopular.

The most important explanation schema in the historical sciences and humanities is the *rational explanation of actions*, in terms of the *subjective* beliefs and goals of the actor. According to Dray (1957, 132–137) and Gardiner (1952, 124f), rational explanations of actions are also based on a *normic* principle, namely the following rationality principle (Rosenberg 2008, ch. 2–4):

(6.4–4) *People normally act purposive-rational*, i.e. if an agent has the goal G and believes that the action A is a suitable means of achieving G, then she will normally try to realize A.

The purposive rationality of an action in the sense of (6.4–4) is understood as *relative* to the agent's subjective goals and beliefs. It is not undermined if these beliefs are false or the goals morally wrong; what counts is only that the agent's action was an adequate *means* for achieving the goals under the condition that the agent's beliefs are true. Thus, the rationality principle (6.4–4) is very broad. It nevertheless has exceptions. It is violated when the action was not caused by reasons of the actor, but by unconscious motives, irrational affects, or schizophrenic cognitive processes. In this case the action does not have a rational explanation. Admittedly, in many cases human thoughts and actions come about in such a non-rational way. There is, however, a traditional principle of *hermeneutics* that asserts a prima facie preference for rational over non-rational explanations. The principle is also called the principle of *charity* (Wilson 1959), of *rational acccomodation* (Davidson 2001, 152), or the hermeneutic *rationality presumption* (Scholz 2001, part II). It says that in the interpretation of (linguistic or non-linguistic) actions one should prima facie, i.e. for want of good counter-reasons, try to explain the action rationally. Only if a rational explanation persistently fails should we draw on non-rational explanations.

Let us come back to the role of covering laws in rational explanations of actions. As explained in sec 4.5.2, from a contemporary viewpoint there is no reason to deny normic generalizations the status of law hypotheses. But in the 1950s, when Dray wrote his book, the dominant opinion was different. Dray (1957, 132) did not consider normic principles as laws and therefore regarded the rational explanations of actions, in *opposition* to Hempel's covering law model, as a kind of explanation which works *without* law premises. Dray's viewpoint led to a serious misunderstanding of his explanation model: Hempel (1965b, 469ff) argued that because laws which connect goals-&-beliefs with actions are missing, Dray's account is *not* an account of the explanation, but of the normative justification of actions. Hempel's interpretation of Dray was inadequate since Dray understood the normic principle (6.4–4) as expressing a *factual* rationality disposition of humans. For him the task of a historical explanation was clearly *not* to justify the historical action, but to explain why it *actually* occurred. The only problem behind the Hempel–Dray dispute was that both Dray and Hempel were unaware that the principle (6.4–4) provided exactly that kind of uncertain connection between goals-&-beliefs and actions which is needed in an account of the explanation of actions.[5] We therefore suggest as an accompaniment to the numeric-probabilistic explanation model the following *normic explanation* model.

(Prop. 6.4–1) A *normic explanation* is a quasi-argument of the form "$L_1,\ldots,L_n$, Aa // Ea" such that:

1   Form condition: $L_1,\ldots,L_n$ are normic laws; Aa, Ea are singular sentences.
2   *Consequence condition:* $\{L_1,\ldots,L_n\}$ entails by probability logic (see note 3 in Chapter 5) the "minimal" normic law Ax $\Rightarrow$ Ex (i.e. "As are normally Es"), together with the probabilistic constraint $p(Ex|Ax) > 0.5$.
3   *Acceptance condition* as in prop. 6.3–1(3).
4   *Maximal specificity* of Aa for Ea: (MS1): For every A*a in S for which $\forall x(A^*x \rightarrow Ax)$ is in S, no opposite normic law A*x $\Rightarrow$ ¬Ex is in S, and (MS2): no A**x in S is maximally specific for ¬Ea according to condition (MS1).

Normic explanations differ from IS-explanations only in the replacement of statistical by normic laws and in the less complicated maximal specificity condition (cf. prop. 6.3–2). The structural similarities between the deductive-nomological, probabilistic and normic explanation models support once more the unity of the methods in natural and human sciences.

6.5 Expectation, Causation and Unification: Explanation as a Prototype Concept

It emerged from the previous sections that there exist different ideas or "paradigms" in regard to the essential features of scientific explanations:

1 *The expectability paradigm:* The key property of the explanation of an explanandum E consists in making E expectable, in one of the following four ways (or "versions" of this paradigm):

  i   by deductively implying E (Hempel 1965b, 337; Halonen/Hintikka 2005); or
  ii by making E more probable than non-E (Tuomela 1981, 276; Stegmüller 1969ff, vol. I, 972); or
  iii by making E more probable than all of E's competitors in a given partition of alternative outcomes (van Fraassen 1980, 141ff); or
  iv by simply increasing E's probability (Gärdenfors 1980, 413).

2 *The causality paradigm:* The crucial property of an explanation consists in delivering a conjunction of causes $C_E = C_1 \wedge \ldots \wedge C_n$ of E which is as complete as possible, together with causal laws connecting C_E with E. C_E has to change E's probability, but it is irrelevant whether C_E increases or decreases E's probability (Jeffrey 1971a; Salmon 1984, 1998; Hempel 1977, 99f).

The expectation paradigm leads to a very *broad* notion of explanation which applies to the explanation of singular and general facts. But it does not capture the narrow aspect of explanation as delivering not mere reasons for believing, but causes. Versions (iii) and (iv) of the expectation paradigm are weaker than the prediction paradigm of explanation, because an explanans which raises E's probability to a value below 1/2 increases E's expectability without being potentially predictive. The expectation paradigm gets in conflict with the causal paradigm in all situations of the following two sorts: (a) probability-raising explanations that do not deliver causes, and (b) causal explanations that do not raise E's probability.

A third paradigm of explanation which has not been introduced so far is:

3 *The unification paradigm:* The main goal of explanations is to provide a deeper *understanding* of the phenomena (i.e. the empirical facts) by *unifying* them, i.e. by reducing a variety of phenomena to a few basic principles and initial conditions in the sense explained in sec. 5.11.2. Approaches to explanation and understanding based on unification or coherence have been developed, among others, by Friedman (1974), Kitcher (1981), Thagard (1992, ch. 4), Schurz/Lambert (1994) and Schurz (1999a). Neither the expectability nor the causal approach can account for the fact that an explanation is satisfying only if its premises are *not less in need of explanation* than the explanandum.[6] For instance,

"Peter is flying past the window in the third floor, because one second ago he was flying past the window in the fifth floor" is a causally and predictively adequate argument, but not a satisfying explanation, because the cause is here just as much in need of explanation as the effect. Similarly, predictively successful scientific laws are only explanatory if they are in conformity with the accepted background theory. An example of non-explanatory laws were Bohr's stability postulates for electrons in an atom in the year 1913: these postulates could successfully predict the hydrogen spectrum, but they were incoherent with classical mechanics and thus were, themselves, strongly in need of explanation, hence most scientists at that time did not view them as a satisfying explanation.

Schurz and Lambert (1994) propose to explicate the unification paradigm via the following condition, which can be *added* to the models of explanation as a logical or probabilistic argument described so far:

(Prop. 6.5-1) *Unification condition:* An explanatory argument which satisfies the conditions of a DN- or IS-explanation is a cognitively *satisfying* explanation of the explanandum E in the sense that it provides *understanding* of E, in a given belief system S, *iff* the addition of the argument's premises to S leads to a successor belief state S* which is more unified than S, according to the criteria C1–3 in sec. 5.11.2.

The unification approach shows how the *local* component of an explanation, namely the presentation of a deductive or probabilistic connection, and its *global* component of unification can be put together. In this way, it avoids van Fraassen's objection (1980, 109ff) that unification is a global notion, while explanation is a local matter. Critical remarks on the explanation as unification account of Schurz and Lambert are found in Weber/van Dyck (2002), de Regt (2006) and Gijsbers (2007, 499). For de Regt, causality and unification are complementary paradigms of explanation.

The unification requirement can come into conflict with both the prediction and the causality accounts, insofar as a predictively successful law (e.g. Bohr's stability postulates) can be incoherent with an accepted background theory and thus decrease its unification. On the other hand, a highly unificatory theory, e.g. quantum mechanics, may produce explanations that stand in conflict with accepted causality principles.

In conclusion, the explanation debate has produced three mutually incompatible paradigms of explanation. This does not seem to be a very satisfying result. However, a little reflection may turn this seemingly negative result into a *positive* insight about the nature of the concept of explanation. For note that in *most* instances of scientific explanations, all three paradigms coincide, i.e. all three corresponding properties of explanations are simultaneously realized: probability increase, causal information and unification. First, causal explanations are normally also predictively the most efficient and robust, and vice versa. Even low-probability laws convey a high probability value to most observed sample frequencies (recall sec. 3.13.2). Second, explanatory premises which are predictively most powerful are normally exactly those explanations which offer the highest degree of unification, and vice versa. So the three features which each of the three paradigms takes to be the "essence" of scientific explanations *normally go together*, and depart from each other only in *exceptional* cases.

This situation does not imply that the notion of "explanation" is not a reasonable one, but merely, that it has a semantic property which it shares with many other natural language concepts, namely that it is a *prototype* concept (cf. Margolis/Laurence 1999). The meaning of a prototype concept (e.g. "bird") cannot be sharply defined by a list of conditions, but is more or less vaguely given, either by way of prototypical examples ("this is a typical bird") or by a list of prototypical properties ("normal birds have wings, can fly, …"). The concept of explanation is a prototype concept which is characterized by the three prototypical properties of expectability, causation and unification. Normally these properties go together, but as there exist birds without wings and birds with wings that cannot fly, there exist predictive explanations that are neither causal nor unificatory, causal explanations that are not predictive nor unificatory, and unificatory explanations that are neither causal nor predictive.

COMPLEMENTARY AND ADVANCED TOPICS

6.6 Lawlikeness

According to Hume's *regularity theory*, laws of nature are nothing more than true generalizations. This position, which was held by the early logical empiricists, is hardly tenable in the view of the counter-examples discussed in sec. 3.6. The following sections present some major attempts to explicate the notion of lawlikeness.

6.6.1 Laws of Nature versus System Laws

An important distinction is the one between *laws of nature* versus *system laws* (Schurz 2002b, sec. 6.1; 2005c). Laws of nature are the fundamental laws of physics which express physical necessities that hold for all physical systems in every possible universe. In classical physics, the Newtonian axioms (N1, 2, 3) are laws of nature (recall sec. 5.2). Axiom N1 is a differential equation with a *variable* total force function defined as the sum of *all* forces acting in a given physical system *without* saying what these forces are. The analogue in quantum mechanics is the general Schrödinger equation with a *variable* energy operator. Laws of nature hold strictly true, *without* any exclusive ceteris paribus clause—but at the cost of being per se not *applicable* to *real* systems, because they do not specify *which* forces are active in the given system.

System laws, in contrast, do not apply to the whole universe, but hold for particular systems of a certain kind. In physics these systems are described by their *system conditions* as explained in sec. 5.2, i.e. the *specification* of *all* forces which act within or upon the given system. Therefore, physical system laws are always subject to an exclusive ceteris paribus clause which is usually definite (recall sec. 5.6.1).

Theoretical system laws of classical physics are obtained by replacing the variable total force function in N1 by the definite sum of all relevant forces. *Empirical* system laws describe the observable time-dependent behavior of a system given its initial conditions. It is only for *simple* systems of physics that the empirical system laws are literally derivable from the theoretical system laws, which are in turn derivable from laws of nature and system conditions. For systems of moderate complexity and, in particular, for evolutionary systems, derivations of this sort are usually impossible (recall sec. 2.6.2). However, as we have seen in sec. 4.5.2, the behavior of evolutionary systems is governed by *normic* system laws which result from their self-regulatory capacities that have been selected through evolution. The system laws of complex or evolutionary systems are usually discovered by empirically inductive means in combination with computer simulations.

There are only a *few* laws of nature, and they are found in physics. Almost *all* laws in scientific textbooks are system laws. Examples of physical system laws are the laws describing planetary orbits, oscillators, mechanical waves, electric circuits; system laws in chemistry describe the behavior of molecules, in biology the behavior of biological organisms (etc.).

The difference between laws of nature and system laws does not coincide with that between strictly universal versus spatiotemporally restricted laws, because some system laws hold everywhere in *our* universe. An example is the law that all stable substances in our universe are composed of matter and not of anti-matter; this system law resulted from spontaneous symmetry breakings in the early stages of our universe which were not prescribed by the laws of nature.

The crucial difference between laws of nature and system laws is that while the former are physically necessary, the latter depend on physical necessities *and* on *contingent* system conditions, which could have been otherwise. This brings us directly to the topic of *lawlikeness*.

6.6.2 Lawlikeness in the Wide versus Narrow Sense

In sec. 3.6 we arrived at the result that the lawlikeness of spatiotemporal restricted general sentences is of a *gradual* nature. We speak here of lawlikeness i.w.s. One the other hand, general sentences that express *physical necessities* are called lawlike i.n.s. The characteristic difference between lawlike sentences i.w.s. and i.n.s. is that laws i.w.s. depend not *only* on physical necessities, but also on physically *contingent* or *accidental* conditions of our world. To avoid misunderstandings, the notion of physical or nomological necessity must not be confused with logical or analytical necessity: physical necessity and contingency are logically contingent properties of facts.

Not only spatiotemporally restricted general sentences, but also the system laws introduced in the preceding section depend on contingent conditions and are therefore lawlike merely in this wide sense. For instance, "All ravens are black" is not a physical necessity (see Armstrong 1983, 18), because apart from albino ravens, evolution could possibly produce white ravens due to some environmental change. Nevertheless, we consider this as a biological law i.w.s., i.e. as a system law. The same is true for other biological laws such as "All higher life is based on DNA-replication" or "Birds can normally fly." On the other hand, that all masses attract each other, or that all bodies with positive rest mass move with a velocity lower than light velocity are laws i.n.s., i.e. laws of nature, which according to the accepted theories express physical necessities that cannot possibly be broken.

Unfortunately, the difference between these two kinds of lawlikeness is usually neglected in the literature on lawlikeness, and this neglect has repeatedly caused misunderstandings. For example, those authors who argue that no genuine laws can be found in the special (non-physical) sciences (Schiffer 1991, Earman/Roberts 1999, Woodward 2002), understand laws in the narrow sense of laws of nature, while those authors who argue that each special science has its own laws (e.g. Fodor 1991, Lange 2009,

Schurz 2002b, Reutlinger et al. 2011), understand laws in the wide sense of laws which are subject to ceteris paribus clauses, i.e. as system laws. Or when van Fraassen (1989, ch. 8–9) makes his radical claim that physics contains no laws but only symmetry principles, he understands laws i.n.s. of physical necessities (which he rejects), while his symmetry principles are of course still lawlike i.w.s. The same holds for Woodward's "invariant generalizations" (2002, 197) and Glennan's "mechanisms" (2002).

6.6.3 Lawlikeness i.w.s., Counterfactuals and Inductive Projectibility

A useful *indicator* for the lawlikeness of a general (strictly or normic) sentence "All As are Bs" is that we accept the corresponding *counterfactual* conditional "If this were an A, it would be a B" as true. That counterfactuals indicate lawlikeness has been observed by Goodman (1946; 1955, sec. 1). It is important to observe, however, that the truth or acceptability of a counterfactual is an indicator for lawlikeness i.w.s., but not a specific indicator for physical necessities. For instance, we agree to the counterfactual conditional sentence "If the bird were a raven, then it would be black" (Nagel 1977, 273), because "All ravens are black" is lawlike i.w.s., although not a physical necessity. By contrast we would not say that this green apple would be red, if it were in this basket (cf. 3.6–7). This indicates that we consider the universal sentence "All apples in this basket are red" not as lawlike i.w.s. but as *accidental*.

Although the truth (or acceptability) of a counterfactual is a useful indicator for lawlikeness i.w.s., it is of little use for the explication of the *meaning* of lawlikeness i.w.s., because the truth conditions of counterfactuals themselves presuppose an independent concept of lawlikeness. This can be seen by inspecting the possible world semantics for counterfactual conditionals that goes back to Stalnaker (1968) and Lewis (1973b). According to this semantics, the counterfactual "if p would obtain, then q would obtain" (abbreviated as p ~> q) is true in the real world w* iff q is true in every possible world w in which p is true and which is otherwise as *similar* to the real world w* as possible. This idea leads semantically to the conception of a similarity relation over the set of possible words, and syntactically to the logic VC for counterfactual conditionals (Lewis 1973b, 132f). For an adequate interpretation of the similarity relation, however, one must already know which true propositions express laws and which contingent facts.[7] To recognize this, consider the following counterfactual:

(6.6–1) If this match were struck, it would light, or formally Sa ~> La, where "a" denotes this match. Assuming that the match a satisfies the so-called *normal conditions* Na, i.e. that the match is dry and oxygen is present, then in the actual world, the following four statements are true:

(6.6–2) w^*: $\neg Sa, \neg La, Na, \forall x(Sx \land Nx \rightarrow Lx)$.

To evaluate the truth of counterfactuals with antecedent Sa, we have to consider w^*-closest worlds w_i in which Sa is true. We obtain these worlds by minimal and logically *consistent* changes of the true facts in w^*. There are three minimal and consistent changes of this sort:

(6.6–3) *Minimal changes of w^*-facts which make Sa true:* Replace $\neg Sa$ by Sa and

 i World w_1: $\neg La$ by La, or
 ii World w_2: Na by $\neg Na$, or
 iii World w_3: $\forall x(Sx \land Nx \rightarrow Lx)$ by $\neg \forall x(Sx \land Nx \rightarrow Lx)$.

In order to obtain the desired result that Sa ~> La is true in w^* we must assume that:

1 w_1 is closer to w^* than w_3, based on the assumption that similarities in laws count more than similarities in singular facts, and
2 w_1 is closer to w^* than w_2, based on the assumption that similarities in facts expressing normal conditions weigh more than similarities in facts expressing events.

So the semantics of counterfactuals presupposes, besides the distinction between facts and laws, the even more difficult distinction between facts expressing normal conditions and facts expressing events. Without these two assumptions we would obtain strange results about counterfactuals: considering w_2 as the w^*-closest Sa-world would verify the counterfactual "if this match were struck it would be wet," and considering w_3 as the w^*-closest Sa-world would verify "if this match were struck, the laws of inflammation would be violated."

Another indicator of lawlikeness i.w.s. is *inductive projectibility*. This connection was also first observed by Goodman (1955). We believe that a regularity is inductively projectible from an observed sample to unobserved individuals if we regard this regularity as lawlike i.w.s. (cf. Spohn 2005). This does not mean that our belief in laws i.w.s. can be used to justify inductive inferences, as some authors seem to suggest (e.g. Armstrong 1983), because a justified belief in a law presupposes our trust in the method of induction. Rather, the relation is a conceptual one: considering a regularity as lawlike i.w.s. *means* that we consider this regularity as inductively projectible—either unrestrictedly or spatiotemporally restricted.

6.6.4 Spatiotemporal Universality and Maxwell's Condition

To avoid the graduality of the wide concept of lawlikeness, many philosophers of science are more attracted by the concept of lawlikeness in the narrow sense of a law of nature, or a physical necessity. Recall that according to the naive Humean regularity theory, laws of nature are nothing but true generalizations. In the face of accidental generalizations such as "All apples in this basket are red," this position is untenable. Logical empiricists cherished the hope that at least all spatiotemporally *unrestricted* universal sentences are lawlike i.n.s. But this hope turned out to be an illusion. This has been shown by example (3.6–9): the universal (or negated existential) sentence "No lump of gold has a diameter of more than one kilometer" is (presumably) true and spatiotemporally universal but still does not reveal a physical necessity. Therefore, spatiotemporal universality is not a sufficient condition for lawlikeness i.n.s. It is, however, a plausible *necessary* condition for lawlikeness i.n.s.

Hempel (1965b, 341f) objected to the concept of spatiotemporal universality, noting that it is not invariant with respect to logically equivalent transformations: "All apples in this basket are red" is L-equivalent with "All non-red objects are not apples in this basket," but the antecedent of the latter implication ("non-red objects") is spatiotemporally unrestricted. This problem is solved, however, by the following definition of spatiotemporal universality that has been suggested (in a different but equivalent formulation) by Earman (1978, sec. 1):

(Def. 6.6–1)

i A predicate $Px_1...x_n$ is *spatiotemporally universal* iff there exists no instantiation $Pa_1...a_n$ of this predicate whose truth value follows mathematically from the spatiotemporal localization of the individual constant $a_1,...,a_n$ in the instantiation.

ii A universal or statistically general sentence (fig. 3.5–1) is spatiotemporally universal iff its antecedent and consequent predicates are spatiotemporally universal.

In def. 6.6–1 it is presupposed that defined predicates are replaced by primitive predicates. For instance, for all individuals a that are *not* in this basket, the truth of the instantiation "If a is an apple in this basket, then a is red" (formally $Ba \wedge Aa \to Ra$) follows already from the spatio-temporal localization of a and this basket, which entail mathematically that a is *not* in this basket ($\neg Ba$), and hence that the implication is true (via the logical rule $\neg p \; ||\!\!\!— \; p \wedge q \to r$). Of course, this remains true if one replaces the implication by its contraposition "All non-red objects are not apples in this basket" ($\neg Ra \to \neg(Ba \wedge Aa)$). So Hempel's problem is solved and definition def. 6.6–1 works fine. Based on this definition we formulate the following universality condition (U):

> (Prop. 6.6–1) *Spatiotemporal universality (U):* Only spatiotemporally unrestricted general sentences are lawlike in the narrow sense.

Let us call the *strong* Hume thesis the view that lawlikeness (i.n.s.) coincides with strict or statistical (spatiotemporal) universality. We know that this thesis is incorrect. Condition (U), however, implies a *weak* Hume thesis, according to which strict or statistical universality is at least a *necessary* condition for lawlikeness (i.n.s.).

Some authors have doubted even the weak Hume thesis and argued that there exist irreducibly *singular* physical necessities or causal connections that do not entail any form of (strict or statistical) generality (e.g. Ducasse 1968, 3f; Tooley 1990). However, irreducibly singular necessity claims are entirely untestable, and therefore epistemically inaccessible (cf. Psillos 2002; Maudlin 2007). Suppose an avalanche descends and a magician asserts that he has caused this event by the power of his mind, though he succeeded only in this individual case. Such an assertion borders on absurdity. In conclusion, the weak Hume thesis in the sense of the *reproducibility* of lawlike connections is a fundamental rationality principle of scientific lawhood and causality.

As the universality condition is too weak to characterize lawlikeness i.n.s., Carnap (1947) and Hempel (1965b, 267) suggested a stronger condition which was intended to explicate *fundamental* (i.e. non-derived) laws of nature and goes back to the physicist Maxwell. In the formulation of Carnap and Hempel, the Maxwell condition requires that fundamental laws of nature do not analytically refer to particular individuals or space-time points, i.e. they are formulated in terms of purely *qualitative* predicates. Carnap thought that the universality condition and the Maxwell condition are more or less equivalent. Wilson (1979) and Schurz (1996a, sec. 3) have shown, however, that Maxwell's condition (M) is substantially *stronger* than the universality condition (U). For example, Goodman's law "All emeralds are green until the year 3000 and blue thereafter" is spatiotemporally universal in the sense of (U), but it does not fulfill Maxwell's condition. Wilson (1979, 111) demonstrated that the Maxwell condition, correctly understood, is a *physical principle of symmetry* which implies the following:

> (Prop. 6.6–2) *Maxwell condition (M):* Physical fundamental laws are invariant under translations (i.e. linear shifts) of their time coordinates and under translations and rotations of their spatial coordinates.

The physical significance of these symmetry principles lies in the fact that the most basic *conservation* laws of physics (for energy and momentum) can be derived from them (Feynman et al. 2005, sec. 17; van Fraassen 1989, ch. 9–10). Philosophically, these symmetry principles assert that the lawlike behavior of closed systems is the same everywhere in space and time. A similar condition is implied by Armstrong's account of laws as an implication relation between universals (sec. 6.6.6).

Physical symmetry principles, however, do not exist a priori but are dependent on the established physical background knowledge (Feynman et al. 2005, sec. 52–2; Earman 1986, ch. vii). If Dirac was right in assuming that the gravitational constant of the universe is temporally changeable, then (M) would not be fulfilled anymore. Therefore, as a general condition on lawlikeness the Maxwell condition (M) is perhaps too strong. At the same time, (M) is too weak, because the counter-example (3.6–9) concerning lumps of gold satisfies (M) and is still contingent.

6.6.5 The Best System Account

According to the best system account, those sentences express true laws of nature i.n.s. which are axioms of the best deductive *system* of truths, in the sense that this system provides the most economic or unified axiomatization of truths. The account goes back to Mill, Ramsey and Lewis and is therefore also called the MRL account.[8] According to Lewis, a good deductive system provides an optimal balance of simplicity and strength: it is the better, the fewer and simpler its axioms and the more and the stronger its consequences are. Since ties between different best systems, i.e. different axiomatizations providing an equally optimal balance are possible, the earlier Lewis (1973b, 1986b) suggested that we regard those sentences as lawlike i.n.s. which appear as axioms in *all* best deductive systems of truths. In (1994, 233) Lewis changes his position: if nature is so unkind that it allows for ties, then one should better say that there are no "laws" in an objective sense of this word.

As Lewis (1983a) (and later Cohen/Callender 2009) points out, the best system account is language-dependent, i.e. dependent on a given system of primitive predicates. A best system formulated in terms of the predicates "green" and "blue" will no longer be a best system if it is reformulated in terms of Goodman's pathological predicates "grue" and "bleen." In sec. 5.11.3 we saw that the choice of an adequate system of primitive predicates is a general problem in philosophy of science to which there exist partial solutions. So we do not regard this problem as a decisive objection. A more fundamental objection to the best system approach consists in the fact that *even if* it is relativized to a given system of primitive predicates in which all truths are formulated, the best system account does not lead to the right results. The two basic objections are the following:

- *Objection 1* (van Fraassen 1989, 47): Why should the accidental universal sentence (3.6–9) regarding the size of lumps of gold never be added to the best system? After all a lot of true consequences are derivable from it. So what guarantees that the best system will not contain a lot of non-lawlike generalizations?
- *Objection 2* (the inverse of objection 1): If a true law L is logically not as densely connected to the other true laws as they are connected among each other, then removing L from a deductive system may improve its balance of simplicity and strength. So what guarantees that the best system contains all the true laws?

To make these objections more precise, first observe that the best system account expresses the idea of *unification* as explained in sec. 5.11.2: a multitude of true statements (expressing facts) are derivable from a small number of simple axioms. As explained there, to measure unification one has to conjunctively decompose consequences into their smallest relevant elements (in short: elements) by the methods introduced in sec. 3.12. So let us represent a deductive system as a pair (A,D) where D is the set of all elements following from axiom set A, and A is an irreducible representation (def. 3.12–4), i.e. a non-redundant set of elements of

D which is L-equivalent with D. We have $A \subseteq D$, where a "good" system will have many fewer elements in A than in D. A basic way to measure the goodness g(A,D) of a deductive system is to attach to each element $S \in D$ a *weight* w(S) and to define g(A,D) as $\Sigma_{S \in D} w(S) / \Sigma_{S \in A} w(S)$, i.e. the sum of the weights of all elementary consequences, divided by the sum of the weights of all elementary axioms. The larger this quotient (which may range between 1 and ∞), the better the unification. Observe that independently from its weight w, an element S produces a *gain* if it is added only to D but not to A (since d+w/a > d/a); and it produces a *cost* if it is added to both A and D (because (d+w)/(a+w) < d/a whenever a < d).

Let T be the set of all truths, $L \subset T$ be a set of all true laws which are accepted by commonly agreed standards (either by standards of physics, or according to our intuitions), and let $C \subset T$ be a non-empty set of general sentences which are accepted as contingencies by commonly agreed standards. Let (A,D) be a best deductive system of T. We ask, under which conditions will the axiom set A of (A,D) contain the set L but exclude the set C?

If one assumes that the weights are determined in a *subjective* manner, then it is easy to see that "anything goes": there exist weight-assignments for which the best system contains not only all laws in L, but also all contingent generalizations in C, and there exist weight-assignments for which the best system contains almost no laws in L. So let us forget the assumption of subjective weights and assume some fixed "objective" method of weight-assignment. Even under this assumption there exist highly plausible situations in which an "objective" best system account is guaranteed to yield wrong results.

The above objection 1 can be implemented with objective weights in the following *situation 1:* Assume a predicate Px, which occurs in many of the true laws, is strictly but contingently correlated with another predicate Cx. So $\forall x(Px \leftrightarrow Cx)$ is a true contingent generalization, for example "For all x: x is a DNA-replicating system (Cx) iff x is a living organism on earth (Px)." If (A,D) is a best system, then the uniform replacement of P by C in A and D will preserve the truth and all consequence relations. So the replaced deductive system (A*,D*) will be as good as (A,D), but it will turn all P-containing laws in the axiom set into contingent generalizations.

To implement objection 2 with objective weights, we assume the following *situation 2:* a subset of the true elementary laws is less densely connected to the other laws than the rest of the true laws. As a simple example, assume the true laws are $P_1 \to P_2$, $P_2 \to P_3$, $P_3 \to P_4$ and $P_5 \to P_6$, $P_6 \to P_7$. If all these laws have equal weight, then the goodness quotient of the first three laws is 6/3 = 2 (because the laws $P_1 \to P_3$, $P_1 \to P_4$, $P_2 \to P_4$ are derivable), and the goodness quotient of all five laws is 9/5 (because from the fourth and fifth law in addition $P_4 \to P_6$ is derivable). So the goodness increases from 9/5 to 2 if the less densely connected laws $P_5 \to P_6$, $P_6 \to P_7$ are omitted from the axiom system. Thus, in situation 2 the best system will not contain all laws in L.

Lewis (1994, 479) was aware of the arbitrariness of our standards of balance. He expressed the hope that nature may be so kind that one deductive system is much better than all others independently from our standards. In view of the above objections Lewis' hope seems illusionary. It is highly probable that the above situations 1 and 2 obtain, which implies that the best system account fails for *all* standards of balance. The reason for this failure is, in my view, that the conceptual essence of laws i.n.s. is not that they yield an optimal axiomatization of factual truths. This might well be true, but if so it is an epiphenomenon. The conceptual essence of laws i.n.s. is, rather, that they express physical necessities, in the sense of general truths that cannot be *broken* by any physically possible process or intervention. This idea is discussed in the next section.

6.6.6 Physical Necessity and Independent Possibility Knowledge

How can one distinguish laws that express physical necessities from contingent generalizations? The universality condition and Maxwell's condition are too weak, and the best systems account does not work. Of course one may characterize the concept of necessity within possible worlds semantics. This is logically highly useful (Hughes/Cresswell 1996), but leads into a semantic explication circle, since in this account one defines a proposition P as *physically necessary* in the actual world w* iff P is true in all worlds w which are *physically possible* from the point of view of w*, i.e. no truth in w contradicts the physical necessities of w* (van Fraassen 1989, 44f).

A more refined explication of laws i.n.s. has been developed by Lange. According to Lange's idea (2009, 20ff), a true sentence S expresses a law i.n.s. if its truth is preserved under all counterfactual suppositions P that are consistent with all laws i.n.s. Lange correctly observes that this definition is circular (ibid., 25–28). He therefore proposes the following more complicated definition (ibid., ch. 2): a sentence S expresses a law iff S is a member of a non-maximal stable set Γ, i.e. a set of true statements Γ which does not contain all factual truths and whose elements remain true under all counterfactual suppositions that are consistent with Γ. However, Reutlinger et al. (2011, sec. 6.1) point out that in order to produce the right laws i.n.s., Lange's semantics of counterfactuals must already presuppose an independent knowledge of laws i.n.s., by similar arguments as in sec. 6.6.3. So in the end Lange's refined explication also turns out to be circular.

Metaphysicians have suggested that we regard the concept of physical necessity as logically primitive, i.e. incapable of being defined. Armstrong (1983, 78ff), for example, advocated the thesis that laws of nature are necessitation relations between *universals* of the form "P necessitates Q," where P and Q are natural properties. These necessitation relations entail the corresponding strict generalizations "For all x, if Px then Qx." Armstrong's necessitation relations are of a contingent nature, i.e. they can differ in different possible worlds, and thus correspond to our concept of physical (as opposed to conceptual) necessity. Maudlin (2007, 15), however, argued that Armstrong's necessitation relations are epistemically *inaccessible*: it is completely unclear how one can distinguish on empirical grounds between generalizations that express necessitation relations and those that do not.

Let us ask: what is our epistemic access to physical possibility and necessity? Here our accepted physical theories come into play—what follows from them is (accepted as) physically necessary (cf. van Fraassen 1980, 199ff):

> (Prop. 6.6–3) A sentence S is *physically necessary* if it is logically entailed by the system of true or accepted fundamental laws of physics.

The important thing to note is this: if one understands prop. 6.6–3 in the *epistemic* sense (i.e. related to the *known* fundamental laws), then it is merely a sufficient but *not* a *necessary* condition for physical necessity. Recall from sec. 2.6.2 that the fundamental laws of physics (e.g. the Schrödinger equation) are unsolvable for systems of modest complexity. We do not know what the true fundamental laws entail; we can only speculate. There are numerous laws that we regard as physically necessary even though we cannot de facto deduce them from the fundamental physical theories, as for instance

(6.6–4) An oxygen molecule can attach itself to red blood cells.

But how do we then distinguish accidental universal sentences such as "All apples in this basket are red," or "All lumps of gold are smaller than 1 kilometer in diameter," from physical necessities like (6.6–4)? The intuitive key feature of accidental generalizations consists in the fact that one *could defy* them. Why are we so sure about that? I suggest the following answer: because our scientific theories are equipped with *independent knowledge* about *physical possibilities*.

How is such independent possibility knowledge achieved? I see two possible ways. First, possibility knowledge flows from our knowledge that our own actions are controlled by our "free" will, which means that they are causally independent of many (though not all) events. Second, it follows from our knowledge about random processes that certain events are causally independent of each other. Both kinds of knowledge can be acquired by means of empirical induction. We know, for instance, that we can put this green apple into this basket, and that the color of this green apple will not change because of the fact that the other apples in the basket are red. Therefore, we know that "All apples in this basket are red" is not a law of nature, even if nobody has actually put a green apple into this basket. In order to argue that the example of the lump of gold (3.6–9) is not a law of nature we have to think about the combinatorial random possibility that enough gold comes together in our galaxy to form a lump of gold that has a diameter of 1 kilometer.

6.7 Causality

Evolutionary theorists tell us that causal modeling is a highly successful capacity of *Homo sapiens* (Tomasello 1999). This diagnosis stands in stark contrast to the perennial difficulties philosophers had when trying to justify causality. According to David Hume's skeptical challenge, the classification of correlated events into causes and effects does not correspond to anything real out there in the world—only the correlations are real, while causality is a mere habit of our cognitive system. In this section we investigate the most important answers to Hume's challenge.

6.7.1 Singular and General Causality

Causality is prima facie a relation between singular events or facts, i.e. event- or fact-tokens. We assume a factlike concept of event, i.e. the event of *a being A* corresponds to the fact that *a is an A*, in symbols "Aa." It seems that the only way that causal claims can become empirically significant is by a connection to empirical regularities, or in Woodward's words (2003, 71f), by being reproducible. Therefore, we suggest the following connection between singular and general causality:

> (Prop. 6.7–1) *Connection between singular and general causality:*
> Event-token Aa is a (positive) cause for event-token Ba iff
>
> i   Aa and Ba occurred in (completely described) causal circumstances Ca, and
> ii   under conditions C, event-type A is a (positive) causal factor for event-type B, where
> iii this analytically entails the regularity that A increases the probability of B given C, $p(B|A \wedge C) > p(B|C)$.

Note: "Aa" in prop. 6.7–1 abbreviates a complex formula, possibly with function symbols, and "a" may stand for a sequence of individual constants.

Example: "Aa" abbreviates "A(a,t)" and stands for "Peter jumps off a bridge at t," "Ba" abbreviates "B(a,t+ε)" and stands for "Peter falls into the river ε-seconds after t." The circumstances "C(a,[t,t+ε])" (abbreviated by "Ca") exclude that interfering factors occur between t and t+ε, which would block the causal process from Aa to Ba.

In prop. 6.7–1 and throughout this section, "cause" always means *a partial* cause, i.e. some causally contributing factor, but not necessarily the *total* cause, i.e. the complete set of all causally relevant factors. For this reason, prop. 6.7–1 relativizes causal claims to the set of *all* other causally relevant conditions—the "causal circumstances" Ca.

Condition iii asserts that singular cause-effect relations imply regularities. This is a *weak Hume thesis* for causality (similar as in prop. 6.6–1 for lawlikeness). This condition excludes empty singular causality assertions such as "Judy the mentalist can cause a thrown coin to land heads by means of her mind, but she succeeds only in 50% of the cases."

We understand regularities not in the narrow deterministic, but in the broad *probabilistic* sense, as probabilistic *dependencies* or correlations (recall sec. 4.1.2), thereby interpreting probabilities in the objective-statistical sense (recall 3.9.1). These probabilistic dependences are assumed to be inductively projectible and thus lawlike i.w.s. (sec. 6.6.2).

Because of our probabilistic setting, causal factors do not always produce their effects (just significantly often). Therefore, the general causal claim in prop. 6.7–1(ii) "A is a positive cause of B in circumstances C" do not necessarily imply the corresponding singular causal claim that Aa is a positive cause of Ba (cf. Eells 1991, 8ff).

Most philosophical accounts to causality attempt to explicate causality by providing definitions. Depending on the nature of the defining condition we distinguish between (a) empirical, (b) metaphysical, (c) physical and (d) interventionist accounts. In the next subsections we present the major representatives of these accounts and their problems.

6.7.2 Regularity Accounts

Prototypes of empirical accounts are regularity accounts. According to these accounts, cause-effect relations do not "produce" regularities among events, but are *identical* with these regularities. Regularity accounts face the following problems:

1 Causal regularities between events appear to be forward-directed in time—the earlier causes the later, but not vice versa. Correlations, on the other hand, are always symmetric (if A correlates with B, then B correlates with A). In reply to this problem, regularity theorists have suggested defining causation as forward-directed regularity (Psillos 2009, 131). But the justification of the *objective* direction of time flowing from the past towards the future is itself highly difficult (sec. 6.7.5). For this reason, Reichenbach (1956) proposed to go the opposite way and define the direction of time by the direction of causal relations. Moreover, the identification of causal relations with forward-directed regularities fails because of problems 2 and 3 below.

2 If two temporally consecutive events are correlated, they do not necessarily stand in a cause-effect relation; they may also be effects of a *common cause*: recall the examples given in sec. 4.4.1, e.g. the barometer-storm example. In such cases the preceding event (the barometer reading) is merely an *indicator* but not a cause of the effect (the coming storm).

3 Directed causal dependencies also appear to hold between coexisting properties of stationary systems. Their correlation is simultaneous in time, i.e. A-at-t correlates with B-at-t. It is nevertheless an accepted practice in science to distinguish between (causally) independent and dependent properties or variables. For example, the height of a tower is the causally independent, and the length of its shadow the dependent variable (Bromberger 1966, 92). Especially in the life and social sciences one discovers dependencies between coexisting dispositional properties, e.g. between the average prosperity and birth rate in a nation. Note that by assuming causal relations between coexisting variables, one does *not* imply that there exist instantaneous physical interactions. Rather, the meaning of these causal relations is coined in terms of possible inter-

ventions: we can change the value of the dependent variables (e.g. the shadow's length) by changing the values of the independent variables (the tower's height), but not vice versa.

Some philosophers have argued that the assumption of cause-effect relations is needed to explain why observed regularities are *inductively projectible* (Armstrong 1983, part 1; Fales 1990, ch. 4). In my opinion these arguments are not sound. As explained in sec. 6.6.3, *lawlikeness* and inductive projectibility are semantically connected. But causality goes *beyond* lawlikeness and inductive projectibility: Regularities that connect the effects of a common cause, for instance, may be perfectly lawlike, but they are obviously not causal.

6.7.3 *Counterfactuals and Causal Powers*

Two prominent metaphysical approaches to causality are counterfactual accounts and causal power accounts.

Counterfactual accounts go back to Lewis (1973a/1986). He suggested explicating the causation relation between singular events thus: an event A(a,t) has caused a later event B(a,t+ε) iff B(a,t+ε) *would not* have occurred in case that A(a,t) *had* not occurred. To obtain the desired results, Lewis constructs the "closest" possible world w in which the antecedent A(a,t) fails as follows: (a) w's history must be identical with that of the actual world w* until immediately before the time t of the putative cause A(a,t), and (b) from time t onwards w departs minimally from the actual world w* inasmuch as A(a,t) does *not* obtain in w. Lewis observes that if one assumes determinism, then world w involves a small "miracle" at time t, i.e. a violation of w's laws which it shares with w*, because A(a,t) does not happen in w although it is causally determined by w's laws and history up to t.

Several problems are associated with Lewis' account. First, his assumption of "miracles" seems to be ad hoc. Second, his account is one of *singular* causation, and there is no clear connection with empirical regularities. The counterpart of the "circumstances" in our prop. 6.7–1 in Lewis' account is the complete history of the actual world immediately before the time of the antecedent. However, this "complete history" is not reproducible and therefore statistically inaccessible.

Most importantly, by Lewis' *own* criteria of closeness between worlds his account does not always produce the right results. These criteria are as follows, in order of preference (Lewis 1979, 47f): (1) avoid widespread violations of laws, (2) avoid widespread violations of facts, (3) avoid local violation of laws, and (4) avoid local violations of facts. Now assume that at most 100 (or fewer) local fact violations are preferred to positing one miracle. The actual world w* is deterministic and contains 100 local events E(i) mediating between cause A(0) and effect B(101), ordered in time:

(6.7-1) E(−1), A(0), E(1),...,E(100), B(101),

where E(−1) is the event immediately before A(0). Then the world w which differs from w* only in replacing A(0) by ¬A(0) involves one event-change and two miracles: one between E(−1) and ¬A(0) and one between ¬A(0) and E(1). This is preferable to the world w': E(−1), ¬A(0), ¬E(1),...,¬E(100), ¬B(101), which involves only one miracle but 102 event-changes. But only w' yields the desired outcome that ¬A(0) *would* have led to ¬B(101). So Lewis' account fails. Another strong inadequacy-argument is found in Woodward (2003, 139f).

Power accounts explain lawlike regularities by postulating causal powers. In distinction to counterfactuals, causal powers are claimed to be situated in the actual world and to make up the essences of fundamental properties (Mumford 2009). For example, that the electron is negatively charged means that it has the power to attract other positively charged particles in the vicinity. Since causal powers entail lawlike regularities, the weak Hume thesis is typically satisfied by these accounts. But entailing regularities is not sufficient for being empirically significant. For every regularity, a causal power can be postulated that "explains" this regularity *post-facto*. Post-facto "explanations" of this sort amount to a mere metaphysical post-facto *duplication* of the regularities among facts, but they can never generate novel predictions by which they are independently testable, nor do they achieve a genuine unification of regularities. In other words, purely metaphysical power accounts fail to meet the criteria for empirically significant theoretical concepts (sec. 5.4.2, 5.10.4).

6.7.4 Causation and the Direction of Time

Intuitively we experience that time elapses, i.e. flows from the past to the future. This time flow is presumably the reason why we conceive causal processes as forward-directed in time. But physically speaking the time coordinate is a dimension, like the space coordinate, without any inbuilt direction. The question thus arises: does it have any objective-physical sense when we say that time elapses?

Some authors have doubted that physical time has a subject-independent direction (e.g. Price 1996). Grünbaum (1969) argued that the direction of time is a psychological phenomenon, which can be explained by the difference between *memory* and *prediction*. However, that there is such a distinct difference between memory and prediction seems itself to be in need of a physical explanation.

According to a famous proposal, the direction of time is determined by the *law of entropy*, which says that the entropy of a closed system increases but never decreases over time. But there exists an equally famous objection to this proposal: all presently accepted *fundamental* physical laws are invariant with respect to time inversion (Feynman et al. 2005, vol. I, 52–2). The law of entropy is not a fundamental but a macroscopic law about the probable developments of large ensembles of particles. The entropic direction of time can only be justified by adding a *contingent* assumption that goes beyond the entropy law, namely that our universe has started from a relatively *low* entropy state. A universe in a state of high entropy could indeed occasionally pass over to a lower entropy state.[9] It is therefore questionable whether one should reduce the direction of causation to the direction of time, instead of doing it the other way round, as proposed by Reichenbach (1956).

6.7.5 Causal Processes and Mechanisms

According to physical accounts, cause-effect relations are the result of a physical process that is initiated by the cause event A (in circumstances C) and propagated through space in time until it terminates in the effect event B. Different kinds of process theories have been developed (cf. Dowe 2009). For Fair (1979, 220) a causal process consists of the continuous spatiotemporal propagation of energy or momentum. In Salmon's account (1984, 179f), two kinds of physical "processes" are distinguished. By a causal *process* i.n.s. Salmon understands the transmission of a physical quantity (e.g. light) through space and time. A causal *interaction* is conceived as the intersection of two causal processes at which the transmitted quantity is altered. An example would be a light ray hitting an object, whereby photons with certain frequencies are absorbed and others reflected.

Salmon (1984) attempted to explain the difference between real processes such as the motion of light and pseudo-processes such as the movement of a shadow, based on Reichenbach's *mark* criterion. Because of the critique of this criterion by Dowe (1992) and Kitcher (1989), the later Salmon (1997, 1998) has modified his theory: building upon Dowe (1992, 2000), he now defines a causal process as the *worldline* of an object that transmits a *conserved quantity*, and an interaction as an intersection of worldlines which involves an exchange of a conserved quantity (Salmon 1998, 253–255). However, Salmon's improved process account also fails to avoid some kinds of pseudo-processes (cf. Hitchcock 2004; Psillos 2002, 123–127).

In spite of their technical difficulties, causal process theories are supported by theories of classical or relativistic physics, since every causal process involves some form of energy propagation. Causal process theories serve as valuable heuristics for conceiving the physical basis of causal relations. But they are violated in the domain of far-distance correlations in quantum mechanics (so-called "EPR" correlations after Einstein, Podolski and Rosen 1935). Here two photons are emitted by a common light source and fly in opposite directions. They can be lightyears away from each other, but are still entangled in the following sense: before the measurement the spin state (up vs. down) of the two photons is undetermined ("superposed"), but when one of the two photons is measured and results in "spin up," the state of the other photon is simultaneously transformed into "spin down," without any physical process between the two photons taking place (cf. Herbert 1985; Penrose 2007, ch. 23).

The main problem of causal process accounts is not quantum mechanics, but rather that their scope is *too narrow*. In order to ascertain that a physical process led from A to B by propagation of a conserved physical quantity, one must possess a *microphysical description* of the events A and B (cf. Hitchcock 2004). For most macro-physical events such a microphysical description is unknown or perhaps unknowable. Most special science disciplines have a good grasp of their relevant *causal mechanisms* without the possibility, or need for, a microphysical description. A causal mechanism (e.g. the mechanisms of digestion) is simply understood as a *system* of entities and processes which together are causally responsible for a certain phenomenon (cf. Glennan 2002). In conclusion, there seems to exist a cognitively significant concept of causality which is *independent* of specific theories about the true physical micro-ontology of the word.

6.7.6 Interventionist Accounts

Because of the failure to define causality in statistical terms, empirically oriented philosophers proposed to explicate causation in a *non-reductive* way, by conditions that themselves contain causal concepts. Prominent non-reductive explications are interventionist accounts of causality. Historically they go back to the *action-theoretic* conception of causality developed by Collingwood (1940), von Wright (1971, sec. II.9) and Menzies/Price (1993). According to this account, an event-type A is the cause of B if B can be brought about by the realization of A by means of an action. Since many events cannot be influenced by human actions, contemporary proponents of this account such as Haussman (1998) and Woodward (2003) have suggested replacing the action-theory of causality with abstract intervention theory.

Intervention theory is explicated in terms of mathematical variables (sec. 3.1.4). An intervention on a variable X is considered as another variable, abbreviated as I_X, which when set to its value "on" acts as a cause of X which is usually conceived as being deterministic, i.e. I_X *fixes* X to some particular value x (cf. Pearl 2009, 23, fig. 1.4). For example, the intervention I_X = "switch on" leads to the effect X = "light on." It is required that I_X is "free" in the sense of not being caused by any other variable of the considered system.[10]

Based on this conception of an intervention, Woodward (2003, 53) defines a variable X to be a *direct cause* of another variable Y *iff* the following holds: there exists a possible intervention I_X on X that by changing X's value changes the probability distribution over Y's values, provided the values of all other variables Z in the considered system are held fixed by suitable interventions I_Z. Obviously this explication is *circular*, insofar as the notion of an intervention is itself a causal notion. This circularity is no problem for Woodward because he rejects the view that causality is reductively definable.

Independent from this question, the major problem with interventionist accounts is that they work only under the assumption that for every variable X in our world there exists an intervention variable I_X by which X's value can be manipulated independently from the other possible causes of X (cf. Haussman's assumption I, 1998, 64). However, this assumption fails, as many variables cannot possibly be *manipulated by interventions*: think, for instance, of the gender of a person as determined by their chromosomes, or of the radioactive decay of an atom, or the big bang (cf. the criticism in Glymour et al. 1991, 166). In reply to this objection Woodward (2003, 132) proposes that we posit "physically impossible" interveners. But such a step makes causal claims empirically untestable or even meaningless. In conclusion: whenever interventions are possible, they provide an important clue to causality, but they do not *exhaust* the meaning and cognitive role of causality.

6.7.7 *Causality as a Theoretical Concept*

Schurz and Gebharter (2013) argue that the attempt to provide definitions of causality is a shortcoming of most philosophical approaches to causality. Causality should, rather, be understood in a similar way to force in Newtonian physics, as a *theoretical* concept whose meaning is not given by explicit definitions, but by the core axioms of a *general theory of causality*, henceforth abbreviated as *GTC*. In what follows we present a brief outline of this approach, which is expressed in the framework of mathematical variables.

Recall from sec. 3.1.4 that a variable X is a function X: D→ Val(X) from a given domain D to a value space of X, Val(X). For example, if X denotes color, then Val(X) = {red, green, …} and X assigns a color X(d) to every d in D. For sake of simplicity we assume all value spaces Val(X) are finite (if X represents a real-valued quantity, Val(X) consists of sufficiently fine-grained intervals). Note that properties or event-types are not variables, but values of variables. Simple dichotomic property-pairs are represented by binary variables X_F with the value space $\{F, \neg F\}$. We use the following abbreviations:

- $X, X_1, \ldots$ are variables, and $V, V_1, \ldots$ are sets of variables.
- Lower-case letters x, x_i and y, y_i, (…) stand for values of upper-case variables X and Y (…), respectively.
- p is a statistical probability distribution over (an algebra over) the domain D.
- p(x) ("the probability of X-value x") is short for $p(\{d \in D: X(d)=x\})$, i.e. the probability of D-individuals whose X-value is x.
- Likewise, p(S) stands for $p(\{d \in D: X(d) \in S\})$, where $S \subseteq Val(X)$.
- $p(\neg x)$ for $p(\{d \in D: X(d) \neq x\})$, p(x,y) for $p(\{d \in D: X(d)=x \wedge Y(d)=y\})$.
- $p(x|y) =_{def} p(x,y)/p(y)$, i.e. the *conditional* probability of x given y, provided p(y) > 0 (recall def. 3.9–2, fn. 3 of ch. 3).

The notion of a probabilistic dependence between two variables X and Y, abbreviated as DEP(X,Y), is a weak notion: it asserts the existence of *some* (positive or negative) probabilistic dependence between *some* values of X and Y. Conversely, probabilistic independence between X and Y, abbreviated as INDEP(X,Y), is a strong notion. DEP(X,Y) is defined as follows:

(6.7–2) DEP(X,Y) *iff* $\exists x,y: p(x|y) \neq p(x)$ and p(y) > 0.
INDEP(X,Y) *iff* not DEP(X,Y), i.e. $\forall x,y: p(x|y) = p(x)$ or p(y) = 0.

In empirical applications "≠" should be interpreted as "statistically significant difference." The corresponding notions of *conditional* (in)dependence (between two variables X and Y, given fixed values of other variables $Z_1, \ldots, Z_n$), are defined as follows:

(6.7-3) DEP(X,Y|$Z_1,...,Z_n$) *iff*
∃x,y,$z_1,...,z_n$: p(x|y,$z_1,...,z_n$) ≠ p(x|$z_1,...,z_n$) and p(y,$z_1,...,z_n$) > 0.
INDEP(X,Y|$Z_1,...,Z_n$) *iff* not DEP(X,Y|$Z_1,...,Z_n$).

Unconditional (in)dependence is obtained as the special case (IN)DEP(X,Y|∅), where "∅" denotes the empty set.

The advantage of the notion of probabilistic dependence between variables is that it is more directly related to causal connections between variables, than probabilistic dependence between *values* of variables is related to causal connection between values of variables. On the other hand, the notions of *positive* and *negative* probabilistic dependence are prima facie only defined for the values of variables, as follows:

(6.7-4) POSDEP(x,y) *iff* p(x|y) > p(x),
NEGDEP(x,y) *iff* p(x|y) < p(x);
DEP(x,y) *iff* POSDEP(x,y) or NEGDEP(x,y), and
INDEP(x,y) *iff* ¬DEP(x,y).

Only if the values of variables X and Y are ordered according to size, does it make sense to say that X is positively dependent on Y *iff* an increased Y-value leads to an increased mean value of X. If X is positively dependent on Y for all possible increases of Y-values, then X is *positive-monotonically* dependent on Y (likewise for negative-monotonic dependence). Otherwise, X is non-monotonically dependent on Y (e.g. positively dependent in one range and negatively in another range of Y-values).

In order to be empirically significant, the theoretical concept of causality as explicated in GTC must have two features (recall sec. 5.4.2): (i) it offers unifying explanations of empirical phenomena which cannot be generated without it, and (ii) these explanations are not entirely post-facto, but generate potentially novel predictions by which they are independently testable. The decisive question is: *What* does causality explain? In sec. 6.7.3 we saw that the answer to this question cannot simply be that causality "explains" all sorts of probabilistic dependencies post-facto. We will argue now that the assumption of directed cause-effect relations is needed because it yields the *best explanation* for two empirical (in)stability properties of probabilistic dependencies in regard to conditionalization: *screening-off* and *linking-up*. Moreover, cause-effect relations do not merely explain these properties post-facto, but they generate independently testable novel predictions. We will characterize these two properties in a purely statistical way, without presupposing causal knowledge.

Screening-off has already been characterized in prop. 4.4–1. In terms of variables the definition is:

(6.7–5) Two variables X and Y are *screened off* by Z *iff* (i) DEP(X,Y) and (ii) INDEP(Y,X|Z) holds.

Examples: (a) Barometer reading (X) storm coming (Y) atmospheric pressure (Z).
(b) Young male (X) car accident (Y) car speed (Z).

Thus, the probabilistic dependence between X and Y disappears when one conditionalizes on arbitrarily chosen but *fixed* values of a third variable Z. Conditions (i) and (ii) imply the probabilistic dependencies DEP(X,Z) and DEP(Y,Z), where usually (but not always) these dependencies are not screened off by the third variable Z. We focus on robust (or "faithful") cases of screening-off which are stable under small numerical changes of the probabilistic parameters (we will see in sec. 6.7.8 that most cases of screening-off are faithful).

Intuitively we interpret the dependencies in (6.7–5) immediately as produced by causal relations: we think we "know" that screening-off occurs because variable Z is a common cause in (a) and an intermediate cause in (b). However, in order to achieve a philosophical justification of causality we must free our mind from causal intuitions and assume for a moment that we know nothing about the variables apart from their probability distributions. If we do that, we are confronted with a riddle: *Why* does the correlation between X and Y disappear when Z is fixed to a certain value? The best available explanation of robust screening-off phenomena—in fact, the only good explanation we can think of—is the following: Only the two probabilistic dependencies between X and Z and between Z and Y reflect a direct causal connection (relative to {X,Y,Z}). In contrast, the probabilistic dependence between X and Y is the indirect result of these two connections and is thus *mediated* by Z. This causal scenario is displayed in fig. 6.7–1: X-values can influence Y-values only by influencing the values of the mediating variable Z. Hence if we conditionalize on a subdomain of individuals with fixed Z-values,

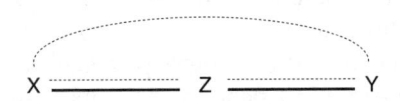

Figure 6.7–1 Explanation of screening-off by binary causal relations (. . . for probabilistic dependence, — for direct causal connection)

individuals with changed X-values will no longer have changed Y-values. This explains screening-off.

To avoid misunderstandings, note the following points: (1) We assume in this explanation that there are no further causal paths between X and Y, i.e. *all* probabilistic influences of X on Y are mediated by Z. (2) We assume that the screening-off case is robust (faithful); otherwise the best explanation would be more complicated.

One may object that the postulate of binary "causal" connections is trivial because it merely reiterates the fact that probabilistic dependence is a binary relation. But this is not true: probabilistic dependencies supervene on unconditional probabilities and thus need not have any independent existence at all—this is the probabilistic generalization of Hume's constant conjunction argument. So probabilistic dependencies do not *by themselves* justify the assumption of ontologically real connections which explain them. What justifies this assumption is the phenomenon of screening-off.

Our explanation of screening-off merely requires the assumption of an *undirected binary* "causal" dependence relation (—); no direction of causation is needed so far. This fact is remarkable, because followers of Reichenbach (1956) often argue that directed causal relations are needed to explain screening-off relations. Our considerations reveal that this is not true: directed causation is not required for explaining screening-off phenomena, but for discriminating screening-off from linking-up phenomena. Linking-up is exactly the opposite of the phenomenon of screening-off and statistically defined as follows:

(6.7-6) Two variables X and Y are linked-up by a variable Z *iff* INDEP(X,Y) and DEP(X,Y|Z) holds.

Example: Position of the Sun (X) length of a tower (Y) length of its shadow (Z).

Thus, two independent variables X and Y are linked-up by Z iff they become dependent when conditioning on (some or all values of) a third variable Z. The position of the Sun is obviously not correlated with the height of a tower, but if we conditionalize on fixed values of the shadow's length, we can compute the height of the tower from the position of the Sun. Again, the conditions INDEP(X,Y) and DEP(X,Y|Z) imply DEP(X,Z) and DEP(Y,Z), and we focus on robust cases of linking-up.

If we put aside any causal intuitions, then we face a second riddle: *why* do two formerly independent variables X and Y become correlated when one conditionalizes on fixed values of a third variable Z? Undirected causal relations cannot explain *both* screening-off and linking-up. This can be seen via the following consideration: the variable Z on which we conditionalize must, again, act as a *mediator* between X and Y. So the structure of undirected causal relations in the linking-up scenario must have the same form as the structure in the screening-off scenario depicted in fig. 6.7–1. But the causal structure underlying screening-off and linking-up cannot have the same form, because these two phenomena involve opposite probabilistic (in)stability effects.

The best available explanation for screening-off *and* linking-up—the only good explanation we can think of—is to assume that binary causal relations are *directed*. From now on X→Y means that some values of X exert a direct causal influence on the (probabilities of the) values of Y (relative to a given set of variables). The way that this influence is physically realized is left unspecified. We are inclined to understand the exertion of causal influence X→Y as a local physical process that takes some time; but in principle, the exertion of directed influence could also take place instantaneously (which may be needed in the domain of quantum mechanics).

In screening-off and linking-up scenarios, the variable Z mediates between X and Y. So we have three possible directed causal structures as candidates for explaining these phenomena:

a   X→Z→Y: Z is an intermediate cause (between X and Y).
b   X←Z→Y: Z is a common cause (of X and Y).
c   X→Z←Y: Z is a common effect (of X and Y).

The first two structures explain screening-off and the third one explains linking-up. Again, our explanations assume that there are no further causal paths connecting X and Y, and that the explained cases of screening-off and linking-up are robust.

(6.7–7) *Explaining screening-off*: We assume for simplicity that the probabilistic dependencies are monotonically positive.

a   *Z is an intermediate cause* (X→Z→Y): Y is positively dependent on X because (i) high X-values cause high Z-values, and (ii) these high Z-values cause high Y-values.
b   *Z is a common cause* (X←Z→Y): Y is positively dependent on X because (i) high X-values are caused by high Z-values, and (ii) these high Z-values cause high Y-values.

For a and b, the disappearance of the X-Y dependence after conditionalizing on Z is explained as before (fig. 6.7–1), since in both causal structures, all influence of X on Y is mediated via Z.

In Search of Causes • 395

Observe that the above explanations assume certain causal principles that will be axiomatized in the next section. The argument in a(i) assumes that a direct causal connection X→Y produces a probabilistic dependency, at least if competing causal X-Y connections are absent—in sec. 6.7.8 this is called the "productivity axiom." The argument in b(i) is a consequence of the same axiom and the fact that probabilistic dependencies are symmetric. The argument in a(ii) and b(ii)—that in the subdomain of high X-values high Z-values cause high Y-values—relies on the productivity axiom and the causal Markov condition (sec. 6.7.8): Y's probability, conditional on its causal parents, is not changed by conditionalizing on non-effects of Y.

(6.7–8) *Explaining linking-up in terms of common effects* (X→Z←Y): We assume that the probabilistic dependencies are monotonically positive. Then high X-values cause high Z-values. But these high Z-values do not influence the Y-values, because value-changes are only propagated *along* the causal arrows, but never from effects to their causes. So no probabilistic dependence of Y on X is produced by the common effect structure, and since X and Y are otherwise causally unconnected, they must be probabilistically independent (this is an instance of the "causal connection axiom" of sec. 6.7.8).

The explanation of the emergence of a probabilistic X-Y dependence conditional on fixed Z-values works as in the Sun-tower-shadow example.[11]

Note finally that two independent variables X and Y may not only be linked-up by common effects, but also by effects of common effects, as in the causal structure of fig. 6.7–2.

$$Z'$$
$$\uparrow$$
$$X \rightarrow Z \leftarrow Y$$

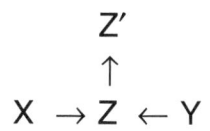

Figure 6.7–2 Linking-up: X and Y are linked-up by Z and by Z'

6.7.8 *Axioms of Causality: C-connection, Productivity and Faithfulness*

The given justification of causality as the best explanation of screening-off and linking-up leads exactly to the axioms of causality which have been stated in equivalent ways by Spirtes, Glymour and Scheines (2000) and Pearl (2009). What is new here is our justification of the axioms by an inference to the best explanation of screening-off and linking-up, and our results on their empirical content (sec. 6.7.9). To explicate these axioms we must first introduce certain notions from the theory of causal graphs. A *causal graph* or causal *structure* is a pair (V,E), where V is a set of variables $X_1,...,X_i,...$ (the "vertices"), and E is a set of directed arrows $X_i \rightarrow X_j$ (the "edges" or ordered pairs, $E \subseteq V \times V$). A graph (V,E) together with a probability distribution p over V is called a *causal model* or *system*, (V,E,p). We understand causal structures and systems as parts of the world, while causal graphs (CGs) and models (CMs) are conceptual representations of causal structures and systems, respectively. Further important notions (where $X \neq Y \neq Z$, $X_1 \neq X_n$, and the two paths attaching to Z are disjoint):

- X→Y: X is a direct cause of Y (Y is a direct effect of X).
- X→→Y: X is a (direct or indirect) cause of Y (Y is an effect of X), i.e. there is a *directed path* $X \rightarrow Z_1 \rightarrow ... \rightarrow Z_n \rightarrow Y$ from X to Y.
- X–Y: X→Y or X←Y, i.e. X and Y are adjacent.
- X_1—X_n: an (undirected) *path* $X_1 - ... - X_{n-1} - X_n$ between X_1 and X_n; we say that this path *connects* X_1 and X_n, and that X_i *lies* on this path.
- X→→Z→→Y or X←←Z←←Y: Z is an *intermediate cause* (between X and Y).
- X←←Z→→Y: Z is a *common cause* (of X and Y).
- Y→→Z←←X: Z is a *common effect* (of X and Y).

The first core axiom of the general theory of causality GTC as developed in Schurz/Gebharter (2013) says that every probabilistic dependency is the result of some causal connection. It is defined as follows: ("−" for set-theoretic difference):

(Def. 6.7–1) *Causal connection axiom (C)—GTC's first core axiom:*

A causal model (V,E,p) satisfies axiom (C) *iff* for all variables X,Y in V and subsets V' ⊆ V−{X,Y}:

If DEP(X,Y|V'), then X and Y are *causally connected* (in short: "*c-connected*") by V' in the following sense:

X and Y are connected by some path π such that no intermediate or common cause on π is in V', while every common effect on π is in V' or has an effect in V' (we say in this case that X and Y are c-connected by V' *via* π).

If X and Y are not *c*-connected by V', X and Y are said to be *c-separated* by V'. Our notions of c-connection/separation are identical with the notions of d-connection/separation that go back to Pearl (1988) and were adopted by Spirtes et al. (2000, sec. 2.3.4). We prefer "*c*" for "causal" over Pearl's "*d*" for "directed" because this avoids misunderstandings: that X and Y are c-connected via path π does not imply that π is a directed path.

Axiom (C) asserts that every probabilistic dependence is the result of some causal connection. Its formulation takes into account all possible combinations of screening-off and linking-up phenomena, the archetypes of which are illustrated in fig. 6.7–3. In fig. 6.7–3(a), X and Y are connected by one path: this path generates probabilistic dependence conditional on a subset V' of variables only if *no* common or intermediate cause on this path is in V' and *all* common effects on this path are in V' or have an effect in V'. So we have DEP(X,Y|E) and DEP(X,Y|Z), but INDEP(X,Y|V'), when $M \in V'$ or $C \in V'$ or ($E \notin V'$ and $Z \notin V'$). In fig. 6.7–3(b) and (c), X and Y are connected by two paths. In this case they are probabilistically dependent iff at least one of these paths generates a probabilistic dependence. So in fig. 3(b) X and Y are screened off only when conditioning on both of their common causes, and in (c) X and Y become dependent by conditioning on at least one of their common effects.

Axiom (C) entails that unconditional dependence implies causal connection simpliciter, i.e. c-connection by ∅. Moreover, it implies the phenomena of screening-off and linking-up as explained in the last section.

A CG (causal graph) (V,E) is *acyclic* if it contains no cyclic path (i.e. a path of the form X→Y_1→...→Y_n→X). Under the assumption that causation is forward-directed in time, cyclic CGs are impossible. Cyclic CGs are nevertheless important for causal relations between simultaneous properties of stationary systems (recall sec. 6.7.2), especially of *self-regulatory* systems containing feedback loops (e.g., outside temperature

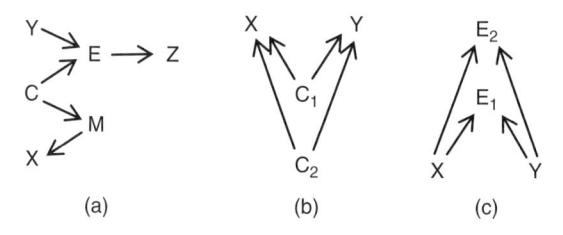

Figure 6.7–3 Three combinations of screening-off and linking-up

→ room-temperature ⇄ thermostat). We agree with Spirtes et al. (2000, sec. 12.1.2) that condition (C) is also reasonable for cyclic graphs; we therefore do not restrict GTC to acyclic CGs.

For acyclic CGs, axiom (C) is provably equivalent with the following two well-known conditions which are labeled after Markov. In def. 6.7-2 "par(X)" denotes the set of direct causes ("parents") of X. We write "INDEP(X,V|Z)" *iff* INDEP(X,v|Z) holds for *all* value instantiations v of the variables in V (i.e. v = $(z_1,...,z_n) \in Val(Z_1)\times...\times Val(Z_n)$).

(Def. 6.7-2) *Causal Markov condition (cM) and Markov-compatibility (Mc)* (Pearl 2009, 16, 19; Spirtes et al. 2000, sec. 2.3.1, 3.4.1):

1. (V,E,p) satisfies (cM) *iff* INDEP(X,V'|par(X)) holds for every set V' ⊆ V of non-effects of X.
2. A finite CM ($\{X_1, ...,X_n\}$,E,p) satisfies (Mc) *iff* $p(X_1,...,X_n) = \Pi_{1 \leq i \leq n} p(X_i|par(X_i))$.

(Prop. 6.7-2) For every acyclic finite CM: (C), (cM), and (Mc) are pairwise equivalent.[12]

We understand (C) as a *synthetic* axiom that holds for (almost) all physically possible worlds or physically closed systems. Moreover, (C) provably holds for every subsystem of a (C)-satisfying causal system that is *causally sufficient*, i.e. one that contains every common cause of variables it contains (cf. Spirtes et al. 2000, 22). Because causal structures and probability distributions depend on contingent conditions and may change over time, we apply (C) not only to actual, but also to physically possible systems.

Various objections against condition (C) or the equivalent causal Markov condition have been raised. Most of these objections are convincingly resolved in Spirtes et al. (2000, sec. 3.5.1). We recapitulate three important arguments:

1 *Interactive forks:* They describe situations in which a common cause C has two simultaneously correlated effects E and E', and these effects are not fully screened off from each other. But in all given examples it turns out that either (a) by more fine-grained specification C* of the

common cause, or (b) by finding a more proximate common cause C* that intervenes between C and {E,E'}, the screening-off can be restored. Salmon's "counter-example" in (1984, 168ff) about the two pool balls entering opposite holes is of kind (a), and Cartwright's (2007) counter-example—which is discussed below—is of kind (b). The only problematic cases for axiom (C) are EPR-correlations in quantum mechanics (recall sec. 6.7.5): but even here, what is violated is not the causal connection principle itself, but only its combination with the physical *locality* assumption, which says that no causal arrow can propagate an influence with a speed greater than the velocity of light.

2 *Time series:* This counter-example of Sober (1988) assumes two independent causal systems that produce a continuous increase of two variables X and Y at successive time points t_1, t_2, ... An example is the sea level X at various places in Venice and the bread price Y in various shops in London. We have INDEP(X_t,Y_t) at each given time point t, but when we unite the populations over all time points we get a probabilistic X-Y-dependence that seems to be causally unexplained. However, a (C)-compatible explanation is possible by considering the causal systems that produce the steady increases of X and Y, with help of certain "influx-outflux" mechanisms represented by variables F_X and F_Y (F_X would be the demand for bread, and F_Y the amount of water in the Adriatic sea). Throughout the considered time interval the values of F_X and F_Y have been fixed to certain values which lead to a continuous increase of X and Y. If the influx variables F_X and F_Y are allowed to vary, the correlation will break down, because the two are causally independent from each other.

3 Non-causal *dependency relations:* A causal interpretation of arrows is only justified if the variables in V are pairwise analytically independent. If two variables are analytically dependent, then the c-connections that are (C)-entailed by probabilistic dependences will not be causal, but analytical. Hitchcock (2010, sec. 2.3, 2.10) gives an example of two binary variables defined in terms of three independent binary items as follows: $F = B_1 \wedge B_2$ and $G = B_2 \wedge B_3$. Then DEP(F,G) holds and F and G are "c"-connected for analytic reasons.

As explained, axiom (C) entails that probabilistic dependence implies c-connections. But (C) does not entail the converse implication, which is called faithfulness (Spirtes et al. 2000, sec. 3.4.3). We define faithfulness as follows:

> (Def. 6.7-3) *Faithfulness condition (F)*: A causal model (V,E,p) satisfies (F) iff it satisfies the converse of (C), i.e.: if X and Y are c-connected by $V' \subseteq V-\{X,Y\}$, then DEP(X,Y|V').

In other words, a CM (causal model) is faithful iff its probability distribution p contains only those independence relations that are entailed by (C). Spirtes et al. (ibid.) define "faithfulness" as the conjunction of (C) and our (F). We prefer our definition since it logically separates (F) from (C). Moreover, (F) does *not* belong to the core of GTC because it may be violated in exceptional cases. There is, however, a logical weakening of faithfulness which belongs to the core of GTC, the axiom of productivity, which is defined as follows:

> (Def. 6.7-4) *Productivity axiom (P)—GTC's second core axiom:*
> A causal model (V,E,p) satisfies axiom (P) *iff* for all $X,Y \in V$: If $X \to Y \in E$ and V' consists of all common and intermediate causes that lie on a path different from $X \to Y$ that connects X and Y, then DEP(X,Y|V').

Axiom (P) is known in the literature as the equivalent principle of *minimality*. A CM (V,E,p) is called *minimal* iff no arrow can be *omitted* from E without violating condition (C) (cf. Spirtes et al. 2000, 31). Schurz/Gebharter (2013, th.2) prove:

> (Prop. 6.7-3) For CMs without immediate causal cycles ($X \rightleftarrows Y$):
> a   Minimality and productivity (P) are equivalent.
> b   Faithfulness (F) implies minimality.

Woodward (2003, 53) assumes productivity, but not the stronger axiom of faithfulness. Axiom (P) guarantees that causal arrows have probabilistic effects, provided other possibly compensatory causal paths are blocked. In virtue of our weak Hume thesis for causality (prop. 6.7-1(iii)), axiom (P) and minimality hold true without exceptions. Faithfulness, however, may be violated in three kinds of exceptional cases.

An important kind of non-faithfulness is (1) *non-faithfulness because of compensation of influences*. This situation is given when X causally influences Y along at least two different paths, but in opposite ways, so that the positive and negative influences transported along these paths compensate each other exactly to zero. Fig. 6.7–4 depicts the situation.

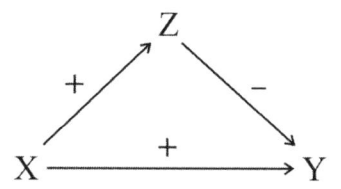

Figure 6.7–4 Non-faithfulness due to compensation of influences: INDEP(X,Y)

The X-Y-independence in fig. 6.7–4 vanishes when one conditionalizes on Z. An example is the "spurious independence" in fig. 4.4–3.

Two further kinds of non-faithfulness explained in Schurz/Gebharter (2013, sec. 3.4) are (2) non-faithfulness because of *non-transitivity*, and (3) non-faithfulness because of *deterministic dependence*.

An important feature of unfaithful CMs is that their spurious probabilistic independencies can be destroyed by minimal changes of their *parameters*, i.e. their conditional probability distributions $p(X_i|par(X_i))$, without violating condition (C). The parameters of acyclic CMs can be varied independently from each other without destroying the independencies that are entailed by (C).[13] A CM (V,E,P) that satisfies (C) is called *parameter-stable* iff it does not possess any probabilistic independencies INDEP(X,Y|V') that are lost by arbitrarily small changes of some of its parameters (Pearl 2009, 48, def. 2.4.1). Schurz/Gebharter (2013, th. 3) prove that faithfulness and parameter-stability are equivalent conditional on (C) (which is stated without proof by Pearl ibid.):[14]

(Prop. 6.7–4) A (C)-satisfying causal model (V,E,p) is faithful iff it is parameter-stable.

The fact that non-faithful models are parameter-unstable is of high philosophical importance. Hitchcock (2010, sec. 3.4) argued that faithfulness is a mere methodological principle. Contrary to this claim, the following physical assumption (N) implies that parameter-unstable CMs are ontologically rare.

(6.7-9) *Noise assumption (N)*: The parameters of causal structures in our world are usually modulated by a multitude of minor independent causal disturbances, so-called "noise"; these noise influences fluctuate more or less randomly over time.

Since minimal parameter changes are sufficient for turning a non-faithful into a faithful causal structure, (N) implies that the probability of finding a parameter-unstable causal structure is very small (cf. Spirtes et al. 2000, th. 3.2, 68f; Steel 2006, 313).

6.7.9 Causal Discovery

Most work in causal graph theory has been concerned with the problem how to infer from an empirically given probability distribution p over a set of variables V something about the underlying causal structure (V,E). This is the so-called "causal discovery problem." Oftentimes, the discovery problem leads to *empirical underdetermination*, i.e. an empirical probability distribution can be explained by more than one causal structure satisfying (C) and (P). The set of empirically equivalent causal models is significantly reduced if one assumes the condition of faithfulness. Important in this regard is the following result of Spirtes et al. (2000, sec. 5.4.1), which forms the basis of their causal discovery algorithm:

(Prop. 6.7–5) *Causal discovery algorithm:* If an (empirically given) distribution p is faithful over an acyclic and causally sufficient causal graph (V,E), then:

i X–Y holds in (V,E) iff DEP(X,Y|V') holds for every V' $\subseteq$ V–{X,Y}.
ii If X–Y–Z holds in (V,E), then X→Y←Z holds iff DEP(X,Z|V') holds for every V' $\subseteq$ V–{X,Z} containing Y.

On the basis of prop. 6.7–5 one can construct all (C)-satisfying, acyclic, sufficient and faithful causal graphs for any given probability distribution. These graphs are also called *strongly* statistically indistinguishable. In fig. 6.7–5 this is illustrated by an example from Pearl (2009, 15). The fact that only the left graph is causally correct follows from additional causal knowledge, e.g. about temporal direction.

In Search of Causes • 403

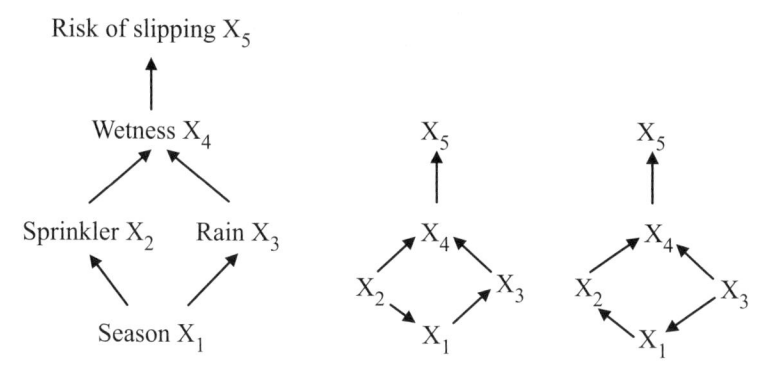

Figure 6.7–5 Three strongly statistically indistinguishable graphs

Spirtes et al. (2000, sec. 6.7) and Pearl (2009, 55, def. 2.7.1–2) also prove some discovery results about CGs which are *not* causally sufficient. Their results show that by embedding a set of variables in a larger *context* of variables—especially into a context of *intervention* variables in the sense of sec. 6.7.6—causal discovery procedures become more informative.

6.7.10 Empirical Content of GTC

In regard to the question of empirical content it is important to distinguish between (i) the empirical content of the general theory GTC and (ii) the empirical content of particular CMs of this theory. While GTC contains those causal principles that hold for all physically possible domains, particular CMs describe domain-specific applications of GTC (e.g. a causal weather model), thereby presupposing GTC. The distinction between GTC and particular CMs is analogous to the distinction between the general force-theory of physics and particular force-models such as a Sun-planet model.

Particular CMs clearly have empirical content, because they entail probabilistic independencies by principle (C). In this section we ask the philosophically "deeper" question of whether GTC has empirical content *itself*. Axioms (C) and (P) constitute the *core* of GTC. But there are further *general* principles, such as acyclicity, faithfulness (F), and temporal conditions. When added to GTC's core they generate *extended versions* of GTC, just as the addition of special force laws constitute extended versions of classical physics (recall sec. 5.2).

A version of GTC has empirical content *iff* it forbids some analytically possible empirical models. An *empirical model* is a pair (V_e, p_e), where V_e is a set of empirically measurable variables and p_e is a probability distribution over V_e. Here is the precise definition:

> (Def. 6.7-5) A version of GTC has empirical content *iff* there exists a logically possible empirical model (V_e, p_e) that is *excluded* by GTC, in the sense that it cannot be *expanded* into a causal GTC-model (V, E, p) such that $V_e \subseteq V$ and p_e is the restriction of p to V_e.

The question whether GTC has empirical content is highly significant. For if GTC had no empirical content, the content of all particular CMs would be entirely *post-facto*. For every empirical model (V_e, p_e) one could then invent a "causal explanation" in accordance with GTC, i.e. a GTC-model (V, E, p) that expands (V_e, p_e). In this case, one could never *predict* a new probabilistic (in)dependence R_{n+1} from already known (in)dependencies $R_1, \ldots, R_n$ via the construction of a GTC-model that verifies $R_1, \ldots, R_n$. For then, for every new R_{n+1} which is mathematically consistent with $R_1, \ldots, R_n$ one could find a GTC-model verifying $R_1, \ldots, R_n, R_{n+1}$. With the consequence that GTC would be nothing more than scientifically superfluous metaphysics.

Schurz/Gebharter (2013, th. 4) prove that, indeed, the core of GTC does not have empirical content, even when acyclicity is added:

> (Prop. 6.7-6) Every analytically possible empirical model (V_e, p_e) can be expanded into a minimal and acyclic CM (V, E, p) that satisfies axiom (C).

It is well known that philosophers have set up alleged counter-examples to axiom (C). How is this possible in the light of our result that (C) does not even have empirical content? The answer is that these authors presuppose independent causal knowledge. Consider Cartwright's alleged counter-example (2007, 122): A chemical X and a pollutant Y are always produced together by a chemical factory C, "but occur only for 80% of the time the production process is in place." Cartwright assumes that the causal system consists of the causal structure $X \leftarrow C \rightarrow Y$ together with a probability distribution including DEP(X,Y|C). So (C) seems to be violated. A defender of (C) must argue that the underlying causal structure is a different one. Based on knowledge about chemical processes, the most plausible causal structure is X←Z→Y, with C→Z, where Z is an intermediate reaction product which causes both X and Y, and occurs during 80% of the time the production process is in place. Since Z screens X off from Y, (C) is satisfied in this reconstruction.

Is it a problem that GTC's core is empirically empty? It seems not: empty theory cores are a rather typical situation for scientific theories. We have seen in sec. 5.2 that even the core of classical physics is empirically empty, but that the empirical content "explodes" if this core is conjoined with further general principles such as the law of gravitational force. A similar situation holds for GTC: Schurz/Gebharter (2013, th. 5) prove that GTC gets empirical content when the faithfulness condition (F) or the noise-condition (N) is added to GTC:

(Prop. 6.7-7)
a   Axioms (C) + (F) exclude empirical models with the following logically possible (in)dependencies: DEP(X,Y), DEP(Y,Z), INDEP(X,Z), and INDEP(X,Z|Y).
b   (C) + (N) make the above (in)dependencies highly improbable.

One advantage of the GTC approach to causality is that it yields the direction of causation independently from an assumed *direction of time*. This opens up the possibility of reducing the direction of time to the direction of causation between events in time—an idea that goes back to Reichenbach (1956, ch. IV). For this purpose it must be assumed that all causal processes point in the same temporal direction, which is defined as the direction "from the past to the future."

The assumption of temporal forward-directedness together with (C) + (F) excludes the possibility that two variables are screened off by a third variable which lies in the future of both, since otherwise at least one causal arrow would point from a future to a past event. To make this precise, we define a *causal event-model* (V,E,P,t) as a causal model (V,E,P) in which the variables are event-variables, together with a given time function t: V→ℝ, so that t(X) is the time point at which the possible X-values (events) x occur. Such a causal event-model satisfies condition *(T)* of *temporal forward-directedness iff* X→Y implies t(X) < t(Y). Schurz/Gebharter (2013, th. 6 and 7) prove:

(Prop. 6.7–8)
a   (C) + (F) + (T) entail that the following is impossible: two variables X, Y are screened off by a variable Z that is in the future of both.[15]
b   If (F) is not assumed, the result holds under the additional assumption that there is no variable Z' in the past of X and Z that screens them off.

Schurz/Gebharter (2013, th. 8) show that GTC's content is further enriched by the addition of *intervention assumptions*, according to which some variable I_X is an intervention variable for X in the sense explained in sec. 6.7.6.

6.7.11 From Variables to Events: Overdetermination and Causal Pre-emption

The explication of cause-effect relations between the values of variables (e.g. event-types) leads to additional complications. Intuitively, the right definition seems to be this:

(Def. 6.7–6) Assume a causal model (V,E,p) satisfying (C) + (P) together with an actual *context* c, in which all variables Z in V take the *actual* values z_c. Then x_c is a *positive cause* of y_c in context c iff (i) X is a cause of Y in (V,E) and (ii) x_c increases the probability of y_c, given all other variables that are non-effects of X are fixed to their actual value.

Consider the deterministic common effect structure X→Z←Y with *binary* variables X, Y, Z. If we apply def. (6.7–6) to this structure, then depending on the *kind of interaction* between the two causes X and Y, we obtain the following causal arrows between the $2^3 = 8$ possible value instantiations of these variables displayed in fig. 6.7–6.

Situation (A) of a disjunctive interaction is also called *causal overdetermination*. According to def. 6.7–6, in situation (A) the event X=1 has only a causal influence on Z=1 in a context when the second possible cause is off, i.e. when Y=0, since p(Z=1|X=1, Y=1) = p(Z=1|Y=1) = 1, so X=1 cannot further increase the probability of Z=1. Intuitively,

Deterministic causal graph with binary variables:

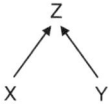

```
      Z
     ↗ ↖
    X   Y
```

Related causal graphs of values (events):
(A) Disjunctive interaction (+X∨+Y→ +Z) – causal overdetermination:

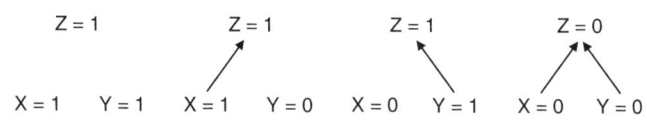

```
  Z = 1        Z = 1        Z = 1        Z = 0
   ↗            ↗            ↖            ↗ ↖
X = 1  Y = 1  X = 1  Y = 0  X = 0  Y = 1  X = 0  Y = 0
```

(B) Conjunctive interaction (+X∧+Y→+Z):

```
  Z = 1        Z = 0        Z = 0        Z = 0
   ↗ ↖          ↖            ↗
X = 1  Y = 1  X = 1  Y = 0  X = 0  Y = 1  X = 0  Y = 0
```

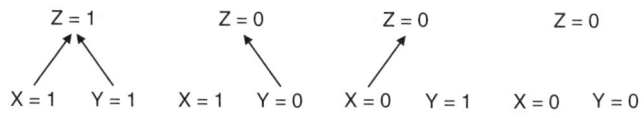

Figure 6.7–6 Causal graph of variables and related graphs of values

however, one would be inclined to say that in a situation of causal overdetermination, *both* causes are influencing the effect Z=1.

Moreover, def. 6.7–6 cannot discriminate between the situation of causal overdetermination and that of *causal pre-emption*, in which one of the two causes, say X=1, comes *first* and thereby blocks the second cause Y=1, even if it is "on." A popular example is a shooting scenario in which bullets (X,Y) are targeted at a person and cause his death (Z). In the case of overdetermination both bullets hit the person simultaneously, while in the case of causal pre-emption bullet no. 1 hits the person first (Haussman 1998, 49–52; Lewis 1973a/1986). Because of these problems, alternative definitions have been developed that fix the remaining variables not to their actual, but to merely possible, values. However, these alternative definitions have problems of their own, and the debate is still ongoing (Hitchcock 2009, 311–313; Woodward 2003, 74ff).

6.8 Introductory Literature and Exercises

6.8.1 *Introductory Literature*

Introductions to Hempel's explanation models are provided by Hempel (1965b, 1977) and Stegmüller (1969ff, vol. I). For overviews on explanation see Salmon (1989), Schurz (1996a) and Psillos (2002). Manninen/Tuomela (1976) is a reader on the explanation of human action. More on the problem of lawlikeness can be found in Armstrong (1983), Earman (1986), van Fraassen (1989) and Maudlin (2007). Introductions to causality are Woodward (2003), Spirtes et al. (2000) and Pearl (2009); Beebee et al. (2009) is a comprehensive handbook.

6.8.2 Questions and Exercises

Sec. 6.1–2

1. Recapitulate the conditions of Hempel's DN-explanation model.
2. Consider the following arguments (the law hypotheses are omitted): (a) Peter came because he wanted to come and see me. (b) Peter will come because he said to me "I will come." (c) Peter will come because he wants to come and see me. (d) Peter wanted to come to me because he came to see me. (e) Peter will come because I believe this.—Which of these arguments provides a justification, which a prediction and which a retrodiction? Which provide an (actual) explanation and which a potential explanation?
3. (a) Which kinds of DN-justifications exist that are not DN-explanations?
   (b) Which DN-explanations cannot function as DN-predictions or DN-justifications?
   Give an example in each case.

Sec. 6.3–4

1. Recapitulate Hempel's IS-model of explanation.
2. Consider the following IS-explanation (law premise omitted): "Mr. Mueller died because he was 82 years old." What does my background knowledge have to be like for the explanation to be maximally specific for me?
3. Someone predicts: "Mr. Mueller will soon die because he is 82 years old." Thereupon someone counters "But Mr. Mueller is in the best of health!" Explain the non-monotony of IS-arguments by referring to this example.
4. Give examples of probability-decreasing explanations in the sense of Salmon.
5. Explain the hermeneutic principle of charity. Give an example.

Sec. 6.6-7

1. Explain the connection between lawlikeness i.w.s. and counterfactual conditionals using an example.
2. Are the following counterfactual conditionals true? Explain the problem of closeness relations between possible worlds in the context of this question. (a) If Verdi and Bizet were countrymen, Verdi would be French (Quine's example). (b) If I could float free in the air, there would be no gravitation.
3. Which of the following sentences is spatiotemporally universal and which fulfills Maxwell's condition: (a) All apples are green. (b) All apples in Goodman's barn are blue. (c) All apples are green except for the apples in Goodman's barn which are blue.
4. Which of the following sentences is physically necessary and which is contingent? (a) Our universe contains energy. (b) Our universe contains life. (c) Life consumes entropy. (d) Life is based on DNA.
5. Explain the interventionist account of causation and its problems.
6. Explain the causal connection and the productivity axioms.
7. Assume that the *only* (conditional or unconditional) independence relation satisfied by a probability distribution p over three variables X, Y, Z is INDEP(X,Y). Which is the only Markov-compatible and faithful causal graph over {X,Y,Z} that generates p? Which alternative Markov-compatible but non-faithful causal graph generates p?
8. What is understood by causal pre-emption and what by causal over-determination? Give an example of each.

Notes

1. We speak of background "system" instead of "knowledge" because in epistemology "knowledge" is meant to entail "truth", but scientific "knowledge" is fallible.
2. Cf. Nagel (1961, 79ff), Friedman (1990), Alston (1971, 14).
3. a may also be sequence of constants. Ax results from Aa by replacing "a" by "x".
4. $p(Ex|Ax)$ is not a true single case propensity, but a repeatable statistical probability (sec. 3.13.3).
5. Another unsuccessful attempt to explicate the rational explanation of actions without covering laws is von Wright's *practical syllogism* (1971); for critical discussion cf. Manninen/Tuomela (1976), 183-207, 335-368.
6. Cf. Stegmüller (1969ff, vol. I, 70), Scriven (1959a, sec. 3), Kutschera (1972, 331).
7. This insight has been stressed by many authors (e.g. Rescher 1964; Stegmüller 1969ff, vol. I 2nd ed., sec. V.7; Woodward 2002, 134), including Lewis (1973b, 163f).
8. Cf. Ramsey (1931,138), Lewis (1973b, 73; 1986b, 124), Earman (1986, 88). In (1994, 480), Lewis extends this explication to include propensity laws; they don't entail truths but should make them as probable as possible.
9. Cf. Reichenbach (1956, 136ff) and more recently Savitt (1996, 353), Albert (2000), Frisch (2007).
10. This definition follows Spirtes et al. (2000, 50), who call I_X a "policy variable". Woodward's definition (2003, 98) is more complicated.

11. Often X and Y become dependent only when one conditionalizes on *certain* values of Z. For example, if X and Y are binary (±) positive causes which combine disjunctively, we have DEP(Y=1,X=0|Z=1); if they combine conjunctively, we have DEP(Y=0,X=1|Z=0).
12. *Proof:* For (C) ⇔(cM) cf. Geiger *et al.* (1990), Spirtes et al. (2000, 44); for (cM) ⇔(Mc) cf. Pearl (1988, 20; 2009, 19).
13. For cyclic CMs, Markov-compatibility (def. 6.7-2(2)) does not hold, whence not all parameters can be varied independently of each other.
14. Direction ⇐ of prop. 6.7-4 is only proved for acyclic CMs and is a conjecture for cyclic CMs.
15. A more complicated impossibility result is proved for linking-up by past events.

BIBLIOGRAPHY

Achinstein, P. (1968): *Concepts of Science*, Johns Hopkins Press, Baltimore, MD.
Adam, M. (2004): "Why Worry About Theory-Dependence?," *International Studies in the Philosophy of Science* 18, 117–132.
Adams, E. W. (1975): *The Logic of Conditionals*, Reidel, Dordrecht.
Adorno, T. W., Albert, H., Dahrendorf, R., Habermas, J., Pilot, H., and Popper, K. (1976): *The Positivist Dispute in German Sociology*, Harper & Row, New York (German original 1969).
Albert, D. (2000): *Time and Chance*, Harvard University Press, Cambridge, MA.
Albert, H. (1985): *Treatise on Critical Reason*, Princeton University Press, Princeton, NJ.
Albert, H. and Topitsch, E. (1971): *Werturteilsstreit*, Wissenschaftliche Buchgesellschaft, Darmstadt.
Alston, W. P. (1971): "The Place of the Explanation of Particular Facts in Science," *Philosophy of Science* 38, 13–34.
Anderson, A. R., and Belnap, N. D. (1975): *Entailment: The Logic of Relevance and Necessity*, Princeton University Press, Princeton, NJ.
Anderson, J. R. (2000): *Cognitive Psychology and Its Implications* (5th ed.), Freeman and Co., New York.
Andreas, H. (2010): "New Account of Empirical Claims in Structuralism," *Synthese* 176, 311–332.
Apel, K.-O. (1984): *Understanding and Explanation: A Transcendental-Pragmatic Perspective*, MIT Press, Cambridge, MA.
Aqvist, L. (1984): "Deontic Logic," in Gabbay and Guenthner (1984, eds.), *Handbook of Philosophical Logic. Vol II,* Reidel, Dordrecht, 605–714.
Armstrong, D. M. (1983): *What Is a Law of Nature?*, Cambridge University Press, Cambridge.
Armstrong, D. M. (1989): *Universals. An Opinionated Introduction*, Westview Press, Boulder, CO.

Armstrong, D. M., Martin, C. B., and Place, U. T. (1996): *Dispositions*, Routledge, London.
Arnold, E. (2010): "Can the Best-Alternative-Justification Solve Hume's Problem? On the Limits of a Promising Approach," *Philosophy of Science* 77, 584–593.
Ausubel, D. et al. (1978): *Educational Psychology: A Cognitive View*, Holt, New York.
Ayer, A. J. (1956): *The Problem of Knowledge*, Penguin Books, Harmondsworth.
Bacchus, F. (1990): *Representing and Reasoning with Probabilistic Knowledge*, MIT Press, Cambridge, MA.
Balzer, W. (1985a): "On a New Definition of Theoreticity," *Dialectica* 39, 127–145.
Balzer, W. (1985b): *Theorie und Messung*, Springer, Berlin.
Balzer, W., and Moulines, W. (1980): "On Theoreticity," *Synthese* 44, 467–494.
Balzer, W., and Mühlhölzer, F. (1982): "Klassische Stoßmechanik," *Zeitschrift für Allgemeine Wissenschaftstheorie* 13, 22–39.
Balzer, W., Moulines, C. U., and Sneed, J. D. (1987): *An Architectonic for Science*, Reidel, Dordrecht.
Balzer, W., and Moulines, U. (1996, eds.): *The Structuralist Theory of Science*, W. de Gruyter, New York.
Bauer, H. (1996): *Probability Theory* (transl. by R. Burckel), de Gruyter, Berlin.
Bayes, T. (1763): "An Essay Towards Solving a Problem in the Doctrine of Chances," *Philosophical Transactions of the Royal Society of London* 53, 370–418.
Bechtel, W. (1988): *Philosophy of Science. An Overview for Cognitive Science*, Lawrence Erlbaum Associates, Hillsdale, NJ.
Bechtel, W., and Abrahamsen, A. (2005): "Explanation: A Mechanistic Alternative," *Studies in the History and Philosophy of Biology and Biomedical Sciences* 36, 421–441.
Beebee, H., Hitchcock, C., and Menzies, P. (2009, eds.): *The Oxford Handbook of Causation*, Oxford University Press, Oxford.
Bergmann, M., Moor, J., and Nelson, J. (1998): *The Logic Book*, McGraw-Hill, New York.
Berlin, B., and Kay, P. (1999): *Basic Colour Terms: Their Universality and Evolution*, CSLI Publications, Stanford (Orig. 1969).
Bernstein, R. J. (2001): *The Pragmatic Turn*, Wiley, New York.
Billingsley, P. (1995): *Probability and Measure* (3rd ed.), John Wiley & Sons, New York.
Bird, A. (1998): *Philosophy of Science*, UCL Press (2nd ed., Routledge, 2002).
Bird, A. (2007): *Nature's Metaphysics*, Clarendon Press, Oxford.
Bishop, M. A., and Trout, J. D. (2005): *Epistemology and the Psychology of Human Judgment*, Oxford University Press, Oxford.
Black, M. (1974): "Self-Supporting Inductive Arguments (1)," in: Swinburne (ed., 1974), 127–134.
Böhler, D., Nordenstam, T., and Skirbekk, G. (1986): *Die pragmatische Wende*, Suhrkamp, Frankfurt am Main.
Boogerd, F. C., Bruggeman, F. J., Richardson, R. C., Stephan, A., and Westerhoff, H. V. (2005): "Emergence and its Place in Nature: A Case Study of Biochemical Networks," *Synthese* 145, 131–164.
Bortz, J. (1985): *Lehrbuch der Statistik* (2nd ed.), Springer, Berlin (6th ed. 2005).
Bourbaki, N. (1961): *Topologie Générale*, Hermann, Paris.

Bovens, L., and Hartmann, S. (2003): *Bayesian Epistemology*, Oxford University Press, Oxford.
Boyd, R. (1984): "The Current Status of Scientific Realism," in: Leplin (ed., 1984), 41–82.
Brainerd, C. (1978): *Piaget's Theory of Intelligence*, Prentice-Hall, Englewood Cliffs, NJ.
Braithwaite, R. B. (1953): *Scientific Explanation*, Cambridge University Press, Cambridge.
Braithwaite, R. B. (1974): "The Predictionist Justification of Induction," in: Swinburne (ed., 1974), 102–126.
Branch, G. (2011): "Introduction," *Synthese* 178/2, 171–176.
Brewer, W. F., and Lambert, B. L. (2001): "The Theory-Ladenness of Observation and the Theory-Ladenness of the Rest of the Scientific Process," *Philosophy of Science* 68 (Proceedings), S176–S186.
Brewka, G. (1991): *Nonmonotonic Reasoning. Logical Foundations of Commonsense*, Cambridge University Press, Cambridge.
Bridgeman, P. W. (1936): *The Nature of Physical Theory*, Princeton University Press, Princeton, NJ.
Broad, C. D. (1925): *The Mind and Its Place in Nature*, Trubner & Co, London.
Bromberger, S. (1965): "An Approach to Explanation," in: R. J. Butler (ed.), *Analytical Philosophy* (Second Series), Oxford, 72–105.
Bromberger, S. (1966): "Why-Questions," in: R. Colodny (ed.), *Mind and Cosmos*, University of Pittsburgh Press, Pittsburgh, 86–111.
Brown, H. I. (1993): "A Theory-Laden Observation Can Test the Theory," *British Journal for the Philosophy of Science* 44, 555–559.
Brown, J. R. (2008): "The Community of Science," in: M. Carrier et al. (eds.), 189–215.
Bruns, G. (1992): *Hermeneutics: Ancient and Modern*, Yale University Press, New Haven, CT.
Bueno, O. (1997): "Empirical Adequacy: a Partial Structures Approach," *Studies in History and Philosophy of Science* 28/4, 585–610.
Bueno, O., French, S., and Ladyman, J. (2002): "On Representing the Relationship between the Mathematical and the Empirical," *Philosophy of Science* 69, 452–473.
Bühler, A. (2003, ed.): *Hermeneutik*, Synchron, Heidelberg.
Bühler, C., and Allen, M. (1973): "Introduction to Humanistic Psychology," Brooks, Cole Publishing Co., Belmont, CA.
Bunge, M. (1967): *Scientific Research, Vol. I+II*, Springer, Berlin.
Bunge, M. (1974): *Semantics I: Sense and Reference*, Reidel, Dordrecht.
Campbell, D. T. (1984): "Evolutionary Epistemology," in: G. Radnitzky, G. and W. W. Bartley III, (eds.), *Evolutionary Epistemology, Rationality, and the Sociology of Knowledge*, Open Court, La Salle, IL.
Campbell, S., and Franklin, J. (2004): "Randomness and the Justification of Induction," *Synthese* 138, 79–99.
Carnap, R. (1928a): *The Logical Structure of the World*, in: Carnap (2003), 5–300.
Carnap, R. (1928b): *Pseudoproblems in Philosophy*, in: Carnap (2003), 301–343.
Carnap, R. (1932/33): "On Protocol Sentences," *Nous* 21, 1987, 457–470: Engl. transl. of "Über Protokollsätze," *Erkenntnis* 3, 215–228.
Carnap, R. (1936/37): "Testability and Meaning," *Philosophy of Science*, Vol 3, 419–471 and Vol 4, 2–40 (independently published with New Haven 1954).
Carnap, R. (1937): *The Logical Syntax of Language*, Routledge & Kegan Paul, London.

Carnap, R. (1939): "The Interpretation of Physics," in: Carnap (1967), 56–69.
Carnap, R. (1947): "On the Application of Inductive Logic," *Philosophy and Phenomenological Research* 8, 133–147.
Carnap, R. (1950a): "Empiricism, Semantics and Ontology," *Revue Intern. de Phil.* 4, 20–40; reprinted in Carnap (1956b), 205–221 (pages quoted hereafter).
Carnap, R. (1950b): *Logical Foundations of Probability*, University of Chicago Press, Chicago.
Carnap, R. (1956a): "The Methodological Character of Theoretical Concepts," in: H. Feigl, and M. Scriven (eds.), *Minnesota Studies in the Philosophy of Science Vol. I*, University of Minnesota Press, Minneapolis, 38–76.
Carnap, R. (1956b): *Meaning and Necessity*, University of Chicago Press, Chicago (1st ed. 1947).
Carnap, R. (1958/75): "Observation Language and Theoretical Language," in: J. Hintikka (ed.), *Rudolf Carnap, Logical Empiricist*, Reidel, Dordrecht (German original in *Dialectica* 12, 1958).
Carnap, R. (1963): "Carl G. Hempel on Scientific Theories," in: P. A. Schilpp (ed.), *The Philosophy of Rudolf Carnap*, La Salle, 958–965.
Carnap, R. (1966): *Philosophical Foundations of Physics*, Basic Books, New York.
Carnap, R. (1967): *Foundations of Logic and Mathematics*, University of Chicago Press, Chicago (Orig. 1939).
Carnap, R. (1971): "Inductive Logic and Rational Decisions," and "A Basic System of Inductive Logic, Part I," in: Carnap/Jeffrey (1971), ch. 1 and 2.
Carnap, R. (2003): *The Logical Structure of the World and Pseudoproblems in Philosophy*, Open Court, Chicago, IL.
Carnap, R. and Jeffrey, R. (1971, eds.): *Studies in Inductive Logic and Probability*, University of California Press, Berkeley.
Carrier, M. (2003): "Experimental Success and the Revelation of Reality: The Miracle Argument for Scientific Realism," in: P. Blanchard et al. (eds.), *Science, Society and Reality*, Springer, Heidelberg.
Carrier, M., Howard, D., and Kourany, J. (2008, eds.): *The Challenge of the Social and the Pressure of Practice. Science and Values Revisited*, University of Pittsburgh Press, Pittsburgh.
Cartwright, N. (1979): "Causal Laws and Effective Strategies," *Nous* 13, 419–437.
Cartwright, N. (1983): *How the Laws of Physics Lie*, Clarendon Press, Oxford.
Cartwright, N. (1989): *Nature's Capacities and their Measurement*, Clarendon Press, Oxford.
Cartwright, N. (2007): *Hunting Causes and Using Them*, Cambridge University Press, New York.
Causey, R. (1977): *The Unity of Science*, Reidel, Dordrecht.
Cevolani, G., Crupi, V., and Festa, R. (2011): "Verisimilitude and Belief Change for Conjunctive Theories," in: Kuipers/Schurz (eds.), 183–202.
Chakravartty, A. (2001): "The Semantic or Model-Theoretic View of Theories and Scientific Realism," *Synthese* 127, 325–345.
Chalmers, A. F. (1986): *What Is This Thing Called Science?*, University of Queensland Press, Queensland (2nd ed.).
Chisholm, R. M. (1946): "The *Contrary-to-Fact* Conditional," *Mind* 55, 289–307.
Christensen, D. (1990): "The Irrelevance of Bootstrapping," *Philosophy of Science* 57, 644–662.

Church, A. (1940): "On the Concept of a Random Sequence," *Journal of Symbolic Logic* 1, 40–41, 101–102.
Coffa, J. (1974): "Hempel's Ambiguity," *Synthese* 28, 141–163.
Cohen, J., and Callender, C. (2009): "A Better Best System Account of Lawhood," *Philosophical Studies* 145, 1–34.
Collingwood, R. G. (1940): *An Essay on Metaphysics*, Clarendon Press, Oxford.
Copi, I., Cohen, C., and McMahon, K. (2010): *Introduction to Logic* (14th ed.), Prentice Hall, Englewood Cliffs, NJ.
Craig, W. (1953): "On Axiomatizability Within a System," *Journal of Symbolic Logic* 18, 30–32.
Craig, W., and Vaught, R. L. (1951): "Finite Axiomatizibility Using Additional Predicates," *Journal of Symbolic Logic* 18, 30–32.
Cramér, H. (1946): *Mathematical Models of Statistics*, Princeton University Press, Princeton, NJ.
Crombie, A. (1959): *Augustine to Galileo*, Harvard University Press, Harvard.
Crupi, V., and Trentori, K. (2010): "Irrelevant Conjunction: Statement and Solution of a New Paradox," *Philosophy of Science* 77, 1–13.
Curd, M., and Cover, J. A. (1998, ed.): *Philosophy of Science*, Norton, New York.
Dahms, H.-J. (1994): *Positivismusstreit*, Suhrkamp, Frankfurt/M.
Dancy, J. (1985): *An Introduction to Contemporary Epistemology*, Basil Blackwell, Oxford.
Darden, L., and Craver, C. F. (2000): "Thinking About Mechanisms," *Philosophy of Science* 67/1, 1–25.
Davidson, D. (1970): "Mental Events," in: L. Foster, and J. W. Swanson (eds.), *Experience and Theory*, University of Massachusetts Press, Amherst, 79–101.
Davidson, D. (2001): *Inquiries into Truth and Interpretation* (2nd ed.), Oxford University Press, Oxford.
De Finetti, B. (1937): "Foresight: Its Logical Laws, Its Subjective Sources," reprinted in H. E. Kyburg and H. E. Smokler (eds.), *Studies in Subjective Probability*, Wiley, New York 1964, 93–158.
De Finetti, B. (1974): *Theory of Probability*, John Wiley, New York.
De Regt, H. (2006): "Wesley Salmon's Complementary Thesis: Causalism and Unificationism Reconciled?," *International Studies in the Philosophy of Science* 20/2, 129–147.
Demopoulos, W., and Friedman, M. (1985): "Critical Notice: Betrand Russell's *The Analysis of Matter*," *Philosophy of Science* 52, 621–639.
Denzin, N. K., and Lincoln, Y. S. (2000): *Handbook of Qualitative Research* (2nd ed.), Sage Publications, Thousand Oaks, CA.
Doppelt, G. (2007): "The Value Ladenness of Scientific Knowledge," in: Kincaid et al. (eds.), 188–217.
Douglas, H. (2000): "Inductive Risk and Values in Science," *Philosophy of Science* 67, 559–579.
Douven, I. (2002): "A New Solution to the Paradoxes of Rational Acceptability," *British Journal for the Philosophy of Science* 53, 391–410.
Dowe, P. (1992): "Wesley Salmon's Process Theory of Causality and the Conserved Quantity Theory," *Philosophy of Science* 59, 195–216.
Dowe, P. (2000): *Physical Causation*, New York, Cambridge University Press.
Dowe, P. (2009): "Causal Process Theories," in: Beebee et al. (eds.), 213–233.

Dray, W. (1957): *Laws and Explanation in History*, Oxford University Press, Oxford.
Ducasse, C. J. (1968): *Truth, Knowledge and Causation*, Routledge, New York.
Duhem, P. (1908/1991): *The Aim and Structure of Physical Theory*, Princeton University Press, Princeton, NJ.
Dupré, J. (2007): "Fact and Value," in: H. Kincaid et al. (eds.), 28–41.
Dürr, H. P. (1985): *Dreamtime. Concerning the Boundaries between Wilderness and Civilization*, Blackwell Publishers, Oxford.
Eagle, A. (2004): "Twenty-One Arguments Against Propensity Analyses of Probability," *Erkenntnis* 60, 371–416.
Earman, J. (1978): "The Universality of Laws," *Philosophy of Science* 45, 173–181.
Earman, J. (1986): *A Primer on Determinism*, Reidel, Dordrecht.
Earman, J. (1992): *Bayes or Bust? A Critical Examination of Bayesian Confirmation Theory*, MIT Press, Cambridge, MA.
Earman, J., Glymour, C., and Mitchell, S. (2002, eds.): *Ceteris Paribus Laws, Erkenntnis* 57, No. 3 (special issue).
Earman, J., and Roberts, J. (1999): "Ceteris Paribus, There Is No Problem of Provisos," *Synthese* 118, 439–478.
Eells, E. (1991): *Probabilistic Causality*, Cambridge University Press, New York.
Einstein, A., Podolski, B., and Rosen, N. (1935): "Can Quantum-Mechanical Description of Reality Be Considered Complete?," *Physical Review* 47, 777–780.
Estany, A. (2001): "The Thesis of Theory-Laden Observation in the Light of Cognitive Psychology," *Philosophy of Science* 68, 203–217.
Etchemendy, J. (1990): *The Concept of Logical Consequence*, Harvard University Press, Cambridge, MA.
Evans, J. St. B. (1982): *The Psychology of Deductive Reasoning*, Routledge & Kegan Paul, London.
Fair, D. (1979): "Causation and the Flow of Energy," *Erkenntnis* 14, 219–230.
Fales, E. (1990): *Causation and Universals*, London, Routledge.
Fara, M. (2006): "Dispositions," *Stanford Encyclopedia of Philosophy, (Spring 2006 Edition)*, E. N. Zalta (ed.), http://plato.stanford.edu/archives/spr2010/entries/dispositions/.
Feigl, H. (1970): "The Orthodox View of Theories: Remarks in Defense as well as Critique," in: *Minnesota Studies in the Philosophy of Science*, Vol IV, University of Minnesota Press, Minneaolis.
Feyerabend, P. (1975): *Against Method*, Verso, London (3rd ed. 1993, repr. 2002).
Feynman, R. P., Phillips, R., and Leighton, R. D. (2005): *The Feynman Lectures on Physics*, Vols I–III, Addison-Wesley Publ. Comp. (2nd ext ed.), London (orig. 1963).
Field, A. (2009): *Discovering Statistics Using SPSS* (3rd ed.), Sage, Los Angeles, CA.
Field, H. (1980): *Science without Numbers*, Princeton University Press, Princeton, NJ.
Fine, T. (1973): *Theories of Probability*, Academic Press, New York.
Firth, R. (1952): "Ethical Absolutism and the Ideal Observer," *Philosophy and Phenomenological Research* XII/3, 317–345.
Fisher, R. A. (1956): *Statistical Methods and Scientific Inference*, Hafner Press, New York (ext. ed. Oxford University Press 1995).
Fitelson, B. (1999): "The Plurality of Bayesian Confirmation Measures of Confirmation," *Philosophy of Science* 66, S362–S378 (Proceedings).
Flach, P., and Kakas, A. (2000, eds.): *Abduction and Induction*, Kluwer, Dordrecht.
Flanders, N. A. (1970): *Analysing Teaching Behavior*, Addison-Wesley, Reading, MA.

Flyvbjerg, B. (2006): "Five Misunderstandings about Case-Study," *Qualitative Inquiry* 12/2, 219–245.
Fodor, J. (1974): "Special Sciences, or the Disunity of Science as a Working Hypothesis," *Synthese* 28, 77–115.
Fodor, J. (1984): "Observation Reconsidered," *Philosophy of Science* 51, 23–43.
Fodor, J. (1990): *A Theory of Content*, MIT Press, Cambridge, MA.
Fodor, J. (1991): "You Can Fool Some of the People All of the Time," *Mind* 100: 19–34.
Foley, R. (1992): "The Epistemology of Belief and the Epistemology of Degrees of Belief," *American Philosophical Quarterly* 29/2, 111–121.
Follesdal, D. (1979): "Hermeneutics and the Hypothetico-Deductive Method," *Dialectica* 33, 319–336.
Forbes, E. G. (1983): "The Pre-discovery Observations of Uranus," in: G. Hunt (ed.), *Uranus and the Outer Planets*, Cambridge University Press, Cambridge, 67–79.
Forster, M., and Sober, E. (1994): "How to Tell when Simpler, More Unified, or Less Ad Hoc Theories will Provide More Accurate Predictions," *British Journal for the Philosophy of Science* 45, 1–35.
Frankena, W. K. (1963): *Ethics*, Prentice-Hall, Englewood Cliffs, NJ.
Frege, G. (1948): On "Sense and Reference," *The Philosophical Review* 57/3, 209–230 (German orig. 1892).
Frege, G. (1984): "Thought: A Logical Investigation," in: Frege, G., *Collected Papers on Mathematics, Logic, and Philosophy* (ed. B. McGuinness), Basil Blackwell, Oxford (German orig. 1918).
French, S. (2008): "The Structure of Theories," in: S. Psillos and M. Curd (eds.), *The Routledge Companion to Philosophy of Science*, Routledge, London and New York, 269–280.
French, S., and Ladyman, J. (2003): "Remodelling Structural Realism: Quantum Physics and the Metaphysics of Structure," *Synthese* 136, 31–56.
Friedman, M. (1974): "Explanation and Scientific Understanding," *Journal of Philosophy* 71, 5–19.
Frisby, D. (1972): "The Popper-Adorno Controversy. The Methodological Dispute in German Sociology," *Philosophy of the Social Sciences* 2, 105–119.
Frisch, M. (2007): "Causation, Counterfactuals and Entropy," in: H. Price and R. Corry (eds.), *Russell's Republic*, Oxford University Press, Oxford, 351–395.
Fumerton, R. A. (1980): "Induction and Reasoning to the Best Explanation," *Philosophy of Science* 47, 589–600.
Gabbay, D. M. et al. (1994, eds.): *Handbook of Logic in Artificial Intelligence, Vol. 3*, Clarendon Press, Oxford.
Gadamer, H. (1975/2005): *Truth and Method*, Continuum (2nd rev. ed.), London 2005 (German orig. 1975).
Gähde, U. (1983): *T-Theoretizität und Holismus*, Peter Lang, Frankfurt/M.
Gaifman, H., and Snir, M. (1982): "Probabilities Over Rich Languages," *Journal of Symbolic Logic* 47, 495–548.
Gärdenfors, P. (1976): "Relevance and Redundancy in Deductive Explanation," *Philosophy of Science* 43, 420–432.
Gärdenfors, P. (1980): "A Pragmatic Approach to Explanation," *Philosophy of Science* 47, 404–423.
Gärdenfors, P. (1988): *Knowledge in Flux*, MIT Press, Cambridge, MA.

Gardiner, P. (1952): *The Nature of Historical Explanation*, Oxford University Press, Oxford.
Garnham, A., and Oakhill, J. (1994): *Thinking and Reasoning*, Basil Blackwell, Oxford.
Garson, J. W. (2001): "Quantification in Modal Logic," in: D. Gabbay and F. Guenthner (eds.), *Handbook of Philosophical Logic*, 2nd edition, vol. 3, Reidel, Dordrecht, 267–323.
Geiger, D., Verma, T. S., and Pearl, J. (1990): "Identifying Independence in Bayesian Networks," *Networks* 20, 507–534.
Gemes, K. (1993): "Hypothetico-Deductivism, Content, and the Natural Axiomatization of Theories," *Philosophy of Science* 54, 477–487.
Gemes, K. (1994): "A New Theory of Content I: Basic Content," *Journal of Philosophical Logic*, 23, 595–620.
Gemes, K. (1998): "Hypothetico-Deductivism: The Current State of Play; The Criterion of Empirical Significance: Endgame," *Erkenntnis* 49, 1–20.
Gemes, K. (2007): "Verisimilitude and Content," *Synthese*, 154, 293–306.
Giddens, A. (1982): *Profiles and Critiques in Social Theory*, University of California Press, Berkeley.
Giere, R. (1988a): *Explaining Science*, University of Chicago Press, Chicago.
Giere, R. (1988b): "Laws, Theories, and Generalizations," in: A. Grünbaum and W. Salmon (eds.), *The Limitations of Deductivism*, University of California Press, Berkeley, 37–46.
Giere, R. (1999): *Science without Laws*, University of Chicago Press, Chicago.
Gijsbers, V. (2007): "Why Unification is Neither Necessary nor Sufficient for Explanation," *Philosophy of Science* 74, 481–500.
Gillies, D. (2000): *Philosophical Theories of Probability*, Routledge, London.
Glasersfeld, E. v. (1995): *Radical Constructivism*, Routledge, London.
Glennan, S. (2002): "Rethinking Mechanistic Causation," *Philosophy of Science* 9, S342–S353.
Glymour, C. (1980): "Hypothetico-Deductivism is Hopeless," *Philosophy of Science* 47, 322–325.
Glymour, C. (1981): *Theory and Evidence*, Princeton University Press, Princeton, NJ.
Glymour, C., Spirtes, P., and Scheines, R. (1991): "Causal Inference," *Erkenntnis* 35, 151–189.
Gödel, K. (1947): "What is Cantor's Continuum Problem?," *The American Mathematical Monthly* 54; reprinted in P. Benacerraf and H. Putnam (1964, eds.): *Philosophy of Mathematics*, Prentice Hall, Englewood Cliffs, NJ, 258–273 (quoted therefrom).
Godfrey-Smith, P. (2003): *Theory and Reality: An Introduction to the Philosophy of Science*, University of Chicago Press, Chicago.
Goldman, A. (1986): *Epistemology and Cognition*, Harvard University Press, Cambridge, MA.
Goldman, A. (1999): *Knowledge in a Social World*, Oxford University Press, Oxford.
Goldszmidt, M., and Pearl, J. (1996): "Qualitative Probabilities for Default Reasoning, Belief Revision and Causal Modeling," *Artificial Intelligence* 84, 57–112.
Good, I. J. (1983): *Good Thinking. The Foundations of Probability and its Applications*, University of Minnesota Press, Minneapolis.
Goodman, N. (1946): "A Query on Confirmation," *Journal of Philosophy* 44, 383–385.
Goodman, N. (1955): *Fact, Fiction and Forecast*, reprint: Harvard University Press, Cambridge, MA, 2005.

Bibliography • 419

Goodman, N. (1978): *Ways of Worldmaking*, Harvester Press, Hassocks/Sussex.
Grice, H. P. (1975): "Logic and Conversation," in: P. Cole and J. Morgan (eds.), *Syntax and Semantics* Vol. 3, Academic Press, New York, 41–58.
Grimes, T. R. (1990): "Truth, Content, and the Hypothetico-Deductive Method," *Philosophy of Science* 57, 514–522.
Grünbaum, A. (1963): "Temporally Asymmetric Principles, Parity between Explanation and Prediction, and Mechanism vs. Teleology," in: B. Baumrin (ed.), *Philosophy of Science. The Delaware Seminar. Vol. I*, John Wiley, New York, 57–96.
Grünbaum, A. (1969): "The Meaning of Time," in: N. Rescher (ed.), *Essays in Honor of C.G. Hempel*, Reidel, Dordrecht, 147–170.
Grünbaum, A. (1973): *Philosophical Problems of Space and Time* (2nd ed.), Reidel, Dordrecht.
Grünbaum, A. (1976): "Ad hoc Auxiliary Hypotheses and Falsificationism," *The British Journal for the Philosophy of Science* 27, 329–362.
Habermas, J. (1966): "Knowledge and Interest," *Inquiry* 9, 285–300.
Hacking, J. (1965): *On the Logic of Statistical Inference*, Cambridge University Press, Cambridge.
Hájek, A. (1999): "Fifteen Arguments against Hypothetical Frequentism," *Erkenntnis* 70, 211–235.
Halonen, I., and Hintikka, J. (2005): "Towards a Theory of the Process of Explanation," *Synthese* 143/1–2, 5–61.
Hanson, N. R. (1958): *Patterns of Discovery*, Cambridge University Press, Cambridge.
Hare, R. (1952): *The Language of Morals*, Oxford University Press, Oxford.
Harman, G. (1965): "The Inference to the Best Explanation," *Philosophical Review* 74, 88–95.
Harré, R. (1986): *Varieties of Realism*, Blackwell, Oxford.
Hart, W. D. (1996, ed.): *The Philosophy of Mathematics*, Oxford University Press, Oxford.
Haussman, D. (1998): *Causal Asymmetries*, Cambridge University Press, Cambridge.
Hawthorne, J. (2005): "Degree-of-Belief and Degree-of-Support: Why Bayesians Need Both Notions," *Mind* 114, 277–320.
Hawthorne, J., and Fitelson, B. (2004): "Re-Solving Irrelevant Conjunction with Probabilistic Independence," *Philosophy of Science* 71, 505–514.
Hays, W., and Winkler, R. (1970): *Statistics: Probability, Inference, and Decision*, Holt, New York (2nd ed. 1975).
Helmholtz, H. von (1896/1910): *Treatise on Physiological Optics* (German orig. 1896) (http://poseidon.sunyopt.edu/BackusLab/Helmholtz/).
Hempel, C. G. (1942): "The Function of General Laws in History," *The Journal of Philosophy* 39; reprinted in Hempel (1965b), 231–243 (quoted therefrom).
Hempel, C. G. (1945): "Studies in the Logic of Confirmation," *Mind* 54, reprinted in Hempel (1965b), 3–51 (quoted therefrom).
Hempel, C. G. (1951): "The Concept of Cognitive Significance: A Reconsideration," *Proceedings of the American Academy of Arts and Sciences* 80; reprinted in Hempel (1965b), ch. II.1 (quoted therefrom).
Hempel, C. G. (1958): "The Theoretician's Dilemma. Studies in the Logic of Theory Construction," in: H. Feigl, M. Scriven, and G. Maxwell (eds.), *Minnesota Studies in the Philosophy of Science 2*; reprinted in Hempel (1965b), 173–228 (quoted therefrom).
Hempel, C. G. (1962): "Deductive-Nomological versus Statistical Explanation," in: H.

Feigl and G. Maxwell (eds.), *Minnesota Studies in the Philosophy of Science*, Vol. III, University of Minnesota Press.

Hempel, C. G. (1965a): "Science and Human Values," in: Hempel (1965b), 81–96.

Hempel, C. G. (1965b): *Aspects of Scientific Explanation and Other Essays in the Philosophy of Science*, Free Press, New York.

Hempel, C. G. (1966): *Philosophy of Natural Sciences*, Prentice Hall, Englewood Cliffs, NJ.

Hempel, C. G. (1968): "Maximal Specifity and Lawlikeness in Probabilistic Explanation," *Philosophy of Science* 35, 116–133.

Hempel, C. G. (1969): "Reduction: Ontological and Linguistic Facts," in: S. Morgenbesser (ed.), *Philosophy, Science, and Method*, St. Martin's Press, New York, 179–199.

Hempel, C. G. (1977): "Postscript: More Recent Ideas on Statistical Explanation," in: C. G. Hempel, *The Philosophy of Carl G. Hempel* (ed. by J. Fetzer), Oxford University Press, Oxford 2001 (German orig. 1977).

Hempel, C. G. (1988): "Provisos: A Problem Concerning the Inferential Function of Scientific Theories," in: A. Grünbaum and W. Salmon (eds.), *The Limitations of Deductivism*, University of California Press, Berkeley, 19–36.

Hempel, C. G. and Oppenheim, P. (1948): "Studies in the Logic of Explanation," *Philosophy of Science* 15, 135–175; reprinted in Hempel (1965), 245–290 (quoted therefrom).

Hendry, R. F. (2008): "Chemistry," in: S. Psillos and M. Curd (eds.), *The Routledge Companion to Philosophy of Science*, Routledge, London and New York, 520–530.

Herbert, N. (1985): *Quantum Reality*, Anchor Books, Doubleday.

Hesse, M. (1970): "Theories and Transitivity of Confirmation," *Philosophy of Science* 37, 50–63.

Hilgendorf, E. (2000): "Das Problem der Wertfreiheit in der Jurisprudenz," in: E. Hilgendorf and L. Kuhlen (eds.), *Die Wertfreiheit in der Jurisprudenz*, C. F. Müller, Heidelberg, 1–32.

Hilpinen, R. (1976): "Approximate Truth and Truthlikeness," in: M. Przelecki et al. (eds.), *Formal Methods in the Methodology of Empirical Sciences*, Reidel, Dordrecht, 19–42.

Hintikka, J. (1966): "A Two-Dimensional Continuum of Inductive Methods," in: J. Hintikka and P. Suppes (eds.), *Aspects of Inductive Logic*, North-Holland Publ. Comp., Amsterdam, 113–132.

Hirsch, E. D. Jr. (1973): *Validity in Interpretation*, Yale University Press, New Haven, CT.

Hitchcock, C. (2004): "Causal Processes and Interactions: What Are They and What Are They Good For?," *Philosophy of Science* 71, 932–941.

Hitchcock, C. (2009): "Causal Modelling," in: Beebee et al. (eds.), 299–314.

Hitchcock, C. (2010): "Probabilistic Causation," *Stanford Ecyclopedia of Philosophy (Winter 2011 Edition)*, Edward N. Zalta (ed.) (http://plato.stanford.edu/archives/win2011/entries/causation-probabilistic/).

Hitchcock, C., and Sober, E. (2004): "Prediction Versus Accommodation and the Risk of Overfitting," *British Journal for the Philosophy of Science* 55, 1–34.

Howson, C. (1990): "Fitting Theory to the Facts: Probably not Such a Bad Idea After All," in: C. Savage (ed.), *Scientific Theories*, University of Minnesota Press, Minneapolis, 222–224.

Howson, C. (1997): "A Logic of Induction," *Philosophy of Science* 64, 268–290.

Howson, C. (2000): *Hume's Problem: Induction and the Justification of Belief*, Clarendon Press, Oxford.

Howson, C., and Urbach, P. (1996): *Scientific Reasoning: The Bayesian Approach* (2nd ed.), Open Court, Chicago.
Hoyningen-Huene, P. (1993): *Reconstructing Scientific Revolutions: Thomas S. Kuhn's Philosophy of Science*, University of Chicago Press, Chicago.
Hrbacek, K., and Jech, T. (1999): *Introduction to Set Theory*, Marcel Dekker, New York.
Huber, F. (2008): "Hempel's Logic of Confirmation," *Philosophical Studies* 139, 181–189.
Huff, D. (1954): *How to Lie with Statistics*, Norton, New York.
Hughes, G. E., and Cresswell, M. J. (1996): *A New Introduction to Modal Logic*, Routledge, London.
Humburg, J. (1971): "The Principle of Instantial Relevance," in: Carnap/Jeffrey (1971), ch. 4.
Hume, D. (1739/40): *A Treatise of Human Nature. Vol. II, Book III: Of Morals* (ed. by A. D. Lindsay), Oxford 1911, reprint 1966.
Hume, D. (1748/2006): *An Inquiry Concerning Human Understanding* (ed. by S. Butler), Echo Library, Fairford.
Humphreys, P. (1989): *The Chances of Explanation*, Princeton University Press, Princeton, NJ.
Humphreys, P. (1993): "Greater Unification Equals Greater Understanding?," *Analysis* 53/3, 183–188.
Hunter, J. E., and Schmidt, F. L. (1990): *Methods of Meta-Analysis*, Sage Publications, London.
Hüttemann, A. (2004): *What's Wrong With Micro-Physicalism?*, Routledge, London.
Hüttemann, A., and Reutlinger, A. (2013): "Against the Statistical Account of Special Science Laws," to appear in: V. Karakostas and D. Dieks (eds.), *Recent Progress in Philosophy of Science (3rd EPSA Proceedings)*, Springer, New York.
Ioannidis, J. (2005): "Why Most Published Research Findings are False," *PLoS Medicine* 2/8, e124, 696–701.
James, W. (1907): *Pragmatism*, Harvard University Press, Cambridge, MA, 1979.
Jaynes, E. T. (1976): "Confidence Intervals versus Bayesian Intervals," in: W. L. Harper and C. Hooker (eds.), *Foundations of Probability Theory. Vol II*, Reidel, Dordrecht, 175–257.
Jeffrey, H. (1973): *Scientific Inference* (3rd ed.), Cambridge University Press, Cambridge.
Jeffrey, R. C. (1956): "Valuation and Acceptance of Scientific Hypotheses," *Philosophy of Science* 22, 337–346.
Jeffrey, R. C. (1971a): "Statistical Explanation vs. Statistical Relevance," in: Salmon et al. (1971), 19–28.
Jeffrey, R. C. (1971b): "Probability Measures and Integrals," in Carnap and Jeffrey (1971), 167–224.
Jeffrey, R. C. (1983): *The Logic of Decision*, (2nd ed.), McGraw-Hill, New York.
Joseph, G. (1980): "The Many Sciences and the One World," *Journal of Philosophy* 77/12, 773–790.
Kamlah, W., and Lorenzen, P. (1984): *Logical Propaedeutic: Preschool of Reasonable Discourse*, Rowman & Littlefield Publishers, Lanham, MD.
Kanitscheider, B. (1981): *Wissenschaftstheorie der Naturwissenschaft*, de Gruyter, Berlin.

Kelly, K. (1996): *The Logic of Reliable Inquiry*, Oxford University Press, New York.
Kelly, T. (2010): "Hume, Norton, and Induction without Rules," *Philosophy of Science* 77, 754–764.
Kelsen, H. (1960/2002): *Pure Theory of Law*, The Lawbook Exchange Ltd., New Jersey.
Ketland, J. (2004): "Empirical Adequacy and Ramsification," *British Journal for the Philosophy of Science* 55, 287–300.
Keuth, H. (1998, ed.): *Karl Popper. Logik der Forschung*, Akademie-Verlag, Berlin.
Keynes, J. M. (1921): *A Treatise on Probability*, MacMillan, New York.
Kim, J. (1963): "On the Logical Conditions of Deductive Explanation," *Philosophy of Science* 30, 86–291.
Kincaid, H. (1996): *Philosophical Foundations of the Social Sciences*, Cambridge University Press, Cambridge.
Kincaid, H. (2004): "Are There Laws in the Social Sciences?: Yes," in: C. Hitchcock (ed.), *Contemporary Debates in the Philosophy of Science*, Blackwell, Oxford, 168–187.
Kincaid, H., Dupré, J., and Wylie, A. (2007, eds.): *Value-free Science?*, Oxford University Press, Oxford.
Kirkham, R. L. (1992): *Theories of Truth*, MIT Press, Cambridge, MA.
Kitcher, P. (1981): "Explanatory Unification," *Philosophy of Science* 48, 507–531.
Kitcher, P. (1985): "Two Approaches to Explanation," *Philosophy of Science* 48, 251–281.
Kitcher, P. (1989): "Explanatory Unification and the Causal Structure of the World," in: P. Kitcher and W. Salmon (eds.), *Scientific Explanation*, University of Minnesota Press, Minneapolis, 410–505.
Kitcher, P. (2007): *Living with Darwin*, Oxford University Press, New York.
Klenk, V. (1989): *Understanding Symbolic Logic* (2nd ed.), Prentice Hall, Englewood Cliffs, NJ (4th ed. 2001).
Koertge, N. (2000): "Science, Values, and the Values of Science," *Philosophy of Science (Supplement)* 67, 45–57.
Kolmogorov, A. N. (1933): *Foundations of the Theory of Probability*, Chelsea Publ. Comp., New York 1950 (German orig. 1933).
Kornblith, H. (1994, ed.): *Naturalizing Epistemology*, MIT Press, Cambridge, MA.
Körner, S. (1947): "On Entailment," *Proceedings of the Aristotelean Society* 21, 143–162.
Krantz, D., Luce, R. D., Suppes, P., and Tversky, A. (2006/1971): *Foundations of Measurement, Vol I*, Dover Publications, New York.
Krebs, D. L. (1998): "The Evolution of Moral Behaviour," in: C. Crawford and D. L. Krebs (eds.), *Handbook of Evolutionary Psychology*, Lawrence Erlbaum Associates, Mahwah, NJ, 337–368.
Kripke, S. (1972): *Naming and Necessity*, Basil Blackwell, Oxford (2nd ed. 1980).
Kriz, J., Lück, H. E., and Heidbrink, H. (1990): *Wissenschafts- und Erkenntnistheorie*, Leske Verlag, Opladen.
Kuhlen, L. (2000): "Wertfreiheit in der Jurisprudenz?," in: E. Hilgendorf and L. Kuhlen (eds.), *Die Wertfreiheit in der Jurisprudenz*, C. F. Müller, Heidelberg, 33–49.
Kuhn, T. S. (1962): *The Structure of Scientific Revolutions*, University of Chicago Press, Chicago (3rd edition 1996).
Kuhn, T. S. (1977): *The Essential Tension: Selected Studies in Scientific Tradition and Change*, University of Chicago Press, Chicago.
Kuipers, T. A. F. (1987, ed.): *What Is Closer-To-The-Truth?*, Rodopi, Amsterdam.

Kuipers, T. A. F. (2000): *From Instrumentalism to Constructive Realism*, Kluwer, Dordrecht.
Kuipers, T. A. F., and Schurz, G. (2011, eds.): *Belief Revision Aiming at Truth Approximation*, Erkenntnis 75/2 (special volume).
Kutschera, F. v. (1972): *Wissenschaftstheorie, Vols. I and II*, Fink, Munich.
Kutschera, F. v. (1976): *Philosophy of Language*, Reidel, Dordrecht.
Kutschera, F. v. (1982): *Grundlagen der Ethik*, W. de Gruyter, Berlin.
Kyburg, H. E. (1961): *Probability and the Logic of Rational Belief*, Wesleyan University Press, Middletown, CT.
Ladyman, J. (1998): "What Is Structural Realism?," *Studies in the History and Philosophy of Science*, 29/3, 409–424.
Ladyman, J. (2002): *Understanding Philosophy of Science*, Routledge, London.
Ladyman, J., and Ross, D. (2007): *Every Thing Must Go. Metaphysics Naturalized*, Oxford University Press, Oxford. (With D. Spurrett and J. Collier.)
Lakatos, I. (1970): "Falsification and the Methodology of Scientific Research Programmes," in: I. Lakatos and A. Musgrave (eds.), *Criticism and the Growth of Knowledge*, Cambridge University Press, London, reprinted in Lakatos (1978), 8–101 (quoted therefrom).
Lakatos, I. (1971): "History of Science and its Rational Reconstruction," in: R. Buck and R. Cohen (eds.), *Boston Studies in the Philosophy of Science Vol. 8*; reprinted in Lakatos (1978), 102–138 (quoted therefrom).
Lakatos, I. (1977): "Science and Pseudoscience," in: Lakatos (1978), 1–7.
Lakatos, I. (1978): *Philosophical Papers Vol. 1*, Cambridge University Press, Cambridge.
Lamnek, S. (1988): *Qualitative Sozialforschung, Vol. 1*, Psychologie Verlags Union, Munich.
Lange, M. (2009): *Laws and Lawmakers*, Oxford University Press, Oxford.
Langley, P. et al. (1987): *Scientific Discovery. Computational Explorations of the Creative Process*, MIT Press, Cambridge, MA.
Latour, B., and Woolgar, S. (1986): *Laboratory Life: The Construction of Scientific Facts*, Princeton University Press, Princeton, NJ.
Laudan, L. (1977): *Progress and its Problems*, University of California Press, Berkeley.
Laudan, L. (1981/96): "A Confutation of Convergent Realism," *Philosophy of Science* 48, 19–49, reprinted in Papineau (1996b), 107–138.
Laudan, L. (1983): "The Demise of the Demarcation Problem," in: R. S. Cohen and L. Laudan (eds.), *Physics, Philosophy, and Psychoanalysis*, Reidel, Dordrecht, 111–127.
Lazarsfeld, P. F. (1955): "Interpretation of Statistical Reasonings," in: P. Lazarsfeld and M. Rosenberg (eds.), *The Language of Social Research*, Free Press, Glencoe, IL, 115–125.
Lazarsfeld, P. F., and Barton, A. H. (1951): "Qualitative Measurement in Social Sciences," in. D. Lerner and H. D. Lasswell (eds.), *The Policy Sciences*, Stanford University Press, Stanford, CA, 155–192.
Lehrer, K. (1975): "Induction, Rational Acceptance, and Minimally Inconsistent Sets," in: G. Maxwell and R. M. Anderson (eds.), *Induction, Probability, and Confirmation*, University of Minnesota Press, Minneapolis, 295–323.
Lehrer, K. (1974): *Knowledge*, Clarendon Press, Oxford (2nd ed. Westview Press).
Leitgeb, H. (2004): *Inference on the Low Level*, Kluwer, Dordrecht.
Lenzen, W. (1974): *Theorie der Bestätigung wissenschaftlicher Hypothesen*, Holzboog, Stuttgart-Bad Cannstatt.

Leplin, J. (1984, ed.): *Scientific Realism*, University of California Press, Berkeley.
Levi, I. (1967): *Gambling with Truth*, Knopf, New York.
Levi, I. (1977): "Direct Inference," *The Journal of Philosophy* 74, 5–29.
Lewis, D. (1970): "How to Define Theoretical Terms," *Journal of Philosophy* 67; reprinted in: Lewis (1983b) ch. 6 (quoted therefrom).
Lewis, D. (1973a/1986): "Causation," *Journal of Philosophy* 70; reprinted in Lewis (1986), 159–171, with a new postscript 172–213 (pages quoted therefrom).
Lewis, D. (1973b): *Counterfactuals*, Basil Blackwell, Oxford.
Lewis, D. (1979): "Counterfactual Dependence and Time's Arrow," *Nous* 13; reprinted in Lewis (1986), 32–52 (pages quoted therefrom).
Lewis, D. (1980): "A Subjectivist's Guide to Objective Chance," in: R. C. Jeffrey (ed.), *Studies in Inductive Logic and Probability*; reprinted in Lewis (1986a), ch. 19.
Lewis, D. (1983a): "New Work for Universals," *Australasian Journal of Philosophy* 61, 343–377.
Lewis, D. (1983b): *Philosophical Papers Vol. I*, Oxford University Press, New York.
Lewis, D. (1986a): *Philosophical Papers Vol. II*, Oxford University Press, New York.
Lewis, D. (1986b): *On the Plurality of Worlds*, Basil Blackwell, Oxford.
Lewis, D. (1994): "Humean Supervenience Debugged," *Mind* 103, 473–490.
Lewis, D. (1997): "Finkish Dispositions," *The Philosophical Quarterly* 47, 143–158.
Lipton, P. (1991): *Inference to the Best Explanation*, Routledge, London.
Losee, J. (2001): *A Historical Introduction to the Philosophy of Science*, Oxford University Press, Oxford (orig. 1972).
Loux, M. J. (1998): *Metaphysics*, Routledge, London and New York.
Mach, E. (1883/2009): *The Science of Mechanics*, BiblioBazaar, Charleston 2009 (German orig. 1883).
Machery, E., Mallon, R., Nichols, S., and Stich, S. (2004): "Semantics, Cross-Cultural Style," *Cognition* 92, B1–B12.
Machover, M. (1996): *Set Theory, Logic, and their Limitations*, Cambridge University Press, Cambridge.
Mackie, J. (1980): *The Cement of the Universe*, Clarendon Press, Oxford (orig. 1974, reprint 2002).
Maddy, P. (1997): *Mathematical Naturalism*, Oxford University Press, Oxford.
Makinson, D. (1965): "The Paradox of the Preface," *Analysis* 25, 205–207.
Manninen, J., and Tuomela, R. (1976, eds.): *Essays on Explanation and Understanding*, Reidel, Dordrecht.
Margolis, E. and Laurence, S. (1999): "Concepts and Cognitive Science," in: E. Margolis and S. Laurence (eds.), *Concepts*, MIT Press, Cambridge, MA, 3–82.
Martin, C. B. (1994): "Dispositions and Conditionals," *The Philosophical Quarterly* 44, 1–8.
Maturana, H. R., and Varela, F. (1992): *The Tree of Knowledge*, Shambhala, Boston (German orig. 1984).
Maudlin, T. (2007): *The Metaphysics within Physics*, Oxford University Press, New York.
Maxwell, G. (1962): "The Ontological Status of Theoretical Entities," in: H. Feigl and G. Maxwell (eds.), *Minnesota Studies in the Philosophy of Science Vol. III*, University of Minnesota Press, Minneapolis, 3–27.
Maxwell, G. (1970): "Structural Realism and the Meaning of Theoretical Entities," in: S. Winokur and M. Radner (eds.), *Analyses of Theories and Methods of Physics and*

Psychology (Minnesota Studies Vol. 4), University of Minnesota Press, Minneapolis, 181–192.
Maxwell, N. W. (1998): *The Comprehensibility of the Universe*, Clarendon Press, Oxford.
Mayntz, R., Holm, K., and Hübner, P. (1976): *Introduction to Empirical Sociology*, Harmondsworth, Middlesex.
McCarthy, T. (1981): "The Idea of a Logical Constant," *Journal of Philosophy* 78, 499–523.
McMullin, E. (1970): "The History and Philosophy of Science: A Taxonomy," *Minnesota Studies in the Philosophy of Science* 5, 12–67.
Melia, J., and Saatsi, J. (2006): "Ramsification and Theoretical Content," *British Journal for the Philosophy of Science* 57, 561–581.
Mellor, H. D. (1980): "Necessities and Universals in Natural Laws," in: D. H. Mellor (ed.), *Science, Belief and Behavior*, Cambridge University Press, Cambridge, 105–126.
Mendelson, E. (2009): *Introduction to Mathematical Logic* (5th ed.), Chapman and Hall, London.
Menzies, P., and Price, H. (1993): "Causation as a Secondary Quality," *British Journal for the Philosophy of Science* 44, 187–203.
Mesoudi, A., Whiten, A., and Laland, K. N. (2006): "Towards a Unified Science of Cultural Evolution," *Behavioral and Brain Science* 29, 329–347.
Mill, J. St. (1865): *System of Logic*, Longmans, Green & Co, London.
Miller, D. (1974): "Popper's Qualitative Theory of Verisimilitude," *British Journal for the Philosophy of Science* 25, 166–177.
Miller, D. (1978): "The Distance between Constituents," *Synthese* 38, 197–212.
Miller, D. (1994): *Critical Rationalism: A Restatement and Defense*, Open Court, Chicago.
Millikan, R. G. (1984): *Language, Thought, and Other Biological Categories*, MIT Press, Cambridge, MA.
Morris, C. W. (1946): *Signs, Language, and Behavior*, Braziller, New York.
Morris, M. (2006): *An Introduction to the Philosophy of Language*, Cambridge University Press, New York.
Mortimer, C. E. (1986): *Chemistry*, Wadsworth Publishing Company, Belmont.
Moser, P. K. (1989): *Knowledge and Evidence*, Cambridge University Press, Cambridge.
Mumford, S. (1998): *Dispositions*, Oxford University Press, Oxford.
Mumford, S. (2009): "Causal Powers and Capacities," in: Beebee et al. (eds.), 265–278.
Musgrave, A. E. (1974): "Logical versus Historical Theories of Confirmation," *British Journal for the Philosophy of Science* 25, 1–23.
Musgrave, A. (2002): "Karl Poppers kritischer Rationalismus," in: J. M. Böhm, H. Holweg, and C. Hook, (eds.), *Karl Poppers kritischer Rationalismus heute*, Mohr Siebeck, Tübingen, 25–42.
Nagel, E. (1961): *The Structure of Science*, Routledge & Kegan Paul, London.
Nagel, E. (1970): "Issues in the Logic of Reductive Explanations," in: M. K. Munitz (ed.), *Contemporary Philosophic Thought*, Vol. 2, Albany, New York, 117–137.
Nagel, E. (1977): "Teleology Revisited," *Journal of Philosophy* 74/5, 261–279.
Nagel, E. (1979): *Teleology Revisited and Other Essays*, Columbia University, New York.
Neurath, O. (1916): "On the Classification of Systems of Hypothesis," in: Neurath (1983), 13–31 (German orig. 1916).

Neurath, O. (1931): "Sociology on the Framework of Physicalism," in: Neurath (1983), 58–90 (German orig. 1931).

Neurath, O. (1934): "Radical Physicalism and 'the Real World'," in: Neurath (1983), 100–114 (German orig. 1934).

Neurath, O. (1983): *Philosophical Papers 1913–1946*, Reidel, Dordrecht.

Newman, M. H. A. (1928): "Mr. Russell's Causal Theory of Perception," *Mind* 37, 137–148.

Neyman, J. (1937): "Outline of a Theory of Statistical Estimation," *Philosophical Transactions of the Royal Society*, Vol. 236A, 333–380.

Niiniluoto, I. (1981): "Statistical Explanation Reconsidered," *Synthese* 48, 437–472.

Niiniluoto, I. (1987): *Truthlikeness*, Reidel, Dordrecht.

Niiniluoto, I. (1998): "Verisimilitude: the Third Period," *The British Journal for the Philosophy of Science* 49, 1–29.

Niiniluoto, I. (1999): "Defending Abduction," *Philosophy of Science* 66 (Proceedings), S436–S451.

Norton, J. (2003): "A Material Theory of Induction," *Philosophy of Science* 70, 647–670.

Norton, J. D. (2009): "Is there an Independent Principle of Causality in Physics?," *British Journal for the Philosphy of Science* 60, 475–486.

Novak, J. (1980): "Eine Alternative zu Piagets Psychologie für den naturwissenschaftlichen und mathematischen Unterricht," in: W. Jung (ed.), *Piaget und Physikdidaktik. Physica Didactica* 7, 17–46.

Nowak, L. (1980): *The Structure of Idealization*, Reidel, Dordrecht.

Oddie, G. (2011): "The Content, Consequence and Likeness Approaches to Verisimilitude: Compatibility," to appear in *Synthese*, online version May 2011 DOI: 10.1007/s11229-011-9930-8.

Oppenheim, P., and Putnam, H. (1958): "Unity of Science as a Working Hypothesis," in: H. Feigl et al. (eds.), *Minnesota Studies in the Philosophy of Science*, Vol. II, University of Minnesota Press, Minneapolis, 3–36.

Otte, R. (1981): "A Critique of Suppes' Theory of Probabilistic Causality," *Synthese* 48, 167–189.

Pap, A. (1978): "Disposition Concepts and Extensional Logic," in R. Tuomela (ed.), 27–54.

Papineau, D. (1993): *Philosophical Naturalism*, Blackwell, Oxford.

Papineau, D. (1996a): "Theory-dependent Terms," *Philosophy of Science* 63, 1–20.

Papineau, D. (1996b, ed.): *The Philosophy of Science*, Oxford University Press, Oxford.

Patry, J.-L. (1991): *Transsituationale Konsistenz des Verhaltens und Handelns in der Erziehung*, Lang, Bern.

Paulßen, J. (2012): *Das Problem der Kurvenanpassung*, Peter Lang, Frankfurt/M.

Pearce, D., and Rantala, V. (1985): "Ramsey Eliminability Revisited," in: J. Hintikka and F. Vanaamme (eds.), *Logic of Discovery and Logic of Discourse*, Plenum Press, New York, 161–180.

Pearl, J. (1988): *Probabilistic Reasoning in Intelligent Systems*, Morgan Kaufmann, Santa Mateo, CA.

Pearl, J. (2009): *Causality* (2nd ext. ed.), Cambridge University Press, Cambridge.

Peirce, C. S. (1878a): "Deduction, Induction, and Hypothesis," in: Peirce (1931ff), Vol. 2, §§619–644.

Peirce, C. S. (1878b): "How to Make Our Ideas Clear," in: Peirce (1931ff), Vol. 2, §§645–668.
Peirce, C. S. (1903): "Lecures on Pragmatism," in: Peirce (1931ff), Vol. 5, §14–212.
Peirce, C. S. (1931ff): *Collected Papers*. Vols 1–6 (ed. by C. Hartshorne and P. Weiss), Harvard University Press, Cambridge, MA, 1931–35.
Pennock, R. T. (2011): "Can't Philosophers Tell the Difference between Science and Religion? Demarcation Revisited," *Synthese* 178/2, 177–206.
Penrose, R. (2007): *The Road to Reality*, Vintage Books, New York.
Piaget, J. (1974): *The Child's Construction of Quantities: Conservation and Atomism*, Routledge and Kegan Paul, London (orig. 1946).
Pietroski, P., and Rey, G. (1995): "When Other Things Aren't Equal: Saving *Ceteris Paribus* Laws from Vacuity," *British Journal for the Philosophy of Science* 46, 81–110.
Pigden, C. R. (1989): "Logic and the Autonomy of Ethic," *Australasian Journal of Philosophy* 67, 127–151.
Pigden, C. R. (2010, ed.): *Hume on "Is", and "Ought"*, Palgrave Macmillan, Hampshire.
Popper, K. (1935/2002): *Logic of Discovery*, Routledge, London (German orig. *Logik der Forschung* 1935).
Popper, K. (1959): "The Propensity Interpretation of Probability," *British Journal for the Philosophy of Science* 10, 25–42.
Popper, K. (1963): *Conjectures and Refutations*, Routledge, London.
Popper, K. (1979): *Objective Knowledge. An Evolutuionary Approach* (2nd ed.), Clarendon Press, Oxford.
Popper, K. (1983): *Realism and the Aim of Science*, London, Hutchinson.
Popper, K. (1990): *A World of Propensities*, Thoemmes, Bristol.
Popper, K. (1994): *Myth of the Framework*, Routledge, New York.
Popper, K., and Miller, D. (1983): "A Poof of the Impossibility of Inductive Probability," *Nature* 302, 687–688.
Price, H. (1996): *Time's Arrow and Archimedes' Point*, Oxford University Press, New York.
Priest, G. (1976): "Discussion: Gruesome Simplicity," *Philosophy of Science* 43, 432–437.
Prim, R., and Tilman, H. (1979): *Grundlagen einer kritisch-rationalen Sozialwissenschaft*, Quelle & Meyer, Heidelberg.
Prior, A. N. (1960): "The Autonomy of Ethics," *Australasian Journal of Philosophy* 38, 199–206.
Prior, E. W., Pargetter, R., and Jackson, F. (1982): "Three Theses about Dispositions," *American Philosophical Quarterly* 19, 251–257.
Psillos, S. (1995): "Is Structural Realism the Best of Both Worlds?," *Dialectica* 49/1, 15–46.
Psillos, S. (1999): *Scientific Realism. How Science Tracks Truth*, Routledge, London and New York.
Psillos, S. (2002): *Causation and Explanation*, Acumen, Chesham.
Psillos, S. (2009): "Regularity Theories," in: Beebee et al. (eds.), 131–157.
Psillos, S., and Curd, M. (eds., 2008): *The Routledge Companion to Philosophy of Science*, Routledge, London and New York.
Putnam, H. (1962): "What Theories are Not," in: E. Nagel, P. Suppes, and A. Tarski (eds.), *Logic, Methodology and Philosophy of Science*, Stanford University Press, Stanford, 240–251.
Putnam, H. (1975a): "What is Mathematical Truth?," in H. Putnam, *Mathematics, Matter and Method*, Cambridge University Press, Cambridge, 60–78.

Putnam, H. (1975b): "The Meaning of 'Meaning'," in: H. Putnam, *Mind, Language and Reality. Philosophical Papers, Vol. 2*, Cambridge University Press, Cambridge, 215–271.
Putnam, H. (1977): "Realism and Reason," *Proceedings and Addresses of The American Philosophical Association* 50/6, 483–498.
Putnam, H. (1978): *Meaning and the Moral Sciences*, Routledge and Kegan Paul, London.
Putnam, H. (1982): *Reason, Truth, and History*, Cambridge University Press, Cambridge.
Putnam, H. (1995): *Pragmatism. An Open Question*, Blackwell Publishers, Cambridge.
Quine, W. v. O. (1951): "Two Dogmas of Empiricism," *Philosophical Review* 60, 20–43.
Quine, W. v. O. (1960): *Word and Object*, MIT Press, Massachusetts.
Quine, W. v. O. (1974): *The Roots of Reference*, Open Court Publ., La Salle, IL.
Quine, W. v. O. (1992): *Pursuit to Truth*, Harvard University Press, Cambridge, MA.
Rahman, S. et al. (eds., 2004), *Logic, Epistemology, and the Unity of Science*, Dordrecht, Kluwer.
Raiffa, H. (1968): *Decision Analysis*, Addison-Wesley Publ. Comp., Reading, MA.
Railton, P. (1978): "A Deductive-Nomological Model of Probabilistic Explanation," *Philosophy of Science* 45, 206–226.
Ramsey, F. P. (1926): "Truth and Probability," reprinted in Ramsey (1990).
Ramsey, F. P. (1929): "Theories," reprinted in Ramsey (1990) (pages quoted therefrom).
Ramsey, F. P. (1931): *The Foundations of Mathematics*, Kegan Paul, London (reprint 1978).
Ramsey, F. P. (1990): *Philosophical Papers* (ed. by H. D. Mellor), Cambridge University Press, Cambridge.
Rawls, J. (1971): *A Theory of Justice*, Harvard University Press, Cambridge, MA.
Reichenbach, H. (1938): *Experience and Prediction*, University of Chicago Press, Chicago.
Reichenbach, H. (1949): *The Theory of Probability*, University of California Press, Berkeley.
Reichenbach, H. (1956): *The Direction of Time*, University of California Press, Berkeley.
Rescher, N. (1964): *Hypothetical Reasoning*, Van Gorcum, Amsterdam.
Rescher, N. (1973): *The Coherence Theory of Truth*, Oxford University Press, Oxford.
Rescher, N. (1980): *Induction*, B. Blackwell, Oxford.
Rescher, N. (1998): "Pragmatism in Crisis," in: P. Weingartner et al. (eds.), *The Role of Pragmatics in Contemporary Philosophy*, Hölder-Pichler-Tempsky, Vienna, 24–38.
Rescher, N. (2001): *Cognitive Pragmatism*, University of Pittsburgh Press, Pittsburgh.
Reutlinger, A., Schurz, G., and Hüttemann, A. (2011): "Ceteris Paribus Laws," *The Stanford Encyclopedia of Philosophy* (Spring 2011 Edition), Edward N. Zalta (ed.) (http://plato.stanford.edu/entries/ceteris-paribus).
Ridley, M. (1993): *Evolution*, Blackwell, Oxford.
Rips, L. J. (1994): *The Psychology of Proof*, MIT Press, Cambridge, MA.
Rock, I. (1984): *Perception*, Scientific American Books, New York.
Rorty, R. (1982): *Consequences of Pragmatism*, Harvester Press, Brighton.
Rosenberg, A. (2008): *Philosophy of Social Science* (3rd ed.), Westview Press, Boulder, CO.

Rosenthal, R., and Jacobson, L. (1968): *Pygmalion in the Classroom*, Rinehart & Winston, New York.
Ross, A. (1996, ed.): *Science Wars*, Duke University Press, Durham, NC.
Rott, H. (1994): "Zur Wissenschaftsphilosophie von Imre Lakatos," *Philosophia Naturalis* 31/1, 25–62.
Rott, H. (2001): *Change, Choice and Inference*, Clarendon Press, Oxford.
Rudner, R. (1953): "The Scientist Qua Scientist Makes Value Judgements," *Philosophy of Science* 20, S. 1–6.
Russell, B. (1903): *The Principles of Mathematics*, Cambridge University Press, Cambridge.
Russell, B. (1905): "On Denoting," *Mind* 14, 479–493.
Ryder, J. M. (1981): "Consequences of a Simple Extension of the Dutch Book Argument," *British Journal for the Philosophy of Science* 32, 164–167.
Salmon, W. C. (1957): "Should We Attempt to Justify Induction?," *Philosophical Studies* 8/3, 45–47.
Salmon, W. (1971): *Statistical Explanation and Statistical Relevance* (with contributions by R. C. Jeffrey and J. G. Greeno), University of Pittsburgh Press, London.
Salmon, W. (1974): "The Concept of Inductive Evidence," in: Swinburne (1974), 48–57.
Salmon, W. (1984): *Scientific Explanation and the Causal Structure of the World*, Princeton University Press, Princeton, NJ.
Salmon, W. (1989): *Four Decades of Scientific Explanation*, University of Minnesota Press, Minneapolis.
Salmon, W. (1997): "Causality and Explanation: A Reply to Two Critiques," *Philosophy of Science* 64, 461–477.
Salmon, W. (1998): *Causality and Explanation*, Oxford University Press, New York.
Savitt, S. F. (1996): "The Direction of Time," *British Journal for the Philosophy of Science* 47, 347–370.
Schiffer, S. (1991): "Ceteris Paribus Laws," *Mind* 100, 1–17.
Schlesinger, G. (1974): *Confirmation and Confirmability*, Clarendon Press, Oxford.
Schlick, M. (1930/31): "The Turning Point in Philosophy," in M. Schlick, *Philosophical Papers. Vol. II* (ed. by H. Mulder and B. van de Velde-Schlick), D. Reidel, Dordrecht 1979, 154–160 (German orig. 1930/31).
Schmidt, P. F. (1959): "Ethical Norms in Scientific Method," *Journal of Philosophy* 56/15, 644–652.
Scholz, O. (2001): *Verstehen und Rationalität* (2nd ed.), Vittorio Klostermann, Frankfurt/M.
Schrenk, M. (2010): "The Powerlessness of Necessity," *Nous* 44/4, 725–739.
Schurz, G. (1982): "Ein Logisch-Pragmatisches Modell von Deduktiv-Nomologischer Erklärung (Systematisierung)," *Erkenntnis* 17, 321–341.
Schurz, G. (1985): "Denken, Sprache und Erziehung: Die aktuelle Piaget-Kontroverse," *Zeitschrift für Semiotik* 7/4, 335–366.
Schurz, G. (1990): "Paradoxical Consequences of Balzer's and Gähde's Criteria of Theoreticity," *Erkenntnis* 32, 161–214.
Schurz, G. (1991a): "Relevant Deduction," *Erkenntnis* 35, 391–437.
Schurz, G. (1991b): "How Far Can Hume's Is-Ought Thesis be Generalized?," *Journal of Philosophical Logic* 20, 37–95.
Schurz, G. (1994): "Relevant Deduction and Hypothetico-Deductivism: A Reply to Gemes," *Erkenntnis* 41, 183–188.

Schurz, G. (1996a): "Scientific Explanation: A Critical Survey," *Foundation of Science* I/3, 1995/96, 429–465.
Schurz, G. (1996b): "Kinds of Unpredictability in Deterministic Systems," in: P. Weingartner and G. Schurz (eds.), 123–141.
Schurz, G. (1997): *The Is-Ought Problem. An Investigation in Philosophical Logic*, Kluwer (Studia Logica Library), Dordrecht.
Schurz, G. (1998a): "Koexistenzweisen rivalisierender Paradigen," in: G. Schurz and P. Weingartner (eds.), 1–52.
Schurz, G. (1998b): "Kinds of Pragmatisms and Pragmatic Components of Knowledge," in: P. Weingartner et al. (eds), *The Role of Pragmatics in Contemporary Philosophy*, Hölder-Pichler-Tempsky, Vienna, 9–22.
Schurz, G. (1999a): "Explanation as Unification," *Synthese* 120/1, 95–114.
Schurz, G. (1999b): "Tarski and Carnap on Logical Truth," in: J. Wolenski and E. Köhler (eds.), *Alfred Tarski and the Vienna Circle*, Kluwer, Dordrecht, 77–94.
Schurz, G. (2001): "What Is 'Normal'? An Evolution-Theoretic Foundation of Normic Laws and Their Relation to Statistical Normality," *Philosophy of Science* 28, 476–497.
Schurz, G. (2002a): "Karl Popper, Deduktion, Induktion, und Abduktion," in: J. M. Böhm, H. Holweg, and C. Hook, (eds.), *Karl Poppers kritischer Rationalismus heute*, Mohr Siebeck, Tübingen, 126–143.
Schurz, G. (2002b): "Ceteris Paribus Laws: Classification and Deconstruction," in: Earman et al. (2002), 351–372.
Schurz, G. (2004): "Normic Laws, Nonmonotonic Reasoning, and the Unity of Science," in: S. Rahman et al. (eds.), *Logic, Epistemology, and the Unity of Science*, Dordrecht, Kluwer, 181–211.
Schurz, G. (2005a): "Non-monotonic Reasoning from an Evolutionary Viewpoint: Ontic, Logical and Cognitive Foundations," *Synthese* 146/1–2, 37–51.
Schurz, G. (2005b): "Kuipers' Account to H-D Confirmation and Truthlikeness," in: R. Festa (ed.), *Logics of Scientific Discovery. Essays in Debate with Theo Kuipers*, Rodopi, Amsterdam.
Schurz, G. (2005c): "Laws of Nature versus System Laws," in: J. Faye et al. (ed.), *Nature's Principles*, Kluwer, Dordrecht.
Schurz, G. (2008a): "Patterns of Abduction," *Synthese* 164, 201–234.
Schurz, G. (2008b): "The Meta-Inductivist's Winning Strategy in the Prediction Game: A New Approach to Hume's Problem," *Philosophy of Science* 75, 278–305.
Schurz, G. (2009a): "When Empirical Success Implies Theoretical Reference: A Structural Correspondence Theorem," *British Journal for the Philosophy of Science* 60/1, 101–133.
Schurz, G. (2009b): "Meliorative Reliabilist Epistemology: Where Externalism and Internalism Meet," *Grazer Philosophische Studien* 79, 41–62.
Schurz, G. (2012): "Meta-Induction in Epistemic Networks and Social Spread of Knowledge," *Episteme* 9/2, 151–170.
Schurz, G. (2013a): "Bayesian Pseudo-Confirmation, Use-Novelty, and Genuine Confirmation," to appear in *Studies in History and Philosophy of Science* 2014.
Schurz, G. (2013b): "Criteria of Theoreticity: Bridging Statement and Non Statement View," to appear in *Erkenntnis*.
Schurz, G. (2013c): "Ceteris Paribus Laws as Assertions about Causal Influence," to appear in *Erkenntnis* 2014.
Schurz, G., and Weingartner, P. (1987): "Verisimilitude Defined by Relevant Consequence-Elements," in: Kuipers (1987), 47–78.

Schurz, G., and Lambert, K. (1994): "Outline of a Theory of Scientific Understanding," *Synthese* 101/1, 65–120.

Schurz, G., and Weingartner, P. (1998, eds.): *Koexistenz rivalisierender Paradigmen*, Westdeutscher Verlag, Opladen/Wiesbaden.

Schurz, G., and Leitgeb, H. (2008): "Finitistic and Frequentistic Approximations of Probability Measures with or without sigma-Additivity," *Studia Logica* 89/2, 258–283.

Schurz, G., and Weingartner, P. (2010): "Zwart and Franssen's Impossibility Theorem Holds for Possible-World-Accounts but not for Consequence-Accounts to Verisimilitude," *Synthese* 172, 415–436.

Schurz, G., and Votsis, I. (2011): *Scientific Realism Quo Vadis?*, *Synthese* 180/2 (special volume).

Schurz, G., and Thorn, P. (2012): "Reward versus Risk in Uncertain Inference: Theorems and Simulations," *Review of Symbolic Logic* 5/4, 574–612.

Schurz, G. and Gebharter, A. (2013): "Causality as a Theoretical Concept with Empirical Significance," to appear in *Synthese*.

Scriven, M. (1959a): "Truisms as Grounds for Historical Explanations," in P. Gardiner (ed.), *Theories of History*, The Free Press, New York, 443–475.

Scriven, M. (1959b): "Explanation and Prediction in Evolutionary Theory," *Science* 130, 477–482.

Shao, J. (1997): "An Asymptotic Theory for Linear Model Selection," *Statistica Sinica* 7, 221–264.

Shapere, D. (1982): "The Concept of Observation in Science and Philosophy," *Philosophy of Science* 49, 485–525.

Shapiro, S. (2000): *Thinking About Mathematics. The Philosophy of Mathematics*, Oxford University Press, Oxford.

Sher, G. (1991): *The Bounds of Logic*, MIT Press, Cambridge, MA.

Shoemaker, S. (1980): "Causality and Properties," in P. Inwagen (ed.), *Time and Cause*, Reidel, Dordrecht, 109–136.

Shoenfield, J. (1967): *Mathematical Logic*, Addison-Wesley, Reading, MA.

Shogenji, T. (2005): "Justification by Coherence from Scratch," *Philosophical Studies* 125/3, 305–325.

Siegel, L. (1978): "The Relationship of Language and Thought in the Preoperational Child," in: L. Siegel and C. Brainerd (eds.), *Alternatives to Piaget*, Academic Press, New York, 43–67.

Simon, H. (1954): "Spurious Correlation: A Causal Interpretation," *Journal of the American Statistical Association* 49, 467–479.

Skyrms, B. (1963): "On Failing to Vindicate Induction," *Philosophy of Science* 30, 252–261.

Skyrms, B. (1999): *Choice and Chance: An Introduction to Inductive Logic*, Wadsworth Publishing, Belmont, CA (orig. 1975).

Smart, J. J. C. (1963): *Philosophy and Scientific Realism*, Routledge & Kegan Paul, London.

Sneed, J. D. (1971): *The Logical Structure of Mathematical Physics*, Reidel, Dordrecht (2nd rev. ed. 1979).

Snow, C. P. (1960): *The Two Cultures*, Cambridge University Press, Cambridge (2nd ed. 1993).

Sober, E. (1988): "The Principle of the Common Cause," in: J. Fetzer (ed.), *Probability and Causality*, Reidel, Dordrecht, 211–228.

Sober, E. (1993): *Philosophy of Biology*, Westview Press, Boulder, CO (2nd ed. 1999).
Sokal, A., and Brickmont, J. (1998): *Fashionable Nonsense. Postmodern Intellectuals' Abuse of Science*, Picador, New York.
Sperber, D., and Wilson, D. (1986): *Relevance: Communication and Cognition*, Basil Blackwell, Oxford.
Spielmann, S. (1977): "Physical Probability and Bayesian Statistics," *Synthese* 36, 235–269.
Spirtes, P., Glymour, C., and Scheines, R. (2000): *Causation, Prediction, and Search*, MIT Press, Cambridge, MA (rev. ext. 2nd ed. of 1993).
Spohn, W. (2005): "Enumerative Induction and Lawlikeness," *Philosophy of Science* 72, 164–187.
Stadler, F. (2001): *The Vienna Circle*, Springer, New York.
Stalker, D. (1994, ed.): *Grue! The New Riddle of Induction*, Open Court, Chicago, IL.
Stalnaker, R. (1968): "A Theory of Conditionals," reprinted in E. Sosa (ed., 1975), *Causation and Conditionals*, Oxford University Press, Oxford, 165–179.
Stanford, K. P. (2006): *Exceeding Our Grasp. Science, History, and the Problem of Unconceived Alternatives*, Oxford University Press, Oxford.
Steel, D. (2006): "Homogeneity, Selection, and the Faithfulness Condition," *Minds and Machines* 16/3, 303–317.
Stegmüller, W. (1969ff): *Probleme und Resultate der Wissenschaftstheorie und Analytischen Philosophie*, Springer, Berlin (Vol. I: 1969, 1983 2nd ed.; Vol. II.1: 1970; Vol. IV.1, Vol. IV.2: 1973; Vol. II.3: 1986).
Stegmüller, W. (1976): *The Structure and Dynamics of Scientific Theories*, Springer, New York.
Stegmüller, W. (1977): *Collected Papers on Epistemology, Philosophy of Science and History of Science* (Vols I and II), D. Reidel, Dordrecht.
Stegmüller, W. (1979a): *Rationale Rekonstruktion von Wissenschaft und ihrem Wandel*, Reclam, Stuttgart.
Stegmüller, W. (1979b): *The Structuralist View of Theories*, Springer, Berlin.
Stich, S. (1990): *The Fragmentation of Reason*, MIT Press, Cambridge, MA.
Strawson, P. F. (1952): *Introduction to Logical Theory*, Methuen, London.
Strevens, M. (2000): "Do Large Probabilities Explain Better?," *Philosophy of Science* 67, 366–390.
Strevens, M. (2004): "Bayesian Confirmation Theory: Inductive Logic, or Mere Inductive Framework?," *Synthese* 141, 365–379.
Strevens, M. (2008): *Depth. An Account of Scientific Explanation*, Harvard University Press, Cambridge, MA.
Strevens, M. (2013): "Ceteris Paribus Hedges: Causal Voodoo That Works," to appear in *Journal of Philosophy*.
Suppes, P. (1970): *A Probabilistic Theory of Causality*, Amsterdam, North-Holland.
Suppes, P. (1985): "Explaining the Unpredictable," *Erkenntnis* 22, 187–195.
Suppes, P. (1999): *Introduction to Logic*, Dover Publications, New York (orig. 1957).
Swinburne, R. (1974, ed.): *The Justification of Induction*, Oxford University Press, Oxford.
Swinburne, R. (1979): *The Existence of God*, Clarendon Press, Oxford.
Tarski, A. (1936a): "The Concept of Truth in Formalized Languages," in: Tarski (1956), ch. VIII, 152–278 (quoted therefrom; German orig. 1936).
Tarski, A. (1936b): "On the Concept of Logical Consequence," in: Tarski (1956), ch. XVI, 393–400 (quoted therefrom; German orig. 1936).

Tarski, A. (1956): *Logic, Semantics, Metamathematics*, Clarendon Press, Oxford.
Tarski, A. (1986): "What are Logical Notions?," *History and Philosophy of Logic* 7, 143–154 (manuscript of 1966).
Thagard, P. (1992): *Conceptual Revolutions*, Princeton University Press, Princeton, NJ.
Thagard, P. (1996): *Mind. An Introduction to Cognitive Science*, MIT Press, Cambridge, MA.
Tichý, P. (1974): "On Popper's Definition of Verisimilitude," *The Bristish Journal for the Philosophy of Science* 27, 25–42.
Tomasello, M. (1999): *The Cultural Origins of Human Cognition*, Harvard University Press, Cambridge, MA.
Tooley, M. (1990): "The Nature of Causation: A Singularist Account," *Canadian Journal of Philosophy*, suppl. vol. 16, 271–321.
Toulmin, S. (1950): *The Place of Reason in Ethics*, Cambridge University Press, Cambridge.
Triplett, T. (1990): "Recent Work on Foundationalism," *American Philosophical Quarterly* 27/2, 93–116.
Tuomela, R. (1973): *Theoretical Concepts*, Springer, Berlin.
Tuomela, R. (1976): "Morgan on Deductive Explanation: A Rejoinder," *The Journal of Philosophical Logic* 5, 527–543.
Tuomela, R. (ed., 1978): *Dispositions*, Reidel, Dordrecht.
Tuomela, R. (1981): "Inductive Explanation," *Synthese* 48, 257–294.
Unwin, S. T. (2003): *The Probability of God*, Crown Forum, New York.
Van Cleve, J. (1984): "Reliability, Justification, and Induction," in P. A. French et al. (eds.), *Causation and Causal Theories*, Midwest Studies in Philosophy 4, 555–567.
Van Dalen, D., de Swart, H., and Doets, H. (1978): *Sets. Naive, Axiomatic and Applied*, Pergamon Press, Oxford.
Van Fraassen, B. (1980): *The Scientific Image*, Clarendon Press, Oxford (new ed. 1990).
Van Fraassen, B. (1985): "Salmon on Explanation," *Journal of Philosophy* 11, 639–651.
Van Fraassen, B. (1989): *Laws and Symmetry*, Clarendon Press, Oxford.
Van Fraassen (2002): *The Empirical Stance*, Yale University Press, New Haven, CT.
Van Fraassen, B. (2006): "Structure: Its Shadow and Substance," *The British Journal for the Philosophy of Science* 57, 275–307.
Vickers, J. (2010): "The Problem of Induction," *The Stanford Encyclopedia of Philosophy (Spring 2010 Edition)*, Edward N. Zalta (ed.) (http://plato.stanford.edu/archives/spr2010/entries/induction-problem/).
Von Mises, R. (1964): *Mathematical Theory of Probability and Statistics*, Academic Press, New York.
Von Savigny, E. (1976a): *Juristische Dogmatik und Wissenschaftstheorie*, C. H. Beck, Munich.
Von Savigny, E. (1976b): *Grundkurs im wissenschaftlichen Definieren* (4th ed.), dtv, Munich (5th ed. 1980).
Von Wright, G. H. (1971): *Explanation and Understanding*, Cornell University Press, Ithaca, NY; reprint Routledge & Kegan Paul, London 2008.
Votsis, I. (2011): "Everything you Always Wanted to Know about Structural Realism but Were Afraid to Ask," *European Journal for Philosophy of Science* 1/2, 227–276.
Watkins, J. W. N. (1964): "Confirmation, the Paradoxes, and Positivism," in: M. Bunge (ed.), *Critical Approaches to Science and Philosophy*, Transaction Publishers, New Jersey, 92–115.

Watkins, J. W. N. (1984): *Science and Skepticism*, Hutchinson, London.
Weber, E., and van Dyck, M. (2002): "Unification and Explanation," *Synthese* 131, 145–154.
Weber, M. (1949): *On The Methodology of the Social Sciences*, Free Press, Glencoe, IL (German orig. 1922).
Weinberg, J., Nichols, S., and Stich, S. (2001): "Normativity and Epistemic Intuitions," *Philosophical Topics* 29, 429–460.
Weingartner, P. (1978): *Wissenschaftstheorie I: Einführung in die Hauptprobleme*, problemata 3, frommann-holzboog, Stuttgart (2nd ed.).
Weingartner, P. (1983): "Definition of Value-Judgment," *Epistemologia* 6 (special issue), 79–86.
Weingartner, P. (2000): "Reasons for Filtering Classical Logic," in: D. Batens et al. (eds.), *Frontiers in Paraconsistent Logic*, King's College Publications, London, 315–327.
Weingartner, P., and Schurz, G. (1986): "Paradoxes Solved by Simple Relevance Criteria," *Logique et Analyse* 113, 3–40.
Weingartner, P., and Schurz, G. (1996, eds.): *Law and Prediction in the Light of Chaos Research*, Springer, Berlin.
Whewell, W. (1837): *History of the Inductive Sciences*, John W. Parker, London.
Whorf, B. L. (1956): *Language, Thought and Reality*, MIT Press, Cambridge, MA.
Wilholt, T. (2009): "Bias and Values in Scientific Research," *Studies in History and Philosophy of Science* 40, 92–101.
Williamson, J. (2010): *In Defence of Objective Bayesianism*, Oxford University Press, Oxford.
Wilson, M. (1979): "Maxwell's Condition—Goodman's Problem," *British Journal for the Philosophy of Science* 30, 107–123.
Wilson, N. (1959): "Substances without Substrata," *Review of Metaphysics* 12, 521–539.
Winnie, J. A. (1967): "The Implicit Definition of Theoretical Terms," *British Journal for the Philosophy of Science* 18, 223–229.
Wittgenstein, L. (1921): *Tractatus logico-philosophicus*, Dover Pub. Inc., New York 1998 (English orig. 1921).
Wittgenstein, L. (1945/2001): *Philosophical Investigations*, Blackwell Publishing, Oxford 2001.
Woodward, J. (2002): "There Is No such Thing as a Ceteris Paribus Law," in: Earman et al. (2002), 303–328.
Woodward, J. (2003): *Making Things Happen*, Oxford University Press, Oxford.
Worrall, J. (1989/97): "Structural Realism: The Best of Both Worlds?," *Dialectica* 43/1–2, reprinted in Papineau (1996b), 139–165.
Worrall, J. (2006): "Theory-Confirmation and History," in: C. Cheyne and J. Worrall (eds.), *Rationality and Reality*, Springer, New York, 31–61.
Young, H. D., and Freedman, R. A. (1996): *University Physics* (9th ed.), Addison-Wesley Publ. Comp., Reading, MA.
Zahar, E. G. (1973): "Why Did Einstein's Programme Supersede Lorentz's," *British Journal for the Philosophy of Science*, 24, 95–123, 223–262.
Zeh, H. D. (1989): *The Physical Basis of the Direction of Time*, Berlin and Heidelberg, Springer.

SOLUTIONS TO SELECTED EXERCISES

(Note: Solutions to exercises which are not mentioned here can be retrieved directly from the text of the corresponding sections.)

Sec. 2.2–4

3 A sentence is fallible if it is possible that it is false; a sentence is falsifiable if it is possible to design an empirical test by means of which, if it were false, we could find out that it is false.

Sec. 2.5–6

3 If political correctness means merely that scientific facts have to be stated in such a way that non-experts will not misunderstand the message and draw illegitimate value-consequences from them, then political correctness and value-neutrality are compatible. If political correctness is understood in a stronger sense, implying that certain facts must not be stated, because given accepted background beliefs they imply unwanted value-consequences, then political correctness and value-neutrality are incompatible.

Sec. 2.7

1 (a) inductive-statistical specialization, (b) deductive inference, from general to particular, (c) inductive prediction, (d) abductive inference.

Sec. 2.8–9

3 (a) psychological (truthfulness), (b) biological, (c) psychological, (d) physical.

Sec. 3.1

1. (a) individual term (proper name), (b) one-place function symbol, (c) functional singular term, (d) two-place relation (1st order), (e) intensional sentence operator, (f) truth-functional sentence operator, (g) quantifier.
2. (a) value concept, (b) observation concept, (c) theoretical concept of physics, (d) empirical disposition concept of physics, (e) theoretical concept of psychology, (f) empirical disposition concept of biology, (g) normative political concept, (h) theoretical concept of legal science with normative implications.
3. (a) nominal scale, (b) absolute scale, (c) nominal scale, (d) ordinal scale, (e) interval scale, (f) interval scale, (g) ratio scale.

Sec. 3.2

1. (a) descriptive, (b) mixed, (c) prescriptive, (d) descriptive.
2. (a) theoretical sentence (singular), (b) observation sentence, (c) empirical disposition sentence, (d) observation sentence, (e) empirical sentence (general), (f) theoretical sentence (general).

Sec. 3.3–6

1. (a) log. true, (b) def. true, (c) synth. true, (d) def. true, (e) log. true, (f) synth. true.
2. (a) statistically general, restricted, (b) strictly general, unrestricted, (c) singular, (d) statistically general, unrestricted (qualitative statistical), (e) strictly general, restricted (localized), (f) existential, restricted, (g) strictly general, unrestricted.
3. Lawlike are (b), (g), and maybe even (d); (a) and (e) are accidental.

Sec. 3.7–9

1. (a) neither-nor, (b) verifiable and falsifiable, (c) neither-nor, (d) falsifiable, but not verifiable, (e) verifiable and falsifiable.
2. (a) Most persons who had as little sleep as you had today will be tired tomorrow. (b) Most persons who had contact with some other person who was as infected with the flu as he was, and whose contact was similarly close as your contact, will catch the flu from this other person. (c) On most days, it won't be clear up in the mountains, if the weather conditions on the days preceding that day are similar to weather conditions observed over the last three days.
3. $V \wedge M$: $100 - (20+30+27) = 23\%$, V: $27+23 = 50\%$, U: $20+30 = 50\%$, M: $30+23 = 53\%$, F: $20+27 = 47\%$, $U \vee M$: $20+30+23 = 73\%$, $V \vee F$: $20+27+23 = 70\%$, $M \vee F$: 100%, $V \wedge U$: 0%; V given M: $23/53$, V given F: $27/47$, F given U: $20/50$, M given $V \vee F$: $23/70$, since $(M \wedge (V \vee F)) \leftrightarrow (M \wedge V)$; $V \vee M$ given M: 1, since $(V \vee M) \wedge M \leftrightarrow M$.

Sec. 3.10–13

1. (a) If a body x is distorted by a force acting on x within a short time interval, then: x is elastic iff x retains its previous form shortly after the distortion. (b) If x is asked for help in a standard situation where help is needed, then normally: x is helpful iff x helps in this situation.

Solutions to Selected Exercises • 437

3   (a) valid, irrelevant ("female" replaceable *salva validitate*), (b) valid, relevant, (c) valid, irrelevant ("is a social being" replaceable s.v.), (d) invalid, (e) valid, irrelevant ("human" and "wants to be alone" replaceable s.v.).
4   According to the binomial formula, $\binom{10}{5} \cdot 1/2^5 \cdot 1/2^{(10-5)} = \binom{10}{5} \cdot (1/2^{10})$ is the probability to obtain exactly 5 heads in 10 tosses. So the result is: $(1/2^{10}) \cdot \Sigma_{5 \leq k \leq 10} \binom{10}{k}$. It is well known that $\binom{n}{k} = \binom{n}{n-k}$ and $\Sigma_{0 \leq k \leq n} \binom{n}{k} = 2^n$, which implies $\Sigma_{5 \leq k \leq 10} \binom{10}{k} = (2^{10} + \binom{10}{5})/2^{11})$. So we obtain the result $1/2 + (\binom{10}{5}/2^{11})$, which is slightly greater than 1/2.

Sec. 4.1-2

1,2 With "±" for "unnegated or negated" (variables and quantifiers omitted): True and relevant are: H→F, H→G, F→G, and the contrapositions of these implications ¬F→¬H, ¬G→¬H, ¬G→¬F. True and irrelevant are (irrelevant antecedent factors underlined): H∧±G→F, H∧±F→G, F∧±H→G, ¬F∧±G→¬H, ¬G∧±F→¬H, ¬G∧±H→¬F.
3   corr(M,V) = p(M|V) − p(M) = 46/100 − 53/100 = −7/100, corr(F,V) = p(F|V) − p(F) = 54/100 − 47/100 = +7/100, corr(M,U) = p(M|U) − p(M) = 60/100 − 53/100 = +7/100, corr(F,U) = p(F|U) − p(F) = 40/100 − 47/100 = −7/100.

Sec. 4.2

1   (a) (L1) is confirmed by samples 1 and 2, (L2) is confirmed by sample 1, and (L3) is falsified by sample 3. (b) (L2) is irrelevant in its antecedent factor "over 40," by comparison of sample 1 with 2. (L2) relevant in its antecedent factor "male," by comparison of sample 1 with 3. (L1) is relevant (in its only antecedent factor) by comparison of sample 2 with 3.
2   Ask yourself: in which respects (which are potentially relevant for allergies) do your two residences differ? Change them successively (if you can) and find out whether this makes a difference to your allergic symptoms.

Sec. 4.3

1   Sample frequencies between 282 and 318 smokers out of 500 beer drinkers would weakly confirm the hypothesis; all other sample results would strongly disconfirm it.
2   [283, 347].
3   For a significant difference smaller than 16%.
4   By $\sqrt{10}$.

Sec. 4.5

1   (a) Assertions (i) and (ii) are exclusive; (iii) and (iv) are comparative. (b) CP assertion (i): Wood must have normal chemical composition; no force besides gravitation and uplift may act on the wood. CP assertion (ii): If we would know such an interpretation, nuclear reactors could be built in a safe way (…).
2   According to the formula $\mu(X) \pm 1.96 \cdot \sigma_{s_n}^{corr}/\sqrt{n}$, the acceptance interval is $80 \pm 1.96 \cdot 12/\sqrt{30}$ = (approx.) [76, 84]. The hypothesis can be retained.

3   According to the formula $\Delta_{sign} = 1.96 \cdot \sigma^{corr} \cdot \sqrt{(1/n) + (1/m)}$, the significant difference is $1.96 \cdot 11 \cdot \sqrt{(1/30) + (1/34)} =$ (approx.) 5.4. The difference is significant. The effect strength is $6/11 = 0.55$.

Sec. 5.1–2

1   (a) An anxious person is often frightened in unperilous situations, and if she has children, she will more often than normal be worried about them. (b) If voltage is applied to a metallic substance, an electric current will flow through it, and if the substance is heated, it will conduct the heat quickly.—Implied empirical predictions: (a) A person who is often frightened in unperilous situations will, if she has children, more often than normal be worried about her children. (b) If an electric current flows through a substance upon application of voltage, this substance will quickly conduct heat when it is heated.

Sec. 5.5–6

2   Such an ad-hoc hypothesis could say that, unlike Modus Ponens, Modus Tollens involves the operation of negation, and this operation is learned very late in the cognitive development. This hypothesis is not very plausible, though, since in many situations the operation of negation is already grasped by the infant.

Sec. 5.7–9

3   Because (and under the assumption that) T's Ramsey sentence asserts everything about T's theoretical concepts which is known about them. By the same reasoning, T's Carnap sentence expresses T's total analytic content.

4   Concerning Piaget's theory: the concepts "logical-structural abilities," "concrete-operational stage" and "formal-operational stage" are T-theoretical, while the concepts "change of perspective," "reversibility of operations" and "invariance" are pre-T-theoretical.

Sec. 5.10–11

3   The regularities, to which this curve has been fitted post-facto, reflect accidental contingencies in the first 100 spinnings of the roulette wheel. They are not use-novel and will not be preserved in further spinnings.

4   "x is blite $\leftrightarrow_{def}$ x is black and has been observed before a given future time point t_k, or otherwise it is white," and "x is whack $\leftrightarrow_{def}$ x is white and has been observed before a given future time point t_k, or otherwise it is black." Since all so-far observed ravens have been observed to be black before t_k, they are all blite.

5   The person should consider all of her dice roll results; this constitutes the total relevant evidence for the question of her "magical power" to influence dice rolls.

Sec. 6.1–2

2   (a) actual explanation, (b) prediction (and justification), but not a potential explanation because Peter's wanting-to-come but not his uttering-the-sentence is the

cause of his coming, (c) prediction and potential explanation (compare with (b)), (d) retrodiction (and justification), but not a potential explanation because the justificandum occurs earlier than the antecedent, (e) neither a justification nor an explanation, since there is no law which together with the antecedent would entail the conclusion.

Sec. 6.3–4

2   I know nothing relevant about Mr. Mueller's state of health except that he is 82 years old; the probability that someone will die soon given he is older than 82 is quite high.
3   The additional information that Mr. Mueller is in the best of health despite his advanced age reduces the probability that he will soon die to below 50%; therefore the IS-argument is no longer rationally acceptable in the minimal sense.

Sec. 6.6–7

2   (a) If the antecedent were true, the worlds in which Verdi was French and in which Bizet was Italian would be closer to the actual world than any others. However, it is hard to tell which one is closer. If both are equally close, standard semantics for counterfactuals give the result that neither one of the two counterfactuals is true. (b) If I could float free in the air, then either the law of gravitation would be violated, or I would have an extremely light material constitution, which—given I retain some essential properties of humans—would violate other laws of nature. Worlds of this sort would involve so many "radical" changes (compared to ours) that it is hardly possible to tell reasonably which of these world(s) would be closest to the actual one.
3   (a) universal and Maxwell, (b) neither universal nor Maxwell, (c) universal but not Maxwell.
4   (a) necessary, (b) contingent, (c) necessary, (d) contingent.
7   By assumption the four dependencies DEP(X,Z), DEP(X,Z|Y), DEP(Y,Z) and DEP(Y,Z|X) hold. By prop. 6.7-5 this gives us the undirected causal graph X–Z–Y. If the graph is faithful for the given p, the directions must be X→Z←Y. A non-faithful graph which explains this p would be the graph in fig. 6.7-4.

INDEX OF NAMES

Abrahamsen, A. 412
Achinstein, P. 312, 411
Adam, M. 64, 87, 411
Adams, E. W. 347, 411
Adorno, T. W. 14, 38, 411
Albert, D. 409, 411
Albert, H. 3, 38, 85, 87, 411
Allen, M. 44, 413
Alston, W. P. 409, 411
Anderson, A. R. 145, 411
Anderson, J. R. 13, 411
Andreas, H. 96, 411
Apel, K.-O. 14, 411
Aqvist, L. 39, 411
Aristotle 3, 50, 86, 114, 348
Arló-Costa, H. xix
Armstrong, D. M. 11, 56, 83, 138f, 171, 293, 375, 377, 381, 385, 408, 411f
Arnold, E. 85, 412
Ausubel, D. 277, 412
Ayer, A. J. 81, 412

Bacchus, F. 148, 164, 412
Bacon, F. 4
Bacon, R. 4
Balzer, W. xviii, 13, 16, 96, 104, 251, 257, 266, 293, 302, 304, 307, 310, 347, 412
Barton, A. H. 37, 423
Bauer, H. 133, 148, 171, 221, 224, 225, 241, 412

Bayes, T. 133, 135ff
Bechtel, W. 362, 412
Beebee, H. 408, 412, 415, 420, 425, 427
Belnap, N. D. 145, 411
Bergmann, M. 122f, 171, 412
Berlin, B. 70f, 412
Bernstein, R. J. 12, 412
Billingsley, P. 133, 241, 412
Bird, A. 3, 11, 15, 55, 83, 138f, 171, 412
Bishop, M. A. 14, 412
Black, M. 82, 412
Böhler, D. 12, 412
Böhm, J. M. 425, 430
Boogerd, F. C. 48, 412
Bortz, J. 99, 104, 191–3, 197, 226, 241, 327, 412
Bourbaki, N. 31, 412
Bovens, L. 23, 340, 413
Boyd, R. 11, 291, 296f, 413
Brainerd, C. 272, 276f, 413, 431
Braithwaite, R. B. 82, 299, 413
Branch, G. 3, 413
Brewer, W. F. 68, 87, 413
Brewka, G. 413
Brickmont, J. 62, 432
Bridgeman, P. W. 98, 413
Broad, C. D. 48, 413
Bromberger, S. 351, 353, 354, 384, 413
Brown, H. I. 64, 413,
Brown, J. R. 3, 44, 413
Bruggeman, F. J. 412

440

Bruns, G. 15, 413
Bueno, O. 13, 293, 413
Bühler, A. 14, 413
Bühler, C. 44, 413
Bunge, M. 287, 293, 345, 413, 433

Callender, C. 378, 415
Campbell, D. T. 13, 15, 413
Campbell, S. 197, 413
Carnap, R. xvii, 5–7, 10, 22, 31, 45, 50f, 53, 59, 63, 65, 70, 72, 94, 96, 99, 104, 109, 117, 123, 133, 136–8, 140–2, 149, 160, 163–6, 168f, 171, 182, 233–5, 243, 251, 291f, 300f, 305, 312, 332f, 343–7, 376, 413f, 421, 438
Carrier, M. xviii, 76, 85, 296, 413, 414
Cartwright, N. 47, 208, 211, 215f, 220, 238, 241, 261, 293, 364, 399, 404, 414
Causey, R. 47, 414
Cevolani, G. 339, 414
Chakravartty, A. 13, 414
Chalmers, A. F. 72, 87, 109, 414
Chisholm, R. M. 123, 414
Christensen, D. 314, 316, 414
Church, A. 154, 415
Coffa, J. 361, 362, 415
Cohen, C. 415
Cohen, J. 378, 415
Collingwood, R.G. 388, 415
Copi, I. 91, 113, 168, 415
Cover, J. A. 345, 415
Craig, W. 271f, 299, 303, 415
Cramér, H. 156, 415
Craver, C. F. 362, 415
Cresswell, M. J. 91, 380, 421
Crombie, A. 4, 415
Crupi, V. 319, 414f
Curd, M. 345, 415, 417, 420, 427

Dahms, H.-J. 38, 46, 415
Dahrendorf, R. 411
Dancy, J. 60, 66, 415
Darden, L. 362, 415
Darwin, C. 4, 8, 114
Davidson, D. 48, 366, 415
De Finetti, B. 133, 149, 158, 161, 164f, 235, 415
De Regt, H. 269, 415
de Swart, H. 433
Demopoulos, W. 302, 415

Denzin, N. K. 14, 37, 415
Descartes, R. 4, 258, 347
Dilthey, W. 14
Doets, H. 433
Doppelt, G. 41, 415
Douglas, H. 76f, 415
Douven, I. xviii, 415
Dowe, P. 387, 415
Dray, W. 219, 349, 365–7, 416
Ducasse, C. J. 376, 416
Duhem, P. viii, 268f, 347, 350, 416
Dupré, J. 76, 416, 422
Dürr, H. P. 173, 416

Eagle, A. 158, 171, 416
Earman, J. 55, 133, 138, 159–61, 164–6, 171, 214f, 219, 232, 234–8, 241, 320f, 329, 345, 372, 375, 377, 408f, 416, 434
Eells, E. 208, 383, 416
Einstein, A. 263, 388, 416
Estany, A. 68, 416
Etchemendy, J. 140f, 416
Evans, J. St. B. 277, 416

Fair, D. 387, 415
Fales, E. 385, 416
Fara, M. 139, 416
Feigl, H. 340, 414–6
Festa, R. 414, 430
Feyerabend, P. 10, 63, 416
Feynman, R. P. 377, 387, 416
Field, A. 133, 416
Field, H. 31, 416
Fine, T. 133, 416
Firth, R. 78, 416
Fisher, R. A. 133, 189, 192, 199, 226, 228f, 416
Fitelson, B. 319f, 416, 419
Flach, P. 55, 416
Flanders, N. A. 40, 416
Flyvbjerg, B. 37, 417
Fodor, J. 47, 67, 94, 143, 217, 241, 372, 417
Foley, R. 333, 417
Follesdal, D. 14, 417
Forbes, E. G. 68, 417
Forster, M. 241, 417
Frankena, W. K. 39, 87, 417
Franklin, J. 197, 413
Freedman, R. A. 257, 434
Frege, G. 31, 94, 417

French, S. 13, 61, 96, 413, 417
Friedman, M. 302, 341, 368, 409, 415, 417
Frisby, D. 38, 417
Frisch, M. xix, 409, 417
Fumerton, R. A. 58, 417

Gabbay, D. M. 59, 411, 417f
Gadamer, H. 32, 417
Gähde, U. 310, 317
Gaifman, H. 236f, 241, 417
Galilei, G. 4
Gärdenfors, P. 356, 363, 368, 417
Gardiner, P. 366, 418, 431
Garnham, A. 71, 101, 418
Garson, J. W. 304, 418
Gebharter, A. 389, 396, 400f, 404–6, 431
Geiger, D. 410, 418
Gemes, K. xviii, 145, 312, 316f, 321, 339, 418
Giddens, A. 37, 418
Giere, R. 13, 16, 63, 69, 87, 418
Gijsbers, V. 342, 369, 418
Gillies, D. 129, 133, 150, 152, 158f, 164–6, 169, 171, 199, 233f, 241, 418
Glasersfeld, E. v. 61f, 418
Glennan, S. 362, 373, 388, 418
Glymour, C. xix, 144, 283, 314–6, 327, 345, 389, 396, 416, 418, 432
Gödel, K. 31, 418
Godfrey-Smith. P. 33, 418
Goldman, A. xix, 14, 82, 342, 418
Goldszmidt, M. 181, 418
Good, I. J. 167, 418
Goodman, N. 22, 124, 171, 322, 331–3, 342f, 345, 347, 373f, 377f, 409, 418f,
Grice, H. P. 145, 419
Grimes, T. R. 316, 419
Grünbaum, A. 205, 262f, 386, 418–20

Habermas, J. 14, 38, 76, 87, 411, 419
Hacking, J. 226, 419
Hájek, A 155f, 171, 419
Halonen, I. 368, 419
Hanson, N. R. 9, 63, 66, 419
Hare, R. 96, 419
Harman, G. 56, 83, 419
Harré, R. 293, 419
Hart, W. D. 30, 419
Hartmann, S. xviii, 23, 340, 413
Haussmann, D. 389, 407, 419

Hawthorne. J. xviii, 162, 164, 320, 419
Hays, W. 133, 171, 179, 192, 198f, 221, 224f, 227–9, 231, 235, 238, 241, 419
Heidbrink, H. 422
Helmholtz, H. v. 65, 419
Hempel, C. G. xvii, 6f, 17, 47, 70, 76, 109, 114, 121–4, 167f, 171, 175f, 185, 238, 241, 251, 261–3, 267, 270–2, 291, 301, 311–5, 331, 341, 345, 348–68, 375f, 407f, 419f
Hendry, R. F. 11, 47, 420
Herbert, N. 61, 388, 420
Hesse, M. 314, 420
Hilgendorf, E. 34, 76, 420, 422
Hilpinen, R. 340, 420,
Hintikka, J. 235, 368, 419f, 426
Hirsch, E. D. Jr. 14, 420
Hitchcock, C. 206, 211, 327, 329, 388, 399, 401, 407, 412, 420, 422
Holm, K. 425
Holweg, H. 430
Hook, C. 425, 430
Howard, D. 414
Howson, C. 53, 87, 133, 149, 155–61, 166, 169, 171, 179, 198f, 228f, 234f, 238, 241, 320, 323–5, 345–7, 420f
Hoyningen-Huene, P. 9, 15, 421
Hrbacek, K. 92, 168, 421
Huber, F. xviii, 315, 347, 421
Hübner, P. 425
Huff, D. 202, 421
Hughes, G. E. 91, 380, 421
Humburg, J. 171, 421
Hume, D. 4f, 12, 50, 77f, 80f, 84, 87, 209, 331, 370, 376, 382f, 386, 393, 400, 421
Humphreys, P. 342, 365, 421
Hunter, J. E. 179, 421
Hüttemann, A. xviii, 48, 220, 421, 428

Ioannidis, J. 201, 421,

Jackson, F. 427
Jacobson, L. 203, 429
James, W. 12, 421
Jaynes, E. T. 228, 421
Jech, T. 92, 168, 421
Jeffrey, R. 235, 414, 421
Jeffrey, R. C. 77, 148, 166, 241, 368, 421, 424, 429

Jeffrey. H. 235, 421
Joseph, G. 215, 241, 421

Kakas, A. 55, 416
Kamlah, W. 25, 421
Kanitscheider, B. 421
Kant, I. 4, 40, 62
Kay, P. 70f, 412
Kelly, K. xix, 150, 422
Kelly, T 83, 422
Kelsen, H. 33, 422
Ketland, J. 293, 301–3, 347, 422
Keuth, H. 15, 422
Keynes, J. M. 133, 234, 422
Kim, J. 356, 422
Kincaid, H. 85, 241, 415f, 422
Kirkham, R. L. 24, 60, 422
Kitcher, P. 45, 260, 341f, 368, 387, 422
Kleiter, G. xviii
Klenk, V. 85, 91, 168, 422
Koertge, N. 76, 422
Kolmogorov, A. N. 54, 134, 149, 156–8, 161, 238, 422
Kornblith, H. 13, 422
Körner, S. 144, 422
Kourany, J. 414
Krantz, D. 99, 102–4, 168, 422
Krebs, D. L. 255, 422
Kripke, S. 10, 88, 422
Kriz, J. 62, 75, 422
Kuhlen, L. 33, 420, 422
Kuhn, T. S. 6, 8–10, 15–18, 21, 63, 66f, 69, 250, 279f, 422
Kuipers, T. A. F. xviii, 57, 63, 69, 87, 284, 293, 314–6, 345–7, 414, 422f, 430
Kutschera, F. v. 70f, 78, 87, 93, 107, 161, 165, 168, 171, 241, 270, 301, 332, 409, 423
Kyburg, H. E. 335f, 415, 423

Ladyman, J. xviii, 15f, 45, 48, 55, 61, 82, 87, 139, 296, 305, 345–7, 413, 417, 423
Lakatos, I. 8f, 18, 184, 241, 260–3, 276–81, 284, 288f, 315, 345–47, 423
Laland, K. N. 425
Lambert, B. L. 68, 87, 413
Lambert, K. 247, 280, 340–2, 368f, 431
Lamnek, S. 14, 37, 423
Lange, M. 373, 380f, 423
Langley, P. 17, 52, 523

Latour, B. 61, 423
Laudan, L. 3, 9, 11, 16–8, 294–7, 346, 423
Laurence, S. 370, 424
Lazarsfeld, P. F. 37, 206f, 423
Lehrer, K. 336, 340, 423
Leibniz, G. W. 4, 184, 347, 363
Leighton, R. D. 416
Leitgeb, H. 150, 347, 423, 431
Lenzen, W. 314f, 423
Leplin, J. 291, 345, 413, 424
Levi, I. 51, 335, 424
Lewis, D. 11, 107, 139f, 157, 161, 293, 303–6, 373, 377f, 380, 385f, 407–9, 424
Lincoln, Y. S. 14, 37, 415
Lipton, P. 56f, 83, 424
Locke, J. 4, 333, 335f
Lorenzen, P. 25, 421
Losee, J. 3, 15, 181, 291, 348, 424
Loux, M. J. 293, 424
Luce, R. D. 422
Lück, H. E. 422

Mach, E. 5, 59, 291, 340, 424
Machery, E. 14, 424
Machover, M. 94, 168, 424
Mackie, J. 174, 424
Maddy, P. 31, 424
Makinson, D. 335f, 424
Mallon, R. 424
Manninen, J. 408, 424
Margolis, E. 370, 424
Martin, C. B. 140, 412, 424
Maturana, H. R. 61, 424
Maudlin, T. 376, 381, 408, 424
Maxwell, G. 70, 291, 294, 301, 419f, 423f
Maxwell, J. C. 375–77, 380, 409 439
Maxwell, N. W. 425
Mayntz, R. 197f, 206, 208, 253, 425
McCarthy, T. 141, 425
McMahon, K. 415
McMullin, E. 16, 425
Melia, J. 305, 425
Mellor, H. D. 15, 425, 428
Mendelson, E. 168, 425
Menzies, P. 388, 412, 425
Mesoudi, A. 221, 425
Mill, J. St. 4, 83, 181, 377, 425
Miller, D. 157, 320, 337–9, 344f, 425–7
Millikan, R. G. 221, 252, 425
Mitchell, S. 416
Moor, J. 412

Index of Names • 443

Morris, C. W. 92, 425
Morris, M. 94, 168, 425
Mortimer, C. E. 47, 243, 252, 425
Moser, P. K. 56, 425
Moulines, C. U. 412
Moulines, U. 13, 412
Moulines, W. 310, 412
Mühlhölzer, F. 307, 412
Mumford, S. 11, 136, 139, 169–71, 386, 425
Musgrave, A. xix, 54f, 423, 425
Musgrave, A. E. 324, 347, 425

Nagel, E. 47, 64, 123, 251, 267, 373, 409, 425-7
Nelson, J. 412
Neurath, O. 5f, 46, 66, 269, 425f
Newman, M. H. A. 302–4, 426
Newton, I. 4, 55, 80, 250, 256f, 259f, 280
Neyman, J. 192, 229, 426
Nichols, S. 424, 434
Niiniluoto, I. xviii, 56, 340, 344, 347, 357f, 426
Nordenstam, T. 412
Norton, J. 83, 426
Norton, J. D. 426
Novak, J. 277, 426
Nowak, L. 261, 426

Oakhill, J. 71, 101, 418
Ockham, W. v. 4, 31, 271, 311,
Oddie, G. 340, 426
Olsson, E. xviii
Oppenheim, P. 121, 348, 356, 420, 426
Otte, R. 209, 426

Pap, A. 171, 426
Papineau, D. 13, 82, 84, 303f, 306, 345, 423, 426, 434
Pargetter, R. 427
Patry, J.-L. 40, 426
Paulßen, J. 329, 426
Pearce, D. 347, 426
Pearl, J. 163, 181, 210, 389, 396–8, 401–3, 408, 410, 418, 426
Peirce, C. S. 12, 25, 55f, 426f
Pennock, R. T. 3, 45, 427
Penrose, R. 61, 427
Phillips, R. 416
Piaget, J. 254, 272–7, 346, 351, 354, 427, 438
Pietroski, P. 215, 241, 427

Pigden, C. R. 77f, 427
Pilot. H. 411
Place, U. T. 412
Plato 3
Podolski, B. 388, 416
Popper. K. 7–10, 15–7, 38, 42, 52–4, 57, 63–6, 81, 108f, 128f, 146, 155–7, 168, 171, 183f, 199, 234f, 263, 278, 283, 288, 314, 320, 337–9, 352, 411, 427
Price, H. 386, 388, 417, 425, 427
Priest, G. 331, 427
Prim, R. 76, 79, 427
Prior, A. N. 78, 427
Prior, E. W. 138, 427
Psillos, S. xviii, 11, 61, 82, 84f, 291f, 294–6, 299, 305, 345, 347, 376, 384, 388, 408, 417, 420, 427
Putnam, H. 10–2, 47, 87, 97, 109, 271, 291, 293f, 346, 418, 426–8

Quine, W. v. O. 7, 11, 13, 71f, 97, 109, 138, 141f, 169, 268f, 288, 295, 346, 409, 428

Rahman. S. 85, 428, 430
Raiffa, H. 39, 428
Railton, P. 362, 364, 428
Ramsey, F. P. 133, 158, 251, 293, 298–306, 345f, 377, 409, 428, 438
Rantala, V. 347, 426
Rawls, J. 22, 428
Reichenbach, H. xvii, 5, 59, 84, 124, 132f, 155, 157, 168, 206–10, 243, 359, 384, 387, 393, 405, 409, 428
Rescher, N. 12, 24, 87, 409, 419, 428
Reutlinger, A. 214, 220, 373, 380, 421, 428
Rey, G. 215, 241, 427
Richardson, R. C. 412
Ridley, M. 115, 428
Rips, L J. 145, 428
Roberts, J. 215, 219, 372, 416
Rock, I. 66f, 69, 85, 428
Rorty, R. 12, 428
Rosen, N. 388, 416
Rosenberg, A. 15, 32, 75, 366, 423, 428
Rosenthal, R. 202f, 429
Ross, A. 33, 429
Ross, D. 15, 45, 48, 82, 139, 296, 305, 347, 423
Rott, H. xviii, 278, 429

Rudner, R. 76f, 429
Russell, B. 92, 429
Ryder, J. M. 159, 429

Saatsi, J. 305, 425
Salmon, W. 81, 155, 168, 171–7, 206, 244, 348, 357, 360–4, 368, 387–9, 408, 418, 420–2, 429
Salmon, W. C. 82, 429
Savitt, S. F. 409, 429
Scheines, R. 396, 418, 432
Schiffer, S. 372, 429
Schleiermacher, F. 14
Schlesinger, G. 328, 429
Schlick, M. 5f, 429
Schmidt, F. L. 179, 421
Schmidt, P. F. 41, 429
Scholz, O. xviii, 14, 366, 429
Schrenk, M. xviii, 11, 429
Schurz, G. 9, 12f, 39, 46, 52–61, 76–8, 84–7, 96, 104, 141–4, 150, 171, 181, 203, 214–21, 244, 247, 268f, 272, 276f, 280, 286, 296–9, 304, 310–2, 316f, 322–9, 338–48f, 354–7, 361, 368f, 371–3, 377, 389, 396, 400–8, 414, 423, 428–31, 434
Scriven, M. 119, 355, 363, 409, 414, 419, 431
Shao, J. 329, 431
Shapere, D. 87, 431
Shapiro, S. 31, 431
Sher, G. 140f, 169, 431
Shoemaker, S. 10, 431
Shoenfield, J. 117, 431
Shogenji, T. 340, 431
Siegel, L. 276, 431
Simon, H. 205, 431
Skirbekk, G. 412
Skyrms, B. 84, 171, 238, 431
Smart, J. J. C. 294, 431
Sneed, J. D. 12, 98, 256f, 291–3, 303, 309–11, 347, 412, 431
Snir, M. 236f, 241, 417
Snow, C. P. 29, 33, 431
Sober, E. 241, 323, 327–9, 399, 417, 420, 431f
Sokal, A. 62, 432
Sperber, D. 145, 432
Spielmann, S. 432
Spirtes, P. 396–400, 402f, 408–10, 418, 432

Spohn, W. xviii, 374, 432
Stadler, F. 5, 38, 432
Stalker, D. 332, 432
Stalnaker, R. 373, 432
Stanford, K. P. 432
Steel, D. 402, 432
Stegmüller, W. xvii, 7, 12f, 16–8, 32, 78, 85–7, 95, 136, 147, 168, 171, 199, 251, 301, 309–12, 345, 348, 352, 356, 362, 364, 368, 407–9, 432
Stephan, A. 412
Stich, S. 12, 424, 432, 434
Strawson, P.F. 81, 432
Strevens, M. 155, 162, 216, 364, 432
Suppes, P. 12, 95, 115–7, 168, 171, 209, 238, 356, 420, 422, 427, 432
Swinburne, R. 85, 87, 323, 412f, 429, 432

Tarski, A. 22, 94, 111, 140f, 427, 432f
Thagard, P. 13, 368, 433
Thorn, P. xviii, 181, 347, 431
Tichý, P. 337–40, 433
Tilman, H. 76, 79, 427
Tomasello, M. 382, 433
Tooley, M. 376, 433
Topitsch, E. 38, 85, 411
Toulmin, S. 79, 433
Trentori, K. 319, 41
Triplett, T. 3, 433
Trout, J. D. 14, 412
Tuomela, R. 14, 107, 271f, 300f, 345–7, 356, 362, 368, 408f, 424, 426, 433
Tversky, A. 422

Unwin, S. T. 323, 433
Urbach, P. 133, 149, 155–9, 161, 166, 169, 171, 179, 198f, 228f, 234f, 238, 241, 320, 323, 345–7, 421

Van Cleve, J. 82, 433
Van Dalen, D. 92, 116, 433
Van Dyck, M. 369, 434
Van Fraassen, B. 6, 11–3, 57f, 70–2, 85–7, 107, 124, 165, 291–3, 300, 351, 354, 363f, 368f, 373, 378, 380f, 408, 433,
Varela, F. 61, 424
Vaught, R. L. 303, 415
Verma, T. S. 418
Vickers, J. 84f, 433

Index of Names

Von Mises, R. 133, 154–7, 171, 433
Von Savigny, E. 33f, 116, 433
Von Wright, G. H. 14, 388, 409, 433
Votsis, I. xviii, 61, 345, 431, 433

Watkins, J. W. N. 55, 347, 433f
Weber, E. 369, 434
Weber, M. 37–9, 41, 434
Weinberg, J. 14, 434
Weingartner, P. 19, 26, 30, 78, 143, 171, 268, 280, 338–40, 347, 355, 428, 430f, 434
Werning, M. xviii
Westerhoff, H. V. 412
Whewell, W. 314, 340, 347, 434
Whiten, A. 425
Whorf, B. L. 70f, 434
Wilholt, T. 335, 434
Williamson, J. xviii, 162, 241, 434

Wilson, D. 145, 432
Wilson, M. 377, 434
Wilson, N. 366, 434
Windelband, W. 14
Winkler, R. 133, 171, 179, 192, 198f, 221, 224–31, 235, 238, 241, 419
Winnie, J. A. 306, 434
Wittgenstein, L. 63, 66, 110, 140, 171, 350, 434
Woodward, J. 210, 372f, 386, 389, 400, 407–9, 434
Woolgar, S. 62, 423
Worrall, J. xviii, 61, 296f, 324, 434
Wylie, A. 422

Young, H. D. 257, 392, 434

Zahar, E .G. 324, 434
Zeh, H. D. 434

INDEX OF SUBJECTS

abduction 55–8, 294–6, 349
acceptance 76, 199, 333–6, 349, 358, 367
– interval 188–94, 223–6
Locke's rule of –333f
– of theories 288–90
shortest – interval 228f
– threshold 157, 333
acceptability (rational) 278–80, 288–911, 333f, 350, 359
action 32f, 42, 77f, 167, 252, 334, 366, 388f
explanation of –s 365f
anomaly 9, 278f
antecedent 118f, 124, 131, 135–7, 172–89, 193–5, 203, 216–8, 348–65, 374f, 385
approximation 261, 267, 326f, 336f
argument 49–58, 110–2, 143–6, 348ff
abductive – 55
deductive – 49f, 110f
inductive – 5, 49–54, 198f, 235–8
quasi– 359, 367
average s. mean value

background 56f, 71–4, 79f, 116f
– knowledge 69f, 171, 207–13, 231, 377
– system 168, 263, 283, 213f, 318, 324, 335, 349, 354–61,
– theory 7, 65, 244–50, 261, 268, 272, 369

Bayesianism 133, 158–64, 226–38, 314–20
objective – 232–5
subjective – 235–8
best system account 377–80
betting quotient 158–60

Carnap-sentence 320
causal
– connection axiom 396
– discovery 402–3
– direction 211–3, 352f, 386f
– graph 395–407
(a)cyclic – graph 397
– graph of values 427
– graph of variables 427
– mechanism 212, 354, 362, 373, 387f
– minimality 400
– model 354f, 396f, 400–7
– overdetermination 407
– power 385f
– pre-emption 407
– process 387f
– productivity axiom 400
causality 174, 180, 186, 200, 204–14, 305, 352–55, 382–407
– as a theoretical concept 389ff
general – 383
empirical content of – 403–6
singular – 383
spurious – 205, 209f

448 • Index of Subjects

cause
   (in)direct – 416
   common – 245f, 416
   counter– 210, 364
   deterministic – 383
   intermediate – 207, 416
   probabilistic – 383
   total – 383
central limit theorem 225
ceteris paribus law 214–219
   comparative – 214, 216
   exclusive – 214–9, 261, 278, 288, 371–3
chaos s. unpredictability
circularity 11f, 64, 80–4, 153f, 211, 340f, 380, 389
   – of definitions 116, 251, 308, 311
   – of arguments 64, 82–4, 197, 294f
   rule – 82
coherence 159f, 340
complexity 47f, 261, 341, 371, 381
complementary theories 37, 285f
concept 88–104
   atomic – 88
   classificatory – 99f
   comparative – 100–2
   descriptive – 97
   disposition – 98
   empirical – 98, 264
   general – 89
   logical – 90
   non-logical – 88ff
   observation – 72–75, 97
   prescriptive – 97
   pre-theoretical – 264, 307–9
   qualitative – 56f, 99f
   quantitative – 56f, 102–5
   singular – 88
   speculative – 309, 311
   theoretical – 98, 244, 264, 307–9
   T-theoretical – 264, 307–11
conditionalization 163–7, 180, 215, 298, 391
Condorcet jury theorem 23
confidence interval 191–3, 198f, 227f
confirmation 26, 128f, 181–98, 200–4, 217–20, 226–38, 281–91, 313–36
   Bayesian – 226ff, 318–20
   genuine – 329–31
   hypothetico-deductive – 181f, 314–18
   measures of – 319

   pseudo – 320–3
   relevant – 317, 349f
conjunction 90, 268–70, 319f
   rule of – 335f
   – problem 289, 341f, 351,
consequence 19f, 24f,
   – -element 282, 338f
   logically-deductive – 112f, 126f, 146f, 314f, 348
   monotonic – 78f
   non-monotonic – 78f
   relevant – 145
consequent 118f, 124, 131, 172f, 185, 188, 193, 216–8
conservation law 257, 377
consistent 111, 121
constructivism 61f
content 126f
   – cutting 238, 320–2
   – element 146f, 321, 329f, 341f
   empirical – 126
   excess – 276, 279, 282, 289, 340
   logical – 126
   model-theoretic – 127
   probabilistic – 127
   relevant – 147
content-rich 19f, 22, 24, 26f, 41, 60, 158
context
   – of application 42f
   – of discovery 17, 42f, 52
   – of justification 17, 42f, 52
   – dependence 98, 270, 283, 290, 360f
continuity argument 70
contradictory (inconsistent) 111, 298, 335
convergence of opinions 235–8
correlation 135, 178, 193ff, 202–14, 253f, 383f, 392, 399
   – measure 178f, 224
   conditional – 180
   significant – 193–6
   spurious – 205
correspondence
   – law s. law
   – relation 266f, 296–9
   – theorem 297
corroboration s. confirmation
counterfactual 124, 137, 373–5, 385f
Craig's theorem 271f, 299
Critical Theory 14, 38
curve
   – fitting 326–9

Index of Subjects • 449

polynomial – 327
simplest – 328

data 17, 27, 32–5, 64, 69, 109, 261, 296, 313–5, 326–9
default assumption 181, 253
definability 135–8, 141–3, 156, 175, 271, 305
definiendum 115
definiens 115
definite description 89, 220, 306
definition 113–7
   chain of –s 6, 24, 116, 251f
   eliminability of –s 116, 137, 299f
   empirical adequacy of –s 114
   empirical non-creativity of –s 116f
   explicit – 115
   implicit – 115
   Lewis – 305–7
   non-circularity of –s 116
   recursive – 116
degree of belief 130–3, 158–87
   actual – 163–6
   a-priori – 163–6
demarcation 8, 44–6, 311
determinism 118, 125f, 175, 209, 362, 355, 385f, 401
   in– 125f, 155, 204, 362
differential equation 258–61, 371
disconfirmation s. confirmation
disjunction 90, 109, 134, 146, 228, 269, 316, 340
distribution 54, 150f, 189ff, 217, 221f
   (a)symmetric – 222f, 227f
   binomial – 150–2, 154
   – of sample frequencies 152, 189
   – of sample differences 193f
   – of sample means 224f
   normal (Gaussian) – 222
   posterior – 235
   prior – 163f, 235
   uniform – 230–4
domain
   – of applications 277, 281, 288
   – of individuals 91, 94, 99–102, 104, 111, 119, 128, 130–2, 140f, 148, 165, 176, 188, 201, 216, 237f, 390
   – of inquiry 19, 30f, 35
   (in)finite – 8, 99, 130–2, 181, 323, 345
   – specific 83, 403
   empirical – 302f

mathematical – 302f
theoretical – 303
double blind test 202f
duck-rabbit 66, 68
Duhem's thesis 268–70

effect 4f, 174, 185–7, 204–14, 382ff
   common – 394–7, 406
   (in)direct – 207, 416
empirical creativity 260, 270f
empiricism 155, 291
   classical – 4f
   logical – 5–7, 11, 18, 54, 63, 251
   minimal – 20, 23f, 50, 63
   value – 78
epistemology 2, 10, 13, 59–61, 80–4
equivalence (material) 90, 101, 115–8, 291
error 23, 200ff, 213, 262, 335
   kinds of – 229
   random – 225, 326
   risk of – 77
   sources of – 200–3
essential sentence types 107, 121–3
essentialism 114, 138f
evidence 53–9, 122, 133, 161–7, 182, 226–36, 243, 271, 283, 295f, 313–34, 340, 343, 349, 355, 358
evolution theory 13, 67, 114, 219–21, 268, 323, 354, 371f, 382
exchangeability 164–6, 234–6, 322, 332
expectation value 163, 165, 223f, 227–9
experimentum crucis 269
explanandum 56, 348–69
explanans 348, 349–69
explanation 2, 14, 21, 25–8, 32f, 56f, 120, 348–69
   – as expectation 368
   – as unification 291, 368f
   – of events 348, 358
   – of laws 351
   causal – 355f, 361f, 368
   covering law thesis 349, 365–7
   deductive-nomological – 348–56
   post-facto – 282, 313, 341
   inductive-statistical – 358f
   inference to the best – 56f, 61, 83f, 294f
   (ir)relevant – 175, 356f
   mathematical – 31
   normic – 219, 366f
   probability increasing – 363

explanation (cont:)
  pseudo – 323, 350, 376
  rational – 366
  self – 350, 356
  ultimate – 350
explication 20
extension 90f, 94f, 111, 136, 140–3, 148, 167, 175, 293, 302–4, 310f, 360

fact 94
faithfulness 400–5
fallibility 3, 20, 23f, 30, 43, 51
falsifiability 8, 128f, 219f, 282
falsification 7f, 21, 112, 181f, 187–9, 199, 120, 128, 262, 282
  holism of – 262
  quasi – 199
falsificationism 8
  naive – 284
  refined – 279
fitting
  curve – s. curve
  over– 327f
  parameter – 322–4, 330
  post-facto – 323f
frequency limit 119, 130–2, 148, 151–7, 165, 234f, 325
foundationalism 3–5, 11

Gaussian s. normal distribution
general sentence s. generalization
generalization 49–53, 83f, 117–29, 370, 375–81
  anti-inductive – 322, 331f
  (un)restricted – 119, 122–5
  accidental– 123–5
  ceteris paribus – 119, 214–8
  empirical – 246, 258, 271, 291
  inductive – 49–53, 322, 331f
  localized – 108
  mixed-quantified – 128f
  normic – 119, 219f, 275
  statistical – 119, 176–81
  strict – 118, 173–5
globality 260, 270, 300f, 369

Hempel's dilemma 270–2
hermeneutic (s. understanding) 14, 32, 36
  – circle 32
  – paradigm 75f
  – presumption 346

heuristics 184, 279, 388
holism
  – of empirical content 255, 268–70
  – of meaning 71f, 142, 268–70
  – of theory testing 129, 261f, 269
homogeneity
  – of reference class 168, 361f
  – of theoretical concepts 253f
  – of theories 289f
humanities (human sciences) 1, 14, 21, 29, 32f, 35, 219, 365–7
Hume-thesis 4f, 376, 383, 386, 400
hypotheses 122, 181ff, 314ff
  ad hoc – 8f, 72, 262f, 278, 346
  auxiliary – 261–3, 269, 278, 282, 289,
  discovery of – 17, 52, 185–8, 191–3, 402f
  testing of – 181–200, 314–331
hypothetically-deductive 181, 314–318

idealism 59–62, 292
  intersubjective – 60
  possibilistic – 60
  subjective – 60
idealization 53, 130, 261, 280, 336
immunization thesis 278
implication (material) 90, 117f, 136–9, 175, 183, 339, 362, 375f
inaccuracy 101f, 261, 326f
incommensurability 9f
independence argument 78–80
indicator 243, 247, 252–4, 273–6, 353, 384
  biased – 254
indifference, principle of 166, 230–8
individual
  – case 14, 33, 203f, 359, 365
  – constant 89, 94f, 123, 133, 161–4, 332, 358, 375, 383
  – variable 91, 115, 150, 163, 172, 176
induction 8, 12f, 49–51, 181, 198ff, 227, 260, 294, 331, 373–6
  assumption of – 150, 165, 233–8
  epistemic – 54, 57f, 198
  logical – 53, 233
  meta – 54, 84f
  methodological – 52, 185, 198f
  problem of – 5, 80–5
inductive
  – deductive scheme 51
  – learning 165, 234f
  – projectibility 373–5

inference
  – to the best explanation 55–8, 83, 294–6, 349, 396
  monotonic – 58f
  non-monotonic – 58f
initial condition 125, 258–62, 356, 368, 371
  sensitive dependence on –s 355f
immediate rationality 279, 284
instrumentalism 5–7, 57f, 291–4, 301–6
intension 89, 91, 124, 137, 366f
interpretation 9, 32–4, 63–9, 80
  – function 94, 111
  logical (extensional) – 94f, 110–2, 141f, 200f
intersubjectivity 23–5, 32, 59f, 63, 78f, 130–2, 160–2, 232, 236, 319
intertheoretical
  – comparisons 284–91
  – relations 266–8, 296f, 307
intervention 230
  – account of causality 338f
interview (questionnaire) 32, 37, 101f, 201f, 252, 255
introspective report 72f
invariance 164, 273–6, 310, 332
  – criterion 140f
  logical – 121, 175f, 317, 339
  translation – 342–5
irreducible representation 147, 175, 264, 312, 317, 357, 378
irrelevance assumptions 181, 253, 347
is-ought 77f
  – bridge principles 77f
  – thesis 77f

justification 352–9, 367
  ex ante – 352
  ex post – 352, 359

language dependence 70f, 233f, 333, 342–5
law 2, 11, 14, 21, 24, 26–8, 32f, 55, 84, 117–22, 172–6, 349f, 370–81
  ceteris paribus – 119, 174, 214–19
  – of coexistence 212, 353, 384
  – of correspondence 242–53, 263–5, 273–5, 327–33
  – of large numbers 150–6, 225
  – of logic 113, 372
  – of nature 11, 84, 122–5, 371f, 375–7, 380–2
  – of succession 172, 353

derived – 123
fundamental – 47, 123–5, 260f, 371, 376f, 381
indicator – 47, 252–4, 273–6
normic – 33, 119, 181, 219–21, 366f
system – 47, 371–3
lawlikeness 98, 122–6, 137f, 155, 174, 215, 260, 307, 355f, 370–381
  – i.n.s. 372
  – i.w.s. 372
likelihood 162f 226–32
  – expectation 227
  – intuition 200, 226
  – maximization 226f
  – ratio 230
linking up 393
logical
  – consequence 49f, 58, 126
  – form 110
  – formalization 93f
  – proof 113
  – truth 131f
  – validity 132

magnitude 103–5
  extensive – 103
  intensive – 103
mathematical structuralism 31
mathematical realism 31
maximal specificity 168, 358–61
Maxwell's condition 375–7, 380
Markov condition 398
mean value 193, 217, 222–7, 391
meaning 7, 10, 24f, 71–3, 93–8, 105,
  – postulate 115, 117, 142, 243–5, 300
  convention of – 113f
  holism of – 71f, 142, 268–70
means 39f
  necessary – 40
  optimal – 40
  sufficient – 40
  – end inference 39–41, 44f, 75f
measurement 32, 36, 69, 102–5, 109, 117, 248–52, 307–11
  chain of –s 251
  T-dependent 307–11
mechanics
  classical – 255–68, 369
  Newtonian – 255–7, 350, 364
  quantum – 21, 41, 61, 102, 247–50, 267, 280, 306, 354, 369, 388, 394, 399

meta-ethics 2, 42, 44, 77f
method of agreement 182f, 188f
method of difference 183, 191f
methodological dualism 14, 33, 350, 365
meta-induction 54, 84f
   optimality of – 84f
   pessimistic meta– 294f
metrization 104f
   fundamental – 104
   theory-dependent – 104
model 88, 147, 348
   minimal – of science 20–7
   logical – 32f, 95f, 302–6
   causal 396f, 400–7
   measurement – 310
   probability – 134, 147–50
   theoretical – 258f, 280
Mueller-Lyer-illusion 66

natural
   – axiomatization 264, 289, 312f
   – kind 10, 94, 114
   –ism 13f, 61
necessity 91
   analytical – 113–5, 141–4
   logico – 110f, 140f, 372
   physical – 372–6, 380–2. 398
   metaphysical – 10f, 184
necessitation 11, 381
Newman's problem 302–4
noise assumption 402
no miracles argument 11, 294–6, 299
nominalism 292f
non-monotonicity 58, 119, 131, 180f, 203, 269, 359f
norm s. value
   categorial – 40
   derived – 39–41
   fundamental – 39–41
   hypothetical – 40
   – sentence 97, 105f
normal form 175
   conjunctive – 146
   irreducible – 147
   prenex – 146
normality 219f, 366

objectivity 3, 20–5, 54–8, 61–4, 77–9, 99, 103, 125, 129f, 140, 155, 160–2, 232, 308, 315, 337, 361f, 378f, 384
   pseudo – 57

observation 2, 6, 8–10, 21–8, 35f, 51–5, 63–74, 78, 97f, 102, 107–9, 122f, 127f, 157, 209, 332, 340f, 343–5
   normal conditions of – 74, 79
   theory-dependence of – 63–71
   theory-neutral – 63–75
Ockham's razor 4, 31, 271, 313
ordering 92, 99, 101f
   Archimedean – 104
   connex – 101
   partial – 285
   quasi – 101
   random – 130
ostensive learning 71–5, 97, 117, 143, 343–5

paradigm 8–10, 187, 240, 279–81, 286, 291
   coexistence of –s 280
   critical-dialectic – 75
   empirical-analytic – 75
   hermeneutic – 75
paradox 78, 143–6 158, 210, 234
   – es of confirmation 144, 315f, 320
   Carnap's – 136
   Goodman – 322, 331–3, 343
   – of truthlikeness 146, 344
   preface – 147, 335f
   lottery – 335f
   Simpson – 211
   tacking – 288f
partition 99, 134f, 166f, 231, 325, 368
perception 23, 25, 61f, 65–9, 72, 79
Piaget's developmental psychology 272–78
place selection 153–5
Popper's asymmetry 7, 128f, 182
population 148, 176, 188–99, 217–27, 324, 399
Positivism 6, 34, 292
   – debate 38
   legal – 33
   logical – 45
possibility knowledge 382
possible world 10f, 49, 58, 95, 111f, 156, 199, 236f, 306, 339f, 373–5, 380f
   similarity ordering between –s 373–5, 385f
Pragmati(ci)sm 25
pragmatics 12, 92
   internal – 12
   external – 12

predicate 89f
  nomological – 132f, 167f, 172, 360
  pathological – 332, 343, 378
  positional – 332, 343
  qualitative – 332f, 343f, 376f
prediction 26–8, 32, 54, 77, 84f, 112, 153, 164–7, 172–4, 204, 218, 236f, 246f, 262, 269, 274–8, 335, 351–59, 363, 368f
  confirmatorial surplus of – 282, 323f, 328f
  – in the epistemic sense 352
  – in the temporal sense 352
  novel – 246f, 250, 260, 270f, 296, 323f, 342, 386, 391,
  potential – 27, 296, 352, 355, 368, 391
  – without explanatory value 352f
predictive function 296, 352, 355f
principal principle 51, 54, 127, 161f
  single case – 161
  statistical – 161–6, 229–31, 358
probability 49–54, 77, 118–21, 129–35, 147–67, 188–211, 221–38, 357–65
  a-priori – 163–6, 319
  axioms of – 134
  – density 221–3, 231–5
  – of hypotheses 199f, 226–38, 318–20
  conditional – 131
  dualist account of – 156f, 161–168
  epistemic – 129f, s. subjective
  evidence-independent – 163–6, 232
  logical – 53, 130, 133, 166, 233–5
  – model – 134, 147–50
  objective – 129f, 157f, s. statistical –
  posterior – 163, 230–2, 236, 323
  prior – 164f, 230–8, 319–23, 330, 363
  non-dogmatic– 165, 237, 319, 332
  statistical – 130–3, 152–8, 161–3, 188–204, 221–26
  subjective – 130–3, 158–68, 226–238, 318–20
  theorems of – 134f
  zero – 130f
propensity
  generic – 155
  single case 157f, 161, 362, 409
property
  categorial – 138
  dispositional – 98, 136–40, 242–6
proposition 94, 96, 121f, 132

quantifier 91, 93, 107–9, 118–20, 127, 137, 146, 218, 301–5

Ramsey-sentence 299f
  – in instrumentalist interpretation 301–3
  – in realist interpretation 303–5
random experiment 148–58, 199, 210, 217–30
randomness 154f
rational reconstruction 18–22, 85
rationalism 4f
  critical – 7f, 18, 45, 52
realism 5–7, 10f, 59f, 291–4, 304–6
  abductive – 57f
  constructive – 61, 63, 293
  (in)direct – 62f, 66f
  hypothetical – 61, 293
  metaphysical – 10f, 60, 293
  minimal – 20–4, 30f,
  naive – 63
  property – 293
  scientific – 11, 291–7
  structural – 297f
  universals – 292
reason(s)
  – for being 351f
  – for belief 351f
reduction sentence 136f, 243–5, 248–51
reductionism xviii, 4–7, 46–9
redundancy 146f, 282, 312, 338, 356f, 378
reference 10–2, 93f, 297f, 301f, 303f
  – shift 297f
reference class 132, 158, 167f
  homogeneous – 68, 361f
  narrowest – 59, 132f, 160, 166f, 180, 203, 359–61,
reflective equilibrium 22
regularity account 4f, 11, 209, 370, 375, 384
rejection s. acceptance
relation
  equivalence – 101
  ordering – 101
relevance 143–6, 173–81, 361–4
  causal – 174, 184–6, 204f, 361–4, 383
  logical – 143–6, 264, 282, 289, 312–8, 338f, 356f
  – of strict laws 173–6
  – of statistical laws 176–81, 193–6, 203f

Index of Subjects

relevant (consequence) element 146f, 317, 320, 325, 329f, 338–41, 378
research program 9, 260, 278–83, 289
retrodiction 352

salva validitate 164f, 175, 338,
sample 52, 54, 181ff, 193ff,
    control – 183, 193–6, 201f
    – size 151, 190f, 196, 224f, 235,
    distribution of – parameters 152, 189, 193f, 222
    random – 151f, 162f, 188f, 197f,
    representative – 183f, 196–8
    stratified – 198
scale 99–105, 179
    absolute – 104
    categorial – 100
    ordinal – 100
    interval – 102f
    Likert – 253
    ratio – 102f
    – transformation 104
science
    classification of the –s 28f, 34–6
    cognitive – 10, 13f, 63–75, 110, 145, 161, 272–8, 342, 366, 382
    dissecting – 35f
    empirical –s 31f, 35, 44–6
    epistemological assumptions of –s 22–5
    experimental –s 35
    formal –s 30
    human –s 14, 29, 32–5, 268, 272–8, 365–7
    mathematical –s 30f
    methodological features of –s 25–7
    natural –s 14, 29, 32, 36, 44, 242, 255–63, 268, 280
    normal – 9, 60, 281
    physical – 46–9, 220, 255–63, 266f
    revolutionary – 9, 60, 281
    social – s 29, 242, 254, 268
    special – 46–9, 220, 266–8, 371–3, 388
scientific community 9, 283, 288, 349
screening off 206f, 209, 216, 392–7
selection, evolutionary 13, 67, 220f, 371
self regulatory 371, 397
semantics 93–6, 141–4, 373, 380f
    logical – 94f
sentence
    analytic– 4, 7, 71, 105, 114, 141–3, 251, 268, 300

    basic – 109
    descriptive – 106f
    empirical – 107–9, 126, 265, 301
    existential – 120f
    general – 118f, 122–6
    mixed-quantified – 120, 128f
    observation – 6, 8, 10, 25–8, 65f, 71f, 78f, 108f, 122f, 127f, 157
    prescriptive – 106f
    pre-(T)-theoretical – 264f,
    singular – 26, 108f, 118–21, 133, 163, 348
    synthetic – 4, 7, 71, 78, 105f, 114, 141f, 246, 251, 268, 300–2, 398
    (T-) theoretical – 108, 265, 292, 301
    universal – 108–28, 172, 180, 373–5, 381
sentence operator 89, 106, 141
    intensional – 91, 106
    truth-functional – 89–91
set 92, 95f
    sub– 92
    – theory 95
sigma-additive 149f
significance
    – coefficient (level) 189f, 193f, 241
    cognitive – 311f, 388
    empirical – 311–3
    statistical – 189–96, 201, 203, 224–6
simplicity 13, 286, 328, 340–2, 377f
solipsism 60
speculation 8, 35, 45, 98, 158, 270, 309–11, 340f
    rational – 322f
    post-facto – 321
SSD-minimization 327
standard deviation 190, 193, 222–6, 326–8
statement view 12f, 95f
    non – 12f, 95f
state of affairs 94
statistics 150–2, 188–203, 221–29
    Bayesian – 229–38
    inference – 198f
    test – 198f
structuralism 6, 12f, 16, 95f, 259, 266, 293, 301f, 309–11
supervenience 48
supreme epistemic goal 19f, 25, 41, 59f
syntax 92f, 95f, 110, 121, 128f
system

Index of Subjects • 455

background – 56, 90f, 116, 123, 168, 263, 349, 354–361
belief – 59, 61, 116f, 142, 146, 340, 389
best – 377–80
complex – 47f
– character 255, 259–61, 268–70
– conditions 257–61, 278–80, 350
evolutionary – 220
– law 47, 371–3
logical – 113
stationary – 384, 397

test person (tp) 68f, 73, 101, 200–3, 253–5
testability 129, 217,
   independent – 63, 247, 271, 296, 313, 326, 342, 386, 391
test(ing) 26f, 31–4, 37, 129f
   – of quantitative laws 326–9
   – of strict laws 181–5
   – of statistical laws 188–200,
   – of theories 268, 281–91
   severe – 183f
theoreticity 264, 266, 271, 307–11
theory 109, 242ff
   – core 247, 255–66, 273–84, 290, 297, 405
   – dynamics 278–81
   – element 259, 261, 266, 279, 300, 307
   – evaluation 281–291
   – dependence 65–72, 79f
   – lattice 259, 266,f 279, 307
   linguistic – representation 95f
   model-theoretic – representation 95f
   – net 266–8
   – periphery 255, 261f, 265f, 273, 276, 278f, 281, 284
   – progress 278–81, 285, 337
   – revision 276, 278–81
   – statics 263–68
   – version 262, 269, 278–85, 288–10
time
   direction of – 384–7
   – series 234, 399
total evidence 59, 133, 182, 318, 333
trope 97, 293
truth
   analytic – 113f, s. sentence
   contingent – 47, 111f, 123, 141, 300, 315f, 319, 372f, 377–81, 387, 398

correspondence theory of – 22–5, 60–2
criteria of – 24–6
definitional – 113f
definition of – 24–6
logical – 110f
metaphysical neutrality of – 60
synthetic – 114, 125f, 141f, s. sentence
truthlikeness 53, 58, 283f, 336–40, 344f
   dynamical – 284
   epistemic – 53, 283f, 340
   semantic – 282, 340
turn
   cognitive – 13
   historical – 16
   linguistic – 7
   pragmatic – 12

uncorrelatedness 224
underdetermination
   empirical – 269, 288, 295f, 402
   semantic (ontological) – 11, 141, 298
understanding 14f, 21, 32, 365, 368f
unification 246f, 260, 264, 270–2, 340–3, 368–70, 378f, 386
unity
   – of science 16ff, 44ff
   methodological – xviii, 14, 46–9, 268, 367
   ontological – 46–9
universality 118, 122f, 375
   spatiotemporal – 119, 375–7, 400
unpredictability 355f
use-novel evidence 246f, 271, 296, 324–31
utilitarianism 78
utility
   epistemic – 335
   expected – 167, 334
   practical – 334

value 2, 14, 23, 29, 33f, 37–44, 75–80
   categorial – 40, 97
   derived – 34, 39–41, 75
   external (non-epistemic) – 41–4, 76f
   – freedom 37–9
   fundamental – 39–41
   hypothetical – 40, 77f
   internal (epistemic) – 41f
   – neutrality 37–44, 75–7
   – sentence 34, 97–9,105f
   – loaded 76

variable 88–91, 110
  bound – 91, 132
  continuous – 190, 221–6
  criterion – 179
  free – 91
  hidden – 201–6, 254f, 276, 296
  (in)dependent – 212, 255, 385
  individual – s. individual
  latent (theoretical) – 236, 242f, 296, 301f, 322–31
  mediating – 207f
  predictor – 179
  statistical (mathematical) – 100f, 179, 216, 326–9, 389–407
  –s and events 390, 407
variance 223–7
  co– 178, 224
vector addition 256
verification 7f, 127–9, 159 182f, 349
verisimilitude s. truthlikeness
Vienna circle 5–7, 15, 38, 109

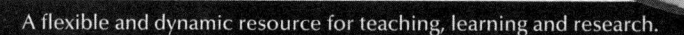